To Annie & Lachie

Christmas 2012

Love Anja

dansk design

Thomas Dickson

dansk design

Photography by Dorte Krogh a. o.

MURDOCH BOOKS

Contents

Preface

This book is about Danish design. To a great degree design is about aesthetics, about beauty. But when you look closely at individual examples, it almost always turns out that other considerations also lie behind their appearance. Design is very rarely only a beautiful surface or an attractive form. A few of the interesting questions which arise when you look more closely at design are: Why do things look the way they do? What has determined the form of a certain everyday article? And how did the designer come to this result? Often design is about finding solutions to users' and manufacturers' problems and thereby developing a better product. In other words, with this book I wanted to introduce the readers to what could be called 'the designer's point of view'. Based on my own background as an architect and designer, I have tried to describe products and the designed surroundings from the point of view that many designers adopt when they work.

Of course this is not to say that aesthetics and the history of style are insignificant. In many cases, the very fascination and beauty of a product's design are what have made it a popular and commercial success. The same can be said about technological breakthroughs. They too have had a great influence on the appearance and use of products. It has merely been important to me to supplement these points of view with yet another: the one that has its origin in the designer's work, and which also involves aspects of the social, innovative and commercial nature in the creation of new solutions.

This book is an attempt to describe Danish design in its entirety. That is why, on the one hand, the book goes as far back in time as possible in order to describe design in Denmark. On the other hand, as many design areas as possible are included – from the ships of the Viking Age, the painted coats of arms of the Middle Ages and the classic furniture of the early 20th century to fashion in the beginning of this millennium. The purpose has been to describe a long Danish tradition in the fields of innovation and good design. Furthermore, an important objective of this book is that it is meant to be read and used by everyone who is interested in design. Therefore esoteric terminology has been avoided as much as possible.

The book offers different approaches to the material. First and foremost, it can be read from cover to cover as a book that gives a general view of Danish design. However, it is also possible to go directly to a specific subject, since apart from a few introductory chapters, the book is divided into product types, such as product design, furniture design, graphic design, public design etc. Moreover, it can be used as reference book by searching the index to find information on specific designers, companies or works. Since the contents are as up-to-date as has been possible, the book can also be seen as a current inventory of Danish design. My goal has not been to describe Danish design as something that is better than any other designs. One could definitely write similar book about Dutch, English, Japanese or Italian design. The decisive point has been to write about the distinctiveness of Danish design at its best and worst, but mostly best.

Although a wide definition of what design is has been used in this book, I have naturally had to be selective, as well as limit the area of design in relation to other creative fields. Before industrialisation, much design was manufactured as craftsmanship. In recent times, things are still made by hand, but this work has increasingly achieved the status of an artistic discipline called arts and crafts. Today, objects from these handicrafts are often made in a single copy – that is, unique specimens – or in very small series, and they're often exhibited and sold as objects of art and collectors' items at higher prices than conventional industrial products. This type of design, such as hand-woven textiles, hand-thrown pottery, glassware blown by mouth and the like cannot be seen as articles for everyday use and thus fall outside the scope of this book.

Despite the justified argument that design and architecture are linked professionally, I have chosen not to give a detailed description of Danish architecture. In many ways, other premises apply to architecture than to design. Among other things, as in the case of objects of art, architecture has had a tendency to create unique specimens, where one house is built at a time. Furthermore, architecture is by its very nature confined to a locality and has usually been designed specifically for the landscape or town where the building was to be built. Even though I use examples from architecture to illustrate a point or a trend in this book, I have refrained from delving into an actual narrative about Danish architecture.

The criteria for my selection have been that the design has actually been manufactured and used. In history books or exhibition catalogues, many projects can be found that haven't amounted to more than a single prototype or mock-up. In this book it's been important for me to use examples that have existed and have been something Danes at one point or another have been able to buy, use or see in the public domain. And naturally it's been crucial that the examples used in this book have an essentially Danish aspect. For example, that a Danish company has manufactured the article or a Danish designer has designed it.

In writing this book I have had great assistance from a number of people. Without their help and advice this project would never have been finished. I am greatly indebted to the following: Curator Max Vinner from Roskilde Viking Ship Museum, design teacher and product designer Henrik Lund-Larsen, design teacher and graphic designer Peter Gyllan, design teacher and furniture designer Erik Krogh, all from Denmark's Design School, Curator Jakob from the Royal Naval Museum, fashion designer Mads Nørgaard, fashion designer Tine Dwinger, fashion designer Mette Hornsleth, costume historian and Master of Arts Viben Bech, textile designer Vibeke Riisberg, museum assistant Solveig Kirstine Kristensen from the National Open Air Museum of Urban History and Culture, Assistant Professor and Architect Steen Ejlers from The Royal Danish Academy of Fine Arts, School of Architecture, Assistant Professor and Architect Flemming Skude from The Royal Danish Academy of Fine Arts, Library of the School of Architecture.

For their reviews and criticism I would like to thank interior designer Marianne Frandsen, Architect Hans Haagensen, Director Peter Meyer from Trapholt Museum, Curator Mette Stromgaard Dalby from Trapholt Museum and designer Pil Bredahl. Special thanks go to head librarian at Aarhus School of Architecture Maia Vonsbaek, who helped with many literature searches. The book's photographer Dorte Krogh, has been very supportive in making the written material come alive with new photographs. Obtaining historic illustrations has been safe in the hands of Lilja Hardt and especially Annette Ekstrand from Gyldendal. Finally, the inspiration, angelic patience and positive support of my editor Lil Vad-Schou ensured this book saw the light of day.

Thomas Dickson, September 2006

What is design?

WE ARE ALL DESIGNERS

From when we open our eyes in the morning till we lay our head on the pillow again at night we are all designers. We each make countless choices that contribute to forming our lives, easing our day to day existence and creating our identities. Although we often don't make these decisions consciously, they influence not only ourselves, but our surroundings and self-image.

This has been the case throughout the history of Man. The ability to change the world purposely, shape the surroundings and manufacture tools is one of the significant things that separates us from animals and make us human. Ever since the intelligent prehistoric ape in Stanley Kubrick's *2001: A Space Odyssey* picks up a femur and uses it as a club against a group of hostile apes, we have been designers.

Most people in Denmark sleep in a bed, and when the alarm clock goes off, they get up. The very arrangement of our bedroom with the choice and combination of bed, bed linen, pillow and curtains is design. These things take part in determining whether we sleep well. Whether the mattress is suitably soft, the pillow is really comfortable, and the curtains keep out the light – all these things have an influence on whether the rest of the day turns out as it should. It is these two aspects, the products and the combination of them, which to a great extent is what design is about. As humans we organise our surroundings so they're as practical and comfortable as possible, so that for instance we wake up refreshed in the morning. Some of the decisions were made a long time ago. After all, most of us only buy a new bed a few times in our lives. On the other hand, every night we decide if we want to wake up the next morning to the sound of the clock radio's buzzer or our favourite radio station.

▲ *A bone club, circa 10,000 years ago, from the Maglemose Period of the late Stone Age. It was found in the Ringsted area and is from an auroch (a Stone Age wild ox). The picture might portray a family of hunters with two men and three women. A sharp flint knife was used to engrave the weapon. It is one of the oldest Danish finds that portrays people.*

HOTELS ARE SOME of the most designed things in the world. To a great extent, the comfort of the guests depends on other people, like designers who have arranged the hotel practically and made the rooms nice to stay in. One of the most famous hotel rooms in the world is the Radisson SAS Royal Hotel, better known as the Royal Hotel. The hotel was one of Copenhagen's first proper high-rises in the modern glass-and-steel style. It was designed by architect Arne Jacobsen and opened in 1960. An amazing attention to detail typifies the building from top to bottom.

This continues throughout the day and throughout our lives. A vast number of decisions and creative actions shape our lives. It's about choosing clothes, shoes, wristwatches, jewellery, hair style, purse, calendar, make-up, car, bike, cellphone, furniture, lamps and the adjustment of an office chair. It extends to your personal things and professional equipment on your desk at work, what you buy on the way home, where you buy it, what kind of food you cook when you have guests and when you're alone, where you go on vacation, where you live and how you live.

This list could go on forever, but it's just meant to illustrate all the alternatives we as human beings have in a modern world and how they contribute to creating our lives and identity. "Show me your home, and I'll tell you who you are" could be the joint title of the many Danish TV programs which since the mid-90s have let marketing experts and sociologists guess the identity of celebrities based on the latter's home or some personal possessions. And when you see how often they "guess" correctly, you're impressed by their abilities, but also puzzled by how much our worldly goods reveal about our personality.

Even when we think we're not making a decision, we're making one anyway. A non-choice is also a way of making up your mind; it just leaves it up to other people, like a designer, to decide what's going to happen. Or was it your sweetheart who decided what bed you were going to sleep in for the next 15 years? Perhaps it was a favourable offer from the hotel supplier that determined which bed a guest would sleep in? When all is said and done, the success of a hotel can depend on its guests not leaving the next morning with aches and pains while thinking, "I'll never stay at that hotel again."

▸ *Room 606 at the Royal Hotel in Copenhagen.*

Everything from the overall line of the building down to the design of door knobs, lamps, furniture and curtain material and even the cutlery in the restaurant was designed by Arne Jacobsen's architectural office.

In this, one of the world's first 'designer hotels', you could find the famous chairs called the Egg and the Swan for the first time. Both were later put into production and can now be bought by anyone who can afford them. On the other hand, the small chair called the Drop has never been mass produced; it could only be found at the Royal Hotel until the rooms were refurbished and the many 'drops' were discarded. Today only room 606 has been retained in the original style. The other rooms have been subjected to some heavy-handed renovations and do not have the original design. But 606 is a coveted room to stay in for visiting architects and designers who want to experience the real Jacobsen deal when visiting Copenhagen. The room has been pictured in several international magazines and there is even a book called *Room 606* by Michael Sheridan. The Royal Hotel is an example of how design works at many levels.

It is distinctive architecture, which even today is a landmark and advertisement for the large Scandinavian airline. The furnishings are made of excellent materials to a consistent quality. Most guests probably enjoy staying at the Royal Hotel. And for connoisseurs who move into room 606 there is the added advantage of living in the closest thing you get to a design museum. It's design that has been totally orchestrated.

THE SUSPENSION BRIDGE over the Great Belt. There is no doubt that it is extremely well-designed since it functions as intended. Thousands of cars cross it every day, and it is rarely closed due to weather conditions or accidents. Some might question whether it's actually beautiful. Others might think it disfigures the landscape. And yet others might stress that it's a handsome design and actually accentuates the magnificence of the location while giving many people an opportunity to experience a part of Danish nature which they wouldn't ordinarily see.

Whether something is experienced as beautiful or not is one of the few aspects of design that can be discussed with some fairness from a personal and subjective point of view. Nonetheless, it is indisputable that the Great Belt Bridge, after a stormy debate during its construction, has become a great success, adding a new dimension to the identity of Denmark. Regions have been closely linked, transportation time cut and, as the world's second longest main span, it has increased awareness of Denmark as a country characterised by enterprise.

DESIGN IS MORE THAN JUST FORM

Our lives and world have to function in a practical manner. We need to use a chair without it collapsing beneath us. The chair should preferably be comfortable to sit in, have good ergonomics and have the right height compared to the table we're sitting at. In other words, the chair has to function correctly and also give us a good physical experience when using it. The same applies to other implements and the tools we use, whether at work or in our spare time. Things have to work so well that we feel better off having them than doing without them. Why buy a shovel if it doesn't dig better than a cooking spoon? Or why print a book with such a small typeface that only a few can read it? First of all, design is about functionality.

'Form follows function' was the motto of the American architect of skyscrapers, Louis Sullivan, in the late 1800s. This statement became a beacon for several generations of architects and designers of the functionalistic school. It was important to them that the houses and products they designed didn't have excess adornments. The idea was purity, sober-mindedness and efficiency. But functionalism did not remain a philosophy about how an architect or designer should work, it became a style in its own right that could be applied to practically any product. The most obvious example is the architecture and products from the German design school Bauhaus in the era between the two world wars. After World War II, the electronics company Braun in particular carried on the aesthetic legacy of Bauhaus. But also Bang & Olufsen subscribed to the same philosophy of design for many years, as was stated in their brochures. Sullivan's 100-year-old statement still stands strong and applies, but several other functions have become increasingly important since then.

Design also functions on a different and more emotional level. Many and perhaps most of the things we surround ourselves with give us emotional experiences in addition to the purely functional. Often we don't just buy a chair in order to sit in it, but also to enjoy its appearance, well-proportioned dimensions and the exquisite treatment of materials. We experience things when we encounter architecture, the furnishing of a room, products and graphic communication. These experiences can be pleasant, fascinating, surprising, provocative or downright repulsive. We almost always prefer the positive, aesthetic experiences when we're choosing a home, clothes, a car, furniture, cellphone etc. But the aesthetic that appeal to a grown woman when she buys a cellphone can be radically different from those that fascinate her seven-year-old son when he builds a plane out of Lego. The Aesthetic experiences don't only apply to our sense of sight, but also to our other senses. Just think of the smell of leather or newly cut wood, or how you sometimes let your hand slide over the armrest of a good chair and you almost feel a rush because it feels so nice. Good design is much more than things just working satisfactorily.

Thirdly, design can give us a sense of belonging – to a group, a culture, a country or a company. Your identity can be confirmed by well-designed products and communications because every thing has a symbolic value. If you belong to the exclusive subculture of people who own and drive a Nimbus motorcycle, it's a part of your self-awareness. You belong to a specific tribe that sometimes meets to share experiences, swap spare parts and go on trips together. Many people are proud to have something that is exclusively designed whether it's a new Bang & Olufsen stereo, a spokeback sofa by Børge Mogensen or some old jewellery by Georg Jensen.

Identity is not only created inside the individual but also by the signals we send in the way we dress and accessorise. Many of us stand in front of the mirror for a long time before going for a job interview, a date or an important meeting. Not only individuals but also most companies consciously work on staging themselves through design and creating an image and thus branding themselves. This covers everything from the architecture of their main office to their logo, the appearance of their products, their packaging and their employees' apparel and behaviour. Finally, on a national level, you can also observe how countries try to design their own image. The Danish Tourist Bureau tries to lure foreign tourists to Denmark by emphasising Danish culture, including architecture and design. In other words, design is something that goes far beyond meeting our fundamental material needs.

The sensual or poetic function is communicated through our choice of products and accommodation. Take for example a track suit, which in principle is some of the most functional clothing you can wear. However, part and parcel of this type of clothing is a certain identity and personality which translate into a *social* function, hence the name 'camping suit'. A packet of biscuits is no longer just a packet of biscuits, it's much more. It has a lot of connotations which say something about how you see yourself and how you want others to see you: Are you into organic food? Are you into fibre? Do you buy the diet biscuits? Is your taste classic or do you have the courage to try something new?

Society today is very divided, and the market is extremely segmented, which means that as consumers we have a lot of goods to choose between. These products are basically identical in contents and quality, but not in image and certainly not in the identity they give the buyer. In the past all umbrellas were black, and you could 'have a Ford T in any colour, as long as it is black', as Henry Ford said. Back then it was about satisfying basic practical needs, and industrial products were popular because mass production guaranteed uniform and reasonably good quality at a sensible price.

Today we want the exotic; the homemade apple vinegar from the Danish star chef Claus Meyer, the hand-cut tortilla chips and the special box of organic vegetables from a company called Aarstiderne (The Seasons). We want something special, something that is the result of consideration and feelings. We want some immaterial qualities and values that come with the product. We don't use products only to satisfy physical and practical needs, as one might deduce from Louis Sullivan's statement, but also to paint a picture of ourselves as unique people, with an identity. Until recently, there has been a tendency for people to buy high-quality furniture and save up for it for a long time. Now, in the new millennium, certain circles are looking for a new intensity, simplicity, clarity – and something original.

Strictly speaking, it doesn't *have* to be expensive design for that reason. For example, IKEA and Hennes & Mauritz both use really good designers to make what is in fashion now, but they manufacture things inexpensively. And that doesn't really matter, because in 3–4 months the fashion has changed, so the clothes don't have to be hard-wearing – they have been artificially outdated before they're worn out. The cheap but trendy Swatch watch is another example. Whether this way of designing and selling products is sustainable as regards resources and the environment is another matter.

THE NETTO SUPERMARKETS started in 1981 with a public image of big discounts, poor service, shabby-looking stores and a small product range. However, the graphic design was especially consistent, and the company focused on the yellow and black discount colours and the Scottie as its logo. Over the years it's become trendy to shop 'sensibly' at Netto, even for clientele that wouldn't normally shop there. According to popular legend, even upper-class ladies shop at Netto but they bring a carrier bag from a high-street supermarket to put their shopping in. Thus, the exclusive brands aren't the only ones who use design to brand themselves and communicate with their customers. If it's done well, systematically and with humour, as is the case here, then design can contribute to opening the market to new client bases.

THE CONCEPT OF DESIGN

If you leaf through glossy magazines or watch the many programs about interior design on television, you can easily get the impression that design is very superficial and only about making clothes, designing expensive furniture and painting your living room in new colours. But design, not least Danish design, is much more than that ...

The Danish language has imported the word 'design' from English where it means many things. It can mean to plan, construct, make a draft, devise, outline a solution, invent, intend, execute a plan or arrange elements or details in a product or work of art. Besides this, there is the meaning that we in Denmark often associate with design – to fashion objects with special regard to the aesthetic aspect.

While a Stone Age family had to make everything themselves – from clothes to shelter to tools and weapons, today's world is so complicated that society has had to develop an extremely far-reaching division of labour. Even the most prolific designer has to use objects and stay in surroundings that others have fashioned and engineered. So even though we're all designers in the sense that we furnish and decorate our own homes, design work has still become a profession for some people. Throughout time, the best and most typical Danish design is often, but not always, created by professional designers.

The Shaker chair is classic design that was developed and refined throughout the centuries by the Puritan sect, the Shakers, who still live in northeastern U.S.A. Since their establishment in 1774, they have worked at developing and making furniture with a high quality of craftsmanship.

WHEN IS A CHAIR designed? Is it when a well-known designer has drawn up the lines? Or when there is consensus on it being good design? Or are all chairs designed simply because there is a human intention behind their creation?

▲ *A modern copy of an original Shaker chair. The model is still manufactured by Shaker Workshops in the USA.*

BØRGE MOGENSEN WAS one of Kaare Klint's best apprentices in cabinetmaking at the Royal Academy of Fine Arts in the years around 1940. He also studied Shaker furniture and in 1947 he designed one of the best selling chairs from that period, Model J39, with the byname 'The Shaker Chair'. Unlike many designers today who like to copy others, but would rather not admit it, it was in good taste back then to elaborate on well-known designs. Is this chair plagiarism? Is it design? Judge for yourself.

Their goal is to be self-sufficient in every way and thus they also design and manufacture their own furniture in a way which complies with their pious, puritan beliefs. So that means simple furniture they can make without the use of machines or materials that have to be bought outside their community. The furniture is devoid of everything but its function. Nonetheless it is very beautiful, as well as being durable. But the design does not bear the designer's name so he can't take credit for it. The form has been inspirational for many designers, even Danish ones.

There is often talk about designer clothes, designer lamps, designer kitchens and designer furniture. This is how the impression arises that some things are designed, while others are not. But every product is designed since someone has come to a decision about its appearance and execution. Design isn't dependent on belonging to the designers' union or having a recognised education or whether the product has been manufactured by a particularly design-oriented company. It's more interesting to talk about what is good and what is bad design. We all have to use our heads and decide what we like and don't like. Naming something as good design just because a well-known designer or a well-renowned company is behind it, only leads to keeping a lid on the personal choice of what good design actually is.

The Church Chair was designed by Kaare Klint circa. 1930 for the Grundtvig Church and the Bethlehem Church in Copenhagen. The form, materials and quality are inspired by the Shaker chair even if it's not an exact copy of one. Now a famous designer can be credited, but the question is whether the chair is more or less designed for that reason.

THERE ARE WORKS of art that in one way or another move into the realm of design. It can be in the form of products, graphic design, branding or other types of concepts. The point is that they draw attention to a global or social problem and make the viewer think by sketching a practical solution to a problem. Thus it becomes art that is functional and generates debate as in the case of Superflex' biogas plant (left). Superflex is a Danish art group that consists of Rasmus Nielsen, Bjørnstjerne Christiansen and Jakob Fenger, and they often work with this type of political design. The artists take solutions to significant problems out into the real world in order to make people think along new lines. In 1997 the group designed an inexpensive biogas unit for poor rural areas near the equator. Manure from live stock is poured into the orange plastic containers and enough natural gas is produced to run a stove and one or two lamps.

DESIGN AND ART

Design is often associated with art, and there are several reasons for this. The main reason is that many designers are educated at art schools or art academies. This isn't a Danish phenomenon – it has been this way and still is in many countries. It used to be that many of the skills you had to have as a designer, artisan or architect were the same ones artists had to have; that is, the ability to imagine something that doesn't exist yet, the ability to sketch, draw, colour and sculpture, and the ability to complete a project, whether it was a statue, a building or a product design.

Today art and design only have something in common on the surface. Previously, design was largely seen as having to do with decoration, and the designer was an artistic and aesthetic consultant in the industry. Today design has developed into something completely different and so has art. The Nobel prizewinner in Economics in 1978, Herbert Simon, once came up with the following definition: 'Everyone designs who devises courses of action aimed at changing existing situations into preferred ones.' This definition goes far beyond what art and decoration can be said to be. A good designer focuses on the product, but also on the solution, and good design is planning and concretising ideas into products, communications, services and experiences. Therefore design is not just about aesthetics; it goes far beyond that.

Similarly, most of today's art isn't focused on aesthetics in a traditional sense. On the contrary, modern art deals with exploring the human condition and challenging our sense of reality without always offering solutions or pat answers.

Art does not, by definition and unlike design, have any use-value, however it must be experienced and possibly interpreted, though it's actually the opposite of what design is. In a very simplified way you could say that design is everything man-made that isn't art. Sometimes design has a distinct element of aesthetics and beauty, while today's avant-garde artist often doesn't aim to create 'fine art' in the old-fashioned romantic sense. Avant-garde art today seldom has aesthetic beauty as its goal.

In saying that design isn't art doesn't mean that it is without spiritual substance. On the contrary, Danish design has a lot of merit that reflects its thousands-of-years-old history, which is about using the resources at hand in the best possible way under the physical, technical and political conditions of the time. This is how Danish design has evolved, obviously not in isolation from the outside world, but in a relationship of mutual influence. Danish design is still something unique as Johannes V. Jensen expresses in his poem and song *How fair the smile of the Danish coast* from 1925: 'What the hand has wrought is in spirit birth.'

Jewellery design is an example of art and design sometimes being mixed. Much jewellery does not have a direct function. On the other hand, both belt buckles and cuff links have very practical uses. On another level, a wedding ring signals to others that the bearer has a special relationship to another person. In a general sense, jewellery is a symbol of the bearer's status and wealth. Today, modern jewellery also signals that one is aware of the times, and avant-garde jewellery is often a symbol of cultural capital rather than material wealth.

AROUND 1370 BC a young woman around the age of 17 was buried in a barrow in Egtved near the town of Kolding. We don't really know who she was or how she died, but she must have been someone special for otherwise she wouldn't have been buried so carefully and with such expensive burial gifts. She had a special piece of jewellery called a belt disc. It looks like a miniature shield and is worn, as the name indicates, on the waist. It's made of bronze and is beautifully decorated with spirals.

The belt plate does not seem to have a practical function, but the value of the metal alone, not to mention the intricate tooling, means that it must have been very valuable at the time. Thus it probably gave the wearer a lot of prestige and was a symbol of wealth in her society. Burying it with her must have been a great sacrifice for her family. From a distance of 3000 years we see evidence of the amount of resources that were used on identity and status. For more on this, see page 174.

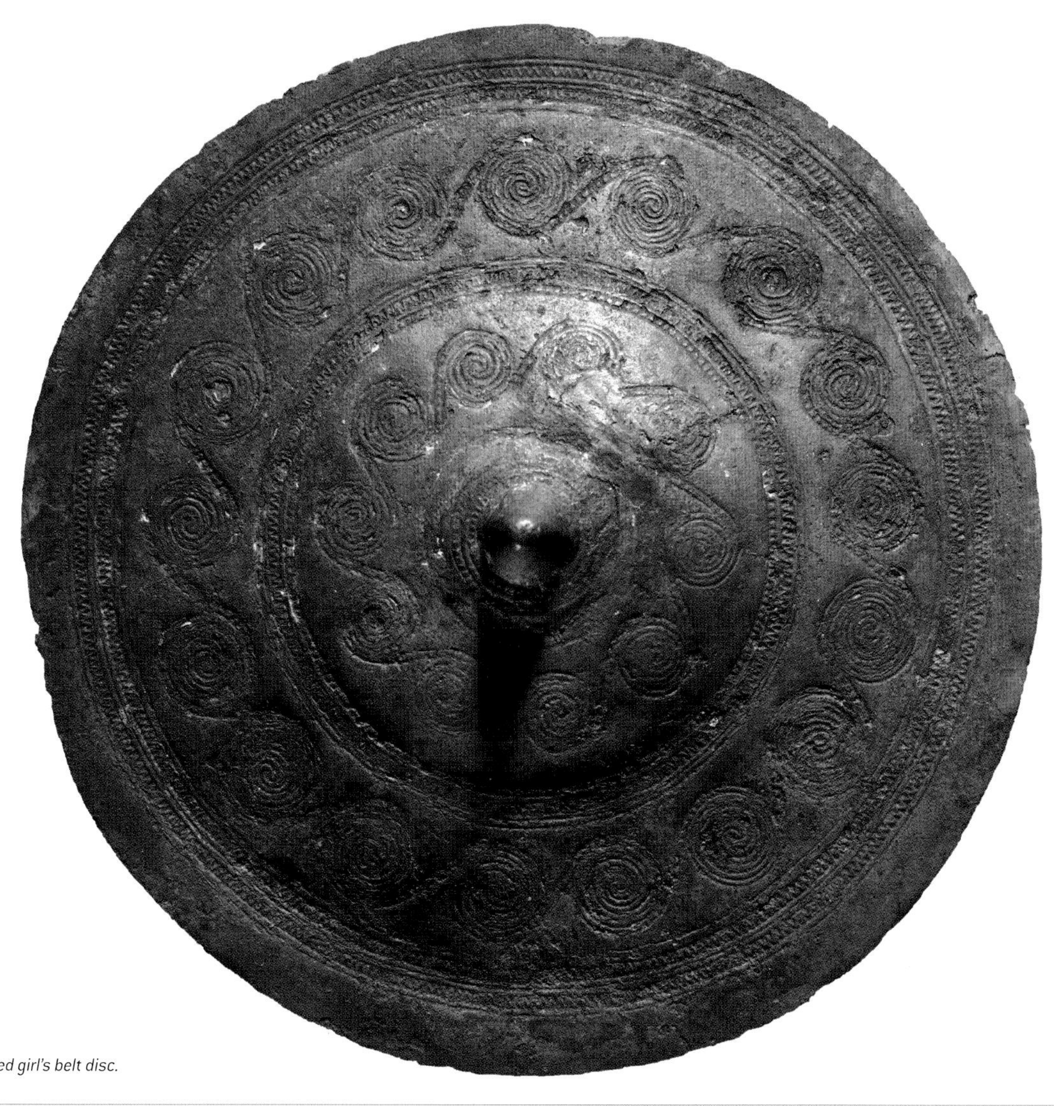

▲ *The Egtved girl's belt disc.*

GEORG JENSEN (1866-1935) was first apprenticed as a goldsmith and later on attended the Royal Academy of Fine Arts in Copenhagen where he became a sculptor and later worked as a potter. In 1904 he established the Georg Jensen Silversmith. Although some people today think that Georg Jensen's jewellery and other silverware from around World War I seem a bit 'convoluted', back then it was new and modern and very popular in well-to-do circles. Especially in the beginning, the jewellery was characterised by being Art Nouveau and often had organic motifs like plants, animals and insects. Wearing Georg Jensen jewellery then was synonymous with being fashion-conscious and indicated that you had money. Georg Jensen became famous and coveted in the rest of the world, and the company opened stores in New York, among other places. Georg Jensen Silversmith became the first splash of Danish design that was later to become a much bigger wave.

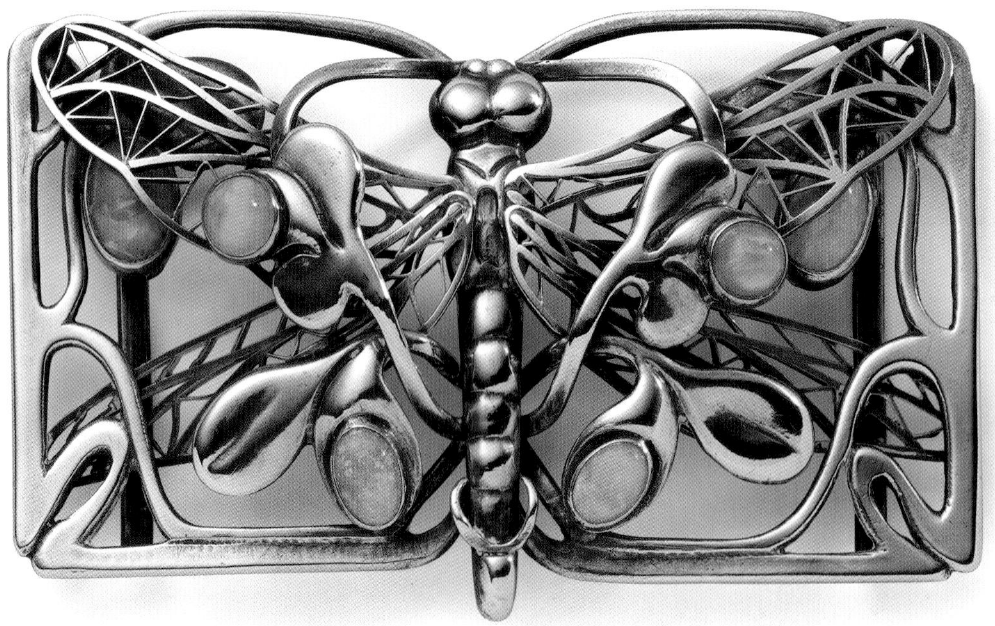

▲ *A belt buckle from 1903 – designed and executed by Georg Jensen. It's called the Dragonfly buckle and is made of silver and opals. The style is Art Nouveau.*

DURING THE PROSPERITY boom and the youth rebellion in the 1960s, the world changed. Values changed. Wealth wasn't something that everyone found important, on the contrary, it was fashionable to be an inverted snob and drive a Citroen 2CV even though you could afford a better car. In the field of jewellery, 'ready made' was a new phenomenon. These were everyday articles that originally had another use, but could be used to adorn oneself and were ingenious and cheap.

One example is this series of bracelets, which according to history was made by the young designer Ketty Dalsgaard. She found these nylon rings for fishing nets in a little fishing harbour north of Copenhagen in 1972. Originally they were white, but by soaking them in tea overnight, they turned golden. Later on she used tie-dye colours. A few years later the jewellery company Buch + Deichmann marketed her design which became very popular. Part of their collection can be seen here at left.

▲ *Throughout the 20th century, Georg Jensen worked with a vast number of designers, most of them Danes. One of them, Nanna Ditzel, created many original pieces of jewellery, using relatively simple shapes. This is a different artistic idiom than the traditional Georg Jensen style and much more modern. These pieces of jewellery are admired by a different set of people from those who prefer the original Georg Jensen design, which however still sells well.*

DROPS OF DEW is the name of this piece of jewellery by goldsmith and designer Mette Saabye. It is a work that sits on the border of design and art. Saabye belongs to a group of new, young Danish jewellery designers that works with very artistic designs, but also makes series productions like the rings with the joint name 'Mokume'.

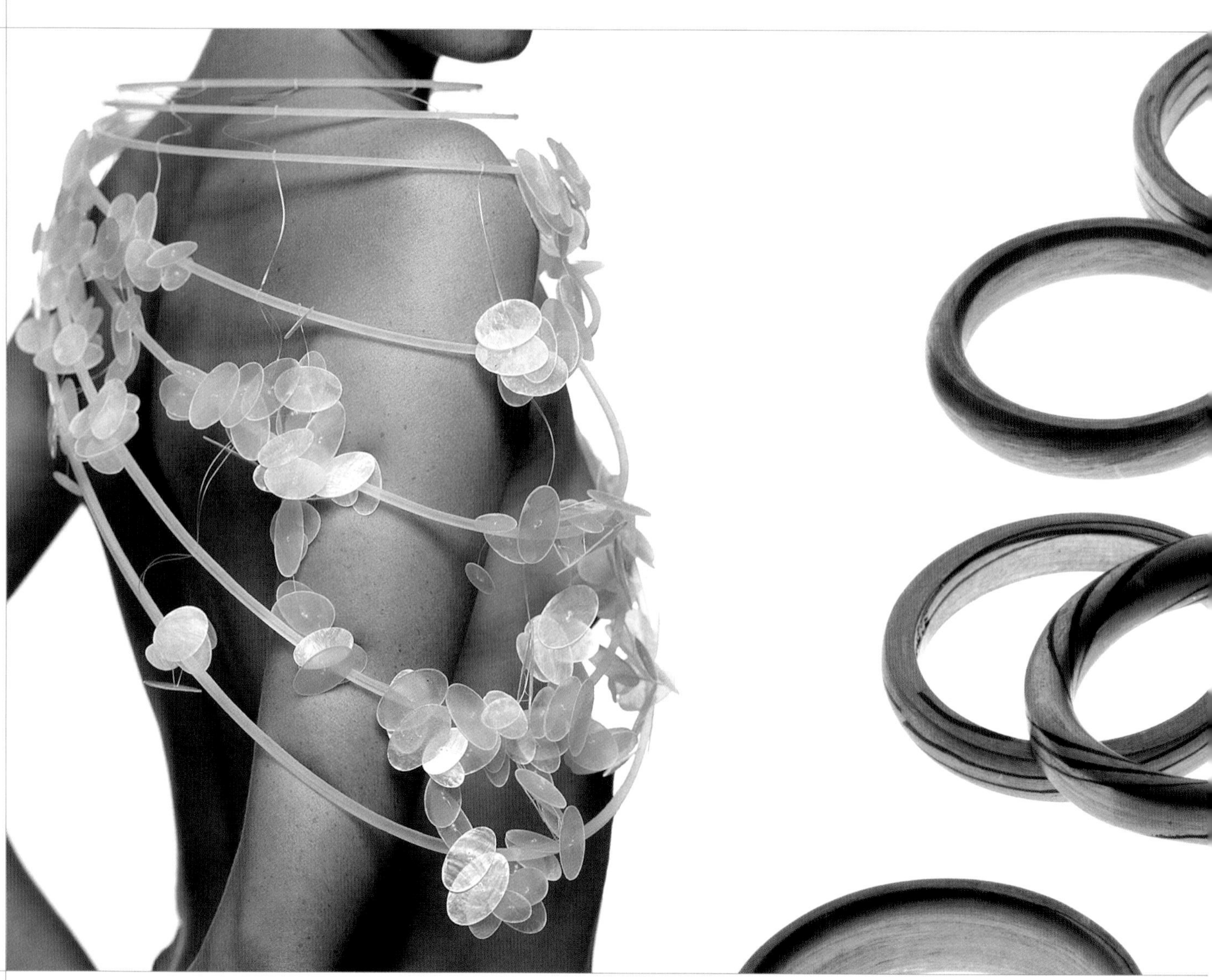

ON HER HOMEPAGE Mette Saabye says of her work, 'Jewellery is ornament, and an ornament is based on the art of jewellery whether it is limited to basic form or designed with rich detail. For decades the word ornament has been a naughty word because it is associated with superfluous decoration, frippery without content. For me the great challenge is to create jewellery with content, it is a story that has to be told. At the same time I want to relate to the basic criteria for the definition of jewellery – that it is something worn on the body, that it marks social status, represents a material value and is part of a functional context'.

▾ *Mette Saabye's rings with the joint name 'Mokume'.*

Where does Danish design come from?

First of all it's debatable whether there is something that definitely can be called Danish design. Of course there is design that's from Denmark because it was made by Danes, Danish designers and Danish companies. But there are those who claim that there's no point in distinguishing between the design of various countries anymore. In short, their opinion is that practically all design in the last 50–70 years belongs to an international style. Since almost every company sells their products on the global market, they can't afford to be national in their design. And since most designers and design schools have a very international outlook, they don't feel they have a reason or need to cultivate a specific national style.

Nonetheless, many people, both Danes and foreigners, claim that there is something special about Danish design. There is something that gives you the impression that, for example, a product, a building or a living room is typically Danish. For most people it's difficult to point out the exact aspect of the object or environment that makes them say, "Exactly here you can see what makes it Danish".

Many people will recognise this when they're out travelling. Then you unconsciously realise that you're not back home anymore. It could be the change in the landscape or the language of the street signs that brings it about. But even in towns where you can't see the landscape and in areas where there aren't many street signs you clearly sense a different culture in the design. And if you visit a private home, company or institution abroad, you sense a different and distinctive way of arranging things. Something as commonplace as an outlet can be among the revealing factors.

Of course the cosmopolitan aspect has come to the fore in recent years. Now there's a McDonalds on every other street corner, IKEA is found in almost every country in the world, and the EU tries to harmonise everything it can get its hands on. Yet there still seems to be something you can't avoid calling Danish design. Among other things, landscape, climate and available resources have a great influence on people and are contributory factors in shaping the architecture and design of a country.

DANISH DESIGN HAS SPRUNG FROM THE LANDSCAPE

Go to a typical place in the Danish countryside such as South Funen and you will see the rolling landscape with softly undulating hills. There is nothing sharp here, no cliffs, no gorges, no high mountains – only rich and fertile soil. It's a typical Danish landscape formed thousands of years ago by the glaciers of the last Ice Age. At one point in time, a kilometre-thick layer of ice covered this area that was later to become part of Denmark. The ice had travelled heavily and relentlessly from northern Scandinavia, bringing huge amounts of rock, gravel and clay with it. The result is the moraine formation we know today.

Then go to Svendborg and visit Erik Jørgensen's Furniture Factory. Since 1995 they have manufactured a special sofa called Waves, which was designed by Anne-Mette Jensen and Morten Ernst for a competition arranged by the classic furniture makers themselves. Does something strike you? The landscape and the sofa are practically reflections of each other. Lying on Waves is almost like lying in a meadow and looking up at the clouds in the sky. This piece of furniture is obviously not a copy of the landscape – it's not naturalism and not upholstered in artificial grass. It is a creative example of poetic design.

THE DANISH DESIGNER Verner Panton, who mostly designed furniture, lamps and textiles, designed Panton Dish in 1988. Like the sofa below it also has a wave motif, but it is said that Panton was inspired by a drawing that had been crumpled up and thrown away. When it had been picked up and smoothed out again, the idea for this dish arose.

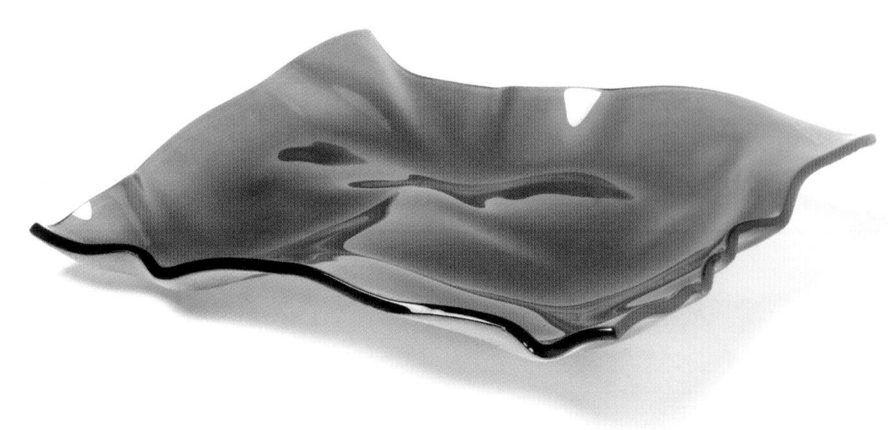

▼ *The lounge sofa Waves from Erik Jørgensen's Furniture Factory, designed by Anne-Mette Jensen and Morten Ernst in 1995.*

THE SHAPE OF the landscape is accentuated when winter snow covers the land. In Henning Koppel's organic design in silver made in the post-war era for Georg Jensen you can almost envision the snowy landscape in the cold material. Henning Koppel was a trained sculptor and very fond of nature. His watercolours of snow landscapes are characterised by the same shapes and cold tones as his works in silver.

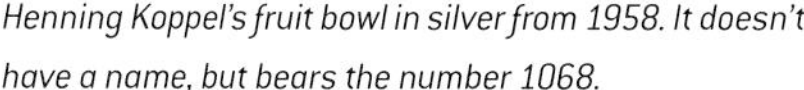

Henning Koppel's fruit bowl in silver from 1958. It doesn't have a name, but bears the number 1068.

Perhaps the two designers weren't thinking of the landscape when they created Waves? Possibly the ocean was their inspiration? Perhaps they just wanted to make a piece of furniture that would be nice to lounge and talk in? No matter what thoughts or inspiration are behind the work, just like many other pieces of Danish furniture, it reminds us of something familiar, something we find pleasant. Of course there is something universally human in our fascination of these round and soft contours, and quite a number of designers in other countries have also used them. Nevertheless, there are many examples of Danish designers and companies that have used this artistic idiom, for example the logo for the Royal Copenhagen Factory with its three wavy lines and Arne Jacobsen's chair the Egg and the Swan.

The landscape is not the only thing that has contributed to forming the Danish national mind and Danish design. People have also shaped the land, so that much of what we today believe is nature is actually man-made, albeit from generations ago. Agriculture has left its mark on the landscape everywhere in Denmark. There is hardly a patch of land in this kingdom that hasn't been cultivated and regulated in one way or another. Today it can be almost impossible to say what is cause and what is effect or even imagine what the country looked like millennia ago.

The prehistoric 'Danes' began marking the land not only by deforestation and plowing, but even more distinctively by creating memorials in the form of burial mounds. It is impressive to think how much earth, stone and peat had to be moved by hand to make the 85,000+ burial mounds of all sizes that have been registered in Denmark. Apart from marking one or more burial sites, the mounds seemingly had no other purpose than to be a vantage point and a place where signal fires, the so-called beacons, could be lit.

The reshaping of the land has sometimes even been adapted as a grand national strategy, as when Dalgas said 'What was lost abroad must be won at home' and headed the reclamation of the great moors in Jutland after the war in 1864. Since then, Danes have advocated for the preservation of nature and it has in modern times become much more difficult to build in the open countryside or close to the coast. The designer and social critic Poul Henningsen spoke in the 1930s against having an overly romanticised view of nature. PH, as he was called, and others saw railway bridges, power pylons and other similarly big works as symbols of progress and better times. New views of eco-friendly design have been put forth since then, and the public's view of nature has become more protective over time.

Nonetheless plants must be built and roads must be planned where nature is, too. But now when a motorway is going to be built, it might as well be done beautifully by routeing the road as gently as possible through the landscape. In the US as well as other countries with a pioneer mentality there is a tradition of using a ruler to plan roads and then let loose the bulldozers. You'll often see a road that cuts right through a hill instead of going around it. In Denmark there is a tradition of letting major roads wind between hills and go around bogs and hollows. Thus you don't have to move as much earth, plus you get roads that are more varied to drive on, which also makes it less likely that the driver will fall asleep at the wheel on the long stretches.

◀ One of the Superellipse tables that Piet Hein designed together with the Swedish furniture designer and manufacturer Bruno Mathsson in 1964. Today the table is produced by Fritz Hansen. The most common version of the table is in white laminate with aluminium edging, but this version, with its obligatory and very popular self-clamping legs, has a walnut top.

▶ A Piet Hein Superellipse Egg in silver lying among rounded stones at the water's edge.

▼ A stretch of a motorway in Eastern Jutland. It winds its way gently through the landscape, which was formed by the Ice Age.

The effect of the Ice Age can be seen in places other than the great landscapes. After a trip through the hilly countryside on Funen, you can walk down to the water and find a myriad of stones that have been ground down by the glaciers of the past and then polished smooth by the water's movement. Some of the stones are very round while most just don't have sharp edges. A few even look like Piet Hein's Superellipse Egg.

Piet Hein constructed the Superellipse by using a mixture of applied intuition and mathematical work. The result was the equation for a figure that is described as a curve that lies between the ellipse and the rectangle. Originally the task was to solve a city-planning problem. On the 200-meter long rectangular Sergel's Square in Stockholm, two traffic arteries were to meet in a very large roundabout. The idea was to find the best and smoothest way of getting the heavy traffic to flow. The end result was this form, which also became a basin with several hundred fountains and beneath it a square for pedestrians and a restaurant in the same shape.

The shape has been used for many purposes, the most well-known is probably the Superellipse table, which was first produced by the Swedish firm Bruno Mathsson in 1964, and from 1968 by the furniture company Fritz Hansen. Furthermore it's been used for serving trays and platters, cutting boards and board games. Concurrently, a three-dimensional form was made, the so-called Superegg, in many sizes with many purposes: as a silver replacement for ice cubes, a series of china bowls, lamps made out of glass, candlesticks etc. Some of the products are certainly more successful than others. A good solution to one problem can't necessarily be transferred to other purposes.

THE GIFTS OF NATURE

In earlier times, it was often emphasised during environmental studies at elementary school, that Denmark wasn't blessed by very many natural riches, by which is was implied that we didn't have coal and iron, and therefore we had to use our brains. This was before oil was found in the North Sea, but it doesn't change the fact that historically we have had to import many raw materials from abroad.

Of course the country has had natural resources, otherwise people wouldn't have settled here in the Early Ice Age. The first migrants came from the south in the summer to hunt reindeer on the woodless tundra, which covered southern Scandinavia at that time (circa 12,000–14,000 years ago). Since then, that is about 3000–4000 years later in the Early Stone Age, more permanent settlements were established. People lived as hunters and gatherers. There was abundant animal life in the woods, plenty of fish and shellfish in the fjords and bays, not to mention the possibility of gathering eggs, berries, roots and nuts.

In addition to the edible resources, the Stone Age family also needed materials from which to fashion weapons, tools, vessels, shelter and clothing. Weapons and tools were made of stone, bone and wood. Especially those made of stone have been found in abundance. Many farmers have found interesting flint tools in or even on top of the dark topsoil.

In 1997, the leader of the Danish Liberal Party, Uffe Ellemann-Jensen, wrote an essay for the anthology *Design Essays*, compiled by The Association of Danish Designers. Unfortunately they were never able to find a publisher for the book.

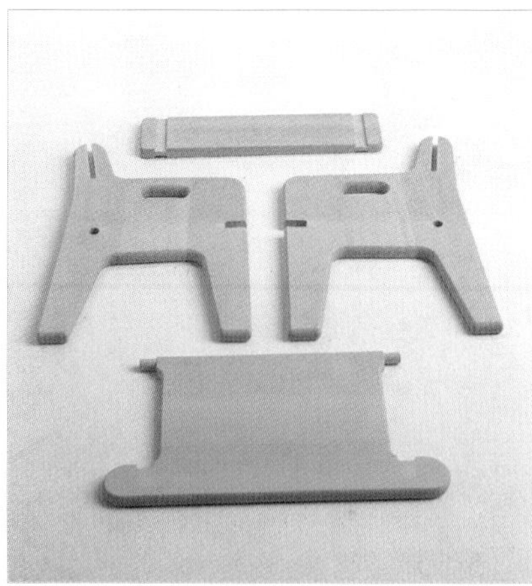

IN 1944, THE furniture architect Hans J. Wegner lived in Aarhus and worked at Arne Jacobsen's architectural practice, designing the interior and furnishing the city's new town hall. In 1937, Arne Jacobsen and Erik Møller had submitted the design of the building in a competition and won. When Wegner was told that his good friend Børge Mogensen, who was the head of FDB Furniture (the Danish co-op movement's design office), had had a son, Peter, he went looking for a christening present for Peter. But as this was

The former Foreign Minister begins his contribution with, 'On my desk lies an old stone axe that was found by my grandfather near my birthplace on Funen. I often pick it up and hold it. It lies comfortably in my hand. It's beautiful to look at. Elegant shapes. Brilliant use of the material. It has a good balance. It must also have laid well in the hand of the ancestor who used it and made the dents in the axe's blunt edge.'

It might sound pretentious, but these flint tools were some of history's first Danish designs and were certainly some of the most long-lasting. But implements weren't only made of stone. Stone Age man often lived at subsistence level, and every possible resource had to be used in order to survive. Energy and ingenuity had to be mobilised to wrench an existence out of nature. They couldn't afford to let anything go to waste which might make the difference between life and death in the cold of winter. Therefore the finds that have been made show that everything on a killed animal was used. Bones became tools, clubs, sewing needles and much more. The hide was obviously used for winter clothing, but also for tent canvas. The meat was dried and saved. Tendons were used as thread. Even parts of the reindeer's antlers were used as chisels when flint tools were made. And what can we learn from this today when evaluating Danish design in hindsight?

From early times, the Danes have been inventive with the raw materials they had at their disposal. Truly valuable minerals have never been found in the Danish subsoil. Due to our geography, amber is about the closest we have to something precious. The climate was seldom good enough to produce luxuriant vegetation on the farmer's field. It took hard work to make ends meet. Denmark may well lie at the mouth of the Baltic Sea and at times could demand Øresund-tariff from the passing ships, but in spite of this, Denmark was seldom rewarded handsomely by the trade that passed through the region. Danish citizens, craftsmen, farmers and companies had to import materials such as coal, iron and other metals to make modern and effective implements, tools and machines. And they had to pay for it dearly, so one can't blame them for being careful. Danes soon learned to be creative and make much of very little. When the Danes were victorious, whether it was on the world market or in other forms of competitions, it was usually a victory based on hard work.

Stone Age people were masters of working with stone since it was the material that was best suited and available for their hunting tools and other implements. In our eyes, the most beautiful examples are the carefully tooled axe heads from the Neolithic Period, 4000–6000 years ago. This is a 22 cm head from a battle-axe that was found in a stone cist grave on Vroue Hede (heath), south of Skive in 1974. The axe head was made by a very talented stone worker in greenstone, which is easier to work with than flint.

near the end of World War II, there was nothing to be found in the shops.

On a Sunday, Wegner went to a cabinetmaker's workshop, which he had been given permission to use. He made a chair for Peter, and it consisted of only four parts that didn't need screws, nails or glue to be assembled. The chair's parts fit ingeniously together, so when the back rest is slid into the grooves of the two sides, the parts are firmly joined, and the chair is a completely stable construction. Later on he designed a small table for it. When Børge Mogensen received the chair in Copenhagen, he immediately said, 'We can make this at FDB'. And that's what happened, and as Hans J. Wegner once said on a television program, 'Back then it cost about 11 or 12 kroner. It is still sold today, but now it costs a fortune'.

Peter's chair is a recent example of how strict rationing of resources can force designers to be imaginative and creative. Perhaps this lack of natural resources more than anything else is what has made the Danes a design-orientated society? Danish common sense certainly resulted in clean lines of design using natural materials and led to the Danish breakthrough in furniture after WW II. The American film icon, Orson Welles, put it another way, 'The enemy of art is the absence of limitations'.

The Hjortspring boat – a 2400-year-old war canoe

Wood is the material that more than anything else is associated with Danish design. Just like today, there was clay under the Danish topsoil, and obviously beautiful cloth was woven from Danish wool and flax. But nonetheless it was wood that has promoted Danish design, whether we're talking about good furniture and interiors or sought-after Danish sailboats. Very early on wood and good craftsmanship played a significant role in society. Perhaps not so much in furniture making as it is today, but definitely so in the making of boats.

There isn't much left of Denmark's first boats. But the remains we have of the few excavated vessels have been patiently cleaned, dried and assembled like a three-dimensional puzzle of something we can learn from today. That's how we know quite a bit about how our forefathers built ships and the significance these vessels had in their time. This knowledge is sometimes used to tell vivid stories about how events unfolded.

One of these stories is written in several archeological works about the landing and battle at Als around the year 350 BC. A small invasion army of about 100 warriors paddled their way to the shore in big, open boats, went ashore and were defeated by the local warriors. Today we have an idea of what happened because one of the boats along with quite a few weapons and other equipment was sunk in the Hjortspring bog, presumably as a celebration of victory.

The sunken boat, a type of war canoe that the attackers arrived in, was an impressive vessel of about 19 metres in length and nearly two metres wide at its broadest point. Weighing only 530 kg it was very light in comparison to its size. As well, it had a flat bottom, so that when 20 warriors propelled it forward, it shot through the water and could practically glide up onto the beach.

Previously it was thought that the boats in the early Iron Age were primitive and only suitable for short trips near the coast. But several copies of the Hjortspring boat have been built, and after many voyages it has proven to be a fantastic vessel. With a full crew, that is, the 20 men who paddled it and at least a helmsman and maybe a leader, it could sail long distances with a speed of 4–5 knots (about 8–9 km per hour). It is so seaworthy that it has been possible to sail across the Baltic Sea to and from Northern Germany, or from Northern Jutland to Sweden via Læsø in 12 hours. Even in bad weather it does quite well.

The boat, which archaeologists have excavated from Hjortspring Bog, was made of lime-wood. The trees used for its construction must have been sizeable since only five planks were used for the boat's hull. The bottom plank is the longest and was over 15 metres long. Since the planks were 65 cm wide, the lime trees must have been about 20–25 metres high in order to have the necessary diameter of 65–70 cm. There aren't such big lime trees in Denmark anymore, so in order to build a copy of the boat, it was necessary to import lime tree trunks from Poland.

The boat is different from boats from a later period in that it doesn't have a proper keel. The bottom plank constitutes a kind of platform for the rest of the construction, and all the other load-bearing elements are built up around this plank. There are two planks on each side that are sewn to the bottom plank with lime bast rope.

Then there are the stem blocks that constitute the stem and stern, to which each side is sewn. Thus it is a shell construction that has been stretched to its final shape by ingenious lattice constructions. These battens, as they're called, hold the frame and the small, well-shaped thwarts which the crew sat on. The hull was caulked with a type of putty that was possibly made of beef tallow as a binding agent.

At both ends there are two trunk-like pieces of wood that protrude from the bottom plank and gunwale, respectively. Their purpose is not known. Perhaps they were like handles that made manoeuvring close to coast and handling on land easier, and possibly they were a kind of ornament. The upper and lower 'trunks' were joined by an oak branch with an engraved pattern. Apart from that the boat wasn't decorated.

All in all, this constitutes a very sturdy boat. And even though it doesn't have a single bit of metal in it, it's an advanced construction that bears comparison to our wooden vessels today. At this time in history, the use of sails was unknown in our neck of the woods. Manual power was the only propellant, and if you look at the design of the 1.5 meter long, slim ores, they're not much different from those we use today. The seaworthiness of the vessel is very good and indicates great experience in building boats as well as an intuitive understanding of the forces of water and weather that are to be overcome.

The design qualities of the boat lie partly in its clean lines, which are a result of the long planks, and partly in the excellent craftsmanship. Saws were not used in constructing it; only various axes and knives and drills that made it possible to bind the hull together. The most impressive thing is that it was possible to create a very light and seaworthy vessel out of wood with the tools that were available at that time.

The round chair

Throughout history wood has been Denmark's greatest resource. At times so much forest was cleared to give room for farm land that the Crown put its foot down and ordered re-forestation. And when the British in 1807 took off with the Danish fleet, there was a wood crisis in Denmark since there wasn't enough wood, especially oak, with which to build new ships for the Navy. So after the war in 1807, 90,000 oak trees were planted in Northern Zealand. However, since oak grows slowly, it wasn't until recently that the oak trees were big enough to be used as lumber for ships.

Wood continued to be an important material, so much so that it had to be imported, which is still largely the case today. The Danish furniture designers definitely didn't stick to Danish types of wood. For example, teak furniture became the trademark abroad for Danish design around 1960. However, it's the cabinetmakers' and designers' work throughout the first half of the 20th century that became the basis of the identifiably Danish design that made its international breakthrough after World War II.

A good example of the organic artistic idiom, the unique carpentry and the modern, simple design typical of Danish work is Hans J. Wegner's 'Round Chair' from 1949. On the one hand, this chair was very simple, yet on the other hand, characterised by very sophisticated carpentry. The first four chairs were made of oak with a woven cane seat for the annual exhibition of the Cabinetmakers' Guild in 1949. It was produced by Johannes Hansen Cabinetmakers from 1950 and later went on to be

▸ The Hjortspring boat was made of lime wood. At the time of its construction planks weren't riveted together with iron rivets as was done in the Viking Age. Instead the Hjortspring boat is sewn together with lime rope bast.

▾ In 1999, the Hjortspring Boat's Guild from Nordborg on the island of Als finished a copy of the original vessel and has since gone on short and long voyages every summer. In honour of the photographer, they dressed in the clothes of that time – though, during the surprise attack on Als in about 350 BC, one would have presumed that the warriors would have been dressed in more subdued colours and had rowed the boat in a more energetic fashion.

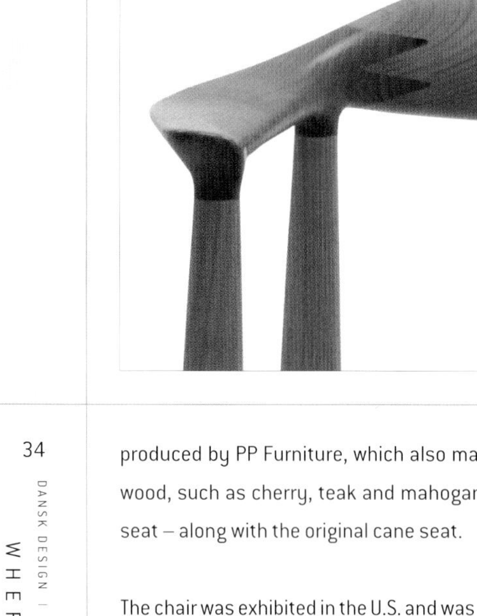

◂ In 'The Round Chair', Wegner used so-called zigzag joints, which formerly had only been used in hidden joints, such as doors that were veneered afterwards. This honest way of joining would also be a characteristic of Danish design in general – we don't hide the construction behind veneer, but make it as beautiful a form as possible.

produced by PP Furniture, which also manufactured it in other types of wood, such as cherry, teak and mahogany with an upholstered leather seat – along with the original cane seat.

The chair was exhibited in the U.S. and was featured on the cover of a major design magazine and got the nickname 'The Chair', since the Americans thought it was the ultimate chair. The highlight of the chair's progress was when it was used for the last, great TV debate between the presidential candidates John F. Kennedy and Richard Nixon in 1960. The Chair became the symbol of the golden age of Danish design when the economical use of wood as a resource was combined with the meticulous craftsmanship that gave Danish design an extravagant head start in the post-war world of furniture and design.

▸ Hans J. Wegner's 'The Round Chair' has four identical legs that bear the seat as well as the beautifully formed combination of arm and back rest. The joint between the armrest and backrest has been praised in professional circles ever since. Look how the arm rests have the flat, broad side upwards, so you can rest your arms, but then are transformed into the vertical backrest. The organic transition between armrest and backrest, almost like a sentient being, expresses the beauty of the post-war era's competence and respect for materials in a time when there was still a shortage of them.

Parts of the Flora Danica service are still made today and can be bought by anyone, of course, at sky-high prices since the edges are covered in real gold and much paint work is done on every piece. Some of the illustrative decorations can seem a bit stiff and out of proportion as they're transcribed unedited and in full size from the botanical work Flora Danica.

Fixed nature

As regards design, nature did not only manifest itself through the use of wood. Sometimes it happened through the use of motifs. Porcelain in particular has been a popular and suitable medium for this type of design. One of the first national design projects was the dinner service 'Flora Danica'. The development of it began around 1790 at the Royal Copenhagen Factory as a prestigious project. The first service for about 100 people was to be given by the Danish king to the Russian Empress Catherine II.

The Flora Danica service's many decorations are taken directly from the botanical work of the same name on a scale of 1:1. Thus the service, which amounted to 1802 pieces, became a national manifestation. The reason why it was to be given to the Russian empress was to mitigate the strained political climate between the two nations. The production was halted by royal decree in 1802, when the empress had been dead for six years. The service never made it to Russia, but the more than 1500 extant pieces are to be found among the collections of the various castles.

Today, nature is not a rare design motif. Often articles for everyday use in the kitchen or on the dining room table are inspired by the imagery of nature. One example of this is Arje Griegst's 'Ocean Tureen', which just like Flora Danica was made at Royal Copenhagen. This soup tureen was designed in 1975 and is also a preliminary study for a coffee service called 'Konkylie' (Conch).

▸ The original Ga-Jol logo is from 1933 and has on the whole remained the same ever since. That's when Galle & Jessen introduced their licorice and menthol lozenges, hence the name Ga-Jol: Ga for Galle, J for Jessen and OL for menthol. A throat lozenge that is appropriate for the Danish weather. Today Galle & Jessen is owned by Toms. Exactly who designed the logo and packaging has been lost in the company's history, but it was most likely an anonymous employee. The blue Ga-Jol box was awarded the Danish Design Center's prize for 'classic design' in 2001.

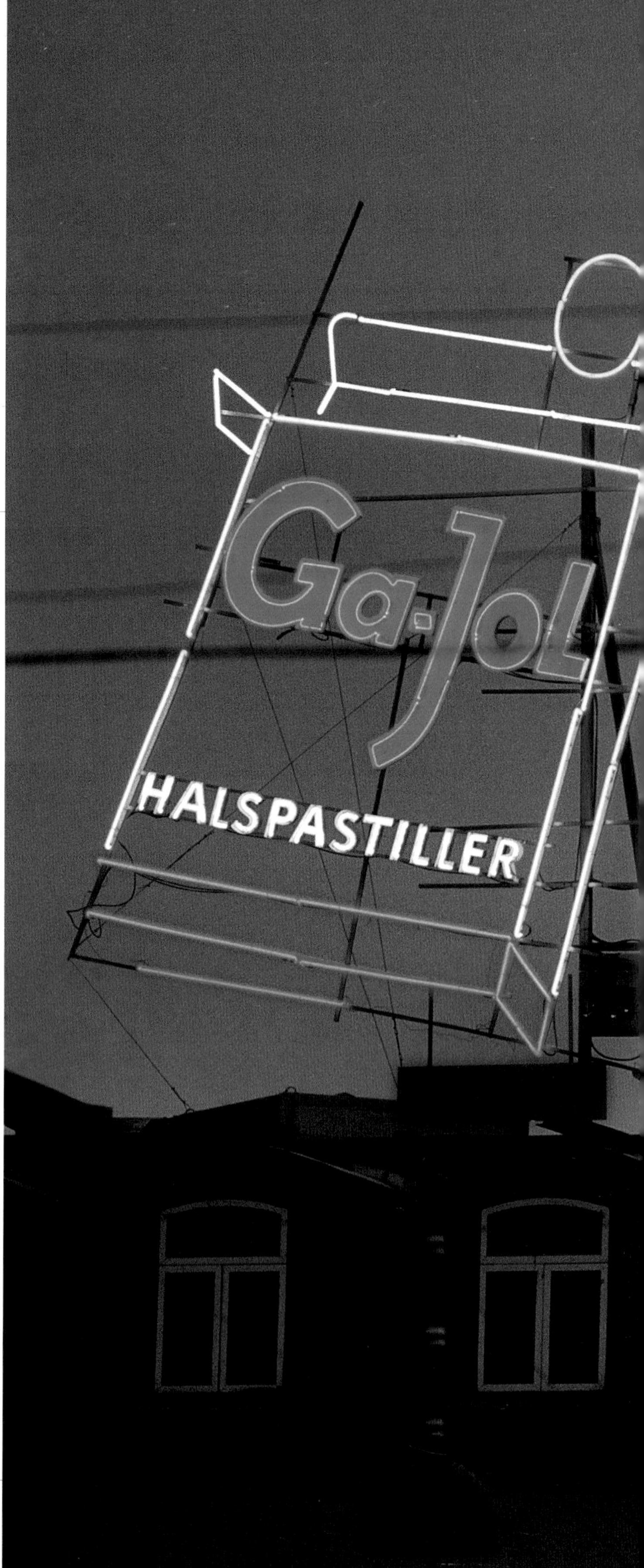

IN STIFF WINDS AND RAIN

'The Danish weather is Ga-Jol weather' could be read for many years on one of Copenhagen's many neon signs. Ga-Jol is a Danish throat lozenge. The sign was on the façade of the company's building on Vibenhus Runddel from 1969, but when the original factory was torn down a few years ago, the sign was moved to Vesterbrogade. The advertisement plays on the idea that the Danish climate is very changeable and that cold, rain and rough weather can be hard on Danish throats.

The climate has always been a significant factor in the design of many things, from the way we construct our houses to apparel and even how some companies sell their throat lozenges. Symbolically, many older homes turn their backs on the predominant west wind and look like they're hunkering down while it whistles around them. And then there are those who don't seek shelter, but live in harmony with nature. They take advantage of the wind and build windmills, which has been a Danish speciality for many decades.

But of course the Danish climate is determined by its northerly location, and thus the little sunlight we have in certain seasons. And we react like other nationalities that live in the north. We enjoy living boisterously outdoors in summer, and when it gets dark in winter, we snuggle up indoors and take great pains in designing our homes. If you go to southern Europe, you'll find a completely different lifestyle. There it's much too hot in the middle of the day, so the locals prefer to stay out of the sun. But if you go to a Greek restaurant in the evening, you come in from the pitch-black night and are perhaps puzzled by the glaring fluorescent ceiling lights which are the only source of light. Foreigners who have lived in Denmark

Det danske vejr
r Ga-Jol - vejr

for a while say that the most typical thing about Danes is our concept of cosiness. We love to have a cosy time, and this is evident in the way we furnish our homes and particularly in our use of lighting. We have many sources of light, which we like to supplement with candles and a wood-burning stove. The light should preferably be indirect and warm, not cold and fluorescent. It's not just about getting light, it has to be pleasant too. It's about furnishing your lair, turning your back on the cold, dark winter and virtually going into hibernation in winter.

One of the first pioneers in lighting, electric lighting, was Poul Henningsen. He was a young man in the 1920s, a self-taught architect, and was interested in the new incandescent light bulbs, which were replacing candles and oil and gas lamps. PH's mother was the author Agnes Henningsen, and she was a bit vain and thought the new-fangled lamps gave a harsh light that revealed all her wrinkles. It's said that this was PH's motivation for designing lamps more suitable for the electric bulbs than the hat-like lampshades on the market.

Poul Henningsen's solution was to construct a different type of light fittings with a system of shades that allowed the light to shine but not blind you, since the bulb couldn't been seen from any angle. The light radiated in the directions it was needed. Furthermore, the new PH lamps were painted red and blue on the inside in order to counteract the incandescent bulb's yellow light. Danish cosiness had a new light source that suited Danish living rooms and the way we like to arrange things.

YOU'RE NOT ALONE, DENMARK – THE FOREIGN INFLUENCE

As a counterbalance to the typically Danish, partly derived from the above-mentioned natural conditions, is a great exchange with other countries. Not only with our neighbouring countries, but at times with other continents. Originally, Danish design was not particularly unique in that the first settlers had migrated here from the south and colonised the country bringing their own weapons, tools and customs. Probably hundreds or even thousands of years went by before an independent culture arose in the Danish region, and Denmark as a nation was still thousands of years away.

Yet even after a permanent settlement was established and one can begin to talk about a kind regional distinctiveness, there continues to be a great spillover effect from the lands beyond. Foreign influence in technological areas alone has been crucial to our development. Just think of the progress in the Bronze and then Iron Ages which definitely must have come from abroad as the raw materials needed to cast and forge tools, weapons and other implements were not very abundant in Denmark. So all the necessary know-how must also have been imported. But there is no doubt that the locals made their mark in design and ornamentation once they learned the techniques.

Maybe we need to go to the Viking culture to find something characteristically Danish or Nordic. And yet during this very expansive period, the Danes became Christians, albeit reluctantly, and thus imported a religion with its own new culture. So perhaps especially when the Vikings went abroad on expeditions, they were open to learning new things and seeing the world in new ways.

◂ *The house in Taagense on the island of Lolland was constructed so it gets maximum protection from the strong west wind. The roof on the gable, which faces west, has been extended and shaped so it looks like a snow plough that's attached to the house. It also serves the purpose of providing a place to store wood and the like.*

▾ *The traditional Danish concept of cosiness often includes things like wooden furniture in classic designs and many small sources of light. By lighting candles, intimate areas are created in a large room.*

It seems that both in times of adversity and good fortune there has been a lot of contact with the outside world, yet it did not lead to an obliteration of Danish culture. Quite the opposite, for when ideas, culture, technologies and thus design were introduced, they became an integrated part of Danish culture and were further developed into something unique.

The story of the stools

Just outside the village of Vamdrup, a good ten kilometres southeast of Kolding, a burial mound was excavated in 1891 revealing Scandinavia's oldest preserved piece of furniture. It was a folding stool from about 1400 BC, that is from the Bronze Age. It was made of ash, and the remains of a seat made of otter skin was also found. This little piece of furniture with a seat height of 24 cm was a symbol of the deceased's high status and dignity. In all probability it wasn't customary for ordinary people to use furniture and certainly not of this type.

The two wooden frames were held together by rivets, probably made of bronze, but we don't know for sure since they weren't found. Before the stool was buried in Guldhøj we know it was used, since the spindle on one of the frames had been replaced. There is only a single decoration on the top of the two frames, three long rows of line ornamentation on each crossbar. This stool was made locally, but where does the style come from? Is it also local or at least northern European?

In Thebes in ancient Egypt a similar stool was found from around the same time as the one in Guldhøj, that is 1450–1400 BC. It's made of cedar and is a little slimmer and the woodwork is more elegantly executed than the Danish one.

◂ *The Guldhøj stool, 1400 BC*

WHERE DOES DANISH DESIGN COME FROM?

This is not the only or oldest stool of this design to be found or pictured in ancient Egypt, but it's the best preserved. This type of chair, which was first used as a ceremonial piece of furniture, can actually be traced even further back in time to Mesopotamia. When the stool from Guldhøj was made, the model was common as a chieftain's or commander's chair all over Europe and the Middle East. It was almost as international as IKEA furniture is today, but the first Danish version is one of the best preserved examples in Europe.

As a type, the folding stool is a very old piece of furniture. Many Danish furniture designers have since used this archetype to create their own personal interpretation of it. Taking an older model and revising it was typical of a whole generation of Danish designers from the beginning of the 20th century. These new interpretations often began with simplifying the original, but could also entail using a new technique or new material. It's safe to say that the folding stools at high prices didn't sell like hotcakes. Most of them weren't even made with a view to selling them, but were rather seen as a challenging task in design and they were used for exhibitions and teaching.

A beautiful example of a new interpretation of the folding stool is Kaare Klint's propeller-like version from 1930. Originally it was made as one or two prototypes for the annual exhibition organised by the Cabinetmakers' Guild in 1965. The principle behind the shaping of the frames, which are made of ash, was that a pole was cut with a fine-bladed band saw in a spiral pattern. So even when the stool was folded, it would be a beautiful piece of furniture.

Unfortunately a saw blade takes off too much wood for the two propeller halves to fit together nicely again. So each half had to be made separately and create the illusion that they originated from one piece of wood. The seat could be made of ox hide or canvas. A limited number of the stool has since been produced.

A generation later, the furniture designer Poul Kjærholm took the idea one step further when he switched from using wood to matt, chrome-plated flat steel. In 1961, he ingeniously retained the propeller motif when he drafted the stool that was given the model name PK 41. The sublime thing about his design is that when the steel is twisted 180 degrees, it ends up turning in just the right places. The steel rests perfectly on the floor, distributing the weight of the construction equally, and the same is true of the seat. In the middle of the frame, where the hub goes, the two steel pieces are completely flat, which is also optimal. Everything forms a synthesis on this stool, which like Klint's is made with a canvas or leather seat.

In the course of time, many Danish furniture designers have made their own version of the Mesopotamian folding stool. The last version to be mentioned in this context was designed in 1965 by Jørgen Gammelgaard, who later became a professor at the Royal Academy of Fine Arts, Furniture School. It resembles Klint's and Kjærholm's in that it also uses the propeller motif, even if it isn't as obvious. Gammelgaard's frame is made of matt chrome-plated steel wire that has been soldered together so that wires revolve like propellers around each other. The hub that holds the two frames together are cleverly integrated in the wires. The seat is made of woven nylon.

▸ *Jørgen Gammelgaard, 1965*

◂ *Kaare Klint, 1930*

▴ *Poul Kjærholm, 1961*

The white gold

While the influence from the outside world regarding the folding stool could have been spontaneous or happenstance, another example from history was more controlled. This is the introduction of porcelain in Denmark and the establishment of the Royal Copenhagen Factory. Many Danes today probably think that blue fluted porcelain is Danish. The truth is that the pattern originates from China, and so does porcelain itself.

Today, porcelain products don't stand out very much. They're just merchandise like much else, but over 250 years ago it was a more serious business. The manufacturing of porcelain began in about the year 900 and for centuries was a special Chinese craft. The recipe for porcelain clay was a strictly guarded secret. Porcelain was first introduced into Europe when the Portuguese opened the seaway south of Africa to the Far East, and in the beginning it was therefore very rare and extremely expensive – almost worth its weight in gold. It was hard to manufacture, and the cost of transport was shocking. Perhaps that's why it was so coveted by European courts where 'the white gold' was a symbol of design perfection.

It was natural for the European monarchs to begin manufacturing porcelain themselves. The first one to master it would gain great prestige and make a fortune at the same time. However, the Chinese weren't willing to cough up the recipe. So for many years, it was a mystery how one could make a substance that was bright white, semitransparent and also harder than any kind of ceramic. Around 1600–1700, the hunt for the secret porcelain formula was a race between the European royal houses. The Danish royal house wanted terribly to jump on the bandwagon but didn't have the resources or connections to the proper scientists.

In 1708 the German pharmacist and alchemist Johann Friedrich Böttger succeeded in figuring out the secret, which is a special mixture of clay called kaolin, feldspar and quartz, and the high firing temperature of 1450 degrees Celsius. This was the foundation for the breakthrough of porcelain-making in Europe, with the first porcelain factory in the Saxon town of Meissen. From here the blue fluted porcelain came to Denmark, and at first it was almost completely copied by the Royal Copenhagen Factory from 1775.

The blue fluted dinnerware has been the most popular in the history of the factory, and its design has been renewed several times, most successfully by the architect Arnold Krog, who in 1885 became the artistic manager when the factory was dwindling. He redesigned the blue fluted porcelain and developed quite new and different decorations, in which Japanese-inspired nature motifs were integrated into the Danish tradition. Soon the factory's wares went from strength to strength in Denmark and abroad.

It's interesting that the social classes in Denmark, for long periods of time from the Viking Age and up to the beginning of the 20th century, have lived in parallel cultures: an imported upper-class culture and a more local and regional peasant culture.

The result of this is that much of the fine and elegant design has been imported or inspired from the south or other parts of the world, among other things furniture, jewellery, clothing and also porcelain. Meanwhile the common people made their own more down-to-earth designs, although they also looked up to the upper-class finery and copied their furniture. Gradually in the wake of a rising prosperity, the blue fluted dinnerware

▾ Many Danes would think that blue fluted porcelain is one of the most Danish designs, but it's really an originally Chinese pattern that has been copied in many places in Europe since the 1700s. The pattern has been redesigned several times since then and adapted to the production at Royal Copenhagen. The latest instance of its development is Karen Kjældgård-Larsen's version, called Mega. She uses a type of graphic sampling in her approach, just like in the world of modern music. The blue fluted Mega is also manufactured in black as a supplement to the blue decorations.

from 'the Royal' came into the homes of ordinary people and became 'grandmother's plates', as some of us remember from our childhoods.

The blue fluted dinnerware was radically redesigned once more by Karen Kjældgård-Larsen (b. 1974). As a young student of design at Denmark's Design School in 1999, she contacted the Royal Copenhagen Factory with her drafts of a new interpretation of the old pattern. That led to the blue fluted Mega, which was launched in the fall of 2000 and has become the company's biggest success in recent times. Since then the pattern has been used for tablecloths and napkins and many other products in the company's portfolio.

Karen Kjældgård-Larsen has practically sampled the pattern in a very modern way and then magnified it in fragments in the way many graphic designers do today. In this way she creates a new and very modern whole. The idea was extended to the bottom of the plates where the company logo, the three wavy lines representing bodies of water Øresund, the Little Belt and the Great Belt, were also enlarged. This adds a note of irony and humour to the design. It's a new way of taking an old Chinese pattern and transforming it into something typically Danish.

KAARE KLINT (1888-1954) was an architect and furniture designer and was apprenticed by his father P.V. Jensen-Klint whose main work, Grundtvig Church, was completed by Kaare in 1930–40. At first he was interested in the same romantic architecture as his father was, but gradually he developed the forerunner of Danish functionalism. Klint drafted his first furniture in 1914 for the Faaborg Museum together with Carl Petersen. Klint's furniture was often typical of older types of furniture from other countries, not least England. Klint also tried to explore the human needs behind the use of furniture. Klint passed on this working method in his teaching at the Royal Academy of Fine Arts' Furniture School from 1924–44. He was professor of architecture from 1944–54. 'The Klint School' reacted especially to German functionalism's rejection of tradition. Klint also designed textiles, lamps for Le Klint and some memorials. He received the Eckersberg Medal in 1928 and the C.F. Hansen medal in 1954.

WE STAND ON THE SHOULDERS OF PAST MASTERS

In the past, Danish architects and designers have often adopted the statement by scientist Isaac Newton, 'If I have been able to see farther than others, it was because I stood on the shoulders of giants.' By that he meant that you don't have to reinvent the wheel every time you begin a new project. Instead you can proudly build upon the experiences of your predecessors.

In past times this was a matter of course, but unfortunately it isn't today when everything has to be new and innovative. The fact that the results of these efforts can end up being farfetched and not very useful doesn't worry anyone. But a generation or two ago, designers who had a degree in architecture were very aware of the history they were a part of. You could learn from your predecessors whether they were Danish or foreigners.

An architect and furniture designer, Kaare Klint often took an older foreign design as his starting point when he drafted his own works. The understanding that an older type of furniture had become a tried and true concept through the ages and could be used as a model was inherent in Klint's way of thinking. If anyone could crystallise a piece of furniture's advantages and discard the unnecessary bits, it was Kaare Klint. And since he and his students made up their minds about what was suitable and what had to be changed in the old model, any discussion about plagiarism or copying became irrelevant. Had anyone less talented attempted to do the same, they would probably have been in big trouble.

Klint was particularly, but not only, interested in working with classic English types of furniture. One of them was the Chippendale chair from the mid-1700s. Several variants were made and simplified over the years. But especially the back rest continued to be decoratively executed, often with intertwining flower-like motifs. Kaare Klint decided to redesign this chair when the old Frederiks Hospital in Bredgade in Copenhagen was converted to the Museum of Art & Design. A lot of chairs were needed and that's how the Chippendale chair came into the picture and became known as 'The Red Chair' due to the colour of the leather seat and back rest.

In Klint's version the underframe of the chair and the seat remain intact, but the carved wooden back is replaced by a back rest upholstered with leather like the seat. He also made the back a bit shorter than the original. According to Klint, this simplification of the chair made the bottom and top more harmonious. As Klint writes, 'What we need is a cheaper underframe and a comfortable back.' The only kind of decoration on this chair is the visible tacks used to mount the upholstery. However, the chair was still exclusive, since it was made of Cuban mahogany and upholstered with red goatskin from Nigeria. Later on, The Red Chair was manufactured in various versions and different sizes.

▸ *For the conversion of Copenhagen's old Frederiks Hospital from 1752 into the Museum of Art & Design, Kaare Klint designed a lot of the furniture in 1927, primarily showcases but also this chair designated for meetings and for use in the museum's auditorium. Originally the chair was upholstered with red-tanned goatskin from Nigeria, hence the name The Red Chair. Today Rud. Rasmussen Cabinetmakers still manufacture it in oxhide in a brownish tone.*

◂ *An example of the original Chippendale chair. The back rest can be found in many versions.*

▲ *An original Chinese chair.*

▲ *Wegner's first Chinese-inspired chair.*

▸ *Wegner's second version of a Chinese chair.*

Four versions of the same thing

While Klint often took his starting point in well-tested furniture and took an analytical approach to making sensible and functional new furniture, his successors and former students went in other directions. One of the most productive furniture architects who made it big after World War II was Hans J. Wegner. He experimented a lot with all the materials of his time: solid wood, steam-bent wood, laminated wood, metal and the many ways of padding and upholstering furniture. He was not particularly inspired by foreign furniture with the notable exception of 'The China Chair'.

Exactly how Wegner became interested in the Chinese chair remains uncertain. The Danish Maritime Museum in Elsinore exhibited some small models of this chair from the Danish China Expedition in 1731. It was also described in literature, for example in Ole Wanscher's book 'The Art of Furniture' from 1932. Anyway, Hans J. Wegner was contacted by Fritz Hansen in 1943 about designing a chair that could be manufactured by steam-bending wood. The same year he designed The China Chair out of cherry and with a removable leather seat cushion. The chair is still in production, but it's very detailed and demands a lot of working hours and meticulousness, so it isn't cheap to put it mildly.

Wegner apparently became especially interested in this type of chair, because two years later, in 1945, he made a simpler version of The China chair. At first it was meant for Fritz Hansen, but later the production went to PP Furniture. The design of this version is mostly based on elements that can be made of round sticks, and it has a woven seat. PP Furniture still produces a revised version of the model.

Four years later Wegner had a new proposal for this theme. It was 'The Round Chair', as previously mentioned. The Round Chair is a simplification of the China Chair, since there are fewer individual parts. On the other hand, it calls for more workmanship and precision and looks even more sophisticated, which has caused the price to go up. This was the chair that generated attention in the US. Yet Wegner's view of the chair was very phlegmatic, 'It could have been made hundreds of years ago, there's nothing new in it.' He also referred to the construction of a traditional side chair. The Round Chair is still produced by PP Furniture in several types of wood and with either a woven seat or padded leather upholstery.

A year after the Round Chair, a more popular version of the China Chair was made. It's called 'The Y-chair' and it became more popular than the others. The individual parts are easier to manufacture, and therefore the price is more affordable. Carl Hansen & Son produce about 17,000 of them a year, which is good for a chair by Wegner. Its Asian roots might be the reason why a fourth of the production goes to the Japanese market – perhaps it's the joy of recognition of a simple and well-proportioned design.

It is thought-provoking and impressive that Wegner succeeded in working his way through a design theme based on an antique Chinese chair and made it such a success. He managed to create the first classic versions (1943, 1945) and the chair that the Americans called The Chair, as it was the ultimate chair, to finally design a chair that achieved widespread popularity and was accepted in the region where its ancestor came from.

As Wegner said in the catalogue for the design exhibition in Philadelphia 1983, *Design Since 1945:*

HANS JØRGENSEN WEGNER (1914–2007) was a furniture architect and trained cabinetmaker in 1931. He studied first at a technical school in Copenhagen and later at The School of Arts and Crafts (1936–38). Afterwards he worked in several architectural practices, among them Arne Jacobsen's in 1940–43. Then he became an independent furniture designer and initially designed furniture for FDB, which was headed by Børge Mogensen. Wegner designed more than 500 chairs. About 100 of them were made, and some are still in production by leading Danish furniture factories. His strength was his deep understanding of carpentry and the qualities of materials. Experiments have often been a driving force for Wegner and his design is characterised by sculptural functionalism. Among his many distinctions are the Lunning Award 1951, the Eckersberg Medal 1956 and the Prince Eugen Medal 1961.

'From an artistic point of view the architects built on and were inspired by the experiences and traditions of the past; they did not want to copy specific styles, but on the other hand, they thought it would be absurd not to learn from what had existed for generations. Many younger architects were especially attracted to the simple rusticity of Danish furniture, to the structural elegance of Windsor chairs, to the honest and restrained expression of Shaker chairs, and to the brilliance of Thonet's bentwood chairs from the middle of the last century. The great historical styles were of interest only when sound structural details could be found, for example in English eighteenth-century furniture.'

Examining the material

Another of Kaare Klint's successors was Poul Kjærholm. He wasn't old enough to be a student of Klint, but from 1976–80 he took the professorship at the Furniture School, which Klint was the first to hold. Kjærholm had the same cabinetmaker's background as Hans J. Wegner, but developed his talent in a different direction. As one of the first furniture designers not to work with wood, Kjærholm concentrated on flat steel. His most well-known piece is the lounge chair PK 22, which is reminiscent of the German architect Mies van der Rohe's 'Barcelona Chair' and the ancient Greek 'Klismos Chair' (see page 68).

Another of Mies' chairs was the subject of Poul Kjærholm's studies and design. In 1930, Mies created 'The Brno Chair' for a wealthy home which he also designed outside of Brno in former Czechoslovakia. The Brno Chair

▸ *The characteristic backrest gave Wegner's Y-chair its name.*

POUL KJÆRHOLM, 1929–80, architect and furniture designer. He was a skilled cabinetmaker and then graduated from The School of Arts & Crafts in 1952, where he also became a teacher. In 1955 he taught at the Royal Academy of Fine Arts, Furniture School, where he succeeded Ole Wanscher as professor in 1976. Kjærholm worked with matt chrome-plated steel, stone, glass, cane work and leather. He was the most important Danish representative of the cool and minimalist international functionalism. His most well-known works are the lounge chairs PK 22 from 1955 and PK 24 from 1965 and the coffee table PK 61 from 1955. For the concert hall at the Louisiana Museum of Modern Art he designed a lightweight folding chair in woven maple to comply with the acoustics. He was awarded the Grand Prix at the Milan Triennale in 1957 and 1960, the Lunning Award in 1958 and the Eckersberg Medal in 1960.

▲ *PK 13, as Poul Kjærholm's interpretation of Mies' chair was called. In matt chrome-plated steel and black leather. Unlike the Brno Chair, the seat is not attached to the legs.*

▸ *A reproduction from Knoll of Mies van der Rohe's Brno Chair in shiny chrome-plated steel and brown leather.*

is a so-called cantilever chair, which means that like the more well-known barber shop chair, it doesn't have back legs but rests on its front legs. That is why this type of chair in Denmark is known as 'a free swinger' because it looks like the seat and the person sitting on it are floating in air.

In 1974, Kjærholm lovingly takes the Brno Chair in hand, and with this project he goes the whole hog. Like Wegner's simplification of the China Chair, Kjærholm tries to pare anything superfluous away. The original China Chair had much that could be simplified, but Mies van der Rohe, who was the director of the Bauhaus School (see page 50) for a while, was a great minimalist himself. So it was harder for Kjærholm to find anything to get rid of. In its time, the Brno Chair was extremely modern and sophisticated, partly because it was a cantilever chair and partly because of the simple and new-fangled choice of material. As you can see in the picture, only chrome-plated flat steel and leather upholstery were used. Kjærholm adapted this type of chair even more, so while Mies attached the seat to the front legs, the two elements are not attached in Kjærholm's chair, which was called PK 13. Thus it's a very radical version of the cantilever chair as the two long runners are only attached to the seat shell at the arm rests. Furthermore, Kjærholm has removed the cross bar at the bottom of the chair, which Mies felt compelled to add to stabilise the chair. And as was Kjærholm's habit, the small Allen bolts in the joints are invisible. Finally, the bushings put space between the steel runners and the shell – yet another way of emphasising that the chair only has three main parts.

It's interesting to ponder the difference between these three highly competent furniture makers – Klint, Wegner and Kjærholm. All three have modified existing international examples into their own high-class versions. But their approaches were very different. Kaare Klint is the classic functionalist, who gives use-value and sober-mindedness pride of place. He isn't concerned about having a distinct personal style – the furniture is a project that has to be completed in the best possible way, so why not draw on the experience of centuries? On the other hand, Hans J. Wegner chooses to work thoroughly with a thematic type and refine it to perfection, preferably in different versions for different companies at the same time. The only things the various versions have in common are the basic form and material, so other factors like price, finish and production technique are constant variables. Finally there's Kjærholm, who's devoted to a particular type of material, namely matt brushed flat steel. It is tested to its limits in order to find out how much the steel can take while he does what he can to make the furniture simpler and more beautiful.

Bauhaus in Danish

Bauhaus is probably the most talked about architectural and design school ever. It was established in the German town of Weimar in 1919 by architects and artists who returned from the trenches of World War I wanting to revolutionise not only art, architecture and arts and crafts, but also society and the way of life. The school had its heyday in the city of Dessau and was the exponent for functionalism, where aesthetics were subordinate to the practical aspect and use-value of buildings, homes, furniture and other products. The public benefits of better design were mass production and cheaper products. Some of the more well-known Bauhaus notables are: Walter Gropius, Ludwig Mies van der Rohe, Johannes Itten, Lázló Moholy-Nagy, Marianne Brandt, Wassily Kandinsky, Paul Klee and Marcel Breuer. In 1932, the school was moved to Berlin where it was closed the following year due to Nazi pressure.

One of the most famous and popular designs from the Bauhaus School is Marcel Breuer's chair, B33, from 1927-28, also known as the Barber Shop Chair. It was used in Peter Bang's office and was inspirational in the design of Bang & Olufsen's radiophonograph Hyperbo 5RG Steel from 1934.

The radiophonograph Hyperbo 5RG Steel, 1934.

It's debatable whether the school, its teachers and students succeeded in achieving the lofty ideals of building for the working class and manufacturing for the people. At first, many of the building projects the school's architects were hired to draft were mansions for the rich, such as the mansion in Brno by Mies van der Rohe. Much of the furniture and many of the products designed by the people at the school were probably more suited to be looked at than to use. And the price was rarely affordable for the man on the street.

The school's artistic philosophy and teaching, which primarily the first-year students were subjected to, were also problematic. Thus the Bauhaus people often inadvertently prioritised the aesthetic aspect rather than the sensible and rational design that worked and could be manufactured cheaply. But it was through the simple and geometric artistic idiom, devoid of ornamentation and decoration, that enabled Bauhaus to put its great mark on future architecture and design.

Bauhaus also had a great influence in Denmark. In the early days, the style was known, perhaps a little condescendingly, as 'funkis', derived from functionalism. This influence was at first great in the field of architecture, promoted by the architect Edvard Heiberg, who was a teacher at Bauhaus from 1930-31 when the school had moved to Dessau. But also other architects had their eye on inspiration from the new school. Arne Jacobsen was at times greatly inspired by it, which can be seen in the Bellevue complex in Klampenborg on the coast north of Copenhagen.

The inspiration from Bauhaus is also clearly seen in product design many years later such as that by Arne Jacobsen. His series of cylindrical products

▸ *The alarm clock by Braun and the timer, designed by Jan Trägårdh for the Danish company Micro Matic, use the geometric artistic idiom. Both products were issued in various models in the 1960's and up to the 1980's.*

from 1967, Cylinda-Line in stainless steel which includes a pitcher, ashtray and ice bucket for Stelton, are clearly influenced by the early functional period. The same can be said about Vola, a series of plumbing fixtures that Jacobsen designed in 1969 and were used for the first time in the new Danish National Bank.

While Arne Jacobsen never openly admitted that he was influenced by Bauhaus, others didn't hide the fact that they learnt from the German school and the modern, international trends. Bang & Olufsen freely admit this heritage. In the 1920s and 1930s, the factory in Struer was busy with solving problems in the technical and production area – so busy were they that they didn't have the energy to create a modern design. The reviewers in the papers in 1933 criticised the new technical wonders of being encased in outmoded casings ...

B&O promptly answered the following year, luckily not as a futile rejection of the criticism, but by launching a radiophonograph in a completely functional design. The name of the model was oddly 'Hyperbo 5RG Steel', as is written in the history of Bang & Olufsen, which was released as a blockbuster book a few years ago. This device was pictured next to Marcel Breuer's desk chair, which stood in Peter Bang's office at that time. But for many years, B&O continued to produce most of their products in what architects called 'cigar boxes', since that was what many customers wanted. Not until much later did Bang & Olufsen's design change radically (see page 127).

The second wave of functionalism

As mentioned, Bauhaus had to shut down in 1933, when the Nazis came into power in Germany, and most of the teachers had to go into exile. Some of them ended up in the US and resumed their work as practicing architects or designers or as teachers. Not until 1953 did a new school open in Germany and its ambition was to follow in the footsteps of Bauhaus. A former student of Bauhaus, the architect, artist and graphic designer Max Bill was the leader in carrying on the Bauhaus tradition with a new school that was built in the town of Ulm in southern Germany. The official name of the school was Hochschule für Gestaltung.

But before long, a conflict arose between the Bauhaus fundamentalist Bill and the young teachers; represented by his second in command, the Argentinian Maldonado. The young generation wanted to break with the overly aesthetic line that Max Bill represented, in order to introduce more studies in technology, marketing and business science. In the end, Bill lost the battle and left the school while Maldonado took over the leadership. Nonetheless, the school in Ulm represented a very pronounced aesthetic line, which wasn't far from that of Bauhaus, and which was reflected in the many products made by the company Braun.

Many Danish designers and companies owe a lot to Bauhaus or the school in Ulm. This goes for the early works of Arne Jacobsen and Bang & Olufsen, Erik Magnussen's thermos for Stelton, Knud Holscher's d-line doorknobs and Lauritz Knudsen's light switches. One of the most prominent Danish industrial designers in the aesthetic tradition was Jan Trägårdh. His pure geometrical style of design is seen in the machines he designed in the 1970s and 1980s, like Eskofot's repro camera and Micro Matic's timer.

A TREE WITH Chinese roots. Inspiration can come from many things. Sometimes it seems a bit far-fetched when a product or logo refers to something mysterious, because the designer or head of marketing had a fixed idea. But in the case of the logo for the company Gori, there was method in the madness when the Chinese character for a tree was chosen and graphic designer Niels Hartmann developed an identity program for the company. The character for a tree is typically Chinese and thus almost a pictogram in itself. The tree is drawn like an organism with trunk, roots and branches. Transposing this for a Danish company that makes wood-protection products seems both logical and very simple. The logo for Gori, which today is an independent brand in the Dyrup corporation, was designed in the mid-1970s. Even if the idea is good, the graphic seems a bit typical of its time with very thick lines and a heaviness about it. It was replaced a long time ago with another identity.

DSB's English connection

The Danish State Railways, DSB, is one of the most Danish things one could imagine – from steam locomotives to the coffee on the Great Belt ferry. But neither of these exist anymore. From 1971 to 1992, this large and rather heavy government institution's head of design was Jens Nielsen. He began to systemise the way DSB communicated to and addressed its customers. He visited England for inspiration, since British Rail in the 1960s was the first railway company in Europe to develop a so-called design manual. This manual is a tool for the employees that indicates exactly how the company should look and communicate to the outside world.

The manual deals with subjects like logo, typography, which colours are used on signs, products, packaging and much more. In some cases the design manual even prescribes how company letters should be written and what to say when answering the phone. In the case of British Rail, they were very thorough and modernised the whole company's look. This was what designer Jens Nielsen studied so intensely in England that he later had a book about British Rail's design line translated and published by the Danish Design Center.

In many ways, DSB chose to follow their English colleagues, for instance the same typography was used on signs and printed matter, namely Helvetica. This is a very well-known typeface, which was drafted by the Swiss typographer and graphic designer Max Miedinger. Helvetica is a so-called a sans serif typeface, which means it's 'without feet' or 'without cross lines'. It was designed in 1956 and is related to the artistic idiom used by Bauhaus and the Ulm school. It's a modern typeface that, without the classic 'curlicues', indicated that DSB was an organisation that was dynamic and no-nonsense and whose trains ran on schedule.

Helvetica was often used from the 1970s on. For many years it has been one of the standard typefaces on most PCs and word-processing programs. That's why it has become a bit 'stale' in many people's opinion, including designers and other professionals in the graphic industry. In the late 1990s, DSB chose to have its very own typeface designed after 25 years of using Helvetica. It was fittingly called Via and drafted by the graphic design company Kontrapunkt in collaboration with the young type designers from e-Types. DSB's sign and colour system was also redesigned so the lettering was in white on a distinguished dark-blue background. The new typeface is very characteristic compared to Helvetica, for example, note the little 'g'.

▸ Changing day at DSB. The old signs, inspired by British Rail's use of Helvetica typeface, were replaced in 1998 with new signs. The new typeface was jointly designed by e-Types and Kontrapunkt. Now the employee needs only to get a new vest.

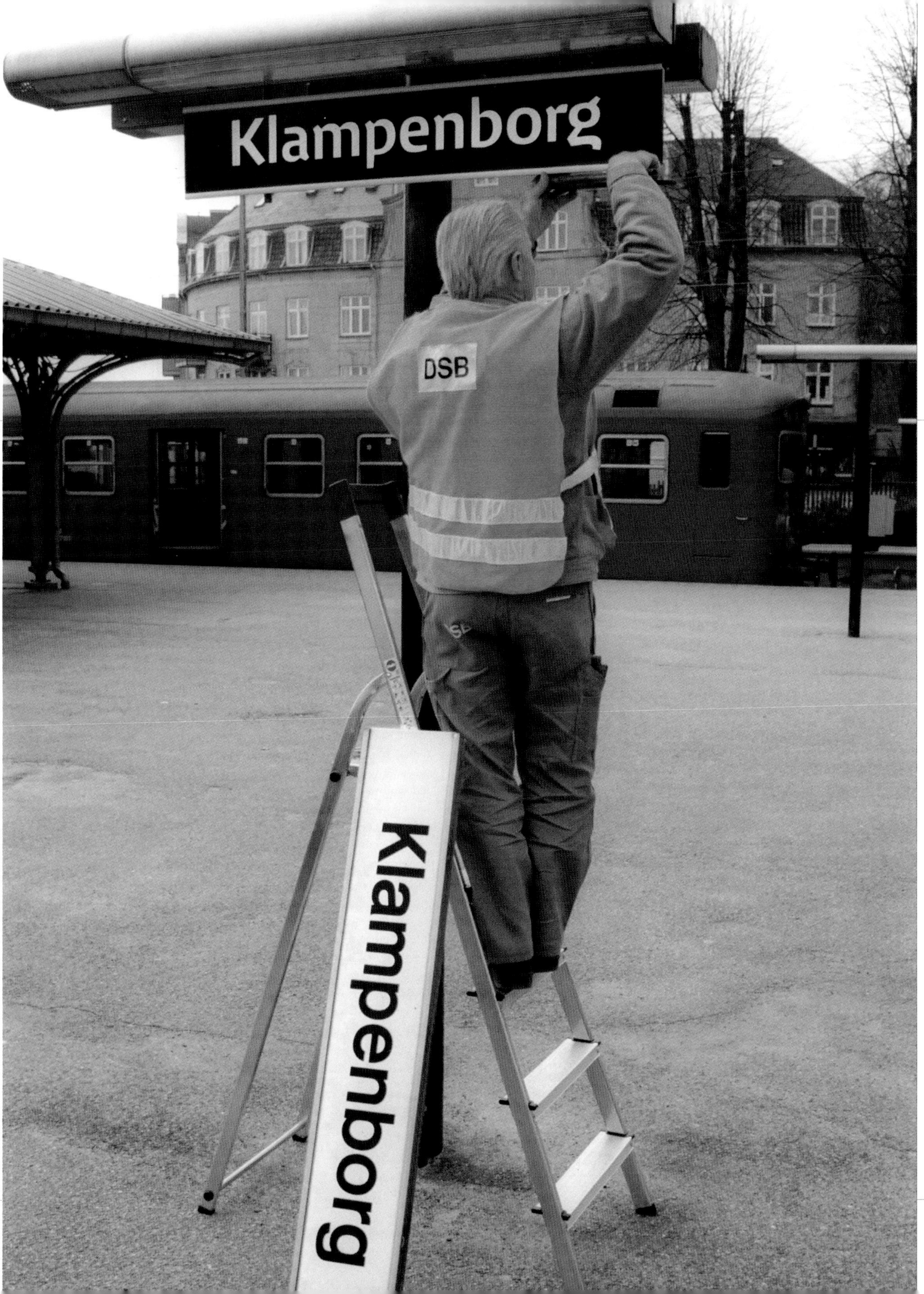
Klampenborg
DSB
DSB
Klampenborg

CHEMIN DE FER DU NORD
A.M.CASSANDRE 27
HACHARD & Cie PARIS.
NEDERLANDSCHE SPOORWEGEN
SOCIÉTÉ NATIONALE DES CHEMINS DE FER BELGES
ÉTOILE DU NORD
DU DÉJEUNER
PULLMAN
AU DINER
PARIS—BRUXELLES—AMSTERDAM
COMPAGNIE DES WAGONS-LITS

banedanmark

WHEN DO YOU get too close? In 1999, the Danish National Railway Agency, now Rail Net Denmark, arranged a competition for a new logo and visual identity. The winning proposal was some lines which in a very stylised way resemble train tracks that converge on an imaginary horizon. So far so good. But then a journalist at 'The Politiken', Henrik Sten Møller, showed the striking resemblance of the new logo, designed by 2 Graphic Design, to a poster for the Paris-Brussels-Amsterdam railway connection from 1927 made by the famous poster artist Cassandre (the creator of 'Dubo, Dubon, Dubonnet'). Is it inspiration? Is it plagiarism? That was pretty much the end of it, so we can make up our own minds about it.

It also works the other way round ...

While Danish designers have been influenced by impulses from abroad, many Danish products and designs have inspired foreign designers and companies. The Danish furniture boom from around 1950 and on through the next 20–30 years is one of the most recognised examples of the internationalisation of Danish furniture, which was trendsetting during that period for avant-garde all over the world. In some cases it's been downright copied, as in the office chair wheel, which the brothers Ib and Jørgen Rasmussen designed for Kevi in the late 1960s.

The new wheel had great practical advantages over the old ones and was more in aesthetic accordance with the design of office furniture of the time. The new Kevi wheels were practical by being much wider and thus rolled better on all types of surfaces. Furthermore, the wheel was divided in two so the vertical axle, which was attached to the chair leg, was much closer to the wheel's vertical centre of rotation and therefore could spin around much easier. The wheels were made of nylon and didn't need to be oiled. Kevi wheels are made in different versions with and without the cover. But what all the versions have in common is that they were a big sales success and this wheel design is practically standard in the furniture industry. Many have been manufactured under license all over the world, although many manufacturers have copied the Kevi wheel without worrying about rights or licenses. In the first ten years alone, at least 30 million wheels were manufactured by Kevi and their licensees, and then there were all the pirated versions.

▸ *The classic office chair caster from the furniture factory Kevi was awarded the Danish Design Council's ID award in 1969.*

POLITICAL DESIGN – FROM PRESTIGE TO WELFARE

Design isn't just fashioning useful articles and necessary tools for everyday use. Design, arts and crafts and architecture have for ages contributed to creating distinctions between people, that is between the haves and the have-nots. The saying that 'clothes make the man' expresses the essence of it very well. The same applies to the interior decoration of homes and official buildings. It's often about staging oneself or one's firm as well as possible. The intention behind these efforts can be manifold, from adapting to a social norm or as a kind of seduction to show how powerful and awe-inspiring one is.

The latter is clearly apparent in the audience hall of Frederiksborg Castle in Hillerød. The arrangement of the room as it looks today originates from 1681–89, when the castle was the royal residence. You can imagine how the king received guests from all walks of society. Some subjects came to ask for permission to do something or other like opening a shop or a business, and some even came to ask to be pardoned. It could also have been a public servant bearing documents. Some of the visitors were welcome, others not.

If not on a proper throne, the king sat in the finely carved and decorated chair against the wall. In the middle of the room is a round table and behind it three high-backed and richly decorated chairs on which ministers and prominent public servants sat. In front of the table are two humble stools for those seeking an audience if they were allowed to sit down at all. Power games have been played in this room. The visitor who sought out the autocratic king did not have an easy time. It is reminiscent of the scene in Hans Christian Andersen's fairy tale 'Clumsy Hans', where the pert princess rejects her many suitors.

The design of this room of power, the audience room, is a textbook example of how it can be done. It's a large room with a high ceiling and plenty of expensive decorations. The placement and arrangement of the chairs indicate a precise rank order, and the king could sit in the background and nap or daydream and only intercede when necessary. A minister could approach the king and discuss a matter in a whisper without the visitors being able to hear them. The king didn't even have to speak directly to the subject. There's nothing intimate or cosy about the arrangement. The room is formal and mighty, the citizen is small.

▸ *Frederiksborg Castle in Hillerød was a proper royal castle where the regent's power was clearly reflected in the architecture, arrangement, design and decoration. Its present appearance dates from Christian IV's time and is in the Baroque style. The castle burned in 1859 so much of what is seen today is cleverly rebuilt and restored under the leadership of the architect Ferdinand Meldahl in the years after 1860. The audience room here was not touched by the fire and looks almost the way it did in the 1680s.*

◂ Trelleborg near Slagelse. A more natural protection would have been provided if the fort's ramparts had followed the width of the streams, so they could function as natural moats. But the ring wall, a perfect circle, is a much more formal and impressive design for a king's castle. Outside the ring wall lay more houses that were protected by an outer and more irregular rampart.

When Denmark was unified

Like other places in the world, Denmark's beautiful castles have had an important representative and prestigious role to play. The intention was to show wealth and be a symbol of the regent's cunning and success. Throughout time, these castles have created exclusive and idyllic scenographies around life at the court and state affairs. But not all castles have been like this. Far back in history, other castles haven't been quite as romantic, but were nonetheless designed as symbols in their time. An especially Danish phenomenon is the circular castle. The most well-known and best preserved is Trelleborg, just outside Slagelse on Zealand. Furthermore there is Nonnebakke near Odense, Fyrkat near Hobro and the enormous Aggersborg near Aggersund. In the city of Trelleborg in southern Sweden there are the remains of one.

The special thing about these castles is that they were built according to strict geometric rules, and it's clear that the same rules were followed for all four in Denmark. They were also built around the same time in the years 980–981. However, they weren't used for more than ten years before they lost their significance and were abandoned. The question is: Why were they built? They were undoubtedly made for prestigious reasons. The short time they were in use also indicates that the military significance wasn't the most important. According to the theory, it's said that the king at the time, Harold Bluetooth, had to manifest himself and show his power over the Danes' region to both foreign enemies and domestic rivals. The background of this impressive construction was primarily to mark the new rise of a Danish nation, a form of political demonstration of power. And meanwhile the four castles functioned as administration and military centres.

APART FROM IMPRESSIVE buildings, the most common ways of showing one's status through design were imported fine furniture, arts and crafts and clothing. But other kinds of dictates have been used – the wooden horse is just one example. The wooden horse was an instrument of punishment used in Denmark to punish recalcitrant copy holders if they had been negligent in the running of the farm or other recalcitrant behaviour. The wooden horse was used from the early 1600s until the late 1700s. It consisted of a thick plank with four legs attached, just like a horse. Sometimes the horse had a head and tail. The victim sat astride the plank with his arms tied behind his back and weights attached to his feet. The punishment was particularly humiliating, and as far as we know, it only rarely led to serious physical damage to the victim. The use of the wooden horse was prohibited in Denmark in 1787.

The circular castles had, as the name reveals, a circular rampart with gates facing the four corners of the earth and an inner area divided by four roads to the gates. In the three smallest forts, every quarter had four, characteristically identical houses of about 30 meters in length with facades that curved outwards. The four long houses were arranged in a quadrangle with an inner courtyard. On the inside of the rampart there was a ring road, and on the outside a moat. The building materials used were oak, turf and dirt.

The three smallest forts were about 120–137 metres in diameter on the inside of the rampart. The largest, Aggersborg, has an impressive inner diameter of 240 metres, which meant there was room for three times as many houses, namely 48 instead of the 16 in the smaller ones. Their special appearance was perhaps an attempt to indicate order and structure in the new society, and that might be why they are so overly well-structured. Due to their special design, the castles and the arrangement of the large, uniform barracks placed in a perfectly symmetrical pattern become a political symbol of budding royal power. They are also imposing examples of how much manpower and how many resources they could mobilise for big projects back then.

The architecture of power

Throughout time, many rulers have made use of the effects of architecture to demonstrate who called the shots. You can see extreme examples abroad of how despots have used city planning, architecture and design to stage their totalitarian messages. This is often called fascist architecture, which refers to both Mussolini's prestigious buildings and the Nazis way of staging the party convention in Nuremberg in the 1930s.

The ultimate plan for using architecture to pay homage to the Führer and suppress any resistance to Hitler was designed by his favourite architect Albert Speer. The plans were already made before the war and included tearing down large areas of Berlin and building a new, monumental capital for The Third Reich. Among other buildings, an enormous palatial chancellery in symmetrical neo-classicist style was to be built. In front of the mammoth building would be a square that was big enough for a million German soldiers to stand in rank and file.

In the models and drawings of the project, you could even see details of how Speer would bring about this manipulation in the building itself. For example, the main doors would be three times as tall as an average person. You can imagine how heavy and difficult they would be to open. In these surroundings, everyone but the dictator and his accomplices would feel small and insecure and thus be easier to suppress and manipulate. There aren't any buildings in Denmark that are even close to resembling these frightful Germanic buildings. Even though we haven't had a dictatorship or anything like it in modern times, it doesn't mean that there aren't tendencies toward authoritarian architecture and design. One of the most interesting and new examples of this is the Danish Police building in Copenhagen.

Design creates companies

The business community uses architectural and design effects to stage itself. Just think of the caricatures in American movies of enormous director's offices resembling that of a dictator. A company's main office is an especially important element in the design of its identity, which the firm tries to surround itself with.

THE DANISH POLICE building is the head office of the Copenhagen police, built in1918–24 and designed by Hack Kampmann and Aage Rafn and others. From the outside, the neo-classicist building has a severe and authoritarian look with a very massive body, which effectively communicates its function. Most of all the building looks like a fort. The grey, plastered façade without projections or variations gives the impression that the large, triangular building is almost cut from one block of stone. It is solid aesthetics that are underlined by the details, such as the grating in front of the window and the gilded morning star. Inside the building it's a little more welcoming with classic pillars and delicate coating. If you get that far, the building has a somewhat milder appearance with a large, round flagged courtyard surrounded by a colonnade and several small, square courtyards. The building is labyrinthine and hard to navigate in, almost like a caricature of the bureaucratic centre of power. Here we're dealing with very controlled and formal architecture, which on its completion was criticised for being a superhuman symbol of power. Furniture was also designed for the building (see page 216).

◂ *The Danish National Bank (circa 1970) is Arne Jacobsen's last great work. Presumably in an attempt to supply the kingdom's money coffers with the appropriate dignity, the architecture and interior became very formal, almost foreboding. From the outside the building looks impregnable, as none of the windows are at street height. Inside, the six-story high vestibule is a continuation of the reserved style.*

The Danish National Bank in Copenhagen is an example of a very formal and closed piece of architecture which corresponds to the institution's desire to be independent of government economic policy and restricted business interests. The building has the appearance of a bank vault which distances itself from the public, and it looks so impenetrable that it's hard to find the entrance. Once you're in the building, you enter a gigantic vestibule that is clearly designed to inspire the visitor's respect for the bank's serious task of taking care of the country's money and economy.

The National Bank was built in 1965–72 and was the last of Arne Jacobsen's big projects before he suddenly died in 1971, barely 70 years old. Unfortunately, many fine town houses on Gammelholm had to be torn down to make room for the big building, which doesn't provide much life to the surrounding city environment. Despite the fact that the National Bank is seen as a noble piece of architecture by Arne Jacobsen, it seems to be a foreign building among other historic buildings. Today, a little more respect would probably have been given to the existing buildings around it.

Other examples are the East Asiatic Company's three headquarters through the ages. From a small, humble building in Copenhagen's free port, the East Asiatic Company moved in 1908 to Holmens Canal in the centre of town to the headquarters that for many years symbolised the East Asiatic Company and its spirit.

The building was designed by Gotfred Tvede in 1906–07, and to the many passers-by the building resembled an old fort with a bridge made of copper at the top. Even after the Ministry of Food, Agriculture and Fisheries moved into the building, it seemed rather reserved and without a lot of architectural merit. Its outer appearance isn't very inviting. However, once you enter the main entrance on the corner, a wonderful spiral staircase is revealed. It's made of teak and the workmanship is beautiful, which makes one think of the distant skies where the East Asiatic Company got its riches. But back in those days, the main staircase was only to be used by the management, board and distinguished guests; the employees and other lowly business connections had to use the side staircases.

After many years' lucrative business, the old company grew too big for Holmens Canal and built a brand new headquarters on Midtermolen, very close to their first offices in Copenhagen's free port. If the Holmens Canal headquarters was big, the new headquarters was huge. One end of the building stretches over the quay and has one leg in the water. While the East Asiatic Company never made use of all 51,000 square metres, since much of the building was rented out to other companies and as residences, the entrance hall succeeds in every way to impress the visitors.

The main entrance is situated at the bottom of the semicircular 12-storey glass tower, with the vestibule towering above you for six stories. At the bottom of this sky-lighted shaft is the reception. Talk about big. The project at Midtermolen was designed by Palle Leif Hansen's architectural practice and emphasised what the East Asiatic Company thought would be a new glorious era in the company's renowned history. Sadly, the company was to meet financial problems in a few years, and the building at Midtermolen is now the head office of an insurance company.

▾ *The East Asiatic Company built a headquarters on Midtermolen in Copenhagen harbour in the beginning of the 1990s. It was meant to impress the outside world. The building consists of a long, compact colonnade of offices, of which one overreaches the quayside and has one leg in the water. Furthermore, there's a 12-storey semicircle that faces Langelinie and Øresund. This is where visitors enter and see the very high vestibule. The building emanates status and capability, which the East Asiatic Company unfortunately couldn't sustain, so now the building belongs to an insurance company.*

FOR LOCAL AUTHORITIES it was and still is important to know the signals you're sending to the citizens and other cities. While the central seat of power set the standard before, in our time also the cities manifest themselves through design and architecture. A city hall is one of the places where you can register the ambitions of the local politicians. Of course this varies according to the municipality and its budget, but the desire for municipal prestige has also changed in the course of time.

The Aarhus City Hall was designed by Arne Jacobsen and Erik Møller for an architectural competition just before World War II. Originally the building was planned without a tower (upper left), but local politicians didn't think that a city as large as Aarhus could do without a tower on its city hall. So the architects had to revise their plans and add a tower (lower left). Around the same time, Arne Jacobsen and Flemming Lassen designed Søllerød City Hall, but the small municipality didn't insist on a tower (below).

◀◀ *The medal designed by Nicolai Abildgaard in 1792 to commemorate the abolishment of the Danish slave trade.*

◀ *One of the reliefs made by Abildgaard for the Freedom Column erected in 1792.*

Free the employees

Oticon, the manufacturer of hearing aids, had financial problems around 1990 and chose to change its working methods and offices as a way of reversing the trend. As one of the first companies in the world they introduced 'the paperless office'. Oticon's vision was to organise their working methods in a new way. First and foremost, they moved into new offices with a new layout. The individual offices were gone. Work assignments were done in temporary groups that met for the duration and then were dissolved. Therefore no one had a fixed desk but instead a portable computer table. Oticon became a 'spaghetti organisation' in that a number of loosely connected working relationships come together on a work assignment and not because they were in a department.

There were no partitions or hierarchies anymore, and professional titles were dropped. Instead they launched a flat structure with open groups that would promote efficiency and creativity. Mobile workstations were introduced so the employees could move to their designated project group. Symbolically, the new offices were arranged so the administration and the director, Lars Kolind, were no longer separated from the other employees. The paperless office was virtually paperless since the mail was scanned electronically and a paper shredder was used to turn all the incoming mail into confetti. The shredded mail could be seen in many places floating down a transparent tube to the dumpster in the basement.

The open-plan office, where not even the director had his own door to close, brought communication into focus in the company. Coffee corners were established to promote networking and informal chats, and the elevators were replaced by wide staircases which made it easier for the employees to meet colleagues on the stairs and quickly solve problems. The changes managed to put Oticon on an even keel again, and the new organisation was a success. This is an example of how thorough interior and furniture design can promote a feeling of community and break down hierarchies.

The democratic movement through design

From the establishment of the Danish kingdom in the Viking Age and for hundreds of years to come, the country was marked by authoritarian forms of government. Denmark was not a democracy, at least not in the sense that in any way is reminiscent of what we today understand as democracy. For long periods of time, the nobility and the Crown fought for power, but basically it was only a question of whom should be the autocratic regent and administrator of a kind of dictatorship. The people's job was to pay their taxes and make men and resources available for the many wars, preferably without complaint, for otherwise they would feel the wrath of the king. But in the late 1700s, things began to change. Enlightened citizens, including a number of artists, architects and designers, were dissatisfied with present circumstances and inspired by the ideas of liberty coming especially from the American and French revolutions. But for a long time it was problematic to voice demands for democracy loudly. In 1799, the satirical author P.A. Heiberg was banished from Denmark. He was the one who wrote the song 'Orders are for hanging on idiots'. So much criticism had to be whispered in corners or written between the lines.

A good example of this hidden criticism is the famous Klismos Chair designed around 1800 by painter Nicolai Abildgaard. How could a chair be so political? The key was that the Klismos Chair was inspired by ancient Greece and was a reference to the world's first democracy there.

NICOLAI ABILDGAARD (1743–1809) was a Danish painter and architect who sought inspiration in the art and culture of antiquity, but also in non-classical literature and Norse mythology. For two periods he was professor at the Royal Academy of Fine Arts in Copenhagen. Like many artists of his generation he went to Rome to study. He led a political double life by, on the one hand, completing artistic assignments for the royal house and being on good terms with Christian VIII, and on the other hand, by expressing his democratic points of view. But Abildgaard quite openly designed the 1792 Freedom Column as a symbol of the abolition of serfdom, and he also designed a medal in commemoration of the abolition of the slave trade in Denmark.

▲ *One of Abildgaard's Klismos Chairs.*

DURING THE GERMAN occupation, subtle ways of criticising the powers that be were again used. Paul Henningsen wrote one of his popular songs to protest in this way. Recorded by Liva Weel, the song 'They bind us hand and mouth' was already popular in 1940. Later on, PH had to flee across Øresund to Sweden in a rowboat with his wife, Arne Jacobsen and the latter's fiancée. PH fled because of his outspokenness and Arne Jacobsen because he was of Jewish descent. In 2004, the group Outlandish rerecorded the same song written by Poul Henningsen and Kai Normann Andersen.

But there were other more understated ways of making one's position clear during World War II. At one point it was popular among young women to knit a round cap in the same colours as the emblems on the wings of English war planes. It wasn't without risk to air one's sympathies. A passing German soldier might give you a shove and tear off your cap. And the Danish police could be forced to write a fine for wearing an RAF cap on the demand of an officious German solider. Some girls counteracted this by switching the colours on the knitted cap so it wasn't a real RAF cap, but the point was still obvious.

The word 'democracy' is Greek. Furthermore, both the type and the design itself were very functional and sober without a lot of frippery and thus the chair was a contrast to the prevailing style of French Empire. One might wonder why Abildgaard and others took exception to the French style, and this was yet another political message. They presumably, but without putting much of it in writing, took exception to the derailment of the French revolution, which they thought Napoleon Bonaparte's regime stood for. The Klismos Chair became a very popular chair, and several other artists and furniture makers designed their own versions of it. It had various looks, such as one made of dark wood with a Greek frieze on the back rest or, like one of Abildgaard's most elegant models, in gold bronzed. Otherwise the chair is characterised by legs that curved outwards, a rounded back and usually an upholstered seat.

The modern rebel

Perhaps Danish design hasn't had very many rebels since then, but the ones it did have were very colourful. The most well-known of them all is undoubtedly the architect and designer Poul Henningsen (known as PH). Apart from being the great designer of lamps and light in Denmark, he was a highly controversial person due to his political and cultural criticism. He was a critic of society and a proponent of living as naturally as possible and avoiding the lies, pretence and bourgeois vanity which he found so abundant in his time.

Poul Henningsen brought out the best possible light from the incandescent bulb through rational observation and experiments. This attitude can be seen also in the way he reasoned in public debate. In actual fact, it was his modern understanding of the expedient in design that was transposed to

◂ *Towards the end of the war, it was almost chic to demonstrate one's defiance of the occupational force by wearing RAF caps. This family is going on a picnic wearing the politically correct headgear of the time.*

▸ *In Copenhagen in 1928, the American singer and artist Josephine Baker performed jazz dance in a banana skirt. The right-wing press was shocked, but the culturally radical architect Poul Henningsen was enthusiastic about this liberated and natural woman, who protested against bourgeois narrow-mindedness.*

understanding the relations between people. For example, he was against romanticising the idyllic peasant life of the past and the environmental preservationists' efforts to curb technology. PH believed in science and rejoiced in the high-voltage lines that crisscrossed the country. To him they were symbols of the new era of progress, industry and greater affluence for the common man.

PH was most controversial in his liberated views on the equality of the sexes and sexual liberation. Everything human was natural to him, and he wrote many feature articles and debate articles against puritanism, hypocrisy and various kinds of prejudice. His defence of free abortion and of Josephine Baker's half-naked jazz dance in a variety theatre in Copenhagen in 1928 made the political right wing and church circles see red. During that time, the PH lamp became a symbol of PH's political views which were either loved or hated. PH voiced his opinions in every possible media – revue songs, movies and the written word. In 1926, he took part in founding the periodical 'Critical Revue', which was a significant mouthpiece for him and other like-minded people.

Colleagues and politicians also bore the brunt of Poul Henningsen's critical activity since he was especially against artificiality in design and construction. Things must be well thought out and clearly fashioned without curlicues and other superfluous decoration. In 'Critical Revue' he writes in 1926, 'This is why we must attack the Social Democrats' imitation of the 18th century's nobility's way of building. It's a thundering lie to copy the foolishness of a deceased class ... But neither is it the architect's job to sugar the tenement house with exterior decorations and artificiality.'

▸ *Kartoffelrækkerne (literally the potato rows) were at first co-operative housing for the working-class as a protest against property speculation in the late 1800s, but ironically they're now some of the most expensive and sought after private homes in Copenhagen. The size and location of the houses appeal to well-off families with children, especially because the roads have no through traffic.*

▸▸ *From the outside Brumleby looks almost like when it was built in 1854–72, but the inside of the two-story ranch-style houses has been renovated. The apartments are still rather small, but they're very popular, not least because of the environment of this little enclave on Østerbro in Copenhagen.*

It was his attacks on the priorities of his day which were that apartment houses should rather be nicer to look at than to live in. As PH so candidly said, 'The future will come of its own accord, progress won't'.

The idealistic home

In the late 19th and early 20th centuries, the home for the common man became a political arena. In the mid-1800s it was well known how important it is for our health to live in sound homes. In 1853, after the cholera epidemic in Copenhagen, The Danish Medical Association took the initiative to build what is known as Brumleby. The official name for these houses in Østerbro was the Medical Association's Housing, which were built in 1854–72. The architects were Gottlieb Bindesbøll and Vilhelm Klein. This enclave in town was an early and very successful forerunner of council housing in Denmark.

The special thing about this unique project was that the rectangular ranch-style houses were two stories, which was unheard of in big cities at that time. However, much inspiration was drawn from the older Nyboder from Christian IV's time. Moreover, there were many recreational spaces between the houses and communal facilities like laundry rooms, shops and public baths. In agreement with the idealistic intentions, the apartments were rented to low-income families. By today's standards, the apartments were rather small (about 25 m^2) and were usually occupied by large families. Brumleby still exists and after extensive renovation in the mid-1990s, which to a certain degree was done in collaboration with the residents, the many apartments were combined to form more contemporary residences.

◂ *The famous one-bedroom apartment built for the annual exhibition of the Cabinetmakers' Guild in 1930 by architects Hans Hansen and Viggo Sten Møller. It was an exact copy of a one-bedroom apartment in the suburbs of Copenhagen and was meant to demonstrate how modern furniture could be used. The authentic touches of this mock-up were the potted plants and the family photos on the walls. Notice that the window glass was replaced by black cardboard.*

The Potato Rows

The initiative behind Brumleby's healthy and sound residences for poor working-class families came from the well-off medical community and could be seen as a form of charity. Some years later, in 1865, the shipyard workers at Burmeister & Wain established a building society and thus took matters into their own hands. This society was inspired by the work being done in enlightening people and the increased focus on the impact of proper housing on public health. In addition, the traditional tenement houses in Copenhagen's former suburbs were the object of widespread speculation resulting in high rent, so the unionised workers also saw the initiative as a way of getting out of the clutches of the slum lords. The building society saved up enough money through the years to build cooperative housing.

In 1873, the society could afford to build the first and largest of these buildings. It lay on the border between the inner city and Østerbro on the Sortedam Lake and was quickly given the name the Potato Rows, partly because the area had previously been potato fields, and partly because the low yellow-brick houses were built in neat rows. The houses are virtually identical, and in 1889, all of the 480 narrow 2.5-storey houses were finished. The architect Frederik Bøttger designed these light and airy houses. They could accommodate two families, but today the wealthy middle class lives in the former working-class homes. The building societies, which were located in several places in Copenhagen, became the beginning of the co-operative housing movement.

The architects' initiative

The various public and social housing projects constitute a few of the buds that later blossomed into today's welfare society. This is how the unionised workers and other layers of society used means other than their vote to create the society they wanted. Just like the co-ops, folk high schools and the peasants co-operative movement, the workers tried to build institutions that could give them and their families better and safer living conditions and more influence over their own lives. The contribution of architects and others in the construction business was to establish the National Association of Better Architectural Design in 1915.

The purpose of Better Architectural Design was to develop a cooperation between architects, craftsmen and building owners and thus improve the quality of architecture and craftsmanship in construction. A committee under the national association was called the Council for Design Assistance, and here the contracted architects designed houses for free for people who were financially hard up. Or as it was written in the annual report from 1919, 'Design Assistance is the architect for the building owner without means and it is the craftsman's colleague'.

The idealistic architects took their starting point in Danish building tradition and designed various buildings, often standard houses cost free. Not only homes for one family were designed, but also agricultural buildings, workshops, dairies, schools and village halls. Better Architectural Design held courses, gave lectures and published pamphlets to make building owners and craftsmen aware of a human and rational building practice combined with high-quality craftsmanship and sound finances. Better Architectural Design was a big success in the 1920s and 30s, but slowly

▸ *An FDB stand full of modern furniture at one of the fairs in 1960.*

faded out as affluence grew and people could afford to design the house of their dreams. The National Association was closed down after its 50th anniversary in 1965.

The social aspect

But the social aspect did not only gain a footing in architecture and the building of homes. In other design disciplines, like interior design and furniture design, there was greater orientation towards the needs of the people. The architect P.V. Jensen-Klint was a co-founder of Better Architectural Design in 1915, and in 1924 the Furniture School was established at the Royal Academy of Fine Arts in Copenhagen by his son Kaare Klint. The latter adopted a rational tack in the new education, where studies of people's needs went hand in hand with new and simpler aesthetics in furniture design. In 1927, the master cabinetmakers in Copenhagen began to exhibit their finest furniture annually.

These two institutions, the Furniture School and the Cabinetmakers' exhibition, inspired and stimulated each other for many years, and together they made a very creative environment. There was a relevant and social aspect in the exhibitions almost from the very beginning. Spurred by the political and social debate in those years, the cabinetmakers, designers and furniture architects began to create basic furniture that the common man could afford. In some of the exhibitions, this sympathetic insight into the housing situation for a large proportion of the Danish population went as far as having a socially relevant theme. It could be designing a proposal for the modern arrangement of, for example, 'the one-bedroom' as was the case of the exhibition of the Cabinetmakers' Guild in 1930. Later on, the exhibitions featured the furnishing of other types of housing.

These initiatives weren't politically inspired in a classic sense. The cabinetmakers were probably good, resolute people, but they hardly saw their activities as part of a Social Democratic building of society. First of all, they were interested in the survival of their own businesses by making the furniture that met people's needs, and secondly in maintaining the professional pride of the cabinetmakers. When the labour movement, cabinetmakers and the socially-minded furniture architects managed to fall into step together, it contributed to strengthening the impact of a better design which symbolised a new age.

From 1939, the annual exhibitions were held at the Museum of Art & Design and practically became an institution until 1966, when the party ended. The social aspect had taken a back seat, and society had changed in 40 years, among other things by a rise in prosperity. In 1981, the tradition of annual exhibitions was reinstated under the name of SE – the Cabinetmakers' Fall Exhibition. However, today the furniture designers set the scene instead of the traditional cabinetmakers, and any political or social ambition for the exhibition is dead and gone.

FDB

At one place in particular, however, work continued on producing furniture for the people, and that was at the Danish Consumers' Co-operative Society, FDB. The idealistic director, Arne Sørensen, wanted to do more than run a co-operative business. Although FDB also had factories and manufactured products for the shops, Arne Sørensen felt the need to be a cultural institution with social obligations. With the help of architect and writer Steen Eiler Rasmussen, FDB put their thoughts into words and contacted one of Kaare Klint's best students, Børge Mogensen.

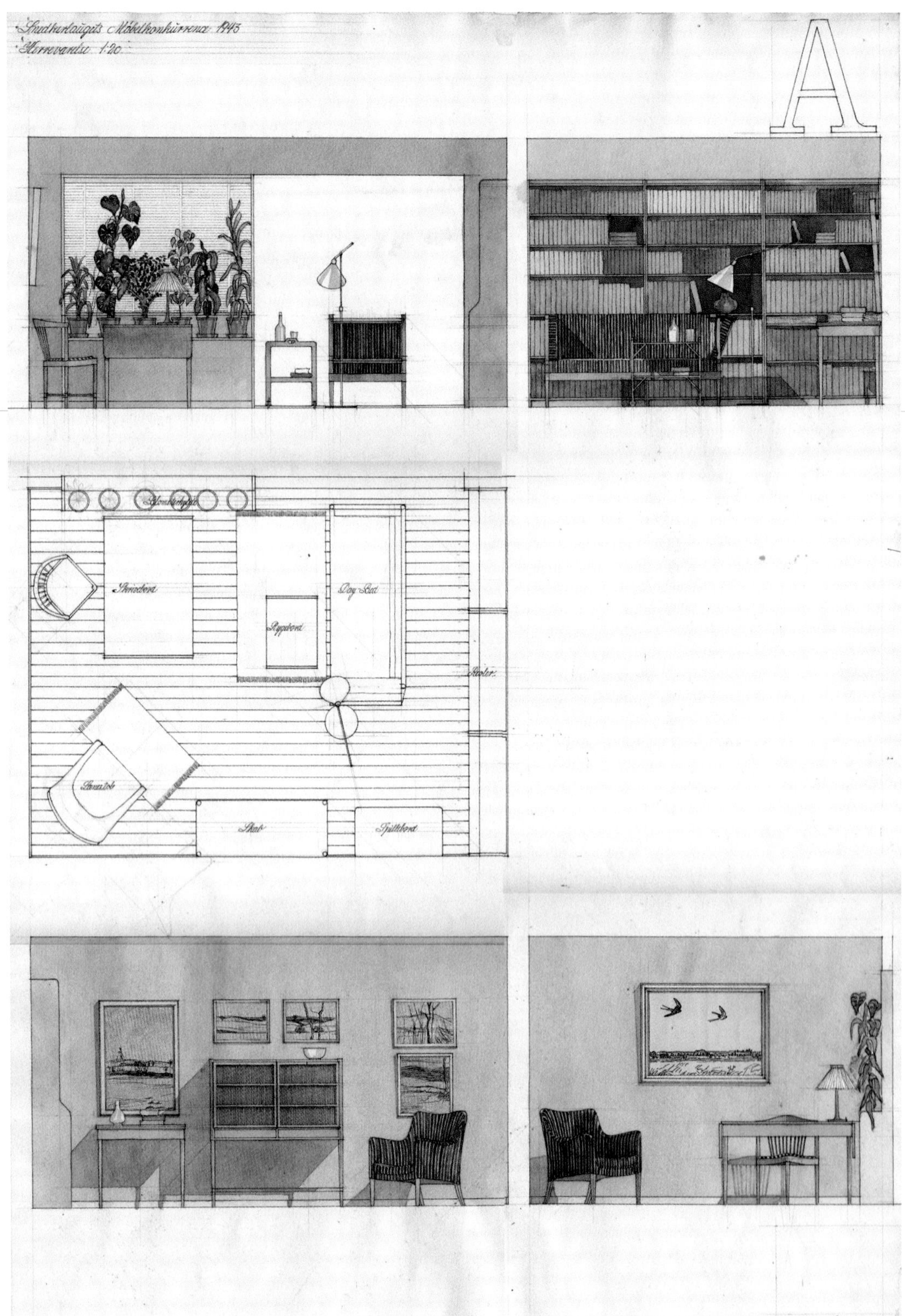
Snedkerlaugets Møbelkonkurrence 1943
Herreværelse 1:20
A

▸ *The low-floor bus, produced by DAB in Silkeborg, is driving through Frederiksberg. There isn't a rear window since this is where the engine is placed in the back of the bus. By moving the engine from its traditional position under the floor, the entrance and exit height was now only a few centimetres above the curb. DAB is no longer an independent company, but many buses today are made using the same approach.*

◂ *Børge Mogensen's display in watercolour of his and master carpenter I. Christiansen's stand at the annual exhibition of the Cabinetmakers' Guild at the Museum of Art & Design in 1943.*

In 1940, FDB began to manufacture quality furniture at reasonable prices, and Børge Mogensen was made head of the design office in 1942. Although there was a war going on, and Denmark was occupied, the project was initiated. These furniture pieces were without frills and were functional versions of old Danish and English types of furniture and were made of wood – the light Danish kinds of wood of course, but that's all they could get during the war. Much of the furniture that was designed in those days at FDB are considered classics today, and Mogensen wasn't the only one who designed them. So did Hans J. Wegner, Arne Karlsen and other younger architects of the time.

FDB organised a distribution system with its own furniture stores called Brugsen Furniture. Otherwise the furniture could be bought in FDB's department store, ANVA, or by mail order. In some cases, sample apartments were built in some of the stores so the furniture could be seen in realistic surroundings. Then people could imagine what their homes would look like with new, stylish FDB furniture. This was a new lifelike way of selling furniture, because until then a piece of furniture was sold out of context with other pieces. This sales method is similar to the one IKEA used later in its catalogues and shops where complete home furnishings are displayed. At FDB, Børge Mogensen often worked with furniture systems, especially bookcases and closets that matched and were designed for the typical room size in homes at that time.

At one point, FDB's furniture production and sales were significant, and with the co-operative society's many members, it should have been possible to think even bigger. But Arne Sørensen left FDB and so did Børge Mogensen in 1950 when he was tired of working on constantly designing new furniture that had to be seriously trimmed with a view to rational production. You can't help wondering: If FDB had concentrated their efforts and thought the matter through, could it have become a serious competitor to the Swedish IKEA?

Design for everyone

Throughout time, Danes have gathered around their interests in various ways in order to solve practical and social problems creatively. Some of the solutions are uniquely Danish, as for instance the folk high schools, while others resemble something our neighbouring countries have done, like the trade union movement and co-operative societies. These experiences have contributed to building the Danish welfare state and creating a tradition of solving problems in a way that includes as many citizens as possible.

One example of this is the development of public transport with solutions that also make it possible for the mobility-impaired to take the bus. In 1994, the bus firm DAB in Silkeborg was awarded the Danish Design Center's ID prize for a so-called service bus. Designer Christian Rosenqvist and the firm got the award because they had solved some problems with existing buses. A traditional bus is built on a truck chassis where the engine is typically between the front wheels. If you want a one-level floor, it has to be built on top of the motor and thus a couple of steep steps have to be negotiated when entering or exiting the bus.

DAB had a good think. What if you moved the motor from the bottom of the bus and also placed the wheels in the corners? Now the floor could be lowered all the way down to the axles and it wouldn't be so difficult for the elderly and the walking-impaired to get on and off. And so it was done.

POLITICAL POSTERS ARE also design. In recent times, there are several good examples of election posters that are remembered long after they were used because of either the text or the graphic strength or perhaps a combination of the two.

The Social Democrats' poster for the parliamentary election in 1935: 'Stauning – or Chaos. Vote for the Social Democrats!' was the first of its kind in Denmark. Until then posters with portraits of a person had not been used as the main motif.

The motor was placed upright over the back wheels, so now there was a gap of only 8 cm from the curb up to the floor of the bus. Since a small ramp could be lowered, wheelchairs and baby carriages could also be taken on the low-floor bus.

There were other advantages to this design. First of all, it was easier to access the motor for repairs, and if necessary, the whole motor could be replaced in 20 minutes. Secondly, time was saved at every stop since it was easier for all passengers to get on and off. Therefore, the bus company could shave some minutes off the bus schedule, to the benefit of both passengers and the company's costs.

The example of the low-floor bus shows that increased accessibility for everyone doesn't necessarily entail difficulty and poor economy. If you think things through from the beginning, lots of things are possible; it's hard to lower the floor of a bus retrospectively. Traditionally, transport companies have considered that handicap design, as it was previously called, was something that just cost them money and they demanded subsidies from the authorities. Today we've found that design for accessibility (as it's now called) makes it easier for everyone to be included and it's becoming an integrated part of a welfare society, although that society still leaves much to be desired.

Perhaps that's why it had such a strong impact on people, but it also played on the motif of the father of the country: You know what you have, but not what you'll get if you vote for one of the others. One would be tempted to associate it with the strong-man syndrome if Denmark weren't such a Lilliputian country.

The hand stealing the house like a thief in the night was a poster printed by the Conservative Party for the referendum on the land laws in 1963. The bill was proposed by the Social Democratic government and was meant to stop land speculation, but it inflamed the non-socialist parties, who saw it as an unnecessary attempt to strengthen the government's power. The message of the poster fulfilled its purpose as a scare campaign and is still singled out for its effective demagogical symbolism. The bill was not passed.

During the anti-establishment rebellion in the late 1960s and 70s, the left-wing parties developed their own peculiar aesthetics. The Left Socialists, listed as Y on the party lists, used this slingshot poster during many parliamentary elections. Traditional non-socialist people probably interpreted this as an incitement to violent revolution while the left-wing people saw it rather as an example of disrespectful and puerile humour. The message of the poster wasn't very convincing and probably esoteric. But it was much more fun than most election posters in the 1970s.

▲ *Three political posters that each manage to communicate their message to their target groups. All three posters were made by anonymous graphic designers.*

GEORG JENSEN STAINLESS
GEORG JENSEN

Product design

We don't give a second thought to many of the products we surround ourselves with every day. We just take them for granted. They're so natural to us because they've always been there and haven't changed much in our lifetime. Take for example a pencil, clothes peg, paper clip or a button. We don't even consider the fact that they could look different. Of course, sometimes a manufacturer who wants to set himself apart will make one of these archetypical products in another colour. Or at times it pays to manufacture clothes pegs in plastic rather than wood, but the shape is rarely changed, and the function never is.

These anonymous products have been gradually developed over the years. Some of them were invented hundreds of years ago and have been slightly improved ever since. These objects have been developed and evolved to become the perfect solution to our everyday problems. Actually, these things have been created through a type of simple and natural design; through designer Darwinism, if you will. There isn't a famous designer behind the fashioning of these objects. Perhaps the encyclopedia doesn't even know the name of the long since dead inventor, but the point is that these things work.

Even today most of the things we have around us are designed by an unknown person. Numerous everyday articles are the result of many years' refinement, or even several generations' small and gradual improvements. This is true of either a pair of scissors or a raincoat. An incredible amount of everyday designed products – like a kitchen knife or a mop – are the result of constant development and modification to the user's requirements for applicability and convenience. Function subordinates form, but usually that doesn't make it uglier.

CERAMICS

One of the oldest handicrafts in Denmark is pottery. The oldest Danish pottery is from about 4600–3900 BC. In the beginning they were crude ceramics in the form of big cooking vessels with pointed bottoms to bore into the coals and small oval bowls that were probably used as lamps. Ceramics was most likely women's work and done without the use of the potter's wheel, which was not introduced in Denmark until just before the Viking Age, around 750 AD. Instead the potter shaped the clay with her hands, perhaps on a board resting on her lap while the work progressed.

The good clay was usually found on the banks of streams, but before it could be used it had to be tempered, that is, mixed with burnt and crushed granite grit, which was often found around the open fireplace. If the pure clay wasn't tempered in this way, the cooking vessels and lamps couldn't withstand the heat they would later be subjected to. The making of a clay pot started with a slice of clay for the bottom and the sides were built by coiling the clay. Then the surface was smoothed so the grit didn't stick out. Finally, before firing, it was decorated by stamping the sides with a stick, a shell or just a nail. A piece of string could also be used to make a pattern on the clay. The firing was done in an open fire and probably didn't take long so the result was a porous pot that was seldom painted or even glazed. Since the very beginning, the decoration of pottery has definitely had significance, and ceramics were made for various occasions such as births, deaths, sacrifices and the like.

Pottery for everyday use without a lot of ornamentation was also made. When agriculture was introduced in Denmark around 3900 BC, ceramics blossomed. Archaeologists even call this era the Funnel Beaker Culture

▾ *Anonymous products that we don't give a thought to are found everywhere in our personal world. If these many objects didn't exist, our lives would be much more difficult. Yet although these things are indispensable, they're usually made by a more or less unknown company, and also the designer is not known.*

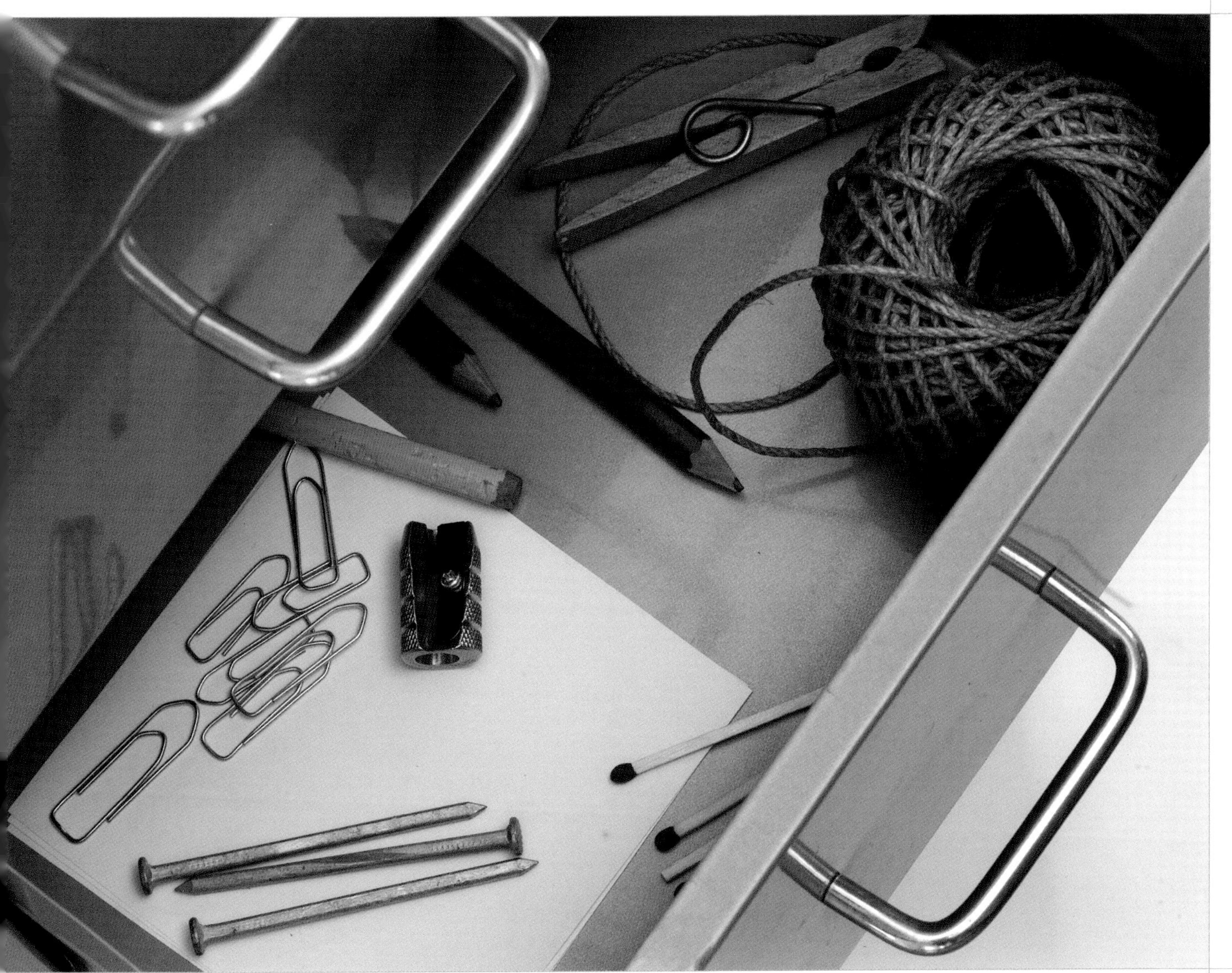

JAN TRÄGÅRDH, 1931–2006, was a Swedish designer who worked in Denmark from the 1950s as an industrial illustrator first, and later as an industrial designer. He was a trained artist and after working and studying in Paris, he headed for Sweden but ended up staying in Copenhagen. He worked for Bjørn & Bernadotte's design office from 1957 before starting his own design company in Copenhagen in 1962. Trägårdh worked in an unsentimental and often geometrical style and was inspired by German functionalism. He often had jobs of a technical nature, such as designing refrigerators for Gram, an emergency case for Ambu, a sign system for Modulex and reproduction equipment for Eskofot. Around 1980, Trägårdh designed one of the first cellphones in Europe for Philips (see page 124). Later on he designed cast-iron kitchenware for the Japanese firm Iwachu. In 1967, Jan Trägårdh was a co-founder of the trade organisation Industrial Designers Denmark (IDD). Jan Trägårdh was also a design teacher at the Academy of Fine Arts, School of Architecture.

because of the most commonly made clay bowl with a rounded belly and a funnel-shaped neck. Small versions of this shape were used in small versions for drinking vessels, and the larger versions show signs of being used as cooking vessels. Apart from these useful ceramics, a lot of pottery for ritual use was also made.

Early on in the Funnel Beaker Culture, when this ceramic tradition was new to the Danes, the design was relatively uniform all over the country. But in the course of 200–300 years, regional deviations arose regarding the shape and particularly in the decoration. From about 3250 BC, the Skarp Salling vessel from Himmerland is known for its minute decoration, and it's considered the most beautiful piece of pottery from the Neolithic Age in Denmark. This earthen vessel, which even by European standards is unique, is basically simple in design, but richly ornamented. The surface of the vessel's rounded belly is harmoniously divided into areas of which some are smooth and others are covered with a regular pattern of grooves that have been made with a cockle shell. The neck is decorated with line patterns, at the top vertical lines, and under them a crisscross pattern. The vessel is from Skarp Salling and is now in the National Museum in Copenhagen. It has two tube-shaped ears through which a string was passed so it could be hung up.

A few hundred years later, around 2800 BC, things started going downhill for fine Danish pottery when ceramics lost much of its ritualistic meaning. The simple pottery for everyday use lived on, but the ceremonial role of the fancier pottery seems to have been replaced by small buckets made of bark or wooden bowls. Even later, in the Bronze Age, other materials and handicrafts probably had a greater value in rituals – these were of course made of bronze. Around the year 0, ceramics once again blossomed. Apart from simple everyday articles, finer things were made, such as large dishes, pitchers and small vessels with ears – a kind of mug – in elegant forms made of thin and well-tempered clay. The pieces were heavily burnished and often fired so the surface was shiny and black. They were decorated with vertical grooves, stamped geometrical patterns and small stamped decorations.

▸ *The Skarp Salling vessel was found in 1891 during an excavation of a passage grave in Himmerland. It's a unique piece of pottery from the most significant period of pottery making in prehistoric Denmark, the Funnel Beaker Culture. The decorations on the sides were made by stamping and scoring the damp clay with a cockle shell, a tubular bone and a thin stick, respectively.*

IN 1975, THE Louisiana Museum of Modern Art arranged an exhibition with the title 'Anonymous Design'. A few older designers still talk about this exhibition with enthusiasm, since for many of them it was a crossroads for Danish design.

This highly respected museum acknowledged that design could be more than teak furniture and silver forks. Design was also making good tools for the carpenter and a practical typewriter for the secretary. Yet it was also about anonymous design that had developed through generations and had passed the litmus test because the users took it to heart.

Jan Trägårdh, one of Danish design's grand old men (see page 84), wrote in the exhibition catalogue that design was becoming a fashionable concept. The word design shouldn't be value-laden as it doesn't say whether the product is good or bad or whether the solution to a given task is good or bad. Design shouldn't be seen as an aesthetic garnish, but rather be seen as product development in the best sense.

At the same time he thought that good design always entails an improvement on something that exists, perhaps not on par with a brand new invention every single time, but still a step in the right direction.

To get his point across Jan Trägårdh suggested that a design award should be given to the best refinement of a Tuborg beer, as he thought it would be better to focus on the contents of the bottle than the shape of the bottle or the design of its label.

AROUND THE YEAR 1900, Jutland pots or black pots were made in the countryside. The black pots were black-fired, unglazed earthenware made in Jutland from around the year 1500 as a subsidiary occupation to agriculture. They were made in roughly the same way as in prehistoric Denmark, that is, by women who crafted the vessel on a board placed in their lap. The black colour arises when the earthenware is fired at a relatively low temperature in an oxygen-deficient firing entailing lots of smoke. Unlike what they did in prehistoric Denmark, when pots were fired in an open fireplace, the black pots were fired in a charcoal stack covered with peat.

The black pots were used in households all over Denmark and the neighbouring countries. They were everyday utensils without notable decorations. The traditional black pot has a round belly and two ears or handles and three studs to stand on. The shape is practical, easy to make and robust in its proportions and sturdiness. The design is frank and unassuming, easy to use. In the mid-1800s, an estimated 1.3 million were made annually, so it was a considerable home industry. Other products were made, among other things candlesticks and pans. For many years, cooking in this type of earthenware was considered better and healthier than using the metal pots and glazed ceramics of that time that could release toxins into the food being warmed. The area around Varde was a prominent pottery region, but Randers and Fjends Herred by the Limfjord also had a large production.

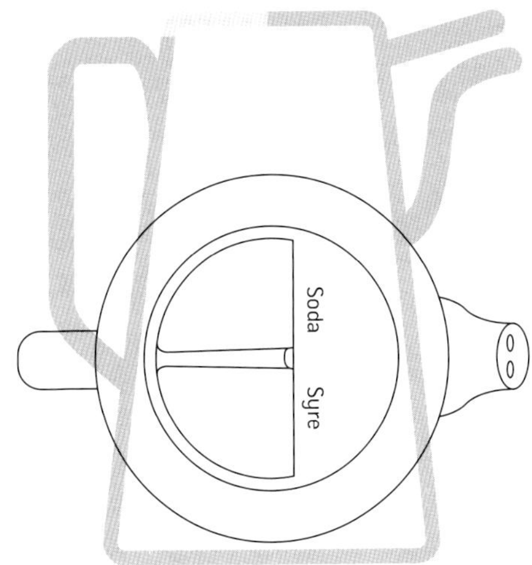

▸ *Many everyday products were manufactured at the faience factory Aluminia, among others this jug from the 1930s. It could be used to make carbonated drinks. The jug has a partition that goes all the way up to the spout. In the one compartment, water, citric acid and sugar were added, and in the other sodium carbonate, water and more sugar. When a glass was poured, equal amounts of the two liquids were combined to form a cheap carbonated drink.*

The Faience Factory in Store Kongensgade

Almost until modern times, ceramics continued to be manufactured locally by mostly anonymous potters who sold their wares at the local market or through travelling salesmen. The architect Viggo Sten Møller, who from 1953–67 was the principal of the School of Arts & Crafts (today known as Denmark's Design School), reports in his book *Danish Applied Arts 1850–1900* that as a child in 1905 he encountered horse-drawn carriages loaded with ceramics peddling the anonymous pots. Until the mid-18th century, most of the finer ceramics for the upper class were manufactured by local workshops or imported.

Not until 1722 was a proper ceramics industry established in Denmark. This was the Faience Factory in Store Kongensgade in Copenhagen, which secured exclusive rights from the king to manufacture faience with a blue decoration. The factory experienced a tumultuous existence with internal struggles, and in 1769 the royal exclusive rights were abolished, and the factory ceased to exist around 1779. This early faience was primarily an attempt to copy the much sought after Chinese porcelain, which Europe hadn't yet learnt how to manufacture. Besides the Chinese inspiration, the style of decoration was also influenced by French and Dutch faience. The most spectacular piece from the factory in Store Kongensgade was a punch bowl shaped like a mitre. Many tiles were also made for, among other places, the staircase of the Eremitage Hunting Lodge to the north of Copenhagen in 1737.

In 1775, Frederik V contributed financially to the establishment of the first porcelain factory in Denmark. Apart from the extraordinarily exclusive Flora Danica dinnerware, most of the production at the Royal Porcelain Factory were copies of foreign porcelain. In particular the Chinese pattern known as blue fluted, but also the popular service called Blue Flower was of foreign origin. The slump at the beginning of the 19th century culminated in national bankruptcy in 1814 and caused a decline in the market for expensive porcelain and ceramic products and therefore very few innovations were made.

Aluminia

Around 1830–50, the royal factory manufactured porcelain in the Classic Empire style, but also made figurines that were modelled on the works of Bertel Thorvaldsen. During this period, the quality of the works of the Royal Porcelain Factory rose to an international level, and the company is still highly respected in Europe. In 1868, the Crown withdrew its commitment to the royal company, which was privatised. During this period, new manufacturers entered the scene, with the most well known being the faience factory Aluminia. It was established in 1863 in Christianshavn, but moved to Frederiksberg in 1869 on the very corner where the Royal Porcelain Factory was later situated for many years.

Aluminia's wares weren't particularly artistic or innovative, but the success of the factory was its production of good and sturdy high-quality faience inspired by English and German stoneware. Aluminia's signature on the bottom of their products was a capital A crossed by three horizontal lines. The owner was engineer Philip Schou, and in 1882, Aluminia acquired the Royal Porcelain Factory, and the two companies were run as one. Philip Schou had invested in new capital goods, including expensive ovens that he had constructed himself, so the newly merged factory had a considerable surplus capacity that couldn't be utilised.

THE WORD CERAMICS actually covers a number of different materials that have one thing in common: they come from the ground – either as a type of clay or as a pulverised form of stone. After being shaped, the material is fired so it more or less melts together (this is also called sintering) and becomes a solid mass.

Porcelain is considered the finest ceramic product. It consists of 50 % kaolin, 25 % feldspar and 25 % quartz, which is mixed with water to the thickness of gruel and then moulded. After several firings of which the last reaches a temperature of 1450 degrees Celsius, the end product is very white and compact, while thin porcelain pieces are translucent. The high firing temperature has made it difficult to decorate the porcelain under the glaze, since only a few colours can withstand the heat. This is why older porcelain is often painted blue.

Philip Schou's answer to this problem was to bank on design and therefore 28-year-old Arnold Krog was hired in 1884. Krog, a young architect, had no background in ceramics. Until he was hired by Schou, he had worked under Ferdinand Meldahl on restoring and decorating the interior of Frederiksborg Castle in Hillerød. But after a short trial period, Krog was permanently employed as artistic head of the old company that had stagnated. He revived the blue under-glazing, and he redesigned and simplified the motifs on the blue fluted porcelain. He also invented new decorations and patterns that were inspired by Japanese nature motifs that were popular at the time in Denmark and abroad.

Aluminia continued to be the company's manufacturer of faience, and particularly in the mid-20th century was productive, making many well-designed services characterised by modern ideas with good everyday design. The artistic leader from 1930-63 was Nils Thorsson (1898–1975), who was trained as a ceramist at the factory and had studied at the Royal Academy of Fine Arts on the side. He designed many faience services, of which Sonja was one of the best. It wasn't experimental design, but a good and sensible everyday service in dusty blue with a white edge. Among other products from that period is a series from the 1930s of white kitchenware, platters and pitchers, and in 1965 Grethe Meyer's dinner service called Blue Line. In 1969, the factory mark was changed to 'Royal Copenhagen Fajance', and the factory became an integrated part of the Royal Copenhagen group in 1985.

▲ *This vase in an example of Arnold Krog's work, inspired by Japanese nature motifs.*

Faience was very common in Europe before the arrival of porcelain. In 1759, the Englishman Josiah Wedgwood produced the stoneware faience that we use today. It's similar to porcelain, but isn't fired at such high temperatures. Faience is also fired twice; the first time at 1100–1200 degrees Celsius. Then it is decorated and glazed before the second firing at 1000–1100 degrees Celsius. The result is slightly more porous than porcelain. The lower firing temperature meant that more colours could be used, and it was cheaper to manufacture. It doesn't make much difference today due to the technical advances in colouring.

Stoneware is made of special types of clay that are greyish or brownish in colour. The pieces are fired at 1200–1300 degrees and thus sinter, meaning they become very tough and dense. Stoneware can be used as durable flooring as tiles or as acid-proof or frost-proof material. Stoneware is also used to make objects of art.

Earthenware is classic ceramics. It has been made since the Stone Age. Objects can either be shaped by hand or on a wheel. The body is porous and brownish or reddish if red clay is used, or buff if blue clay is used. It's fired at a maximum temperature of 900–1000 degrees Celsius.

▲ *The faience dinnerware Sonja was designed by Nils Thorsson while he was the artistic head of Aluminia.*

ARCHITECT AND DESIGNER Grethe Meyer (b. 1918) has mostly worked in architecture and interior design. Together with Børge Mogensen she designed Boligens Byggeskabe (Unit cabinets for the home) in 1954–59. For Aluminia she designed Blue Line (below), which was awarded the Danish Design Council's ID prize. It's simple dinnerware without frills and very much in line with the functional tradition that the cabinets had sprung from. In 1976 Grethe Meyer designed a very different series of ceramic products. This is Firepot (right) which is a type of ovenproof stoneware that can go directly from the freezer into the oven. The design of Firepot is very different from Blue Line in that it's cookware with a very robust look. With time the colours of Firepot change slightly, but the warm, earthy tones age with grace, and Firepot is so well designed that it can be used as a serving dish even if you have company. Firepot was awarded an ID prize in 1976.

◂ *The porcelain tea and coffee service Form 24 from 1962 was extended to a complete service called Form 678 in 1968. Designer Henning Koppel was relentless in his demands of the form and he resisted having it decorated. The ware is so thin that it can hardly survive a cycle in a modern dishwasher without breaking. Koppel's answer to this was, 'Then just wash it by hand.'*

Bing & Grøndahl

In 1853 a new major competitor to the Royal Porcelain Factory arrived on the scene – Bing & Grøndahl. In the beginning they concentrated on figurines and, like Aluminia, they often used Bertel Thorvaldsen's work as their models. Around 1860 the factory also began to manufacture dinnerware. The first artistic director was Pietro Krohn (1840–1905), who in 1888 had designed the Heron service with under-glaze decoration. In 1893 he became the first director of the Danish Museum of Art & Design in Copenhagen. The company's most popular service ever is the Seagull service from 1892 designed by Fanny Garde (1855–1928). In 1895, Bing & Grøndahl made their first Christmas plate, which ceramist August Hallin (1865–1947) was responsible for.

Initially, the factory's designers were much inspired by nature, Japanese motifs and a twining Art Nouveau style. Today many people would think that Bing & Grøndahl's early works, especially the Heron service, are very different and ornate with decorations, figures and ornamentation, but in its time, Bing & Grøndahl came the closest to contending with the Royal Porcelain Factory for dominance as the country's leading ceramics company. The factory's mark was 'B&G' until 1895 when Bing & Grøndahl became a joint-stock company, and from then on the three towers from Copenhagen's town arms were added to the B&G symbol. But then in 1987 all the major ceramic producers became one company, and Bing & Grøndahl merged with the Royal Copenhagen corporation.

In more recent times Bing & Grøndahl has used designers such as Axel Salto, Gertrud Vasegaard (b. 1913), Erik Magnussen and Henning Koppel. Several of the products that resulted from this period have a very simple and modern expression. Among them, Koppel's two services 'Form 24' and 'Form 678', both from the 1960s, reflect the designer's wish to make flawless white service and the factory's desire to indicate its modern outlook on design. Form 24 is a tea and coffee service, and Form 678 is an extension of it to a complete service. Both are white, undecorated porcelain. Koppel used his unerring sense of the tight curves from the hollowware he had worked on so much for Georg Jensen. For example, the whole service is characterised by careful attention to form and balance in the individual pieces. However, Koppel was very opposed to decorative painting since that went against his view of modern design.

▴ *The spice jars were designed by Bo Bonfils in 1969 for Bing & Grøndahl. The mortar is part of the same series and is from the early 1970s. The series was manufactured until 1989.*

CERAMIC ART IS the name of the more experimental type of ceramics that is often made as unique pieces in small workshops or in limited series at specialised companies. In the course of many ceramists' careers they have gone back and forth between ceramic art and mass-produced ceramics. The established companies like Royal Copenhagen and Bing & Grøndahl have also placed their workshops at the disposal of experimental ceramists. Two of the most well known in this area are Axel Salto (1889–1961), who worked with Bing & Grøndahl and the company Saxbo and was known for his pinecone-like, sculptural vases, and Thorvald Bindesbøll (1846–1908), who worked in the Art Nouveau style for several companies, of which Kählers in Næstved is probably the most well known. The platter on the left is from Eifrig in Valby.

ROYAL COPENHAGEN HAS also developed new services and other products in recent years. One of the most talked about is the everyday service Ursula (below left) by Ursula Munch-Petersen (b. 1937). It's made of faience and was developed over a period of years in the 1990s. The service is very popular with its bright colours and distinct almost exaggerated forms which can be seen in the lip of the pitcher. Another modern ceramic designer is Ole Jensen (b. 1958), who also created a series of kitchenware for Royal Copenhagen. It's made of faience and is called Ole (below right) and has very expressive forms. His teapot that was cast in one piece is very characteristic of his surprising ceramics. The series consists of a grater, a citrus squeezer, a unique tipping sieve along with cups, carafes, platters and plates. Finally, Karen Kjældgård-Larsen's blue-fluted Mega (left) must be mentioned (see page 43).

THE COFFEEPOT 'MADAM Blue' (pictured right) was one of the many blue-enamelled kitchen and household wares manufactured by Glud & Marstrand, a factory in Copenhagen, in the 1880s. The coffee pot's design has been changed several times, but the form is thought to originate from an English type of coffeepot. This blue kitchenware was manufactured until the 1960s, but was gradually replaced by other products in stainless steel, aluminium and plastic, which were cheaper to manufacture and more modern to look at.

OTHER THINGS FOR THE TABLE AND KITCHEN

Same function, new materials

Just like in the Viking Age when wood was increasingly used instead of pottery for bowls, mugs and vessels, in our time we have seen new materials replace pottery for this type of kitchenware. Plastic and to some degree also a new robust make of glass have been used more and more in the last 50–75 years instead of ceramic materials.

One of the most familiar examples is the Margrethe bowl. It was created in 1950–51 at the first proper industrial design practice, Bjørn & Bernadotte, in Copenhagen. This design company was established in 1949 by the Danish architect Acton Bjørn and the Swedish prince and industrial designer Sigvard Bernadotte. One of their first employees, who also worked on this project, was the young Jacob Jensen, who later would establish his name as an independent designer for Bang & Olufsen. One of their first jobs was for the company Rosti and led to the series of Margrethe bowls (above). These bowls were made of melamine, which is rather heavy and very durable. The bowls were named after the royal couple's eldest daughter, Princess Margrethe, and before they hit the market, the new constitution was passed and Margrethe became heir to the throne.

At first the bowls were made in three sizes, and in 1965 there were five with volumes ranging from 1.4 to 4 litres. The colours have followed fashion from pastels at first, to brown, orange and beige in the 1970s, black and white in the 1980s, to today's very saturated yet hazy colours. In 1966 another improvement was made – a non-slip rubber base so the bowl would neither slide around the counter nor scratch its surface. The shape is typical of the 1950s, rounded and sensible to ensure its success as a good mixing bowl. The handle and lip are fully integrated in the form, very user-friendly. It's a classic piece of industrial design sold in the hundreds of thousands and still found in the shops today.

Krenit

Around the same time as the Margrethe bowl was launched, you could also buy the new Krenit bowls. They were conceived and designed by mechanical engineer Herbert Krenchel (b. 1922) and his good friend Torben Ørskov from the company Form & Farve, who put them into production. They had realised that Americans ate a lot of salad, so they wanted to make a series of bowls for that purpose. The Krenit bowls, as they were called, consist of a millimetre-thick steel plate that was enamelled black on the outside with a glossy colour inside. Enamel is a very durable surface treatment, and they made a point of maintaining the high quality. One of the great challenges was to retain the sharp edge during enamelling. If the edge had been folded over, the bowl would have been easier to manufacture.

But the sharp edge is part of what gives the Krenit bowl a more resilient appearance than that of the Margrethe bowl, and even today they look extremely sophisticated, which has made them very popular collectors' items. The production was discontinued in 1963; not because there weren't any buyers, but because both sub-suppliers had closed down and no one else could manufacture the quality called for. There were nine different sizes and the smallest was about 10 cm in diameter and the largest about 30 cm. All were black on the outside, but there were eight different colours to choose from on the inside.

BJØRN & BERNADOTTE. In 1949 the Danish architect Acton Bjørn (1910–92) formed a partnership with the Swedish designer Sigvard Bernadotte. They established the first industrial design practice. In their Copenhagen office, designers like Jacob Jensen and Jan Trägårdh experienced much that would be important for their later careers. The practice is especially known for the Margrethe bowl, the Beolit 500 radio for Bang & Olufsen and numerous other everyday products. From 1964 to 1990 the practice was headed by Acton Bjørn.

SIGVARD BERNADOTTE (1907–2002) was a Swedish prince that lost his right to the throne after marrying a commoner in 1934. In 1930 he began working for Georg Jensen Silversmith and designed both classic and modern hollowware in silver. The flatware called Bernadotte from 1939 (see page 111) with its grooved handle is an elegant example of his style that's somewhere in between the old and the new. After he discontinued his collaboration with Bjørn in 1964, Bernadotte worked as a freelance designer.

▲ *The Krenit bowls were a big hit in the US, and in the late 1950s almost 7000 bowls were manufactured every week.*

▲ *A large enamelled pot and lid from the Købenstyle series, which was popular in the US. It was designed by Jens Quistgaard in 1954.*

ERIK HERLØW, 1913–91, was a Danish architect and industrial designer. From 1959 to 1979 he was the first professor of industrial design at the Royal Academy of Fine Arts, School of Architecture. Erik Herløw started his own practice in 1949, and apart from working for prominent companies like Tupperware, he designed factory buildings for Superfos among others. He was also an exhibition designer at home and abroad. In 1954 he was the co-founder of the Danish Society of Industrial Design (SIF), which today is called Danish Designers.

▲ *Aluminium pitchers with Bakelite handles designed by Erik Herløw's practice for the Kløverblad factory in 1955.*

▸ Erik Herløw Design made this salad spinner for Tupperware in 2000 (below left) and a series of containers for flour, grain and sugar etc. The containers are filled from the bottom and emptied through the spout in the top – the principle is first in, first out, and thus the contents in the bottom never become stale.

Købenstyle

Other Danish designers had success with enamelled iron. Jens Quistgaard (b. 1919) was a skilled sculptor and had served his apprenticeship at Georg Jensen before he designed kitchenware after World War II. Among other things he designed a series of lidded pots and pitchers in enamelled sheet iron. The series was called Købenstyle and was developed together with the American businessman Ted Nierenberg, with whom Quistgaard in 1954 established the firm called Dansk Designs. For 30 years they ran the company developing, manufacturing and selling Danish designed cookware on the American market in particular.

The pots from the Købenstyle series are high quality. The sheet iron is rolled in both directions before it's chased into its bowl-like shape. This ensures great stability at high temperatures. The way the handles are formed and spot welded to the body is especially beautiful and characteristically done. Glud & Marstrand, who also enamelled the Krenit bowls and made the old Madam Blue coffeepots, did the surface treatment. Later on, the production was moved to Japan and France, and the company changed its name to Dansk International Designs since Quistgaard didn't want to suggest that the products were made in Denmark. He was also one of the first people to work with laminated wood for cutting boards and in 1960 he designed a large ice bucket in teak.

Tupperware's Danish designers

An example of a designer that worked with the new type of materials is architect Erik Herløw. He established his practice in 1949, and he and his employees worked primarily in architecture. After a while, more industrial design was done, and in 1959, Erik Herløw was appointed Denmark's first professor in industrial design at the Royal Academy of Fine Arts, School of Architecture. He has also written some books and articles about his view on design. Like many of his contemporary architects and designers, he was very preoccupied with giving pride of place to good everyday artefacts at reasonable prices. In the financially lean times after the war, there's a lot of thrifty horse sense in that way of thinking.

Erik Herløw's practice took on many jobs for Danish companies, such as the cookware factory Kløverblad in Copenhagen, for whom they designed various aluminium pitchers. One of the goals of the design was to make the most of the factory's machines and simplify the design so the pitcher could be manufactured as rationally and cheaply as possible. The new pitchers were fitted with a handle of Bakelite, which was easy to mount and was tightly sealed to the sides of the pitcher, making it easier to clean. The pitchers were anodised in various bright colours, and the upper edge was cut and formed so as to make a lip. Back then it was a sensible everyday article, but today the materials seem a bit cheap and 'tinny' to most of us.

But Herløw also had foreign customers, and in 1968 he landed Tupperware as a client. Since then the practice has designed kitchenware for the company that is known for its high quality and its special way of selling them, that is at home parties. Here housewives sell to other housewives and their informal networks lead to coffee parties where the products are demonstrated and sold. The success of Tupperware began in 1947 when its founder, Earl Tupper, patented the special closing mechanism that seals the food in the container. The company has developed this principle in all of its products.

IN 1974, BODUM launched its big seller, the Bodum cafetiere for coffee making. At the same time, this product introduced the company's primary design language, which was similar to Eva Trio's, that is simple design for everyday use that is unsentimental and without frills. The geometrical forms were once again reminiscent of Bauhaus. Today over 60 million cafetieres have been sold. Bodum also entered the market for kitchenware and have their own stores in cities all over the world, and the design has become more colourful and alive. Today, Bodum is an international brand that is still moving into new product groups like desk accessories and electric household products like the popular Ibis electric water kettle.

Ole Palsby's universe

One of the designers who has had a keen eye on the geometrical design of Bauhaus and the design school in Ulm is Ole Palsby (b. 1935). He is a self-taught Danish designer who was originally a stockbroker, but specialised in the design of minimalist, simple kitchenware. Palsby began by designing a system of pots and pans, the Eva Trio products, at the request of Erik Mangor, the director of Eva. This was in 1975, and the main idea was to use the different properties of three metals to give the ideal conditions for any kind of cooking.

The same size pot and pans were manufactured in copper, aluminium and cast iron, respectively. All three metals are suitable for cooking, but have different advantages: copper quickly reacts to a rise or fall in temperature, aluminium is a bit slower, while iron reacts even slower. Once you know these qualities, you can make the most of them when cooking. The copper pan can be used for quick frying, while aluminium is more suitable for boiling, and iron is best for a roast that has to be cooked for a long time at an even temperature.

The handle is made of stainless steel, which doesn't conduct heat very well, and it's riveted to the pan. The lids are also made of stainless steel and in standard sizes, so only four sizes are needed. Since the lids are flat, you can heat things on them while cooking something else in the pot. Eva Trio has since become a well-established brand that includes service, porcelain platters, bowls, flatware, kitchen knives and other cookware. Ole Palsby has been the primary designer, but also other designers have worked on the Eva Trio series lately.

▲ *Pots and pans from Ole Palsby's Eva Trio series. He designed the mixing bowl for Rosti.*

THE BODUM COMPANY is in many ways a Danish company, which people perhaps don't know. It was established in 1944 in Copenhagen by Peter Bodum (1910–67) as a wholesaler company of kitchenware made by Danish manufacturers. The company didn't begin to develop its own products until the 1950s. Industrial design was important to Bodum, and today the company has a R&D department with 30 designers, engineers and graphic designers employed in Lucerne, Switzerland under the leadership of head of design Carsten Jørgensen (b. 1948). In 1980, Bodum moved its headquarters to Switzerland under the leadership of Jørgen Bodum in order to be closer to the Central European markets.

For Rosti, Ole Palsby designed a series of hemispherical kitchen bowls in semitransparent, matt plastic, and for the German company Alfi his very popular spherical vacuum jugs in plastic or metal in an array of colours. Ole Palsby had always had a penchant for geometric shapes, especially the cylinder and sphere, and that's why his works appear very clean, sensible and unsentimental. Despite his fascination for the basic shapes that are reminiscent of the German functional tradition from Bauhaus, his products don't seem old fashioned at all.

Stelton, Arne Jacobsen and Erik Magnussen

The success of Danish design at home and abroad in the 1950s whetted the appetite of several manufacturers. In 1960, the Stelton company was established, and they manufactured mediocre kitchenware for the domestic market at their factory in Fårevejle. They hired a young salesman, Peter Holmblad, who was the son of Arne Jacobsen's wife Jonna. Young Peter finally managed to convince his stepfather to design some proposals for new products for Stelton. The result was the series Cylinda-Line, launched in 1967 after many technical problems with the unmanageable stainless steel. In one stroke Stelton moved up into Danish design's major leagues. The very same year Stelton was awarded the Danish Design Council's ID prize, and the following year, the American International Design Award.

At first Cylinda-Line was composed of 18 pieces, including a coffeepot, teapot, ashtray, serving tray, ice bucket etc. Until his death in 1971, Arne Jacobsen continued to design new products for the series. Once again it's surprising that a Danish architect and designer took his starting point in the early Bauhaus tradition and creatively re-interpreted the form, function and especially the manufacturing conditions. If not exactly cheap, the Cylinda-Line products are far more reasonably priced than the Bauhaus designers' more craft-based products. Arne Jacobsen was a firm believer in industrial production, and he even felt that machines could do a better and more flawless job than people working by hand.

According to Peter Holmblad, who was then the managing director of Stelton, Arne Jacobsen never managed to design the vacuum jug that so many Stelton customers were waiting for. Instead it was made by ceramist and designer Erik Magnussen (b. 1940) and launched in 1977. Magnussen didn't strictly follow Jacobsen's details; among other things he created a different plastic handle than the one on the original pitchers for coffee, tea and ice water. But the cylindrical form in stainless steel remained the same for a while. In 1979, the vacuum jug was also made in a plastic version and in time it also came in a variety of colours. The tall, slim vacuum jug with the special rocker lid was at first harshly criticised for being unable to keep the coffee hot, and a burn specialist demanded that the jug be taken off the market because a number of children were scalded when jugs were knocked over. Nonetheless it was elegant, and Magnussen's jug became a great success for Stelton and is still found in many homes and offices.

THE LAND OF THE VACUUM JUGS. Few other nations drink as much coffee from vacuum jugs as the Danes, and the development in product design of household products is clearly reflected in the fashioning of Danish vacuum jugs over the last 30 years. Before that time, vacuum jugs weren't used much in the home; the coffee was kept hot in Madam Blue on the stove or heating stove.

In the past, vacuum jugs were mostly used for fishing trips, picnics or to bring to work, and they often had a robust, metallic appearance. The Stelton jug from 1977 was one of the first vacuum jugs to be designed for indoor use in the home. Other companies caught on and developed their own distinctive vacuum jugs. The distinctiveness could lie in the aesthetics as in Ole Palsby's jug from 1985 for Alfi. It was also geometrical in form – spherical with a cylindrical lid. Yet it doesn't look 'posh' like Stelton's model, but rather more informal. The geometrical design suggested serenity and deep seriousness through the use of materials like polished chrome, brushed stainless steel and matt, black plastic – a bit like a Bang & Olufsen stereo. Once the plastic came in more and more vivid colours, a hint of humour was added to the noble and formal style, and today the informal aspect is in the form itself. More of nature's curves can be seen in vacuum jugs. In 2003, ceramist Ole Jensen designed a completely different jug for Royal Copenhagen.

▲ *Erik Magnussen's Stelton jug with sugar bowl and creamer. The artistic expression is redolent of Bauhaus, and if you owned this set in 1977, it indicated that you had a serious and conscious sense of style.*

Its soft curves make one think it's made of clay instead of plastic. The jug is very simple: it doesn't have a handle, so you have to hold the neck to pour from it. The simple lid is made of rubber and adds to the feeling that Ole Jensen was inspired by the pottery and leather wine flasks of old – a radical break from geometry. Another organic design is the jug Quack, also from Royal Copenhagen, designed by Maria Berntsen (b. 1961) in 2004. The name refers to the shape of the jug, which looks like a duck.

This vacuum jug was also manufactured in plastic, but with a lip and handle in aluminium. Stelton, too, has begun to develop products like the new vacuum jug with the smiling name of Pingo, designed by John Sebastian (b. 1975). Like Erik Magnussen's predecessor it's made of stainless steel and plastic, but in contrast to the original Stelton jug, the form is hardly geometrical. A creamer in the same form, but naturally smaller, is part of this new series.

The shapes of the designer vacuum jugs have changed, but in terms of function they're the same, and the quality hasn't been improved much. One could rather say that three decades ago, ambitions arose to create new objects of utility and value. For example the rocker lid on the Stelton jug that can be worked with one hand since the lid doesn't have to been loosened. There isn't any more of that. Now innovations are made in the areas of aesthetics and art.

▲ *Ole Palsby for Alfi.*

▲ *Stelton's Pingo by John Sebastian.*

▲ *Quack by Maria Berntsen.*

▲ *Ole Jensen for Royal Copenhagen.*

OLE'S SENSE OF wood. This broom of hand-turned beech with natural bristles, by Ole Jensen, is an example of the recent tendency to return to the natural when designing household products. Until recently, it has been inconceivable to use anything but newfangled materials like plastic or aluminium. The dustpan is made of a semi translucent paper-thin piece of polypropylene. A minimalist cleaning tool whose design takes one back in time. It's manufactured by Normann Copenhagen.

The explosion in the kitchens

In the long Danish history of kitchen utensils, times were often marked by frugality. Money was scarce and most people usually looked for simple, cheap and durable solutions to their needs. This meant that in the kitchen there were fewer, but perhaps more durable utensils in the cupboards than today. The previously mentioned black pots and Madam Blue in enamelled iron are historic examples of these utensils, whose origins are anonymous, but they're characteristic in their design and as a rule excellent to use. A third significant material, once very common, was wood.

Like the black pots and other everyday ceramics, wooden products could be made locally and without a lot of machinery. Products such as cooking spoons, personal flatware, cutting boards, bowls, basins and knife handles could often be carved and shaped by hand with the help of a few simple tools. Not until rather late in the late 1800s to early 1900s, were these types of products more or less industrialised.

One example of this is Ryslinge Trævarer (Wooden Articles) who in 1919 began a machine production of traditional wooden articles. Since the price on the market had to be rather low in order to be competitive with the home-made cooking spoons, the factory's products had a rather rough finish. On the crooked specimens many of us have in our kitchen drawers, the marks left by a band saw or moulding machine are plain to see. On the consumer market of that time, these commonplace articles didn't cost much a piece in contemporary prices.

However, in the second half of the 20th century, you could buy exclusive wooden articles in the design shops. Now the handmade and carefully sanded cooking spoons became a completely different type of product, namely an indication that you appreciated good craftsmanship and beautiful, natural design. A shop called Form & Farve was located in Copenhagen for many years and sold well-designed products. Here you could buy the loveliest wooden kitchen utensils like cooking spoons, but they were sold without specification of the manufacturer or the craftsman. Form & Farve was the buyer and guarantor of quality and good taste; the shop was branded, not the craftsman. Today it's probably cheaper to buy a plastic cooking spoon by Rosti than a handmade wooden one.

▲ *The two wooden spoons are many years apart. The raw one with obvious saw marks is from the early days of industrialisation. The other new one is a carefully sanded lifestyle-spoon made of spindle-tree wood from Form & Farve.*

UPSTAIRS DOWNSTAIRS. In the old days, everyone made coffee in a Madam Blue coffeepot. The difference between ordinary people and the posh people was that most people took their Madam Blue into the living room and put it on the heating stove to keep it hot, while the wealthy poured the coffee into a porcelain coffeepot from The Royal Porcelain Factory before putting it on the table. TV series like 'Matador' and 'Upstairs, Downstairs' portray this difference. Oddly enough, while most of the time was spent explaining the lives and intrigues in the parlour upstairs, the servants downstairs were put in a sympathetic light. Downstairs we find a natural and unpretentious environment where life is actually lived. In many ways, Danish design in the 20th century is a story about longing for the natural and unassuming, wrapped in good design. Madam Blue is considered by many to be more honest and frank than the grand porcelain coffee service. A broom should be natural and turned in wood, but that doesn't mean it won't cost a fortune compared to a traditional industrial model made of plastic.

SILVER HOLLOWWARE ARE large articles like pitchers, platters, bowls, chandeliers, trophies and goblets that in most cases have been chased (hammered into shape and then polished). Especially in the first half of the 20th century this discipline reached new heights in design, and Georg Jensen Silversmith and Crown Jeweller A. Michelsen were the leading firms in this development. Today, Georg Jensen is mostly known for its jewellery, but unforgettable pieces were also made in silver hollowware. In the first decades of the 20th century, the artistic expression was dominated by Art Nouveau and natural shapes, twining vines, flowers, buds and many-fingered leaves. They were all made of silver, but often with precious stones inlaid as flowers in the motifs. One example is Georg Jensen's fruit bowl from 1918 (left) that is all silver and borne by a stylised grapevine with clusters of grapes. Just two years later, in 1920, artist and designer Johan Rohde (1856–1935) designed a silver pitcher for Georg Jensen, and it's

▲ *Johan Rohde's pitcher from 1922.*

▲ *Wine jug by Kay Fisker from 1926.*

perhaps the first step away from the decorative tradition in Danish applied arts towards the modern, simple artistic expression.

The slightly dented pattern is due to the fact that the hammer strokes were deliberately not removed completely by polishing and, according to Rohde's original drawing, it was to be the only form of decoration on the pitcher. But while the work was going on, a little ornament sneaked its way into the bottom of the handle. The modern pitcher cultivates the naked form's sculptural beauty where there's a gradual transition of the line on the edge to the handle. It's no wonder that the pitcher with the model name of 432 caused a sensation when it came on the market.

The hammer strokes became the symbol of the new style and a distinguishing mark for Georg Jensen in the 1920s, but at the end of the decade it was criticised by, among others, Kay Bojesen. The hammer strokes had become a mannerism; now something new was wanted. And Georg Jensen probably felt pressured by A. Michelsen to modernise. In 1925, the Crown Jeweller had teamed up with the young architect Kay Fisker, who had designed a wine jug in silver that was at least as elegant as Rohde's, yet far more simple in its sculptural form. No hammer strokes or ornaments here – only a pure form, although one can see that it was inspired by the classic Greek wine jar.

▲ *Henning Koppel's Pregnant Duck is from 1952.*

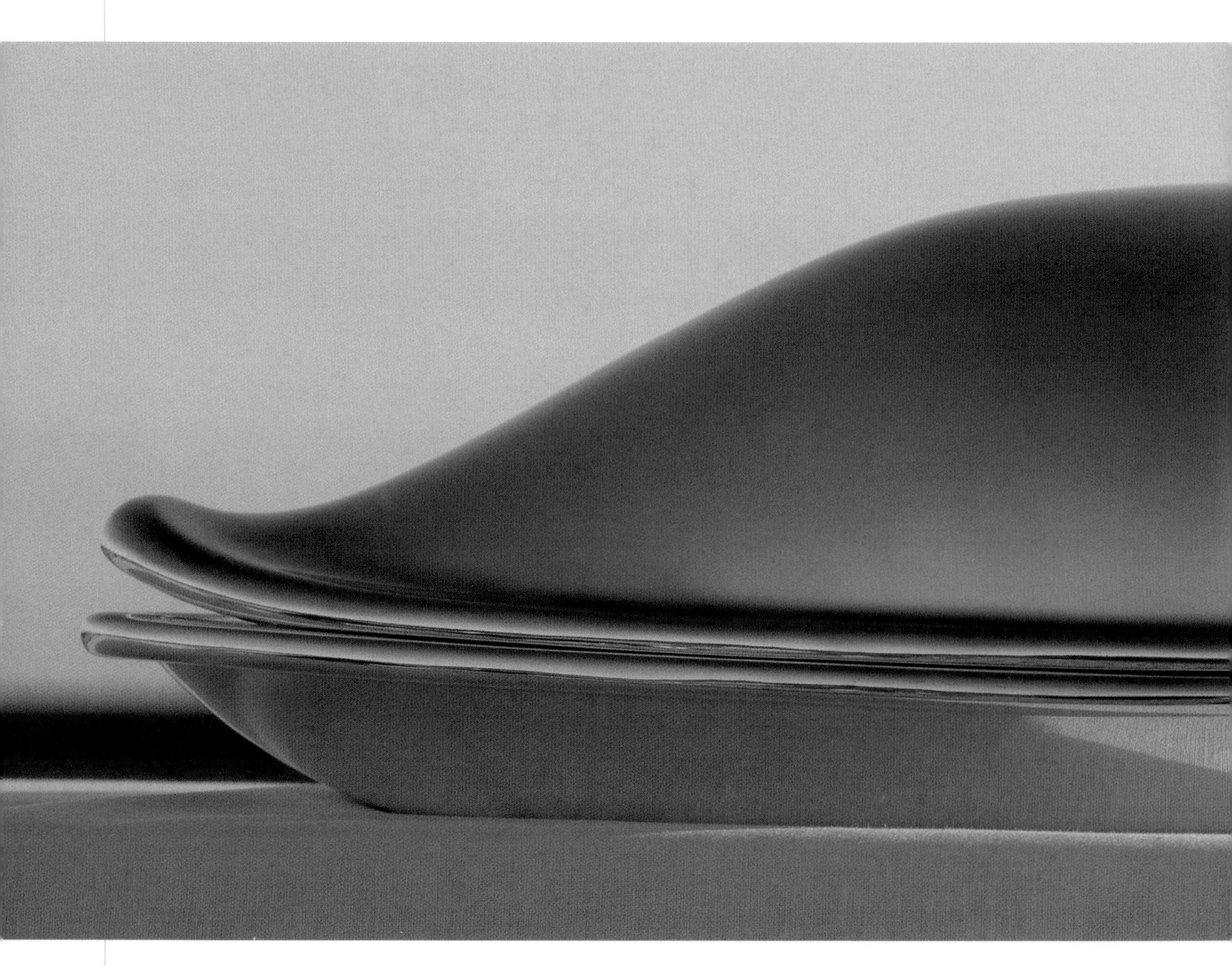

IF WE MOVE about 30 years into the future, we find Danish society entering a time of prosperity, and foreign countries have refreshed their knowledge of Danish design, not least of the Georg Jensen company. In the 1950s, Henning Koppel (see page 111) designs a number of his best products, among them three silver pitchers; one more sophisticated than the other. The most well known is from 1952 and was nicknamed 'The Pregnant Duck', but its precise name is model no. 992. This was sculpture converted to silver and extremely difficult to execute. It takes a seasoned silversmith many months to hammer out one of these pitchers. The price is high and dependent on the going price of silver on the world market. Designed for a well-off upper class, but it's definitely beautiful. Koppel's gigantic fish platter from 1954 is almost as impressive; it takes 500 working hours to hammer out, and half a million kroner to acquire.

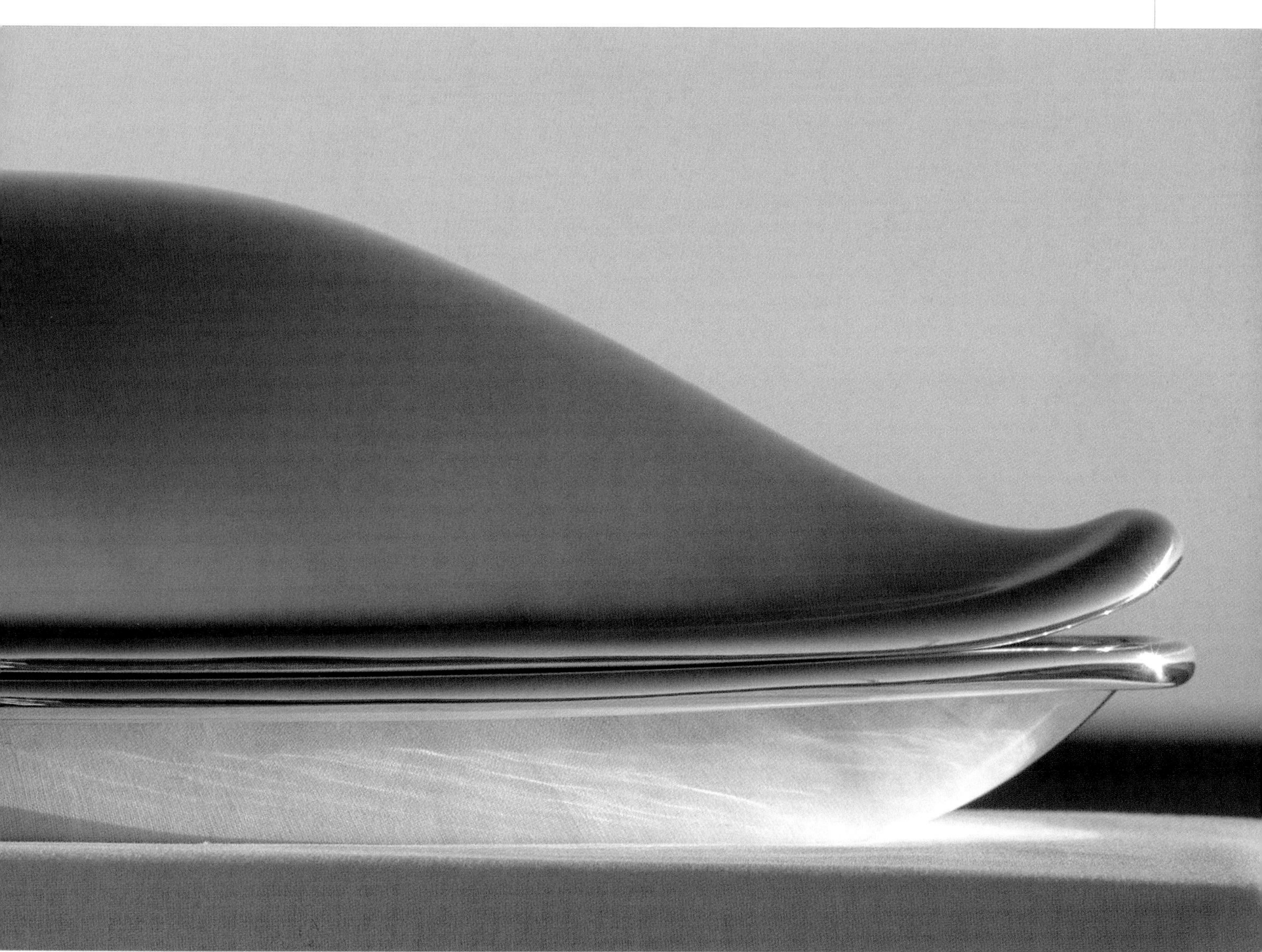

▾ *Frederik IV's personal gold flatware. The design isn't much different from what we can buy today, except for the precious metal and the hinges on the spoon and fork. This flatware was the king's personal possession, which he also took with him on his travels, and therefore it also came with a small salt cellar with a lid.*

KNIFE, FORK AND SPOON

For a long time in our history, most people used flatware made of wood. Apart from the knife blade, wood was the prevalent material at the table. The fork virtually didn't exist as one could easily get by with a spoon, using one's fingers and the help of a knife once in a while. In the early 1700s the flatware we know today came to Denmark; at first only for the nobility. Inspiration came from mighty Europe, and its design was greatly influenced by France and England. The Danish gold and silversmiths of the time mostly incorporated the foreign design, if they didn't downright copy it. One example is Frederik IV's personal cutlery, called, freely translated, 'gold mouth pieces'.

This flatware is from around 1730 and could be identical to the one mentioned in the court's ledgers, which was delivered on March 29, 1729. In that case it was made by Frederik Fabritius (1683–1755), who was a master goldsmith and Crown Jeweller at the time. It's not definite since the flatware isn't stamped with a master stamp. However, in the ledger it says that the Treasury paid 259 rix-dollars and 8 shillings for gold flatware on that day. The fact that flatware was personal can partly be seen with the king's monogram on every piece including the matching salt cellar with a lid in blue, white and rose enamel, and partly by the fact that the fork and spoon have hinged handles. The latter means that the king presumably travelled with his flatware, since you couldn't be certain that flatware was used everywhere, or at least not flatware fit for a king.

For a long time, flatware was exclusively a handicraft where the design of the products could entail more or less ornamentation on the pieces, and local variations could be great. But when industrialisation came to Denmark

▾ *Danish Standard Flatware in stainless steel manufactured by Cohr's Sølvvarefabrikker (Silverware Factory) from 1929 until the late 1960s.*

in the late 1800s, which was late according to European standards, some flatware began to be manufactured in factories. The material wasn't silver anymore, since it was much too expensive for the common man, but it was often made of stainless steel. One of the pioneers in this area was Cohr's Sølvvarefabrikker (Silverware Factory), established in 1860, in Fredericia.

This company, developed Scandinavia's largest silverware factory, very simple stainless steel flatware in the mid-1920s for use in hospitals. The design was fashioned in collaboration with Hospital Director Hans Christian Ridter and it had to be cheap, hygienic and no-maintenance. It's very simple flatware; almost like a template for any kind of flatware. It's big, rounded and without decoration, extra details or joints, so bacteria can't hide. It's almost an anonymous design. In 1929, Cohr's flatware was recognised by the newly established organisation Danish Standard as model flatware for hospital use. Then the actual industrial production began of what was to become known as Danish Standard Flatware.

Grand Prix and others

Other people could also design simple flatware. One of Danish design's early flatware from the time when modern simplicity without decoration began to be popular is from 1938 and was designed by silversmith Kay Bojesen (1886–1958). He was the one who also made the jolly monkey in teak. Originally, the knife in Bojesen's silver flatware came in two versions; one with an ebony handle, and one with a handle made of silver. The latter became the basis for a later version in stainless steel, which was awarded the grand prize at the Biennale in Milan in 1951, hence the name Grand Prix. In almost the same way as Cohr's, Kay Bojesen simplified his design to an

◂ *Henning Koppel's flatware from 1957 called Caravel.*

▸ *Bernadotte's flatware from 1939.*

▾ *Kay Bojesen's Grand Prix flatware, here in stainless steel, from 1950.*

archetypical one. The beauty lies in the sculptural treatment of the forms of the individual pieces, so that each piece is part of a whole, and the familial relation between them is evident and harmonious. That's why a designer like Kay Bojesen searches for uniformity by replacing wood with metal. The difference between this and Cohr's flatware is partly in the material, and partly in the refinement of the dimensions that Bojesen allowed himself, since his original silver flatware was so expensive that it would never have been used in a hospital kitchen or a factory canteen.

Several other designers came in the wake of Bojesen and Cohr in an attempt to design the ultimate flatware. Flatware, like chairs, is something every designer has to try their strength at by designing one chair or one set of flatware in the course of their career; some even do both. One of our first industrial designers, Sigvard Bernadotte, started his career by designing silver hollowware for Georg Jensen. In 1939, the year after Kay Bojesen created Grand Prix, he designed the flatware called Bernadotte for Georg Jensen Silversmith. It's also modern, but not as radically simple as Bojesen's. It was manufactured in silver with grooved handles and is an elegant example of Bernadotte's simple style.

Another great Danish designer of silver hollowware from the mid-20th century was Henning Koppel. He designed several sets of flatware. The silver flatware Caravel is from 1957, and Koppel's great experience as a hollowware designer can't be denied. His earlier work with pitchers, chandeliers and silver fish platters have left their mark on this flatware. This sculptural way of fashioning silver hadn't been and still isn't surpassed. In 1963, Koppel managed to design something almost as good, namely the stainless steel flatware New York. It has many of the same qualities as

HENNING KOPPEL (1918–81) was a skilled sculptor, who later designed silver hollowware and ceramics. From 1945, he designed for Georg Jensen Silversmith with whom he was affiliated until his death. He is famous for his large, elegant silver hollowware, like the fish platter from 1954 and the pitcher 'The Pregnant Duck' from 1952. Despite the simple, organic forms, Koppel was primarily an aesthete, not a functionalist. He also designed silver and stainless steel flatware and porcelain dinnerware for Bing & Grøndahl and glasses for Holmegaard Glassworks.

Caravel, and it's a bit more affordable for us mortals. Both types of flatware are still manufactured by Georg Jensen.

The Blue Shark and the surgical ward

The flatware Blue Shark is unfortunately no longer in production. It was designed by Svend Siune (b. 1935) in 1965 for Georg Jensen, and it's one of the most limited series of flatware ever manufactured. That is, there are very few individual pieces – knife, fork, spoon, a combined tea and coffee spoon and a few more; nine pieces in all. Blue Shark was the result of a competition where it only won third place, but it was the flatware that was put into production. Any feeling of separation between, for example, the knife's blade and handle is not present in this flatware. It's organic and smooth just like a shark.

The name was dubbed by author Kjeld Abell, who added the word 'blue' to give the imagination a little more to work with. Impeccable and sculptural to the utmost. Some years later, in 1971, Svend Siune designed a modified version of Blue Shark in plastic for the co-op chain store FDB. It was probably the most beautiful disposable flatware ever made, but it was only available for a few years. The 1970s weren't the best years for good design, and the way FDB treated this flatware is almost indicative of the great design values that the co-ops created in the course of time and then bungled when everything was all about discount.

While designing the Royal Hotel, architect Arne Jacobsen also designed some special flatware in 1957 called AJ flatware. Similar to Svend Siune, Arne Jacobsen works with creating as smooth a transition between the tool's parts as possible – between the handle and blade. You can't actually tell where one ends and the other begins. You could say that Jacobsen takes the tangent a bit further than Siune does, and to such a degree that a short time later, the flatware was removed from the restaurant at the Royal Hotel and replaced by something more traditional. The guests, most likely the foreign tourists, could not figure out how to use it and complained.

Arne Jacobsen enjoyed being ahead of his time. He often sussed out trends from the best in the trade abroad and then made his own unique version. Jacobsen took his projects a little further than his role models so his was slightly better and a bit different, and therefore he didn't think he was copying. In his design works in particular, Arne Jacobsen frees himself from the foreign inspirations. If he was inspired by anything for his AJ flatware, it was probably the newfangled lightweight flatware that the airlines used back then. But why was the flatware so disliked that people disgustedly compared it to surgical instruments? Jens Nielsen, who later became chief architect at the Danish State Railways, wrote ironically about this radical flatware in 'The Politiken' in 1963 and called Jacobsen's spoon, knife and fork, respectively, 'soup spatula', 'cutlet scalpel' and 'meatball probe'.

American design's high priest from 1930–1970 was Raymond Loewy, who designed numerous products, including the Greyhound bus and the Lucky Strike cigarette package. He used the abbreviation 'MAYA' to explain his design philosophy. It stood for: Most Advanced, Yet Acceptable. His point was, since he was also a businessman, that design should be innovative, but if the users can't understand the product, it will be a commercial failure. Arne Jacobsen's AJ flatware was so advanced that it was used in Stanley Kubrick's science-fiction film *2001: A Space Odyssey*.

Since the 1950s and 1960s there hasn't been any ground-breaking flatware on the market. The ones that have been designed are variations on well-known themes. Bo Bonfils' (b.1941) flatware from 1988, which was awarded the Danish Design Council's ID prize in 1990, differs from Henning Koppel's New York flatware by having slightly different curves, a long knife blade, shorter and more rounded handles, but you can easily see they're related. Bonfils' flatware points further back in time than Koppel's in one way in particular. The extension at the bottom of the knife's handle basically originates from about 200 years ago when there were 'pistol handles' on flatware. Back then you held your flatware like you held the old curved pistols.

Another variation that at first glance is hard to distinguish from the other products on the market is Mads Odgaard's (b. 1960) Odgaard flatware made for Rådvad Knivfabrik (Knife Factory). This design is from 1988 and made of stainless steel. The distinctive things about it are that is has a longer handle and shorter blade, but otherwise it's a little more angular in shape and feel than the organic models Blue Shark and others from the 1950-70 period.

▲ *Bo Bonfils' flatware from the late 1980s was awarded the ID prize in 1990.*

◂ *Left: Arne Jacobsen's AJ flatware, designed for the Royal Hotel, which was opened in 1960. Middle: Svend Siune's Blue Shark from 1965. Right: A set of Mads Odgaard's flatware Odgaard from 1988.*

▾ *The Hogla beer glass from 1928 (left) was one of the first projects that Jacob E. Bang pushed through at Holmegaard. The designer saw it as 'the beer glass for Denmark's common man'. He was inspired by an older porter beer glass from Holmegaard, and Hogla was redesigned (right) in 1951 so that the foot was more simple and thus cheaper to mass produce.*

GLASS

Danish glass design is a new trade compared to ceramics or furniture design. This is because most glassware used to be imported. In the Middle Ages and the Renaissance it came from the south and later from Norway, part of the Danish Realm until 1814. Only then did a large production of Danish glass begin, at first with the glassworks at Holmegaard in the middle of Zealand in 1825. Glass-making requires a high temperature to melt the glass mass, and the energy source here was peat from a nearby raised bog.

Later on, a number of other glassworks arose in Denmark. The number culminated in the late 1800s when there were over 10 factories spread around the country, including Fyen's Glassworks, and the ones in Aalborg, Århus, Hellerup, Kastrup and on Frederiksberg. Much of the production consisted of windowpanes and standard bottles for beverages. The factory's own craftsmen, the glass-workers, were practically the only ones who designed drinking glasses, serving bowls and the like.

In the beginning of the 1900s Thorvald Bindesbøll (1846–1908) and Svend Hammershøi (1873–1948) designed a few carafes and wineglasses for Holmegaard. But it wasn't until 1923 that skilled designers began to be permanently associated with Holmegaard which had begun a collaboration with the Royal Porcelain Factory. In 1927 the glassworks hired architect Jacob E. Bang (1899–1965), and he designed a lot of glassware until he retired in 1941. Bang was a functionalist and as a rule designed simple, pretty and practical products.

In 1942, Bang's job as chief designer at Holmegaard Glassworks was taken over by Per Lütken (1916–98). He was a skilled decorative painter, and for more than 50 years he put his mark on Danish glass design. Initially his style wasn't much different from Bang's, and he fashioned some relatively simple products in a bold design, but with softer forms and a heavier body. Later he became more imaginative in his artistic idiom and experimented a lot with the glass material and design techniques.

Per Lütken worked at Holmegaard till his death in 1998 and managed to design about 3000 glass products. During Lütken's later years, more designers started to work as freelancers for the company, and in 2001, a proper design team was established with the participation of Allan Scharff, Michael Bang (son of Jacob Bang), Torben Jørgensen, Anja Kjær and Per Svarrer. Furthermore, a collaboration was initiated with other glass artists, both individuals and groups of designers.

In the last 35 years there has been a blossoming in the so-called studio glass-making. These glass artists make unique pieces and usually emphasize the artistic aspect rather than that of utility. Now and then some of the glass artists have worked with large manufacturers, but often they have concentrated on glass-making in their own workshops. One of these glass artists is Finn Lynggaard, who was also the driving force behind the establishment of the Glass Museum in Ebeltoft in 1985.

▲ Anja Kjær is a glass designer who works in her own workshop as well as for Holmegaard. Since 1987, she and her husband, the American glass designer Darryle Hinz, have made a series of small glass bowls in different bright colours; all with a narrow edge in a contrasting colour.

▸ Finn Lynggaard graduated from the Painting School at the Royal Academy of Fine Arts in Copenhagen, but became interested in studio glass around 1970 and even built a glass furnace. He has also developed a technique where he practically paints with bars of coloured glass, thus combining his background as an artist with glass-making.

FYEN'S GLASSWORKS GOES back to 1873. The company produced things like pressed glass items, such as drinking glasses. The pressed technique isn't used in Denmark anymore, but involves making glassware by pressing molten glass into a metal mould. Many cheap wares, like children's glasses, are manufactured in this way and are often very durable. In 1902, Fyen's Glassworks took over Aarhus Glassworks and changed its name to De Forenede Glasværker (The United Glassworks). In 1907 the company merged with all the glass-making factories in Denmark, with the exception of Holmegaard Glassworks, under the name of Kastrup Glassworks Inc. In 1965, Holmegaard took over the lot, but during the energy crisis of the 1970s, many of the factories had to close, and today Holmegaard Glassworks in Holme-Olstrup is the only large company in Denmark. However, production didn't stop in Odense until 1990. The pressed 9-centimetre tall children's glasses (left) are from 1924 and were designed by an unknown worker at Fyen's Glassworks. The design is very similar to numerous industrial glasses from that period, and the type is still manufactured in countries like France at very low prices.

◀ *These unconventional brandy glasses were designed in 2004 by Rikke Hagen (b. 1970) for Normann Copenhagen. Rikke Hagen graduated from Denmark's Design School in 1998, and apart from running her own glassworks in Hillerød, she has designed products for Holmegaard Glassworks.*

▶ *Jacob Bang's tradition of developing good, high-quality everyday glasses was carried on by Per Lütken. The drinking glasses called Pearl from 1966–67 make a beautiful and simple series and were the start of several product lines of a similar type, such as Tivoli from 1968 and Ships Glasses from 1971.*

◀ *There are other manufacturers besides Holmegaard that develop and make glass in Denmark. Normann Copenhagen sells a number of glass products including the sculptural Swing vase designed by Britt Bonnesen (b. 1971). Each vase is unique because you can't control the turns the neck makes during production.*

KITCHEN MACHINERY

A natural consequence of industrialisation and the availability of new materials was that not only were traditional kitchen utensils product developed, but also completely new machines for the kitchen were created. Among other things, the introduction of town gas entailed that something that hadn't existed in a Danish kitchen had to be manufactured, namely the gas ring. One of Denmark's first industrial designers, architect Knud Valdemar Engelhardt, took on the job of designing this practical product for the company Tobe in 1919. This gas ring was the predecessor of today's stove and was usually placed on a so-called gas table, which consisted of an iron frame with a surface of inlaid tiles.

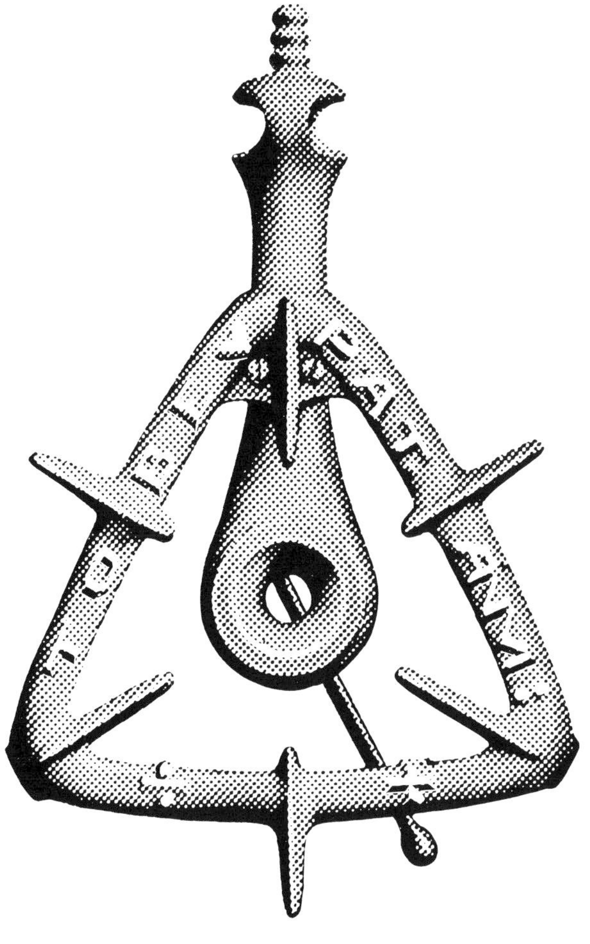

The gas ring was cast in aluminium and then zinc, and Engelhardt made sure to make it easy to clean by making all of the edges rounded. Moreover, he made the most of the casting technique by inlaying the writing on the top of the frame. Apart from the company name of Tobe and that the product was patented, the plus and minus signs indicated how to turn the gas on or off. And then there's a little heart, which is Knud V. Engelhardt's logo, and can be found on all his products and graphic designs. The product is thoroughly businesslike and sensible, but even here one feels the architect's need to make it beautiful and well proportioned.

Another example of the mechanisation of cooking is the many bread slicers that came on the market. Before, you sliced your rye bread with a cutting board and a sharp knife, but in the mid-1800s bread slicers came on the market. It was a burgeoning engineering trade that sensed a market for these machines, and a series of models saw the light of day in the following century. Some of the models were like Heath Robinson tools, for example

▾ *The bread slicer from Rådvad Knivfabrik (Knife Factory). A bold and robust design that commands the respect of children due to its large blade. Notice the little device that determines the thickness of the slice. When the blade is lifted, the bar is raised and determines how far the loaf can be pushed forward. When the blade is lowered, the bar is lowered as well and lets the slice fall in one piece; otherwise the slice would break. Perhaps it's low-tech, but it works.*

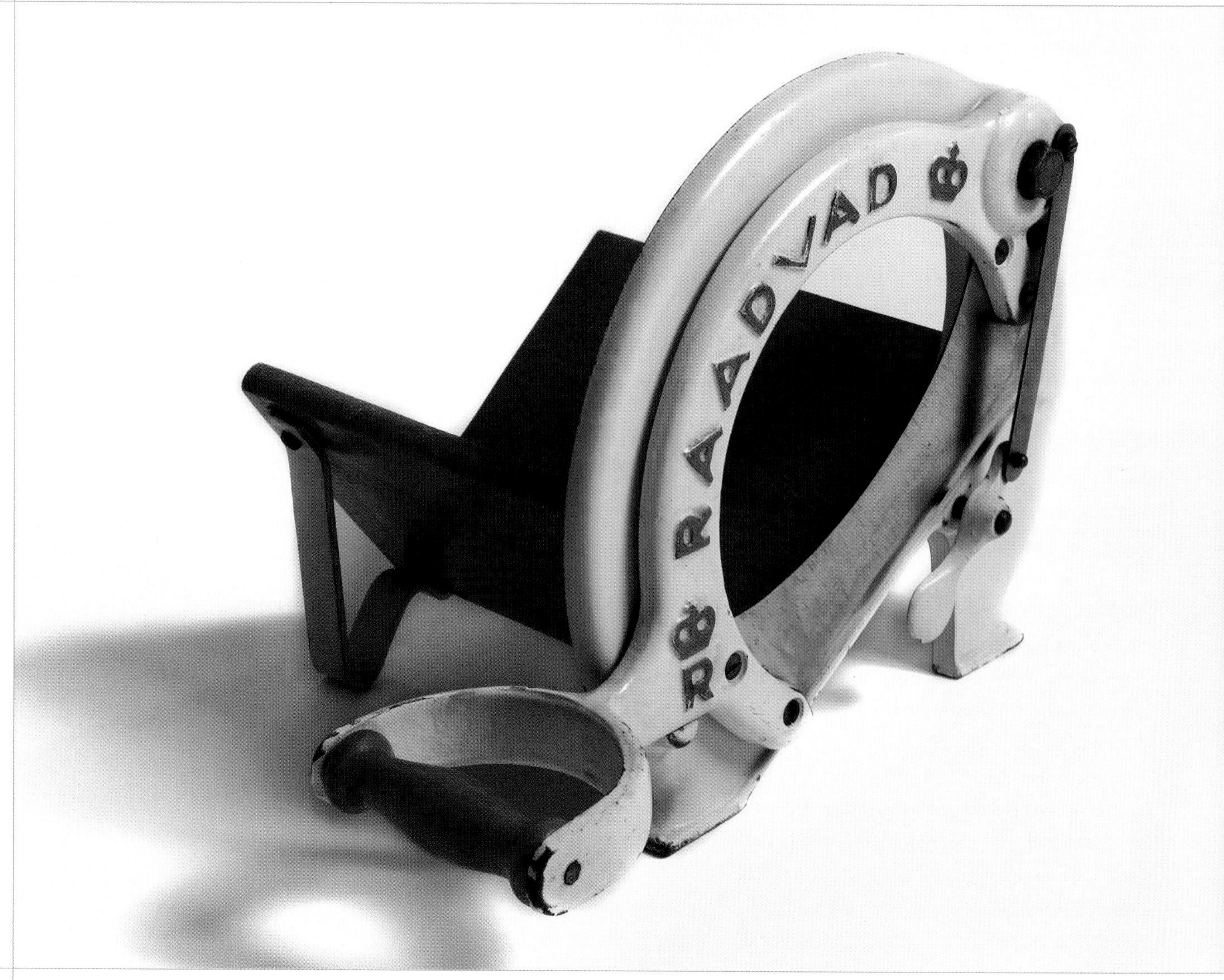

the loaf of bread stood upright and the blade was underneath it in a vertical position, and the slices of bread fell into a drawer at the bottom of the apparatus. The last and most well-known example is the famous guillotine model from Rådvad Knivfabrik (Knife Factory) designed in 1956 by Ove Larsen, who is known for his platters made for Bing & Grøndahl.

The slicer consists of a wooden trough with a cast-iron blade mounted at one end. Just like Engelhardt did with his gas ring, Ove Larsen used the casting technique to inlay the company name and logo in the body. This model has a neat little adjustable lever that determines the thickness of the slice of bread – it's a little wing regulated by a flat piece of iron. With its very robust design, the bread slicer has become a classic. It's a bit heavy and not as elegant as Engelhardt's gas ring, but it could slice bread for generations. In 2005 you could still buy brand-new models as well as used ones. Since then other versions have featured a circular blade and a turning handle, but the guillotine model is the classic bread slicer.

THE ELECTRIC HOUSEHOLD

There are also examples of electric kitchen appliances manufactured in Denmark, although the factories here never managed to assert themselves compared to the German, British and American companies in the business. But especially from 1945 to about 1970 a few companies were relatively successful, particularly on the home market. The basis for this mechanisation of cooking was partly due to the general rise in prosperity in Danish society, and partly due to many women entering the workforce, and therefore the workload in the home needed to be lightened. But there was also some prestige in having these appliances and showing them off on social occasions, just like Dad's car, 'Look what we can afford.'

▲ *The Ballerup mixer.*

For example, in the post-war period, the company Helmuth A. Jensen Inc. manufactured what we today would call food processors, but back then were called mixers. In fact it was a kind of multipurpose machine with many attachments so it could do everything from whipping egg whites to grinding meat and kneading dough. Although the firm was situated in Frederiksberg, all their models throughout the years had names that included the place name Ballerup. The first model was called the Ballerup Master Mixer, and the others all had English surnames like Ideal Mixer, Senior Mixer, Junior Mixer etc.

The design is clearly inspired from abroad, most likely from the USA, where the company's founder had travelled around in his youth and had been inspired to start manufacturing electric fences in Denmark. It's impossible to find out who actually designed the Ballerup mixers; possibly it was the owner of the company, Helmuth Jensen, or perhaps technicians who were employed there. At any rate, the mixers are rather streamlined and exude a modern and high-quality design. The main parts of the machine have rounded edges and corners which make them easy to keep clean. The motor part on the Ballerup Junior Mixer can be removed and used as a kind of hand-held power drill or polisher, so when a housewife in the 1950s wasn't using the mixer, the man of the house could use it to wax the car.

Gram

When you look at a refrigerator or a freezer, you might not think about design. These were probably the kind of products that Jan Trägårdh was thinking of when he wrote about anonymous design in the Louisiana Museum of Modern Art's catalogue (see page 85). The fact that he designed this type of product himself can be seen in the series of refrigerators and freezers that he and his colleague Rolf Andersen designed for the Gram brothers in Vojens. In the early 1960s when these refrigerator freezers were made, the Danish economy was flourishing and the Gram company, which had previously manufactured large refrigerating plants for industry, now entered the home refrigerator market. Earlier, refrigerators, like mixers, had been inspired by the round and sometimes bulky American style. They were large units with rounded corners and chrome on the enormous doors, a bit like American cars.

Trägårdh and Andersen's style was quite different. To them a refrigerator should first of all be practical, and it was important to them that the new units were better suited for the modern fitted kitchens, where the standard measurement of 60 x 60 cm was also becoming the norm. So, seen from the outside, these refrigerator freezers became more anonymous, square, clear cut and with a flat front. Furthermore, the door handle was in the form of a profiled, vertical panel on the whole length of the door that could be altered from being right-hinged to left-hinged and vice versa. The doors were fitted with rubber strips with subjacent magnets, which all in all provided a hermetical seal.

However, the great revolution was on the inside. The design of older refrigerators was very modest and they looked more like laboratory cupboards or industrial bookcases, but Trägårdh and Andersen analysed the needs of a household and renovated Gram's new refrigerators accordingly. The many models were divided into cold zones with movable shelves and hermetic plastic containers for vegetables, cheese and luncheon meats etc. The inside of the refrigerator was lined with a specially designed plastic that was used to make shelves on the door for milk and other beverages.

◂ *Gram's series of refrigerators, Multi-line, was launched in 1963 and designed by Jan Trägårdh and Rolf Andersen. Here it is pictured in one of their catalogues, enamelled in one of the bold new colours of the time.*

▸ *A Nilfisk from the GM200 series. The design was initiated by Hanne Uhlig and later finished by Jacob Jensen Design in the late 1980s.*

▾ *Nilfisk model M20, which was launched in 1924, was made in different versions with small changes in design. The later models, like the one here, had wheels.*

In the top of older refrigerators there was a small freezer compartment that could barely make ice cubes, but in Gram's new refrigerators, this was replaced by a proper deep freezer with a tight-fitting door at the bottom of the unit.

Trägårdh and Andersen's Multi-line refrigerators from 1963 heralded a quiet revolution in the concept of food storage. The design was extremely sensible, close to being boring, but it's a good example of anonymous design that doesn't constantly demand to be seen as a trendy design product. For many years white was the only colour refrigerators came in, and not until the 1970s, at an extra charge, could you get one in a popular colour of the time, such as eggplant, bottle green and curry. This was one of Jan Trägårdh's first major design jobs, but certainly not his last.

Nilfisk

The firm Fisker & Nielsen was established in 1906 as a factory that manufactured electric motors for many uses, but already by 1909–10 one of the owners, P.A. Fisker, developed the company's first vacuum cleaner, which was given the name Nilfisk C1. The Danish vacuum cleaner brand wasn't the first on the market, but over the years some rather singular models were developed. In 1922 the company launched the model L1 that had a slim, upright construction, resembling a sophisticated torpedo in modern stainless steel. Back then, vacuum cleaners were very technical things that augured well for a new period in the home, although in the beginning only wealthy people could probably afford such a newfangled device (for the maid to use).

◀ *In the mid-1970s, GNT Automatic, which lay in Søborg just outside Copenhagen and was the main supplier to KTAS, got the industrial designer Henning Andreasen to design a new series of pushbutton telephones for their company. The first one came in 1978 and was called F-78, but later more functions were added to the telephones, and they were called DanMark 1 and DanMark 2 (the black and red telephones, respectively). In design circles, the model series was given the nickname 'the rolled meat sausage' because of the softly rounded form of the casing, which was sharply cut off at the ends. Kirk in Horsens was the main supplier in the JTAS area. In 1972, Jacob Jensen designed the series of telephones called Comet (the brown one), which was the first pushbutton telephone in Denmark.*

The 1920s and 1930s were a time when hygiene was in fashion. Order and cleanliness were required because people became aware of the harmful effects of bacteria. Among other things, the labour movement participated in campaigns to improve public health by means of exercise, hygiene and cleaning. The modernist architecture without plush and tassels became a characteristic symbol of the trend at that time, and the vacuum cleaner was a suitably rational product for that purpose. Moreover, the early Nilfisk models could be bought on a reasonable instalment plan. In 1924, the M20 came on the market, and many Danes remember it from their grandparents' home. It was a chubby floor model that was furnished with wheels later on. Its upright, barrel-like shape is the general style for almost all the later Nilfisk vacuum cleaners.

In 1932 a low-noise model was introduced and it was called 'the quiet Dane' on foreign markets. Moreover, around this time Nilfisk had a reputation for making vacuum cleaners with a high suction capability. It's said that a 'Nilfisk' is slang for a pickpocket in Holland. Over the years the design was very much characterised by a matter-of-fact machinelike aesthetics. It's impossible to find out who designed the various models up until the present, but it was probably engineers at the factory. For about 60 years the different Nilfisk vacuum cleaners were very much alike; stainless steel was the dominant material, and the upright model was practically the company's landmark. The period after World War II was their heyday and in 1954 their annual sales were over one million vacuum cleaners.

It wasn't until the late 1980s that Nilfisk seriously started using designers. In the development of model GM200, the company first worked with industrial designer Hanne Uhlig, whom they replaced with Jacob Jensen Design. It's not clear why they did that, but perhaps Nilfisk wanted their product to be associated with the more prestigious name of Jacob Jensen. In any case, the result was not the world's most elegant vacuum cleaner. For many years, the major foreign brands had tried to make their models as low, compact and smart as possible so they almost looked like little sports cars. Nilfisk's old tried and true principle of having an upright motor ensuring a higher suction capability made it difficult for the factory and the designers to turn it into something beautiful. Today Nilfisk primarily focuses on making powerful vacuum cleaners for the professional cleaning market.

THE TELEPHONE – A STORY OF DEVELOPMENT

We call and call and take the telephone for granted in our everyday lives. We even make wireless and mobile calls and can hardly remember a time when we couldn't reach into our pocket and call whomever we wanted. Of course a device was required to talk into, and for many years there was one telephone factory in Jutland and one in Copenhagen. There were no other factories in the days of monopoly and before the liberalisation of the telephone market in the late 1980s. The Jutlandish company established in 1892 in Horsens was Emil Møller's Telephone Factories, which in 1937 became Kristian Kirk's Telephone Factories. In Søborg, a suburb of Copenhagen, was an almost equally old telephone factory, best known by the name GNT Automatic.

From the time the Copenhagen Telephone Company, KTAS, was established in 1892 and for the next 20 – 30 years, many telephones were imported from either Bell in the US or from L.M. Ericsson in Sweden. In the beginning, the two Danish factories manufactured most of their telephones under

◀ *Bang & Olufsen entered the telephone market with their BeoCom series in the late 1980s when the telephone market was liberalised. The model on the far left was designed by the designer couple Lone and Gideon Lindinger-Loewy and was later made in many models and colour variations.*

◀ *In the mid-1990s, B&O came out with wireless telephones. Here are BeoCom 6000 (right) by Henrik Sørig Thomsen and David Lewis' BeoCom 2 (middle).*

license from foreign companies or in designs that were very close to being copies of their phones. It wasn't until 1972 that an original Danish telephone was designed. Jacob Jensen designed the Comet telephone in 1972 for Jydsk Telefon-Aktieselskab and Kirk in Horsens. It was one of the first push-button telephones in Denmark, and it was developed into a whole family of products, of which the most expensive telephones had a built-in display and a memory that could be programmed with frequently used numbers.

It was a very advanced telephone for its time; it's said that it was so popular that hotel guests cut the cord and took it with them before checking out. Back then you could only buy the telephone if you were a subscriber in the Jutlandish company's area, and it didn't come to KTAS on Zealand until later. The Comet was probably meant to look like a control panel; very rectangular, very matter-of-fact in its artistic idiom, and all the parts, even the receiver, were rectangular in shape. At that time it was a bold and visionary design from the future; a telephone that you would find in a spaceship or in a nuclear plant. If you had one, you were cool.

DanMark 1

KTAS and GNT Automatic also delved into designing their own product. This was in collaboration with a designer from LK-NES, Henning Andreasen, who was a qualified construction engineer, but later became a self-taught designer. For LK-NES Andreasen had designed switches, wall sockets and other electrical material, but the company let its product developers take on outside projects so they could gain experience elsewhere. One of these projects was the telephone that first was called F-78 (the year it came on the market) but it was later marketed under the name DanMark 1. The design of DanMark 1 was much softer in its expression than the Comet's. There were details that seemed more user friendly: among other things, the receiver lay crosswise and the cord could be attached on both sides of the base, so both right and left-handed people could be accommodated.

DanMark doesn't exude the same fascination for technology that the Comet does. Henning Andreasen also stressed that the basic model in the product line was without extra functions. It was purely an everyday article. It had to be easy to clean, and the buttons were placed in the same way as on a calculator, unlike foreign telephones whose numbers were mounted the other way round (later every telephone followed the foreign system as a result of international agreements). The telephone base consisted of two plastic shells and two flat end panels. The advantage of this construction is that extra functions, like a little switchboard, could be added through the removable end panels.

For a long time, GNT Automatic continued to manufacture the DanMark telephones, but forgot that product development is an on-going process if a company wants to survive in our times. Later on, the company in Søborg never made any really new telephones, and it subsequently become part of the Store Nordiske corporation and now manufactures mostly wireless equipment for offices and measuring instruments for the telephone industry. However, Kirk in Horsens continued developing telephones, among others the very common wall model Kirk Plus, which Marianne Stockholm and Gad Zorea designed in 1987–88, along with a less distinctive table model. Kirk still exists today under the name of Kirk Scantel, but production is done abroad; only development and design are still in-house.

THE DANISH CELLPHONE. Although no major Danish telephone brands have seriously gone down the cellphone road, there are nonetheless Danish designers who have been active in this area. The first one was Jan Trägårdh. In the mid-1980s he designed various models for a little Danish company called AP, which was later bought by Philips. Back then they weren't really called cellphones, but car phones. At that time the technology in batteries in particular wasn't very advanced, so these models looked like small suitcases with handles and weighed several kilos. Nevertheless, Trägårdh managed to create several good designs. On the model on the left, the receiver is beautifully formed, but like many other telephone designers at that time, he experimented with the placement and layout of the buttons, and by putting them in two single rows he didn't make it easy for the user if they were used to the traditional keyboard.

A few years later, designer Anders Smith (b. 1960) designed his version of the telephone suitcase for the Korean company Samsung.

▲ *Bang & Olufsen's latest venture in the field of telephones is Serene from 2006, made in collaboration with Korean Samsung.*

Like Jan Trägårdh, Smith also worked with a big box for the electronics and battery as well as a 'receiver' that was given its own design expression. Because of the size of the technology it was hard to design something very elegant, but the position of the handset on the box was one of the areas of freedom that designers had back then. Practical and ergonomic considerations as well as the aesthetical played a role in the choice of solution. At this time, cellphones weren't for personal use since they were much too expensive and impractical. The market was typically for the professional user who worked in the field, such as salesmen and repairmen, and the artistic idiom was therefore very robust and masculine. A couple of times Bang & Olufsen dabbled in the cellphone market, but did not design their own cellphone from scratch. In the early 1990s the company made a cellphone by designing their own front faceplate for an existing Ericsson model. In 2005, B&O entered into a close collaboration with Samsung from Korea to design a cellphone. As with many previous cases, when Bang & Olufsen design a product, it's very different from what all the other manufacturers make. Serene is a folding cellphone and has an almost square form when it's folded, unlike the other manufacturers' oblong forms. The buttons are placed in a circle, and the display is underneath them. The built-in camera is located in the hinge on the side of the phone. This fact as well as the format and the circular keyboard gave rise to some criticism in the press, who implied that B&O and Samsung had sacrificed the use value for the benefit of being different and exclusive.

Bang & Olufsen's telephones

In the course of the 1980s, the telephone market was gradually liberalised, and this meant that many more companies could sell telephones on the Danish market. Relatively cheap foreign telephones became available in the shops for that reason, but some new players entered the field with their own production.

The best bid from the point of view of design was from Bang & Olufsen. The company had great experience in producing well-designed melodiousness. So in 1987–88, they launched the BeoCom 2000, which was designed by the couple Lone and Gideon Lindinger-Loewy. The design was at that time very different for a telephone and for a B&O product. It came in many colour combinations, often with bright colours on the cabinet and pastels on the oval oblique buttons.

This is probably the closest Danish design has been to the so-called postmodern. Modernism was the characteristically undecorated design from Bauhaus with straight lines and no excessive ornament or colours. Postmodernism was a movement that began in Italy in the late 1970s. The style and the people behind it demanded more joie de vivre in design by using bright contrasting colours, pastels, cheerful patterns and antique architectural elements like pillars and symmetry. If Braun was the home of modernism, then the Italian kitchenware company Alessi was the company that represented postmodernism.

Nonetheless, the BeoCom 2000 and the subsequent variants (BeoCom 1000 and BeoCom 600) were unmistakably Bang & Olufsen products and were on the market for more than ten years. The telephone demanded a period of adjustment from the user; both the telephone and especially the receiver were extremely light, so you wouldn't think that there was any quality electronics inside. It was also surprising that the little panel next to the keyboard could be slid open to reveal a little notepad. It's no wonder that this telephone was standard equipment in American TV series portraying fashionable circles.

The wireless telephone

Later on Bang & Olufsen would focus very much on wireless telephones. In this context, design became a crucial factor in order to indicate the company's distinctiveness and to justify their relatively high prices. In the design of telephones in particular, B&O have worked with designer Henrik Sørig Thomsen (b. 1961), who designed several wireless telephones and an answering machine for them. While the BeoCom 2000 still had a very classic look for a telephone – it stood on a table, had a receiver and visible buttons – the wireless products allowed new opportunities to design spectacularly.

In the mid-1990s, the BeoCom 6000 came on the market, and this wireless telephone was almost like a sculpture. It was very different in its day by not being symmetrical; one side has an oblique curve instead of a straight one. There isn't a functional reason for this and whether it's nice to hold is a matter of taste and also dependent on which hand you use. The keyboard has a central wheel which is used to operate the device in the same way as the Apple iPod, which came on the market several years later. The base station, which is where the BeoCom 6000 is charged, was also given a radically different appearance like a kind of pyramid with a groove for the handset.

◂ In Arena's catalogues from around 1960, you find a judicious mixture of appeal to the new teen and their culture, and exclusivity for those can af maid. The design was rather ordinary, especially you think of the venture that Bang & Olufsen had in at that time.

Bang & Olufsen's strategy in this area was, and probably still is, to make the most of their know-how in sound, which they've acquired in the area of stereos, to make telephones. Furthermore, the design is so distinctive that the company's products differ greatly from those of their competitors. Henrik Sørig Thomsen is still designing telephones for B&O, but so is David Lewis, the most closely associated designer to the company in Struer, and who designed a very distinctive telephone. It's called the BeoCom 2 and looks like a slim banana. It's made of aluminium and is held in place in its semi-spherical base station with the help of powerful magnets. The buttons are in two vertical columns and require some getting used to. Once again B&O have launched one of the most unusually designed products. Even the ring tone is specially designed; it sounds like a bell, like when an aluminium pipe is dropped on the pavement.

PICTURE AND SOUND

In the Danish TV series 'Better Times' the plot revolves around a fictitious Danish radio factory, Bella, in postwar Copenhagen. The newfangled TV media is having a difficult delivery, and several Danish electronics factories are vying for a position on the new market for televisions. In actual fact, many of Bella's characteristics could be found in the radio factory in Horsens called Arena. About 25 radio and television factories have existed in Denmark. Today there's only one left, and that is the national treasure Bang & Olufsen. All the other noteworthy companies have succumbed to the tough competition.

In 1928, 21-year-old Ove Hede Nielsen started manufacturing radios under the make of Herofon in a corner of his father's bicycle factory. Herofon, or Arena as the factory was named in 1955, would become one of the biggest and most tenacious opponents of the factory in Struer. For many years there were between 500 and 1000 employees in the company, but in 1970 it burnt down, and in the ensuing reconstruction 80% of the shares were transferred to the British company Rank, and the company was now called Rank Arena.

Only a few years later, the international recession following the energy crisis led to bankruptcy and the firing of 600 employees. The employees tried to take over Arena, and being inspired by all the talk about economic democracy at that time, they tried to put the company on smaller denomination shares in order to run it under the name of 3-F Folkefabrikken (the People's Factory). But it ended in 1979, and the radio and television factory had to close its doors once and for all. The lesson to be learnt from the very tough competition between the many radio factories in Denmark must be that it not only takes great technical and business talent to survive in this field, but also that one must be able to think creatively and use designers. Bang & Olufsen are proof that it can be done.

If you leaf through Arena's old brochures from the 1950s and on, you'll quickly notice that they often stressed the fact that their radio and TV cabinets were 'designed by architects'. Words like 'tasteful' and 'pure style' are also repeated several times. There is no doubt that their marketing tried to ride on the wave of Danish Design. In some of the brochures, there are posed photographs of living rooms where a typical family is sitting in the best designer furniture of the time and watching an Arena television in 'modern lines'. But if you look closer, Arena's products don't seem especially innovative and are rather ordinary in their design. Stereos and TVs from the factory in Horsens look like classic cellarets in polished

▸ *An Arena P9/FM transistor radio from 1962 for the price of 520 kroner. Height 20 cm, width 32 cm and depth 11.5 cm. It weighed 3.2 kilos, and the model came in six different colours. Neither the price nor the design is very different from Bang & Olufsen's at that time, and it wasn't until the mid to late 1960s that B&O started to surge ahead of their competitors in the area of design.*

laminated walnut or teak. In justice it must be said that B&O took a long time to understand the meaning of innovative design, and Arena never really got it.

BANG & OLUFSEN

In 1925, around the same time that Arena was established in Horsens, a new and, ultimately, more successful industrial adventure began in Struer. The two engineers, Peter Bang (1900–57) and Svend Olufsen (1897–1949), established the company Bang & Olufsen.

Like many other industrial enterprises at that time, technology was the underlying basis for the business. In 1926, B&O sold their first battery-free radio in Denmark. The basis for this was the two engineers' development of the modern power supply. Up until then you couldn't plug your radio into a wall socket; first you had to charge the battery, which then provided the radio with electricity in the proper voltage. Bang & Olufsen radios were sold under the slogan, 'The Danish quality brand', which put them under a certain obligation. In the beginning, the company only concentrated on the inner workings of the radio, the technology and quality of electronics, while factors like appearance and user friendliness took a back seat.

It was often happenstance who actually designed the cabinets at the factory and how the products eventually looked, and in 1933 this led Professor of Architectural History Vilhelm Wanscher to sarcastically criticise Bang & Olufsen's design in an article he wrote for 'The Politiken'. 'Getting the radio to fit nobly in anywhere at all is easily achieved with the help of Caucasian wing nut wood and badger legs, or Chinese functionalism – it's like a piece of theatre scenery that's been designed by the furniture

▴ *The Hyperbo 5 RGF from 1934. Compare this to the more modern B&O Hyperbo 5RG Steel from 1934 (see page 50). Although the company in Struer had begun to discover the new ideas in design, most of their products were still in veneered wood cabinets. Notice that the two radios are identical in construction. The speaker is in the same place as well as the buttons, the tuning display and the large drawer for the shellac records of that time. The record player is also located in the same place, but with different types of covers. Back then, B&O bet on several horses from a design point of view.*

▾ The Beolit 39 from 1938 (below) and a Jet 505 K from 1949 (right). There are 11 years between the two radios; the cabinet is made of different material, the components have switched places, but otherwise they're similar. The contrast between the black cabinet and the ivory buttons and speaker grill makes the Beolit an eye-catcher in the living room; this is something the company got even better at in the years to come.

dealer's youngest apprentice.' Luckily Bang & Olufsen didn't react by being passively insulted, for the next year they introduced a radiophonograph which was the prototype of functional design with a frame made of shiny chrome-plated steel tubes and a cabinet of black lacquered wood.

Although many of the factory's products still followed the style of the day, with the radio and record player often built together with the speakers into a large piece of furniture in the living room, B&O still worked on ideas for a more modern design. In 1938, a contest for listeners was arranged to make a new design for a table model radio. The result was the beautiful Beolit 39. Exactly how this listeners' contest took place is a bit hazy, but the product was still the company's first radio cabinet cast in Bakelite, the slightly primitive plastic of the past. The style was pure and modern for its time. Maybe the inspiration came from the US, where the smooth shapes of streamlined design had been the hottest style for a number of years.

Time for a new scolding

However, Bang & Olufsen had not yet decided which design line they wanted, and as usual it was the chief engineer who took responsibility for the final design. This design job was probably well intended and based on a vague feeling that one should give people what they wanted. And even though the listeners' contest of 1938 should have given Bang & Olufsen an idea of which way the wind was blowing regarding design, after the war they still fell back on the huge veneer eyesores with inlaid wood in contrasting colours and elaborately braided speaker grills. The radios and new TV sets were still considered furniture and were designed like them, which among other things led to a small specialised section for AV equipment at the annual exhibition of the Cabinetmakers' Guild in 1954.

▼ Bang & Olufsen's first so-called AV centre, model TV 509 RG from 1953, which includes a television, radio, record player and speakers. Perhaps it was this device that Poul Henningsen reviewed in 'The Politiken' and suggested that it had been designed by a fishmonger or potato merchant.

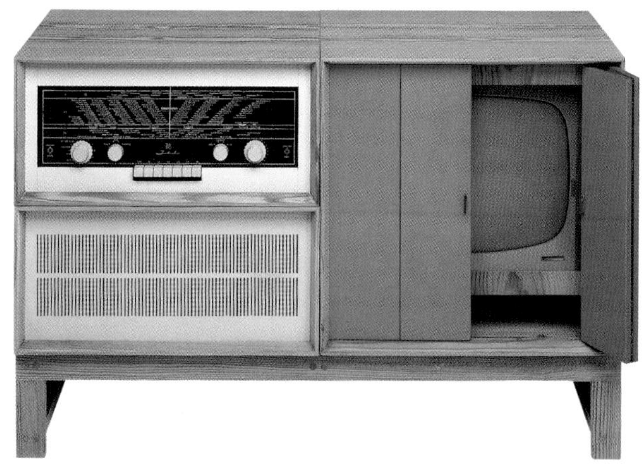

◀ *In 1957–58, architect Ib Fabiansen designed the modular Bang & Olufsen system, which was called unit furniture. The principle was that as a customer you could assemble your own AV centre according to your own needs. The system came in different types of wood and colours including light pine, not traditional at the time.*

▶ *The Beomaster 900 was B&O's first transistor radio and was designed by architect Henning Moldenhawer. At that time, the crisis in the radio and TV business was being felt, and this conscious gamble on design would be put to the test. For the first time, the front of the radio was as wide as the cabinet's width and this pre-empted the design line of the future in that it doesn't have the traditional wooden cabinet as a frame.*

▶▶ *The transistor radio Beolit 500 from 1965 was designed by Acton Bjørn's architectural practice and won an ID prize the following year. It had pushbuttons for the programmed stations so you no longer had to turn the dial to find another radio station.*

Architect and writer Poul Henningsen reviewed the exhibition in 'The Politiken', and he didn't beat around the bush. Here are a few excerpts from his torrent of words: 'Round and pot-bellied artificiality with swing, curves and convolutions, often combined with the most outrageous kinds of wood plastered with plastic and brass, so it makes you sick to see so much lack of talent in one place ... To people who appreciate modern furniture, it's a downright insult to force them to buy these monstrosities in order to enjoy the great cultural benefit of the radio. Are fishmongers or potato merchants dabbling in designing these things in their spare time?'

The criticism wasn't only directed at Bang & Olufsen, but the largest illustration for the article was a B&O television, and that smarted in Struer where the designer was chief engineer Vindeløv himself. On the one hand, he was offended by the criticism of this cultural-radical braggart, but on the other hand, he could see that there was something in it. The long and the short of it is that now they started taking design seriously again. It didn't happen overnight, but things started getting going in design. They still took as their starting point that TV sets in particular were so big that they had to be considered as furniture and designed accordingly. To this end, they hired an architect in furniture design, namely Ib Fabiansen.

Among other things, architect Fabiansen designed unit furniture for B&O. It came in different kinds of wood and was similar to Børge Mogensen's system of the same name. These units were limited to accommodating radio and television equipment. The basic element in this product line was a low table on which B&O equipment could be incorporated according to one's taste and wallet. The system was exhibited at the Danish Arts & Crafts Exhibition at Charlottenborg, Copenhagen in 1958 and went from a modest radio with a separate speaker to the large bureau-sized AV system with a TV and reel-to-reel tape recorder. It takes time for new inventions to find their own artistic idiom. That is also true of radios, hi-fi equipment and TV sets. Ib Fabiansen was the designer in this time of transition when Bang & Olufsen still saw them as furniture. However, he did design a portable reel-to-reel tape recorder or rather a suitcase for that purpose.

Design as a survival strategy

Meanwhile two things happened in the late 1950s that would have a great influence on the world and on the future of B&O. First of all, the EEC (today the EU) was established in 1957, and for agricultural reasons, Denmark negotiated a free trade agreement with the new common market. But what benefited agriculture killed off 10–15 Danish radio and TV factories in the course of few years since they suddenly had to compete on equal terms with German and Dutch giants in particular. B&O realised that design could come to the rescue of the company. Instead of banking on being the biggest fish in the Danish sea, by focusing on high quality and good design B&O could perhaps carve out a lucrative niche on the far bigger European and global markets.

Secondly, during this period the arrival of the transistor gave rise to technological opportunities to create something brand new. While the old tubes, or lamps as they were also called, took up a lot of space and emitted heat, the new technology took up much less space. It opened new possibilities for design, and yet another architect, Henning Moldenhawer (1914–83) was the one who would usher in a new era for the company. In 1964 the Beomaster 900, designed by Moldenhawer in a brand new artistic idiom, was introduced. This stereo radio with built-in speakers

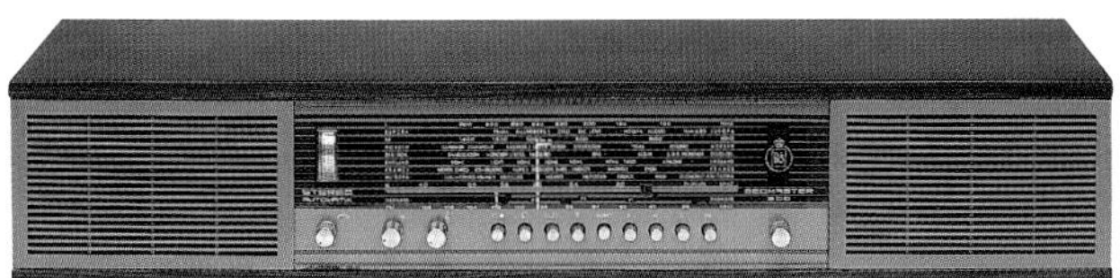

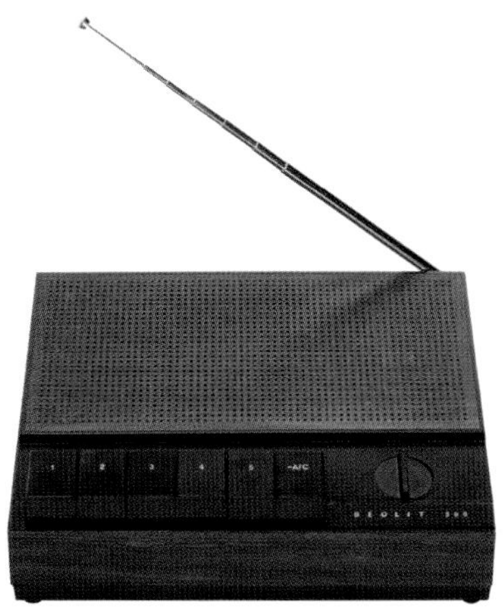

was smaller and lower and therefore looked wider than earlier B&O radios. The horizontal lines were emphasised by the front in grey synthetic material stretching all the way to the sides, which was very new and modern at that time. The Beomaster 900 was a success in the new Europe and not least in Denmark. B&O's idea that design was the way forward was confirmed in earnest.

Moldenhawer, who perhaps never became a world-famous B&O designer, did set his mark in several ways on the development of design at the company. He managed to design a number of products in the 1960s including new transistorised and portable TVs for the company, but he also hired one of the up-and-coming B&O designers in his architectural practice.

This was David Lewis, who set up his own architectural practice in the early 1970s and since then has designed all Bang & Olufsen's television sets. Another architectural practice in Copenhagen, Bjørn & Bernadotte, also designed a couple of B&O products in the 1960s, including some of the company's first transistor radios. However, this architectural practice hired another B&O designer in the making, namely Jacob Jensen, who from 1965 was the company's primary supplier of design with David Lewis as his assistant in the beginning.

The Jacob Jensen era

The first big project that B&O's two new freelance designers produced was the Beolab 5000 radio with the matching Beomaster 5000 amplifier. This project makes the most of the smallness of the new electronics and it is a benchmark for Bang & Olufsen's new ambitions in design. By international standards it is probably a very epochal product where in particular the satin-matt fronts in aluminium and the slide rule-like sliders were very special. The flush-mounted Allen bolts contributed to the feeling of a solid technical quality along with the businesslike Helvetica typeface used in the graphics. There was still a way to go before the factory's heyday in design was reached – the long row of black plastic buttons seems a bit primitive – but they were off to a flying start. The product was a great commercial success and from then on, Bang & Olufsen didn't budge from their strategy of becoming the leader of design in their field.

Jacob Jensen continued to be B&O's primary designer of audio equipment until 1987, and the tone established by the 5000 series from 1967 was continued consistently during that time and even up until today. Slightly less expensive variants of the 5000 series were introduced in the following years – the Beosystem 3000 and the Beomaster 1200 in 1969, the Beocenter 3500 in 1972 etc. In 1976, the Beomaster 1900 was brought onto the market as the first radio amplifier with sensi-touch buttons, and was considered in professional circles to be one of Jacob Jensen's best designs. It was certainly a big sales success for the company.

At this point it's clear that B&O were going their own way. The rest of the industry on a global basis, led by the Japanese manufacturers, adopted another strategy. To them, hi-fi equipment should look like something situated halfway between military hardware and a professional mixing console from a sound studio. Their products were at any rate supplied with plenty of buttons, handles and large instruments with needles. B&O's understated aesthetics seemed refined in comparison to the competitors' products, and the products were always of the best quality and finish.

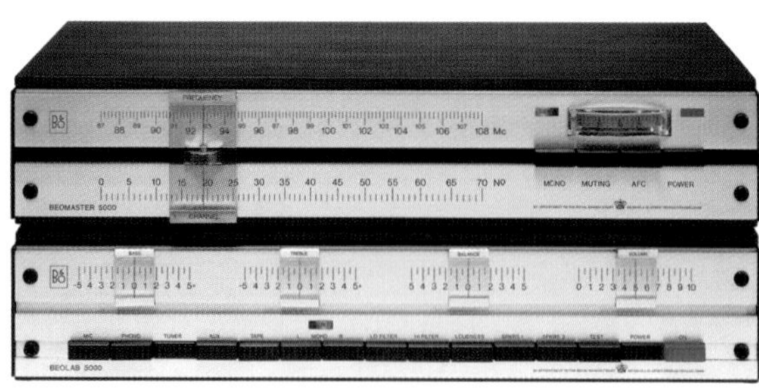

▾ *Beolab/Beomaster 5000 was Jacob Jensen's first job for B&O.*

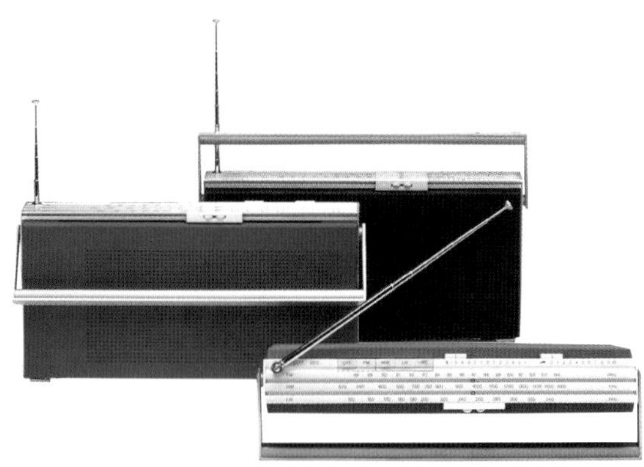

▾ *The Beolit series of transistor radios from 1970 were and still are very popular.*

In time it has become a B&O speciality to manufacture the most exquisite surfaces, such as polished stainless steel. Now it was minimalism in its purest form plus the fact that the products were given that special something which distinguished Bang & Olufsen's products from classic Bauhaus functionalism.

Part of Jacob Jensen's philosophy was that you had to achieve the 'wow effect'. There must always be an element of surprise in the products, such as a panel that pops up, behind which secondary functions are hidden. And when the panel closes, it does so slowly; it doesn't shut with a cheap sounding bang, but slides gently into place.

Jacob Jensen's way of designing put a lot of pressure on the technicians to construct completely new minimal solutions. There's a story about his arrival in Struer to introduce a new design. Everyone stood around the table when the cloth covering Jensen's model was pulled off. A shiver went through the crowd: before them stood an outrageously low radio. 'This is your new radio,' said Jacob Jensen, clearly proud. One of the younger

▴ *The Beomaster 1900 from 1976 by Jacob Jensen immediately became a design icon and was bought by many museums for exhibitions.*

JACOB JENSEN (b. 1926) is an industrial designer, one of the first in Denmark to be educated at the School of Arts & Crafts in Copenhagen in this new subject area. After his graduation in 1951 he was employed by Sigvard Bernadotte and Acton Bjørn. In 1958 he set up his own architectural practice, Jacob Jensen Design. He made his name by designing numerous products for Bang & Olufsen; a collaboration which lasted from 1963 until the late 1980s. What is distinctive about Jacob Jensen's design is the futuristic and super-industrial look with the frequent use of geometric forms executed in materials like plastic, aluminium, Plexiglas etc. He is one of the most prominent Danish designers from the second half of the 20th century, and since 1990 his practice has been carried on by his son Timothy Jacob Jensen (b. 1962). Apart from B&O products, Jacob Jensen Design has designed office chairs, cable drums, telephones, and wristwatches. Jacob Jensen has been awarded countless Danish and foreign prizes.

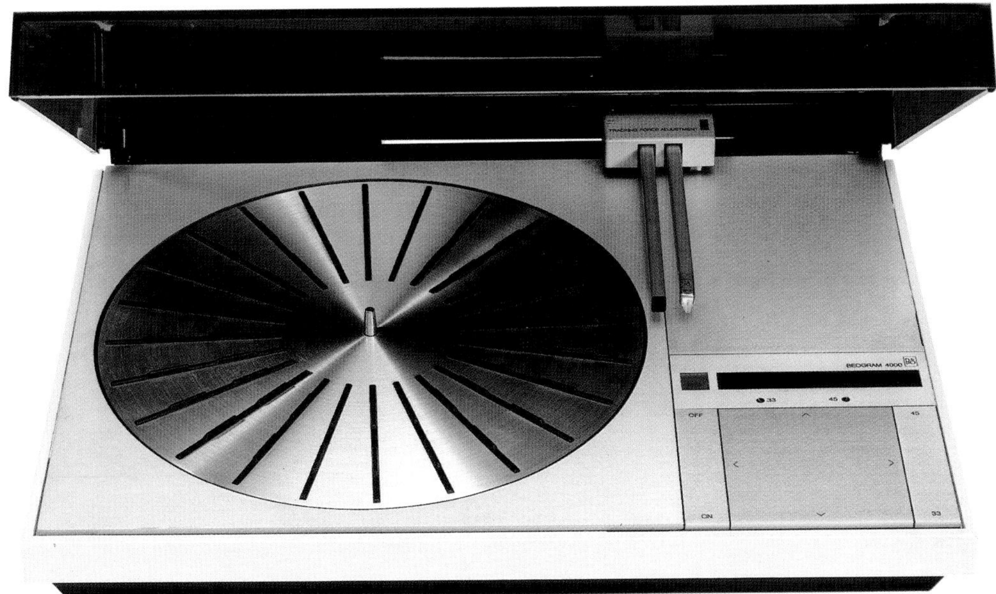

▲ *The Beogram 4000 is one of the products that, worldwide, has been awarded the most international design prizes.*

JUST A FEW years after Bang & Olufsen's gamble in design, they attracted great international attention. In 1972, the Museum of Modern Art in New York ordered seven products from B&O for their permanent collection, which is something that rarely happens. In 1978, MOMA demonstrated its admiration further by arranging a special exhibition of all of the company's 39 products. The museum had only done this three times before, for Olivetti, Braun and the furniture company Thonet. This was a significant accolade in the design world.

▲ *The Beosytem 2500 from 1991.*

engineers spontaneously exclaimed, 'But it's much too low; we can't fit the power supply in it.' Jacob Jensen gave him a frosty stare, 'Didn't you hear what I said? This is your new radio ...' And then they had to construct a new power supply.

At one point, Jacob Jensen expressed the following work philosophy, 'If the right idea is present, then people will figure out how to put it into practice. If the idea is so exciting and viable that people say, "We want one of those", then they'll figure out how to make a chair that can tilt, a lower transformer or a record player with a parallel arm. You name it. The manufacturers don't care if it's difficult. They'll gladly spend money on something they can see is so obviously the right thing to do.' This way of thinking is evident in Jacob Jensen and B&O's masterpiece, the Beogram 4000. This product was revolutionary by being the first consumer record player that played the records in the same way that they were recorded, that is with a parallel arm or tangential arm as it was also called.

The Beogram 4000 wasn't only a technological breakthrough for the company, but design-wise it was yet again proof that it pays off for a niche company to go against the flow. While hi-fi enthusiasts at that time wanted record players that could be adjusted with weights and pulleys and preferably could be taken apart and oiled and calibrated, Bang & Olufsen's design was simplicity itself. Seen purely as a piece of graphics, the product is fascinating with its double arm and turntable with the black contrasting lines. It was futuristic and cool design that expressed 'I know what's hip' and appealed to a particular audience. However, some critics thought that the target group of B&O's products must be reduced to German engineers and other control freaks.

David Lewis

Jacob Jensen, who continued to work for Bang & Olufsen until 1987, only designed audio products. From the early 1970s, the company's visual products were designed by David Lewis, who was educated in the UK. He worked for three years for Jacob Jensen and seven years for Henning Moldenhawer before he worked independently for B&O. One of the most successful televisions that David Lewis designed is the BeoVision MX series. It all began with a 21-inch TV in 1985, the MX 2000, and the series was continually expanded with small and large models over the course of many years. In 2006, the MX 4200 was still on the market.

The MX 2000 was one of the first televisions that was so sculpturally beautiful that it could stand alone on the floor. It was designed so that even seen from behind it's a visually interesting and provocative design. When it was introduced, it became a benchmark for how TV sets could be designed. In addition, it was innovative in that it could be placed directly on the floor; you didn't need the traditional table with wheels. In order to stand on the floor it had a little built-in support underneath it allowing the screen to tilt backwards. The screen could also be put in an upright position if the TV were placed on a table or in a bookcase. Furthermore, there is a little handle on the back of the set so it was also a continuation of the B&O tradition of manufacturing portable TVs.

Bang & Olufsen also left behind their tradition of making cabinets made of either wood or covered in veneer; now the set came in modern materials like metal, glass and plastic. Yet parts of the cabinet on the MX models were replaceable so you could choose between 4 to 5 colours; the traditional black and white or more lively colours like blue and red. Similar solutions

ORTOFON, SUCCESS IN A NICHE. For most people the concept of a pickup on a record player is obsolete. But for the small circle of older vinyl enthusiasts and hip DJs the name of Ortofon is still equivalent to high quality and good design. In the late 1970s, industrial designer Jan Trägårdh and graphic designer Flemming Ljørring designed the Concorde pickup in collaboration with the company. For Trägårdh this was once again not just a matter of aesthetically-pleasing design. The form and construction were optimised for the benefit of the sound quality, the production and the user. The pickup head is pointed like a needle, so it's easy to find a track on the record. The profile is quadratic so there's plenty of room for the small components inside, but only the necessary room, so the size and weight can be minimised. The final result resembled the nose of a Concorde, hence the name. The product was awarded the ID prize from the Danish Design Centre in 1979, and even though the market isn't as big as it has been, the Ortofon factory is still thriving in Nakskov.

▲ *The Beovision MX2000 was designed by David Lewis like a sculpture that even looks good from behind. This design line from the mid-1980s is still alive in 2006.*

▾ *The BeoVision 5 was a 42-inch flatscreen TV that was on the market for a couple of years from 2000.*

can be seen in the later models designed by Lewis, like the BeoCenter AV 9000 and BeoVision Avant from 1995. After Jacob Jensen left B&O in the late 1980s, David Lewis took over most of the design work, including the audio products. The Jensenian line has been carried on to a large degree since the two designers are not that different in nature.

If you look at Bang & Olufsen's design over a long period of time especially in the area of TV, but also at their audio products, you'll see an interesting development. In the beginning they were rather gaudy and tasteless monstrosities. Wanscher and PH's criticism led to a functional and discreet artistic idiom where the design of TVs in particular became very subdued, but also many of Jacob Jensen's designs were rather restrained. This period could be called 'discreet functionalism with a wow effect' because the style was, as mentioned previously, different from that of Bauhaus and the school in Ulm. There was simply more in B&O's products that roused the senses and curiosity than what the traditional modernists could serve up.

In recent years, this ingenuity has led to a more sculptural type of design. The MX televisions are just one example. Some of David Lewis' stereos also bear this mark clearly; the Beosystem 2500 from 1991 is one of them. It's an upright stereo with matching speakers. The wow effect of this product is that an infrared sensor detects the movement of a hand and makes the smoke-coloured Plexiglas panels silently retract and the control panel light turn on. The stereo is more striking than almost all the other systems on the market. In addition you can choose to make your sound system even more of an eye catcher by choosing coloured speakers.

▼ *The BeoSound 9000 is an untraditional radio and CD player that can hold (not to mention show) six CDs that can be played in random order. The acrylic cover opens and shuts mechanically, and the system can be mounted in many ways: on the wall, standing on a shelf or mounted on a pillar. It's an impressive piece of mechanics and electronics that doesn't blend into the background. The BeoSound 9000 is flanked by two BeoLab 8000 speakers from 1992.*

OVER THE PAST 50 years, Danish designers have designed a number of interesting watches ranging from the noble classic to the futurist visionary. The key words are, as is the case with much Danish design: simplicity and innovation. In 1962, the newly qualified Copenhagen master watchmaker Ole Mathiesen (b. 1930) designed a watch that has been in production ever since, and consequently he won the Classics Prize in 2004 from the Danish Design Centre. Its design is pure in style and comes with Roman numerals or simple stroke marks on the face. Georg Jensen has had many designers design watches over the years. One of the more interesting models, the bracelet watch from 1962, is by Viviana Bülow-Hübe (b. 1927). The watch is made of silver and is a combination of a wristwatch and a bracelet, almost a piece of jewellery. The face of the watch doesn't have numbers or any kind of graphics. It was ahead of its time when Georg Jensen put it into production in 1967 after five years' deliberation.

In the early 1990s, designer and goldsmith Flemming Bo Hansen (b. 1955) designed the most simple digital watch the world has yet seen. Placing the numbers two by two, that is, hours and minutes, one above the other, gives it a sophisticated look, which especially at that time differed greatly from the image of the digital watch as something technical and geeky. It was manufactured for a number of years by the Swiss company Ventura, but is sold today in a newly designed version by Rosendahl.

▲ Viviana Bülow-Hübe's watch was designed for Georg Jensen in 1962. ▲ Ole Mathiesen's design from 1962. ▲ Flemming Bo Hansen designed this watch in the early 1990s.

▸ *A piece of children's furniture made in one of the Danish prisons in the period 1950–70 and marketed by the company Dansk Legetøjsfabrik A/S (Danish Toy Factory Inc.) It's a combination model where the child can either sit at the little table, or the chair can be unfolded and used as a highchair.*

David Lewis continued this expressive line a few years later by designing yet another impressive music centre with a wow effect and great visual impact. This is the BeoSound 9000, which is a CD player with an amplifier and radio. The system can be loaded with six CDs at once, and they are visible through the large Plexiglas front. An arm moves from one CD to the next and provides visual entertainment. Despite its size, this system is very flexible and can be mounted in many ways: vertically, horizontally, standing, hanging on a wall or placed on the floor stand that comes with it. The LED writing adjusts to the angle at which the product is placed. This system undoubtedly calls attention to itself.

Buying this system for your living room or office was a clear statement that you like music and are fascinated by what technology can do. The six CDs could have been be loaded in a discreet cassette, and the sound would still be superb, but because of the way the BeoSound 9000 is designed, it looks more like a display window of both the CDs and of Bang & Olufsen and, when all is said and done, of the owner's status. It's like an indoor BMW, just a little more highbrow.

It will be interesting to see how B&O will tackle the new age when the sources of music and pictures are constantly becoming more obscure. Music is downloaded from the internet and isn't recorded on records or CDs anymore. TV sets are ultra-thin flat-screens that hang on the wall like framed pictures. The new 42-inch BeoVision 5 flat-screen TV hits a sore spot. It costs as much as a small car, and its design takes us back to pure minimalism. Bang & Olufsen can probably go far with their high-quality picture, new ingenious and hidden functions, motorised floor stand and enhanced branding. Only the future will reveal if it's enough to make ends meet financially as well.

TOYS

Parents and their children have played since prehistoric times. Unlike work, play is a pastime that isn't one of life's dull chores, although many children and adults can take play very seriously at times. Toys are the tools of play and help stage the game or aid the imagination. Many of the games children play are about emulating the adult world and activities. They're practicing to be adults if you will, although games are often very different from the adult world; they're actually in a world of their own. The commercial manufacture of toys began in the 1500s. Small farmers around the southern German town of Nuremberg made and sold wooden toys in the winter. The area became the centre of the production of cheap wooden toys, the so-called Nuremberg Merchandise. Later tin soldiers were cast, and even later cheap tin toys. Many of the antique toys that are found in Denmark are Nuremberg Merchandise.

Denmark has also had it own production of toys, but did not have the same efficient merchants as did southern Germany. It wasn't until the 20th century that Danish toys were sold and branded systematically, until then they were mostly sold locally. The toys were dolls, different kinds of stuffed animals, wooden and tin copies of everyday things like the farm animals, horse carriages, farms or the inside of a house in the form of a doll house. But toys could also be copies of tools and implements or musical instruments. Ships, tin soldiers and other war toys were also common.

In 1905 a Danish prison reform was implemented which entailed that hard labour for the inmates be replaced by the remunerated production of various things including toys. The Copenhagen company Dansk Legetøjsfabrik (Danish Toy Factory Inc.) was established the same year and for about the

TOYS AND FURNITURE can be combined. It's old news that far back in time, things were designed for children to sit or lie on, and they were toys as well. The rocking horse is just one example. Adults have also had furniture that were toys: just think of chess tables or other game furniture. In 1962, furniture designer Nanna Ditzel designed a piece of children's furniture that looked like an oversized bobbin and was called Toadstool. It has been in production almost ever since; first it was made of Oregon pine at Kolds Savværk (Kold's Lumber Mill) in Kerteminde, and today it's manufactured in oak, beech, teak and gumwood at Snedkergaarden (The Cabinetmaker Farm) in Them. There were three children's sizes and later an adult size was added.

For the toy fair held at Forum in Copenhagen in 1963, Nanna Ditzel designed a nursery. It was a play area for children of all ages, and the bobbins and the hat stands, which were for Kvist Møbler, are part of the installation (see page 141). Poul Henningsen wrote enthusiastically about Nanna Ditzel's nursery in the design periodical Mobilia in November, 1963.

▲ *Wooden toys from Dansk Legetøjsfabrik A/S (Danish Toy Factory Inc.) produced by prisoners in the period 1930–50.*

◂▾ *The die cast aluminium cars from Tekno were very lifelike and rich in detail. Moreover, they were very Danish; the crane truck and fire truck were from Falck-Zonen, the brewery truck from Tuborg, and the moving van is of course from the firm Danmark.*

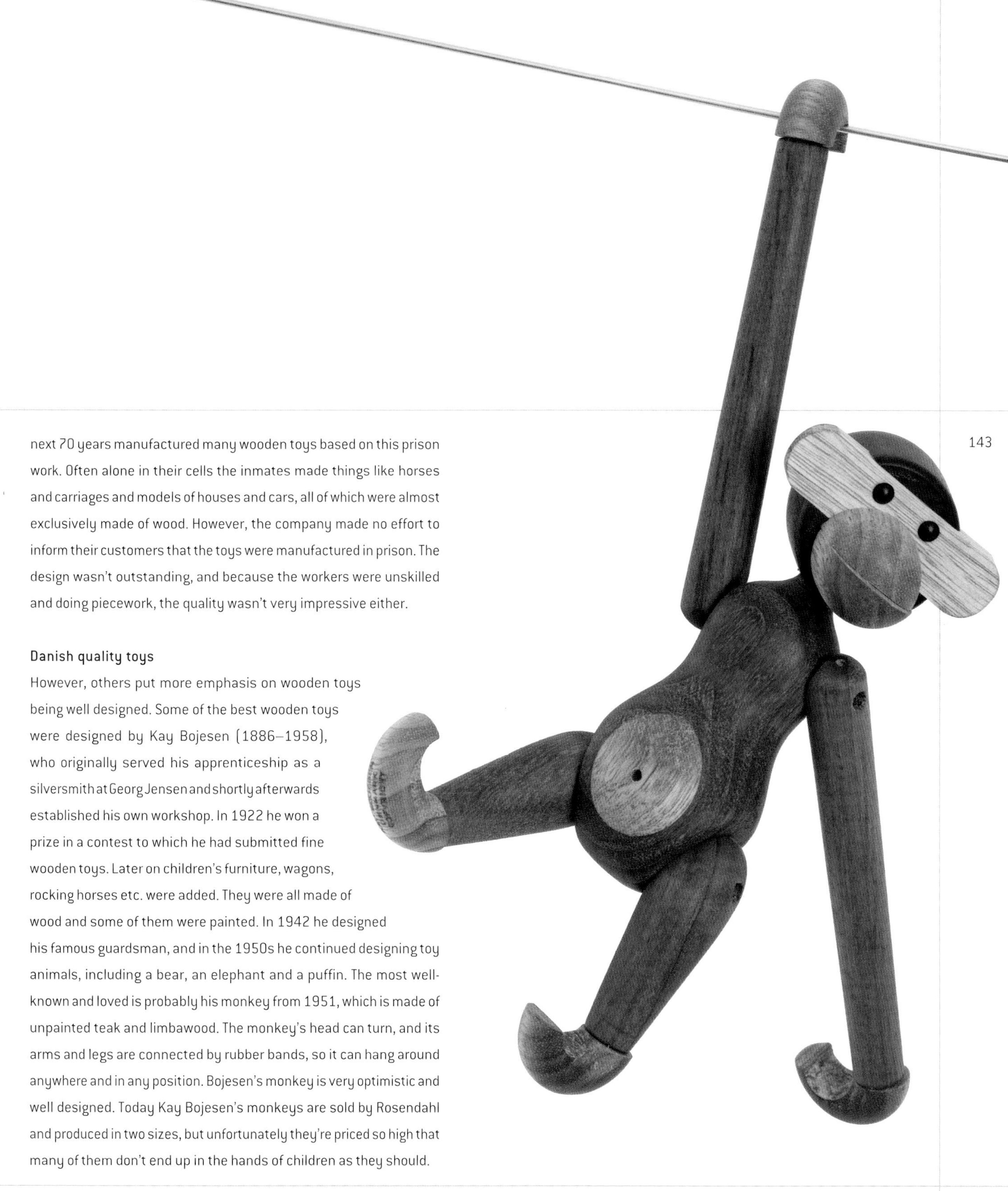

next 70 years manufactured many wooden toys based on this prison work. Often alone in their cells the inmates made things like horses and carriages and models of houses and cars, all of which were almost exclusively made of wood. However, the company made no effort to inform their customers that the toys were manufactured in prison. The design wasn't outstanding, and because the workers were unskilled and doing piecework, the quality wasn't very impressive either.

Danish quality toys

However, others put more emphasis on wooden toys being well designed. Some of the best wooden toys were designed by Kay Bojesen (1886–1958), who originally served his apprenticeship as a silversmith at Georg Jensen and shortly afterwards established his own workshop. In 1922 he won a prize in a contest to which he had submitted fine wooden toys. Later on children's furniture, wagons, rocking horses etc. were added. They were all made of wood and some of them were painted. In 1942 he designed his famous guardsman, and in the 1950s he continued designing toy animals, including a bear, an elephant and a puffin. The most well-known and loved is probably his monkey from 1951, which is made of unpainted teak and limbawood. The monkey's head can turn, and its arms and legs are connected by rubber bands, so it can hang around anywhere and in any position. Bojesen's monkey is very optimistic and well designed. Today Kay Bojesen's monkeys are sold by Rosendahl and produced in two sizes, but unfortunately they're priced so high that many of them don't end up in the hands of children as they should.

▲ *One of Kay Bojesen's monkeys in a typical pose.*

THE PLAYGROUND TRACTOR. In 1980, furniture architects Lars Mathiesen (b. 1950) and Niels Gammelgaard (b. 1944), who run the architectural practice Pelikan Design, designed a tricycle. They made it for the RABO company that used to be located in Fakse on Zealand and who wanted to enter the market of day care products with a safe and robust tricycle. The result, with its thick yellow tubes and black rubber parts, reminds one of an excavator – a really solid piece of playground equipment (opposite). All the sharp edges or small openings where little fingers could get caught were removed in the design.

Pelikan Design designed the first products in the series. Since then the new owner of RABO, the Veksø Taulov company, has taken over the development and design of tricycles, which have remained pretty much unchanged. Today about 30,000 are manufactured a year. As early as the year the tricycle was introduced, RABO was awarded the Danish Design Centre's ID prize.

In the course of the 20th century the materials used for making toys changed. Wood and cheap tin were more seldom used while plastic gained ground. Quality products in metal also become popular for a long time. One example of this is the company Dansk Legetøjs Industri (Danish Toy Industry) which in the 1930s launched constructional toys under the product name Tekno.

We remember something called 'the little chemistry set', and this was the closest you could get to 'the little engineering set' (left). It was a system of about 15mm wide pieces of green-painted flatiron in many different lengths and with three rows of holes. Besides that there were small screws, nuts, washers, axles, gear wheels etc. in yellow chrome. You could also get small electric motors, so you could build anything from mechanical constructions to even vehicles. The design was simple, even though the things constructed could be very complicated. The green colour of the bars, the orange colour of the discs and wheels, and the yellow screws made the system look especially appealing.

Otherwise, people mostly associate Tekno with the small die cast cars on a 1:43 scale that the company began manufacturing after World War II. During the war you couldn't get tin, so toys were made out of wood instead. After the war, tin was still a restricted commodity, but zinc wasn't. Then Andreas Siegumfeldt (1894–1967), a qualified plumber who had established the company Dansk Legetøjs Industri (Danish Toy Industry) in his basement in Vanløse, began casting in zinc. The small precision die cast cars were a big hit and were manufactured in lots of different models, which are collectors' items today.

▲ *Besides the very famous model cars (see page 142), Tekno also manufactured constructional toys for future engineers.*

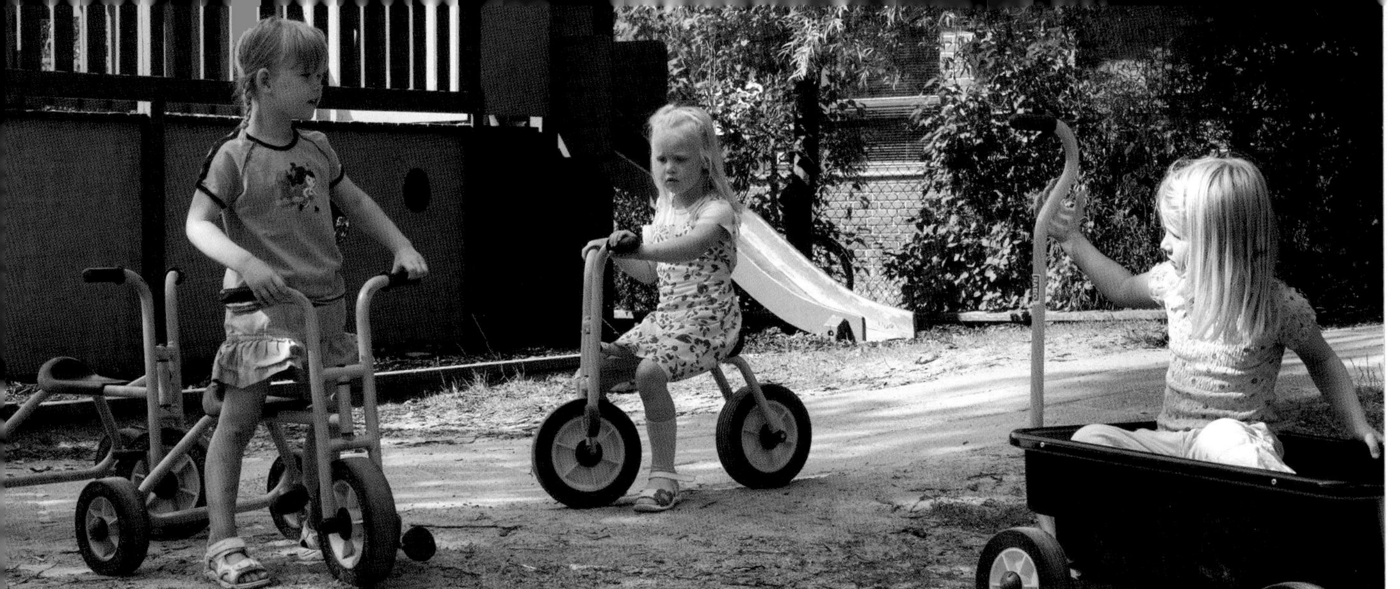

At the peak of their success, over 1 million model cars were sold a year, of which about two-thirds were exported. After Siegumfeldt's death in 1967, the company got into financial difficulties. Tekno was sold to a Dutch firm that presumably still manufactures Tekno cars, but mostly for collectors. It may not sound like there's much design in reproducing cars in miniature, but it's not easy. All the details cannot be included on a 1:43 scale, so getting it right is quite an achievement – something Tekno were good at.

LEGO

'To say, oh, how can such a little plastic brick change the world is like saying how can 26 simple little things like the letters in the alphabet change the world. Oh, it's so naive. The universal language of the world is not English, it's not Microsoft Windows. It's LEGO. A thousand years from now, it will probably have done more to influence the thinking of a lot of people and the look of the physical world than pretty well any other invention.' Douglas Coupland, author of *Generation X* and *Microserfs*, on Radio Denmark TV, December 20, 1995.

Right in the middle of Jutland in the little town of Billund there once lived a carpenter by the name of Ole Kirk Christiansen (1891–1958). He built houses, but around 1930 times were hard, and on the side he started making wooden toys out the ends of beams and boards that were left over in construction. From 1932 he concentrated on toys alone, and in 1934 the company and its products were given the name LEGO, which is made up of the first two letters of the Danish words for 'play' (leg) and 'well' (godt). Later he was told by the local minister that the word 'lego' in Latin means 'I build' or 'I construct'. For many years Lego only made wooden toys, but Kirk was a forward-looking man, and in 1947, the first to do so in Denmark, he imported a machine for plastic injection moulding. In the beginning, many plastic toys were ordinary copies of wooden toys and were made without any major effort as regards design. In 1949, LEGO started to manufacture the first primitive building blocks in plastic according to a British principle called Automatic Binding Brick.

Ole Kirk's son, Godtfred Kirk Christiansen (1920–95) became Junior Vice President in 1950, and four years later he met the purchasing manager of the Danish department store Magasin on the boat to England. The latter thought that toy production lacked a system, and that things were too haphazard in the business. Godtfred latched on to this idea and in 1955, the firm introduced 'The LEGO System of play' and from now on the company focused on the building bricks. At that time, LEGO wasn't the only company that made plastic bricks according to the British principle, but in 1958 the LEGO block coupling system was improved with the invention of the inside tube. The company not only patented the tube, but also every other way of increasing stability. Thus LEGO made it extremely difficult for competitors, and in no time LEGO had a monopoly on that type of brick.

In the following years the company blossomed and launched lots of new construction sets and developed new elements for their range of products. In the 1960s and 1970s LEGO trains were designed, and the company made wheels and axles, invented hinges and introduced electric motors. In 1977 LEGO Technic came on the market with lots of new parts including gear wheels, gear boxes and much more. This was a good construction toy for older boys, but it highlighted the company's sore spot, which was that there wasn't much in the LEGO box that appealed to girls.Later they tried to remedy this with LEGO Scala, Belville and the jewellery system Clikits.

FROM 1930, CARPENTER Ole Kirk Christiansen began making wooden toys, like the duck on wheels on the left. In 1934 he named his company LEGO, but the first building bricks weren't manufactured until 1949. For many years to come, LEGO made traditional building sets – houses, farms, fire stations and much more. When the children had built what was pictured on the lid of the box, they continued building using their own imagination.

As part of the company's branding, the LEGOLAND theme park was initiated in 1968 in Billund. Everything here is designed in LEGO bricks, yet it doesn't feel like direct marketing. The main attraction at LEGOLAND is Miniland where famous buildings and locations are made in miniature. Later, other LEGOLAND parks were established abroad.

In the late 1960s, LEGO also began considering the younger age groups; LEGO Duplo was designed for younger children and later LEGO Primo for the very young.

From 1979, the founder's grandson, Kjeld Kirk Kristiansen (b. 1947), ran the corporation that continued to grow. For long periods of time, LEGO has been the biggest toy company in Europe and a leader on the global market for construction toys. LEGO is a unique system built on the principle that every part can fit any other in the stud system. The principle of LEGO is to let the imagination have full rein. If you have six of the traditional bricks with eight studs, you can, according to LEGO, assemble them in over 900 million ways. And the possibilities of play and combinations increase exponentially the more bricks you have.

LEGO design

The original LEGO brick was a good design in itself and an excellent basis for further development. That's what the designers – of which there have been many according to tradition – have achieved. In the beginning it was mostly about making some good construction sets out of the existing bricks – a house, a farm and a fire station. A need was quickly apparent to form more elements, such as roof tiles, windows, doors, simple wheels and axles etc., all of which complied with the original system.

There are four different eras in the company's development. The first was the simple construction and building era. In the second, in the 1960s, wheels and other moving parts were added for the small motors, among other things. The third era, starting in the late 1970s, is a period when LEGO's mini-figures came into being, and today, in the fourth era it's about adding intelligence and other complicated contents. The distinction between these eras in the company's development is closely linked to the three generations of executives at LEGO and their respective outlooks.

In Ole Kirk's day it was all about quality that is symbolised in the carved wooden sign he made that still hangs in the headquarters in Billund: 'Only the best is good enough.' The second generation of owners, Godtfred Kirk Christiansen, invented and cultivated the system-mentality, and it became his guiding star. During his reign it was extremely important to develop new bricks, new construction sets and to make everything work together in agreement. It was also important to communicate this to the children and their parents, that is, that more bricks meant even more possibilities for intelligent play since everything was part of a system.

For the third generation, Kjeld Kirk Kristiansen, it was important that LEGO understood its customers as much as possible, and that LEGO developed their toys in accordance with children's ages and interests, so that there were LEGO toys from infancy to adolescence. Under his leadership the company has also engaged in research so LEGO could achieve a deeper understanding of the significance of play-to-learn and thus design better toys.

What the three generations have in common is the desire to maintain a high level of quality. Not only regarding product quality, but in addition a set of house rules was drawn up that strictly defines the requirements of new LEGO products and the real play qualities they should give children. Furthermore, as a consequence of the Kirk family's high ethical standards, they have never made war toys.

MANY ADULT FANS of LEGO think that it was much better in the past when there were only simple bricks. But LEGO had to follow the times and change if the company wanted to survive. Therefore newly designed LEGO systems with computer chips that the children could program themselves saw the light of day in the late 1990s. At around the same time, the company began to collaborate with film companies on creating new worlds of play based on things like Star Wars. Finally, LEGO also made Bionicle with figures that children can build and have role-playing games with.

LEGO has also linked its name to licensed products like children's clothes, bags, watches and games. Most of them are relatively well designed and of a high quality. At the turn of the millennium, the LEGO brick was elected the toy of the century by both Fortune Magazine and the British Toymakers' Guild. But then a number of new ventures in the area of computer games and media products went wrong. These were contributory factors to a crisis at LEGO in 2003, and at the time of writing this, they still hadn't turned the tide. However, there's every indication that the company can make good money on the bricks, though their ambition to maintain a high growth rate and be the leading brand in the area has suffered a serious blow.

▾ The well-known LEGO brick did not become LEGO's own private property until they discovered and patented the small tubes inside the bricks. Until then, several companies around the world made bricks that resembled LEGO's, but then the company in Billund got the edge that made them what they are today. The small tubes increased the stability of the bricks so much that you could almost build anything and it wouldn't fall apart.

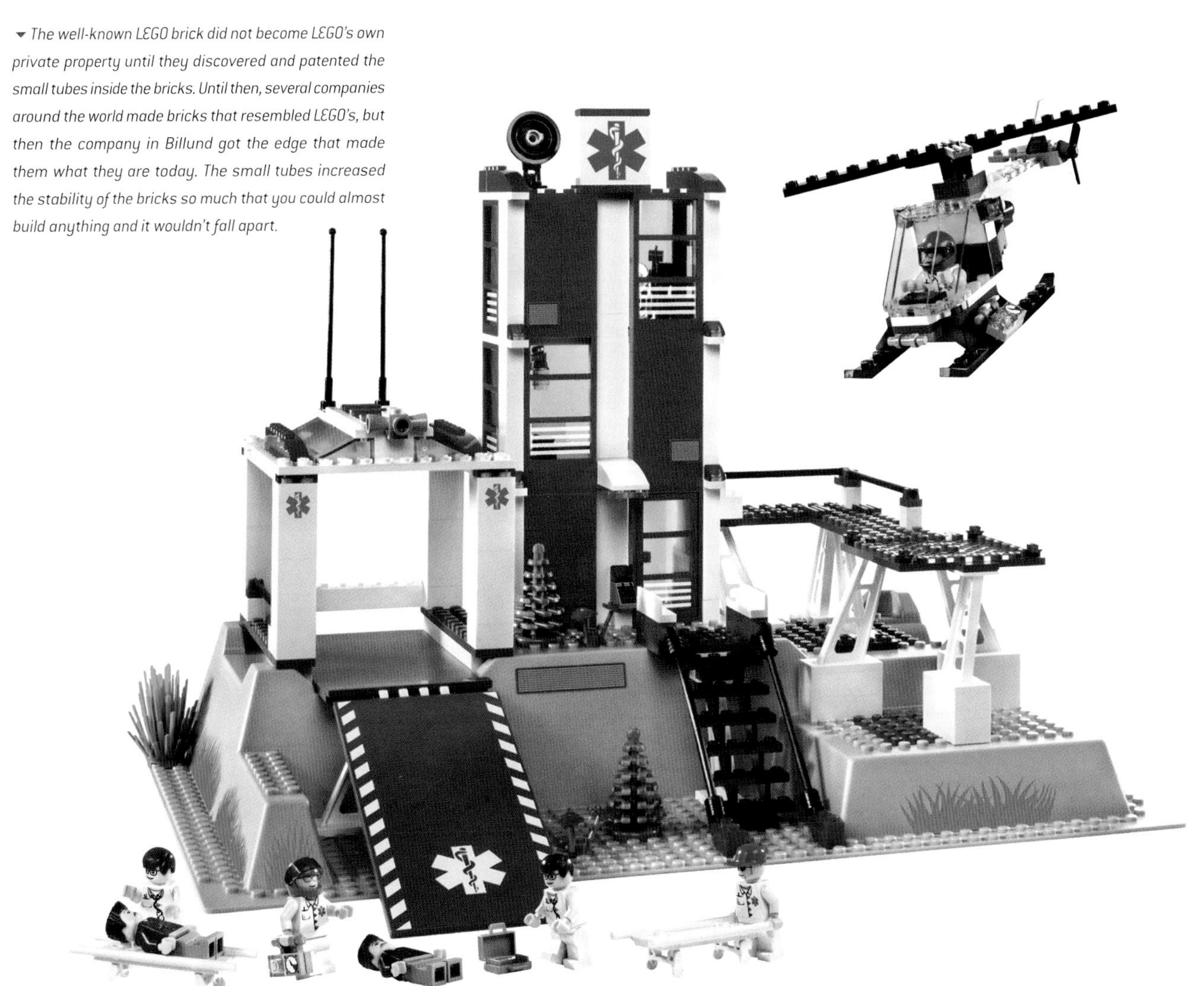

Textile and clothing design

Cloth, fabric, textiles – three words for the same thing – and they're an important prerequisite for making clothes and many other products that entail textiles, such as the interior design of rooms. Of course there are a few things like carpets or curtains where textiles are the products themselves, but fabric is often one step in a development process, where the fabric is a semi-manufactured article that is the basis of the final result. Perhaps it's a bit unfair, but we often take more notice of the end products, like a dress, an upholstered chair or a tent. We acknowledge the fashion designer or the furniture designer, but we may not think about the textile's role in the result.

It's said in the textile and fashion business that if a dress costs between 5,000 and 10,000 Danish kroner, then no more than 100 kroner have been spent on the fabric. The consequence of this fact is of course that Danish textile companies no longer make fabrics for clothing. They can't compete when the price is pushed so low. As a result of the ever increasing globalisation, production first moved mainly to Italy, and later to India and China. But quite a few materials are designed and developed in Denmark although they're manufactured abroad. Furnishing fabrics, namely carpets, curtains and upholstery fabric, are still manufactured in Denmark.

WEAVING IN THE BRONZE AGE

But textile manufacturing hasn't always been so international. If you go back about 3,400 years to the clothes found on the Egtved girl (see page 174), they tell a story about the burgeoning development of a local weaving craft. Before woven material was invented, animal hide was the only material at hand. But as soon as weaving was possible, it seems that fabric was often preferred. Perhaps this is because it was easier to make

◂ A woollen cape with leather applications from Jean Voigt's 1984 collection Fantastic Look in Paris.

◂ *The warp-weighted loom as it looked during the Viking Age, but the principles of construction did not change significantly from the Bronze Age and for thousands of years. This type has been used in northern Scandinavia until the 20th century. Note the loom-weights that were either stone in a suitable size with holes in them or made of clay.*

clothes out of fabric, and the material was more comfortable to wear and maybe more distinguished to own.

The fabric woven during the Bronze Age was very simple wool and probably not dyed, but kept in its original colour. They used looms that were simple upright constructions with two vertical poles and a beam across the top. The loom-weights were often fist-sized rocks with holes that held the warp threads in place. Large finds of these loom-weights plus studies of the preserved cloth have helped archeologists to figure out what looms looked like at that time. The so-called warp-weighted loom has been used for long periods of time and up until our time, and different examples have been reconstructed, among other places at Moesgård Museum near Aarhus where a reconstructed model from the Viking Age is exhibited. A loom was a natural fixture in the home, and one can imagine that it was used whenever there was some spare time.

Even though the woven fabric probably was exclusive in itself, and the looms were simple, the desire to own and to manufacture something special quickly arose. Women's apparel often had fringes, their cloth belts were made of elaborate knotted work, and primitive relief patterns were worked into the woven cloth. So even back then the demand to set oneself apart and maybe even some changes in fashion taught the weavers to vary the appearance of the cloth relatively quickly. As with patterns and ornamentation on ceramics, there have been variations in weaving from region to region and from one era to another. The Egtved girl's short skirt was not made of woven material, but was made by knotting a 1.5 metre long and 38 cm wide piece of braided material made of triple-threaded wool. This wide band of knotted cloth was wrapped around her waist several times. More examples of this type of skirt from the Bronze Age have been found, and some of them had fringes at the bottom to which there were attached little bronze pipes that clinked when the woman moved. Maybe they were the party dresses of the past.

FROM DOMESTIC CRAFTS TO INDUSTRY

Weaving cloth was for a long time a distinctly domestic industry and most often typical women's work. Textiles were also becoming more important, not least practical, since they were used for sail-making from the end of the Iron Age, throughout the Viking Age and onwards. From a cultural point of view, textiles were also important. If you wanted finer cloth, like silk, with which to make more prestigious clothes, it had to be imported. But the Danish weavers did their best to copy the finest foreign fabrics. This was done by improving the weaving quality by using patterns and also by dyeing and other ways of treating the fabrics.

In the beginning of the Middle Ages, around the year 1100, the horizontal foot-powered loom became popular in Denmark and replaced the warp-weighted looms. The foot-powered loom has the great advantage of allowing much better control of the various groups of warp threads up and down, which allows for much quicker weaving, while making patterns in the fabric is also easier. Moreover, the foot-powered loom makes it easier to make long lengths of fabric. The principle of the foot-powered loom is still largely in use in the industry today, but it's of course far more technically sophisticated and faster than its predecessor from the Middle Ages.

At the end of the Middle Ages, spinning and weaving began partly to become a male profession that one could learn, and an actual weavers' guild was established. Now textile workers started to work full time for the market; it was no longer a subsidiary occupation for them. However, weaving cloth at home was predominant up until the late 1600s. Around 1600, what is called a putting-out system gained a footing. Although the weaver stayed at home working on his own loom, the raw materials were delivered to him by an investor. The finished textiles were then delivered to the merchant, who sold them or passed on the textiles for further treatment.

MECHANISATION LEADS TO A NEW DESIGN

Later, factories were introduced. Here the weavers worked in the merchant's workshop with the owner's raw materials on manual looms. But there wasn't a radical change in the way of manufacturing textiles like mechanisation or division of labour. The individual weavers made their own product and were paid per metre of finished cloth. This way of producing fabric and clothing is where the term 'manufactured goods' comes from, at least in Danish. Nonetheless, the production of cloth continued to be rather labour-intensive, and therefore a somewhat expensive process, so one of the first trades to be mechanised during the Industrial Revolution was the production of textiles, and this included spinning and weaving.

In the course of the 1700s, great machines were invented in the textile trade. It started in 1733 with the introduction of the fly shuttle which increased the speed at which the transverse weft thread could be sent through the warp threads. Then the spinning machine was invented in 1760 and the mechanical loom in 1780. Now it was possible to establish proper textiles factories that could mass produce fabric. These inventions were primarily made in England, while in Denmark the industrialisation of the textile production didn't get started until 1825.

The progress from a domestic craft to one produced in a factory also had consequences for design. When a production is co-ordinated and a businessman is in charge of purchasing and sales, then one of his aims was most likely to achieve a great degree of homogeneity in quality and appearance. So making a special design was perhaps not the main reason that a private investor wanted to introduce a putting-out and manufacture system, but in time this became one of the outcomes. And the design aspect was clearly one of the reasons why the state, for long periods of time, had their own factories and later on actual cloth mills.

The king and state as clothing manufacturer

In 1605, at the time of Christian IV, Tugt- og Børnehuset (The Hard Labour and Orphans' House) was established near Helligåndskirken (The Church of the Holy Spirit) in Copenhagen. It was a state mill where both convicts and orphans made cloth for the court, military and civil servants. The children were furthermore taught 'textile skills', as they were called. Here wool was spun, and cloth was woven and dyed, primarily for sewing uniforms for the army and navy. On average about 500 children worked here plus whatever vagrants and beggars were busied in this way. After a serious plague epidemic in 1621, the institution was divided into a proper prison and an orphanage where, in the children's case, more emphasis was placed on education and a little academic learning.

The institution was closed in 1649, but was replaced first by an institution called Børnehuset (The Children's House) that despite its poetic name was in actual fact a prison. It was located near Christianhavns Torv, and later, in 1790, it was replaced by Tugt-, Rasp- og Forbedringshuset (The Rasp and Hard Labour House).

THE WOOL JUTLANDERS. On the heaths around Herning and Ikast in Jutland, there was a long tradition of making homemade textile products, especially knitwear. For a long time they had sheep on the farms that provided the necessary wool as well as giving the shepherd something to do with his hands while watching the flock. Like in other parts of Jutland where they made black pots and sold them on their travels, the wool Jutlanders did the same with socks, caps and sweaters. This painting below, from 1885, is by Frederik Vermehren and depicts one of these knitting shepherds.

▾ The various prisons and orphanages that were run from 1605 until 1860 produced cloth for military uniforms as well as embroidery, lace and other luxury items for the court. The quality is said to have been good although the workers were unskilled prisoners and orphans. The soldier in uniform depicted below is a musketeer from Falsterske Geworbene Regiment, around 1756. As we can see, putting army personnel in uniform was demanding both in regard to the cloth and the work required.

There are several reasons why various kings initiated this public production. First of all, it was a social measure that despite hard labour and bad conditions did provide the orphans with food. But perhaps more importantly was that the initiative supplied clothing in a uniform quality and style for the army and navy. A standing military force hadn't previously existed in the country; the army had been comprised of local forces when there was a war. Therefore it had been up to the individual regiments to sew their own uniforms or have them sewn, but this was eventually centralised. Also the civil servants, who wore clothes resembling uniforms, needed homogeneous clothing.

Throughout the 1600s, the king gained more and more power which culminated in the introduction of absolute monarchy in 1661, and this only increased the need for a systematic and uniform design of textiles. So as an extension of the textile production in prisons and orphanages, a state company was initiated. It started in 1719 as a 'royal military wool manufacturer' that was housed in 'Guldhuset' (the Gold House) on Rigensgade in Copenhagen. Later, from 1801 to 1810, the state took over a number of industrial buildings near Usserød stream close to Hørsholm and turned them into the Military Textile Mill. The production at the factory in Usserød didn't stop till 1981, and the remaining company was renamed the State Clothing Service and was later turned into a state joint-stock company. However, it went bankrupt in 1996 when the old state company was no longer cost-effective among ordinary competition.

▾ Johanne Siegumfeldt wove several copies of this tapestry called Folkevisetæppet (the Folk Ballad Tapestry) in 1917. The motif for the tapestry was designed by Ernestine Nyrop, daughter of Martin Nyrop. It illustrates four different Danish folk ballads. Freely translated from the top: They were seven and twenty-seven; The board game ballad; Song, harp and dance; and Mr. Oluf and his golden sound. The style is Art Nouveau which was the style of the day.

▸ A damask-woven cotton tablecloth in an Arne Jacobsen design, introduced by Georg Jensen Damask (see page 159) in 2002 on the 100th anniversary of Jacobsen's birth.

A third aim of Christian IV's initiatives was to create a Danish textile industry that could compete with the large import of fabric. At the same time, this policy, which was later known as mercantilism, was meant to increase the king's revenue. This should be seen as an attempt to raise and consolidate the nation state after the medieval locally-oriented estates. Therefore trade and industry had to be developed, and privileges (monopolies) were also given to private businessmen who wanted to establish factories and industry. In Denmark this continued long after Christian IV's death in 1648, and according to the Association of Manufacturers' archives there were 54 factories in the textile business that employed 3,844 people in 1746, while in the 1780s there were 150 factories with a total of 12,000 employees.

THE VILLAGE LOOMS WERE BURNT

Throughout the 1800s, industry attracted much interest, not least the textile sector. Companies like Brandts Klædefabrik (Brandt's Cloth Mill) in Odense popped up like mushrooms at the end of the century, and the subsequent mechanisation made part of the labour force redundant. This lowered the price of cloth to a level where working by hand was no longer cost-effective. This resulted in, quite literally, that many of the traditional hand-worked looms all around the country were thrown into the fire or put in the attic and forgotten. Industrialisation produced large amounts of machine-made cheap cloth in a uniform quality and appearance.

This new development corresponded to what was happening in other trades in Denmark, and in Europe the same revolution was taking place. A counter reaction came from many sides.

WOOL WAS NOT the only material. Cloth made of flax has been woven in Denmark since the Iron Age. During certain periods, flax was a contender to wool. Flax yarn is made of fibres from the inner bark of the flax plant, and these fibres undergo several treatments until they can be spun into thread. Flax was difficult to dye with the natural dyes of the time, but it was preferred by the church for things like altar cloth because flax cloth gets whiter every time it's laundered. In the 1700 and 1800s in particular, flax and wool were woven together.

Cotton came into use in the 1700s, arriving first from India and later from America. Both ready-woven cotton cloth and raw cotton for further processing were imported. A great part of the growing textile industry was employed with spinning and weaving cotton fabrics. The royal licensed Cotton Factory was founded outside the Copenhagen ramparts in 1782 and existed until 1795. The fabric made here was bleached and washed in Blegedammene (the bleaching grounds) where Rigshospitalet (The National Hospital of Denmark) now lies.

Hemp fibres have been used since prehistoric times for ropemaking and weaving coarse textiles like canvas, tarpaulin and burlap. Since Christian IV's time, farmers were required to sow hemp on a designated amount of their land in order to supply the navy, but also in the interest of game management. Especially after World War II, new synthetic textiles were developed such as nylon, rayon, viscose and polyester.

◂ *In the 1950s, Paula Trock developed a woven material called Hulgardinet (literally: the hole curtain). Weaving a fabric with this very open and light structure took many experiments. Hanne Vedel, who later took over as head of the textile company Spindegården (The Spinning Mill) used this fabric as inspiration for weaving curtains for the National State Hospital.*

In England, William Morris, one of the leading figures of the Arts and Crafts movement, strove to rediscover the medieval traditions in craftsmanship; among many other things, he designed printed textiles and wallpaper. The Danish reaction to the loss of this craftsmanship was not as ideologically-based as that of the English, but was rather driven by the desire to maintain a high quality. Unlike the forces behind the Arts and Crafts movement, the Danes in the new textile business weren't that interested in the old artistic idioms; they also wanted to design new things.

The new Danish weaving tradition began especially at Askov Folk High School where Jenny la Cour (1849–1928) and Johanne Siegumfeldt (1868–1953) were so inspired by the art of weaving after a study trip to Sweden in 1888 that they imported and had their own looms built. At the same time they began to teach, and Jenny la Cour held weaving courses every summer for the next 25 years at Askov. Later, in 1905, a wooden building was erected at the folk high school for weaving and teaching, and it was called the Weaving House. Many interested people, predominantly women, took the courses and were inspired to revive the tradition on their return home. In the beginning Johanne Siegumfeldt assisted la Cour, and in 1897 they wrote *Vævebog for Hjemmene* (Weaving Book for the Home), which was published in several printings till 1937, and there were even cloth swatches pasted in the book. Of course both of these weavers wove many textiles – some were traditional while others were influenced by the style of the day, Art Nouveau. At times they wove tapestries that were inspired by folk ballads.

Jenny la Cour's main contribution lay in teaching at Askov and in imparting knowledge about weaving in other ways. Johanne Siegumfeldt moved to Copenhagen in 1913 to work and teach at Husflidsselskabets (The Arts and Crafts Association's) school, called Vævestuen (the Weaving Workshop). At this time there was a growing interest, not least among the trendsetting architects of the time, in strengthening the art. Among others, architect Martin Nyrop (1849–1921), who was a professor at the Royal Academy of Fine Arts and had designed Copenhagen's city hall, put himself in the forefront of a new movement in design that called attention to arts and crafts. During that time Nyrop designed quite a few motifs for woven fabrics himself. After a few years in Copenhagen, Johanne Siegumfeldt returned to Jutland and began a collaboration with Georg Jensen Damask in Kolding that lasted for many years.

The Jutlandic branch of the new weaving tradition was continued around Askov Folk High School. One of Jenny la Cour's students was Paula Trock (1889–1979), who took the course at Askov in 1925 and continued her education abroad, visiting schools and weaving workshops in Sweden, Finland and England. In 1928, the same year Jenny la Cour died, Paula Trock returned to Askov, to start the weaving school Askovhus (Askov House) and began to organise a further education in weaving. The following year she admitted students to a new, two-year course with final exams. In 1948, Trock founded the company Spindegården (The Spinning Mill) right next to the folk high school. From here she supplied woven textiles like curtain material and carpets for Finn Juhl's interior design of the UN building in New York, and for the Danish State Railway's ferry 'the Sjolland'. The spinning mill was later converted into an independent institution, and in 1970 it was taken over by weaver Hanne Vedel and moved to Aabenraa where it is today.

▾ Gerda Henning experimented with different weaving techniques. This is her first attempt to weave damask tablecloths on the programmable Jacquard loom. It's a test piece, which in this case is a draft of furniture upholstery. The warp thread is flax, but the weft thread is cotton.

The Copenhagen weaving milieu

The interest in high-quality textiles was now seriously awakened in design and architectural circles in Copenhagen. Architect Anton Rosen (1859–1928), who among other things designed the Palads Hotel on Rådhuspladsen (the city hall square), got involved in the craft and designed patterns. Rosen and other like-minded people saw a future in the development of furniture fabrics, carpets and curtains that could perfect the interiors of their architecture.

For the very same reason, the architects didn't want to be retrospective, but on the contrary wanted to develop new quality textiles that lived up to their special demands more than the mass produced textiles of the time. It was not so much because they were against industrial products as such. In contrast to the English Arts and Crafts movement, they weren't raging against the machines, but only desired textiles of a better design and higher quality.

But the industry couldn't comply with the architects' wishes, or perhaps the companies just couldn't see that there was a market that wanted something new. One of the first people to plunge into the new sophisticated weaving by hand was Gerda Henning (1891–1951). First she was trained at Statens Tegnelærerkursus (The State Drawing Teachers' Course), then from 1910 to 1917 she worked as a porcelain painter at the Royal Porcelain Factory. Afterwards Henning worked with embroidery, and meanwhile she bought her first loom and was taught by the German weaver Schultze, who was working in the basement of Christiansborg Castle because he had been invited to Denmark for a number of years to weave damask tablecloths for the new Folketing (the Danish Parliament).

DAMASK IS CLOTH that is woven so the pattern is revealed in shiny and matt weaves, respectively. Traditionally damask was woven in one colour, often white, and the pattern appears like a relief in the fabric. This effect is also achieved by using glossy thread, traditionally silk. The word damask comes from Damascus and was introduced in Denmark centuries ago. The family that owns Georg Jensen Damask, which has nothing to do with the goldsmith of the same name, have been weavers since the 1400s in the Kolding area. Before the invention in 1808 of the advanced Jacquard loom that can be programmed with special punch cards, damask was extremely expensive and exclusive. They began using flax and later cotton, and nowadays damask is not only woven in one colour, but often in two. Today damask tablecloths and placemats are still luxury items, yet affordable for us mortals. Over the years, Georg Jensen Damask has worked with several Danish designers, including tablecloths designed by Arne Jacobsen and Vibeke Klint. Kim Naver (b. 1940) designed the 'Linie' tablecloth on the left in 1981.

▾ *In 1938, Lis Ahlmann wove this bedspread for Kaare Klint's Kugleseng (spherical bed). The pattern in stripes was inspired by the old Danish duvets in fustian, but Kaare Klint stressed that the colour and the stripes had to go perfectly with the design of the bed and his aesthetics. The material is cotton, a bit unusual at the time when most weavers used wool, but Lis Ahlmann often used cotton, and it became of one of her distinctive marks. Ahlmann also wove dress material.*

▸ *Kirsten Fribert trained at the Design School in Kolding. Since 2002 she has made pillows, tea cosies, handbags, wallets, placemats etc. out of material she made herself. Since then she has outsourced some of the sewing to sub-suppliers and established her own brand called By Fribert. However, she still prints the material by hand in her workshop in Copenhagen. Her prints are in a young and graphic style with plenty of polka dots and stylised flowers that are printed in bright colours on white material. Kirsten Fribert has previously worked with fashion designers such as Baum und Pferdgarten. Among other places, her works are now sold by the design shop at the Museum of Modern Art in New York.*

In 1922 Gerda Henning started her own weaving workshop and began to exhibit her works the following year. Around 1924 she started working with architects Kaare Klint and Mogens Koch, and in 1925 she and Klint designed the carpet for the boardroom at Thorvaldsen's Museum. In 1927, at the initiative of Klint, she started a weaving school in a wing of the Museum of Art & Design in Copenhagen. Gerda Henning became an institution in weaving in Denmark and trained many other weavers at her school. The need for a more formalised weavers' education was highlighted by Henning's work and new initiatives, which brought about the takeover of her weaving school in 1930 by the Technical Society. Henning continued as the head of the school until her death in 1951.

Over the years, Gerda Henning's artistic form developed from weaving pictures with motifs like animals and Oriental figures to a style whose patterns were more unsentimental and abstract. The functionalist architects' influence is apparent in her style from the second half of the 1920s and on, while her earlier works seem to be more inspired by her time working with embroidery. One of Gerda Henning's later students was Vibeke Klint (b. 1927), who completed her training in 1949. Klint took over the workshop after Henning's death. Ea Koch (1905–87) had her first lessons in weaving with Henning, and together with her husband, Mogens Koch, she designed and made a number of interesting carpets with stylised nature motifs. For example, the couple were inspired by bird plumage and sandbanks, often in subdued earth tones.

Among the many, mostly women, who learned the basics about weaving and textile design in Gerda Henning's classes, was Lis Ahlmann (1894–1979). In 1923 she was Gerda Henning's first student and worked for about ten years with her master before opening her own weaving workshop in 1934. Lis Ahlmann worked with both Klint and Koch, but later she had a particularly good and friendly working relationship with Børge Mogensen focusing on the design and production of mostly furniture upholstery, for example for the Wing chair, but also for curtains. She was one of the first textile designers who in the late 1920s collaborated with furniture architects from the Klint school on weaving fabrics whose design and quality were suited to the new types of furniture, architecture and interiors. Ahlmann's style was in a way more unassuming than many of her colleagues' works. Hers were inspired by old rustic materials with stripes and checks. This design line was suited to the English and Shaker inspired furniture that Kaare Klint, and later Mogensen, designed.

TEXTILE PRINTING

Until about 1930 textile printing in Denmark had suffered the same fate as weaving. It had practically been forgotten because of the advance of industry and cheap materials throughout the 1800s. In Denmark there had been the so-called calico printing (the word is 'kattun' in Danish which is derived from the Arabic 'qutun', cotton in English). Since the beginning of the 1700s this technique was known and had been inspired by French textile design. For obvious reasons textile printing is much younger than weaving since some kind of cloth was needed before you could print on it. Cotton fabric was imported from Tranquebar, the Danish colony on the southeastern coast of India. The dyeing and printing of cloth in the late 1700s was a very lucrative industry, and every provincial town had its own dyeing works where textiles were also printed. In the late 1700s, Copenhagen had 16 of these calico printworks which employed about 600 people.

▸ *The fabric Cherries by Marie Gudme Leth was hand-printed in 1946 in her own workshop. This print requires six screens, one screen for each colour, and the screens are 18.5 x 41 cm. So it takes a lot of printing, and the screens have to be moved with extreme precision for each print. In technical printmaking jargon, this careful alignment process is called 'rapport'.*

From the mid-1800s textile printing went seriously downhill because of the industrial production and extensive import of cheap textiles. In the 1920s a new interest in it was awakened partly as a reaction to the bad quality of industrial goods at the time, and partly inspired by the boom and success of weaving. It was Marie Gudme Leth (1895–1997), who was the driving force behind the reintroduction of textile printing in Denmark. She was trained in drawing at the Drawing and Applied Art School for Women and later at the Royal Academy of Fine Arts in Copenhagen, but after a three-year stay in Java, she started to print textiles in 1924.

The School of Arts & Crafts was established in Copenhagen in 1930 by merging the Museum of Art & Design's craftsman's school and the Department of Applied Art under the Technical Societies' schools. Marie Gudme Leth was their first teacher of textile printing.

Back then, as now, they distinguished between block printing and screen printing. In block printing, carved wooden blocks or linoleum carvings are used and the relief creates the pattern. In screen printing, also called silk printing, a stretched piece of silk or other material is used. This is proofed so some areas are impenetrable to the print colour. The printed pattern is created when the colour is pressed through the screen onto the material below with a doctor blade. In modern industrial production both printing methods are used, often with the help of complex machinery. Today textile printing is characterised by many experiments in technique and motifs where, for example, the new inkjet printing technology makes it possible to make exact prototypes and manufacture new patterns in very small quantities at affordable prices.

▸ *Continued on page 167*

▼ *Rolf Middelboe worked with abstract patterns in his screen-printed material, sometimes strictly geometrical, sometimes a little looser – a bit like clouds in the sky. Middelboe often printed on silk or satin. The material here is from the late 1950s.*

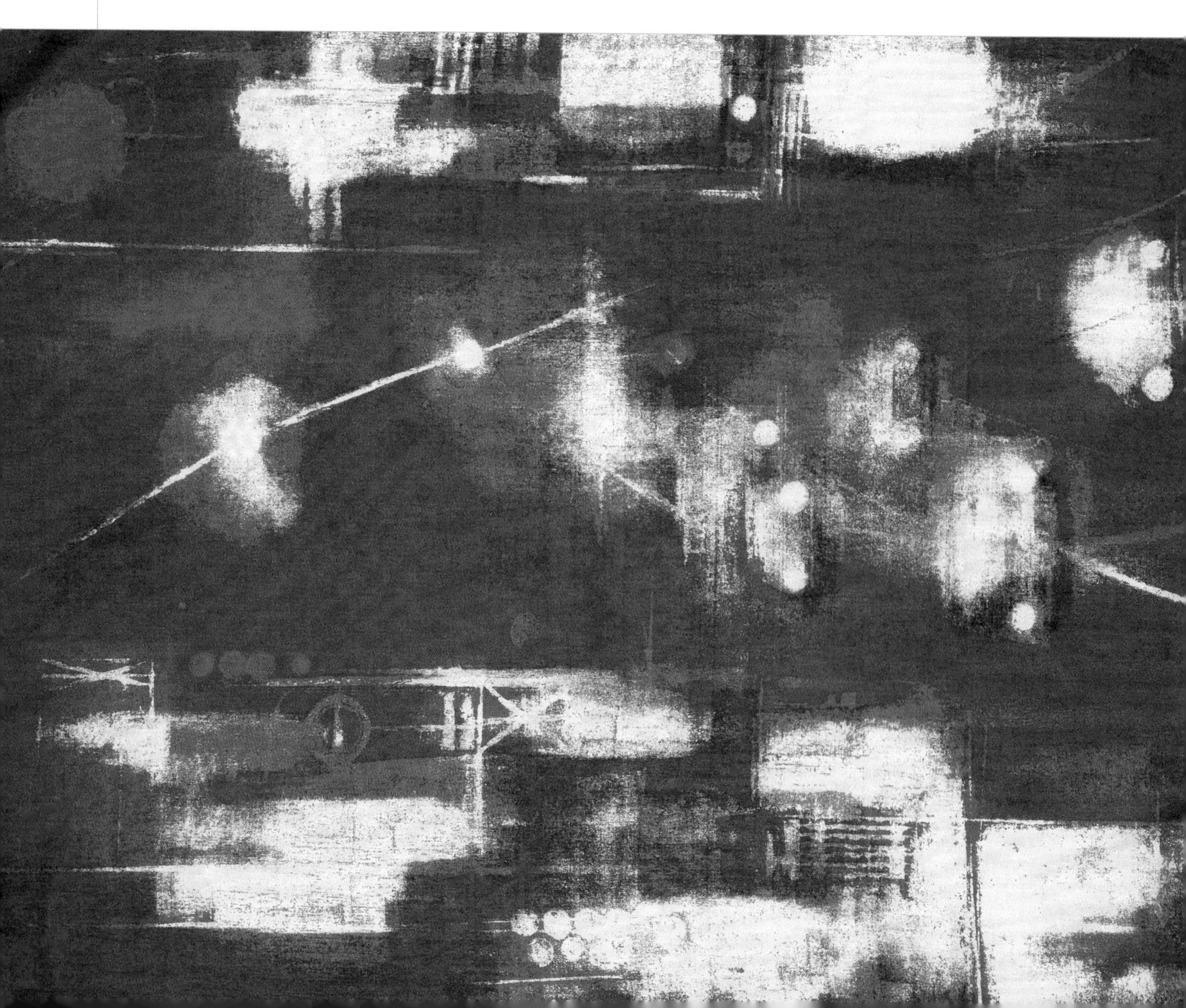

▾ *While a refugee in Sweden during the German occupation of Denmark, Arne Jacobsen made use of his talents as a watercolour painter to design material. Often his motifs were nature's plants, and therefore Jacobsen's textiles from that time were given the nickname 'the wayside textiles'.*

▾ *Verner Panton was inspired by the modern art of his time and by the possibilities of the materials. The artistic inspiration is very clear in his total design for the exhibit 'Geometry 1' in Zurich in 1961 for Plus-linje Furniture. The international school of art which he was influenced by is called op art; it's art that is based on optical illusions. These exhibition milieus were completely covered with textiles.*

At first Marie Gudme Leth worked with block printing, but later, in the late 1930s, she moved on to screen printing. In 1935 she was co-founder and director of Dansk Kattuntrykkeri (Danish Calico Printing Works), but she left in 1940 to start her own workshop for hand-printed fabric. In the beginning, Leth worked a lot with motifs inspired by the Orient or by nature, such as fern leaves, birds and cherries. Later in her career, in the 1950s, she adopted a more geometric abstract style. Marie Gudme Leth achieved the same status as a groundbreaking pioneer in textile printing as Jenny la Cour and Gerda Henning did in weaving. And Leth too taught a whole generation of textile printers while working in education.

Graphic textiles

In the wake of Marie Gudme Leth came a long line of young textile printers. Many of them were former students of Leth, but some had different backgrounds, like painters, and were attracted to the creative possibilities that lay in printing graphic motifs on textiles. The 1950s in particular were very productive times for textile printing in Denmark. One of the people who entered the trade in an untraditional way was Rolf Middelboe (1917–95). First he graduated as a graphic designer from the School of Arts & Crafts in 1937 and then he became a skilled textile printer in 1940. His style was often graphically experimental, and many of his textiles required great precision in the placement of the screen for the pattern to be well executed. He worked as the artistic head or as a consultant for a number of companies, among others Unika-Væv (Unique Weave), Danish Calico Printing Works, Bing & Grøndahl and the Danish State Railways.

Some architects also began to design patterns for textiles with a view to perfecting the interior design of their architecture with things like carpets, curtains and furniture upholstery. One of them was Arne Jacobsen who started painting motifs for textile prints after he fled to Sweden in 1943. The Swedish architects were said to be opposed to Jacobsen working as an architect, since they were afraid that he would land all the best jobs. Instead he learned the basic principles of textile printing from his wife, Jonna Jacobsen, who was a skilled textile designer. So instead of making houses, he designed textile patterns, in particular for curtains. At first he used nature motifs, and in posterity these designs have been often referred to as 'Arne Jacobsen's waysides', since his textiles from his Swedish period were full of flowers and small plants in vivid colours. He sold several of his suggestions to Swedish companies, of which Arnedal was one and the department store Nordiska Kompaniet another.

After his return to Denmark, Arne Jacobsen continued designing fabrics, mainly for curtains and room dividers, but he also designed carpets. It always happened when he needed something special for one of his buildings, for example, the Royal Hotel. Today Georg Jensen Damask in Kolding still weave tablecloths in patterns he designed.

Architect Verner Panton, who incidentally worked at Arne Jacobsen's architectural practice for a short time, didn't build many houses, but worked more with furniture and interiors, which were designed down to the last detail. Panton also designed many textiles for his interiors and for exhibitions throughout the years. Panton saw textiles as materials that were part of a whole. For the German chemical corporation Bayer, which manufactured some of the new synthetic fibres like Dralon, Panton designed some spectacular exhibition milieus for the international furnishing shows in Cologne. Some of his textiles are still made today.

◂ *The printed curtain material Waves, which was launched in 1979 and designed by architect Ole Kortzau (b. 1939) is a product from Kvadrat. The previous year, a design called Moves had been launched without much success. It was a 'positive' version of Waves, i.e. the jagged stripes were white on a coloured background. In its time this fabric was a rather unusual design, as the contemporary styles were characterised by the late and somewhat square modernism and by earthy tones. The material was to a certain degree seen as post modern in its style. Kvadrat still prints and sells the material, which is woven out of a kind of polyester called Trevira CS and which is approved by the fire authorities for use in the public sector.*

▸ *Kvadrat still weave the material called Hallingdal designed by Nanna Ditzel in 1964–65. This was actually the material that was behind Kvadrat's establishment, and it's been in production ever since. The material is 70 % wool and 30 % viscose.*

FROM CRAFT TO INDUSTRIAL PRODUCTION

From the beginning of the renaissance in textile design, that is from about 1900 till about 1950, the field was characterised by small-scale production in workshops with few or no employees apart from the owner. This was the case in both weaving and textile printing, although there were a few companies with more employees who also produced textiles of a good design and high quality. One of the few good examples of this was Den blaa Fabrik (The blue Factory) in Lyngby, which was founded in 1934 by Brita Drewsen (1887–1983) and Gudrun Clemens (1905–53). With its approximately 20 employees Den blaa Fabrik was the largest company in its field and one of the few that had progressed from hand weaving. But for many years most of their production was made by hand.

Den blaa Fabrik was also lucky because in the 1930s, which was about the time the company was founded, import restrictions were introduced on foreign fabric. However, there was a limit to how many companies could make a living by manual production alone. Hand-woven products had the same fate as handmade furniture of the time: they were exclusive products. And as long as the craftsmen's wages were low, you could manage by selling to well-off customers. Some people in the industry gradually realised that their cut-price production didn't have a high quality of design, and by now the power looms could make a good quality product. The time had come to admit that not everyone could make a living by bending over the loom or the printing table.

In the years after the war, weavers like Lis Ahlmann began to work with the company C. Olesen, and they exhibited machine-made textiles at the 400th anniversary exhibition of the Cabinetmakers' Guild in Copenhagen in 1954. She was interviewed on that occasion and has reportedly said that, 'To me there is something very satisfying about working for the industry when the quality can be maintained. A power loom can make the fabric look hand-woven, and by fabric I don't just mean the thread and colour, but the texture ... The furniture fabric of the future should be durable cotton that is colourfast and has a zipper for easy mounting.'

Even though Lis Ahlmann designed for and advised the textile industry, she and others like her never gave up their looms or printing screens. They had the craft in their blood and felt the need to participate actively in the creative process and maintain a hands-on attitude. In 1956, the company C. Olesen Boligtextiler (Furnishing fabrics) and a number of consultants and professionals started a design line called Cotil. For several years, high-quality fabrics were produced, and they were designed by Lis Ahlmann, Arne Jacobsen, Børge Mogensen, Vibeke Klint and many others.

But after World War II, many others saw the opportunity for progress in the areas of design and the production of textiles. The businessman Percy von Halling-Koch (1914–92) drove around on his motorcycle in 1947 to farms out in the Danish countryside and bought old fustian upholstery. The upholstery was then cleaned and sold as furniture fabric. One day he was contacted by some female weavers who asked him to help them sell their textiles. This is how the company Unika-Væv was started and later assisted by Mads Eg Damgaard, who ran Egetæpper A/S (Ege Carpets Inc.). Halling-Koch's own productions began to be made on power looms in Herning in 1951. Unika-Væv was where a lot of the good Danish textile design was made for many years, and this is where Gunnar Aagaard Andersen and others developed textiles and held exhibitions.

IN 1964, HALLING-KOCH was squeezed out of his company by other investors, and he had to start over. He founded Halling-Koch Design Centre and allied himself with designer Nanna Ditzel. Together they developed the concept for a new collection of furniture fabrics called Hallingdal. Nanna Ditzel was given full rein in deciding the design and colours, since Halling-Koch believed that designers should have full creative responsibility. A collaboration on the sales and running of the company was set up with the Kvadrat company that saw the light of day at the same time in Ebeltoft. Hallingdal textile was popular and has been a big seller at Kvadrat ever since. A total of 4 million metres of Hallingdal textile have been produced in the past 35 years. Pictured are a few of the 62 different colours it comes in. It's used in Denmark's IC3 trains, where its great durability comes into its own. When Halling-Koch was about 70, Kvadrat took over the full responsibility for Hallingdal.

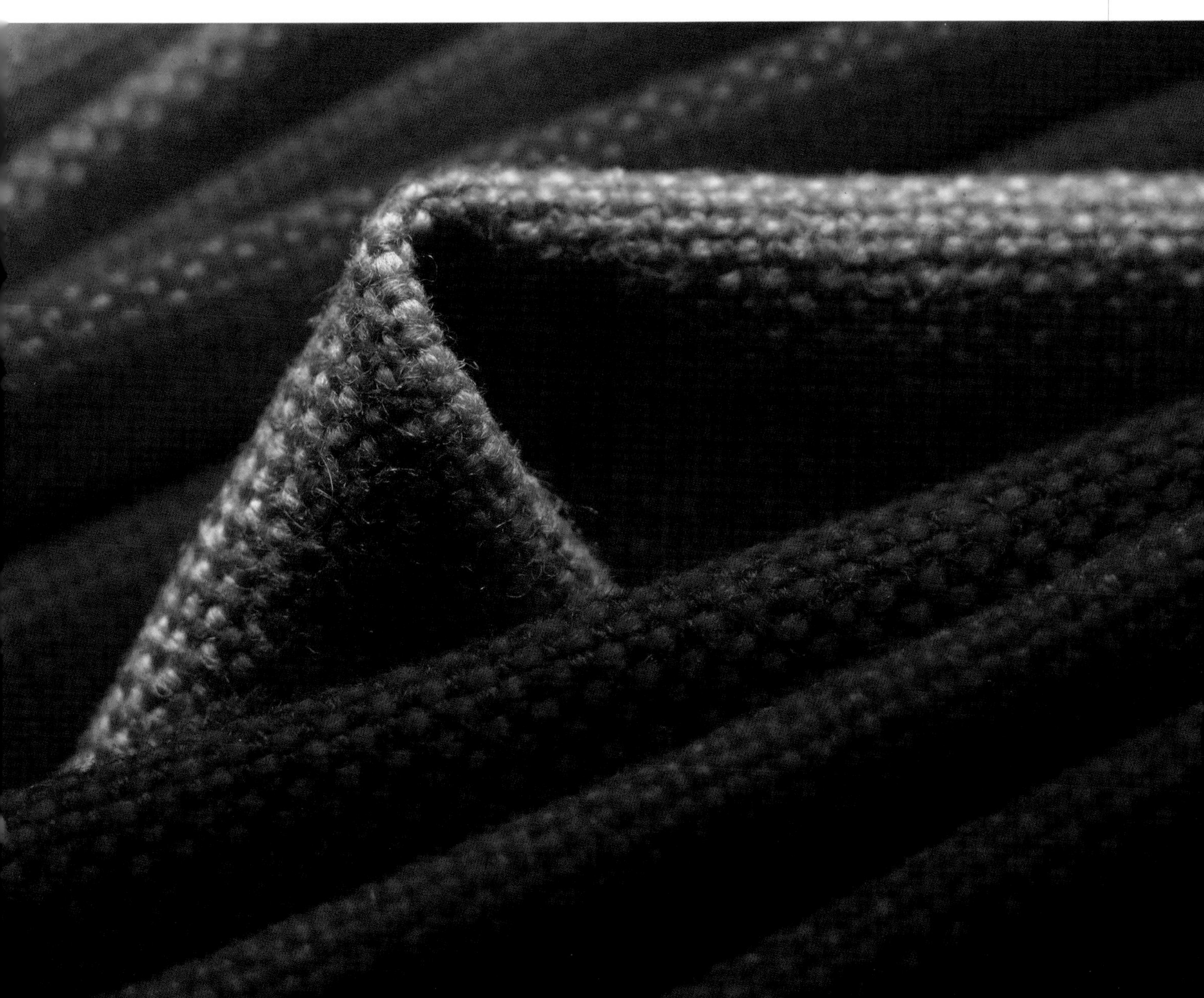

TEXTILE DESIGNER CHARLOTTE HOUMAN (b. 1963) has together with the company Faber developed and designed a number of Venetian blinds with cut-out patterns. The textiles are in light colours, and a laser is used to cut out the small patterns in the linen fabric. This creates a relief effect in the material itself as well as a pattern of light in the drawn blind. The collection was launched in 2003 and is called Nordlys (Northern Lights). It comes in a number of colours and different cut-out patterns.

LINIE DESIGN was established in 1980 by two former employees of Cotil, namely Hugo Anthon and Keld Agerskov. The company has successfully marketed handmade carpets at affordable prices. The carpets are primarily sold in Denmark, but are made in India where Agerskov and Anthon take great pains to ensure that the working conditions of their employees are in order. Linie Design collaborates with several Danish designers such as Kim Naver, Bodil Jerichau and Marie-Louise Rosholm.

▲ *A Venetian blind from the series Nordlys (Northern lights) by Charlotte Houman.*

▲ *Marie-Louise Rosholm has developed the carpet Rapallo in flax and wool for Linie Design.*

TEXTILE DESIGNER ASTRID KROGH (b. 1968) graduated from Denmark's Design School in 1997 and has since had assignments in artistic decoration but she has also had more practical design jobs like making a support undergarment for ostomy patients for Coloplast. On this page is a 3 x 8 m tapestry from 2003 resembling a neon installation in one of Christiansborg's long hallways. The tapestry is not made of textiles; it's made of 'woven' neon tubes that change appearance every few seconds with the help of electronics.

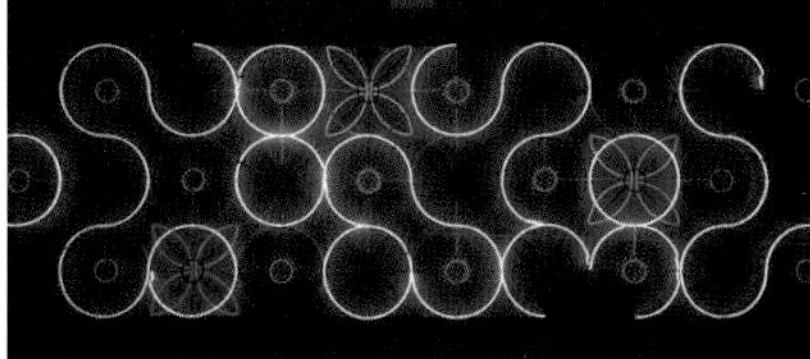

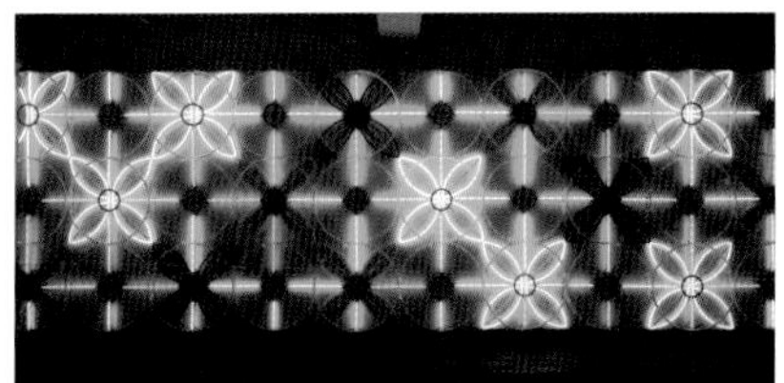

KURAGE. THERE ARE still textile designers in Denmark who do a great deal of the production work themselves. Just outside the town of Odder lies the design and textile company Kurage, which the designer couple Jesper Gundersen and Ruth Fabricius have run for over 15 years. In spite of the fact that they often work at the printing tables themselves, their company is probably the largest of its kind in Scandinavia. They made their name in the world, and especially in the trade, when they took on design work for the coffee bar AMOKKA on Østerbro in Copenhagen. The job included every kind of graphic expression such as logo, stationery, signs and other products such as textiles, packaging, coffee cans etc. They made all the curtains, tablecloths and employee uniforms themselves. The products that have AMOKKA's dancing black women with coffee beans on them were sold in many other places as well, making the brand very well known. This is how Kurage's design job was not limited to the design of a café's textiles.

Kurage also makes other furnishing fabrics, and when the firm started in 1990, quite a bit was manufactured in India, such as hand-woven and hand-printed silks designed by Ruth Fabricius and Jesper Gundersen. But as of 1993, Kurage's collections were only manufactured in Denmark. The small company's strength lies in the direct path from design to production, which intensifies the feeling of authenticity and genuineness in the final expression.

CLOTHING DESIGN

Our clothes are part of what gives us our identity. Unlike our other possessions like our home and car, our clothes are an inseparable part of our appearance in the public domain. No matter whether we're at work, in the garden, on the beach or at a party, we have dressed for the occasion in what we think is appropriate for the situation and our personality. Our clothes are some of the most personal things we own. They're something we have chosen ourselves and are an expression of our distinctiveness. But to be honest, how personal are they really? How big is the selection when we go into a clothes store or a department store? And when it comes right down to it, to what degree do we let ourselves be, consciously or not, influenced by the social conventions of our society? Not to mention the norms that are found in our family, social class or subculture? Can a businessman, say a bank manager, take the liberty of wearing anything but a nice suit to work?

If we take a look at designers and architects, for example, a striking number of them are dressed all in black every day. Does this reflect a professional code? Or is it just a habit? At least you don't have to justify your choice of colour. Furniture architect Verner Panton, who was very fond of colours, had a similar habit. He wore only blue. He said once that it was practical when you travelled as much as he did since all the clothes in his suitcase matched. Throughout the history of clothing, people haven't had equally rational arguments for the clothes they wore. Nonetheless, some method can often be found in the madness when you delve a bit into the whims of fashion.

Fundamentally, people have always worn clothes to protect the body from the weather, cold and heat, and out of modesty. From a historic

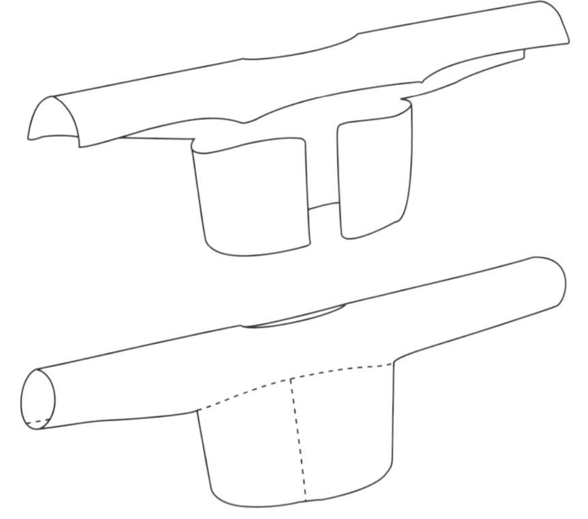

◂ *Reconstructions of several women's clothing have been made, for example the Egtved girl's. A recurring piece of clothing from the period is this little blouse, which is 'cut from one piece', to use a technical term. By cutting the rectangular piece of cloth in an ingenious way, it becomes a blouse without wasting any material. In the reconstructions the wool was dyed brown, which is how the original looked when it was found, but the many years in the ground have given it this colour. Originally the clothes were not dyed, but had the natural colour of wool, white or yellowish.*

point of view, clothing can be divided into two main groups: on the one hand, the draped or loose-fitting clothing that gives the body freedom of movement, and on the other hand, the tailored clothing that hugs the body and practically shapes it according to the fashion of the time. The latter has in general been the predominant one. You can also see fashion as an extension of the European creative urge and dynamic that won't be ruled by the biology of the body, but has wanted to shape not only clothes, but the body itself. But clothes and fashion create distinctions between the masculine and the feminine and between different social classes and communities.

If we go very far back in time, we obviously don't have much that can tell us about the use and appearance of clothing. But from the few fragments that were found we can assume that the first pieces of clothing were made of animal hides, and later fabric was woven of flax and other suitable plant fibres. The Danish climate and soil have supplied some of the best conditions in Europe for preserving textiles over a long period of time. One of the earliest and most well-preserved outfits is from 1370 BC, the Bronze Age, and was found in barrow near the town of Egtved in Jutland. The body of a young woman, about 17 years old, was found. She was wearing a little blouse that was short sleeved and skimpy, so part of her stomach was showing, which funnily enough has been the latest fad among young women in Denmark until recently. She also wore a short skirt of braided string that hung low on her hips and reached just below her knees.

This woollen clothing was rather summery, which fits the time of year she was buried in (this is known because she had summer flowers in her oak coffin). Around her waist she had a knotted belt made of the same

▸ *Frescos depicting clothes from the late Middle Ages, around the year 1500. The motif shows a so-called 'dance of death', where every other figure is a person, and every other one is the person's soul. As we can see on their clothes, each of these people represent a rank or class in contemporary society. There's a king, a bishop, a nobleman and a farmer or craftsman. The fresco is from Nørre Alslev Church on the island of Falster.*

material as her clothes, but its purpose wasn't to hold her skirt up, but to carry her valuable belt disc (see page 19). The find itself doesn't make it easy to determine who this woman was or whether her attire was typical. However, it's presumed that because of her expensive burial presents, among other things, that she belonged to a rich and privileged part of the population although she was rather simply dressed.

When the find was made in 1921, the girl's minimal clothing was considered so racy that it was thought that everyone couldn't have dressed so provocatively. One theory suggests that she could have been a 'lady of the night', perhaps a kind of concubine like in the Far East. But not much is known about prevailing morals in the Bronze Age, so these guesses are more a reflection of posterity's interpretations and norms.

Clothes until the Gothic period

As we approach our time, we naturally know more about clothes, their construction and use, not to mention the culture and the symbolic language they express. We have more finds from the end of the Viking Age and the early Middle Ages to relate to, and furthermore there are frescos in the oldest Danish churches and other descriptions of clothing. According to the grave finds from the Bronze Age and up to the Viking Age, there doesn't seem to be a great difference in men's and women's clothing, at least not in everyday clothing. The men did wear a kind of trousers, while the women wore skirts, but both sexes wore the same blouses and capes or mantles. The material and decorations were usually the same, while there could be a difference in their headgear. At this time, dyes were difficult to obtain and use, so clothes whose colours differed were a symbol of dignity, prestige and wealth. In particular blue and red colours as well as expensive imported silk were status symbols then.

In the Middle Ages, major changes took place. While the everyday clothes of the common man didn't change for a long time, the ruling classes' attire started to follow the general European fashion, which was mainly determined by the court of Burgundy (former duchy in eastern central France) which was a trendsetter in Europe at the time. The Gothic period in Denmark starts around the year 1200 and lasts till about 1500. Another name for this period in Denmark is 'the pointed arc style' because the architecture was characterised by very tall and towering architecture that was pointed at the top, seen in the Danish cathedrals. The formal clothes followed this tall and narrow ideal, especially in the case of women.

In the 13th century, the ankle-length coat or tunic became popular, and men's long hoses were replaced by trousers that were more or less like the ones we have today. The special fashion for men was the chaperon, a long-tailed hood that was commonly used around the year 1300, and it underlined the straight-up-and-down lines in clothing, which were also accentuated by the pointed boots or even peaked shoes. This makes the human body look very tall and narrow.

In the 14th century, fashionable women wore a tunic with large armholes, the so-called 'windows of hell', since you could see the underwear beneath that hugged and revealed the shape of the sinful body. The trendy look for men also clung to the body – the tunic was shorter and had buttons. The clothes of the upper class were particularly colourful during this period.

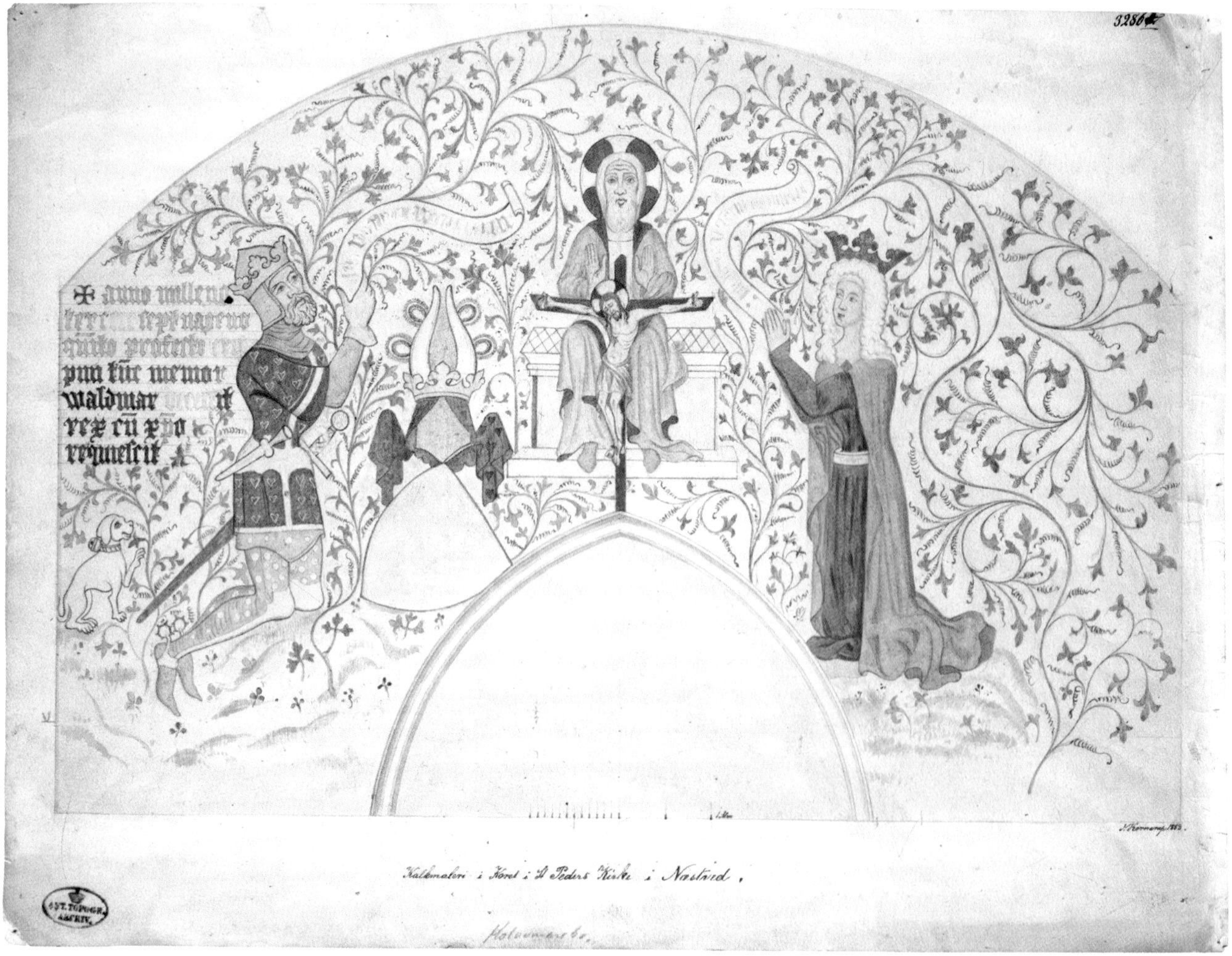

▲ *Medieval dress underlines the tall and the narrow, which also became the ideal for the body. It can be seen on many of the frescos that have been revealed in the last few decades in the many Danish village churches that were built in the early Middle Ages.*

THE CHAPERON. In 1936, a body was found in Bocksten Bog in Halland, a former Danish territory. The Bocksten man was about 25–35 years old at the time of his death, which was probably in the 1330s. He was found fully dressed in an outfit that is well preserved and complete. It consists of a short tunic, a chaperon, a cloak, hosiery and foot coverings, all of which are of wool, as well as leather shoes and a belt. The find is exhibited at Varberg Museum in Sweden. The chaperon consists of a cape that covers the shoulders and chest, and a liripipe or tail that is normally long and wide enough to be used as a built-in scarf.

Dressing in a manner consistent with one's station

At the beginning of the Renaissance and with the growth of towns, a concept of what we call fashion slowly began to develop. When a person adopts a new fashion, it shows that they're developing and following the times and advances in society.

People who don't follow along and adapt, risk being seen as a bit backward. Before the Renaissance, progress was so slow that one can hardly talk about changes in fashion. However, for the upper classes it might have meant something that one's clothes were up to date. When visiting foreign crowned heads it could be important not to make a fool of oneself by looking like a country bumpkin. So in principle, worrying about fashion and style was a matter for the upper classes as long as society was divided and isolated, at least seen from the common man's point of view. In the lower ranks, tradition and functionality reigned, although snobbery did cause some people to want to emulate the ruling classes.

Hence the concept of 'dressing in a manner consistent with one's station', since one of the most significant roles of clothing in society is to indicate the social status of a person or group. Sometimes this could be done by simple means like using a better quality of material or silver buttons instead of bone or horn buttons. Thus it was possible for some people or groups to manifest their wealth and profit. In other cases the clothes of the individual classes looked completely different, which is why especially royalty and the nobility sometimes revelled in furs, silk, bright colours and jewellery. For long periods of time, the establishment tried to prevent people from the lower classes from 'dressing above their station' and autocratic kings issued sumptuary laws that dictated who could wear what.

Long before the Renaissance, during the reign of King Erik Klipping (1249–86), the establishment was dissatisfied because the people had begun to dress lavishly by wearing gold, silver, silk and bright colours. So the king had to issue a decree against the superfluous use of materials, and it said, 'Neither may anyone adorn his clothing with gold and silver except the king and his children ... If someone wants to wear his clothes for a year or more, it shall by no means bring shame upon him.' And this continued for centuries, actually right until the abolishment of absolute monarchy in 1849, when the Danish constitution was adopted.

The establishment often tries to legislate its way to a monopoly on being fashionably and expensively dressed, and the people are equally stubborn in attempting to wear more expensive clothes and finery than permitted. For example, it was prohibited for a period of time for anyone but royalty to wear a train. This led some of the aristocracy to try wearing a short one, while the wealthy but common citizens would try to imitate other privileges the aristocracy had in clothing. Thus all classes tried to dress above their station. During some periods there were import restrictions on expensive silk, so only the king and other high-ranking people could obtain clothes made of this grand material.

And although we don't have any restrictions today on who can wear what, there is still some status in wearing clothes that are expensive, exclusive or different in one way or another. By wearing the latest and most sophisticated fashion that hasn't become popular yet, one can signal that one is upbeat and has cultural capital. Even though some clothes aren't even very expensive, the wearer can achieve status, especially in certain subcultures, by being avant-garde. Ludvig Holberg's comedy *Jean*

▲ *The paintings above are from 1589 and depict the highest official in Denmark and his wife. They are Christian II's first member of the Danish council, Jørgen Rosenkranz, and his wife, Dorte Lange. Their clothes are examples of the very buttoned-down style of the time. It actually looks like their head and bodies are in separate worlds and living separate lives, but the body is far subordinate to the intellect.*

de France from 1722 is an early example of a Francophile fashion snob who is ridiculed by ordinary people because he thinks he's so smart and way ahead of all the other 'peasants'.

At the mercy of religion

For long periods of time, the Christian view of the relationship between man's head and body has resulted in, during the most conservative times, clothing being practically a prison for the body. The high-neck collars are buttoned all the way up, sleeves are tight around the wrists, dresses and trousers go all the way down and cover everything, and sometimes the female body is completely laced in. The body and soul are seen as two very different worlds that should be kept apart, where the spirit and intellect (head) must keep the body's urges and instincts in check. This puritanical attitude is most prevalent during the Renaissance and in the early Baroque period. Afterwards a more secular view is adopted, and the strict codes of dress become more relaxed. But the change in outlook on the body and naturalness undulates back and forth throughout history. For example, today we perceive the Victorians as people who disavowed the body and were very straightlaced, but there's an odd double standard in the clothing of this period. On the one hand, the body is covered, but on the other hand, the feminine shape is emphasised e.g. through the use of corsets and big skirts. The clothing of this period has a 'look but don't touch' aspect to it. And even today we can sense remnants of this religious regime in the style of clothing. Look at a businessman's suit, which might even include a vest, and a white buttoned-up shirt and a tie that seals the constriction. There isn't much physicality in an outfit like this, and for women at the top of the business world almost the same norms apply. Or take for instance the traditional Muslim women's apparel which is taken to the limit by the shrouding burka that hides any manifestation of physicality.

▲ *The world has changed since Rosenkranz' time. When this portrait was painted in 1783, Europe and Denmark were characterised by enlightenment and liberation, and 30-year-old Sibylle Reventlow's looser and more flowing clothes are a testament to that.*

FASHION DOLLS. How did people in, for example, Denmark find out what the fashion was in Paris? Back then they didn't have the know-how to reproduce colour pictures. Instead they used dolls that were sent from the centre of fashion to the major cities of Europe. We know that this already happened in 1391 when a fashion doll was sent from the French court to the Queen of England along with the latest designs in clothing. In 1664 the Queen of Denmark received a doll, and in the Rococo period (first half of the 1700s) the practice was systemised and a doll was sent from Paris once a month. From 1716, Louise Rosset had the exclusive rights to exhibit them in Købmagergade in Copenhagen. Later in the century, the printing process had become advanced enough to publish illustrated fashion journals. This is how European fashion gradually became rather uniform.

▲ The picture above and the one on the right are 18 years apart. The one above was painted in 1759 by J.H. Tischbein and portrays the Duke of Schleswig-Holstein and family. Note the circumference of the dresses, the corseted waists, and that all the members of the family are wearing white-powdered wigs with the exception of the youngest. The painting on the opposite page by Jens Juel is of the 16-year-old Princess Louise Augusta from 1787. The dress is of the chemise-type and the latest fashion of the time. This was a rather daring pose, for only a few years earlier this was considered an undergarment. She is not wearing a corset, her hair colour is natural, as is her hairstyle.

In the course of the 1700s, societies in Europe were polarised and this influenced fashion. These tendencies made their way to Denmark as well. At the court in Paris, especially that of Louis XVI, clothing and hairstyles became spectacular with huge skirts and hair piled high, which were both held up by supports underneath. Silk by the metre and wigs en masse characterised the wanton life at court where social problems and revolutionary thoughts outside the castle walls were paid no heed. This resulted in the French Revolution, and at the same time, new aesthetic norms were created in general and in clothing in particular. The ideal was a much more natural appearance, and the revolutionary ideas of 'Freedom, Equality and Brotherhood' almost automatically removed any class distinction in clothing.

Clothes were more practical and functional and less determined by status. The fashion of this new time was especially different for women. The corset was discarded along with the side hoops and the very elaborate hairstyles. Even though Denmark had not gone to the same extremes, roughly the same change in fashion applied here. And the outlook on the world was changed in the same way, which Nicolai Abildgaard was the exponent of with his Greek-inspired Klismos Chair (see page 68). The clothes that were created after the popular movement, which was kick started by the American Revolution in 1775 and the French in 1789, were also inspired by classic Greek democracy. Later on the fashion leaned more towards the French Empire style, and the inspiration was from classical Rome. The style became slowly more formal again after the wave of freedom had passed, and Napoleon had crowned himself emperor. The citizens' revolt did not come to Denmark until 1849, and it was very peaceful.

▸ *The national costumes, or folk costumes, were 'invented' types of clothing that had their glory days in the mid-1800s. They were examples of romantic nationalism that were used especially for festive occasions and were often meticulously made in colours and patterns from individual regions. They often exhibited characteristic details and were appliquéd with locally manufactured lace and embroidery etc. The national costumes shown here are a man's costume from Amager, two women's costumes from Hedebo and a wife and her child from the island of Fanø.*

INTERNATIONALISATION

For many centuries, fashion in Europe was relatively uniform from country to country, especially for the upper classes. But because communication was slow and there were trade restrictions and wars, the latest trends from Paris could be delayed in reaching the outskirts of Europe. Sooner or later, however, the trends worked their way to the most remote cities. The local communities were not always unequivocally enthusiastic. According to Ellen Andersen's book about fashion in the 1700s, a Danish minister, P.F. Edvardsen, wrote in 1759 'Skelskør has unfortunately become rather 'frenchified'. And those damn hoop skirts only bring more fashions and useless expenses with them.'

After the French Revolution, the inspiration for fashion came increasingly from England, especially as regards menswear. The festivities at the French court were not very typical of the English court. On the contrary, the English nobility lived it up on their estates while enjoying hunting, riding and other physical pastimes. The more natural and sporty clothing was better suited to the new ideals of freeing the body from the trammels of former times and to living a more carefree life on the whole. This change in fashion also signals that the power and influence of the Crown and the nobility were diminished in favour of the new wealthy middle classes. Now, society's wealth stems from Industrialisation and trade.

And it's the new ruling class' requirements of menswear in particular that have set the norm for how clothes should look to this very day: a good cut, discreet colours, durable materials and easy to wear and wash. So the suit loses its status as a symbol and becomes a kind of uniform. For the new bourgeoisie it's more about achieving success in business by means of personal values and qualifications like industriousness, competence and frugality – or 'constant care' in other words. These values were not worn on their sleeves, but manifested themselves in their will to succeed.

Danish clothing

While fashion was increasingly internationalised by new and more efficient ways of communicating, a new national awareness grew. The nation states tried to influence the consciousness of the people, and being a Dane was something one tried to emphasise. After the wars against Prussia and Austria-Hungary in 1848 and 1864, respectively, there was a national and patriotic frame of mind that was also expressed in the national costume, or folk costume as it was also called. In contrast to what the monicker means, folk costumes are not very old. If anything they're artificial, romantic inventions that are part and parcel of the new national consciousness and the quest for something originally Danish or regional.

These costumes had their heyday in the mid-1800s and could even be bought in the department store Magasin du Nord in Copenhagen. Even the bourgeoisie bought them since they wanted to dress their female servants in these outfits. This infused the household servants with a sense of simplemindedness since they looked like they had just fallen off the turnip truck. Art historian R. Broby-Johansen wrote this caustic remark in his book *Krop og Klær* (Body and Clothing) from 1953, 'The newfangled national costume is a true child of its times, since it originates from the century of misleading trade descriptions, the 1800s.'

It would be an exaggeration to say that Denmark has previously been a leading nation in fashion. Some people even believe that Denmark has

▼ *At department stores like Magasin one could buy almost everything from folk costumes for the servants to clothes appropriate for the middle class. Below is an advertisement from Christmas 1885.*

never created fashion, in the sense that Danes have never been among the true trendsetters. This is contrary to Danish furniture design, that in the mid-20th century even lent its name to a style, namely Danish Modern. Historically, Danish clothing production has been a typical domestic market industry that has followed fashion from abroad and to some extent modified it for the Danish public. But this wasn't a hindrance to success.

In 1856 Jacob Moresco opened his first retail store which sold women's fashions and millinery on Østergade in Copenhagen. Moresco qualified as a draper, and the following year, 1857, he went to Paris to take a short course in cutting. The following year he founded his company, which quickly developed into a large wholesale business with dressmakers working in both Denmark and Sweden. In Copenhagen alone he had contracts with 300 dressmakers at one point who supplied his shop. In the 1890s he expanded the business with shops in Malmø and Oslo (Kristiania at the time). Ladies' ready-made clothing was the main basis of his business, that is, clothing that was sewn to be in stock and that hadn't been ordered by a customer, unlike custom-made clothing. Moresco was the largest company of its kind in Scandinavia at that time. In 1900 it became a joint-stock company, and in 1975 the name was changed to Birger Christensen, after the present owner who is also known, perhaps more so, for selling furs. He later opened the fashion store Bee Cee in Pistolstræde in Copenhagen, which was one of the first stores to sell French prêt-à-porter.

Most people who were the slightest bit well-to-do did not buy clothes at the draper's, but had them tailored, especially if the clothes were for a party or for business use. One could go to the tailor's shop or to the stores (that later became department stores) that had their own tailoring departments.

ERIK MORTENSEN, 1926–98, was one of the greatest Danish couturiers. At the age of 15 he was apprenticed to Holger Blom at his boutique in Copenhagen. In 1948 he joined the house of Pierre Balmain in Paris where he continued his education. In 1960 he was the artistic head of the house of Balmain, and in 1982 he took over as head designer and director. In 1990 he left Balmain, and from 1992–94 he was head of the house of Jean-Louis Scherrer. He won the France Haute Couture Golden Thimble award in 1983, 1987 and 1994. His personal interpretation of fashion made his style easily adaptable to theatre costumes, which he did several times. In 1987 Erik Mortensen wrote his memoirs, *Ej blot til pynt* (Not for adornment alone), and in 1990 the novel *77001 Nat* (77001 Nights) was published. Erik Mortensen was once asked whether it was a radical change to move from Holger Blom to Pierre Balmain in Paris. 'Not at all', he is said to have answered. 'The greatest change in my life was moving from Frederikshavn to Holger Blom in Copenhagen.'

Here measurements were taken and the clothes were sewn, and the customer usually had to come by once or twice for a fitting. But where did the tailors get their designs from? Of course, most of them came from Paris, but they weren't stolen copies. They had a system for this.

Haute couture was created in 1858 by the Englishman Charles Worth and the Swede Otto Boberg when they established their couturier Worth in Paris. Later on other couturiers appeared, but it was and still is difficult to make a living on haute couture alone. Therefore a type of fashion export was established where the directors of department stores went to Paris twice a year and bought patterns from the major fashion houses. They took these patterns back home and sold copies of the original couture design for a tenth of the price in Paris. There were naturally very strict agreements on this kind of business.

This continued up till the 1960s and customers in Copenhagen could go to special tailors or department stores and know that this was where they could get a 'real' Chanel or a 'true' Dior. So this is how Danish women could be almost as well dressed as their Parisian sisters. However, the style and the design weren't very Danish.

WHEN DESIGN BECAME DANISH

Eventually we did get our own designers. The first one to be considered a proper clothes designer was Holger Blom (1906–65) in Copenhagen. He was self taught and started out by sewing clothes for his female friends while studying Latin and history at the University of Copenhagen. Rumours about his abilities in fashion travelled from mouth to mouth, with the result that he gave up his studies in 1930, hired seamstresses and opened a boutique on Nørrevold in Copenhagen. Blom quickly became well known and soon had a clientele of wealthy and famous women, many of them actresses, and later on the royal family. He was renowned for not drawing patterns or making sketches, but instead he worked with his customers and draped the material on their bodies. They often had 5–7 fittings before the clothes were finished. Blom's creations were seldom the latest fashion, but he did keep abreast of international fashion. What he was known for was his cultivation of beauty, quality and good workmanship. Blom also made clothes for the cinema and theatre, but the culmination of his career was probably the Danish Princess Anne-Marie's wedding gown in 1964. At the time, other boutiques emerged that worked in roughly the same way. The concept of 'the three big B's' came about because two of Blom's closest competitors and good friends were Uffe Brydegaard and Preben Birch. Blom's boutique was where Erik Mortensen and Jørgen Bender learned their craft.

While Jørgen Bender (1938–99) took over Blom's boutique after his death in 1965 and carried it on in the same spirit, Erik Mortensen became the first Dane to become the head of a Parisian house of fashion. Mortensen, who was born and bred in Frederikshavn, was apprenticed at the age of 15 to Holger Blom in Copenhagen. In 1948 he went to Paris for further education at the house of Balmain, and in 1950 he became his right-hand man.

In 1960 he was promoted to artistic head of the house of fashion, and when Pierre Balmain died in 1982, the job of head designer went to Erik Mortensen, who carried on the exclusive style of the house till 1990. During his time at Balmain he twice received the highest award in

▸ *From Jean-Louis Scherrer's fashion show in Paris 1993 when Erik Mortensen was the artistic head of the house.*

◂ Christian Dior designs from the spring-summer collection in 1963. These sketches of the latest fashions were handed out at open-house parties to the guests who were invited. They could be buyers from Danish department stores and fashionable boutiques. By paying a fee to the Dior company, the Danish boutiques were allowed to copy the models. This is how Danish women could wear something that was almost a real Dior, but without the label, and at a fraction of the price of one in Paris.

▾ Holger Blom in his boutique in Copenhagen in the 1950s accompanied by prima ballerina and actress-to-be Margrethe Sophie Marie Schanne.

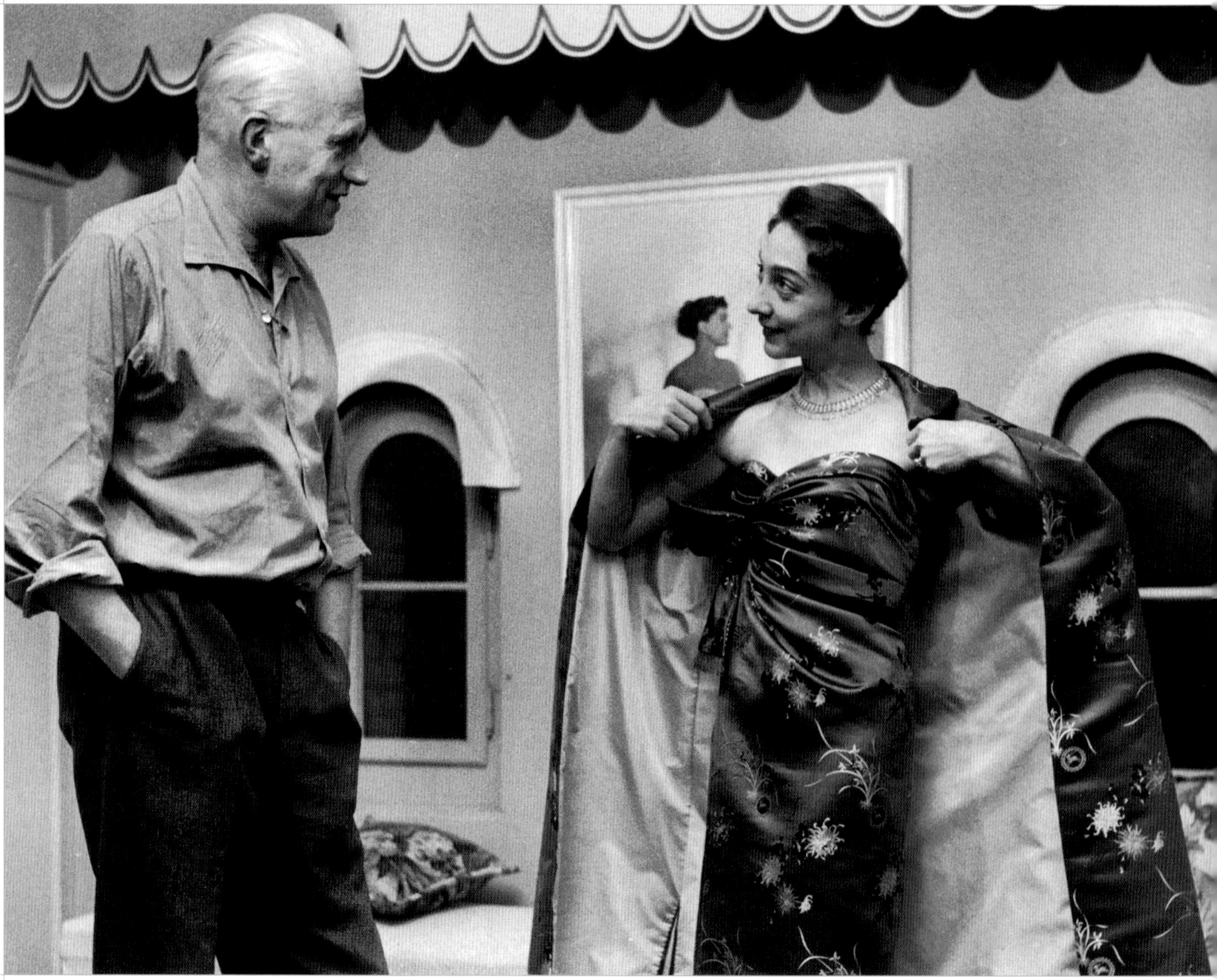

▸ *From the party celebrating the 25th anniversary of Nørgaard's T-shirt no. 101 in 1992. At the time over a million of these popular T-shirts had already been sold. Two of the employees that had worked at the store from the beginning are pictured here along with their daughters. All of them are naturally wearing no. 101 from Nørgaard på Strøget.*

French haute couture, the Golden Thimble, and once again after he left. From 1992 to 1994 Mortensen was head designer and director of the house of Jean-Louis Scherrer. Mortensen was praised for his ability to accentuate the female form. Moreover he has designed costumes for several Danish theatres, one of which is the Royal Danish Theatre.

Back home in Copenhagen there was something brewing at the onset of the 1960s. Young people especially wanted something new, something that looked decent and preferably wasn't too expensive. The rich and famous could go to Holger Blom, and the well-heeled could go to the department store Fonnesbech and buy a knockoff of one of Jacqueline Kennedy's chic little outfits. But everyone else was obliged to buy clothes off the rack at the draper's or the men's readymade clothing stores. The word 'teenager' was making its way into the Danish language, and trendy clothes for young people were in short supply. On Strøget (the pedestrian walking street) in Copenhagen, draper Jørgen Nørgaard (b. 1930) took over the family store Sørgemagasinet in 1958. The store had existed since 1863, and earlier there had been a market for sombre funeral clothes, but this was now outmoded. Instead Jørgen Nørgaard started a new store called Nørgaard på Strøget at the same address. He had lived abroad for a few years and worked in the textile business, and at the time he had probably noticed what the new teenage generation was interested in. The clothes in his new shop were youthful and fresh, and the name was established as the place where you could buy something cool. Nørgaard på Strøget started something new by letting young artists like Kirsten Dehlholm and Susanne Ussing dress their windows. This went on for many years.

Flower power and more

The Danish fashion schools gradually began to gain a footing. Previously, one of the few ways of getting an education in the field was an apprenticeship to a tailor, and if young people had greater ambitions, they had to go abroad for further education. In 1904, Copenhagen's Tilskærerakademi (Cutting Academy) was established, and in 1931 the Margrethe School was also founded in Copenhagen. Ambitious students from these private schools began to assert themselves as designers of Danish fashion. One of the very first was Margit Brandt (b. 1945) who had attended these two schools before going to Paris to work for couturiers Pierre Balmain and Louis Feraud. In 1966 she returned to Denmark, and with her husband, Erik Brandt (b. 1943), she opened the design company Margit Brandt that quickly became renowned for simple and youthful clothes, often in the miniskirt style of the day, as well as accessories like eyeglasses and jewellery. Up till now in Denmark one couldn't find a fashionable clothing store, of which there are so many today, that sold only one brand of clothing. The Brandt couple were greatly responsible for starting this new era with Denmark's first proper fashion label.

In addition to Jørgen Nørgaard and Margit Brandt, there was Ib Drasbæk (1931–97) and Søs Drasbæk (b. 1937) who started their own design company Dranella and its accompanying wholesaler in 1956. Their style and business practice was quite different from the Brandts, for example their design was much more experimental, Danish and Scandinavian; a bit like Marimekko if you will. In the 1960s and 1970s they represented a softer, florid and more hippie-like style with emphasis on textile design (such as red and white striped dresses), but also colourful clogs with shiny studs was one of their big hits at the time.

JEAN VOIGT (1940–96) was a skilled haute couture tailor who went to Paris at the age of 19 to work with the Spanish couturier Balenciaga. He had his own fashion boutique in Copenhagen from 1962 to 1967. Then he went back to Paris to study art, design and stage history at Académie des Beaux-Arts. Meanwhile he worked for Pierre Cardin. From 1970 he was renowned for his picturesque scenography and costumes for numerous performances at Det Ny Teater (The New Theatre) and the Royal Danish Theatre in Copenhagen.

His clothes were elegant, imaginative and theatrical through the use of lace, tulle, silk and velvet that were made into drapings with large graphic appliqués. In 1977 he introduced the fashion boutique Maria Sander, and in 1979 the Fantastic Look Collection was launched for the shop Brothers Andersen. Jean Voigt showed beauty in decline when he exhibited his works at Charlottenborg in Copenhagen in 1982. In 1984, as the only Dane, he managed to get his own house of fashion in Paris accepted in the prestigious syndicate of French houses of fashion, Chambre Syndicale de la Couture Parisienne.

Later their lingerie line X-tase was launched at a time when it was acceptable for women to wear a bra of the soft kind again. They didn't have their own stores like Margit Brandt, but sold their label in others' stores, such as Nørgaard på Strøget and Deres.

Other young Danish designers followed in their wake, among them Ivan Grundahl (b. 1951), who graduated from the School of Arts & Crafts in Copenhagen. After having worked for Birger Christensen for a couple of years, he opened his first store in 1973 with exclusive women's clothing of which the suit coat and the leather jacket in simple, subdued colours were typical. At the onset of the 1980s, subdued colours were what characterised the general state of things in fashion. A designer like Jan Machenhauer (b. 1954) also worked with black, white and grey in his very simple, sculptural and elegant clothes. At times his fashion was also very popular among architects as well. His style and choice of materials are very suited to the Danish weather, which is evident in one of his most well-known products, the dark grey raincoat made of rubber. Jan Machenhauer graduated from the School of Decorative Arts (now Denmark's Design School) in 1976, and he opened his boutique Zone 1 in Copenhagen in 1982.

◀ *Margit Brandt came back to Denmark from Paris in 1966 and established her own fashion empire with her husband Erik Brandt. The recipe was youthful and simple clothes in an internationally inspired style that was customised to the Danish market. After the couple had concentrated on running restaurants and a gallery for a few decades, Margit Brandt again became topical in fashion and in September 2006 received the Golden Button award from the Danish ladies' magazine 'Alt for damerne'.*

▶ *Jean Voigt's silk outfit with matching cape in silk tulle with poppy flower-appliqué from 1977.*

HUMMEL WAS ORIGINALLY German, but is now a major Danish brand of sportswear. It's one of the oldest brands of shoes and clothing for team sports in particular, like football and handball. Hummel was one of the first brands to make sport shoes with rubber soles. In the 1970s and 1980s, several players from the All-Denmark teams in handball and football bought shares in Hummel, and the company gradually fell into Danish hands. Today Hummel is run by Christian Stadil, who brands the label very efficiently, for example by introducing street wear and sportswear in retro design (below right).

Hummel makes use of clothing sponsorships to market themselves, for example, for a number of years they sponsored the All-Denmark football team, and they were the only company to sponsor the All-Tibet football team for the highly publicised match against Greenland in 2001.

▲ *Ib and Søs Drasbæk's Dranella collection from 1976.*

NOT ONLY FASHIONABLE party and business clothing are designed, but so are work clothes. Since 1920, the Danish manufacturer Kansas has produced boiler suits, work jackets and trousers for the working population (below right). The clothes weren't given the name Kansas until the company was reorganised in 1952, but it's been the same ever since, and therefore it won the Danish Design Centre's Classics prize in 1996 for design that hasn't changed for over 25 years. The company still manufactures white trousers and a blue anorak that aren't quite so workmanlike. Clothes from Kansas were a special fashion statement in the 1970s when many left-wing young people wore them to show solidarity with the workers in the industry.

▲ *Hummel's Old School collection with the familiar chevrons on the sleeves and pant legs.*

▲ *Genuine Kansas working clothes that were awarded the Classics prize from the Danish Design Centre in 1996.*

THE STORY OF Ecco is a strange tale about some shoes that many Danes consider a bit too sensible and maybe even geeky, but which are popular abroad, especially in the US where they're considered fashionable and trendy. Ecco was founded in 1963 by Karl Toosbuy and became an almost immediate success with their ergonomic, comfortable and industrially manufactured shoes at reasonable prices. The crisis in the shoe trade in the 1970s made Ecco focus on innovation and, among other things, they developed a special way of integrating the rubber sole with the leather upper of the shoe, which is called direct injection. The company has continued to design and develop, also by means of this technique, and this has recently led to the introduction of the distinctive women's boot called Shark.

FROM 1990 AND ON

Major Danish clothing manufacturers have asserted themselves over the last 20 years by making ready-made garments of a pretty decent quality. The design isn't bad at all, but on the other hand, it isn't the latest fashion or special in any way. Primarily efficiency in production and marketing has made a company like IC Companys into a giant on the Danish/Scandinavian clothing market. The corporation arose in 2001 when InWear and Carli Gry merged. IC Companys comprises the labels Matinique, Jackpot, Cottonfield and others. Other major Danish clothing manufacturers are Bestseller that sells the labels Vero Moda, Jack & Jones and Only; and Brandtex that has Cero, 4you, Fransa, b.young and others. These companies in particular have given the Danish clothing industry a huge volume in recent years, and clothes and other fashion products were some of Denmark's biggest exports in the transition to the new millennium.

Of the designers that were more avant-garde during this period, one of the first that springs to mind is Bruuns Bazaar. It was founded in 1994 by the Bruun brothers, Bjørn (b. 1963) and Teis (b. 1969), who collaborated with designer Susanne Rützou (b. 1965). In no time they created a fashion success that merited design awards, publicity and good sales in Denmark as well as abroad. In the early days, their style was unequivocally that of Susanne Rützou's: very personal, feminine, bohemian, colourful and ethnically inspired with extensive use of beads and sequins. In the late 1990s, Bruuns Bazaar achieved the status of being the first Danish couturiers to be put on the official Prêt-à-porter calendar during fashion week in Paris. In 1999 Rützou and the Bruun brothers went their separate ways, and a small group of designers under the leadership of Bjørn Bruun adopted a more simple and international style. The company has several of its own shops in Denmark and abroad. Susanne Rützou now designs in her own name and has continued her personal style, which is sold across most of Europe.

The fashion company Munthe plus Simonsen is from about the same time as Bruuns Bazaar. Naja Munthe (b. 1968) and Karen Simonsen Shagawi (b. 1966) met at the School of Arts & Crafts in Kolding (now the Design School Kolding). They both graduated in 1994 and opened a fashion shop, but shortly after they started making their own fashion wear. In many ways their style was like Rützou's, but perhaps the colours were a bit more subdued. They too used embroidery, textile prints and a rather 'loose' and imaginative style. Their personal view of fashion is that every piece of clothing must be a work of art. Their marketing is often unusual since they use 'authentic' models, or even actors like Iben Hjejle and Ole Lemmecke, as in their catalogue in 2001. Along the same lines we have Day Birger et Mikkelsen who also subscribe to the sophisticated bohemian style that was typical of the most successful Danish fashion designers in the mid and late 1990s when Danish designed fashion seriously asserted itself in the world, also with some financial success.

The latest

In the new millennium Danish fashion is still prospering. Not only financially, but also design-wise, so that Danish fashion can still assert itself internationally. Even though impressions are collected from foreign countries, as they always have been in any field of design, the design itself is developed in a rather independent direction. There is something indisputably Danish about much of the fashion during these years, in spite of the fact that the chic bohemian style that characterised the last half of the 1990s has been replaced by design of a more international cut.

◂ *Bruuns Bazaar's collection from the year 2000 on the catwalk in Paris.*

◂ *Munthe plus Simonsen's wonderful collection from autumn/winter 2003, when they were just about the hottest thing in Danish fashion design with their extravagant bohemian style with a touch of the ethnic. The colours were dark, and there was a lot of soft leather, velour and angora with silver embroidery, fringes, sequins and beads on the clothes.*

Today, the retro and ethnic look is passé for most designers. If you look at one of the more established designers in Danish fashion like Mads Nørgaard (b. 1961), you'll find a more relaxed and subtle Danish clothing design in his shop. Mads Nørgaard opened his shop in 1986 right next to his father's Nørgaard på Strøget in Copenhagen. The style that Mads Nørgaard has developed over the years is suitable for our times since it's meant to be functional mass produced clothing. He is the company's designer and started out with a men's line years ago, which was followed by a women's line, and now children's clothes are on the way. The clothes he designs aren't very formal, but rather optimistically casual. Apart from being sold all over Denmark, they're found in about 200 stores abroad.

The relaxed, informal and often humorous style seems to be the earmark of Danish clothing design in the early 2000s. Fashion designers like Baum und Pferdgarten are good examples of this. It all started in 1999 when two fashion designers Helle Hestehave (b. 1960) and Rikke Baumgarten (b. 1970) established a joint company and played around with their two surnames and the German language to make their new company name. Their clothes fit their name very well as there's a sense of the big top about it; large textile prints, intricate patterns, plenty of contrasts in shapes and colours, and all of it with a dash of humour. So far they only make clothes for women, but they're sold in exclusive stores all over the world.

Another example of this unpretentious trend was the team Daughters of Style, which consisted of Marianne Eriksen (b. 1964) and Kristina Søndergaard (b. 1969). Like Baum und Pferdgarten, the designers behind Daughters of Style had graduated from Denmark's Design School. Yet the

▾ *Mads Nørgaard works a lot on designing what you could call basic clothing and he has also redesigned the traditional sailor sweater seen below from the fall/winter collection in 2006.*

▸ *Baum und Pferdgarten (Helle Hestehave and Rikke Baumgarten) use a theatrical circus motif in the presentation of their collection from 2004.*

Daughters' style was more inspired by the rock scene of 1970s with lots of glitter and studs, gold and silver and paper clip-like apparel. The clothes from Daughters of Style were often perforated or cut into strips making them semitransparent. In the beginning the two designers had to go to London to sell their avant-garde clothes and accessories, but since then they have even been included in the permanent collection at the Danish Museum of Art & Design.

There is movement in the Danish clothing designers' milieu, which also is reflected in a stronger perception of being an industry. In 2005 an exciting initiative was established with the name of DAFI (Danish Fashion Institute). Because the industry needs a bigger exchange of ideas, it's a network collaboration between companies, designers and educational institutions. Basically it's about meeting and creating these important contacts. It is also the institute's job to co-ordinate the work in marketing the Danish fashion industry at home and internationally, as well as arranging lectures, workshops, competitions and other things in the field of fashion. One of the members of the board of this new organisation is Mads Nørgaard, and according to him the distinctiveness of the Danish fashion industry is not based on special aesthetics or a special look, but on a common ethical point of reference. No matter how wild it may look, there is always a certain amount of Danish horse sense behind it. What Danish fashion companies are good at is marketing and production whether it's in Denmark or the Far East, so in the field of fashion we have embraced globalisation instead of seeing it as a threat.

Mads Nørgaard says that for most people the object is to make clothes for everybody. Not because they'll be very inexpensive, but because they

THE YOUNG DESIGNER Henrik Vibskov (b. 1972) is one to watch. He has been a musician, break-dancer, artist and film-maker before going to Central Saint Martins College of Art and Design in London where his graduation collection caused a sensation and prompted a free place in further education. Instead he returned to Denmark. In 2005 he participated in an exhibition arranged by the Danish Design Centre. His contribution was to dress a number of aeroplane models.

won't be as exceedingly expensive as the exclusive design that comes from many other countries tends to be. He says that in reality we all have a good, functionalist designer inside us.

Although Denmark from a historical point of view hasn't been a pioneer in clothing design, one can say that Danish fashion has changed the fashion world a bit since the early 1990s. This is mainly due to the strong Danish firms in the business, and they haven't been condescending which is the typical avant-garde way of thinking. You could say that they've had a more humble approach to their marketing. Danish fashion has been able to make its mark, so that, for example, Danish female politicians don't look like the women in a typical group picture of EU ministers in Brussels. Many Danish women in politics and the business world wear feminine clothes that they've chosen in order not to resemble a careerist whose trousers have been replaced by a skirt. Danish fashion has chosen a different path than Armani and Calvin Klein. But then again, they would probably claim that Danish fashion is a mess that puts sequins on everything. But this is how Danish fashion has created an alternative to the old minimalists.

◂ *Daughters of Style consisted of two designers, Marianne Eriksen and Kristina Søndergaard, who here exhibit their own leather jewellery design in connection with the fashion exhibition at the Danish Design Centre in 2004.*

▸ Henrik Vibskov's 'The aeroplane project 2005' was exhibited at the Danish Design Centre the same year.

▾ Henrik Vibskov's collection from 2006 was exhibited in the middle of an art installation that he called 'The big wet shiny boobies collection'. Exhibited in Paris in July 2006.

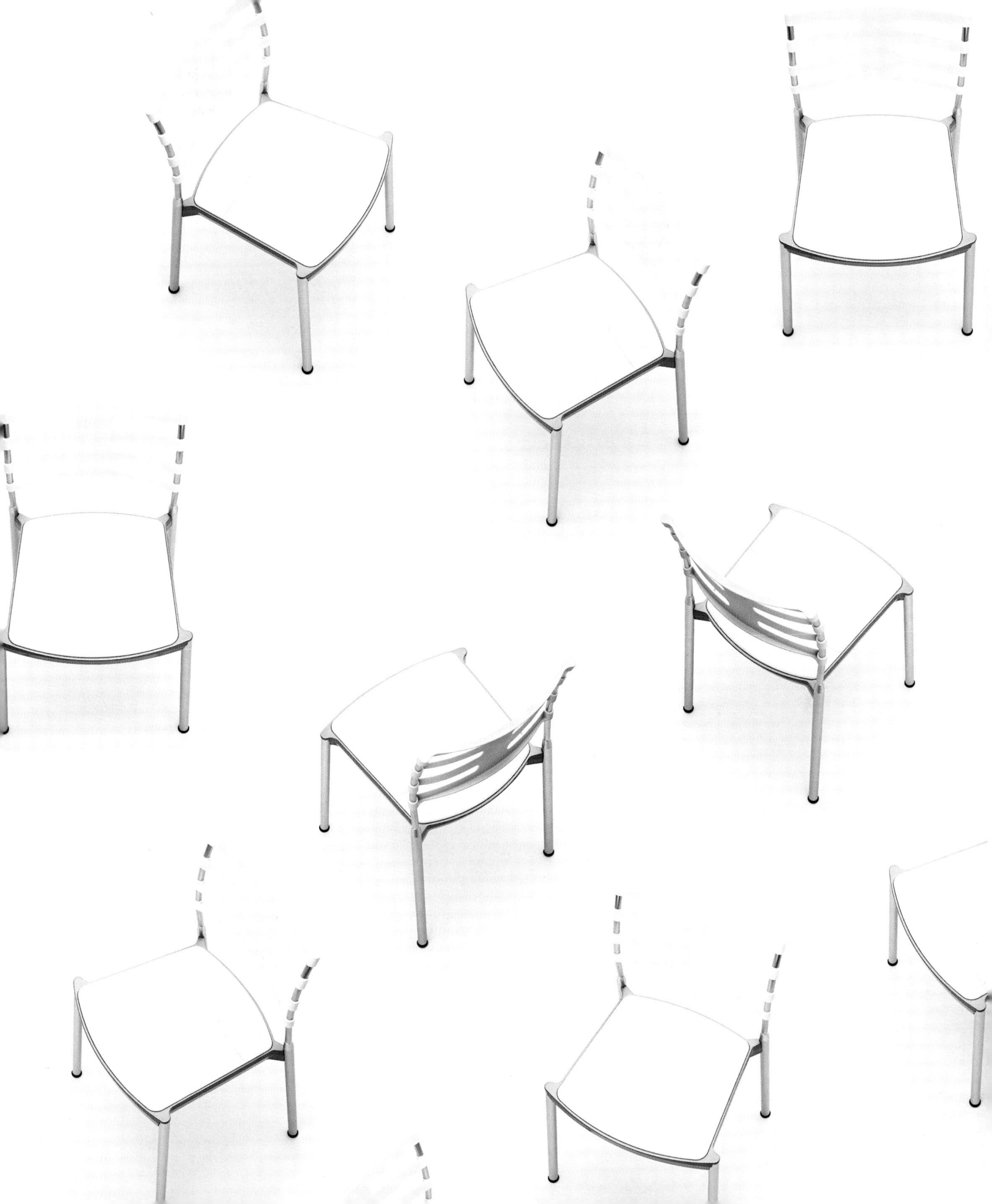

Furniture and interior design

For many years Danish furniture design has had the status of being something very exceptional. In particular the functionalist furniture from the decades after World War II has propagated the concept of 'Danish Design' out in the world. To this very day furniture from the golden age of Danish design is still sold at high prices at auctions in Denmark and abroad. However, questions quickly crop up: Was Danish furniture from that time really unique? And if so, what made it so special? Were the designers back then particularly talented? Or were the schools that educated them especially good? What roles did cabinetmakers and the furniture industry play? Can we learn from history and possibly revive this success?

As in the example of the old folding stools in chapter 2 (see page 39), in the past many of the leading designers have worked with historic and classic foreign models. Time and again they've taken existing and often very old pieces of furniture and made new interpretations of them. The results of these design efforts have often been surprisingly successful and innovative. At other times they've practically been copies, as in the case of the Egyptian-style folding stool that then Professor Ole Wanscher designed in 1958. This stool is almost an exact copy of the original Egyptian pharaoh stool that was excavated in 1934 and exhibited at Staatlische Museum in Berlin. It's debatable how much innovation there was in this stool.

Originality and talent determined whether these pieces of furniture were successful developments based on tradition or whether they were mere copies of the past; like mass produced museum copies. Danish furniture design has almost always resided within this tension field – between cultivation of the past and innovation for the future, but also between the national and the international. While working with things from the past, Danish designers could either indulge in nostalgia or be inspired to develop something new. How this could best be done has been one of the great challenges for which there is no set formula.

Danish functionalism, which had a lot of fame in the post-war years, was based on a Danish and Scandinavian tradition of thorough studies of the masterpieces of the past. Around the same time, German modernism from Bauhaus chose to break radically with the past in an attempt to create something new and epochal. Both strategies were somewhat successful in their separate ways. But if the Danish architects and designers had chosen to follow Bauhaus slavishly in an attempt to be on the ball, one can assume that the result would have been a watered-down and not very successful version of the international trend of the time.

THE CHAIR

In the beginning, the world was without furniture. When people needed to rest, they sat on the ground or on a rock, but in Danish lands that could be quite cold, even with the help of animal hides, so a log was preferable. At some point, they therefore began to make furniture to sit on. Maybe the pieces were similar to the aforementioned folding stools that were found in prehistoric graves all over the ancient world from Mesopotamia and ancient Egypt to Guldhøj near Kolding in Denmark. The fact that these stools were found in the graves of prominent people tells us that the stool was a ceremonial article, a symbol of dignity.

Only kings and military commanders were allowed to use a stool because the stool represented power itself. That is, the right to sit down while talking to others indicates the high rank of the seated person.

OLE WANSCHER, 1903–85, Danish architect, furniture designer and industrious writer. He was influenced by his father, Vilhelm Wanscher, who was a professor of art and architectural history at the Royal Academy of Fine Arts and a staff member of the newspaper 'The Politiken'. Ole Wanscher studied in Kaare Klint's department at the Royal Academy of Fine Arts and was employed in his architectural practice from 1925–27, after which he set up on his own. He was one of the principal organisers of the annual cabinetmakers' exhibitions in Copenhagen. Wanscher's furniture is part of classic Danish modernism, and like Klint he often used English, but also Middle Eastern furniture as models. His furniture is usually made of exquisite wood and manufactured by cabinetmaker A.J. Iversen's. Wanscher took over the professorship after Klint from 1955–71 at the Royal Academy of Fine Arts, Furniture School.

▾ Ole Wanscher's stool, which he originally designed in 1958 for cabinetmaker A.J. Iversen, is an almost exact copy of an Egyptian pharaoh stool. The production was taken over by P.J. Furniture, who still manufacture it in different types of wood including cedar and palisander.

THE GULDHØJ STOOL (see page 40) from about 1400 BC was found in a burial mound near Vamdrup. An exact copy was manufactured by the thousands (about 15,000) in the 1960s by furniture architect Poul Hundevad, who actually lived in Vamdrup. This stool (right) is a direct descendant of its Egyptian forefather; and the two aren't very different. Nonetheless, Wanscher stressed that his inspiration came from the land of the pharaohs and not from a burial mound.

The folding stool was further developed into a larger folding stool with armrests, and some even with backrests. The fact that it was a chair considered only for people of power to sit in, explains the great emphasis that was later attached to the throne as a symbol. We use a phrase like this or that regent 'has taken the throne'. The folding stool in our time has the form of a director's chair; the light and practical folding chair that can be bought and used by anyone, but its name originates from the artistic leader of a film or theatre production.

Among designers and furniture architects, including Danish ones, designing a chair is still seen as the ultimate assignment in the field today. Designing beds or closets isn't as prestigious even though these tasks can be equally important to people's everyday lives and quality of life. The designers' interest in the chair is not only about its prestige as a product, but also about the professional challenge it entails. A good chair has to be sturdy enough to carry the weight of a person, be comfortable to sit on (although some furniture designers seem to forget this), be possible to manufacture, and, not least, be beautiful to look at. All these factors have to come together, which is easier said than done.

◂ *Danish furniture architect Mogens Koch has cleverly developed the folding stool into a real folding chair with armrests and a backrest. It's obvious that the basis for this chair is the little stool, and it's surprisingly comfortable to sit in. The chair is still in production at one of the few authentic cabinetmakers left in Denmark, namely Rud. Rasmussen in Copenhagen. The chair comes in beech and mahogany and with a seat and back in either canvas or leather.*

TODAY FURNITURE IS still used to indicate a difference in status, however, this isn't normally done as clearly as Arne Jacobsen did when he designed the Oxford chair for St. Catherine's College in 1965. Two versions of the same chair were designed; one with a high back that was for the academic personnel, while other people had to make do with the low-backed one. In the great hall the students even sat on long benches without backrests while the professors sat at their own table in high-backed chairs. Today this is also a popular executive chair.

INTERIOR DESIGN IN THE VIKING AGE

It's one thing that special chairs were made for the top dogs, but how did ordinary people furnish their homes back then when they needed a place to sit? If you look at the reconstructions of homes from especially the Viking Age, which are mainly based on excavations, an interesting picture appears. The common people – peasants, fishermen and craftsmen – did not have much furniture in their homes. And they weren't what we would call homes since the buildings they lived in accommodated all of life's doings under one roof. Here they worked, slept and ate, and at one end of the building there was usually a stable with animals. In the middle of the floor of the main room was the open fireplace where the family gathered.

This hearth wasn't just a source of heat and light, but also one of Denmark's earliest conversation kitchens. Everything took place here; they cooked, ate, talked, wove, whittled tools and slept. Almost everything in the room was arranged according to the open fireplace. There wasn't a ceiling in the room, but a hole in the ridge of the roof to let out smoke. The floor was packed earth and was obviously not very comfortable to sit on. So in order to have something to sit on and get off the floor where there probably was a draft, they made a raised area along the walls. These were about 30 cm high and were like wide platforms lined with boards.

The platforms were indeed more comfortable than the floor, but they too were made of packed earth. During the cold and wet season this area could be kept dry because they probably didn't wear outdoor shoes here. To keep warm in winter, the occupants surely kept most of their outdoor clothing on, and as well animal hides were most likely spread out on the platforms. Maybe there were also woven blankets or hides on the walls for insulation.

Three types of movable furniture existed in the average home: the stool, bench and chest. But many homes possibly also had a proper chair with a back that was a seat of honour for the family's guests. The oldest or most distinguished guest was then given the chair to sit on.

The stools resembled the three-legged milking stools that have been used on farms almost to this day and are still available. But otherwise they sat on the edge of the platforms, squatted or sat with their legs crossed facing the open fireplace. They had benches with and without backrests, but probably mostly without. These were used while they worked or sat around the fire. A bench was half as refined a piece of furniture as a chair, and a high-ranking person could not sit on a bench with the commoners, so they had to have their own chair which they often brought with them on their travels. If things were done right, a privileged person would have a servant carrying the chair behind him, and when there was a need to sit down, the chair would be readily available.

Tables weren't used very much, but instead a type of loose board, probably a bit like an oversized cutting board with a border or one that was bowl-shaped could balance on their knees and be used for eating or crafting. Archaeologists have found a few small short-legged tables with a border round the edge; actually a kind of tray table that was used for games perhaps.

In the large royal seats that had banquet halls, some of the fixtures were long tables and benches, so they could have big parties with plenty of food and drink. Once again, the king and other magnates sat in their own ornate chairs at the end of the tables or at a separate table.

▾ The inside of a reconstructed Viking house built at the ring castle Trelleborg near Slagelse. In the middle is the fireplace with a smoke hole in the roof, and everything else in the room is organised around this important source of light and heat. Along the walls are the raised platforms that especially during winter were certainly covered with hides and blankets. Here the occupants could sit and work or sleep. The food was naturally prepared over the fire in this big common room.

The chest: A piece of multipurpose furniture

During the Viking Age and in the Middle Ages as well, one of the most important pieces of portable furniture was probably the chest. Chests had many shapes and sizes; from small delicately made boxes to big roughly hewn crates that were joined with iron fastenings. Often they were furnished with locks since they contained the person or family's most treasured possessions like jewellery, money, amulets, fancy clothes or just the spare clothes they had. These chests were also used for travelling, and in a large Norwegian ship dated from the early Viking Age, namely the Oseberg ship, something special was found. The ship was found in the burial mound of a prominent woman, and a large number of chests were found as well. Besides the fact that the ship didn't have any thwarts, that is seats for the rowers, it suggests that the crew could have used their chests to sit on even when rowing. So maybe what we're talking about is the first multipurpose piece of furniture in history: a chest to keep and transport one's personal items, and at the same time be the owner's workbench. The Danish Viking ships, especially the Skuldelev finds in Roskilde fjord, are about 150–200 years younger than the Oseberg ship, and these ships had thwarts, so whether the 'chest as a chair theory' is also true of Danish ships, we don't know, but it's an interesting theory.

The Viking houses ostensibly functioned very well. They may seem a bit empty but if one analyses the way they utilised the space and considers the materials and heat sources they had at their disposal, they managed to make a good living space of what they had available.

The big open fireplace was of course the unifying aspect of the room, and since there were no windows, it had an even more important role.

▸ The chest is a reconstruction of a find from 800 AD. It's in a similarly reconstructed Viking house at Moesgård Museum, south of Aarhus. The chest isn't very big, about 30 cm high, but it's so well made that it could have been used to sit on whether it was in a home or on a ship's expedition to faraway lands. This type of chest was very common at the time and could also be furnished with a lock.

▾ Nanna Ditzel probably wasn't inspired by the interior design of Viking homes for this arrangement of raised platforms and low furniture, but the feeling that the room is divided into different levels is similar. The picture is from an exhibition stand in 1962 and is a proposal for a dining-cum-living room designed by Nanna Ditzel. The only thing it needs to be a perfect Viking home is an open fireplace.

◂ A circa 200-year-old settle that originates from Årup on western Funen. If you lift up the seat whose hinges are in the back, you can lie down in it. In the old days it might have been filled with straw instead of a mattress. This one isn't very long, so it was used by a child or a very short adult. This type of furniture could also be used to store various possessions when it wasn't used as a bed.

▸ This wedding chest dates from 1605 and belonged to Birgitte Lindenov, who had worked at the court in the queen's maiden chamber. On October 13, 1605 she was married to Otto Skeel and the chest is from their wedding. At the time it probably contained her trousseau: linen, clothes, woven tablecloths, bedding etc. When a young woman from a wealthy family was to be married, she was not only given a lot of homemade equipment, but also the chest to store it in. A chest like the one shown is from the late Renaissance, and it usually had the family crest on the front, as seen here. The chest is at Frederiksborg Museum today.

And the different levels constituted by the platforms were an efficient way of dividing the room into functional zones. Thus the occupants had walkways, and work areas and living areas were established; a bit like today's kitchen-cum-utility room and living room all in one.

TWO DIFFERENT WORLDS – 1100–1777

Throughout the Middles Ages and onwards, furniture and its design naturally evolved. It happens in many ways, just like the progress made in the rest of society, as social conditions change and as a result of the development of craftsmanship and technology. Socially, the difference between rich and poor deepens – a gulf between the nobility and the peasants. This manifests itself clearly in design and architecture. Characteristically, all the fancy furniture is bought and imported from abroad during the High Middle Ages till the end of the 18th century. Royalty, the nobility, landowners and the wealthy town citizens import their furniture in the same way they import clothes, shoes, glassware, ceramics, flatware, jewellery etc. First of all, this is because style and fashion come from the south during this period since Denmark lay outside Europe's cultural focal points. Secondly, there weren't enough skilled craftsmen in Denmark to manufacture the things that met the demands and taste of the upper class.

The commoners lived in a parallel world to the privileged. The peasants developed and made their own furniture, and sometimes they were copies of what the rich had, but the dimensions were bigger, the craftsmanship was cruder, and they were made in local types of wood. But many pieces of furniture were based on their needs and the space available in the home. For example, a simple bench from antiquity became a multipurpose piece of furniture which was used until recently, namely the settle. This piece of furniture solved the problem of living and sleeping in the same room. It functioned as a seat during the day and a bed at night since the seat could be raised. Today's sofa beds are actually a continuation of this tradition.

From chest to chest of drawers

An important piece of furniture from the Viking Age is the chest that continued to be popular among the well off and certainly among the peasants. The chest was used to store all kinds of things, but it also had ritualistic significance as the place where a young woman collected her trousseau – linen, clothes, utensils etc. – for the day she got married and moved to her new home. In time the chest got bigger and bigger in comparison to those of the Viking Age that travelled with their owners. In the Middle Ages, the chests were large pieces of furniture which indicated that the Danes had become peasants and had settled down rather than be nomadic pirates and merchants on the high seas.

Other furniture based on these chests was also developed, such as the chest of drawers. This piece of furniture was developed in the Renaissance, around the year 1500 in Denmark. And the upright, portable cabinet with feet or a base was already prevalent in the 13th century. Some of these cabinets developed into enormous and very heavy pieces that could accommodate the whole family's valuables.

In general the style of furniture during this period was often rather bombastic, and much of the furniture like the big closets could hardly be moved. But also beds and tables became permanent fixtures. The box bed was a fixed piece of furniture; a small closed, cave-like sleeping quarters that often had a curtain at the opening.

▸ A living room in a farmhouse in Pebringe on Zealand. The high wainscoting on the wall are from the 1600s. Compared to houses from the Iron Age when everything was collected around the open fireplace in the middle of the floor, we have here a stove that is connected to a chimney (on the left behind the photographer). The result is that now the furniture is placed along the walls, and the windows shed light on the table.

Notice the round chalk marks on the side of the beam. They are 'sun marks' or weather signs that in the past were used like a type of calendar to predict the weather in the coming year. The 12 circles represent one month each. On each of the 12 days between Christmas and Twelfth Night the farmer would study the weather and see it as a sign of how the weather would be in that same month the following year. The circles are divided by a horizontal line so the weather in the morning corresponded to the first half of the month, and in the afternoon to the end of the month.

The interior design of houses from the Middle Ages and onwards was also characterised by technical developments. Prehistoric homes only received light from doorways, the smoke hole in the roof and the fire, but now windows became the norm. At first they were peepholes made of dim and irregular glass that let light in, but through which you could hardly see. And yet this entailed that the gathering place of the room, the table, was moved over to the window and flanked by benches. Furthermore stoves were made that could be connected to a chimney, so they didn't have to put up with rain and a draft that came from the smoke hole. And now they could make a ceiling that insulated the room and gave them a top storey. The stove was placed by a wall or in a corner, and the other furniture, like beds and closets, were also placed against the walls. The result was an empty space in the middle of the room unlike before when the fireplace was the gathering point for the family.

The rise of craftsmanship

During the long period from the end of the Viking Age, around the year 1100, until 1777, great strides were made in wood craftsmanship. From all woodwork being carried out by carpenters, there gradually arose the specialised cabinetmaker. This was underlined by the establishment of the Copenhagen Cabinetmakers' Guild in 1554. This professional development indicated a refinement in the production of furniture in Denmark that had previously been characterised by crude tools, robust products and over-engineered dimensions in the body and joints.

After the establishment of the guild and for some time afterwards, furniture was something that one ordered from the town cabinetmaker just like some people still use a tailor to order a suit or a party dress today. In principle, it's still possible to order and buy furniture like this, but not many people do so. The advantages of manufacturing in this way are obvious. Seen from the cabinetmaker's point of view, the advantage is that he doesn't have to keep furniture in stock that he might never sell and has to pay for and store. From the point of view of the customer, the advantage is that they can get furniture in the exact size and shape they need. But you have to be patient since the furniture has to be made first. However, in some of the major Danish cities, and especially in the capital, they had so-called magazines, which was another word for shops. Here you could look at and buy models that were readymade furniture.

Nevertheless, when the guild was formed, the cabinetmakers' work wasn't quite up to the standard of quality that made the upper classes order furniture from the Danish cabinetmakers. They still wanted foreign designs and quality. Therefore the Danish cabinetmakers manufactured furniture for the townspeople and people in the environs, but rarely for people in other parts of Denmark and certainly not for export. So fine furniture was imported for the rich people in Denmark. The Danish cabinetmakers weren't good enough, but they did request that the king impose an embargo on the import of foreign furniture. This caused architect G.E. Rosenberg to establish the state-subsidised 'Royal Furniture Magazine' in 1777 on behalf of the Royal Academy of Fine Arts.

The Furniture Magazine was much more than a store. Its purpose was to raise the quality of furniture by introducing a stamp of quality in the form of wax seal on all the furniture that was sold through this new organisation. Moreover, the magazine had its own workshops, but they could only be used to produce for their own store and not for customised furniture.

▸ The Royal Furniture Magazine's wax seal was only used on furniture that was found to be 'very good pieces'. The cabinetmakers who were affiliated with the magazine didn't like being judged by a state authority and being 'stamped'. But the seal was also used on documents and accounts.

▾ A masterpiece of a three-legged round table from the Furniture Magazine's time, that is in the early 1800s. The inspiration for this table is from an English type of table where the tabletop is mounted on the frame with a hinge so it can be raised vertically, as shown here. The tabletop itself is very elegantly made of a combination of mahogany, ivory and lemonwood, and in the middle is a picture made of inlaid wood, by a technique called intarsia. This table was not stamped with the Furniture Magazine's wax seal, but it probably could have qualified to be so.

The Furniture Magazine also supported the cabinetmaker's trade by giving credit and providing good furniture designs as well as stocking and supplying exquisite wood for the individual masters. Although the cabinetmakers and the guild were skeptical at first, not to mention the fact that they were against the idea of a newfangled magazine, the initiative did raise the standard so that after it had existed for 38 years, it was thought that the cabinetmakers could now manage on their own. The sale of Danish furniture skyrocketed during this period, and exports, especially to Sweden, began seriously to make their mark in foreign trade. In 1815 the Furniture Magazine was dissolved by royal resolution.

NATIONAL DANISH FURNITURE

The establishment of the Royal Furniture Magazine in 1777 is reminiscent of the Royal Porcelain Factory that was established two years earlier, and there are obvious parallels between the two companies. Both initiatives were an attempt to raise the quality of the products of the applied arts and arts and crafts. Similar initiatives had been implemented previously in Europe, especially in France. In 1665 the French financial minister Jean-Baptiste Colbert introduced a policy to promote the production of excellent art, design and crafts. He wanted to protect the French manufacturers and the domestic market by introducing an import embargo and issuing privileges to the royal French commercial houses and particularly to outstanding suppliers.

Furthermore, skilled craftsmen and artists from all over Europe were invited to come and work in France. This soon resulted in the country becoming the leader in art, arts and crafts, architecture and fashion; a position that France still holds in several of these fields today.

▸ *This cabinet sofa, which today is in Frederiksborg Castle, is similar to the many other versions of this type of furniture that was made in the first 30–40 years of the 1800s. The cabinet sofa is just over 230 cm long and is made of pine, veneered with mahogany. The inlaid ornaments are yellow wood (possibly lemonwood). The side cabinets have slightly curved fronts, and there are three drawers in the base under the seat. The seat is very deep, so one probably sat on the edge when eating.*

Just over a hundred years later, Denmark reached the same conclusion, that is, that the state had to support certain branches of art and craftsmanship. This was done partly through the establishment of the Royal Danish Academy of Fine Arts, and partly by subsidising the manufacture of porcelain and furniture. This happened around the same time as a national self-awareness grew in Denmark, but also a more critical view of absolute monarchy and a budding yearning for democracy (see page 68). In the time that followed, art and craftsmanship, or design, if you will, are characterised by being more independently Danish. Nicolai Abildgaard's Klismos Chair sets a fashion for a number of other furniture designers, who began to subscribe to this style. One of the most well-known Klismos interpreters was Gustav Friedrich Hetsch (1788–1864), who was a German-Danish architect. Apart from his contribution to architecture, which includes the synagogue in Copenhagen, Hetsch became a professor in 1822 at the Royal Academy of Fine Arts where he also made furniture designs for the craftsmen to use as models. Although the Klismos Chairs were often painted with pictures from Antiquity, these light and simple pieces are indicative of the success of Danish furniture in the 20th century.

The cabinet sofa is one of the few original Danish contributions to the new types of furniture. It appeared for the first time around 1800 in the Empire style, where the cabinets are unattached, but placed on either side of the sofa. A few years later, the cabinet sofa becomes an integrated and complete piece of furniture, and it was evidently rather popular since many of them are still around. How and for what purpose this type of furniture came about has been the cause of some speculation. Art historian Tove Clemmensen has given a very plausible explanation, namely that it's a type of dining room furniture, since the cabinets could accommodate flatware, plates, wine bottles, salt and pepper etc. In England similar cabinets have been used for dining room tables, but not as sofas, and during this time in Denmark, sitting on a sofa was common when having a meal. That's why it was practical to have everything you needed to set the table to be to hand. This type of furniture existed until the second half the 19th century when they stopped sitting in a sofa and eating and started using the dining room table as we know today.

Striving for symmetry

As mentioned earlier, the peasants furnished their homes in a relatively practical manner, given their circumstances and resources, but during most of the 1700s and 1800s, the interiors of the upper class were inspired by the French and were very formal. Among other things, symmetry becomes tremendously popular, and is sometimes taken to grotesque extremes. Not only is architecture symmetrical, as we can see today on the façades of castles, stately homes and mansions, but also the rooms themselves were very formal. A living room should preferably have an axis of symmetry, so if there was a door on one side of the room, there had to be an identical one on the other half, even if it was a fake door. The same was true of ovens, furniture, mirrors and pictures hanging on the walls; everything was symmetrical. However, some people could see how fake and affected this seemed.

The writer and later managing director of the Royal Danish Theatre, Johan Ludvig Heiberg, wrote in 1830 an essay with the title *Æstetisk Moral* (Aesthetic Morals), where he makes sarcastic remarks about the furnishing of the time. He criticises the custom of having a parlour that was only used for entertaining, while 'Large families are crammed into a small room'.

▾ *A well-preserved living room in the pure Victorian style. It's at the Danish National Museum and here we see the opulent use of fringes and little pompoms on the furniture and curtains. This is the overly decorated style that truly irritated the functionalist architects and designers. Note the S-shaped loveseat in the foreground called a tête-à-tête. Around 1930, designers Peter Hiort-Lorenzen and Johannes Foersom took this type up again and designed the Rotor sofa* *(see page 276).*

ONE OF THE leading names in Art Nouveau is Thorvald Bindesbøll, who is probably best known for the Carlsberg beer label, which is still used today, only slightly modified. Bindesbøll's furniture is characteristic of this period when the decorative was emphasised rather than the constructive. That is to say, designers during this period did not try to make new types of furniture or minimise the use of materials in order to make lighter and stronger furniture, which is what happened later on. Instead, the furniture was a background for ornamental symbols.

Heiberg's thoughts about how one could take the family and especially the children's well-being more into consideration when furnishing are rather visionary for his time. It wasn't till about 1900 that someone actually took this problem up again, and many years passed until something was done about it.

The Victorian style and a budding revolt

During the 1800s, Denmark shifted very slowly from being an agricultural country to being an industrial society. Architecture and design are increasingly cultural phenomena that were staggering behind the economic development. This might be the main reason why people today think that the aesthetics of the time seem old fashioned and characterised by outdated norms and ideals. The second half of the century is often called the historicist phase. Here designers borrowed from the earlier Classicist styles that were mixed together and manufactured in the new materials of the day like cement and cast iron. New industrial products appear and are often designed in this older style, for example heating stoves made of cast iron and shaped like little Greek temples with inlaid pillar reliefs and laurel wreaths. Today we find it a bit humorous and see it as odd kitsch, but back then they were serious and thought that these household products should have a kind of cultural covering.

The development that Johan Ludvig Heiberg criticised in 1830 continued relentlessly throughout the 1800s. Of course there were new ideas in the making regarding society's basic structure, for example the king's absolute monarchy was abolished when Denmark won its democratic constitution by referendum in 1849. Nonetheless, the old nobility and the new middle class maintained a view of society that had changed significantly. They saw themselves, perhaps with good reason, as being the ruling class. This was reflected in their lifestyle and aesthetic ideals which were evident in the way their homes looked. There are several thorough descriptions with illustrations of the wealthy homes of this era. Among other places, the National Museum in Copenhagen has a fully furnished luxury apartment that dates from the 1890s and is virtually unaltered.

In historian Søren Mørch's book *Den ny Danmarkshistorie 1880–1960* (The new history of Denmark 1880–1960) there is another detailed description of a luxury apartment on Vesterbrogade in Copenhagen and the life that was led by both the family and the servants. The apothecary Madsen lived in this apartment above the apothecary with his wife and four children and somewhere between five and seven servants. Yet only the cook, maid and governess lived in the apartment. The caretaker and his wife lived in the wing while the coachman and outdoor servant lived in the back building. The apartment was clearly divided into the area for entertaining and then the rest of the apartment contained the bedrooms, kitchen, bath, toilet and the servants' quarters. The family's part of the apartment was furnished in the spirit of the time with three rooms en suite facing the street, a living room, a parlour for guests and a den plus the dining room that faced the yard.

The style of the apartment was grandiose. Lots of gilt, Baroque tables, overstuffed plush armchairs, crystal chandeliers, mirrors, thick carpets on the floor and the stucco and ceilings painted with a grapevine motif. Nowhere was there anything plain one could rest one's eyes on. The rooms were a showroom for everything one owned when one was a wealthy citizen that lived according to one's station.

THE LAST GREAT spasm from Neo-Classicism is the Copenhagen police building that was built in the years 1918–24 (see page 61). In 1923, one of the building's architects, Aage Raffn, designed a number of chairs in an Egyptian-Roman style especially for the building. The chair shown here is an interpretation of the old commander-in-the-field's chair except it isn't at all easy to transport since it's made of bronze and can't be folded. The source of inspiration wasn't chosen for practical reasons, but for its symbolism. Notice the large tassels and the braided covering on the back. Some of these chairs were at the International Exhibition in Paris in 1925, and Poul Henningsen found them reactionary and wrote about them in the 'Critical Revue', saying that 'apparently nothing has happened since the ruin of Pompeii'.

As Søren Mørch writes, 'The furnishing of the home and the use of different rooms reflected partly the way Madsen and his wife and their class structured and understood the world around them, and partly reflected the roles that the world around them attributed to them and that formed their lives.' In other words, the upper class used the design of their homes to create a view of the world and adopt their place in society. If one was as rich as Madsen, who in 1890 was one of the 500 biggest taxpayers in Copenhagen and earned 100 times as much as his coachman, you had to live and surround yourself with extreme luxury, whether it was impractical or not, and which, in our view of design, looked like a traffic accident.

For the progressive cultural elite this style of living was old fashioned and reactionary. In principle they couldn't care less that the middle class lived in a time warp of vulgar Classicism. To them the problem wasn't that the wealthy had an extravagant way of demonstrating their ideals, but that the lower classes tried to copy this interior design. That's how all the new artists, architects and designers saw it. They wanted more honesty, to break with the old and artificial, and to have a clear indication that these were new times, which included the area of aesthetics.

But many working-class families in their one-bedroom apartments preferred to furnish their front parlour like a cheap copy of apothecary Madsen's apartment, and otherwise hunker down in the room at the back. For many of the common or poor people this was a way of maintaining their self-esteem. They held on to the illusion that they had risen above abject poverty. But in the long run it didn't change the fact that various reactions against the ruling classes arose.

ART NOUVEAU

Some of the first people in Europe who tried to formulate an alternative to this confusion of styles was the English Arts and Crafts Movement. This movement, which was headed by historian John Ruskin and artist William Morris, didn't have on their agenda a revolt against the historic motives. In their view, it was the industry that made ugly products by making shabby copies. So instead the Arts and Crafts people revived the true craftsmanship from the Middle Ages and subscribed to a decorative, twining romanticism in nature in things such as printing and beautiful wallpaper. The Arts and Crafts movement had its heyday in the 1890s, but was a slightly reactionary protest against industrialisation itself.

Later on, similar movements emerged in other countries, for example the Jugend style in Germany, Art Nouveau in France and Wiener Werkstätte in Austria. In Denmark this trend was implemented under the name 'Skønvirke' (roughly: aesthetic activity, but Art Nouveau from now on) from about the year 1900 and was as regards style similar to Arts and Crafts but without the ideology behind it. Selskabet for Decorativ Kunst (the Association for decorative art) was established in 1901, and from 1914 it published the periodical *Skønvirke*. The style was Romantic nationalism and was inspired by historical Danish arts and crafts like wood engraving, embroidery and ceramics. Art Nouveau in Denmark was different from the Jugend style, which was the leading style in most of Europe, since mostly Danish and Scandinavian motifs were used here. Later on, Japanese influences were incorporated into the style (see page 88) as regards ceramic art and Georg Jensen's works in silver. The motifs were often flowers, insects, the ocean and fish. Also the Danish practitioners of Art Nouveau preferred arts and crafts to the industrial mass production.

◂ *The Faaborg Chair in the hall at Faaborg Museum on Funen. The very airy cane work on the see-through seat and back makes the chair less dominating and heavy in the room. Carl Petersen and Kaare Klint worked together on designing the furniture for the museum, and their mindsets and personal expressions were so alike that today one can't really say who had the most influence on the final result.*

INCIPIENT FUNCTIONALISM

The 20th century began with the odd sensation that everything was going every which way. And up until World War I, which broke out in 1914, there wasn't much that changed this. In the fields of architecture and furniture design, Classicism was vying for position with Art Nouveau and the Jugend style. However, especially on the political level something was going on. Among other things, a new legislation was passed that limited building speculation in the cities' slum areas. Furthermore, the Workers' Co-operative Housing Association was established in 1912 as an initiative to acquire more good homes for union members and other working-class people.

In the furniture world you could still find Victorian and Neoclassical furniture, some of it inspired by Empire, some by Greek and Roman styles. In what is called art furniture, mostly furniture in the Art Nouveau and Jugend style were manufactured. If you wanted to find furniture design that pointed to the future around and after World War I, then you had to look to some of the most successful buildings from this time. The young architect Kaare Klint designed the furniture for several of these projects.

In Faaborg there's little art museum that was built in 1912–15, and it's one of Danish architecture's most significant works. It isn't very big, but it's a curiously charming mixture of the classic and the modern. On the one hand, it's simple and straightforward when you look at the lines of the architecture. On the other hand, the rooms are rich in colour and have lovely decorative details like the mosaic tiles on the floor. Actually you can compare Faaborg Museum to a large well-proportioned piece of furniture. The chief architect was Carl Petersen, who was a Neoclassicist, and together with the young Kaare Klint he designed the furniture for the exhibition rooms and the winter garden at the back of the museum where you can relax after seeing the landscape painters from Funen.

The most famous chair from Faaborg Museum is known as the Faaborg Chair. Many professionals consider this chair to be the introduction of functionalism in Danish furniture design because of its simplified expression without ornamentation. In the museum these chairs are primarily used in the main exhibition hall. The chair is an armchair where the back and armrests are joined as a whole in what looks like a screen that envelopes the occupant of the chair. The chair is made of oak with open caning on the seat and a back made of rattan fibres. The lines of the seat and back are horizontal in order to make the chair as unobtrusive as possible in the room full of paintings. The front legs are straight while the back ones curve outwards, like a compliment to the Klismos Chair.

At the Museum of Art & Design in Copenhagen we also find a chair from the early 1800s that is reminiscent of the Faaborg Chair in its basic shape and cane seat. Taking an old model and giving it a new design was typical of Kaare Klint. Time and again he made new interpretations of older models from home and abroad, and in the process, nearly all decoration and ornamentation was removed. By eliminating all the stylistic features, Kaare Klint became the one to seriously introduce functionalism along with Knud V. Engelhardt's industrial design and graphic works. From an aesthetic point of view, many of his contemporaries found this design philosophy too puritanical, especially in light of all the styles that had preceded it, but Klint's design turned out to be long-lasting. The chair is still in production at Rud. Rasmussen Cabinetmakers in Copenhagen.

P.V. JENSEN-KLINT (1853–1930) was an excellent architect who first trained as an engineer and later as a sculptor. His major work as an architect was Grundtvigskirken (Grundtvig's Church) in Bispebjerg in Copenhagen. It was conceived in connection with a competition in 1913 and built from 1921 to 1940. When Jensen-Klint died in 1930, the church was finished by his son Kaare Klint. The reason why it took 20 years to build was because it was a public monument in honour of N.F.S. Grundtvig and therefore financed by national subscription, which trickled in so slowly that at times construction had to be halted. In 1927, when the tower was finished, part of the church was opened provisionally, and for that occasion Jensen-Klint had some Italian spindleback chairs imported.

When Kaare Klint took over the project, he designed a chair in 1936 that was based on the Italian chair but was also inspired by the Shaker chairs and traditional Danish peasant furniture. This was his Church Chair made of beech with a woven seat. And since it's a church chair (see below), it has a hat stand under the seat and a shelf for the hymnal on the back. Once again, Kaare Klint adapts an existing model. The chair was also used in the Bethlehem Church, which Kaare Klint also finished for his father, on Åboulevarden in Copenhagen.

This drawing by Carl Jensen for the Danish annual satirical book 'Blæksprutten' (The Octopus) from 1943 has the title, 'An architect crossed the room'. The general public thought that functionalism went too far and was a cold style, and one couldn't understand what was wrong with the old cosy living room with lots of knick-knacks. But in the long run modernism triumphed both in construction and in the design of furniture.

The Klint School of Furniture

Concurrent with the development in architecture where Classicism was gradually replaced by functionalism, new views were also gaining ground at Denmark's only school of architecture at the time, namely at the Royal Academy of Fine Arts. At the end of 1924, 36-year-old Kaare Klint was hired by the Royal Academy's School of Architecture as a part-time teacher at first, but the following year he was given the position of lecturer in 'Interior Design and Furniture'. At the same, the classes at the academy changed in form and content. The school went from only teaching from an artistic perspective to a more technical and down-to-earth method of teaching. More emphasis was put on social and economic questions when the students projects were assessed.

The form changed from one-on-one classes with students supplemented by lectures to scheduled classroom teaching. Klint chose to interpret the new rules rather loosely and started a type of project class where all the students from different years studied together; a bit like being in a real architectural practice. He felt it was better and more fruitful if the students from different years could all contribute and thus everyone could benefit more than they could on their own. Furthermore Klint was fond of practical experiments to train the students' knowledge of understanding materials and the construction of furniture.

This form of teaching did not develop into a traditional apprenticeship with the students having to aesthetically emulate their teacher. This was an easy trap to fall into, but instead Klint's class was like an Exploratorium. In this environment some of the first research in furniture design in the world began. Klint's starting point was facts.

This took place on many levels. First of all by studying and learning from historic furniture and their construction and function. Klint had previously demonstrated how this could be done successfully. Secondly, the students had to collect information on the human body and the purpose of furniture in order to create the most well-functioning furniture possible. Finally, the constructions, joints and materials were to be carefully studied so quality furniture could be designed.

Early ergonomic studies

Kaare Klint summed up the content of his classes in an article in 'Arkitektens Maanedshæfte' (The Architect's Monthly) in October 1930: 'Measurements as preliminary studies for later processing – human objects and movements – the object of articles – constructive relationships with regard to user requirements – ways of joining, treatment of materials, aesthetic considerations, collaboration.' In practice, some classes were spent measuring and making accurate drawings of existing furniture. By doing this, students could get to know the strong and weak points of the furniture, and acquire an understanding of how to do a better job than their predecessors. At other times they measured how much space everyday articles took up, such as 12 dinner plates, 12 dessert plates, 12 wine glasses etc. Based on these facts the students could design the optimal cabinet for the home. In the same manner, an early form of ergonomic studies began at the Furniture School in order to find out how a chair could be made comfortable or how high a bookcase could reasonably be.

In line with his ergonomic views, Klint never used centimetres and metres when designing furniture. He consistently used the old Danish measures: inches, feet and a unit called 'alen', which corresponds to two feet.

FUNCTIONALISM IS A way of thinking, a design and architectural philosophy and also a style. Around 1924 the French painter and architect Le Corbusier was one of the first to use the word functionalism, and the Danish art critic and debater R. Broby-Johansen defined the concept like this: 'The appropriate is the beautiful'. The concept of modernism is often used interchangeably with functionalism, while the Scandinavian term 'funkis' is a bit condescendingly used with regard to the early smooth functional style of furniture made of steel tubing, rectangular cement houses with flat roofs, and undecorated radios in Bakelite. Functionalism was also called 'machine aesthetics'.

From the very beginning, the functionalists saw this style and ideology as suitable for the working class. It was to be the new society's rational way of building and designing. This was how industrial production could fulfil the people's need for healthy housing and good products. That's why superfluous decoration was prohibited in this style since it was an irrational and old-fashioned way of production. The unadorned, simplified and standardised was seen as easier and cheaper to mass produce. In aesthetical terms, the functionalists put content above form. What mattered was the individual's need for shelter and welfare, and not the prestige of the individual imitating the ornamental aesthetics of the upper class.

According to Klint's reasoning, the metric system was an artificial invention, while inches were directly associated to the human body (the width of a thumb), and 'it was always at hand'. Kaare Klint also designed lamps for Le Klint (see page 322) and a number of cenotaphs, memorials etc, many of which were made in collaboration with sculptors like Kai Nielsen and Mogens Bøggild. He was even a rather active building architect.

In contrast to the German functionalists, who were establishing their Bauhaus school at around this time, Klint's school didn't reject the past. The Bauhaus philosophy was that only by throwing all the old things away and starting anew could one create radically new design. The course of Danish functionalism was quite different, among other things because the Royal Academy's Furniture School also leaned on cabinetmaking and for the same reason preferred well-known materials like wood. The school had its glory days in the 1930s and educated many furniture architects during this period, among them were Børge Mogensen and Mogens Koch, who both became rather well known later on. Klint was appointed professor of architecture at the Royal Academy in 1945 and held it until his death in 1954. In his later years he seemed a bit disillusioned about educating furniture architects and subscribed to the opinion that 'no architect can compare with a cabinetmaker that is equipped with a sense of form,' as he said in an interview in 'The Politiken' in 1945.

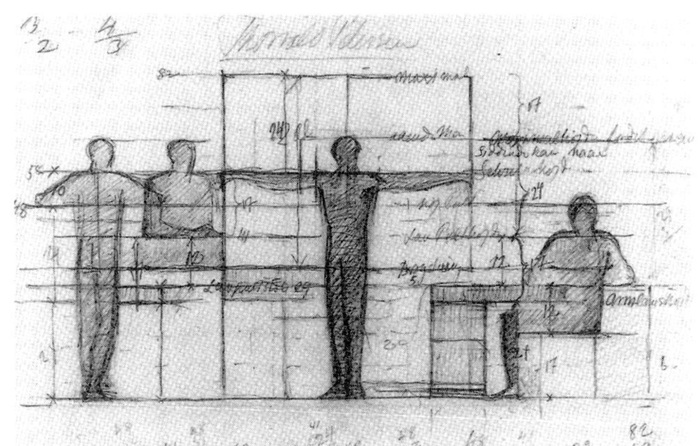

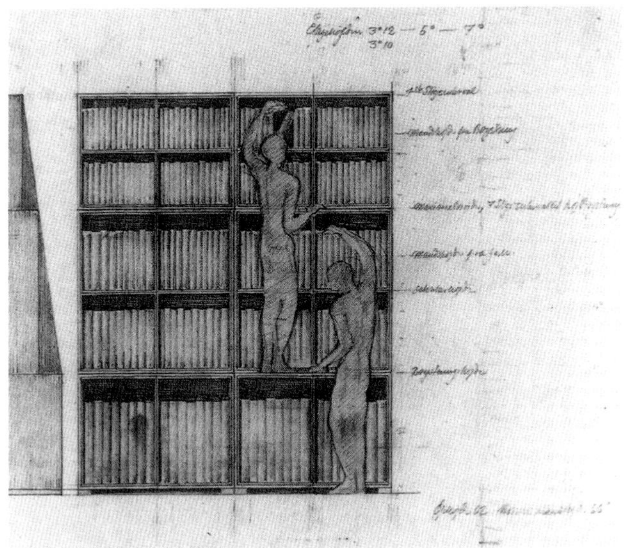

▸ *As early as in 1917 Kaare Klint worked on mapping the proportions of man in his endeavour to become a better furniture designer. In this case it was for designing a system of bookcases that were never manufactured. Note Klint's calculations surrounding the drawing in pencil; especially the note at the top: 'The difference between the eye level of a standing and sitting person is around 3/2 – 4/3.' This shows how early on Klint tried to become aware of the proportions of the human body.*

Zoologisk
HAVE

THE SAFARI CHAIR was inspired by an English camp chair and can easily be taken apart and put together without tools. Therefore the Safari Chair came in a box with 'KK Safari Chair' written on it (right). So this chair pre-empted IKEA furniture where the cost of transport and assembling are significantly reduced since the customers do it themselves. Klint's version was made of teak and goatskin from Nigeria, but now it's made of ash with a seat of canvas or oxhide. The poster on the wall (left) was drawn by Sven Brasch for the Copenhagen Zoo around 1924.

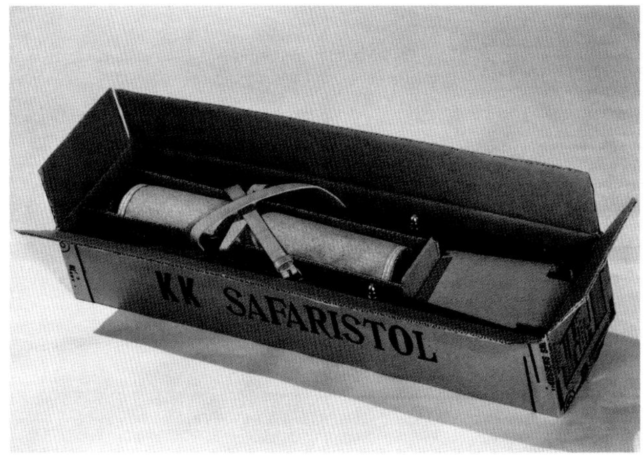

KAARE KLINT AND HIS CIRCLE

Besides teaching, Kaare Klint continued to design his own furniture, but it was often closely connected to the projects his students at the Academy were working on. One example of this is the armchair that was called Mix because it was the result of a collaboration with a student at the Furniture School, namely Edvard Kindt-Larsen. It was typical of the Furniture School for projects to arise through a dialogue between teacher and students or just between students. Mix is also a typical Klint chair since the radius of the curve at the front of the armrest (when seen from the side) corresponds to the curve going the other way where the armrest meets the back. You can find other examples of identical curves on the chair when you look at the drawings. The question is, of course, whether this kind of geometrical refinement makes better furniture.

Occasionally, the geometrical was something that interested Kaare Klint so much that it almost became an obsession. One of the most obvious examples of this was the so-called Kugleseng (spherical bed) (see page 160). It was first shown at the annual exhibition of Cabinetmakers' Guild in 1938 at Rud. Rasmussen's presentation of a bedroom for a lady. The reason why it was called the spherical bed was because the headboard, footboard and sides are geometrically designed so that a giant sphere can rest on top of the bed.

This imaginary sphere, for there never was a real one, would have had a diameter of several metres, and the upper edges of the bed are slanted so it could have rested comfortably there. But what the point of this formal aesthetics was we'll never know, and it wasn't very practical either since the bed required a custom-made mattress with rounded ends.

Kaare Klint possibly dreamed of designing furniture that would be industrially manufactured, but only his church chair has been produced in relatively large numbers. Other pieces were only manufactured in small numbers, but are still in production. One example is his Safari Chair, which like so much of Klint's furniture design takes it reference point in an older piece of furniture; in this case a portable English officer's chair. The chair was originally an armchair for use in the field and is therefore easy to take apart. All the wooden parts of the chair could be rolled up in the two pieces of canvas that constituted the seat and back. Klint found the Safari Chair informal and suitable for outdoor use, and he held on to the principle that it can be assembled without tools and while it's used it can be held together and stabilised by the adjustable straps.

One of the first students at Kaare Klint's Furniture School was Mogens Koch, who later became an employee at Klint's architectural practice and professor of architecture at the Royal Academy of Fine Arts in Copenhagen. Koch's folding chair was described earlier in this chapter, but his most well-known design is perhaps his bookcase system that in architectural circles is legendary. It has been in production since 1932. Mogens Koch began designing it in 1928, and in principle it's a bookcase with a square front. So the bookcase can be turned this way and that depending on how high you want the shelves for your books to be. The system also consists of cabinet doors, bases, drawers and letter trays and even a system of picture frames that fit the size and wood of the bookcases. Kaare Klint had been working on a system of bookcases since 1917, but it never turned out as simple and composed as Koch's. The bookcases are still manufactured by Rud. Rasmussen's Cabinetmakers. It has inspired other manufacturers such as Montana's similar bookcases in spray-painted MDF.

THE ARMCHAIR MIX was designed by Kaare Klint and Edvard Kindt-Larsen, who was a student at the Academy of Fine Arts School of Furniture. The draft is characteristic of Klint's way of working. The drawing shows the chair in a series of projections – from the side, top and the front. Klint hardly ever used perspective drawings, but preferred sketches with accurate dimensions that allowed him to consider the form and function, among other things whether the chair was comfortable or if the bookcase could accommodate what was necessary. The chair is still in production at Rud. Rasmussen's Cabinetmakers in Copenhagen under the name 'Armchair no. 4396'. However, today only Kaare Klint is named as the designer. The differences are very small, for example the leather upholstery is no longer riveted with brass studs.

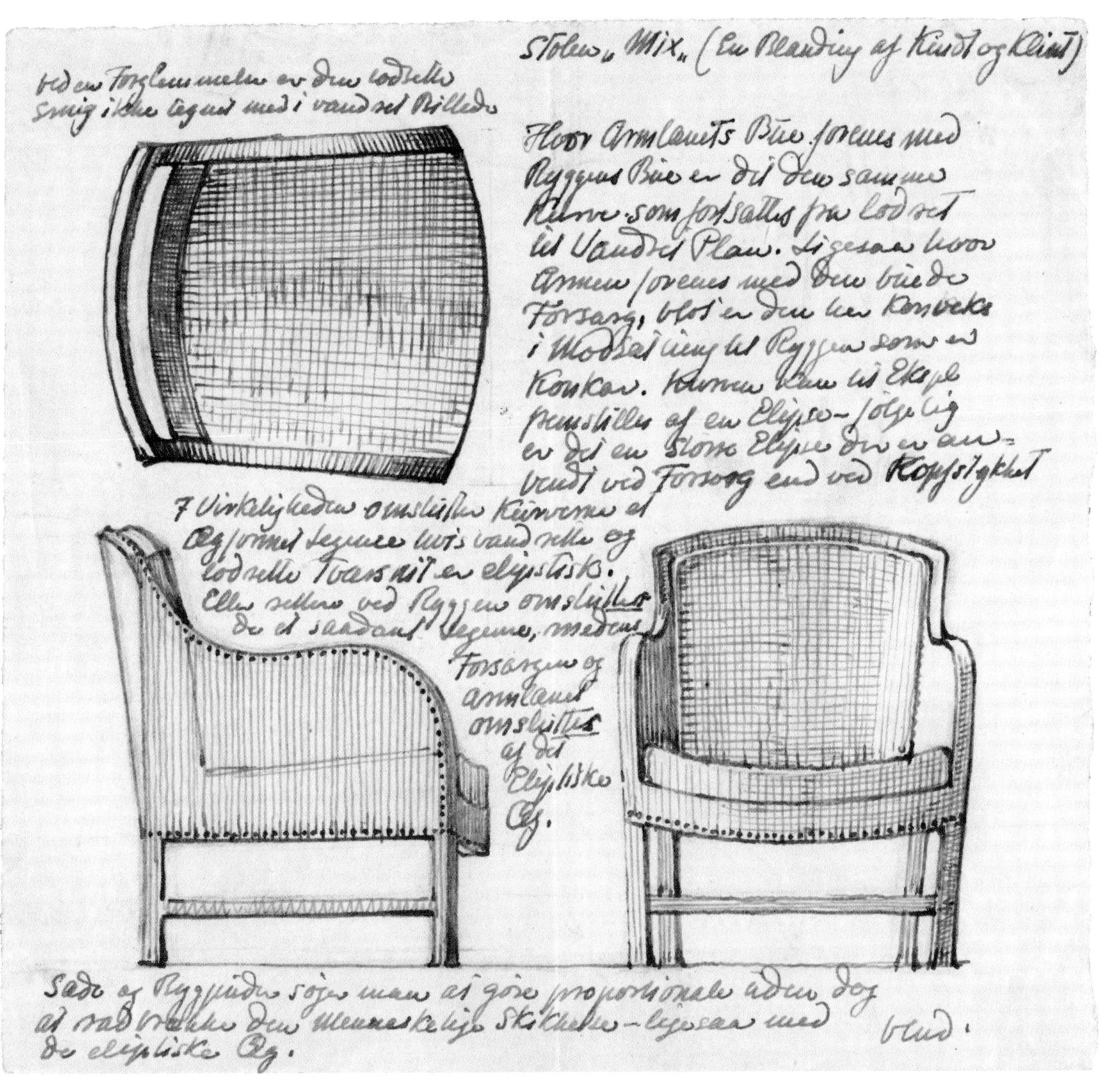

AT AND AROUND the Furniture School high-quality furniture was often made, but frequently for a very select few. In 1937, Rigmor Andersen, a student, designed a modern and functional cabinet for silverware made of palisander and based on the measurements of the flatware. When Kaare Klint saw it, he is supposed to have said, 'that with this clarified and fine piece of furniture she was a step closer to perfection than he had ever been'. However, it was typical that the cabinet was made of an exotic and precious type of wood like palisander. Oddly enough, the ideals of designing user-friendly and functional furniture did not result in reasonable prices. A rational industrial production in less precious types of wood could have lowered the price significantly and ensured a larger distribution of these functionalist ideals. Rigmor Andersen later worked with Kaare Klint at the school and at his architectural practice.

Parallel developments

Establishing the School of Furniture at the Royal Academy of Fine Arts was not an isolated incident. When Kaare Klint became the head of the Furniture School, Kay Fisker became the head of the new department of housing architecture. A teaching position in city planning was also established at the same time under the responsibility of lecturer Steen Eiler Rasmussen. All three of these gentlemen became professors at the Academy later on. Kay Fisker's housing class, as it was called colloquially, had a great impact on a generation of Danish architects and on the notion of creating good housing. Kay Fisker designed many large housing complexes, and in 1922 he designed the apartment block Hornbækhus on Nørrebro in Copenhagen with the help of Poul Henningsen, among others. The special thing about this building was that it was the first one in Copenhagen to have a courtyard landscaped like a large garden. Previously there would have been small industries, bike sheds or just a courtyard covered with asphalt. However, the façade is characterised by a formal and almost Classicist boring regularity in the placement of windows and doors. For a few years Fisker was the editor of the architectural society's members' journal, and he finally made a name for himself as one of the main architects behind the University of Aarhus.

The revolt continued against the old-fashioned way of seeing the home as a place to show off one's prestige and furnishing it according to middle-class ideals. In 1921 a few architects began designing more modern layouts for apartment blocks, for example by placing the apartment's living rooms where there was the most daylight. Previously, the living rooms dogmatically faced the street because that's what one used to do when the façade meant everything. Now one considered putting them in the back if the light and the atmosphere were better there. During this time the Association of Better Architectural Design was also very active in designing well-functioning housing for low-income people (see page 74). Experiments were also made with building townhouses, partly inspired by ones in England, and partly by Nyboder and the early building societies like the Potato Rows in Copenhagen (see page 72).

THE CABINETMAKERS' EXHIBITIONS

Outside academic circles things were also brewing in the field of furniture design. The craftsmen, represented by the Copenhagen Cabinetmakers' Guild, moved into the offensive in 1927 by arranging annual exhibitions of modern furniture in the capital. This didn't happen because the cabinetmakers felt a sudden need to strike a blow for modern furniture design, but more so because they were financially squeezed, in part because of the financial slump, and in part because of the rising competition from the furniture factories. The 1927 exhibition was held with the sole intent of selling. It took place at Axelborg in Copenhagen and was a financial success with its 20,000 visitors and the fact that much of the exhibited furniture was sold. Yet the press reviews and the furniture architects' reaction was a bit lukewarm. On the one hand, the good initiative was praised, but on the other hand, there wasn't much innovation to be found in the stands. There was too much 'wedding cake' to the style.

The architect Tyge Hvass criticised the exhibitors for not taking enough consideration of the housing conditions of the general public. He felt that since most of the cabinetmakers' potential customers lived in one-bedroom or two-bedroom apartments, the cabinetmakers should work with young architects in developing new types of suitable furniture. This criticism

▾ *In 1928 Mogens Koch designed a bookcase and cabinet system for himself, but in 1932 it went into production at Rud. Rasmussen's Cabinetmakers. It's one of the few pieces of furniture that was manufactured in large numbers, although the price is rather high.*

◂ *Hornbækhus is an enormous building that is a whole block long on Nørrebro in Copenhagen. It was designed by Kay Fisker in 1922. The façades facing the street are very compact and classicist in the very regular windows and doors. In architectural circles a little jingle was used to poke fun at Fisker's extreme regularity: Window, pillar, window, pillar, window, pillar, entrance, window, pillar, window, pillar, window, pillar, drainpipe. The style was also called 'the kilometre style' since it went on forever. The façade facing the courtyard has the same regular appearance, but as something quite new, a green area was landscaped where one previously would have built back buildings, small industries or garages. Classicism is on its way to becoming functionalism here.*

▸ *Proposal for the interior of a young family's living room by Hans Wegner and master cabinetmaker Johannes Hansen for the annual exhibition of the Cabinetmakers' Guild in 1947 at the Museum of Art & Design in Copenhagen. For the first time Wegner's Peacock Chair was exhibited; a model of it is standing on the coffee table.*

▸▸ *Proposal for the interior of a two-bedroom apartment by Børge Mogensen and Hans Wegner together with master cabinetmaker Johannes Hansen for the annual exhibition of the Cabinetmakers' Guild in 1945 at the Museum of Art & Design in Copenhagen. Børge Mogensen's Spokeback Sofa was exhibited for the first time. The upholstery was woven by Lis Ahlmann, and the lampshade over the table is Kaare Klint's Fruit Lantern pendant designed for Le Klint.*

made the cabinetmakers think twice, and the following year several of them had allied themselves with designers like Kaare Klint.

But it wasn't until 1930 that the new development really got going. Two architects, Hans Hansen and Viggo Sten Møller, joined forces with two cabinetmakers, H. Wörts and P. Nielsen, to make a complete furnishing suggestion for a one-bedroom apartment (see page 74). It even went as far as the lamps, potted plants on the dresser and pictures on the walls. There was even a budget for the whole package: 1500–1600 kroner for the standard solution. If money was tight, they could shave off a few hundred kroner, or if you wanted to splurge, you could get a better solution for an additional 300–400 kroner.

That was the main attraction at the exhibition that year. And the idea of furnishing an apartment was repeated intermittently, but with other kinds of housing, such as in 1934 when there was 'A small one-family house'. Gradually all the master cabinetmakers collaborated with the furniture architects that either came from Klint's department at the Academy or were building architects who had designed furniture for public housing. Later on the design-educated cabinetmakers from the School of Art & Design joined in, and eventually the Cabinetmakers' exhibition became the biggest furniture and design event of the year in Copenhagen. From 1933 on, this success led to an annual design competition for proposals for new types of furniture as a prelude to the exhibition.

If we go back to the 1500 – 1600 kroner for furnishing a whole apartment, it certainly sounds cheap to us today, but back then it was a lot of money (it corresponds to about US$10,000/Euros 6000 today) and it was much more than if you went to the furniture factories' shops that had shot up in Danish towns since World War I. In many ways the cabinetmakers contributed to clearing the way for the design-based furniture industry that came later on in the 20th century. Very few of the cabinetmakers from back then exist today. Perhaps only Rud. Rasmussen's Cabinetmakers on Nørrebrogade in Copenhagen are keeping up the good work. The exhibitions were held every year until 1966 when the new industrialised times had steadily sidelined the cabinetmakers.

FUNKIS AND FURNITURE OF STEEL TUBING

Naturally the cabinetmakers made their furniture out of wood; that was the very nature of their craft. There was strength in the fact that they made the most of this material, and wood is lovely material. The weakness lay in the fact that the development of products was very much limited by what one could make out of wood and by the craft. Other materials and industrial production were heretical concepts. This meant that architects and designers that had different approaches to the world of furniture had to go elsewhere. And yet there were some who had a special approach to creating modern furniture and functional homes. For example, they wanted to work with furniture made of metal, wicker and with the new synthetic materials.

In particular, young architects such as Poul Henningsen and Mogens Lassen felt inspired by the new technologies and trends in the world, among them the Bauhaus school and the French architect Le Corbusier's works. Mogens Lassen was a talented building architect who worked in the field of international functionalism after World War I. He was employed at Tyge Hvass' architectural practice in the years 1925 to 1934. Tyge Hvass

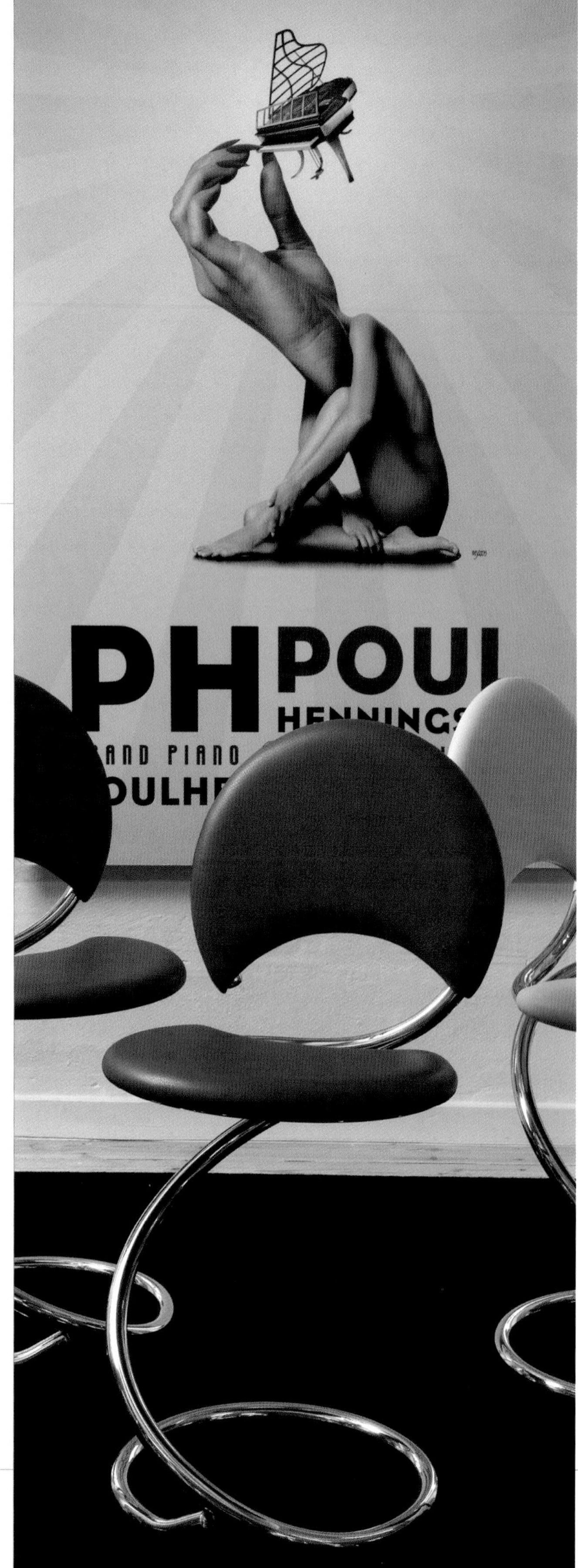

◀ In 1932 Poul Henningsen designed an extensive series of furniture made of steel tubes. These functionalist chairs never really caught on, but the production has been resumed recently. This is the Snake Chair in its new production.

was the one who had criticised the Cabinetmakers' exhibitions for being uninspired, and who had since then become their exhibition architect. During a stay in Paris in 1927–28, Mogens Lassen's interest in Le Corbusier was awakened, and in particular his ideas about the home as a means of having a freer life.

Lassen became one of Denmark's first architects who worked with the technical possibilities of concrete as a material in housing. His curiosity towards new materials also led him to design an armchair in chrome-plated steel tubes with a seat and back of round pith caning. Around 1933 the chair was briefly manufactured by the furniture factory Fritz Hansen, and it was a very direct interpretation of a Bauhaus chair designed by the director of the school, Mies van der Rohe. That was Lassen's short career as a furniture designer, but from 1939 to 1967 he was the exhibition architect for 'The Permanent Exhibition of Danish Arts and Crafts' in Copenhagen, which for many years was known as The Permanent. Here he designed many exhibitions that helped to promote Danish design, also internationally.

The enfant terrible of Danish architecture and design, Poul Henningsen, also tried his hand at steel furniture. Although he had previously been against it, in 1932, at the initiative of the company V.A. Høffding, he did design an extensive series of drawing room furniture. The result of his efforts was shown the same year at 'Dansk Købestævne' (The Danish Fair) in Fredericia, and he got decent press reviews, as far as we know. There is no doubt that PH was inspired by Bauhaus when he designed this furniture in chrome-plated steel tubes and leather upholstery, since the same materials were used by the Bauhaus designers. But the Danish designer had a much more playful attitude to the furniture and the material,

ONE NIGHT IN 1931, Poul Henningsen was at a restaurant with his friend Andreas Kristensen, who made pianos. At one point in the evening, the first sketches were made of a piano of steel, leather and Plexiglas. That became the beginning of a production of about 60–70 of the oddest pianos in music history. It is difficult to say whether they were designed in any particular style. Once again, like PH's steel-tube furniture, they look like something inspired by jazz. The legs curve outwards like a Klismos Chair, while the lid is in the style of Art Nouveau. The frame has a padded leather cushion all the way around it, and the materials are pure functionalism, or rather high tech, as we would call it today. The sound wasn't particularly good although the piano cost about 100,000 kroner – a fortune. Today the used pianos sell for about 300–400,000 kroner. Recently production of them has been resumed, allegedly with a better sound and a price tag of just under half a million kroner. One of PH's few really extravagant designs.

and they also seem to be inspired by the music PH liked so much, namely jazz. The Snake Chair, which is the piece from the series that most often is pictured in literature, almost resembles solidified jazz. But despite the good reviews, the chair wasn't a seller; the design was probably slightly too advanced and expressive even for jazz enthusiasts. In 2004, some of the models are once again being manufactured by a company that calls itself 'Poul Henningsen Inc.'

Critical Revue

Poul Henningsen began his professional life as a critic; first of art. This was during World War I, when he mainly wrote for a modernist culture magazine called 'Klingen' (The Blade). But before long the young PH also became a critic of society, and he took it out on the Academy of Fine Arts, School of Architecture, among others. He demanded that it be closed since it had become 'a home for cripples and old people'. This criticism was directed at the focus on the artistic and aesthetic, which was prevalent at the Academy back then, and the subsequent lack of attention to the housing shortage and social problems caused by bad architecture and inappropriate interior design. This criticism was along the same lines as that which brought young architects like Kaare Klint, Steen Eiler Rasmussen and Kay Fisker to the helm at the School of Architecture.

Between his many duties as an architect and especially lamp designer, Poul Henningsen also took part in social debate all his life, and he did not mince his words. From 1926 to 1928 in particular, while he was the editor of the periodical Critical Revue, he made his mark as the constant critic of everything that smacked of the bourgeoisie, injustice, prejudice and narrow-mindedness. He advocated modern sexual morals, free abortion,

▲ *Poul Henningsen's tribute to the simple beauty of the Vienna chair (bentwood chair) that was reasonably priced.*

THE BENTWOOD CHAIR inspired not only PH, but also the furniture company Fritz Hansen, who manufactured the DAN chair from 1928–48. This chair is based on the same technique that the German-Austrian company Thonet developed in the 1830s: steam-bending beech roundwood in an industrial-like production form. In 1932, Fritz Hansen was licensed by the Thonet factory to manufacture a number of their models. This is how the Danish factory gained access to the necessary know-how to develop its own models. Over the years, almost 15,000 DAN chairs were made, which at the time was a considerable number for a Danish furniture factory. The Danish versions were designed by the 3rd generation of the company's owner, Søren Hansen, and since then by architect Magnus Stephensen (his chair is pictured left). They weren't quite equal in design and comfort to the famous Thonet models, manufactured by the millions over the last 150 years in basically the same form.

equal rights for women and letting go of everything that was old fashioned and that limited the spirit. The periodical was provoking in both its form and content. The editorial staff included people like Edvard Heiberg, Thorkild Henningsen, Ivar Bentsen and Otto Gelsted, and among the writers there were Hans Kirk, Johannes V. Jensen and the Finnish architect Alvar Aalto. The subjects they dealt with polemically, sarcastically and wittily were the confusing mixed style of the time, housing politics, city planning etc.

Furniture design also went through PH's wringer once in a while. For an article criticising Kaare Klint's Faaborg Chair, Henningsen was photographed balancing one of Thonet's famous bentwood chairs on his index finger. In the caption under the picture he wrote, 'This chair does its job to perfection: the light low-backed chair is suitably comfortable. It weighs 3.5 kilos, just like a newborn baby. It costs 16 kroner and 50 ører with a cane seat. By making this chair five times as expensive, three times as heavy, half as comfortable and a quarter as beautiful, an architect can achieve fame ...' This is how PH tried to urge architects and designers to look for simpler and cheaper solutions so more people from the lower classes could enjoy the industry's rational production and get better housing and products.

PH mostly approved of Klint's efforts at the Academy to give pride of place to the unsentimental and sensible. Perhaps the initiative could have been a little more collective, thought PH, and there could have been less Cuban mahogany and fewer silverware cabinets. Three years later, the Critical Revue shut down; the periodical was short of money, and the various employees had thousands of other projects to work on, but the periodical's rebuke against being bourgeois reverberated for many years.

FDB supplies the people with furniture

During the 1930s, several other people advocated the production of good, but relatively inexpensive products, especially furniture. In 1933, the folk high school advocate, a member of the Danish Liberation Council later on, and cabinet member of the liberation government for the Unity Party, Arne Sørensen, wrote a book called *Funktionalisme og Samfund* (Functionalism and Society). In it he challenges the Danish Consumers' Co-operative Society (FDB) to consider the problem of the old-fashioned style of products for the home. He thought that private capitalist companies had no interest in manufacturing proper furniture and fixtures. Apart from the PH lamps and DAN chairs he couldn't find any Danish designed or manufactured products that weren't in bad taste. Now the co-op had to enter the scene.

And it did. Possibly not as a consequence of Arne Sørensen's book, but others were pressuring them as well. The forward-looking first director of FDB, Frederik Nielsen, had used Kaare Klint and not least the architect and writer Steen Eiler Rasmussen as consultants in the late 1930s. Then in the early 1940s, Steen Eiler Rasmussen developed a concept for FDB's new campaign in furniture. And at the same time, Kaare Klint recommended making the recently graduated architect Børge Mogensen, who was his best student at the School of Architecture, the head of FDB's design office. Frederik Nielsen seized the idea, and in 1942 one of the most exciting initiatives in furniture starts in Denmark.

Børge Mogensen was 28 years old at the time and he fearlessly took on the job with gusto. The design office had a few employees and freelance designers, and one of them was Mogensen's friend and fellow student

▾ *A proposal for a room with a bed and a bedside shelf that can be folded into the wall cabinet during the day. Designed by Børge Mogensen for the 400th anniversary exhibition of the Cabinetmakers' Guild in Copenhagen in 1954.*

Hans J. Wegner. Over a period of two years a full collection of furniture was designed in a fit of labour because now Børge wanted to prove what could be done if one considered the industry while designing furniture. In 1944, the first collection of Brugsen furniture was ready to be presented at a newly renovated shop on Frederiksborggade in downtown Copenhagen. The collection created a stir towards the end of the war when the shortage of materials didn't make the job any easier for Mogensen and FDB.

The pedagogical project

As a consultant, Steen Eiler Rasmussen followed the project all the way and described it in an article in Andelsbladet (Journal of The Danish Co-operative Organisations) in 1944, 'To make new furniture that can entail progress, it's not enough to make new curlicues or just get rid of the old ones. It's necessary to study the basic forms of furniture meticulously in order to reveal the 'purebreds' that each represent a type that's most appropriate for its function. Work of this kind takes time and costs money ... Unlike the advertisements that conjure up marvellously large rooms where the wonderful furniture is placed, the Co-operative Society has constructed an apartment of realistic rooms with floors, walls, a ceiling, doors and windows that all have the dimensions and fixtures that you would find in the more humble homes. It's like a housing laboratory.'

In the article Steen, Eiler Rasmussen pedagogically and thoroughly explains to the members and representatives of FDB the project they had embarked on and shows that it was being carried out in a scientific and serious way. This was quite a big gamble for Frederik Nielsen and there was a danger that the members of FDB would turn their back on it and prefer the old-fashioned type of furniture. The furniture was to be sold to the members

▼ *Boligens Byggeskabe (Cabinet Units for the Home) was a modular system of cabinets, bookcases and folding tables which Børge Mogensen developed with architect Grethe Meyer around 1956. The cabinets were made of Oregon pine and had brass fittings.*

either in their local co-op or in the eight furniture stores that FDB had opened in the capital and large provincial towns. Housing consultants, or what we today would call interior designers, were associated with these stores to advise the members on functional furnishing. The marketing was massive in Andelsbladet, whose name was changed to Samvirke in 1945, but also by means of advertisements in 'The Politiken' in particular, and by means of lectures and a 45-minute film about interior design that FDB had made and that was shown in the local co-ops.

Exactly how big a success this gamble was for FDB isn't known, but the turnover was so high that they bought Tarm Furniture Factory in 1947 in order to keep up with demands. Until then the furniture had been manufactured by sub-suppliers, among others at Fritz Hansen. And even after FDB got their own factory, the sub-suppliers still had plenty of work for the co-ops. However, at first it wasn't the working-class who bought FDB's furniture, but instead younger, well-educated people who had embraced the new style and could now afford it. After a while people from other walks of life bought the functional furniture at FDB or at the many places where this type could be purchased. But several decades would still pass before 'Danish Design' was fully accepted by the people.

BØRGE MOGENSEN

FDB's success in furniture gradually waned. Throughout the 1950s the company steadily faced more competition, and furthermore you had to be a member of the co-op to buy the furniture, and not everyone was. In other stores you could also find a completely different assortment. Moreover, the co-ops were typically located in the country, and FDB's furniture was seen by some as being 'city furniture'. And then Børge Mogensen left the design office in 1950. He was sick and tired of all the hard work and having to deal with sub-suppliers and the rigid systems in the co-op organisation. Børge Mogensen's sparring partner, Director Frederik Nielsen, had also quit his job, so now a new leading fireball was needed to fill the void. Børge Mogensen wasn't on the same wavelength as the new management, so he left for a life as an independent designer.

For ten years Børge Mogensen had practically been synonymous with FDB's furniture, and he's especially known for the first unit furniture and the dining room chair in Shaker style that's also called J39. But most of the other furniture that Børge Mogensen is known for was either designed after his time at FDB or was manufactured for others. As mentioned before, Børge Mogensen had been one of Kaare Klint's best students and was probably the one who was the closest to being the professor's heir as regards design. But while Klint designed numerous pieces of furniture that weren't very well known, Mogensen's furniture was. Unlike Klint, Mogensen wasn't such a stickler for perfection. While working at FDB, the young designer learned to work quickly and accept the conditions set by the industry, and among other things that one has to compromise on details if the price is to be kept at a reasonable level.

Børge Mogensen sometimes, but not always, worked in the same way as Klint by using older foreign models for his furniture design. The Shaker chair has been described previously (see page 15), and the Windsor chair was another spindleback chair he designed for FDB. It was inspired by 18th century England. However, the Spanish Chair was the result of a lot of inspiration during a trip to Spain in 1958. Here he saw Spanish officers' chairs as well as traditional Moorish furniture and rooms. His chair is a

THE SPOKEBACK SOFA. The sofa was presented for the first time at the annual exhibition of Cabinetmakers' Guild in 1945, but it didn't sell very well. In 1962–63 it was again manufactured by Fritz Hansen, and this time became a much bigger seller. The special thing about the Spokeback Sofa is the end that can be lowered and the leather cords that are used to regulate how far it's lowered. Børge Mogensen designed it when he and Hans J. Wegner furnished a two-bedroom apartment for the annual exhibition of the Cabinetmakers' Guild in Copenhagen. This two-seater sofa is vaguely reminiscent of the English daybed and the French chaise longue. Today it's manufactured in oak, beech and walnut by Fredericia Furniture.

▼ *The Spanish Chair which Børge Mogensen designed in 1958 was, as the name indicates, inspired by a type of chair he saw during a trip to Spain. The original Spanish model was an aristocratic chair that he saw in palaces and officers' quarters. In Mogensen's version the chair is a simpler, more robust and bold chair.*

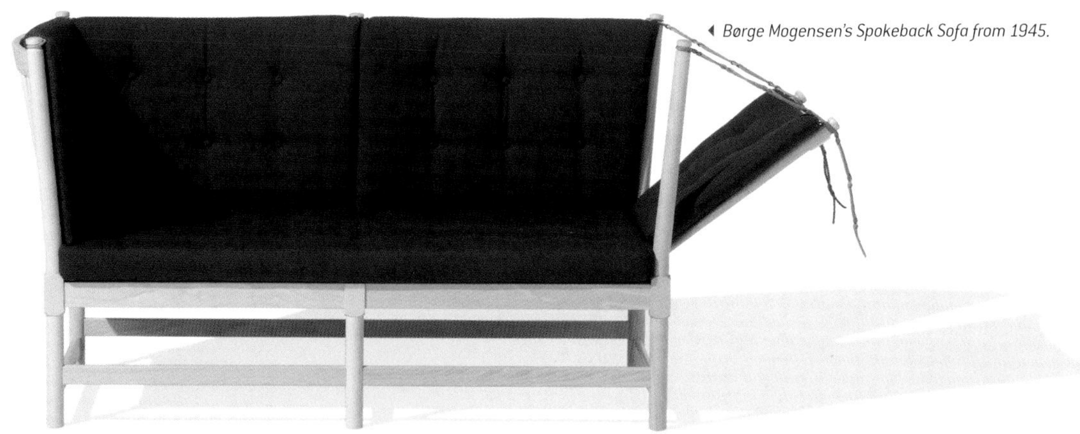

Børge Mogensen's Spokeback Sofa from 1945.

Børge Mogensen's Wing Chair from 1963 with matching footstool.

highly modernised version where the ornamentation and carvings are left out, but the constructive element is maintained. The wide armrests especially give the chair a robust character and have the added bonus of being like little tables where you can place your cup or glass. Fredericia Furniture still manufactures them in oak and full-grain leather.

Børge Mogensen's Spokeback Sofa also has characteristics that could be traced to earlier types, like English spindleback chairs, but they aren't really that closely related. And this is the case with much of Mogensen's pieces of furniture, they're not radically different, yet so innovative and distinct that one can talk about a personal Mogensen style. His Wing Chair from 1963, for which a footstool was also designed, is a salute to the master Kaare Klint and English armchairs. It wasn't often that Mogensen designed upholstered furniture; he wasn't very fond of the big armchair and sofa sets that he and Wegner had given the nickname 'the brawny butcher's set'. Like most people from the Klint school, he preferred simple furniture with visible constructions. And in this case he simplified the chair as much as possible for its type.

BØRGE MOGENSEN, 1914–1972, Danish furniture architect. He got his apprenticeship as a cabinetmaker in Aalborg in 1934 and attended the School of Arts & Crafts and the Royal Academy of Fine Arts, School of Furniture in the years 1936–42. Mogensen studied under Kaare Klint and was head of the design office at FDB Furniture from 1942–50. Afterwards he started his own architectural office. After the war, Børge Mogensen was one of hottest names in Danish furniture design with his simple, robust and masculine style. Starting with the annual exhibition arranged by the Cabinetmakers' Guild in Copenhagen in 1939, Mogensen was a regular participant with his friend and colleague Hans J. Wegner. He was very socially conscious and while working for FDB he designed many pieces of inexpensive, well-made furniture. Among his many distinctions are the Eckersberg Medal (1950) and the C.F. Hansen Medal (1972).

Børge Mogensen has designed an abundance of furniture, and many of these pieces never amounted to more than drawings and a single model at most. He enjoyed constantly challenging the furniture types, the production machinery, the market and his colleagues. He never thought his work was done, and he burned the candle at both ends until it went out. Børge Mogensen died in 1972 at the young age of 58.

HANS J. WEGNER

Børge Mogensen and Hans J. Wegner seem to have lived parallel lives far into adulthood. They were both born in 1914; Børge in Aalborg, Hans in Tønder. They were both skilled cabinetmakers and moved to Copenhagen for further education. Their paths crossed at the School of Arts & Crafts and later at the annual exhibitions of the Cabinetmakers' Guild. Sometimes they worked together, sometimes apart, sometimes with others. Their common point of reference was their pursuit of excellent craftsmanship and their desire to make good functional furniture. However, their paths went in very different directions later on.

Journalist Henrik Sten Møller once called Wegner 'the world's best cabinetmaker'. And it's true that Wegner's command of the craft was huge and without it he would probably have never been able to create many of his best designs. In many of Wegner's projects he challenges the material and the traditional view of what good furniture construction is and what is beautiful. The chair in particular was what Wegner was most fond of. In the course of his career he managed to make 500 different designs, of which about 100 are or have been in production. In a television interview he was asked, again by Henrik Sten Møller, about his view on other types of furniture like tables and cabinets.

▲ *Hans J. Wegner's 'The Round Chair', here in oak with a seat of rattan cane.*

THE SHELL CHAIR. This chair was designed by Børge Mogensen in 1949 and presented at the annual exhibition of the Cabinetmakers' Guild the same year. Back then there weren't any companies that dared manufacture it. It was launched again in 2004 by Fredericia Furniture to mark the 90th anniversary of Mogensen's birth. The chair is an unusual combination of a dining room chair and a light easy chair. The back is a thick piece of plywood that has been cut into a shape that is both beautiful and more flexible. The seat is a thicker piece of laminated plywood. The chair isn't typical of Børge Mogensen, who didn't work much with lamination, and it's sculptural while his furniture is usually more rustic and simple.

Wegner's opinion was that not everything in a room should draw attention to itself; cabinets and bookcases are just supposed to work, but the chair is 'closer' to us and therefore should have character.

While in his final year at the School of Arts & Crafts, Wegner started working for Arne Jacobsen, who at the time was completing the city hall in Aarhus. Therefore Wegner was sent over there from 1940–43 to design the interior and the furniture for this prestigious building and furthermore to supervise the work. Today the interior of the city hall is almost identical to how it was over 60 years ago. After Aarhus City Hall was finished, Wegner started out on his own and in the last years of the war he designed a lot of furniture for FDB where Mogensen was head of design. Wegner continually participated in furniture competitions and the annual exhibitions of the Cabinetmakers' Guild, and together with Mogensen he designed a two-bedroom apartment for it in 1945.

1949 was to become a great year for Hans J. Wegner. At the annual exhibition of the Cabinetmakers' Guild he presented the chair that would make him world famous. He called it 'The Round Chair', and it was made at Johannes Hansen Cabinetmakers like many of Wegner's other designs at the time. Originally the chair didn't get a hearty welcome in the newspapers, but one of the standard-bearers of Danish craft-based products and design, architect Viggo Sten Møller, sent some pictures from the exhibition to the US. The rest is history, as they say, because suddenly the Round Chair was on the cover of the American periodical 'Interior' and proclaimed to be the world's best chair, the ultimate chair, 'The Chair' as the Americans dubbed it (see page 34).

An American restaurant ordered 400 of them. Johannes Hansen had been pleased to sell the four from the exhibition, and now such a big order was a bit difficult for a little cabinetmaker's workshop. Other American companies wanted Wegner to design furniture for them, but he declined for, as he said in the television interview, 'it has to be crafted by Danes'. 'But we can do the same thing by machine,' said the Americans. 'Yes, but it's still not the same,' replied Wegner, 'even though I could have made a lot of money, but no matter. All you have to do is get by.' However in the same interview he did admit that 'today we also make them by machine'. This short anecdote describes, perhaps better than anything else, the prevalent mindset in the milieu at the time. They kept the professional banner flying so high that many designers didn't want to sell out, not even for many dollars. Although one might think that Wegner works very sculpturally, he constantly emphasised in the interview that the sitting quality of a chair and its function were always at the forefront. As one of the first Danish furniture architects, he also realised that people often move around on a chair, and a designer must take this into consideration. It's also difficult to find a Wegner chair that is truly uncomfortable.

The chair with the funny name 'Jakkens Hvile' (literally: the resting place for a coat, but called the Valet Chair) is an example of Wegner's humorous ingenuity. Originally the chair was designed for a large hotel on the Copenhagen waterfront, and it was an assignment that Wegner was given together with Børge Mogensen. The chair is an idea that Wegner had sketched previously but hadn't perfected until now. It's from a time (1953) when mainly businessmen stayed at hotels. The principle is that you first hang your jacket on the hanger-shaped back.

continued on page 245

▼ Hans J. Wegner's Valet Chair was designed for a large hotel in 1953, and it's a chair with en extra built-in function. The back is like a hanger for the businessman's jacket at night, and the seat can be lifted, so the trousers can hang over the edge. A little tray under the seat is for the contents of his pockets.

THE PEACOCK CHAIR was designed by Hans J. Wegner in 1947 and it's natural to compare it to two other chairs. One is the original English Windsor chair that was popular in the 1800s, and which is pictured at left in Børge Mogensen's exact copy. Mogensen later designed a modern version of the chair for FDB. The chair at bottom left, Acton Bjørn's version, was shown at the annual exhibition of the Cabinetmakers' Guild in 1943. While Mogensen and Bjørn don't digress much from the original, Wegner lets his imagination go (below right) and designs a very different chair in a more luxuriant artistic expression, but he doesn't compromise on the use value. Wegner's design always starts with the functional. When furniture architect Finn Juhl saw this chair for the first time, he immediately noticed its singularity and named it the Peacock Chair. The chair was developed and manufactured first by Johannes Hansen Cabinetmakers. PP Furniture continued the production in 1992.

▾ Wegner designed the Ox Chair in 1960. It is one of the few upholstered pieces of furniture that Wegner is known for, but in this case he tried to make something that was expressive in a different way than 'the brawny butcher's set', which he and his friend Børge Mogensen loved to hate. Today it's manufactured by Erik Jørgensen.

▾ The Pelican Chair is from 1940, but looks like it could have been designed in the last decade. It's voluminous upholstery is counterbalanced by the sturdy round legs, which are even rounded at the bottom to underline the soft and teddy bear-like quality of the chair.

Because Finn Juhl wasn't a craftsman, good drawings were important to communicate what he wanted to achieve. Normally a furniture designer would only make a rough sketch, but one of the ways Finn Juhl worked was to paint beautiful watercolours. Chair model FJ45 from 1945 was one of Juhl's most successful armchairs; a type he returned to and redesigned again and again.

When you lift the seat, a little compartment is revealed that can accommodate the contents of your pockets. Finally you can hang your trousers over the straight edge of the upright seat. In the morning everything is ready to put on, and your trousers creases are still there. When you lower the seat, you can sit down and tie your shoes. The Valet Chair is still in production at PP Furniture.

Hans J. Wegner didn't usually get much involved in professional debates, unlike his friend Børge Mogensen. But on the occasion of the opening of a large exhibition for Scandinavian design in Chicago in 1984, Wegner wrote an article for the catalogue about the success of Danish furniture design in the post-war era, stating that 'Paradoxically, one could venture to say that the basic reason for our success was that Denmark was lagging behind in industrial development. Technically there was nothing new in our work, and there was certainly no money to carry out major technical experiments. The philosophy behind it was not to make the process of work more complicated than necessary, but to show what we were able to do with our hands: to try to make the material come alive, to give it a sense of spirit, to make our works look so natural that one could conceive of them in that form only and in no other.' For other examples of Hans J. Wegner's design see pages 46 and 238.

FINN JUHL

Not all contributions to the Danish new departure in furniture design came from people who were educated in the field. Architects who hadn't studied at Klint's School of Furniture, but had a background as building architects, also worked in furniture design. Several of them turned out to be very competent in doing so. One of the best was Finn Juhl. He was born in 1912 and therefore almost the same age as Wegner and Mogensen, but he wasn't a skilled craftsman. In many ways he was actually their opposite since he came from a wealthy background and had originally wanted to study art history, but his father, who was a wholesaler, was against it because it had no prospects. So young Juhl attended the School of Architecture in 1930. For four years he studied in Kay Fisker's Department of Housing Architecture, but before he graduated he started working at Vilhelm Lauritzen's architectural practice and never actually graduated from the Academy.

Instead Finn Juhl worked on big public projects like Radiohuset (the Radio House) on Rosenørns Allé in Copenhagen and the new airport terminal in Kastrup. At Vilhelm Lauritzen's architectural practice he worked on the interior design of rooms, he designed fixtures, door handles, lamps etc. During his 11 years there, he also designed furniture for the annual exhibition of the Cabinetmakers' Guild. But Juhl's approach to designing furniture was different from most of his contemporaries and the people from Klint's school. While Wegner and Mogensen made their own prototypes in a workshop, Juhl had to compensate for not being a skilled craftsman by allying himself early on with the very talented cabinetmaker Niels Vodder. The two worked together for the annual exhibition for 22 years, and when the architect couldn't cope with the construction problems, the experienced Vodder stepped in.

But the way Finn Juhl designed furniture is greatly ascribed to his interest in art. He wasn't nearly as interested as many of his contemporaries were in interpreting old types of furniture. Yet he was somewhat inspired by Egyptian furniture from Antiquity.

◀ *Finn Juhl's proposal from 1956 for the design of the cabin in the new DC-8's for SAS.*

▶ *The Chieftains Chair was executed by Finn Juhl's regular partner, cabinetmaker Niels Vodder, for the annual exhibition of the Cabinetmakers' Guild at the Museum of Art & Design in 1949. It's one of the most extravagant pieces that modern Danish design has produced. It's made of Cuban mahogany with delicate joints and the seat, back and armrests are upholstered in leather. As a sort of comment on the prevalent Klint school's emphasis on human proportions, mathematics and functional ideals, Juhl decorated his booth at the exhibition with art, tools and weapons from primitive tribes. That's why the chair was called the Chieftains Chair. The very slender dimensions of much of the chair's wooden frame is a significant part of the design expression. As if challenging themselves, Finn Juhl and Niels Vodder wanted to minimise as much as possible the materials used.*

But he rarely converted the old types of furniture into modern design, which Klint, Mogensen and Wanscher did. If anything, Juhl used Egyptian furniture in the same way he used modern art – he let his imagination go and invented new furniture forms. He was often inspired by Mondrian's paintings and sculptures by Henry Moore, Barbara Hepworth and Jean Arp, and the Danish sculptor Erik Thommesen's wood sculptures were often included in Finn Juhl's designed interiors.

There are two kinds of Finn Juhl furniture. The light sitting furniture, especially chairs, and then upholstered furniture such as armchairs and sofas. The light armchairs and easy chairs have a distinct construction: a wooden skeleton that supports the upholstered materials. This division of the load-bearing structure and the borne parts of the chair weren't exactly invented by Juhl, but it wasn't very common in Denmark before. Until then the norm was that the seat and back were integrated parts of the construction as one can see in almost every other piece of sitting furniture from that time. Juhl's chairs had a visible sculptural skeleton which was the result of sublime cabinetmaking, and they were almost always made of precious woods like Cuban mahogany or teak. The Chieftains Chair is the Rolls-Royce of Juhl's repertoire, but also the so-called 45 Chair that was crafted by Niels Vodder for the annual exhibition of the Cabinetmakers' Guild in 1945 is a good example of this type.

The large padded pieces of furniture had a different artistic idiom than the slender wooden chairs with limited amount of padding. As early as the late 1930s and early 1940s, Juhl and Vodder exhibited examples of the organically formed padded furniture that exuded a cosy, teddy bear-like quality. These pieces truly had body, and when the exhibition visitors gave them nicknames like 'The Pelican Chair' and 'The Poet' (inspired by a Danish comic strip called The Poet and the Little Woman), it was a sign that people liked Juhl's furniture. But his distinctive design language and his whole approach to design would eventually bring him on a collision course with the main trend in the trade.

In 1945, Finn Juhl quit his job at Vilhelm Lauritzen partly to start out on his own, and partly to become the principal, or senior teacher as it was called, of the School of Interior Design on Frederiksberg. Now he used his great experience in designing interiors to take on big jobs in this area as well as being an exhibition architect. He designed Bing & Grøndahl's store on Amagertorv in Copenhagen. But he got his laurels in 1950 when he was asked to do the interior design of the Trusteeship Council Chamber at the UN headquarters in New York. It was a huge job and a challenge for him as a 38-year-old. From 1952–57 he also designed Georg Jensen's shops in New York, Toronto and London, and as of 1956 he worked on designing 33 SAS offices in Europe and Asia. Furthermore he worked as an exhibition architect for many years both at home and abroad, and among the exhibitions he designed 15 were international ones, many of which were touring exhibitions on Danish design.

Finn Juhl was one of the most internationally oriented Danish architects of the time, and he was the first Danish furniture architect who started an industrial production of furniture in the US in 1951. This was at Baker Furniture. Today the relatively small and young furniture company called Hansen & Sørensen have taken over all the rights to Finn Juhl's furniture.

FINN JUHL, 1912–39, architect and furniture designer. Finn Juhl studied at the Royal Academy of Fine Arts in Copenhagen from 1930 to 1935 under Kay Fisker.

From 1934 to 1945, Juhl worked for Vilhelm Lauritzen on the design of the interior of Radiohuset (the Radio House) in Copenhagen and Copenhagen Airport in Kastrup. In 1945 he started his own architectural practice and also became the principal of the School of Interior Design on Frederiksberg. Juhl designed a few buildings, but it was as a designer of furniture and rooms and as an exhibition architect that he had the most success. He designed the interior and furnishing of the Trusteeship Council Chamber in the UN building in New York from 1951 to 1952 and he designed several SAS offices all over the world. Furthermore he designed the Georg Jensen shops in New York, Toronto and London from 1952 to 1957. Finn Juhl's furniture is sculpturally elegant and characterised by his great interest in art. Among other distinctions, he was awarded the Eckersberg Medal in 1947.

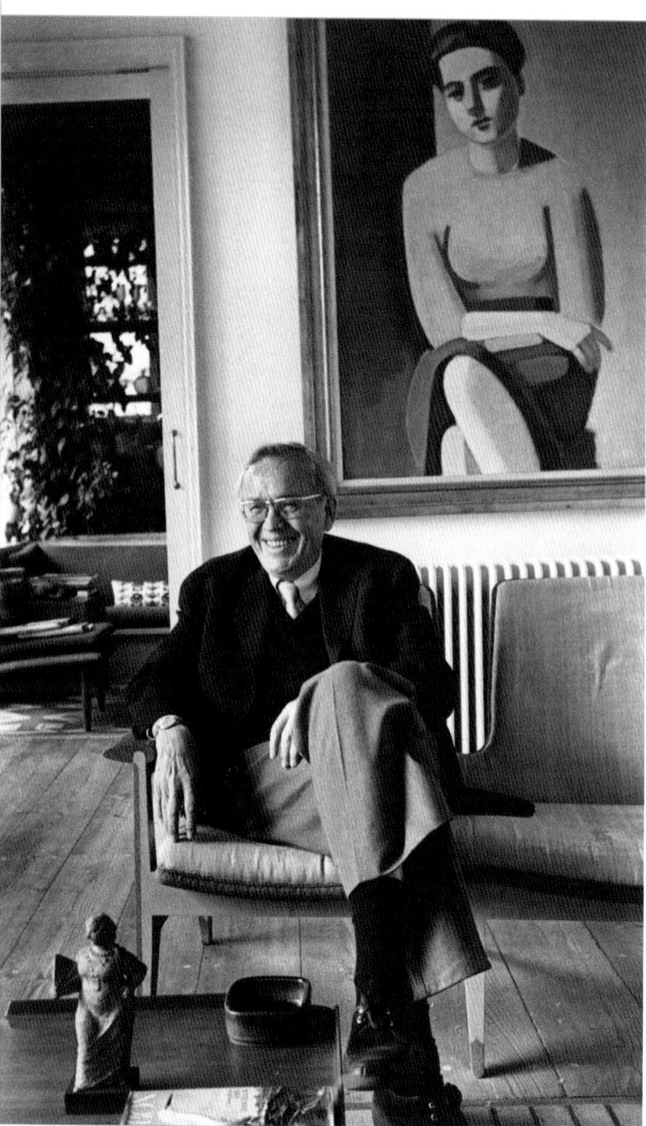

▲ *Finn Juhl photographed in his home in 1982.*

ARNE JACOBSEN

Another architect who like Finn Juhl wasn't educated as a furniture designer was Arne Jacobsen. In contrast to Juhl, Jacobsen was primarily a building architect who saw furniture and other fixtures as a small, but important part of the whole project. In this way he carried on a Danish architectural tradition that includes, for example, Martin Nyrop's city hall in Copenhagen from 1889 for which specially designed furniture was made. Another example is Carl Petersen and Kaare Klint's Faaborg Museum from 1912–15. In some projects Arne Jacobsen took this tendency to the fullest extent. For the Royal Hotel in Copenhagen from the late 1950s he went so far as to design the cutlery for the restaurant.

When the architect designs everything for a building, one often uses the German expression 'Gesamtkunstwerk' or total design. In Arne Jacobsen's case with the Royal Hotel it is said that his desire to control the final design was so great that even after the hotel opened he would gently move the tables in the restaurant into line when he came by. An early example is one of Jacobsen's first projects called the House of the Future from 1929 which he designed with Flemming Lassen for the Architects' Building and Home Exhibition. Not only the house but also the furnishings and technical solutions were designed. A type of helicopter (an autogyro) was placed on the roof, a speedboat was in the underground port and an electric oven was in the basement for burning household waste. Furthermore the house was fully furnished with built-in closets, bunk beds in the children's rooms and other furniture. A chair has been preserved from this project; it's a wicker easy chair from the roof terrace, and its nickname is the Black Slug.

▼ *The easy chair nicknamed the Black Slug was made in several versions, but it wasn't mass produced. It was for the terrace of the House of the Future in 1929 and was awarded third place in a competition that had been arranged the same year by the Basketmakers' Association. Architect and writer Poul Henningsen reviewed Arne Jacobsen's chair critically in a periodical, 'This man doesn't think in terms of chairs and tables but in nice lines. And he did supply the poor master basketmaker with a nice line.'*

ARNE JACOBSEN, 1902–71, was both architect and industrial designer. Jacobsen became internationally famous, also outside professional circles, for his functionalist architecture and his furniture and product design. He graduated from the Royal Academy of Fine Arts in Copenhagen in 1927 and in the course of his long career he designed a number of renowned buildings such as the Bellavista complex in Klampenborg, Aarhus City Hall and the Royal Hotel in Copenhagen. Arne Jacobsen was especially known for his total solutions, designing everything from the building to the door handles. Many of these designs were mass produced, and some of them still are, for instance the chairs the Ant, the Seven, the Egg and the Swan, among others. He also designed the Stelton service Cylinda-Line and the Vola plumbing fixtures. Jacobsen was a professor at the Royal Academy of Fine Arts in Copenhagen from 1956–65, and he was awarded the Eckersberg Medal, the C.F. Hansen Medal and Prince Eugen's Medal.

▾ *Arne Jacobsen furnished the Bellevue Theatre with his own design for the chairs and wall coverings. The row of seats go up and down. The back rest is made of laminated veneer. Notice in the picture on the right how the auditorium ceiling has been rolled back so the audience can get some air during the performance on hot summer nights.*

In the real world, Arne Jacobsen shows his preference for total design for the first time with his white Bellavista buildings from 1934–35 and the adjoining Bellevue Theatre. In the theatre you can still see Jacobsen's undulating line of chair backs going up and down and in and out. The chairs are made of laminated layers of veneer that have been moulded and dried in a specially made tool that gives the shells the desired curve. Afterwards they were sawed into shape, and when they were mounted shoulder to shoulder, they create the characteristic undulating rows.

The walls and ceiling of the auditorium are lined with canvas whereas the balcony is covered by thin bamboo stalks. A section of the ceiling could slide open so the audience could sit under the open sky on warm summer evenings. This is one of many examples of how Arne Jacobsen endeavoured to design a total experience for the users of his architecture. It's almost like scenography that's in front of the stage.

The Ant and the others

Arne Jacobsen was probably the Danish architect who had the most buildings built in the 20th century, and who also consistently tried to characterise the buildings with his design. Only rarely did Arne Jacobsen design furniture that wasn't specified for a particular building. One of these cases turned out to be one of his greatest successes. In 1952 he designed an odd little chair that consisted only of a wooden shell seat and back and three skinny tubular steel legs. He made a model of the chair out of cardboard and wire and took it to Fritz Hansen, one of the few furniture factories at the time in Denmark. They shook their heads and said they'd have nothing to do with it. It would be too expensive to develop, and furthermore they didn't think it would sell very well ...

THE ANT AND the Seven are the two shell chairs by Jacobsen that have been in production since they were first launched in 1952 and 1955, respectively. They have been made in many versions, and the colours have changed with the times. The chairs can, or could, also come with fabric or leather upholstery, and the legs have been varied – shiny chrome-plate was standard from the beginning, while matt chrome-plate and plastic-coated have also been used. A model called Grand Prix with laminated wooden legs was also developed.

Below is a selection of Arne Jacobsen's laminated shell chairs from the 3000 series. From left: The original Ant from 1952 (model no. 3100) with three legs; today four are the norm. The Seven from 1955 (3107), here with armrests. In the middle is the Tongue from 1955 (3102), which is the only one that can't be stacked. Next to the Tongue is The Grand Prix chair from 1957 (3130), which is the only chair that is made completely of wood, but it was also made in a version with steel legs. To the far right is model 3208 from 1970, which is nicknamed the Sea Gull. It was designed for the Danish National Bank and was only in production for a short time since many of the shells had to be rejected by the factory because the curve was too steep for the veneer.

THE SOFA WITH the not very sexy name of 3300 was designed in 1966 and used in Rødovre City Hall, which was finished the same year. It consists of modules that have the width of a person, so in principle it can be extended ad infinitum. This angular artistic idiom isn't typical of Jacobsenian sitting furniture. Like much of Finn Juhl's sitting furniture, one can talk about the load-bearing and borne elements. The seemingly slight frame forms a load-bearing frame for the upholstered elements. This sofa was also used in the rooms and public lounges at the Royal Hotel, and it is still sold by Fritz Hansen. The picture shows the prototypes of the furniture series AJ 3300 photographed at the Round House in Sjællands Odde. Arne Jacobsen designed the house for the smokehouse owner Henriksen in 1956. In its form the house is related to the House of the Future, which Arne Jacobsen designed in 1929 with Flemming Lassen for a housing and building exhibition in Forum in Copenhagen.

The architect put the model in a corner of his practice where it remained until the director of Novo came by shortly after for a meeting about the new factory that Arne Jacobsen was designing for the company. He saw the model and began enthusiastically to ask about it. Jacobsen seized the opportunity and said the chair was designed for Novo's new canteen. Shortly after Fritz Hansen agreed to start a production of the 200 chairs for Novo. Afterwards it came on the market and became a big success. Later on the series was expanded with new models such as the Seven (its product number is 3107 and the back's silhouette looks like the number 7), which is the only chair that became as popular as the Ant. In all, over seven million of Arne Jacobsen's shell chairs have left the factory in Allerød. If anything, this chair is a symbol of the light, poetic and yet practical Danish functionalism that existed after World War II.

The Ant was typical of Arne Jacobsen in that he constantly challenged the technical limits of industrial production. He seldom gave up if he thought he was right about something being feasible. Most likely he wasn't always easy to work with. A chair like the Ant hadn't been made before. In the US, laminated veneer had been used for stretchers during the war, and since then the designer couple Ray and Charles Eames had made furniture using this technology, but no one had made such a large laminated piece that also curved in two directions. And this was the challenge, and that's why both the Ant and later on the Seven had such narrow waists since this was where the wooden layers had to be able to bend when the seat was moulded into shape. Arne Jacobsen wanted the smallest dimensions possible; the thinnest shell and the slimmest legs. When the Ant came on the market it was so sensationally diminutive that especially elderly people refused to sit down on it because they thought it would collapse beneath them.

The Royal Hotel

The Ant and the other shell chairs were not the end of Arne Jacobsen's organic artistic idiom. A few years later, in the late 1950s, Arne Jacobsen started designing one of his greatest works ever, the Royal Hotel for SAS in downtown Copenhagen. Once again there was the opportunity to design new chairs. Except for the relatively angular sofa with the anonymous name of 3300, all the furniture for the hotel project was designed for the occasion. The best known today are the Egg and the Swan. The Pot chair also came on the market while the chairs called the Drop and the Giraffe did not and are only known today in collector and professional circles.

Today the Egg is one of the most coveted easy chairs, both as used copies at auctions as well as new ones from the factory. Once again, Arne Jacobsen started something that was technically unresolved, namely whether it was possible to make such a big shell, upholster it, mount it on a frame and get the whole construction to bear the weight of a human being. It was achieved by casting the shell in hard polyurethane foam, then mounting the swivel foot and finally by padding the chair in a relatively traditional way, and finally upholstering it with fabric or leather. The chair didn't look like anything one had seen before. Some of the furniture that the Eames couple and the Finnish architect Eero Saarinen developed can, in all fairness, be sources of inspiration, and otherwise it's the classic wing chair that Børge Mogensen also made a version of that comes the closest to this type. The Egg feels like a room within a room, a kind of cave that you want to ensconce yourself in, even if you aren't a child, while you waited in the foyer of large, square Royal Hotel.

The Swan can be perceived as the little sister of the Egg. It's manufactured in roughly the same way, but it's a much more open and sociable chair to sit in.

THE EGG AND the Swan are together seen as the climax of Arne Jacobsen's furniture production. The Egg is a cave-like room within the room, modelled like the way a sculptor would make a sculpture, while the Swan is the elegant floating chair whose form to a degree stems from the Seven, especially the narrow waist and the shape of the back. Note the difference between the feet of the two chairs. The Egg, right, has the original solid-cast foot just like Arne Jacobsen designed it, while the Swan has a newer version that the manufacturer Fritz Hansen introduced in the 1970s. In the latter version, a metal cylinder goes down into the cross-shaped foot supposedly because suspension was added to give a little when you sit down. Inveterate collectors of classic Danish designed furniture naturally prefer the original version.

If you should find the Egg a bit too bulky and cavernous, you might prefer the airborne elegance of the Swan. The two chairs together with especially the Pot and the Drop are in their form diametrical opposites of the very functionalist, square and geometrical hotel building that Arne Jacobsen designed for SAS. He had a flair for creating an environment that, on the one hand, was internationally sophisticated, and on the other hand, had a welcoming feel to it. There was an elegant kind of tension between the two facets of the interior of the Royal Hotel. Today the interior has been renovated several times, so although the Egg and Swan are still used, the lobby interior doesn't look the way Jacobsen originally designed it.

FURNITURE CONTROVERSY

Over the years, Danish society had developed. The social indignation and political movements from the 1920s that had led to FDB's policy of better and cheaper furniture as well as the social housing around World War II were slowly being replaced by something else. The one-bedroom apartment that had been shown at the annual exhibition of the Cabinetmakers' Guild in 1930 had in 1934 already progressed to a little one-family house and, despite the world war, into a two-bedroom apartment in 1945. In 1963 it led to Grete Jalk's electronic entertainment unit for the modern living room. The crisis-stricken society, characterised by shortages from the inter-war period, was quickly becoming the welfare society of the 1960s with surplus, if not abundance. Grundtvig's old ideal of 'Few have too much and even fewer too little' was coming true.

During this new period there was also a fierce debate among architects and designers about the developments. While some stuck to the previous social and functionalist ideals, others criticised them. The criticism was especially aimed at the idea that early functionalism had created a kind of congregation and had become formalism. One of the people who wondered whether the Klint school hadn't outlived itself was Finn Juhl. He wasn't blind to the social aspects that had interested the profession especially in the beginning, and he had himself chosen to attend Kay Fisker's department at the Royal Academy. Here the emphasis was put on assignments on designing good housing for people of modest income.

But in the area of furniture, Juhl went his own way as he phrased it in a lecture with the title 'Past, Present, Future' at the Museum of Art & Design in 1949 where Professor Klint was present, 'Almost everyone works for the museum and very few for development and for life. Denmark is becoming one big museum of art and design where everyone is a custodian or an assistant who dusts each other off and categorises.' And he continues in the same lecture, 'The strict and traditionally based education that arts and crafts are given in this country don't leave much room for the personal task of liberating oneself.' He continues, 'Knowledge and taste are prescribed. When there is no development, there is stagnation which is the same as going backwards because everything in life is in motion. You can't keep the artistic idiom of arts and crafts at a 150–200-year-old stage by force and still have the right to claim that you work rationally.'

Finn Juhl went on to praise Kaare Klint for using the English and Chinese models for revision and inspiration since it 'was an artistic feat in itself in light of the exaggerations of Art Nouveau, but Klint's fundamental contribution was the rational study that lay at the root of the design of these furniture types.

GRETE JALK (1920–2005) got her apprenticeship as a cabinetmaker in 1943, then attended the School of Arts & Crafts and continued at Kaare Klint's School of Furniture at the Royal Academy. Grete Jalk's most famous piece of furniture is this little easy chair from 1963. It consists of two laminated shells of Oregon pine that are bolted together (see below). Unfortunately, this chair, which has Japanese affinities, was never produced on a large scale. The same year she designed a special unit that hung on the wall and was called 'Watch and Listen' with two easy chairs to put in front of it. A critic called it 'The entertainment wall of the welfare society'. Grete Jalk had found some of the best designed entertainment equipment of the time and built a unit for it. In the new welfare state, one could sit and enjoy the new media. In 1987 she published the book *Dansk Møbelkunst gennem 40 år* (40 years of the art of Danish furniture).

I am not claiming that this rational work isn't continued haphazardly, but I am claiming that what characterises the craft today is the artistic idiom – that is, pure formalism – which is heading in the complete opposite direction to the original idea behind Kaare Klint's efforts. He is highly responsible for this development since his joy of toying with mathematics has resulted in furniture where the rational has no influence, like for instance a bed whose upper planes and curves can accommodate a sphere.'

Considering how early on this criticism was voiced, it's unusually harsh and clear sighted. It was phrased decades before the first architectural theorists in the US criticised functionalism for being misanthropic, boring and indeed formalistically bound to geometrical aesthetics – this is the criticism that eventually led to postmodernism. In actual fact, Juhl contested the Klint school's monopoly on deciding what was sensible and rational design. Finn Juhl was more sculptural in his expression, which often displeased his colleagues. The debate surged back and forth, and in 1961 the furniture architects Børge Mogensen and Arne Karlsen wrote an article for the periodical *Dansk Kunsthåndværk* (Danish Arts and Crafts) in which they defended Klint and the tradition of the Academy's School of Furniture. They set the tone in the very beginning by going back in time and quoting Poul Henningsen from the Critical Revue in 1927:

'Dear friends in the arts and crafts. How can you expect us to keep our respect for you as long as the swindle goes on in the name of art while all the modern tasks remain undone? We have neither a proper water glass nor a plate nor a water service or a knife, fork or spoon – but the more well-off homes are full of all kinds of rubbish at fantastical prices. Pull yourselves together and take a look at the tasks that entail making things that people can enjoy in their everyday lives. Take off your artistic hat and tie and put your work clothes on. Forget about artistic accomplishments. Just make one single article each that can be used. There's plenty of work to do and there's a huge market for it and lots of money to make.'

Mogensen and Karlsen's point was that PH and Klint were in agreement about functional and decent design. In the article, the designer Jens Quistgaard (see page 97) is criticised as is the advertising business, but also Verner Panton and Finn Juhl get a scolding, and all of them are decadent. As it said in the article, 'There is an advanced decline in the fact that the practitioners of a field of applied arts almost as one turn all their attention to the population's surplus shopping and thus they only seek to fulfil their pipedreams instead of finding and satisfying their actual needs.' Finn Juhl's interiors are described as 'perfumed' in the article and, 'It's the bad habits of the time and not its will to be cleansed that Finn Juhl has latched on to. It surprises us that these pieces of furniture were featured at the exhibition of the Cabinetmakers' Guild – one would have rather expected to see them at Lysberg, Hansen & Therp's show window on Bredgade.'

Børge Mogensen and Arne Karlsen expressed opinions that were very prevalent in their generation of architects and designers, namely that the content and not the form was important both in life and in products and furniture. The suitable content would also show up on the outer fringes of design. Finn Juhl thought that it was an excellent starting point, but what if the furniture was only functional on the surface? Can't other people design furniture that has a sculptural appearance as long as it functions well? Poul Henningsen was unintentionally drawn in to the discussion by

▾ *Poul Kjærholm's chair with the model number PK 12 is made of the same material and with the same technique as those used for the chairs for the concert hall at the Louisiana Museum of Modern Art. The chair is made of maple and the seat and back are woven.*

Mogensen and Karlsen, and he voiced his opinion in a special debate issue of the periodical Mobilia a few months later:

'But as slightly implicated in the dispute I do have some reservations about being appointed a pioneer along with Kaare Klint. We were rather serious opponents, and it was his famous Faaborg chair that I was criticising in Critical Revue in 1927 when I balanced a bentwood chair on my index finger ... The Faaborg chair was an untouchable work of art, a monument of something that has never been sacred to me, a beautiful ruin that you couldn't sit on without a retrospective sadness ... But those of us at Critical Revue had a different opinion of quality. We felt it was wrong to make by hand what could be made by machine. Therefore is must be Verner Panton whose works in modern materials can be manufactured in factories that carries the torch of Critical Revue onward ... Fortune and particularly foreign currency has for a number of years let us play with the noble craft that was so significant to Kaare Klint. For a while we have had the world's rich citizens as our customers. Is it now not time for the big task which has hitherto not been done: Useful furniture for the common man as an applied art?'

In some areas the fronts from the 1920s were still drawn in the same place 35 years later. And in many ways there is still a schism in Danish furniture design today between the elaborately expensive and the common sensical and useful. But this is current history so we'll have to wait and see ...

POUL KJÆRHOLM

Ever since Poul Henningsen and Mogens Lassen's short flirt with furniture made of steel tubing during the 1930s, there weren't any designers that had

◀ PK 25 – Poul Kjærholm's graduation project from 1952 at the School of Arts & Crafts in Copenhagen. The frame of the chair is bent from a steel plate from which all superfluous material is pared away. Afterwards the steel was plated in matt chrome. The seat and back are made of flag halyard, the end of which deliberately hangs down to indicate that it's one long piece of running halyard. The curve of the legs and the feet that are turned outwards are reminiscent of the Klismos Chair.

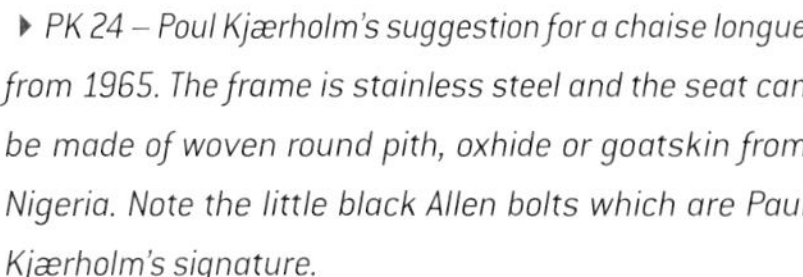

▶ PK 24 – Poul Kjærholm's suggestion for a chaise longue from 1965. The frame is stainless steel and the seat can be made of woven round pith, oxhide or goatskin from Nigeria. Note the little black Allen bolts which are Paul Kjærholm's signature.

designed furniture in metal. The annual exhibitions of the Cabinetmakers' Guild prepared the ground especially for furniture designed in wood. Of course there had been the odd chrome-plated chair leg now and then, but furniture where metal had been the dominant material, no, that had rarely been seen, and the ones that had been weren't very successful. But one day, in 1952, a newly qualified designer and his graduation project from the School of Arts & Crafts would show that it could be done. The skilled cabinetmaker and young designer was Poul Kjærholm.

The chair that he designed at the school in 1951 and that was finished as a prototype the following year was very unusual in its day. It was created around the same time that Arne Jacobsen designed the Ant, which also had legs made of chrome-plated steel, but otherwise was made of wood. Kjærholm's chair, which he called PK 25, had a frame of matt chrome-plated steel but the seat and back were made of one long piece of flag halyard. The special thing about the construction of the frame was that it was made out of one sheet of steel that was first given slits so it could be bent into the final shape of the frame. It was a very different way of making furniture, especially at that time. The finished PK 25 also looked very different from other furniture available then, with both Finn Juhl and Arne Jacobsen working with organic forms as a conscious contrast to the straight lines and flat walls of a house. Young designers, like Kjærholm, tried instead to create simplicity and order in the rooms by making stringent furniture characterised by straight lines.

Poul Kjærholm's graduation project was in many ways typical of his career. Although he was a skilled cabinetmaker and had worked at Wegner's architectural practice as a student, steel was his preferred material. With regard to choice of material and type of chairs, he was strongly influenced by Mies van der Rohe's furniture (see page 47). Kjærholm's most famous and popular chair, PK 22 from 1955, has often been compared to the Bauhaus guru's Barcelona chair from 1929. But the Danish designer adapted PK 22 and all his other furniture in his own way. Kjærholm's method is not only different on a technical level, but also his view of the function of furniture differs. Mies made his Barcelona chair a little bit too big for the human frame (it was designed for the Spanish king so it was a prestigious chair), and he used mirror-like chrome plate and heavy padding. This made his chair look at bit ostentatious. Kjærholm didn't like that at all and made his PK 22 more modest in size and finish.

This modesty is in no way the same as saying that Kjærholm's furniture was poor in quality or ambition. On the contrary, he was practically obsessed with things being perfect regarding his own work, the design and the manufacturer's work. As regards the latter, he found a good partner in the manufacturer Ejvind Kold Christensen, who was just as dedicated as Kjærholm was. In the beginning, the furniture was made of matt chrome-plated steel, but in 1982 Fritz Hansen took over the production of Kjærholm's collection and began to use stainless steel. The difference is hard to see. Kjærholm's signature is the characteristic joints that are visible in the form of little black chromatised Allen bolts.

At the early age of 23 Kjærholm had finished his education at the School of Arts & Crafts in Copenhagen and was almost immediately hired as a teacher at the very same school. Besides teaching he was affiliated with the furniture manufacturer Fritz Hansen as a kind of external product developer, but hardly any of the furniture he made models of at the time

◂ *PK 22 is the most popular of Kjærholm's chairs and is also considered his best and most classic chair. The frame was originally made of matt chrome-plated steel, but today it's made of stainless steel while the seat and back are made of either round pith, canvas or leather.*

found favour at the factory. This disappointment made Kjærholm skeptical about the industry's lack of vision, but luckily he met Kold Christensen. Later on, Kjærholm was employed as an assistant at the Royal Academy of Fine Arts, Furniture School, and in 1974 he took over Ole Wanscher's professorship, which Kaare Klint was the first to hold at the Academy.

Most of his furniture is made of steel rods with a square profile. However, what he subscribed to then and in the future was a very considered, precise and unsentimental minimalism. It was closely related to the international functionalism that prevailed in avant-garde circles. He phrased it this way, as if 'it's the language of the materials that I want to express'. This was also reflected in his choice of unstained leather instead of, for example, black leather since the patination of unstained leather had more charm he thought. His design was never popular, although Fritz Hansen sells about 4000 of his PK 22's a year.

Poul Kjærholm also worked with materials other than steel and round pith. His black shell chair in two parts, PK 0, is made of laminated wood and is very organic. This chair is from 1952, but only a limited number came into production in 1997 by Fritz Hansen. Moreover, Kjærholm worked in 1954 with some interesting outdoor furniture for lay-bys for Hjørring County Highway Authority. The shells were cast in concrete and were meant to suit the landscape beautifully with the frame partly buried in the grass so they looked like they had grown out of the soil. However, only about 100 were actually manufactured.

VERNER PANTON

Another designer who disagreed with the conception that all furniture should be made out of wood was Verner Panton. He was almost the same age as Kjærholm, but that's about all they had in common. Panton graduated as an architect from the Royal Academy of Fine Arts in 1951, and at that time he had already started working at Arne Jacobsen's architectural practice. Among other things, he worked on the development of the Ant chair that was finished and named the following year. In 1952 he started out on his own and worked on furniture made of steel tubing and with ideas about collapsible and portable houses. One result was a chair for Tivoli. His creativity and lack of respect for conventions soon led him away from Europe. He furnished a VW van with a bed and drawing table for a while, so he could work his way through the world although business was slow in the beginning.

In addition to some work with furnishing restaurants, including his parents' Kom-igen Kro (Come Back Inn) on Funen, he got the opportunity of designing some furniture. Panton's first example of really different furniture design was the Cone Chair with a matching table that was presented for the first time to the public in 1957 at the Danish Fair in Fredericia. The chair caused a sensation, and rightly so, but not only because of its unusual design, but because Panton had hung the furniture upside down from the ceiling so the visitors had to look up to see it. His very logical reason for doing so was that since there were so many people, you couldn't see what was on the floor anyway. This desire to play with the creative possibilities of the room was characteristic of Panton. One of the few places in Denmark where this could be seen was in the Copenhagen Circus building, which Panton furnished and chose the colour scheme for in 1984.

▾ *PK 0. – One of Poul Kjærholm's relatively few pieces of wooden furniture. A black-lacquered shell chair in two parts made of laminated veneer. It was designed in 1952 and produced in a numbered series of 600 by Fritz Hansen in 1997 on the occasion of the company's 125th anniversary.*

▾ *Verner Panton's Heart Chair displayed in his own home. It consists of a metal sheet that is shaped into a cone and padded with foam rubber and upholstered with fabric. The first version of the Heart Cone Chair didn't have the Mickey Mouse ears, as some people called them, but looked more like an old-fashioned ice cream cone without the ice cream. A version made of a net of chrome-plated steel lattice was also made.*

VERNER PANTON (1926–98) was an architect and designer who, after graduating from the Royal Academy of Fine Arts in 1951, worked for Arne Jacobsen and others. He started his own architectural practice in 1955 designing furniture, lighting, furnishings, exhibitions, textiles and products for the home. He experimented with new materials, especially plastic, and with new bright colours. His designs appealed to the imagination, the senses and was often humorous. His milieus were often total installations that should preferably be experienced by the body. In 1963 he settled in Basel, Switzerland. His most important partners were the companies Vitra (the Panton Chair from 1967), Fritz Hansen, the lighting company Louis Poulsen (among others, the FlowerPot lamp) and the chemical and textile company Bayer.

Very quickly Panton was responsible for some of the most spectacular furnishings of rooms that had ever been seen, and this opened opportunities abroad as well. For example in Trondheim, Norway, he was given the job of furnishing the Hotel Astoria in 1960. Here he used his newest development of the Cone Chair, namely the Heart Cone Chair, which was given its name because of the big Mickey Mouse-like ears that had been added. His wildest job as a room designer was for the German industrial corporation Bayer. They asked Panton twice, in 1968 and 1970, to furnish their exhibitions at a fair to promote their latest synthetic textile Dralon. This took place on a small ship on the Rhine at Cologne where the annual German furniture fair Orgatec was held. Panton designed some exhibition milieus that went down in history as some of the most psychedelic and hippie-like ever. They were called Visiona 0 and Visiona 2. The rooms were furnished from top to bottom with organically shaped furniture, and the walls were covered in bright and richly coloured textiles and indirect lighting.

One result of these wild exhibitions was the lofty lounging piece of furniture called Living Tower from 1969. It is still manufactured and for sale at Verner Panton's old partner, Vitra in Switzerland. Vitra was also the company that dared to manufacture the chair for which Panton is most famous. It's mostly known as the Panton Chair and is one of the world's first chairs to be made out of one piece of plastic, although it took several years to solve all the technical problems. It wasn't just a chair made of plastic, which back then wasn't as technically well tested as it is today, but it was also a chair without back legs, which caused major constructive problems. The first designs and prototypes began taking shape around 1960, but it wasn't until 1967 that Panton and Vitra could launch the first small series of the chair.

◀ *The Panton Chair, one of the world's first chairs to be made of one piece of plastic, had its difficult beginnings in 1960 and has now been made in a new type of plastic in 1999 (see picture left). At first it was made of fibreglass, but today it's made of 'real' plastic – injection-moulded polypropylene.*

▶ *Living Tower is the closest you can get today to Verner Panton's renowned exhibitions from the 1960s with totally designed rooms and wild experiences of colours, light and organic forms – like reality on LSD.*

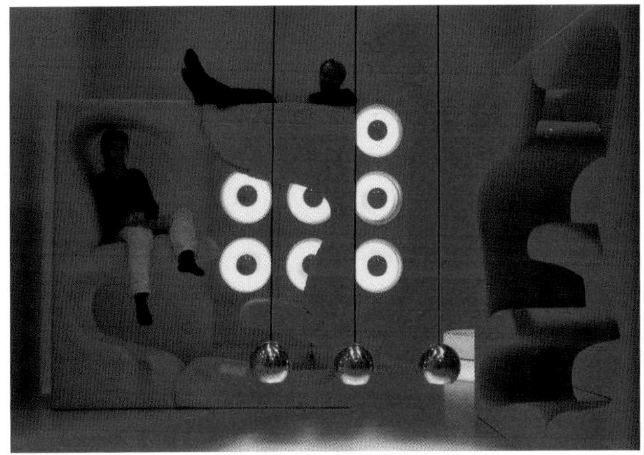

At first it was made of fibreglass and later other plastic types were used. Today you can buy the original but expensive shiny version in fibre-reinforced polyester and the mould-injected version with a matt finish which is even cheaper than the first two.

The prevailing myth about Verner Panton is that he was practically deported from Denmark because of the tall poppy syndrome. And even though he lived in Basel for many years, it's hard to see how this was possible, since he was good friends with Poul Henningsen, Arne Jacobsen and Nanna Ditzel. Of course he was attacked by Børge Mogensen and Arne Karlsen in the previously mentioned article from 1961, but Finn Juhl bore the brunt of their criticism, and Panton was defended by others. His problem and the reason why he left the country so often was rather that he had difficulty in finding companies in Denmark that were big enough to manufacture his designs. Many did not have the necessary technology or access to a market that was big enough to bear the considerable investments in development and machinery. In many ways, Panton was a colourful person that even wrote a book about colours. He wasn't very fond of the colour white; and he thought it was so boring that an extra tax should be imposed on white paint.

NANNA DITZEL

Nanna Ditzel was one of Verner Panton's very good colleagues and also a close friend. In many ways they shared the same professional interests, and although her design isn't as radical and groundbreaking as Panton's, she used colours a lot and experimented with total milieus (see page 207). She was a skilled cabinetmaker before she attended the School of Arts & Crafts from which she graduated in 1946. The same year she married her colleague Jørgen Ditzel, and together they ran a design office until his death in 1961. Nanna and Jørgen were very active participants in the annual exhibitions of the Cabinetmakers' Guild and often presented their newest ideas in this forum. The couple, and especially Nanna, was very inspired by Finn Juhl's artistic idiom and his approach to designing furniture and rooms rather than being inspired by the Klint school's philosophy.

Therefore Nanna and Jørgen Ditzel also cultivated the organic artistic idiom, and to free themselves from the traditional cabinetmaking methods, they designed some wicker furniture around the year 1950. Today we think of wicker furniture as suitable for a garden or a summer cottage, but back then it wasn't unusual to have it in your living room. One of the best examples of Ditzel's use of wicker furniture as innovative design is the egg-shaped and cave-like sitting furniture that can't stand on the floor, but has to be hung from the ceiling or from a tree in the garden. The couple made other projects in wicker, such as low reclining furniture, some of which was almost Japanese in style.

In the 1950s, Nanna in particular designed some characteristic silver jewellery for Georg Jensen, and they were very organic to look at too. After Jørgen Ditzel's death, Nanna ran the design office herself for a few years before moving to London with her new husband Kurt Heide. Here they ran the international furniture house Interspace. Nanna Ditzel was a bit out of touch with the Danish milieu while living in England although she kept her studio in Bagsværd and still had Danish customers. In 1985 Kurt Heide died, and she moved back to Denmark.

In the following years Nanna Ditzel continued designing imaginative and often colourful furniture and room installations. Her furniture was

The Trinidad chair from 1993 became Nanna Ditzel's bestseller. The graphic expression with the routed slots in the back and seat originated from inspirational sources in the Caribbean according to the designer herself. The chair is available in various versions regarding the finish of the steel tube frame and/or stained or painted veneer shells.

Bench for Two has a strong graphic expression that is very different from what Nanna Ditzel had designed before and what was typical of the time (1989). It's made of maple. The back is made of very thin veneer, so-called aeroplane veneer, onto which the graphics are silkscreen printed.

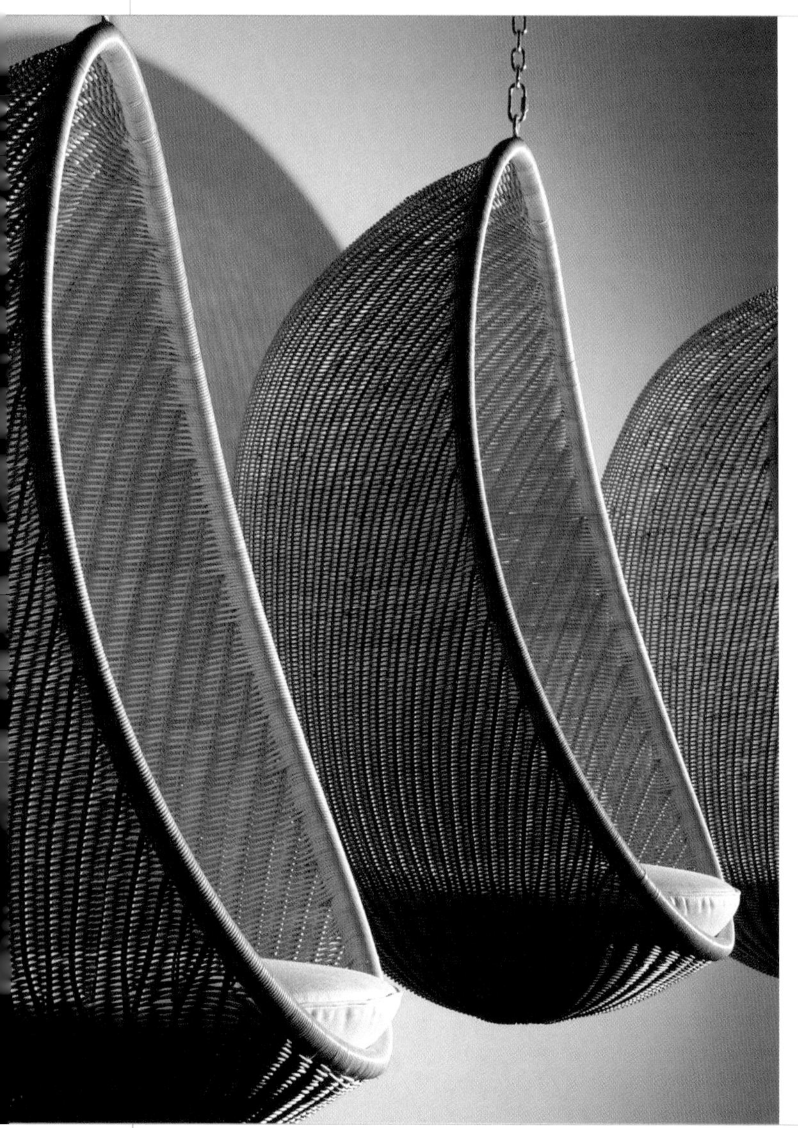

developed mostly with the help of Fredericia Furniture, for example Bench for Two from 1989. It has a strong graphic expression with the bull's eye silk screen print on the thin veneer of the backrests.

This little sofa with a matching table won the gold medal at a furniture exhibition in Japan in 1990. While this project was mainly an experiment that never became a great commercial success, it did lead to a closer collaboration with Fredericia Furniture. In 1993 Nanna Ditzel's most popular furniture ever was launched and that is the Trinidad chair. Its simple steel tube frame and thin veneer shells on the back and seat can be manufactured at an affordable price. With the help of new technology such as the computerised wood router it's possible to make the slots in the veneer shells much easier and quicker than before.

Ditzel has always sought the poetical aspect in her designs and often experimented with new technological possibilities. She has also been a pioneer in children's furniture, for example, see her Toadstools on page 141. There's also her playground furniture, which is a beautiful extension of her well-known 'reclining milieus' for adults. Here her congenial companionship with Verner Panton is apparent since they had a mutual understanding that adults should also play. One of her latest installations of low podiums and foam cushions could be seen at the Museum of Art & Design in Copenhagen in 2002. At that time she was 79 years old and still not too old to play.

Jørgen and Nanna Ditzel's version of the Egg? It was designed in 1957 at around the same time that Arne Jacobsen designed his famous chair, and was manufactured first by the Copenhagen wicker company R. Wengler, and since then in Italy and Japan.

NANNA DITZEL, 1923–2005. Furniture and interior designer educated at the School of Arts & Crafts 1942–46. She married Jørgen Ditzel (1921–61) with whom she designed furniture, textiles and jewellery (for Georg Jensen) in the 1950s. They won the silver medal at the Triennale in Milan in 1951, 1954 and 1957, and a gold medal in 1960. In 1956 they received the Lunning Prize. After Jørgen Ditzel's death she continued designing alone for a number of years until she married Kurt Heide and ran a design company with him in England for some years. She returned to Denmark in 1986 and designed furniture for Fredericia Furniture in particular. She has also designed the fabric Hallingdal, which is manufactured today by Kvadrat in Ebeltoft. Nanna Ditzel's design was characterised by organic forms, colourful milieus and harmonious proportions, often with a surprising or unexpected twist. She received the ID prize for her Trinidad chair and the Classic prize for the fabric Hallingdal (see page 169).

GUNNAR AAGAARD ANDERSEN

Included in the circle around Verner Panton and Nanna Ditzel in the 1950s and 1960s was the sculptor and designer Gunnar Aagaard Andersen (1919–1982). He attended both the School of Arts & Crafts in the late 1930s and the Royal Academy of Fine Arts during the war. He was interested not only in free art, but also in design through the use of experiments with industrial materials and constructions. From 1948 he was a member of the group of artists 'Linien II' with whom the Ditzels were also in contact in the 1950s. Aagaard Andersen, who was a professor at the Academy's School of Visual Arts from 1972 to 1982, also regularly visited the low furniture that Ditzel and Panton were working on. He tried to combine the different art forms on several occasions, for example, at Mads Eg Damgaard's factory (later on called Ege Carpets) in Herning in 1957 where he took on the roles of architect and sculptor. Furthermore he was a co-editor of the design periodical Mobilia for almost 20 years.

Aagard Andersen's own furniture experiments caused a big stir in design and architectural circles. This was particularly true of his bizarre chair made of expanding polyurethane foam. He poured the plastic mass on the floor of the factory and formed the chair without the use of a bearing frame or construction under the plastic mass. He made about ten chairs and a sofa in this way. Most of these pieces are in the art and furniture collections of museums around the world, such as at the Museum of Modern Art in New York. Aagaard Andersen also worked with wood furniture, and here too he tried to test the limits of the material.

▲ *Gunnar Aagaard Andersen experimented with materials and the senses when he worked, no matter whether he was doing art or more design-oriented things. His chair made of expanding foam caused a debate, and some found it scandalous. Is this supposed to be a chair? It looks like something the dog could have made. Nonetheless one of the ten-odd chairs that Aagaard Andersen made in this way is exhibited at the Museum of Modern Art in New York.*

POUL M. VOLTHER (1923–2001) was a furniture architect from the School of Arts & Crafts. Today he is mostly known for having designed the easy chair called Corona, which is still produced by Erik Jørgensen in Svendborg, and it was designed in the early 1960s. First it was made of oak instead of steel. Corona, like Arne Jacobsen's the Swan, has an artistic expression that indicates cool relaxation. For this reason it's been used in many fashion shoots, music videos and TV programs. The four organic upholstered shells are mounted on profiles of stainless steel. Volther also designed furniture for FDB Furniture before and after Børge Mogensen quit his job as head of the design office in 1950.

NEW HOUSING IDEALS

In the 1960s the economic boom heralded good times for most of the population in Denmark and most other countries in Western Europe. The social project, which many furniture designers and architects had become a part of during the lean times in the first half of the century, had been completed in many ways. The housing standard had risen significantly. Many people, skilled as well as unskilled workers, could now realistically dream of having a little house in the outskirts of the capital. Suddenly all these square metres of homes from the building boom in the 1960s and 1970s had to be furnished. How would this be done, and would the average Danish family buy the good architect-designed furniture when they loosened their financial belt?

From the inter-war period's social and political awakening and far into the 1960s, much of the information about housing conditions was characterised by what could be called 'well-intentioned agitation for common sense'. As mentioned before, Poul Henningsen and the periodicals Critical Review, Mobilia and Samvirke expended a lot of energy trying to convince the population of the benefits of the new ideals about simplicity, honesty in design and the functional way of furnishing one's home. All of it was with the best intentions and for the good of the people. But people couldn't shake off the feeling that there were still raised fingers and that the architects and furniture designers were trying to lay down the law.

Today it can be very entertaining to go to the library and read some of the oldest editions of the periodical Bo Bedre (Live Better) from the early 1960s. The first volumes show that there is still a housing shortage in Denmark, and there are many articles about 'how to furnish a two-bedroom apartment in the best way when you're a family of four'. But there are also articles on raising children, consumer rights, proper hygiene in the kitchen, and gradually also a lot of do-it-yourself items like 'How you can get more storage space by lowering the ceiling in your hall'. During the first years of Bo Bedre most people had got rid of the 'parlour', and now it was all about functionality. If the readers couldn't afford to buy furniture from the cabinetmaker, then Bo Bedre gave directions on how they could furnish a room themselves.

Only a few years previously, in the 1950s, even the foremost cultural avant-garde were into Danish handcrafted furniture. The author Klaus Rifbjerg wrote an essay in 1997 called *Tyngdens lethed* (The lightness of weight) about the furniture he and his wife were buying in a fine furniture store in 1955: 'There was an atmosphere of reverence everywhere, and we stood self-consciously quiet in front of every piece while our hands secretly glided over the polished wood, and we didn't want to make up our minds quickly because nothing must be over with quickly. This was our future we were securing in this store; the furniture we bought wasn't only to be a silent witness to our personal scenes from a marriage, it would be part of it. We didn't only marry each other, but also Wegner and Mogensen and all the others. That's the way it was; it couldn't be any other way; you are what you surround yourself with and what you sit and sleep on.'

Rifbjerg's analysis didn't come out of nowhere, it had sprung from the many years of general education of the public in furnishing and setting up house that culminated in the fifties. Magazines and newspaper articles dealt with these subjects, and books had been written to guide the public. For example, in 1953 Radio Denmark published a book called *Bosætningsbogen* –

LOW SLOTTED CHAIR designed by Bernt, whose real name is Bernt Petersen (b. 1937). This minimalist chair from the mid-1980s has a springiness that makes cushions superfluous. The seat and back consist of thin pieces of laminated plywood that taper off almost like leaf springs on a truck, and thus Bernt creates a flexibility that would otherwise have been difficult to achieve. The sides are made of solid wood and all together a minimal and surprising construction is formed. It's spray painted and the final result is a delicate and interesting chair. Bernt is a skilled cabinet-maker and studied at the School of Arts & Crafts. He was an associate professor at the Royal Academy of Fine Arts from 1977–85. In his own design office Bernt has designed furniture, products and exhibitions as well as auditorium furniture for the Bella Centre in Copenhagen, among others.

En grundbog for studiekredse (The book on setting up house – a textbook for study circles). The book was a compilation of articles by mostly architects who pedagogically covered what was needed to make a home cosy and not in the least functional. Similarly, in 1954, a book was published entitled *Hjemmets indretning* (Interior design of the home) written by Finn Juhl, who at the time was the head of the School of Interior Design. In it were a number of examples of how one could design one's home beautifully and appropriately, of course by using some of Finn Juhl's furniture, among other things.

The arrival of the sixties

The sixties brought more changes in Danish society. People had more money in their pockets, but also new norms for life and social intercourse were established. The young generation reacted to the ever-so-nice sofa group, which was also what Panton, Ditzel and Aagaard Andersen had tried to experiment their way out of during this period. As Verner Panton said in an interview with Henrik Sten Møller in 'The Politiken' on November 10, 1995, 'I can't stand entering a living room and seeing the sofa, coffee table and two chairs and at once knowing that this is where I'll be stuck for the whole evening. I made furniture that could be raised and lowered in the room so one could get a different view of the surroundings and a new angle on life.'

And once again the cultural radical Poul Henningsen sees where things are heading, and he doesn't mince his words in a review of the annual exhibition of the Cabinetmakers' Guild in 1961. He questions whether cabinetmaking by hand has any future at all. It still doesn't make sense to him as he writes, 'None of us mortals will pay 1200 kroner for a chair when we can get one that's just as comfortable for 58 kroner ... We must face the fact that any handcrafted work a person wants around him in the future he'll have to make himself if he isn't extremely rich. The rest will be art and priceless. Isn't that fair? Today when machines can even think for themselves and perform any old trick, the hands will be reserved for art.'

Apart from PH's foresight in 1961 when he can glimpse the computerised industrial machines on the horizon, he also heralds the hippie era. He is sick and tired of furniture and TV consoles made of teak and palisander and the constant keeping up with the Joneses as to who has the finest living room. In the end of his review he writes, 'If I were young today, I would find a second-hand furniture shop and buy ugly, but sturdy chairs for 10–15 kroner apiece. My girlfriend and I would agree to paint them a lovely colour – who knows, maybe thunder blue? And then a divan with upholstery in a jolly, solid colour – perhaps up against a white wall with a modern poster on it. For a table, a board and four ready-made legs. What more do two people need? The rest are just things one doesn't feel the right to be without.' A few years later the youth revolution breaks out, and beer crates make their entry into the communes. In light of this, all the fine handcrafted furniture, especially in exotic types of wood, smack of the bourgeois. For many years afterwards this furniture was a bit condescendingly called 'silver wedding furniture' at the design schools.

In 1966, the Cabinetmakers' Guild holds the last of its legendary exhibitions in Copenhagen. As PH had predicted five years before, they had had their day. Industry has taken over. The fine handcrafted furniture of the post-war era had fit the spirit of the times perfectly. After the barbarity of the war, the fine Danish furniture, much of which was designed in organic shapes, came and caressed the body and soul of modern man. A well-off

▸ *Rud Thygesen and Johnny Sørensen's café chairs from the 8000 series that are manufactured by the Magnus Olesen company are an example of the light furniture style of the 1980s.*

▾ *Jørgen Gammelgaard worked on many different projects such as a special bicycle and flatware. Only some of his more conventional pieces of furniture were manufactured, and among them was this armchair for the Schiang company. It's a fine interpretation of a classic dining room chair.*

cultural elite in Denmark as well as abroad loved the style and adopted it as their own. That was then, but now young people wanted something else. The style changes throughout the 1960s and 1970s with flower power, bookcases made of beer crates, tile-topped tables and stripped furniture from grandmother's time. This was a difficult time for functionalist furniture. And for a number of years, the Danish furniture industry is stuck with the dated image of traditional teak coffee tables. During this time, the magazine Bo Bedre functions as a sensitive seismograph. It effortlessly moves away from the aesthetic do-it-yourself solutions in the beginning to becoming the Danish version of *House Beautiful* today. Here we can find help to style our homes so they can really be presentable. It's a far cry from PH's ideals about naturalness.

For the cabinetmakers, manufacturers of designed furniture and especially for the furniture designers this downturn was like going cold turkey. The heart of the matter is that they never really understood why they were successful. Most of them probably believed that their great talent had put the world at their feet. They didn't see the psychological mechanisms behind the great demand for Danish designed furniture. And neither were the social visions of good furniture for everyone realised.

Handcrafted furniture was, as PH indicated, too expensive and much too exclusive for the general population. And since the industry didn't understand this, they hadn't a clue what to do when society and the times changed. One is tempted to use the parting words of the old Danish AFL-CIO boss Thomas Nielsen, 'We have triumphed like hell.'

NIELS JØRGEN HAUGESEN (b. 1936) is one of the few classic skilled cabinetmakers-cum-furniture architects who, like Poul Kjærholm, worked with designing furniture of metal. Haugesen graduated from the School of Arts & Crafts in 1961 and worked for Arne Jacobsen from 1966 until 1971. In 1977 he designed the X-line chair that apart from being metal was also very minimalist in its construction. The frame is made of 8 mm chrome-plated round steel, while the seat and back are made of perforated steel plate that is either chrome-plated or spray painted. This chair is probably the closest Danish furniture design got to the high-tech style of the 1970s and 1980s. It's still in production at the furniture factory Bent Krogh.

THE GENERATION AFTER DANISH DESIGN

In 1980, Professor Poul Kjærholm died at the early age of 51 and with him an era ended. Now almost all of the pioneers from the golden age of Danish design were either dead or retired. On the whole, Panton and Ditzel were the only ones left from that generation that had some good years left to work and create good designs in. Now it was time for the next generation to take over, and they were people like Bernt Petersen, Niels Jørgen Haugesen, Jørgen Gammelgaard, Rud Thygesen, Johnny Sørensen, Peter Hiort-Lorenzen and Johannes Foersom. At the Royal Academy of Fine Arts, School of Architecture in Copenhagen there was a lull and seven years would pass before the professorship in the Department of Interior Design and Furniture was filled again. This happened in 1987, and Jørgen Gammelgaard (1938–91) took the position.

In terms of education, Gammelgaard had gone all the way from a skilled cabinetmaker to attending the School of Arts & Crafts to studying at the Royal Academy. He was employed by Arne Jacobsen and Grete Jalk, among others, before he set up his own architectural practice in the early 1970s. Here he worked primarily on experimental furniture projects and product design, but far from all of them were put into production. He died after only four years as professor, and ever since the Royal Academy hasn't had a professor in this field. Kaare Klint's School of Furniture has been closed down and replaced by a department of design that is primarily related to construction, for example for building components, fixtures, signposting and the like.

Several long-lasting designer partnerships arose during this time. One of them was Rud Thygesen and Johnny Sørensen. Thygesen, who was born in 1932, was clearly older than Sørensen, who was born in 1944. Rud Thygesen attended the School of Arts & Crafts with a business background, while Johnny Sørensen was a skilled ship joiner. They both graduated in 1966 and established their own design office, which existed until 1994. During these years they designed some of the most commercially successful Danish furniture. In the beginning, things didn't go so well. Their 'King's furniture' from 1969 is greatly inspired by Klint's artistic idiom, and their little armchair, which was added to the series in 1985, owes much of its expression to the Faaborg chair. Their greatest success is probably the café chair from 1980 (see page 275) and matching table. The lightness of this chair has been compared to Thonet's bentwood chair, but otherwise it's very different in that it's laminated and made of light beech.

Another successful partnership is Johannes Foersom (b. 1947) and Peter Hiort-Lorenzen (b. 1943), who have pretty much the same educational background as 'Rud and Johnny', but are otherwise much more experimental. In 1977 they established their own design office and a working relationship that still exists. They have made their mark as two of Denmark's most renowned and successful furniture designers from the 1980s and onwards. For Erik Jørgensen's furniture factory they have designed a lot of furniture, and one piece is the interesting and successful little sofa called Rotor.

◂ *Johannes Foersom and Peter Hiort-Lorenzen designed the sofa Rotor. It consists of a seat and two shell backrests. Each shell is mounted under the seat with a swivel joint that allows the sofa to change from an ordinary sofa to a conversational piece of furniture where the two people are facing two different directions but are face to face in a modern version of the classic tête-à-tête.*

The room and furniture

In the history of man there have always been rooms of some type or other, even a primitive cave in the Stone Age. Furniture came shortly after: a well-organised place to sleep or a primitive chair to avoid sitting on the cold ground. Ever since, these two things, rooms and the furniture, have been interconnected. Furniture was often made for specific rooms, and rooms were made according to their use. When houses were built and divided into rooms, the idea of how to furnish the rooms was often a given. Rooms and furniture were like yin and yang, and furniture was made for the location. Not until the 20th century was furniture by and large mass produced to be sold on a market that perhaps was geographically far away. Consequently we have the development in which the individual piece of furniture has its own status that is isolated from the room it's meant to be in. And so it's very much up to the individual user to give the piece its own life by placing it wherever he wants and using it like he wants.

But homes should be furnished appropriately for people to thrive in them. For architects and furniture designers that had organised the many housing exhibitions in the first half of the 20th century it was an old realisation. These people and their exhibitions were perhaps condescending and overly pedagogical at times, but the idea was to introduce the population to alternatives to the old world and the overly decorated Victorian style. And this was the line that FDB adopted when they focused on supplying their members with functional furniture. Through the use of showrooms furnished like test apartments the co-operative company demonstrated what a home could look like. And that's why it's unfortunate that they were only partly successful. The effort was given up after Director Frederik Nielsen resigned and Børge Mogensen indicated he'd had enough.

When you look at the Swedish furniture giant IKEA, which was founded around the same time (1943), you can't help wondering what would have happened if FDB or other clever furniture folk with an industrial way of thinking had made a bigger effort and thought more clearly. Then there could have been a Danish alternative to IKEA that wasn't quite as inexpensive but had a better quality. And IKEA has understood that furniture has to be conceived in a context. Look at the IKEA catalogue that is actually a publication with the world's largest circulation – it even beats the Bible. The catalogue doesn't just picture single pieces of furniture, but gives visions of real living rooms, real bedrooms, children's rooms and kitchens. They do now what originally started with the one-bedroom apartment at the annual exhibition of the Cabinetmakers' Guild in Copenhagen in 1930. They create dreams. What Henry Ford was for the automotive industry, is what IKEA's founder Ingvar Kamprad (b. 1926) has been for the furniture business.

It's as what Verner Panton once said, 'The relationship to the surroundings is much more important than a single chair or some other article. The room, the colours, the furniture, the textiles and the lighting have to be conceived and experienced together. You can only create an attractive milieu if you master the big picture.' And perhaps that's what the furniture business and designers have forgotten. If you go to a Danish furniture show, whether it's in a store or at the annual furniture fair at the Bella Centre or even an exhibition at a design centre or a museum, you'll usually see a group of objects displayed. It's as if the many furniture designers and furniture companies focus so much on their own work or product that they don't give a thought to the big picture, let alone the real people who are actually going to use their furniture.

THE CONCRETE TABLE. A group of self-taught furniture designers are on the rise. They seem to be inspired by the success of Danish furniture and especially the more spectacular aspects of the design, such as the scenographic appeal that is the reason why chairs like the Egg, Swan and Corona have so often been used in photo shoots, music videos etc. One person who makes some very special furniture is Morten Voss (b. 1964) who became well known for his series of concrete tables from 1993. He calls them FlightDeck. The table tops are cast in cement (they come in several sizes) with the designer's logo 'Voss' moulded on the side. The legs come in different lengths, so the users can have both coffee and dining room tables. The legs are made of aluminium in a simplified Rococo style and are screwed onto the concrete slab. These tables are maybe the closest Danish furniture design has come to postmodernism. Morten Voss manufactures them himself, but most of the production is made by sub-suppliers.

IKEA'S DANISH DESIGNERS. For many years IKEA has used quite a few Danish designers. Some of them have only had a few assignments while others have practically been permanently employed by the gigantic Swedish furniture company. The ones who have been there the longest are people from the design office Pelikan Design in the middle of Copenhagen. The design office was established by Niels Gammelgaard and Lars Mathiesen in 1978, and at this point they had already had assignments for IKEA. Since then Pelikan has had lots of jobs for other companies, but IKEA has been there the whole time. While many of IKEA's earlier products didn't have a particularly high quality of design, they have raised the standard in the last 10–20 years. Pelikan has designed many of the products that were part of IKEA's 'Democratic Design' campaign. Items worth mentioning are the popular dining room table Moment (opposite) with its glass top and metal frame, and the little chair called Nevil (below) with a swivel plastic seat.

▾ *Louise Campbell's Casual Cupboards from 1999 were produced for a couple of years in two versions with straight shelves and winding compartments, respectively. The material is laminated veneer of light wood. Two sturdy rubber bands enveloping the oval form secure it from being scratched or tipping over.*

▸ *Kasper Salto's chair Runner consists of a steel frame and a slotted seat and back. The special way of routing the slits in the backrest allows the wood to curve in two directions and thus make a comfortable backrest. The chair was first developed with the Botium company, but was then sold to Fritz Hansen, who has discontinued its production in favour of Kasper Salto's latest chair project called Ice (middle). It's a true industrially manufactured chair with an aluminium frame and injection-moulded plastic pieces for the seat and back.*

▸ *The little table Micado can be taken apart by pulling the legs out of holes in the table top. Designed by Cecilie Manz for Fredericia Furniture.*

In a similar manner, a group of 46 manufacturers, architects and furniture designers began in 1981 to revive the Cabinetmakers' Exhibitions under the name SE (the Cabinetmakers' Autumn Exhibition). These exhibitions aren't thematic like the original exhibitions. There is no longer any ambition to design furniture for the general public. It's on a superficial level that furniture designers and furniture schools are trying to revive 'the good old days' and still hope that if only they're talented and clever enough, then fortune will smile upon them again and people will start buying expensive designer furniture again. The chance of that happening is minimal, at least on a large scale.

BODY HOLDER AND OTHERS

Some of the young furniture designers today get together in exhibition groups. The medium of exhibitions is an important forum for almost all furniture designers. This is where the design trade meets and where the Danish Arts Foundation checks out the talent they want to subsidise. Therefore it's necessary to take part in many exhibitions. One of the more spectacular initiatives in recent years was an experimental forum called Kropsholder (Body holder) which was also the framework around a professional women's network. From 1997 to 2000 these 15–20 young female designers arranged exhibitions and their initiative was the object of much attention. None of the exhibited furniture was much more than extremely artistic drafts that didn't have much of a chance of being manufactured. This initiative, like many other similar exhibitions in the last 10–15 years, was highly influenced by the artistic view of design and some radical experiments with materials, which is especially cultivated at Denmark's Design School in Copenhagen.

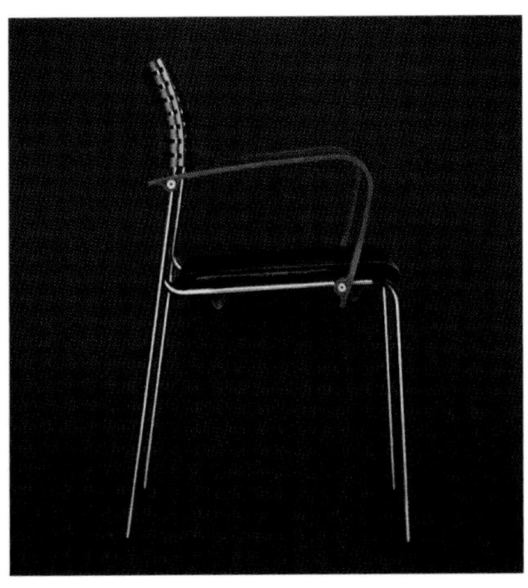

This crossover trend is very much inspired by the Swedish and English design milieus that try to link design and visual art together in a type of artistic installation. The functional qualities take a back seat. Whether the exhibited chairs are comfortable to sit in does not concern the designers very much; to them it's more important that the furniture looks good in an exhibition.

Today all the designers from Kropsholder make a living in their profession and have since then designed furniture that is more useful and production-friendly. One of them is Louise Campbell (b. 1970) who at times has been the unofficial spokeswoman for the group. She was one of the young designers that got the most exposure around the turn of the century. Today Louise Campbell's lamps and furniture are in production at places like Bahnsen, Hay and Stelton.

A typical furniture project by Louise Campbell is the 'casual cupboard' that, as she says herself, is for young people who live in a different way than previous generations. They move around more, and then they can tuck their closet under their arm and carry it. The cupboards are in production and come in two versions, one with straight shelves and one with curved ones. The wood can be either maple, ash or cherry, and there are two sturdy grey rubber bands around the laminated cupboard, so it doesn't scratch or get scratched from tumbling around the room. The cupboards can also be hung on the wall, but then they look more like a cabinet for CDs.

Cecilie Manz (b. 1972) is another member of Kropsholder that has made her mark, but perhaps not as imaginatively as Louise Campbell. Her design expression is more minimalist. One of her new pieces of furniture is the table Micado that won the Danish Design Centre's ID prize in 2004 and is now manufactured by Fredericia Furniture. It consists of a circular table top and three legs, and it can be assembled without tools or screws. The table top and the three legs lock in place when the table is set upright. Micado is available in solid ash, oak or cherry, and the table top is also available in black lacquered MDF.

There are other designers from the generation born in the 1960s and early 1970s. One of them is Kasper Salto (b. 1967). He got his apprenticeship as a cabinetmaker before attending Denmark's Design School from which he graduated in 1994. He also attended a design school in Switzerland before being employed by furniture architect Rud Thygesen. Kasper Salto's first success was the Runner chair with a relatively ordinary steel tube frame, while the seat and back are of wood. The backrest is special and demands a cabinetmaker's insight to construct. After it's been laminated, the slots are routed into the backrest so that it can bend in two directions. This is how the designer gets a visually interesting form and a backrest that is comfortable for the seated person. Later on, Runner was taken over by Fritz Hansen who also launched Salto's next chair project called Ice. This chair has a cast aluminium frame and mould-injected plastic shells for the seat and back.

Another example is Hans Sandgren Jakobsen (b. 1963) who was also a skilled cabinetmaker before heading for the furniture department at Denmark's Design School. In 1991 he started working as an assistant to Nanna Ditzel, who thought it was fine that he worked on his own furniture on the side. Since the mid-1990s Jakobsen has concentrated on his own design office in his hometown Grenaa.

◀ *Designer Pil Bredahl (b. 1971) was a member of the Kropsholder (Body Holder) group and has made this flexible storage unit that can quickly be packed away and functions like a light, sculptural divider in the room. It consists of eight thick cardboard tubes with different diameters that are held together by two bands. The system is an alternative bookcase and can easily be stowed away using the Pandora's box principle.*

He has designed an abundance of furniture and also other products like lamps, but a project like his screen wall Viper is very interesting. It's a room divider made of cardboard tubes with an oval profile. This came about through a collaboration with the firm Art Andersen & Copenhagen, which primarily makes Venetian blinds, but also room dividers. Later on the project was purchased by Fritz Hansen. A luxury version of Viper was also made in perforated aluminium.

It seems like Danish furniture design has been in a transitional phase for many years now. The classics from the 1950s have been given a lot of attention, and new and used versions are sold on the various Internet auctions. Meanwhile the young Danish furniture designers are working in several directions. Like Hans Sandgren Jakobsen and Kasper Salto, others seem to be continuing the classic way of developing furniture, although to a great degree it's an extension of the tradition that calls for imagination and experiments. Other young designers whom Louise Campbell, Cecilie Manz and Morten Voss represent, seem to want to create a niche with very artistic furniture whose quality lies in the surprising and spectacular in their experiments with materials and forms.

▶ *Hans Sandgren Jakobsen's two screen walls with the joint name of Viper were designed in 1996. The first version was made of cardboard tubes, next came the aluminium version. The cardboard version is manufactured in the same way as poster tubes.*

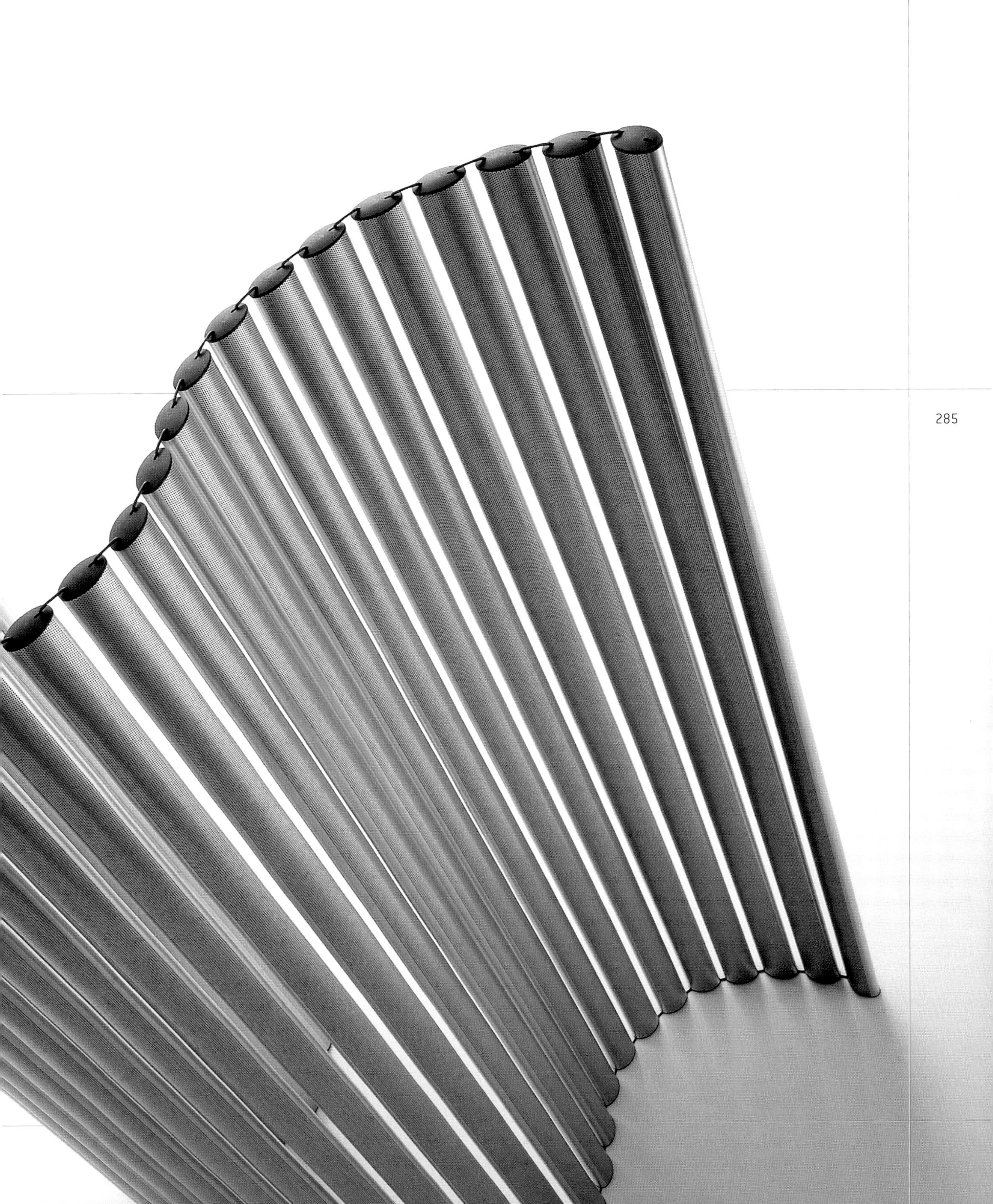

Building and design

It is not my intention to describe Danish architecture since that field has to a great degree its own independent history. Therefore the building culture is only included in this book when there is a clear reason for it as regards design or because an example of architectural design has been a good example of the general tendency of the time. Having said that, you can't get round the fact that architecture and design are very interconnected. A great deal of the Danish design tradition is an extension of our building culture. The way we have built our houses also has an effect on the way we furnish our homes, and not least the design of all sorts of products, such as the cabinetmaker's furniture and the Danish lamp designs. But the influence also works the other way round; from the design of articles to the design of houses. When the Vikings became masters of building ships of wood, they probably also got better at building their homes.

When we talk about design in relation to building houses, there are at least two ways in which design comes into the picture. The first is through the design of various building materials and components that are part of the building process itself. This could be anything from the old medieval bricks to today's prefabricated elements that arrive on a flatbed truck and only have to be lowered in place by a crane and mounted. The other way that design comes in close contact with a building is when it's finished and the house is supplied with fixtures that make it inhabitable and comfortable. Here we can choose between a wealth of various designed products that are manufactured by the industry. These are things like wood-burning stoves, kitchen elements, light sockets and door handles.

◂ *Grundtvigskirken (Grundtvig's Church) is an excellent display of the use of bricks and the closest we get to a cathedral in honour of bricklaying. All the yellowish bricks were carefully cut on site so they would have sharp and precise contours. At the end of the workday, the bricklayers were white from top to bottom from all the dust. And therefore the piecework was much lower than for ordinary bricklaying. It also took 20 years to finish the church, which is located in northwest Copenhagen.*

THE MATERIALS

The oldest Danish houses that we know of have almost exclusively been made of wood. House building from the Stone Age and almost to our time has been based on building materials that could be procured or manufactured locally. And this has often been wood, which was at hand in abundance. In certain regions of Denmark, such as northern and west Jutland, there have at times been such a shortage of wood that substitutes had to be used. The outer walls of a house could be partly or completely made of peat or dirt. Later, when deforestation made room for arable land, timber framing was used in houses in most parts of the country. With this technique much of the wood in the outer walls was replaced by mud and wattle, so only the load-bearing framework of the house consisted of wood.

If you want to see local variations in the supply of building materials, you can visit the Open-Air Museum in Lyngby, north of Copenhagen. Here you can clearly see that in some regions there was a lack of the traditional reeds from lakes and bogs used in thatching the roofs. Instead they used straw, heather or even seaweed as roof covering. But even though the building materials were local in the past, and some of their solutions showed a necessary creativity, a certain standardisation did arise. In the course of time, craftsmen learned the exact dimensions that the wooden posts had to have to bear the weight of the roof and the impact of nature. This is how building materials were gradually made in standard sizes that are more or less the ones we use today. So when people today still talk about a piece of wood as a 4x4, then they're talking about the cross section of a post in inches. These old units, like inches and feet, have been an easy way for craftsmen to denote measurements since olden times. Even in the 20th century there were furniture architects who found these units more natural to use than the metric systems when designing furniture. This is true of Kaare Klint, for example.

A traditional way of building prevailed, and this was passed on from generation to generation in the form of tacit wisdom that was conveyed through training. This created an intuitive understanding of how houses were built. Drawings or explanations were hardly necessary when building a new house. All there had to be were enough available materials, since the craftsmen already knew what to do. They needed wood in certain dimensions, clay for caulking, reeds or straw of a certain length for the roof, and that was about it. They often got by without the use of iron which was an expensive imported commodity. But in the course of the 11th century, at the end of the dynamic Viking Age, something new happens in the supply of building materials, for this is when brick building reaches Denmark.

The Danish brick

At first granite boulders found in the fields were used to build the growing number of churches after the introduction of Christianity in Denmark. We can still see quite a few village churches around the country that were partly or completely built of these irregular unhewn stones. From Italy the Danish monks had imported the necessary knowledge of how to burn lime to make the mortar for the brickwork. About 100 years later, in the mid-12th century, the monks also introduced the method of baking clay into bricks – hence the name 'monk stones'. They were usually no smaller than 27.5 x 13 x 8.5 cm and often larger.

The master builders were the skilled tradesmen and thus the architects of that time. They were responsible for construction and now they had a

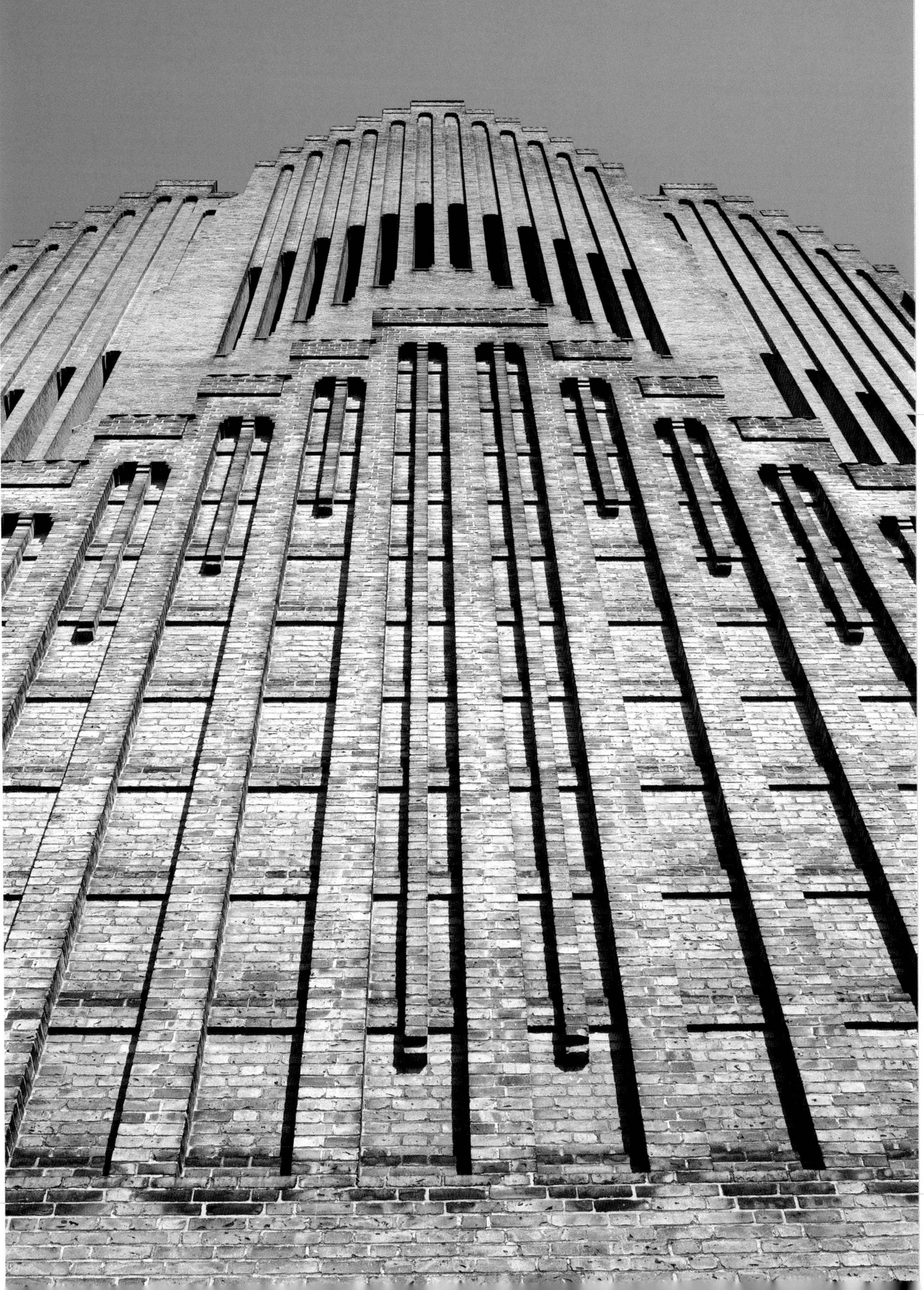

▸ On the façade of a restored office building that used to belong to the porcelain factory Bing & Grøndahl on Vesterbro in Copenhagen you can see an untraditional use of facing bricks. Not only were new dark bricks laid on the façade, but a special awning system using blinds made of larch wood was mounted that gives shade and life to the façade. Notice that the bricks are not mounted in cross bond. In other words, they didn't try to make the brickwork look like it was bonded. The architects are the architectural practice JJW Arkitekter.

new flexible building component. And even today this man-made brick has formidable qualities. It's both impenetrable and porous so that rain and wind can be kept out of the house, but at the same time these bricks let the house breathe and give off moisture. Bricks are also so strong that the bottom ones in a 5 or 6 storey building aren't crushed by the great weight of the floors above them. Finally they are virtually imperishable so even hundreds of years after a castle or monastery has been abandoned and all the other building materials have rotted, burnt or crumbled, the bricks are still there. Just look at the ruins of Hammerhus on Bornholm or the restored Koldinghus in Kolding.

For many hundreds of years bricks were so expensive that they were reserved for prestigious buildings like monasteries, churches, castles and fortresses. In the buildings that have survived from the Middle Ages one can also see how much freedom bricks have given. These new building materials were phenomenal building blocks since now they could build tall and solid constructions with round or pointed arches over the doors, gates and windows. At first they had to have clay nearby in order to build with the new bricks since transporting them was troublesome. So a temporary little brickworks was established near the building site. Everything was done by hand, and in the beginning the bricks were rather crude and varied a bit in size, which can be seen in the first churches built in Ringsted and Sorø from circa 1150. The bricks here vary from 25 to 30 cm in length, from 11 to 15 cm in width, and 7 to 10 cm in thickness. Naturally, this great difference in size gave the buildings a slightly irregular but charming appearance.

This non-uniformity in quality and size wasn't very practical, so gradually a standard size of this building block was aimed for. After a while, Denmark, like many other parts of Europe, established it own traditions and designs in this field. Bricks were suitable for the Danish climate, and the raw materials were at hand, but the 'monk stones' were large and hard to hold with one hand, so the size of bricks reduced over time. However, the dimensions of bricks varied a lot until 1896 when associations of engineers, architects, master bricklayers and the brickworks made the joint decision to make the standard Danish brick 23 x 11 x 5.5 cm. Later on the measurements were adjusted to 22.8 x 10.8 x 5.5 cm. The reason why these odd measurements were chosen was because the joint, that is the layer of mortar between the bricks, is 1.2 cm thick. So when the joint is added to the length or breadth of a brick, two halves of a brick correspond to a whole brick. This is important when laying bricks because you can alternate between using whole and half bricks and thus design a beautiful, practical and stronger brickwork.

During the 850 years that bricks have existed in Denmark, many beautiful buildings have been constructed with the help of them. Christian IV's many magnificent buildings are all a display of what the field of bricklaying can achieve. In our time, magnificent buildings aren't the only ones made of brick. The many one-family houses of red brick that were built in the first half of the 20th century in Denmark are called 'master builder houses', which is often synonymous with a well and solidly built house. Apartment houses from the same period are also often popular places to live, although they're usually rather plain, but of a solid quality.

▸ There are 900 years between the brickwork in the first and last picture, but the brick itself hasn't changed much. There are many ways of varying the pattern of the bricks, the so-called bond. When a whole brick is laid, it's called a stretcher, while a half brick is called a header, and most of the patterns of bricklaying have a name in the trade. From left to right we have: Frue Kirke (the Church of our Lady) from circa 1100. Here the large bricks are laid in Flemish Garden Wall bond – three stretchers plus a header. The next picture is from the central railway station in Aarhus where the bricks are laid in English Cross bond, i.e. alternate layers of headers and stretchers. The soft clay was stamped with the construction year on some of the bricks. The third is from a building on Åboulevarden in Copenhagen from 1930. This is also laid in English Cross bond, but with an intricate pattern of yellow and red bricks. This is why the building has been nicknamed the Linoleum House. On the far right we have Raking Stretcher bond on the museum ARoS in Aarhus from 2004. Here a relief effect is achieved by every other course protruding a bit.

In the inter-war era, one of the major works in Danish brick architecture was built. This is Grundtvigskirken (Grundtvig's Church), designed by architect P.V. Jensen-Klint, who won a competition in 1913 to build a memorial for N.F.S. Grundtvig. The construction was funded by collections from the Danish population. Construction started in 1921, but the church was not completed until 1940 since the collection was a bit slow. Jensen-Klint designed the church with a tall, three-part tower, and everything inside and outside the church consists of light, almost whitish yellow hand-moulded bricks. Jensen-Klint died in 1930, and his son, Kaare Klint, designed and furnished the rest of the church. Both father and son were meticulousness itself, and everything in the church was minutely designed including the many brick patterns that are called bond in the trade.

Although Danish bricks have been industrially standardised, there are today more than 20 different bricks in production. In addition there are all the colour variants and many special products available in small series. The latter are either used when repairing or restoring old buildings or, which is increasingly common, as specially designed bricks for facing. These facing bricks usually don't serve any construction purpose but are mounted on the façade on top of concrete panels for decoration. Often there isn't even a mortar joint between the bricks to create the illusion of brickwork. We are still waiting to see examples that are really successful of this new way of designing façades. Up to now, most of them look like products that are trying to look like brickwork but aren't.

Building with industrial design

The brick is a good example of an early standardisation of building materials. Other materials followed suit: timber was gauged, and roof tiles

made of brick or slate were given norms. And this continued throughout time and once in a while there would be new materials: iron to make into fittings, handrails and nails; copper for roofs, eaves gutters and drainpipes; glass for windows. Later, more synthetic materials were produced such as concrete, asphalt roofing and eternit. The number and quantity of these new materials rose drastically in connection with industrialisation in the late 1800s and gave builders and architects brand new possibilities.

In the beginning of the 1900s, especially after World War I when functionalism arrived, it became an architectural ideal to industrialise construction. This shouldn't be understood as just a more rational way of building, but also as a particular attitude towards types of housing and aesthetics. Some of the avant-garde architects, especially some of the foreign ones like Le Corbusier, went so far in their thinking that they began to talk about seeing the home as a machine in the same way that the factory was a machine filled with machines. In this light, it's no wonder that the new industrial types of construction appealed to these circles. Therefore the buildings should also look like they were manufactured by machines. Reinforced concrete became popular as well as flat roofs covered with asphalt roofing and windows with factory-made steel frames.

In Denmark this new style was only partly a success. The funny thing is that sometimes they only embraced the style, but the rational factory methods often couldn't be realised. For example, Arne Jacobsen's modern Bellevue complex in Klampenborg looks like it's built of the then very modern white concrete. But behind the smooth, white plaster are ordinary bricks. Later in this period the Danish construction tradition and the Danish architects, horse sense triumphed over the functionalist ideals, and a more Danish type of functionalism prevailed. They didn't go back to the old Classicism; it had been eradicated once and for all, but now they worked with simple building forms without ornamentation and decoration. This new simple style could also be executed using yellow bricks, which the many buildings in the University of Aarhus' park-like area are a testimony to. They were built between 1932 and 1943.

Although functionalism didn't industrialise building construction from one day to the next, the tendency gradually penetrated. The demand for more and better homes, especially in the cities, combined with periods when skilled craftsmen were in demand, led to rationalisations gradually making their entry in the construction sector. One result was that the number of different building materials skyrocketed. Around the year 1900 there were hardly more than a couple of scores of different materials, and they were all very basic, such as brick, mortar, boards, beams, glass, slate, zinc etc. At that time there were certain and rather simple ways of building, and the working-up of the materials often took place on the building site.

A hundred years later, architects have many thousands of different types of materials and industrially manufactured components to choose between when a house is to be designed. This is a consequence of the fact that large elements of a building are today prefabricated at a factory and arrive ready to be installed at the building site. This applies to everything from balconies and sections of the outer wall complete with insulation and wiring systems for electricity to ready-made windows and doors. It's tempting to say that our buildings today almost exclusively consist of a number of designed industrial products that are assembled to make an architectural whole.

▾ *Since 1941 the VELUX company has made billions worldwide by focusing on a mass production of well-designed skylights. At first they manufactured roof windows for the top storey, but in the last few decades other types of windows have been added to their range. Initially the skylight was a creative solution to the housing shortage in Denmark, since the top storey or attic could be converted into a liveable area.*

This new industrialisation has never been unproblematic – we recall the 1980s and 90s when the Danish Eternit's crumbling roof tiles cost the factory huge amounts in damages. And this is just one example.

VELUX

One of the first Danish companies that seriously started a mass production of specialised building components was the window company VELUX. The name is a contraction of the words 'ventilation' and 'lux' (light). The company was started in 1941 by engineer Villum Kann Rasmussen (1909–93) and was based on the idea that in a time of housing shortage one could get more inhabitable rooms if the top storey with its sloping walls could be furnished with windows. The tilting roof window was for many years VELUX' most significant product. One of its most important properties is that it was not only designed for new buildings but could also easily be installed in existing buildings since the width of the window corresponded to the traditional distance between the rafters in Danish roofs.

When the VELUX window is closed, it's virtually flush with the roof and gives the top storey a lot of light. The window tilts on a axis on the middle of the frame and is opened by pulling a panel on the top of the window. That makes it difficult for young children to open and perhaps fall out. The whole window can, at least in most models, be turned 180 degrees so it can be cleaned. Besides the successful roof window, VELUX also sells accessories like special blinds and shades. The company furthermore manufactures solar panels and other types of windows, among other places at their subsidiary company VELFAC.

VELUX-OVENLYSVINDUER	DK 69.028.36 September 1936	138

Solafskærmning med markiser.

MARKISETTEN

I sommermåneder bliver lokaler med store glasflader betydeligt og ofte ubehageligt opvarmet, hvis solstrålerne får lejlighed til at ramme glasfladerne. Denne opvarmning kan reduceres ved anvendelse af persienner, rullegardiner o. lign., men den bedste kontrol over situationen får man med anordninger, som kan forhindre solstrålerne i at nå glasset.

Selv om glasfladerne i Velux-ovenlysvinduer som regel er relativt mindre end de, der kræves for at opnå tilsvarende lysmængde gennem lodrette glasflader (man får 2-3 gange så meget lys pr. arealenhed gennem skrå glasflader end gennem lodrette) er problemet ofte aktuelt, og vi har derfor udviklet en særlig markise for Velux-ovenlysvinduer: **Markisetten.**

Markisetten skærmer effektivt for sollyset, er let at betjene og har en dekorativ virkning.

Beskrivelse

Markisetten, som er patentanmeldt, består af en zinkskærmkasse, der indeholder en selvoprullende stok, hvorpå markisedugen er monteret.

Markisettebeslagene monteres foroven på ovenlysvinduet med 4 skruer, og på disse fastsættes skærmen med fløjmøtriker, således at den derefter kan nedtages og opsættes uden brug af værktøj, d.v.s. det hele kan let afmonteres om vinteren. Forneden på ovenlysvinduets ramme monteres en krog i hver side. (Se omstående illustrationer.)

Der er ingen markisearme eller anden mekanik, så betjeningen sker ganske enkelt ved at svinge rammen op i pudsestilling og påkoble kanten af markisedugen til krogene. Når rammen svinges ned i ventilationsstilling, trækker den selv markisedugen frem. (Se nedenstående illustrationer).

Markisetten bør, ligesom almindelige markiser, ikke anvendes i stærk blæst.

Specifikation

Markisetten leveres i farverne gul og orange og i to standardstørrelser

Type 02	stofbredde 70 cm, passende til Velux-ovenlysvinduer af typerne FV1, FV2 og FVK2 (med udvendig karmbredde 78 cm).
Type 22	stofbredde 140 cm, passende til Velux-ovenlysvinduer af typerne FVS11 og FVS22 (med udvendig karmbredde 156 cm).

Andre størrelser eller farver kan leveres på bestilling.

Ved bestilling bedes ved standardmodeller opgivet følgende:
Antal, Markisettetype 02 eller 22, ovenlysvinduets bredde og højde samt den ønskede farve.

Ved bestilling på specialstørrelser bedes skitse af ovenlysvinduet medsendt eller en henvisning til vort fakturanummer på ovenlysvinduesleverancen. Markisetten kan kun bruges til Velux-ovenlysvinduer med vipperammer.

Markisetten i brug:

Vinduet åbnes og drejes til pudsestilling (lodret).

Markisetten trækkes ud af dækkassen og hægtes til krogene på vinduet.

Vinduet drejes tilbage og markisetten ruller ud.

V. Kann Rasmussen & Co., Civilingeniører, Maskinvej 4, Kbh.-Søborg. Tlf.: *Søborg 6570. Station: Buddinge

DURING THE LAST many years of efforts in urban renewal, one of the desires was to add a new amenity value to existing homes. One way of doing this was to put balconies on old apartment buildings. One solution was this prefabricated balcony, which BBP Architects developed with the DAN-LUK company in the early 1990s. The whole balcony is lifted in place with a crane after the mounting has been installed along with space for a door and fortifications on the outer wall. The product was given the ID prize from the Danish Design Centre in 1993.

Espansiva

The dream of building a house in much the same way as playing with LEGO bricks was one that lived in the hearts of many architects after the industrialisation of construction had come. Just after World War II, the American designer couple Ray and Charles Eames had inspired many architects by building a legendary house for themselves in a Los Angeles suburb. It was made solely of standardised building materials that were stock goods in the building industry. Pictures in periodicals of the poetic, light and pavilion-like house were carefully studied in professional circles, but no one in Denmark dared to proceed so radically. In the late 1960s Jørn Utzon (b. 1918) began to work on an interesting concept called Espansiva.

A group of timber merchants asked Utzon to devise an additive building system that could be sold at DIY centres. They established the firm Espansiva Byg A/S in order to realise the project. Utzon's proposal consisted of a number of small rooms and pavilions in different sizes that could be assembled in many ways. In 1970 he wrote about the project in the periodical Architecture: 'A consistent utilisation of industrially manufactured building components can only be achieved when these components can be added to buildings without having to trim or adjust them. So they are like building blocks that can be assembled in many ways without having to use force. This is how a one-family house can be extended or rebuilt according to the family's needs.'

Espansiva was an architectural system with unlimited possibilities of variation, and the load-bearing construction was laminated wood. All the components of the small pavilions could be prefabricated, and every unit had its own roof with a gradient of 17 degrees, which was enough for many

▸ Espansiva was an attempt to make a flexible building system with standard components that could form many different and varied solutions. Three module sizes were designed with a common width of three metres; the length could be 2 m, 3.2 m or 5 m. By assembling the modules, almost any kind of room or home could be created. The floor was made of lightweight concrete, and one could choose almost any type of wall lining or roofing.

types of materials, for example tiles, asphalt roofing, eternit or metal could be used.

Utzon emphasised that the system could be seen as an extension of the Danish tradition of timber-framed houses and would give a vivid and varied expression. The intention was that one could either buy the components at the DIY retailer and build one's house according to wishes and wallet, or go to an architectural consultant and have one's house designed.

Jørn Utzon's goal for the system was, as he wrote further on in the aforementioned article: 'not only to give the individual builder total freedom in the layout of his house, total freedom to extend or change it at any time, but also to give the builder the opportunity in large building complexes to create a common expression as we know from our old, organically connected timber-framed villages, and nonetheless allow the individual family to have their own unique house, be it big or small. Here there's no stiff, military repetition that characterises many towns with standard houses or the haphazard expressions we see in the new residential areas.' However, Espansiva was never a success. Perhaps most people wanted a house with a traditional and individual appearance.

THE ARCHITECT-DESIGNED STANDARD HOUSES

Unfortunately, prefabricated building has been given a bad reputation. Perhaps because it emerged at a time when quantity was put before quality. The rational ideals that prevailed in Danish society from the early 1960s to about 1980 were characterised by the notion that growth was good, almost at any price. But much of the industrialised construction from this time was later hit by extensive building damages.

A significant problem for the mass produced building from this time seems to be that entrepreneurs and builders wanted to make the most of the advantages of a large-scale operation. That gave rise to some large and monotonous housing areas that many today consider grey and dismal neighbourhoods that have become concrete slums and ghettos.

Industrialised construction has, in other words, been compromised in the eyes of the general public. And this applies not only to the social housing from the time, but also to a great deal of the vast residential areas with very identical standard houses that were built in the 1970s, in particular. These were seen by professionals, but perhaps not so much by the residents themselves, as non-adventurous neighbourhoods without architectural quality. For many years the standard house was in the doghouse according to architects, but today it's as if there's an interest in the advantages of large-scale production in construction, also of one-family houses. Among others, the construction firm M2 launched in 2005 a series of different standard houses that were designed by well-known Danish architectural firms like CEBRA, 3XN, Schmidt, Hammer & Lassen, Dorte Mandrup and Bjarke Ingels Group.

The express thought behind the project is to challenge the traditional view of what a standard house could look like. In contrast to the standard house from the 1970s where the architect was anonymous (if the houses had been even been designed by an architect), M2 uses architects to brand the project. This was done with the understanding that the lack of architectural qualities is the sore point of traditional standard houses. However, in the presentation of M2's projects there is no special emphasis on developing a more industrial way of building. This is probably because they don't want to give the buyers the impression that they're buying a mass produced house. They accentuate the unique and architect-designed aspects in this case.

DESIGN THAT COMPLETES THE HOUSE

Apart from the many mass produced components that are used to build a house nowadays, designed products are used to a great extent to make the buildings usable and inhabitable. If we compare with earlier times, buildings need more installations and functions than before. For example, we have running water, both hot and cold that require installations, not to mention the plumbing fixtures and mixer taps needed to enjoy this luxury. There are many examples of the need for good designs in order to just finish a building and to be able to use a house optimally.

For most architects, it's a dream to be allowed so much influence that they are allowed to design the minor details, such as wall sockets and door handles. This dream was fulfilled for Arne Jacobsen in the Royal Hotel from 1960, but there are other examples of total design before that. Martin Nyrop was given the big assignment of designing Copenhagen City Hall, and he gave it his all, mainly with regard to decorations. Furthermore, the architect designed the furniture, the recessed doors and the tall-as-a-man wood wainscoting in the conference rooms as well as the door handles, stucco ceilings and tile patterns on the floors. Not even the sinks and wastepaper baskets escaped the architect's attention. And way up on the roof there are even large and small figures, some of which can hardly be seen with the naked eye from the square in front of the building. It took 13 years to build the city hall, which was completed in 1905. Much of the fixtures and decorations are still there today.

▾ *The architectural practice 3XN has designed three of the fifteen tract house projects, which the firm M2 began to offer in 2005. The pictures here show the house Kip (below) and Flower House (top). In the spring of 2006 the construction of the first house was commenced.*

Heat in the living room

Houses don't have to be as grandiose as Copenhagen City Hall to benefit from some designer attention. Around and just after World War I, quite a few apartment buildings were erected, especially in Copenhagen, and they needed a heat source. At that time, central heating was still a thing of the future, so the heat source was the heating stove. A number of companies manufactured these stoves, and most of them used architects, designers or visual artists when constructing their products. Among this group we find architects like Kay Fisker, Vilhelm Wanscher, Kaare Klint and Knud V. Engelhardt.

The latter designed in 1921–22 one of the best heating stove systems of the time. It consisted of a number of modules that could be assembled into a big or small stove, depending on the size of the room and its heating requirements. The stove was a square pillar with a base that curved outwards, almost in the same way as Engelhardt's advertising pillars made for Gentofte municipality (see page 446). The result was easy to clean. The stove could consist of a number of modules on top of the base, from four to seven, and thus more than 30 different stoves could be constructed from the modules. The height of a module was 22 cm, so the total height of the stoves could vary from 100 cm to 166 cm. Units for warming plates or water evaporation on the top could be included. The stoves were convection stoves, that is, the cold air was drawn in via air canals at the bottom and was let out as warm air at the top. It was a relatively modern principle at the time. The stove series was called Dana and was manufactured for a number of years by H. Rasmussen & Co. A/S in Odense. They were made of cast iron, and Engelhardt had the artists Niels and Joakim Skovgaard design a stallion and a bull, respectively, that were made in relief on the top module.

Copenhagen City Hall was finished in 1905 after 13 years of construction. It's full of details, which the architect Martin Nyrop designed in order to make the biggest project of his life as perfect as possible. Both inside and out, nothing is left to chance. Everything from the figures on the roof to the sinks in the bathrooms have been designed or approved by the architect.

◂ *Knud V. Engelhardt's cast-iron stove built of modules. It was called Dana and was designed for H. Rasmussen & Co. in Odense. The Skovgaard brothers, who were both artists, designed the decorations.*

Although the design was made to be functional, Engelhardt still used decorations. Besides the bulls or stallions, all the handles are shaped like pears on a branch. On one of the modules, Engelhardt's logo, a little heart, is cast. The aesthetics are relatively simple even though the smooth functionalism hadn't yet made its mark. But the principle of modules, in particular, makes this series of heating stoves interesting and innovative.

Around World War II, central heating was introduced, and for many years open fireplaces weren't fashionable, but rather old fashioned, in the modern home. In the old patrician homes there were still open fireplaces, and in the country they would light the wood-burning stove on a chilly evening in late summer before the heating season started in earnest. Yet many people thought an open fire was cosy and began to miss a fireplace in the modern single-family house with its oil furnace and radiators beneath the windows, so there was a market for new solutions to the age-old need to warm oneself at an open fire. One of the more elegant solutions to this problem was the Cubus fireplace designed by Nils Fagerholt (b. 1933), who later became professor of industrial design at the Royal Academy of Fine Arts, School of Architecture. This fireplace is very simple and constructed to be mounted on the wall. It's made of 2 mm thick steel plate and fireproof tiles. The fireplace was designed in 1971 and was awarded the ID prize the same year.

LIKE K.V. ENGELHARDT, Kaare Klint also designed a cast iron stove (below). That was in 1944 and the client was Morsø Iron Foundry. The stove isn't built of modules like Engelhardt's, but it's well proportioned with slightly curved sides that slope inwards at the top. The decoration on the side of the stove is a verse written by Johannes V. Jensen at the instigation of Kaare Klint: 'At Morsø Iron Foundry I was baptised/Cast for the hearth, and not for weapon/Stay out of strife, cold and fog/I spread warmth in your house.' The reference to the non-belligerent use of iron was probably a reference to the ongoing war.

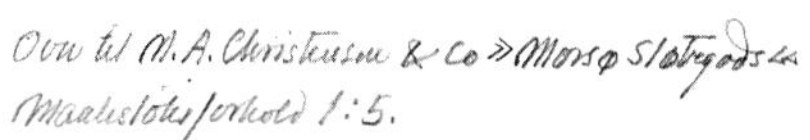

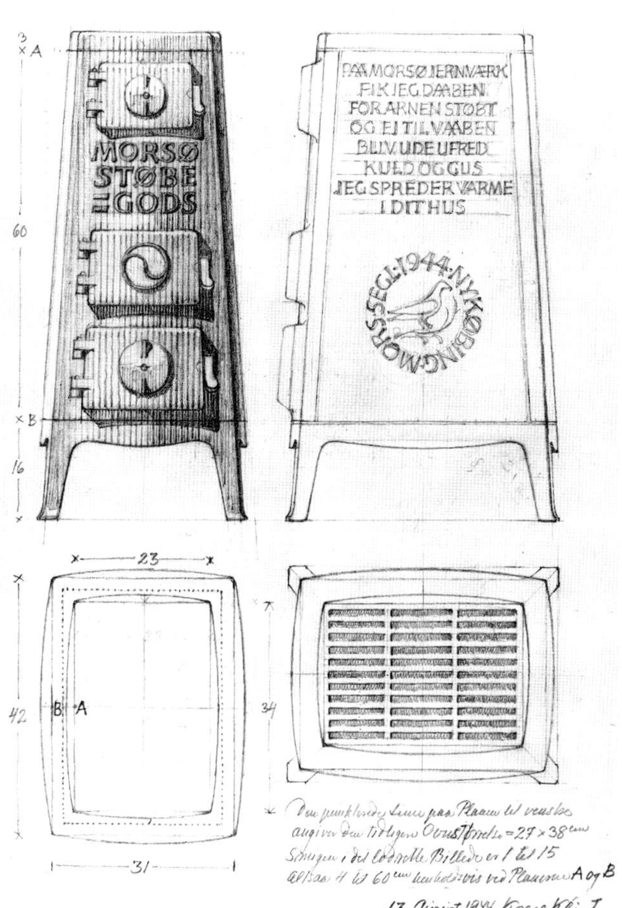

◂ *Nils Fagerholt's Cubus fireplace is made of simple steel plates and is one of the first fireplaces that isn't decorated in one way or another. It complements the modern functional construction.*

▾ *Bent Falk's wood-burning stove that was designed for Rais was one of the Danes' answers to the energy crisis in the mid-1970s. It was designed for practical, daily use with room for wood at the bottom and a hotplate for the teapot at the top. Having a stove like this in the living room indicates that, 'We're having a cosy time even though times are tough.'*

An open fireplace may be a very cosy thing, but it's not the most heat economical way of burning wood, since most of the heat is pulled out of the room and up the chimney. But in 1971 when Fagerholt designed his fireplace, there hadn't been an energy crisis yet. This came a few years later, and then the more efficient fireplaces and wood-burning stoves became popular.

One of the first of this kind was designed in the early 1970s by architect Bent Falk (b. 1938) for the luxury townhouses Gassehaven in Gammel Holte. When the energy crisis really set in, this stove was redesigned for mass production by the Rais company in 1975. In just a few years production reached 4–5000 a year, and some were exported.

In contrast to Fagerholt's simple and almost refined fireplace, Bent Falk's wood-burning stove had a good heat economy, but also very robust expression. The sturdy hinges that were riveted on the coarse plates that constituted the fire chamber express a more rural and rustic style as well as a very sensible approach to having a wood-burning stove in the living room. While the aesthetics of Fagerholt's fireplace are an extension of the unsentimental and minimal modernism of the 1960s, Bent Falk's wood-burning stove is much more a product of the 1970s. There is a 'back to the countryside' feel about it, and it's a good gutsy stove for everyday use.

Hot and cold water

In the second half of the 1800s, running water began to be installed in Danish cities. Previously citizens had to pump water by hand, but now there was a need for taps that could turn the water on and off. One of the old fixtures is still in production, albeit in a newly redesigned version.

RADIATORS HAVEN'T BEEN the object of the same attention that manufacturers and architects have given fireplaces and wood-burning stoves. To many people an open fire is cosy and fascinating, but the radiator isn't half as sexy. However, a few people have tried to make radiators in a more interesting design including the Hudevad company. In the mid-1990s, they had industrial designer Annette Krath Poulsen (b. 1966) design various products, one of which was the radiator Radius. Radius was originally designed for a large building project in Berlin and was awarded two German design prizes. Radius is especially used in front of glass façades since it doesn't ruin the view and at the same time it prevents the fall of cold air from the large windows.

This is the so-called Christiansborg tap that was originally conceived for the reconstruction of Christiansborg Palace after the fire in 1884. In 1930 it was redesigned and modernised by engineer Crone from the engineering company Crone & Koch. Today it's a classic tap that is still used in Christiansborg and in other old buildings.

When the Christiansborg tap was originally designed, there wasn't hot water in the tap, only cold. Hot water didn't come till later and thus another tap was added to the sink. But today most people find two taps impractical since you can't mix the water and get a comfortable temperature to wash your hands in. Then the mixer tap was invented and in the beginning this was just what it looked like; two taps and a spout that were joined. Therefore Arne Jacobsen's Vola tap caused a stir when it was presented in 1969. It was designed to be built into the wall so there was only one tap and one spout that were visible to the user. There was only one handle to pull out to start the flow of water and then to turn to regulate the temperature.

Vola was first used in the Danish National Bank, which Arne Jacobsen's architectural practice also designed at the time. Since then the mixer tap has become very popular, especially in new constructions and other modern milieus. Subsequently many other versions of Vola have been designed, among others a more traditional deck-mounted version. Finally, a few years ago, one came to realise that the principle of pulling the handle outwards wasn't user friendly, so now a rocker lever was introduced as well as ceramic discs in the valves, which make it easier to use. The new thing about Vola, apart from the radically new artistic idiom, was that it was part of a module system where different elements could be combined; for example, a shower head could be added, or you could choose between a long and a short spout. Furthermore Vola eventually came in 18 epoxy enamel colours and not only in chrome like most taps.

Door handles

In the attempt to make everything fit the overall aesthetic in the building of a new house, quite a few architects began designing much of the accessories that were necessary in a new home. Previously in this book it was emphasised how architect Arne Jacobsen was very interested in assembling the design puzzle for the Royal Hotel from 1960. Apart from furniture, lamps, textiles and flatware for the hotel restaurant, Arne Jacobsen also designed the door handles for the new building. This wasn't his first time, but this door handle was the only one that was mass produced then as well as today. The AJ handle, as it's called, is related as regards form to the Swan and the Egg that were also designed for the Royal Hotel. It's a very organic handle with taut lines that make it look a bit like a propeller wing. It's very comfortable to the touch and it's as if it fills the void in your hand when you close your fist around it. The AJ handle comes in two versions, with either a polished brass or satin nickel finish. These door handles are indicative of the way Arne Jacobsen worked with furnishing a building. Normally it was only some of the freestanding furniture, like his chairs, that were designed in an organic artistic idiom while the fixed articles were designed with a more geometric look like his Vola tap and wall lamps.

▸ While the Christiansborg tap looks like the classic and almost old-fashioned tap, Arne Jacobsen's tap is still ultramodern even though almost 40 years have passed since it was designed. Here is the model with the ceramic discs and rocker handle.

PRESSALIT. NORMALLY YOU wouldn't associate toilet seats with groundbreaking design, but in Ry just outside of Silkeborg, there's a company that has worked with designers for many years. Pressalit started in 1956 as an entrepreneurial company that in 1966 contacted Denmark's leading design company of the time, Acton Bjørn and Sigvard Bernadotte. The result of this collaboration was the modern toilet seat Pressalit Comfort, which was a big success. The company continued working with the renowned architectural practice, and in 1975 the model Scandinavia came out. This model became Pressalit's big breakthrough on the export market, especially in England and Germany. Today the company in Ry has its own design department and manufactures hundreds of thousands of toilet seats a year with the help of robots at its modern factory. Since the mid-1970s, Pressalit has also focused on developing and manufacturing bathroom equipment that's specially designed for the handicapped.

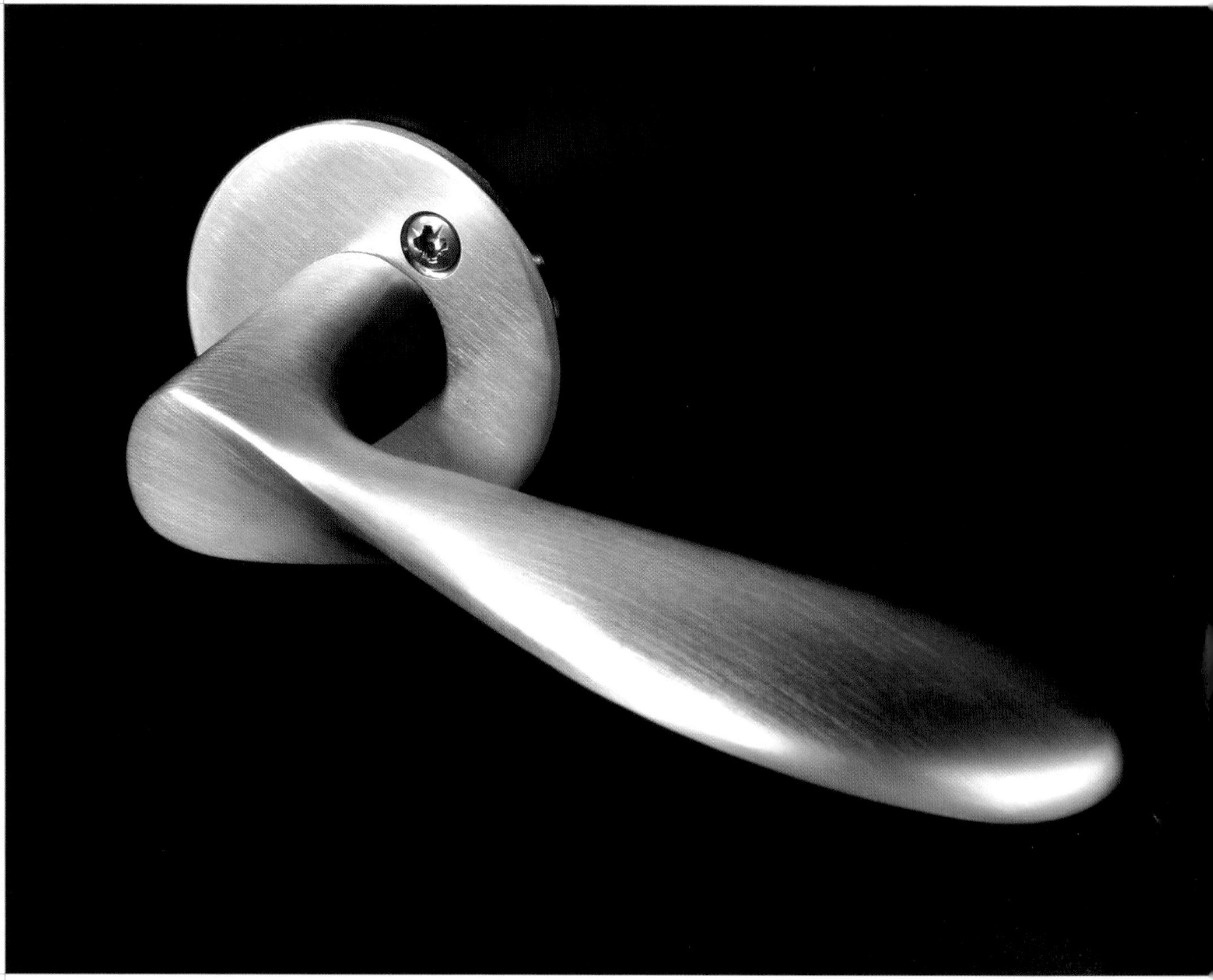

▸ *The hardware series d-line by Knud Holscher is pure geometry transformed into door handles and hundreds of other practical solutions in the building environment.*

▾ *Opposite page, bottom: Arne Jacobsen's door handle that was designed for the Royal Hotel in the late 1950s is a small organic article in a big square building.*

One of Arne Jacobsen's many co-workers was the architect Knud Holscher (b. 1930), who was the supervising architect for the construction of Oxford's St. Catherine's College, which Jacobsen designed in the early 1960s. The young architect, who later became professor of architecture at the Royal Academy of Fine Arts in Copenhagen, had trouble finding hardware like door handles and the like for the building. Together with the English designer Alan Tye he designed a series of handles and hardware in aluminium tubing that suited the new college. After Holscher returned to Denmark and started his own architectural practice, he began to work with the Carl F company on a new series of hardware that was similar to the English one, but was made of stainless steel instead of aluminium.

D-line was the name of the new series and it's characterised by consistently using brushed stainless steel tubing. The whole series is made of this material although tubes of various diameters are used for the different products. There is also another rule in the system that says that at the point where the tubes bends 90 degrees, the inner radius of the bend has to be equal to the radius of the tube. It's a rather sharp bend that normally isn't possible to make without deforming or breaking the tube. Carl F solved this problem by inserting a cylinder of synthetic material inside the tube just before the bend, so the pressure is counteracted from the inside.

In the beginning, d-line's door handles were L and U-shaped, and since then the assortment as grown enormously, so today there are over 400 individual elements. These can be combined in more than 3000 useful solutions for all kinds of things, from soap dispensers to toilet paper holders in the bathroom, to door stoppers and coat hooks. D-line is also used in private homes, but the slightly formal geometric and metal appearance makes it more suitable for public areas and modern office architecture. In recent years, the rather dogmatic requirement for perpendicular geometry has been modified to include door handles that are either slightly curved, wavy or have sharp bends.

ELECTRIC LIGHTING

The general use of electricity was not only a child of industrialisation in the late 19th century, but it was also the basis for the further development of industrialisation. That electricity was installed in every company and private home was a prerequisite for the proper functioning of the burgeoning towns and for the further growth of industry. Finally, electrical energy made it possible for numerous products and machines to be developed and contribute to the growth of society and to the comfort of man. Many of the inventions from that time that we still use today are dependent on electricity.

Where new technologies and products arose, there came a need for designing them properly. Many of these articles had never been conceived nor seen before, and now they had to be given a form that suited their use and function. But there is a natural inertness in the design of new articles. It takes time to comprehend the scope of new things and how they should be designed. Let's take an example. For many years, cars looked like horse carriages, but just without the horses. And for years the body of the car was made by coachbuilders.

The first power stations appeared in large Danish cities in the course of the 1890s, but the Danish electricity sector wasn't built up and organised until around 1910.

UNO FORM. THE industrialisation of construction also meant that much of the fixtures that had previously been specially manufactured for an individual house, like kitchens, could now be manufactured more easily and inexpensively at a factory. As a builder, you used to have to hire your own craftsmen to build a kitchen from scratch, but today you can choose elements, counter tops, sinks and lighting from a catalogue. Often you can see a similar kitchen in the factory showroom or at a retailer. In many cases you can get help to design your kitchen from an interior designer that is employed by the kitchen company, and at no extra cost.

This development follows a general trend seen all over the world in the 20th century where standardisation is seen as a quality. First of all, you can manufacture it more cheaply when the work and purchasing of raw materials is rationalised, and secondly you can supply a more uniform quality that the customers can count on. Thirdly, it easier to market the company's products and brand yourself.

In the area of kitchens this development really got going in the 1960s, and several Danish manufacturers came onto the market in the last half of the decade. One of these was Tectum Køkkenet (the Tectum Kitchen) that was designed in 1967 by architects Inger and Hans Zachariassen and Børge Kjær. The Tectum Kitchen has changed much in the 35 years it's

existed. Even today it is a very functional kitchen system that may seem a bit anonymous.

Another company, Uno Form, started in 1968 and has branded itself much more aggressively and has also tried to keep up with developments in design. This kitchen was designed by the advertising man Arne Munch who spied a new and interesting market. In time, Uno Form became a symbol of good and tasteful interior design. Housing ads emphasised the fact that a house for sale had a Uno Form kitchen. Instead of writing that you had a well-furnished kitchen, it was easier and more effective just to write that you had installed a Uno Form kitchen. This is how you could increase the market value of your house by adding branded products. Today the market for kitchens has virtually exploded, and numerous companies, including Danish ones, design and manufacture kitchens to suit any taste.

In the beginning, it was mainly various industrial machines that were powered by electricity. In private homes and in offices electricity was primarily used for lighting. The new lamps with incandescent bulbs looked at first like the well-known paraffin lamps. Chandeliers were also converted from gas to electricity, and basically the old designs were maintained. The first electric light sources had carbon-filament bulbs in transparent glass. The matt metal-filament bulbs we know today as ordinary incandescent bulbs were not introduced until many years later. In comparison to paraffin lamps, candles and gas lights, these bulbs gave off a strong and very bright light. Therefore they started putting fabric lampshades on the new lamps, and they were often designed in the Victorian style with fringes or tassels at the bottom.

POUL HENNINGSEN

The author Agnes Henningsen (1868–1962) had a son, Poul Henningsen, out of wedlock. In her writings she fought for equal rights for women for many years. She imagined that a free, erotic life could be combined with a career, as well as being a mother and wife, and it needn't be perceived as scandalous by society. She tried to live by this philosophy and moved in artistic and political circles where her point of view was accepted. This was the environment in which the young Poul Henningsen, who was later known as PH, grew up.

PH wanted to be an artist at first; he dabbled at painting when he was young. Through his mother's circle of friends he came into contact with some of the leading architects and wanted to try his hand at it. He attended a technical college and at the early age of 18 he was given little architectural jobs by friends of the family. PH became interested in light at the age of 13–14, especially electric light. He grew up during the time when electricity was introduced. The family didn't have electric lighting until they moved from Roskilde and its paraffin lamps to Copenhagen and its carbon-filament lamps in 1907. His mother was rather vain and felt that the new light wasn't flattering, so at that time PH began to design some lampshades.

The existing products on the market were also very old fashioned. It wasn't hard to find coloured silk shades with trimmings and fringes, but proper reading or working lamps barely existed. So here was a task for the young PH, who had ambitions of being an inventor. Gradually he began to work more seriously with the design of lamps, but ten years passed before he set down the principles for the lamps that would be famous later on. At the age of 30 he participated in a lamp competition which the Committee for Exhibitions Abroad had arranged in 1924. The results would be exhibited at the World Exhibition in Paris the following year, and Poul Henningsen won all six prizes for his new lamps. The lamps caused a commotion in Paris, and PH won even more recognition there in the form of a gold medal. These lamps were the forerunners of the ones we today know as PH lamps.

In the meantime, the lamp designer had come into contact with Director Sophus Kaastrup-Olesen, who owned a business called Louis Poulsen. This company had previously imported wine, but had since switched to selling tools and electrical equipment. Now they began to construct Poul Henningsen's lamps, first of all for the World Exhibition in Paris in 1925.

PH continued working on his ideas, and the following year he and the company Louis Poulsen won the competitive bidding to make lamps for the newly built exhibition building Forum in Frederiksberg. These lamps whose diameter was 85 cm got good reviews in the press and a lot of publicity. PH was becoming known as more than the provocative writer he also was.

New models were then designed in smaller sizes that were more suitable for homes and offices, and then the production went on for many years on a large scale. Thus PH and Louis Poulsen created a joint destiny in which they both achieved huge success by developing and manufacturing one of Denmark's first and biggest design successes ever. And today the company is a major industrial business that in particular sells lighting, much of which are the old models designed by PH.

Offhand it sounds like it took PH a long time to develop the principles for his lamps. Did it really take ten years? But if you look at what he was up to, it's perhaps easier to understand why it wasn't so simple. First of all, PH was a keen observer. He looked at the existing lamps and analysed their pros and cons. He looked at the light bulbs that were on the market back then, and not least he studied the rooms that needed lighting and the purpose of that lighting. He compiled all this information in the decade from 1914–24 when he was in this 20s. Then he thought things over, made experiments, cut lampshades, looked at light and shadows and sketched the reflection of light beams on the shades. Finally, one evening in late 1925 he sat down and drew the first sketches of what became the prototype of the PH lamp.

As mentioned before, Poul Henningsen was born into the cultural-radical milieu, and all his life he continued to champion the progressive points of view with body and soul. He was an inveterate supporter of scientific truths, reason and authenticity, and his efforts to design lighting and lamps are characterised by this outlook. He began his work by noting that the new electric lamps dazzled one if they weren't shaded and you could see the light bulb. It was this glaring light that made Agnes Henningsen realise that she looked all wrinkly in the mirror. The conclusion was that no matter what, the bulb had to be shaded so you couldn't see it.

The problem with shades is that, on the one hand, they swallow some light that remains within the fixture so we don't benefit from it, and on the other hand, lampshades also create unpleasant transitions in the surroundings; between the bright light and shadows. Many of the lampshades that were available then originated from the paraffin lamps of the past. These fabric-covered shades cover the bulb in principle, but according to PH they emitted the wrong light in the wrong places. If this kind of lamp hung over a table, it would make a well-defined circle of light in the middle of the table, and if the shade were open at the top, there would also be a circle of light on the ceiling. The people sitting around the table would be in semi-darkness and so would the rest of the room if there weren't other sources of light there. If the tablecloth was light in colour, the dinner guests could be hit by reflected light from below like grotesque footlights in a theatre.

▾ *The first PH lamp that was mass produced and came on the market was PH 5/5 from 1926. It was a success from the word go, and 12,000 were sold during the first year. The opalescent glass shade lets about 12 % of the light shine through, and thus PH could create the light he wanted in order to illuminate a room in a good way.*

◂ *One of Poul Henningsen's last redesigns of his principle for lamps resulted in the popular PH 5 lamp from 1957. It gives off all four types of light that PH found necessary for a lamp in a dining room. Notice that most of the light falls on the table and how the light fades into the surroundings without harsh transitions from light to darkness. PH 5 was the first lamp that was designed especially for incandescent bulbs with matted glass. PH preferred the original bulb with transparent glass since the light was emitted from an exact point from which it was easier to design shades. When the PH 5 was launched, he wrote: 'After 33 years of fairly good Christian behaviour, I have converted to Mohammedanism, as you'll see, with regard to the manufacture of the incandescent bulb. All my life I have believed that my regard for the users and for my sense of reason would triumph, but now I've become a fatalist. I bow to my fate and with Louis Poulsen's permission I have constructed a PH lamp that you can put anything in – a glowworm, Christmas lights and 100-watt metal-filament bulbs. A fluorescent tube is too long in its present size.' Later on, Louis Poulsen redesigned PH 5 so now it can also accommodate a compact fluorescent light bulb, which in principle is a little fluorescent tube.*

Light and shadow

Based on his observations, PH listed a number of criteria for good lighting. He differentiated between four types of light and shadow that should be present and which he, in experiments with loose lampshades, designed most of his lamps to give off. If we look at a lamp, a so-called pendant that hangs above a dining room table, then it first of all has to give off a lot of light so that you can see the food you're eating or read your newspaper at the table. When you're writing, it's also an advantage that the light creates precise but not too harsh shadows so you can see the pencil approaching the paper. If the light is too diffuse and without shadows, it's too difficult to determine distances when trying to pin down peas on a plate or writing a letter.

The second type of light doesn't have to be as bright as the first type. This light should be directed more diffusely around the table so you can see the other people around it. It mustn't create harsh shadows on the faces of your dinner guests, but preferably be a warm, comfortable and soft light. And thirdly, a little bit of light should be emitted around the table. You should be able to see the floor so you don't trip over the dog when you're going to get dessert in the kitchen. But otherwise the floor isn't very interesting unless you're showing off your oriental rugs. The fourth type of light seems to be the least important, but it helps to define the room by sending a little bit of light upwards. This gives one a feeling of how high the ceiling is and how big the room is.

PH spent a lot of time and conducted numerous experiments to reach the final result of the task he had set himself, namely to construct a modern lamp for the new electric lighting. His goal was a lamp that could spread the electric light out in four different kinds of light and create correspondingly nice shadows.

The design that PH arrived at was based on a system of curved shades that partly shaded the bulb so one wasn't blinded, and partly directed the light in the directions and in the amount that met the requirements of the desired four types of light. In order to make the light fade from bright to weak in the room and on the table, the shades had to be curved. The curve that PH calculated followed a logarithmic curve. Thus the light is reflected differently the further away from the bulb it hits the shades, and harsh transitions in luminosity are avoided.

Quality instead of quantity

The principle behind PH's lamps is that none of the main areas of a room in the home is in complete darkness. No harsh shadows are created by the lamp itself, and there are soft transitions from the bright to the weak light. The light in PH's lamps is directed where it's needed, where attention should be focused and not everywhere else.

PH criticised many of the standard lamp types in his time. Spotlights often create big contrasts and dazzle the eyes. And the so-called uplights that have been very popular at times, most recently in the 1980s, did not find favour with PH because they sent light in directions where it wasn't needed at all. How interesting is the ceiling of a room anyway? And the light that was reflected from the ceiling came down again so diffusely and imprecisely that it didn't even make proper shadows. To be in a room like that, as Poul Henningsen once said, was like sitting on the bottom of an aquarium.

POUL HENNINGSEN ALMOST always used collages while designing lamps, and they were always split down the middle. On the one side was the finished lamp, and on the other was a cross section of the lamp where you could see the placement of the bulb and the painted surfaces of the inside of the lamp. This is PH's collage for the design of the Contrast lamp.

While engineers who specialised in lighting concentrated on quantity, on getting as much light as possible out of the fixtures, PH focused on improving the quality of light. Heated debates took place in professional journals about who was right, and PH's arguments were based on the technical aspect of his ideas, on usage and aesthetics. The light should be pleasant, and a lot light all over wasn't necessarily good lighting. He was adamantly against the fluorescent lights that came on the market in the inter-war era. This was mainly because the fluorescent lights of the past rendered colours very poorly. They produced a lot of light and consumed very little power, but they could only do so by emitting light in a very small part of the colour spectrum, especially in the blue-green and yellow part of the spectrum. Therefore the red colours took on a greyish hue, and people could look rather pale and ashen in that light.

But light from an incandescent bulb wasn't perfect either; it's rather yellowish, as many have probably noticed when taking a colour photo indoors without a flash. And taking this fact into consideration, PH coloured some parts of the insides of his lampshades blue and dark orange to compensate for the yellow light. Some of the lamps were made of glass, either milky opalescent glass or frosted glass, so they couldn't correct for the colours. But many PH lamps with metal shades are painted on the inside in the colour-adjusting blue and red tones. PH's work in forming a theory of light is some of the first research done in the area of design. And not only in Denmark, but also on a worldwide scale this is a unique achievement. To the layman it may appear to be a complicated system, but as PH said when he concluded an explanation of this ideas and the design of his Contrast lamp, 'It's easier to put light in a ladies' hat. But Burgundy requires loving care.'

Various PH lamps

The first proper PH lamp that came on the general market was the white opalescent glass lamp 5/5 from June 1926. The numbers 5/5 indicate the size of the fixture and a system that PH's constructions follow thereafter. The first number 5 indicates the diameter of the largest shade in decimetres, that is 50 cm. The next number 5 states that the 'normal' lower shades are used, in this case, and a 31 cm middle shade and a 16.5 cm lower shade. The proportions between the three shades are 3:2:1. If smaller lower shades were used, then they were denoted PH 4/3, for example, which is PH 5's little brother and still available today.

When Poul Henningsen had his lighting principle and the shape of his shades mastered, he continued constructing new lamps. Since the shades were individually manufactured and were made using the same formula, they could be used on different fixtures. PH took advantage of this by designing innumerable lamps for many purposes. At first he varied the size of the pendants, but soon he made table lamps, floor lamps and wall-mounted lamps. At first his customers were mainly private companies, government offices and institutions. Among others, Kaare Klint, who was finishing the reconstruction of the Museum of Art & Design in Copenhagen in 1926, chose the new PH lamps for the whole museum.

Shortly thereafter, PH lamps also came in the form of chandeliers with small PH lamps mounted on the arms. There was also a great variation in the materials, from different types of glass in various colours to an assortment of metal shades that were either enamelled or in untreated copper. PH was so resolute in his principle that he continued developing new lamps for Louis Poulsen for many years.

▾ *The Contrast lamp was developed by PH from 1958 to 1962. The special thing about it is that you can decide whether the light has a bluish or reddish tone or just neutral. The lamp consists of ten shades that are painted on the inside with the colour-correcting blue and red colours. The light-bulb socket can be raised and lowered easily within the fixture, so you can decide whether you want the red or the blue inner shades to be illuminated and thereby decide the colour of the light. The system required around 130 separate paintings of the ten shades which made the Contrast lamp rather expensive, and therefore it's not in production any more.*

▼ *The Artichoke is an extravagant lamp for large rooms with high ceilings. The 72 'leaves' in the original fixture are made of copper and are painted light pink on the inside. Later on Louis Poulsen made two smaller and one larger version of this lamp. The Artichoke also comes with leaves of brushed stainless steel and in a white lacquered version. Below is Poul Henningsen's original collage of the Artichoke lamp from 1957.*

▶ *The AJ Royal pendant lamp, like so many of Arne Jacobsen's other industrial designs, was made for the Royal Hotel in the late 1950s. The original lamp was black, dark brown and light grey, but now it only comes in white. It has powerful light sources as the little model has three sockets for 100-watt bulbs, while the large model also has a top mirror 100-watt bulb in the middle, so in all it has 400 watts of light.*

▶ *Arne Jacobsen's wall and ceiling light that he designed for St. Catherine's College in Oxford. At first it was called the Sailor Hat because of its special shape. Today it's marketed under the name AJ Eklipta by Louis Poulsen. The shade is made of triple-layered mouth-blown white opalescent glass with a clear glass outer edge which makes a halo of light around the lamp.*

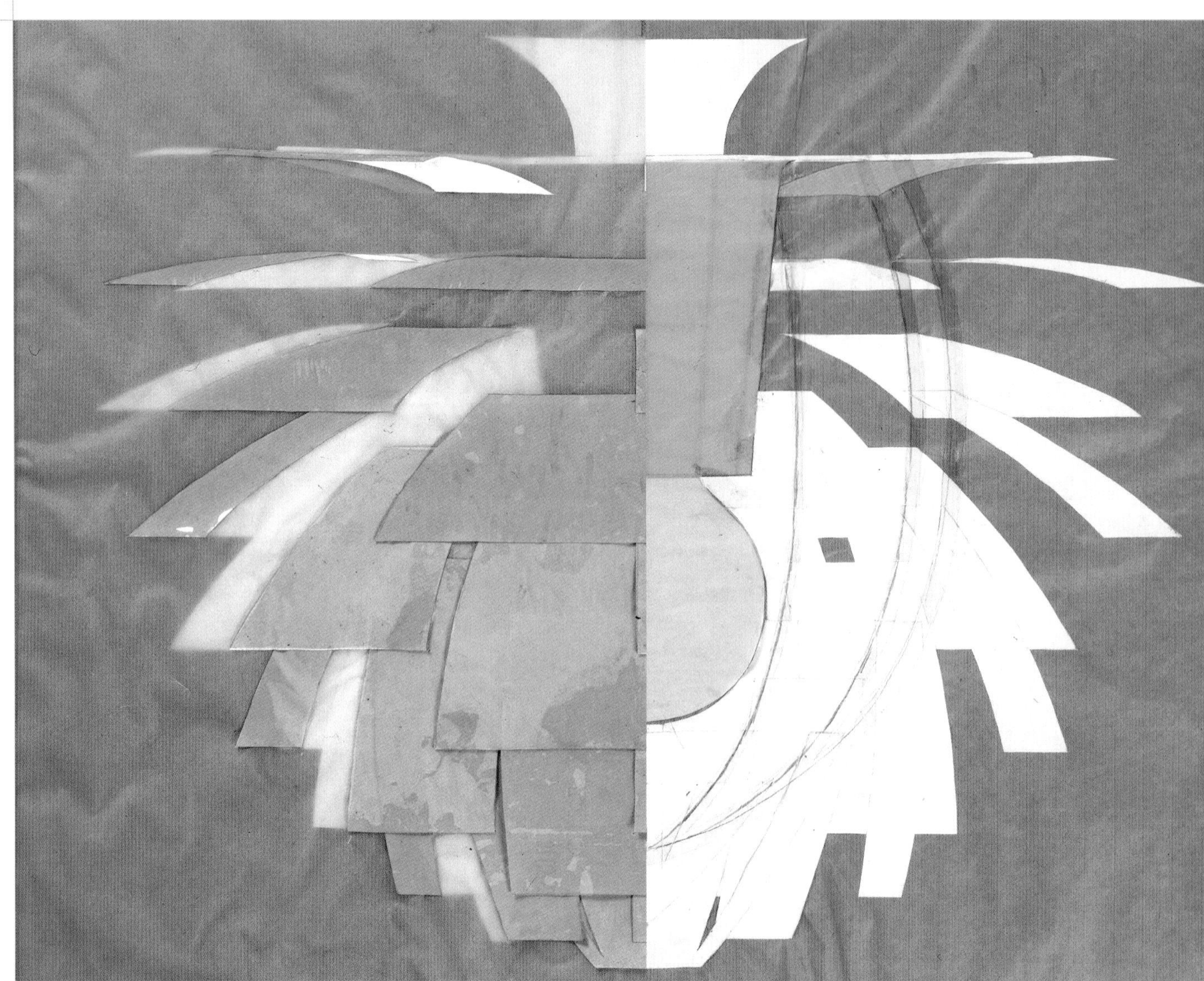

Among the curious models in the archives, you can find pictures of dentist's lamps, lighting for operating rooms, growth lamps for greenhouses and not least the Tennis lamp that was designed for KB-Hallen (concert hall and sports centre in Copenhagen) in 1927.

During World War II people had to be creative because of the blackouts and the shortage of materials, especially metals. In 1941 Poul Henningsen was appointed the architect for the Tivoli Gardens in Copenhagen, and one of his first assignments was to solve the problem of blackouts. The Germans demanded that the city be blacked out so the Allies' planes couldn't get their bearings. But it would be very detrimental to the Tivoli's economy if the garden had to close at dusk, so PH had to design a special metal lamp whose light couldn't be detected from above. Because of the metal shortage during the occupation, Poul Henningsen constructed his lamp models in pleated paper. While he was working on this, he had to flee to Sweden because his revue lyrics had provoked the Wehrmacht. One evening in the autumn of 1943 he and his wife, along with Arne Jacobsen and his fiancée, Jonna, rowed across Øresund to Sweden. Arne Jacobsen wasn't politically active like PH, but he was of Jewish descent, so the place was getting too dangerous for him too. In Sweden PH managed to get other Danish refugees to fold the pleated shades for PH lamps, but it was never a big business.

After the war, PH designed one of his oddest lamps for the Tivoli. Some of them still exist down by the Tivoli lake. They have spiral-shaped shades that revolve with the help of a little motor. Even later, in 1956, PH was responsible for the reconstruction of the Tivoli's concert hall, which the Nazis had blown up in 1944 to avenge the sabotage of the resistance movement. In the post-war period, PH continued tirelessly to design lamps for Louis Poulsen such as the P-hat, PH Louvre and not least the Artichoke that was developed for Langeliniepavillonen in 1957. Instead of round shades, the latter has rectangular copper leaves, 72 in all, that make the lamp look like an artichoke. Now it is also available in stainless steel.

ARNE JACOBSEN

The lighting company Louis Poulsen had for many years been synonymous with Poul Henningsen's lamps, but gradually other designers' products were included in their range. Today the company with its headquarters in downtown Copenhagen is practically the epitome of Danish lamp design. Although they don't reign supreme on the market, at times they have managed to gather some of the country's best lighting designers into their fold. In quite a few instances, the development of new lamps took place in connection with large building projects where the architect approached Louis Poulsen with drawings of a new lamp for the construction in question. If the design was up to scratch, the specially manufactured product was further developed for mass production and ended up in stores and in electrical shops.

Arne Jacobsen is an example of an architect who was good at using his building projects as a lever to design other products such as lamps that are still popular today. At first Arne Jacobsen designed lamps that didn't look at all like PH's. The oldest of these that is still in production is called the Munkegaard lamp because it was designed for the Munkegaard school that was completed in 1957 in Gentofte. But already in 1955 Jacobsen had designed this built-in lamp whose visible parts consist of a circular plate of opal glass framed by brass edge.

THE AJ LAMP is also from the Royal Hotel project and was designed in three versions: a table, floor and wall lamp. Louis Poulsen started manufacturing them in 1959 and still does so today in white, dark grey or black (left). The aesthetics of these lamps is an interesting combination of the geometrical and the skew. The tilting lampshade consists of a cylinder and a cone that are cut obliquely and mounted on a stand that tilts. Finally, the foot has a special hybrid form, but it has a circular hole in it that corresponds to the diameter of the bottom of the shade. Arne Jacobsen played with forms in this lamp.

This disc protrudes about 3 cm from the ceiling and is mounted to look like it's floating. It comes in three sizes from 26.5 cm in diameter to 52.5 cm.

Arne Jacobsen designed another similar lamp for St. Catherine's College in Oxford in 1962. The lamp can be mounted on the ceiling or wall and was called the Sailor Hat, but now it's sold under the name AJ Eklipta by Louis Poulsen. Like the Munkegaard lamp it's a flat fixture in white opalescent glass that is mouth-blown into a flat disc-like shape. This lamp is made in several sizes, as well. AJ Eklipta protrudes more from the wall since the base isn't built into the wall or ceiling behind it, but is contained in the fixture itself. The design of these two wall and ceiling lamps complies to a much greater degree with the premises of the architecture than PH's lamps do. They were to fit the overall architectural concept that Arne Jacobsen wanted to promote in his buildings. And they don't comply with PH's principles for lighting either.

However, one can say that Arne Jacobsen's pendant lamp called AJ Royal from 1959 does comply with PH's ideas. It was designed for the café and lounge areas of the Royal Hotel, and just like many of his other designs, it is kept in a stringent geometrical artistic idiom. The AJ Royal's shape is a hemisphere made of white lacquered aluminium. It's geometrical outer shade is interrupted by a row of louvres that give ventilation as well as emitting diffuse light. This light emitted at the top has in principle the same function as the top shades of PH 5 that ensure a general lighting of the room in addition to the bright, downward-directed light. AJ Royal comes in two sizes.

VERNER PANTON

While PH subscribed to good light in theory and practice, and Arne Jacobsen was interested in lighting as an architectural component, Verner Panton had a completely different starting point for designing his lamps. He wanted to create some powerful and transcendent spatial experiences for his audience and in order to do that he concentrated on forms and colours. To him light was an effect that was part of a total experience, and often at exhibitions that only existed for a short time. Nonetheless, some of his lamps were mass produced and still are. However, the only one that is still sold by Louis Poulsen is his lamp series Panthella that consists of a table and floor lamp.

If the Panthella resembles anything, it must be a luminous mushroom. And this suits Panton's general artistic idiom very well with all its organic shapes, new plastics and bright psychedelic colours. But it is one of the few products by Verner Panton that is white; a colour which he otherwise thought should be taxed because it's so boring. Panthella also came in a polished chrome version in 1971, but today it has been removed from the collection. The lampshade is cast in milky white acrylic and emits a rather diffuse light to its surroundings. It became one of the symbols of the beginning of the cool 1970s.

The little pendant called FlowerPot is similar to Panthella. Louis Poulsen put it on the market three years before Panthella. This lamp became one of Verner Panton's biggest successes since its price and size were reasonable for the general public. Back then it consisted of two enamelled metal bowls, a little one and a big one that shielded an ordinary 60-watt bulb.

▾ The shining mushroom, which Verner Panton designed in 1971 for Louis Poulsen, was a big success for both parties. Both the table and the floor model are still manufactured in semi-transparent milky white acrylic. The floor model has a larger shade than the table one, but both have the characteristic spherical switch on the base.

▸ The FlowerPot lamp from 1968 was Panton's popular breakthrough. It was affordable and fun without being too peculiar. Many Danes bought a lamp in one of the eight bright colours that were typical of the time. After having been in the doghouse for a number of years, it is now in production again and also a table lamp is available.

It came in numerous colours, which was typical of Panton. The inside of the big shade was white and in the little one it was orange. This construction didn't emit a very bright light, but it had a warm glow. After having been out of fashion for a number of years, the production has been resumed by Unique Interieur. A table version of FlowerPot has been developed, and besides the eight original colours, a polished and a matt metal version have been added.

LE KLINT

There were indeed people other than Louis Poulsen who were interested in developing lamps early on. One of these early birds was the architect behind Grundtvigskirken (Grundtvig's church), P.V. Jensen-Klint (1853–1930). He had made his own lampshades from before lighting was electric. Jensen-Klint was a versatile gentleman,; he was an engineer, had attended the Royal Academy of Fine Arts, School of Painting and was an artist before making his mark as an architect around World War I. In 1901 he made a paraffin lamp in the style of Art Nouveau for his own use, out of stoneware. He needed a lampshade for it and began folding parchment paper in the shape of a pleated cone. But the problem was that the top was too close to the hot lamp glass, and a lot of his family and friends were consulted to solve the problem.

The solution was to give the shade a perpendicular fold by turning the pleats crosswise in the longitudinal direction. And this became the family's pastime: to fold lampshades for their friends and acquaintances. During the occupation, when there was a shortage of practically everything, P.V. Jensen-Klint's eldest son, Tage Klint, decided to make a business out of this. Electric lighting was now the norm, and the market was big.

DESIGNER LOUISE CAMPBELL (b. 1970) began in 2004–5 to design for Louis Poulsen. One of her lamps is the glass pendant called Campbell. The lamp project began with a number of prototypes in polyester that were exhibited at the Furniture Fair in the Bella Centre in May 2004. Here the visitors could vote on which model they liked best. This feedback was integrated into Louis Poulsen's decision-making. The result is a lamp of two layers of mouth-blown glass with a traditional incandescent bulb inside. Sandblasted stripes help make the light more diffuse. This is a type of design that cultivates the artistic feeling for the materials, but it's a far cry from Poul Henningsen's sophisticated treatment of light and Louis Poulsen's original functional starting point.

POSTMODERNISM NEVER REALLY made itself felt in Denmark. Only a few houses and the interior design of a few cafés and restaurants bore the stamp of this style that used simplified classic motifs from ancient Rome and Greece. The style was often symmetrical, and pillars and classic grandiose furniture were a part of it. Postmodernism borrowed from every era and style and sampled them under the motto 'less is a bore'.

Around 1980 there was a little lamp company called Focus that launched a series of lamps whose simple geometrics flirted with this style, albeit discreetly. Two architects, Claus Bonderup (b. 1943) and Torsten Thorup (b. 1944) designed a number of lamps for Focus in a matt white; a simple artistic idiom that suited the slightly prestigious and formal architecture of the time.

The Quatro lamp was one of these fixtures. Shaped in a hemisphere, it could be mounted on a wall so it either lit upwards or downwards. It was made of metal and could accommodate a single bulb that was shielded by a piece of white opalescent acrylic. Alfred Homan designed an almost identical lamp for Louis Poulsen at that time. This lamp is called Homan Wall and is mounted on a square base. The lamp is conceived as outdoor lighting.

◂ *The pendant Undercover from Le Klint is a rather atypical product for a company that otherwise only made pleated shades. Designer Philip Bro Ludvigsen invented a system where transparent foil can easily be inserted behind the acrylic glass shade. There's enough room for four foils which gives the owner the opportunity to combine different patterns and thereby design his own lamp.*

▾ *The Le Klint company is named after one of the family members, the granddaughter of P.V. Jensen-Klint, who started the whole thing of folding paper into pleated lampshades. One of his sons, Kaare Klint, designed one of the company's first successes, Frugtlygten (the Fruit Lantern), while his other son, Tage Klint, headed the company and invented the special shade collar that keeps the shade supple.*

The company Le Klint, which was named after Tage's daughter, was started in 1943, and several models were put on the market the following years. Not only were the relatively ordinary shades for the floor lamp developed, but also more untraditional spherical pendants. Kaare Klint designed a pendant in 1944 called Frugtlygten (literally: the Fruit Lantern).

In the late 1960s, a young student of architecture by the name of Poul Christiansen (b. 1947) sat at his drawing board and played with his compass on a piece of paper. He scratched some sine curves, and when he picked up the paper, he noticed that he could fold it into some interesting shapes. That was the beginning of a new type of Le Klint lamp that wasn't folded in straight lines and at right angles, but in wavy lines. The forms were far better suited to the trends of the time, and the new lampshades, called Sinus, were a big success for the company. Le Klint had already worked with designers and architects for a long time, so it was no longer the family's home industry that drove the business forward.

A new Le Klint pendant series in a brand new material saw the light of day in 2004. The concept called Undercover was designed by Philip Bro Ludvigsen (b. 1962) and consists of a pendant of clear acrylic under which you can place coloured or patterned foil. So then you can change the motifs of the lamp as often as you want. From the beginning it came in both solid coloured foil and patterns that were designed by Danish textile designers. Later they entered into a collaboration with the Finnish clothing and textile company Marimekko to use their patterns for the shades. The various foils can be combined since it's possible to mount up to four foils on the inside of the clear shade.

▼ *The Sinus shade was designed by Poul Christiansen while he studied at the School of Architecture in Copenhagen in the late 1960s. The wavy lines fit the flower power style of the hippie era better than the traditional Le Klint shades.*

LK LIGHT SWITCHES. For 100 years, Lauritz Knudsen has dominated the Danish market for electrical equipment. In 1968 the company merged with Nordisk Elektricitets Selskab (the Nordic Electricity Company) and became LK-NES, but today it's called Lauritz Knudsen or just LK.

The Danish factories, including LK, had some advantages on the home market, since there are special standards for electrical equipment in Denmark, but that doesn't change the fact that LK has used design to create sturdy and characteristic products.

In 1910, Lauritz Knudsen began to design and manufacture light switches, and the first one was the rifled one in brass. The model was launched again as a new classic in 2005. In 1924 the rifled switch was replaced by one with a smoother and more functional appearance with a cap in either brown bakelite, brass or white porcelain. In 1934 another variant of the 1924 model came on the market, and the main visible difference was the missing ball at the end of the toggle. Yet another new LK switch arrived in 1938 and it was even better suited to be built into a wall or doorframe. It didn't stick out as much either and came in black, brown or white bakelite. An updated version came in 1948 – at first only in brown bakelite, but from the late 1950s also in a white version.

In 1959, their future fusion partner, NES, put a light grey pushbutton model on the market that also came in a version with a white/red indicator

1924.

for on/off. LK's very widespread 'Smal Minitangent' (narrow mini-tangent) switch came out in 1961 in grey bakelite.

In 1975, the company's chief designer Henning Andersen (b. 1923) designed the Plantangent switch that was awarded the ID prize. The large switch came in fancy colours, and the design was rather new since people had been used to little grey buttons. The product was sharp and geometric in its design and without superfluous details. Aesthetically it's related to B&O's products from that time. LK has continued producing similar switches that are known today as FUGA; the design has more rounded corners and a larger frame around the switch itself.

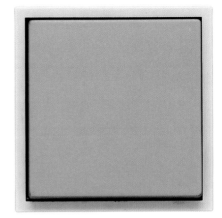

1975.

1934.

1938.

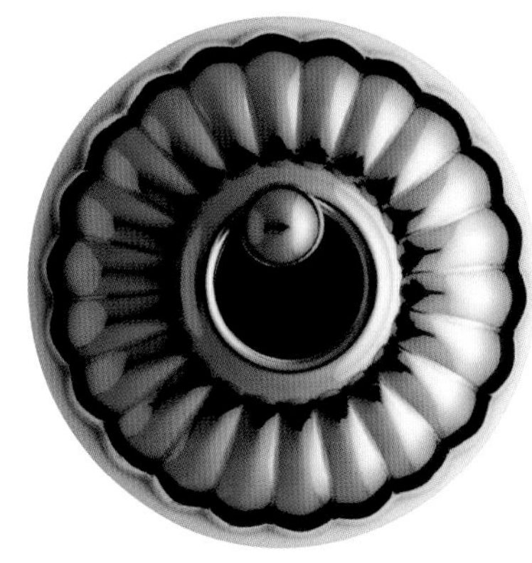

(1910) 2005.

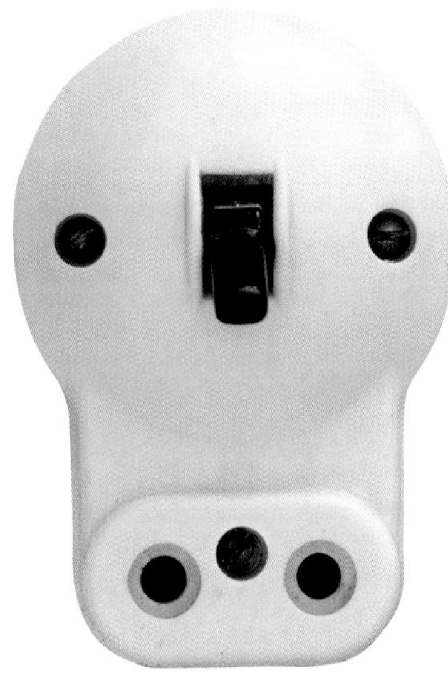

1948.

1959.

1961.

Design for the workplace

In the beginning of time, survival was of the utmost importance, and that was without a doubt hard work. It probably didn't occur to primitive man that there could be a difference between work and leisure time. During all his waking hours he tried to meet his basic needs. Therefore the first manmade objects were things that could increase his chances of survival. This means that some of man's oldest designs have been tools for things like hunting or defending oneself from enemies or the raging elements. Not until later did man begin to make things whose purpose was to make life more comfortable, such as furniture or games or things that had a symbolic or decorative function, such as cave paintings or the patterns on ceramics or fabric.

When we talk about design today, we have a tendency to focus very much on the interior design of the home and personal consumer products like clothes, cars and jewellery. On the other hand, many of the nameless products we use at work are not given the same attention. Yet we are also dependent on design that functions well in the workplace. This could be many things from the layout of the computer keyboard to the furniture and lighting of the workplace.

It is indeed thought-provoking that even though we have an increasing amount of aids and machines that can raise productivity, it doesn't seem to have reduced the workload. On the contrary, many of us actually define ourselves by our work and thus design in the workplace is also very significant to the welfare of modern man. Companies have also become increasingly aware of the significance of design in their everyday lives, and not just in the form of ergonomically designed workplaces that are meant to prevent deterioration of the body, but also in the form of designed

▾ A large number of many different types of Viking axes have been found in Denmark. The one called Telgjaøx looks the most like the axe called a broadaxe. The Telgja axe, like the broadaxe, has a 'crooked' handle that makes it possible to cut long and wide shavings off a plank.

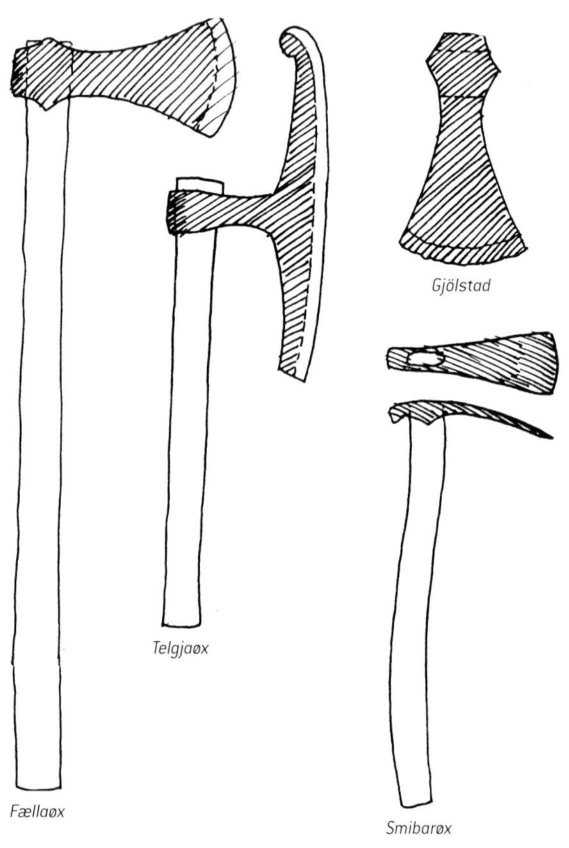

surroundings that create identity and job satisfaction for the company and its employees.

THE HISTORY OF THE AXE

One of history's oldest tools is the axe that has been used for war, hunting, tree felling and building ships and houses. Richly ornamented versions have also been made, such as in bronze, for ceremonial use and as a symbol of power and dignity. The axe can be traced back at least 100,000 years, and the first primitive axes were probably developed by an inventive Stone Age man who combined a hunting club and splits of flint. Originally axes were like other tools, very simple, but gradually different types emerged. Throughout history the axe has followed in the footsteps of man's development and that of society in general in that the division of work and the specialisation of tasks have led to various solutions in the design of axes. The discovery and use of new materials, such as metals, have led to even better and more sophisticated types of axes.

The initiative to develop new types of tools has especially come from the craftsmen themselves. For instance, carpenters had to make new types of axes when new challenges and special tasks were in the offing. Each individual craftsman in every trade often had to make his own personal tools that could, however, be passed on from father to son. The tool represented both expensive raw materials, like costly iron, and the time-consuming task of making the tool. Therefore much care was taken in the making and adaptation of a craftsman's tools. This design has resulted in some beautiful tools that people collect even today. As one of the fathers of modern English design, Sir Terence Conran, founder of the furniture chain store Habitat, has put it, 'how difficult it is to find an ugly working tool. Ordinary implements such as hammers, planes and wrenches, which have been designed to fit the hand and fulfil the function required of them with little or no thought of styling, have a natural beauty of their own.'

The axe is a good example of how hand tools have developed throughout history. During the transition from the Iron Age to the Viking Age in Denmark, around the year 800 AD, carpenters and shipbuilders had developed the axes that were necessary to build good ships. And it was the axe that was the primary tool for shipbuilding then since saws were hardly used. When they felled trees, split the trunks and made planks for the ships' sides, the axe was used. In the rest of the shipbuilding process, different axes were used. One of the most special and interesting types from this time is the so-called broadaxe, which was also used far into the 20th century. The Danish name, bredbil, comes from Low German and means the same thing. The broadaxe is used in the process of shaping beams and making large pieces of wood plane.

The broadaxe – a story about thorough ergonomics

When beams were made for houses or for large parts of ships, the first thing to do was to cut down a tree with a woodcutter's axe, which resembles the long-handled axes we know today. When the trunk was to be shaped into a square beam or a ship's keel, the carpenter first marked the places to chop with chalk. Then the woodcutter's axe was used to make some V-shaped cuts very close to the chalk line with intervals of about 50 cm. The broadaxe has a wide blade and a short handle, so it was easy to use this to remove the rest of the wood along the trunk. The advantage of this type of axe is that it can split plane surfaces, especially in wet wood. It's the only axe that is asymmetrical, that is, the blade is mounted at a 'crooked' angle in relation to the handle, so the carpenter doesn't hit his knuckles while working on a wide piece of wood. Unlike most other axes, the broadaxe is only bevelled on one side so it can allow a flush stroke when hewing a flat plane on a log, almost like a big plane. A skilled carpenter could work his way along the trunk and chop off a shaving as long as the trunk.

On the famous Bayeaux tapestry from the late 1000s, which has been called the world's oldest comic strip, you can see how the ships were built for the Norman invasion of England in 1066. Here it's clear to see that three or four different types of axes were used for the initial felling of trees as well as for shipbuilding. We know from archaeological finds that the Vikings built their ships in exactly the same way. And Viking descendents who lived in Normandy built the ships depicted on the Bayeaux tapestry for William the Conqueror. It is clearly illustrated here how each axe had its specific purpose, and they couldn't do without any of them in their toolbox. You can also see the broadaxe at work both in turning the felled tree into lumber and in the shipbuilding process. Normally it's held with both hands and worked with short, vertical chopping motions. The blade has to be very sharp for the lumber to be cut plane and smooth and not frayed.

The broadaxes of the past were smaller than the later versions that have a bigger and broader blade. In the 1700–1800s the axe heads were often industrially manufactured, but carpenters put their own handle on them and sharpened the edge. Some craftsmen even had several of each individual axe type with different handles or degrees of sharpness. And that's even if an axe could cost up to two months' wages.

▾ *The broadaxe is a cutting axe that doesn't split the wood like other axes, but cuts off shavings like a plane. The broadaxe has a very thin blade that is flat on the side that faces the beam or plank you're working on. It usually had a slightly curved edge, but the shape varied according to the craft it was used for. The important thing was that one side was flat so that the axe could glide along the wood, and the bevelled edge has to be very sharply honed for the axe to cut. The pictures show that the handle is 'crooked', so there's room for your knuckles when you use it.*

The design of the broadaxe is a story about sensible ergonomics based on experience and practical use. Today the band saw and circular saw of the sawmill and lumberyard have taken over the work of the axe, and the broadaxe is now only used in jobs involving restoration. Once a part of an old tradition in building, this axe was extremely widely known and has today sunk into oblivion apart from a small circle of professional experts. Today, industrialisation has radically changed the way we treat wood. The irregularities and little faults that one put up with earlier have been replaced by precise cuts of wood. Everything that can't be cut into homogeneous standard products ends up as MDF and chipboard.

THE DESIGN OF TOOLS AND EQUIPMENT

Developing and designing new tools and implements is not always an easy art. Craftsmen are often conservative, demanding and particular. They have learned their craft through years of practical experience, and these tried and true methods of doing things do not change like the fashion in Paris. It can be very hard for an outsider to sell a whole new solution to a seasoned craftsman. The DIY people are often much more liable to buy a new, smart gadget that can solve next weekend's problem of getting the carport to stand erect. On the professional tool market it's often from craftsmen's own ranks that new ideas are presented of how tools and equipment can be improved or even redesigned.

More than just a drill

Steen Mandsfelt Eriksen (b. 1958), who has a background as a craftsman, was given an assignment while attending the School of Architecture in Copenhagen to design an ergonomic power drill. As he saw it, the problem wasn't that the existing drills were bad from an ergonomic point of view, but that both professional craftsmen and DIY people often had to switch between different uses of the machine. For example, first you have to drill a hole in a wall, and then you have to fasten the object with screws. Many people have two drills that they alternate between where one has a drill bit in it, and the other a screw bit. But it's a bother even with the cordless battery-driven machines. Couldn't one combine the two machines, he thought?

Steen Mandsfelt thought about this now and then while finishing his studies. His graduation project was a backpack vacuum cleaner for professional use, and later it was produced (see page 547). In 1999 he once again seriously started working with his idea of constructing a combination tool. Originally he thought to use the principle of the revolver, so you could turn the various drill or screw bits into place, but the concept would be too technically complicated. Then one day Mandsfelt saw a so-called turret lathe in a machine shop. It's a lathe where the various tools are mounted on an angled swivelling head so you can quickly alternate between them. This was something he could use.

His idea was elaborated on in 1999, and design models were built. The idea was to have a swivelling head with room for two tools; a kind of two-headed power drill. By activating a simple button on the side of the machine you could turn the head and use the other bit. This way it would be easy to alternate between the two functions when you were standing at the top of the ladder installing a new ceiling. Steen Mandsfelt got a design prize from the Danish Design Centre for his visionary idea the same year. But the setback was that when he had to find a tool factory, no one would buy the idea nor develop or even manufacture it for him.

◂ *Like most of Jacob Jensen's designs there's something fascinating about the cable drum from J.O. Madsen. Practical functionality combined with the designer's sense of aesthetics makes you want to grab one of the many black and red cable drums and fiddle with it. The products were developed in the early 1980s and are sold today by JO-EL, a firm in Odense.*

So he had to do it himself, but even after he had solved all the technical problems and patented the idea, none of the 14 power-tool factories he contacted would have anything to do with the new product. Luckily, in 2003 Mandsfelt met a visionary businessman, Stig Gamborg, who could see the product's potential, and together they put it into production in a factory in China.

'The world's biggest cable drum factory'

In the town of Bogense lives J.O. Madsen. He is a keen inventor and a real entrepreneur. For many years he's been interested in tools and accessories for craftsmen. In the late 1970s he realised that there was a good market for sturdy extension cords for building sites as well as for hobby use. This resulted in some metal cable drums, but he thought the product could be improved and be even more functional. So he contacted designer Jacob Jensen to initiate a collaboration for the development of new products. This led to a number of different cable drums in the early 1980s. They were made in the characteristic colours of red and black and can easily be spotted as places where you can access electricity for a drill or work lamp. The principle is very simple – you can roll out metres of cord and plug in a number of electrical appliances to the plastic box, and afterwards you can roll up the cord easily with the help of the built-in handle.

In 1993, Jacob Jensen explained on a TV program how many different things had to be taken into consideration in the design of the new cable drums. Besides being able to wind and unwind the cable easily, the cable drum had to withstand being thrown on the floor without breaking. It also needed thermal fuses to prevent the drum becoming overheated. It had to be easy to clean and a practical handle was also factored in. The product was a huge success not only in Denmark, but also on the export market, especially in England at first. In the TV program, Jacob Jensen concluded by stating what a delight it was to have the world's biggest cable drum factory in Bogense. It's not known if this is still true, but the cable drums are still selling like hotcakes to both professionals and all the DIY people. And J.O. Madsen? He has continued developing equipment for craftsmen, such as special toolboxes that can also be used as stools and foldaway workbenches for building sites.

JO-EL's Goliath

The Department of Industrial Design at the School of Architecture in Copenhagen no longer exists, but in the late 1980s and mid-1990s it was a creative milieu. Classes often took their starting point in solving concrete everyday problems and designing solutions based on innovation. Quite a few students in this department have since become trendsetters in developing practical, useful products for industrial manufacture. Some of the ideas, like Steen Mandsfelt's drill, began as study projects that were put into practice later. Another example of a study project from around 1985 was Anders Smith's worklight that was put into production some years later under the name of Goliath by JO-EL.

The assignment at the department was to design a worklight, and Anders Smith took his starting point in the very new flat and square fluorescent lamps of the time. Could these strange tubes be transformed into proper lighting? Back then, energy-saving bulbs weren't common, but Smith sketched a flat fixture that was furnished with a good reflector.

In this way, a 38-watt neon tube could emit the same light as a 300-watt halogen lamp, which was traditionally used on building sites. Moreover a

▾ *Industrial designer Steen Mandsfelt Eriksen discovered a problem that craftsmen had when alternating between different machines. His solution was to design a two-headed drill and screwdriver machine. But since none of the companies could see what a good idea it was, the designer put his machine into production himself.*

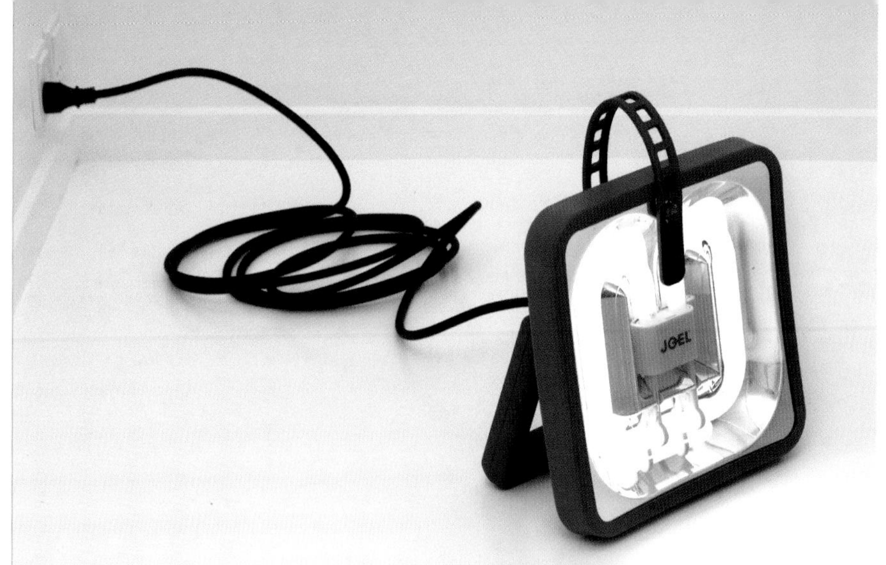

◂ *Anders Smith's Goliath lamp has changed the working conditions for professional construction workers and the DIY people. It is a well-designed example of a robust worklight that emits plenty of light without using lots of electricity or being something you could burn yourself on. This is the latest version of the worklight called Goliath 250 – the first version was designed while he attended the Royal Academy of Fine Arts, School of Architecture in the mid-1980s.*

big bar was mounted that could be used as a handle, to hang the lamp up on a wall or as an adjustable foot if the lamp were placed on the ground. When the lamp was further designed and manufactured by JO-EL, the parts were moulded in plastic. All the components could be assembled and taken apart without the use of tools, which was an advantage when having to change the tube and also when the fixture was eventually discarded and the parts sorted for recycling.

In the first year JO-EL marketed the lamp, which was called Goliath, they made over 25 million kroner in sales. About 85 % were exported, and more models were designed such as smaller lamps and some that were designed for indoor hobby use. In 2004, Anders Smith designed a successor to his original lamp, and it was called Goliath 250. The new lamp has a thicker rubber frame, so it can be dropped on the floor without breaking. Furthermore, the fixture has a neoprene strap that makes it easier to hang up where it's needed. Just like Jacob Jensen's cable drum, Goliath is a sturdy product with cool details that make it hard to keep one's fingers off it when visiting a DIY centre. A variant of the model called Goliath 250+ has two electric sockets on the back, so now the cable drum and the worklight are combined in one product.

The Knudsen Wedge

When craftsmen encounter a problem that irritates them, some of them can't help trying to solve it once and for all. This was what a carpenter foreman experienced in the late 1960s when he was tired of all the trouble he had with blocking up floors. During the post-war building boom, a lot of houses, institutions and office buildings were built, and many needed a wood floor. When laying a wood floor on top of something like concrete, you have to place something under the joists to make the floor plane and level. Previously, carpenters used bricks, bits of board and small wooden discs to get the correct thickness, and this was what Johannes Knudsen was tired of. There had to be an easier way of doing it.

The solution he reached became known as the Knudsen wedge. It's a little yellow plastic wedge with serrated sides that work like barbs. When you put two of these wedges together under a floor, they can't slide apart. If you press them together, you obviously get a thicker layer. So this is how laying floors became much easier – a couple of wedges under the joists at regular intervals, and now the carpenters didn't have to make provisional solutions. Moreover, plastic is moisture resistant, unlike wood, so the problems of the blocking-up wood expanding was also solved on this occasion.

When the idea was to be put into production, Johannes Knudsen contacted his son-in-law, who was in plastics. Take out a 50,000 kroner loan on your house, was his answer, and we'll start production. Lots of sizes and shapes have since been designed for various purposes, but the little yellow wedge is something we all know since it's often used as a doorstop. The patent on Knudsen's wedge expired in 1994, so now there are many copies on the market, but the original model is still manufactured in copious amounts at the factory in Frederiksværk.

A bucket can also be designed

Tools and work implements are many things. For the carpenter, a circular saw is indispensable. In other trades a good bucket is a tool just as important. The Vikan company, which is located in Skive, manufactures

PLYFA BOXES. For many years there was a company in Glostrup, outside Copenhagen, that manufactured crates for many purposes. They're made of thin, waterproof plywood with metal edging on the edges and corners. The company was previously called Kristian Stærk, and most of the boxes were used as sturdy packaging that could be reused several times, for example, for the delivery of bakery goods. But many craftsmen used the Plyfa boxes for their tools. These special toolboxes had handles and locks and loose drawers for bits and bobs. There was plenty of room beneath these drawers for bigger items. The robust look of these boxes can take a blob of paint and a couple of scratches without looking scruffy. Kristian Stærk was taken over a few years ago by a Finnish firm, and now it's called Moelven, but the boxes are still called Plyfa.

▸ The Knudsen wedge is an industrially manufactured solution to the problem of blocking up floors. Due to its flexible design and serrations that work like barbs, the necessary thickness can be achieved. The wedges can also be used for other purposes, for example when you have to put a whole window section in place or you need a doorstop.

◂ The new bucket from the Vikan company designed by the design office Spektre. New functions were incorporated in the design process such as the built-in handle on the bottom, the option to use a lid and several other functional details.

▾ Although the Vipp pedal bin is also used in many homes today, it was developed for professional use. Holger Nielsen (1914–92) was a smith, and his wife, who had a hairdressing salon, asked him in 1939 to make a proper bin. Then the doctor and dentist also wanted one, and that's how a large production started. Today Vipp is still a family-run business, and several sizes and models have been manufactured as well as other products for their line like soap dispensers and toilet brushes.

all kinds of cleaning equipment including buckets. In 2005 they asked the Aarhus-based design office Spektre to redesign the traditional 12-litre industrial bucket. Some improvements were made on the old model, and the freedom of design in using injection-moulded plastic has been utilised to the fullest.

For example, the rim is reinforced and smoother in shape so it's easier to grab hold of and keep clean. And for hygienic purposes, Spektre designed a handle near the bottom, about 3–4 cm above the floor, so that the user doesn't have to touch the bottom that has stood on the dirty floor to empty it. Furthermore, the lip of the bucket is quite wide and shaped so that the liquid flows in one jet when poured instead of sloshing all over and sometimes down the side of the bucket. They also designed a straight back so you can both carry it without bumping your leg and hang it on the wall in a stable manner. Finally there's a sturdy rim that lifts the bottom of the bucket 24 mm off the floor and makes it stiff and stable even when the bucket is full of a very hot liquid that often makes ordinary plastic buckets bulge. All in all, every aspect has been studied in the design process, and much thought has been put into the many details that have been improved. This is an example that an everyday article like an industrial bucket can be redesigned and improved.

DESIGNING TECHNOLOGY

Craftsmanship is very much based on crafting with the hands and using one's muscles. Only in the last 100-odd years have we come to take electric hand tools for granted. That's one of the reasons why the carefully crafted, smooth axe heads from the Stone Age impress us so much today. We're so used to pushing a button to start a 1000-watt power drill that the thought of grinding a flint stone by hand makes us shudder. Almost all types of work in ancient times have most certainly been laborious. To a certain extent, draft animals have delivered some raw power, but mainly in field work and as transportation. But when different types of mills were developed, mechanical power began to play a role. The oldest mills in Denmark were watermills and were introduced around the year 1000, and at least 250 years passed until the first windmills were mentioned in written sources.

Watermills were geographically dependent on water, while the wind blows everywhere, so in time, windmills played a dominant role. The oldest Danish windmills were the so-called post mills. They were built of wood and were relatively small since the whole millhouse had to be turned to bring the sails into the wind. The post was a thick beam that was dug into the ground and supported by crosstrees that the rest of the mill rested on and revolved around. This construction required that the miller stayed on his toes and figured out the direction of the wind, and if it had changed, he had to go out and turn the mill. The weak point of this type of mill was the place where the house sat on the post, and faulty use or a powerful storm could easily knock over the whole mill.

Around 1620 another type of mill could be found in Denmark, the so-called smock mill, which can still be seen in the Danish countryside. In contrast to the post mill, the smock mill could be partly made of brick since only the mill cap and sails turned. Not only was this construction far stronger, but the machinery could be more powerful. The cog wheels and axles were normally made of wood, but later on cast iron was also used. In the late 1700s this type became common all over Denmark. The mills

▸ *From the late 1700s the smock mill was the most widespread type of mill in Denmark since it was more sturdily built, and only the mill cap and sails were able to rotate. It could also produce more since the machinery inside could be heavier and more powerful than that of the post mill.*

▾ *The post mill was the most common type of mill in Denmark from the Middle Ages and up to the 1700s. Its size was limited by the fact that the whole millhouse had to be turned when the wind changed direction.*

were primarily used to mill grain, but during the great damming projects in the late 1800s, mills were constructed that could pump water out of the dammed areas with the help of spiral pump. No matter the type, mills gradually became a characteristic part of the Danish landscape in the same way the village churches had become so centuries before.

The experimental mill at Askov Folk High School

At the end of the 1800s about 30,000 small windmills of the wind wheel type were built in Denmark. They can still be seen in a few places and they resemble very much the little wind wheels with lots of short blades that we see out on the prairie in American westerns. These wind wheels were actually developed in the US in the 1850s, and the advantage was that they turned around at even very low wind speeds. In Denmark they were often used to pump water, but also to mill animal fodder and to power small machines in workshops. Until this time, special Danish mills hadn't been developed. The windmills in Denmark were built here, but they were copies of foreign models. Special Danish-designed mills didn't exist, but that would soon change. In the early 1880s, physicist, meteorologist and folk high school teacher Poul la Cour began to work on windmills and the possibility of producing electricity in this manner.

It was a very visionary idea because the first motorised electricity plants didn't open until 1891 in Denmark. But the very same year, he built the world's first wind-powered electricity plant at Askov Folk High School where he was a teacher. His first mill looked a lot like the wind wheels that had shot up all over the place at that time, but the wings on this mill were larger and more angular. And the wings were the focus of la Cour's attention because this is where he thought the most progress could be made by

▾ *Poul la Cour's experimental mill at Askov Folk High School in a traditional design that resembled that of the smock mill. On the right is his first attempt that looks more like a wind wheel. La Cour was mostly interested in the efficiency of the mills so he concentrated especially on the design of the wings. Therefore one of the world's first wind tunnels was constructed. On the whole, a lot of experiments with wind power took place at Askov until la Cour's death in 1908.*

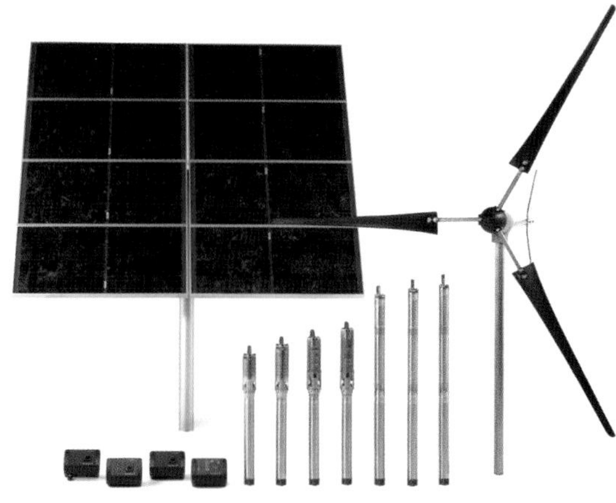

improving the design. He studied modern aerodynamics, and the wings were partly self-regulating in that the sections or flaps that constituted them would bend away when the wind was too strong and threatened to damage the mill.

In 1891 Poul la Cour was awarded a Civil List pension and in 1897 he got a special appropriation of 27,000 kroner for his next experimental mill. Back then it was an astronomical sum for such a purpose. With this mill, research in using wind power for the production of electricity could continue at Askov Folk High School. La Cour's windmill was built on top of a research centre that had been designed by architect P.V. Jensen-Klint, who later became famous for designing the Grundtvig church (see page 288). This research station contained one of the world's first wind tunnels, which in this case was used for aerodynamic experiments on the design of mill wings. The new mill actually looked older than the first one since it was built in the smock style. The experiments at the folk high school focused on making the best possible technique to produce electricity whereas the design of the towers of the mills was of secondary importance.

Poul la Cour's efforts made Askov Folk High School self sufficient in energy. He also worked on the problem of the wind not blowing all the time. He solved this problem by using surplus electricity in windy periods to split water into hydrogen and oxygen. The hydrogen could be used in special lamps at windless times. Later la Cour also tried to use hydrogen in some motors that would keep the production of electricity going for up to 24 hours when the wind wasn't blowing, and after that a gasoline-driven emergency generator had to be started. Poul la Cour was a proper inventor, but his work also had important aims in the fields of general education

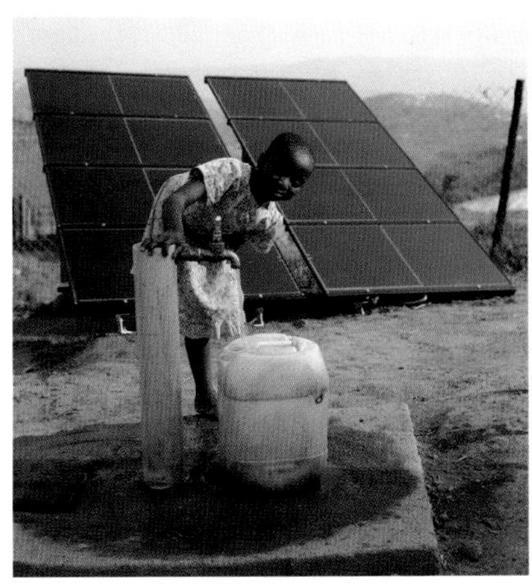

GRUNDFOS. IF YOU see design as something that has a particularly good appearance, you might have difficulty understanding why a company like Grundfos has been awarded ID prizes from the Danish Design Centre so many times over the years. The merit of design in this case is to make a technological product like a pump understandable, manageable and easy to use. Furthermore, good design can make a product easier and cheaper to manufacture or more environmentally friendly to use or to dispose of. One of the more obvious examples of how Grundfos is good at designing is the drinking water pump SQFlex that got the ID prize in 2003. This pump was designed to secure drinking water in isolated areas since it's either powered by electricity from a solar panel, a little windmill or a generator. Along with the pump Grundfos can supply the energy source(s) that the customer finds most suitable to his needs. The pump has built-in electronics so it's both easy to use and the motor continually adjusts to the energy supplied.

and industrial policy. He worked with Grundtvigian persistence in getting electricity to the rural areas, and until his death in 1908, about 100 small wind-powered electricity plants had been built in the manner of the Askov mill, but often in a more modern design that resembled the wind wheels more than the smock mills. Furthermore, Askov Folk High School became the centre for educating technicians that could use and maintain these plants; they were like rural electricians. The falling oil and gasoline prices, especially after World War I, made these mills unprofitable, and apart from a blossoming during the occupation, la Cour's initiatives died out.

Posterity and the Gedser turbine

Some of la Cour's collaborators did continue on a small scale to develop and build windmills in the first half of the 20th century. Among others, quite a few la Cour mills were built by the Funen-based company Lykkegaard. The design was very simple: a four-winged mill mounted on a mill tower that was a simple grating construction made of steel sections. Other companies experimented with the number of mill wings and a better aerodynamic design of the wings, for instance Hans L. Larsen's Factories in Fredericia that manufactured the Agricco Mill. They made six different sizes of mills and the smallest had four wings, the medium model had five, and the largest mills had six wings. All of these mills were almost without exception used in rural areas on either farms that had to pump water or workshops that needed to power their machinery.

Not until the German occupation did a large company start building mills, and that was F.L. Smidth, who together with the aeroplane factory Kramme & Zeuthen built electricity-generating mills to replace the diesel oil and coal that the war had caused a shortage of. The mill towers were built in concrete, which was due to the shortage of iron as well as the fact that F. L. Smidth owned a cement factory. The towers turned out to be a little awkward and badly proportioned, especially since only two short wings were mounted on the big concrete towers. During the war, about 20 of these mills were built, and they supplied a necessary but not significant supplement to the production of electricity. After the war, the big companies lost interest in wind power.

However, in 1947 an enthusiast began working on windmills. His name was Johannes Juul, and at the age of 17 in 1904 he was the youngest participant ever at la Cour's courses for rural electricians at Askov Folk High School. For many years Juul had worked for SEAS, the electrical company on Zealand, and when he was hired, one of his conditions was that he could simultaneously do research and development in electricity. Throughout the years he worked on developing a number of technical improvements on electrical material and, among other things, in 1930 he invented a low-volt stove that was patented. The management at SEAS supported Juul's work by developing a new generation of windmills for the production of electricity, and in 1950 the first experimental wind turbine was erected in Vester Egesborg on southern Zealand. The following year SEAS took over an older mill from F.L. Smidth on the island of Bogø before the big Gedser turbine was finished in 1957. In the meantime, the government had granted 300,000 kroner for research purposes.

Johannes Juul's construction in Gedser had a 200 kW generator. The idea was that it was only meant to generate electricity directly to the grid, and with a good wind it could supply electricity for all of south Falster even if this was just an experimental turbine. The construction became the

▼ *The Tvind wind turbine was built in concrete from 1975 to 1978, primarily by enthusiastic amateurs that were students and teachers at the Travelling Folk High School and the Necessary Teaching Training College in Ulfborg. Back then and for a number of years, it was the world's biggest wind turbine. The checked pattern is relatively new, from 1999, and was designed by architect Jan Utzon.*

basis for the future wind turbine industry in Denmark. It had three wings, which was the most cost-effective construction, and several other features that made the mill cap turn in the optimal direction and prevented the mechanics from being overloaded at high wind speeds. The tower that held the wings and the generator house was 25 m tall and cast onsite in cement with three sturdy supporting struts. Compared to the wind turbines of today, the Gedser turbine seems a bit oversized and not very elegant, but the pilot project in wind energy caused a great stir abroad. The turbine ran for ten years, until 1967, and when the energy crisis hit in the early 1970s, so much experience had been gained from this project that a new Danish wind turbine industry had valuable knowledge to build on.

The new Danish wind turbine industry

The oil crisis in the 1970s kick-started the development of new energy sources. While many politicians and businessmen thought along the lines of atomic energy, a new grassroots movement in the field of energy policy arose like the one at Askov Folk High School had done about 100 years earlier. In the beginning the new wind turbine builders were driven by pure enthusiasm, and the ones at Tvind Folk High School were the most spectacular. From 1975–78, the teachers and students at Tvind constructed the biggest wind turbine in the world at that time. The turbine was cast onsite in concrete using a process called gliding formwork. This means that the tube-shaped tower was cast bit by bit, and the formwork, that is the casting mould, was gradually moved upwards as the work progressed. This is done because the cement mustn't cure completely before a new layer was added, otherwise cracks and fractures could arise in the structure. And this is why the work was done in back-to-back shifts until the top was reached.

Johannes Juul's Gedser wind turbine from 1957 generated electricity for ten years on an experimental level. The turbine with its massive concrete construction seems a bit oversized compared to the size of the wings, but Johannes Juul was a careful man and wanted to avoid wrecking the construction. The Gedser wind turbine was used again from 1977–1979, especially to record measurements that formed the basis of the construction of new turbines and their location. Below is the Gedser turbine during its deconstruction in 1992. The drawing shows the technique behind the turbine's adjustable wings.

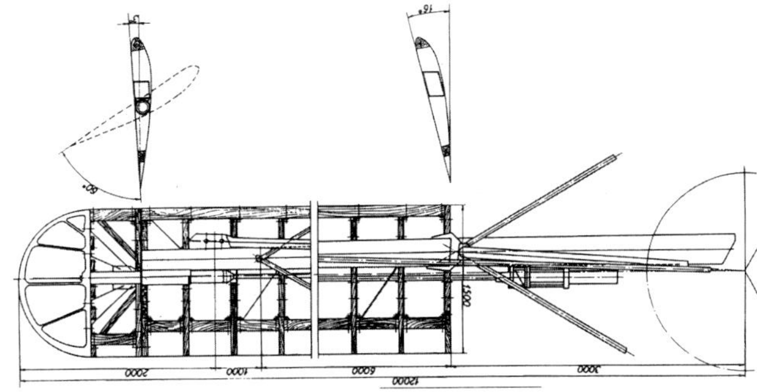

The Tvind wind turbine is still running merrily and has only been stopped for maintenance and repairs in the almost 30 years it's been running. It runs a 900 kW generator, which is more than four times the amount of the Gedser turbine. The tower is also twice as high, namely 53 metres, and the wing diameter is 54 metres. The Tvind turbine is atypical by being a downwind turbine, which means that the wings turn behind the tower in comparison to the wind direction. Like other cement turbines, the Tvind turbine looks a bit more awkward that the more common steel turbines we know today. On the other hand, in 1999 it was painted in red and white checks, like a huge piece of pop art, according to specifications made by architect Jan Utzon. By completing the project and running the turbine, Tvind has proven that it's possible to build big wind turbines that could cost-effectively generate energy.

Concurrently with Tvind's project there were innumerable other pioneers in the field that built different kinds of turbines. Many of these small turbines were household turbines designed to supply hot water to one or a couple of ordinary households. Heat was sometimes generated with the help of a dynamo, but you could also utilise the friction energy by letting a kind of whisk heat the liquid that was circulated in the radiators of the house. Other pioneers built smaller turbines that were merely meant to generate electricity, and they sold surplus electricity to the power plants, although the latter weren't always pleased about having all these small-time amateurs as suppliers.

These experimental years were a mixed bag of designs. All kinds of constructions were attempted, from cement towers to steel lattice towers. Many shapes of wings were also experimented with – short, wide wings

◀ *The Middelgrund Wind Farm Guild was established in 1997, and the turbines were officially opened on May 6, 2001. More than 8,000 consumers bought turbine-shares in the project, and today it supplies 3 % of Copenhagen's collective electricity. The 20 turbines, which each supply 2mW, were built by Bonus Energi, a company that was bought in 2004 by the German industrial magnate Siemens, who wanted to get a foothold on the international market for wind turbines. Since then the number has dropped to 5,500, but on the other hand, the size of the turbines has increased, so wind energy today (2005–6) covers 20 % of the collective Danish electricity consumption. In 2008 it is estimated to reach 25 %.*

and long, narrow ones. In the late 1970s there were dozens of small and medium-sized manufacturers of which some had previously produced agricultural equipment, but had now switched to making wind turbines. Around the year 2000, there were a handful of factories left, and after a number of mergers, there was only one Danish wind turbine factory left, namely Vestas. The constructions had now become much bigger than the household turbines of the 1970s, and idealism was no longer the driving force, but also share prices and the world market had entered the picture. For example, Danish wind turbines were already being exported in the 1980s to wind parks in places like California.

The design has also undergone great changes in the last 25 years, for not only do the giant turbines of today make demands for more solid constructions, but the economy of the projects also demand a rational production. Last, but not least, the public demands that considerations are taken to the places where the turbines are erected by requiring aesthetic designs that mar the landscape as little as possible. All these things are factored in the construction, design and colouring of the new turbines. The tall, slim and white turbines are far more elegant than the Gedser turbine's grey cement block from 1957. And the wind farm that was built in 2000–01 on Middelgrunden, off the coast of Copenhagen harbour, is today a beautiful symbol of a visionary energy policy – something that brands Copenhagen and Denmark for our visitors.

PERFECT

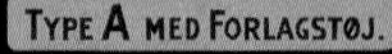

KRAFTCENTRIFUGEN

BURMEISTER & WAINS

MASKIN & SKIBSBYGGERI KØBENHAVN C.

CREAM SEPARATORS. Just like Poul la Cour's rural electricians who spread technical knowledge and thus contributed to the mechanisation of agriculture and the starting of small industries, the co-operative dairies' production of butter resulted in greater demands on dairy machines. The most important machine was the cream separator or centrifuge. It could quickly and hygienically separate raw milk into cream and skimmed milk. The cream was turned into butter, which was one the first big export successes of the co-operative dairies. The separator was originally a German invention, but the late 1870s saw large-scale production of them in Denmark with strong competition from the Swedish factory Alfa Laval. Maglekilde Maskinfabrik (Machine Factory) patented their centrifuge in 1878 and three years later sold the rights to Burmeister and Wain. Mikael Pedersen, who was later known for his Pedersen bicycle, took part in developing the Maglekilde separator, but he wasn't included in the patent, so he went to Roskilde Machine Factory where he developed an improved version. Later, Pedersen took the rights to this centrifuge to England, where he made a fortune in collaboration with the Lister factory. For 20 years, Burmeister and Wain continued the production of their Perfect Kraft centrifuge, selling some 10,000 of them. Rapid distribution of cream separators to co-operative dairies had a great impact on the quality of dairy products and on the organisation of Danish agriculture in co-operative projects.

DESIGN FOR BETTER WORK

In a society where the demands for efficiency on the job are ever increasing, the way work is organised also becomes more important. There are simple, physical limits as to how fast we can complete our work tasks. Therefore the tools, machines and systems we work with have great importance not only for our efficiency, but also for our work satisfaction and in terms of how quickly we get tired and worn down. For example, in the old days in Denmark refuse workers carried the garbage can on their shoulder or back to the garbage truck and emptied it by turning it upside down. Later, paper sacks were introduced and they were lighter than the cans and saved the refuse workers the return trip with the empty can. In some places, large fibreglass dumpsters on wheels are used, but that's mostly in large building complexes with good terrain. In residential neighbourhoods the paper sack method is still used.

But if you're a supplier of paper trash sacks, it might be a good idea to study how your sacks are used. Maybe the system of collecting trash wasn't quite as well thought out, and perhaps it could be made easier and more environmentally healthy. This is what the company Bates Kornäs did in the mid-1990s, and they did so together with a large Danish design office, namely Christian Bjørn Design. Together they developed a sorting and transport system that won an ID prize in 1995. The system still uses the classic paper sacks, but a special holder makes it possible to sort the garbage into two categories: kitchen waste and other waste.

There are three stands on the holder, and one is always empty. So when the refuse collector comes to collect the garbage, he already has an empty stand with him, and it's put in the empty slot.

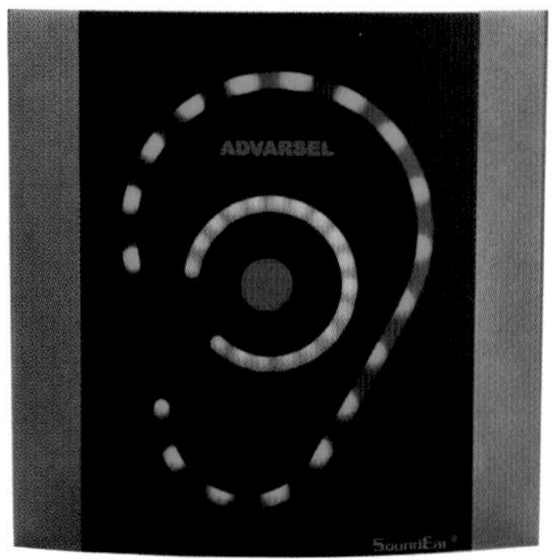

Using a specially designed transport cart, he takes the first full sack to the truck. Here a special lifting device empties the stand in the garbage truck and a new sack is inserted on the way back down, and the process is repeated. The transport cart is robust and made of stainless steel with two disc wheels that can navigate small obstacles easily. The design is ergonomic, and the modern refuse collector is spared constant lifting and great strain. The system is still in use in some Danish municipalities.

THE SOUND OF DESIGN

Noise is a big nuisance in many people's everyday lives, and the number of cases of hearing damage is also large. Many are greatly afflicted by it at work, and the traditional industrial workplaces are no longer the worst places; here many resources have been spent on reducing machine noise. Yet there are a lot of musicians who get tinnitus, and among daycare workers there are many whose hearing is damaged. A project worker at the Danish Music Council, Lars Boldt, knew how great the acoustic problems were in concert halls and rehearsal rooms, and he realised that there wasn't an inexpensive sound level meter on the market. Together with a friend from Copenhagen Business School, Ole Juul, he decided to solve this problem. The result was that they founded SoundShip in 1998 and developed a sound level meter called SoundEar.

This is a noise indicator to hang on the wall in rooms where there are noise problems. Originally it was meant for rehearsal rooms to prevent musicians from getting their hearing damaged or complaints from the neighbours, but the music industry was only 20 % of the market – 80 % of the customers are daycare centres where the sound level is just as ear splitting. When SoundEar is turned on, the green ear lights up, but when the noise level reaches a certain level, the yellow ring lights up, and at even higher noise levels the red dot in the middle of the ear lights up as well as the word WARNING. The sound level has two settings, 85 dB, which is the maximum level in ordinary rooms, and 105 dB, the limit for rehearsal rooms and concert halls. The device can be supplemented with a SoundBuster that turns off the power of a stereo, for example, when the sound level has been in the red zone for more than ten seconds. Later on, the SoundEar 2000 was launched, and here you can choose your own warning level on a 16-step scale.

SoundShip soon started a collaboration with designer Anders Heger (b. 1958), who developed the SoundEar casing, which is raised from one piece of sheet metal without welded joints. The facing is made of PVC and can easily be switched, for example, to other languages. The purpose of the design was to indicate that SoundEar wasn't an extremely precise device, but rather a guide for its users. SoundEar was put on the market in 1999 and won the ID prize the same year. Since then, several products have followed, such as PocketEar, which is a personal noise meter that you can carry in your pocket with a set of earplugs. Many of SoundShip's products are exported.

The big sound level meter

While SoundShip is a rather small, new company in phonometry, Brüel & Kjær is an older and much bigger firm in the field. It was founded in 1942 by engineers Per Brüel (b. 1915) and Viggo Kjær (b. 1914) and was based on their common interest in acoustic measurements when they were students. This led especially to the development and manufacture of noise meters and advanced microphones that are so first-rate that they were used in the first American lunar probe.

◂ *SoundEar is a relatively inexpensive type of noise alarm that in a very educational way warns you when the noise level is too high. When the green light is on, all is well, when the yellow one lights up, it's getting critical, and when the red light goes on, the safe noise level is exceeded.*

▸ *The three sound level meters from Brüel & Kjær are from, respectively, 1965 (top right), 1993 (top left) and 2004 (below). Together they fairly well represent development in design in the last 40 years in the 'device' industry, going from a casing of raised and pressed sheet metal to a smooth and streamlined design in mould-injected plastic to an ergonomic design with slip-resistant rubber surfaces.*

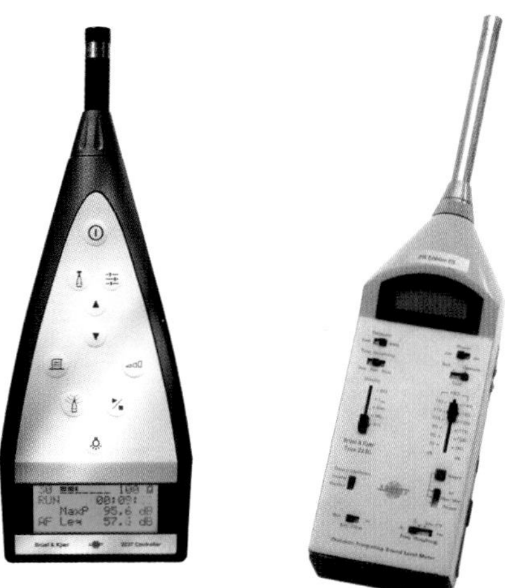

Otherwise the firm's products are mainly used as tools by acoustic engineers, the Danish Working Environment Authority and environmental authorities. The first time Brüel & Kjær were recognised for their industrial design was in 1965 when they got their first ID prize from the Danish Design Council, now known as the Danish Design Centre.

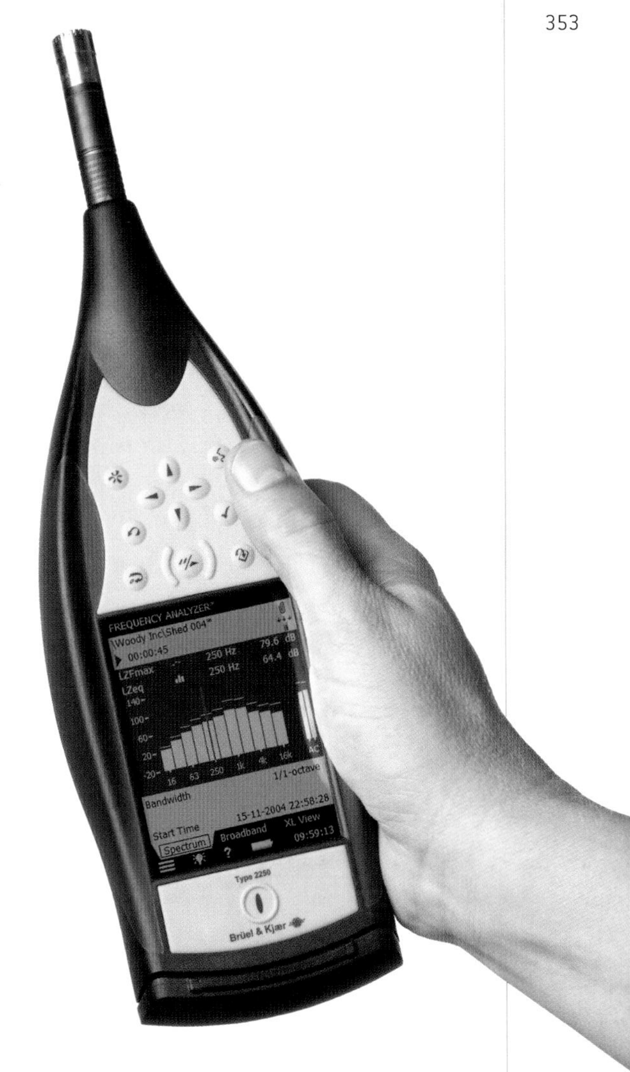

The acknowledgement was for a hand-held sound level meter, model 2203, that was the firm's first development of this type of equipment. The form was determined by the technology of the time in raising and pressing thin metal sheets and by the electronics inside the device. Furthermore, the microphone had to be placed in an undisturbed place like the end of the casing. The pale, faded green colour was haphazardly chosen by the in-house development team that designed model 2203. One of the founders, Per Brüel, stated a few years later in a publication from the Danish Design Centre that they probably wouldn't choose that colour if they had the chance to choose another. But this was the colour that Brüel & Kjær became known for in the business, where they were responsible for some the most advanced sound equipment at the time.

But the random choice of colour shows how significant a company's decisions can be in the field of design. Suddenly you're stuck with a colour that you later realise that you don't really like, but perhaps it was a fashionable colour at the time. Later on, Brüel & Kjær used professional designers because, as Per Brüel said in the aforementioned interview, 'There is a connection between the design of a product and its technical quality. The two things affect each other. It's about being one step ahead all the time regarding technology and design and predicting what people who work in acoustics will want in 20 years.'

◂ *Despite the fact that R. Malling-Hansen's various versions of the Writing Ball from the 1870s were faster than the American Remington typewriter, it still lost the battle of becoming the archetype of the future typewriter. The Remington system with a cylindrical rubber roller was used for over 100 years until the computer gradually took over.*

For a number of years, Brüel & Kjær had a lucrative niche on the world market, and for a while it was the Danish company which had the highest number of engineers employed. However, the company had financial problems in the 1980s and was taken over by foreigners in 1992.

In 1992–93, the second generation of hand-held sound level meters was developed by Brüel & Kjær and designed by a team headed by industrial designer Steve McGugan (b. 1960). A series of meters with model numbers in the 2230s were made. This second generation had a much more aerodynamic look than the earlier model. Phonometry is very dependent on there not being acoustic reverberations from the casing. A square casing would give erroneous readings, and therefore the new series of meters should preferably have the shape of a ship's hull for the sound waves to glide undisturbed along the device. New, smaller and more modern electronic components made it possible to make the new meters smaller than the old one, and also more streamlined. The control buttons are located on the top and can be used in roughly the same way as a remote control.

In 2003–4 yet another generation of sound level meters was developed, still with Steve McGugan as the chief designer, and it was even more streamlined. Naturally the new series was technologically updated, but more emphasis was given to ergonomics than in the previous models that could be slippery, especially if the user wore gloves. The new models, whose type numbers are in the 2250s, have a kind of ridge on the sides, and the gripping areas are of rubber. Both of these features give the meter a better grip and greater sturdiness if you should drop it. This design was given the ID prize in 2004, and together the three generations of sound level meters are an interesting study in design development in the technical industry in the last 40 years. In the beginning it was mainly a piece of technical equipment that was scantily designed and randomly coloured. In the next round the design was used to optimise the acoustic capabilities and the instrument panel. But in the latest generation of sound level meters, user-friendliness has been prioritised even more by using ergonomic design and more suitable materials.

BEHIND THE DESK – OFFICE EQUIPMENT

Alongside the development of industrial production methods in large companies there also arose the need for a corresponding administration in the new enterprises as well as in the public sector. The office is where these new tasks took place, and much of the work was about registering what happened in the company and what came in and what went out. Many of the very basic tasks were accounting, filing and corresponding with customers and suppliers. Long after industrialisation, this was done by hand; letters were written by hand and accounts were written in ink in large ledgers. Like many other tasks in modern times, one tried to improve these procedures and rationalise the work.

R. Malling-Hansen (1835–90) was a teacher, minister and inventor, who after certifying as a teacher was employed by the Royal Deaf-Mute Institute in Copenhagen in 1859. Later, he got a degree in divinity and became the principal of the institute in 1865. Malling-Hansen was very enthusiastic about breakthroughs in education in his time especially with regard to teaching the deaf-mute, and he also did research in the area. Among other things, he tried to improve sign language, and that quickly led him to develop a kind of communication apparatus that could speed

THE ERGONOMIC FLOOR. Since 1990, the firm Ergomat, located near Søndersø on northern Funen, has designed special ergonomic rubber matting. These floorings were developed by Arne Rex Bræmhøj and are especially used as anti-fatigue mats where people stand and work for long periods of time, such as while working a machine or packing goods. The matting is very flexible and made of polyurethane, which is a lot like firm foam rubber, and it alleviates many of the problems of stationary work, such as bad circulation and tired legs and feet. The mats are available in many types and patterns depending on the industry in which they are used, for example there are special requirements in the food industry for easy-to-clean products. You could call these mats a kind of artificial grass that the employees can stand on instead of cement floors. An almost overlooked design for a better working environment.

up the rate of communication. In 1865 he made his first prototype of a typewriter which he then got assistance in developing, making more reliable and production friendly.

R. Malling-Hansen's typewriter was called the Hansen Writing Ball because of its appearance. It looked a bit like a mechanical porcupine with the keys placed in the form of a sphere. The principle of the Writing Ball was that when you pressed a key, the rod on which it was placed descended and hit the carbon paper, which then hit the paper underneath it. On some of his models the paper was fastened to a semi-cylindrical roller, but on other models the paper was on a flat mechanical frame. In 1870, Malling-Hansen patented the Writing Ball for a period of 15 years, and it was the world's first typewriter that was mass produced. In 1872 this model was presented at the Nordic exhibition in Copenhagen where it attracted a lot of attention and was then exhibited at world exhibitions in Vienna the following year and Paris in 1878; in both exhibitions it was awarded a medal. Here licensing rights were sold to manufacturers abroad, but the Writing Ball was quickly outmatched by the American typewriter brand Remington, although it is said that it was not as fast to write on.

The businessmen's interest in Malling-Hansen's typewriter had little to do with their interest in deaf-mutes, but rather in the economic potential of typewriters in rationalising office work. Before his time, if you wanted a text printed on a piece of paper, you had to send the handwritten manuscript to a printer where it was first typeset. Afterwards you could have it duplicated in large numbers. Throughout his life, R. Malling-Hansen worked with solving problems that arose in his own everyday life. In 1872, he introduced xerography or dry photocopying, which was an invention for the mechanical copying of letters and drawings by means of a system of carbon paper and rollers. Xerography was also the focus of international interest, but it was never widespread.

The mechanisation of the office

The interest in Malling-Hansen's Writing Ball illustrates that the time was ripe for new breakthroughs in office technology. The continuing development of new office machines, and the rising number of manufactured versions indicates that the administrative tasks skyrocketed in the private and the public sector. While Malling-Hansen's Writing Ball appears to have been a technical apparatus almost without any design considerations, attention would soon be paid to the aesthetic aspect as well as the practical design of these machines. If you take a closer look at the Writing Ball, you'll see that the mechanics can cause problems such as getting wide sleeves caught in the keys, rods and paper holder. Some of the first designs in this area are simply about surrounding all the mechanics in suitable, but maybe also beautiful, casings.

This is the kind of design that is often called styling among professional designers. The word isn't uttered with respect, but rather with contempt. For many seriously functionalist designers and architects it corresponds to putting make-up on a corpse and hiding the technical problems behind fancy screens. To a great degree, styling is a concept that arose with the automotive industry and especially the American automobile designers' yearly job of doing a facelift on last year's model.

In contrast to this are the designers whose ideal it is to work seriously with their trade and to feel that design must be innovative and improve the product, also functionally. Enveloping an office machine or an automobile in colourful, lacquered casing is deceiving the consumers; it's like putting frosting on a cake that has no nutritional value.

In Europe, and perhaps especially in the Nordic countries, designers have for long periods of time had a hard time accepting the American way of styling, which originates from the fields of industry that makes cars, consumer electronics, kitchen appliances and the like. The design was often inspired by the big companies' marketing departments whose interviews of customers and questionnaires resulted in their knowing 'what consumers want'. Their surveys asked car owners if they liked chrome on their cars, and if they did, this information was relayed to the design department, and in many cases more chrome was put on the fenders or around the headlights.

Unlike the American philosophy of design, many Danish designers subscribed to the unsentimental and cool artistic idiom, often with slightly angular lines like those of the German design tradition from the Bauhaus and Ulm schools. In this way they stressed the common sense aspect of their design. Although in many of these cases you could also talk about encasing machinery, yet in angular and lacquered metal, it seemed to be more 'intelligent' and rational. These designers believed in the American architect William Sullivan's motto 'form follows function', which despite its American origin sounds very European. Here follows the story of two very different ways of designing office equipment.

The 'American' model

The first and one of the most successful and internationally oriented design offices ever to exist in Scandinavia was established in 1949. It was located in downtown Copenhagen, and the two designers were the Danish architect Acton Bjørn (1910–92) and the Swedish artist and industrial designer Count Sigvard Bernadotte (1907–2002). They were both inspired by the American way of running a design office where they were the bosses who led the team and authoritatively told the employees what to do. Their design style was to a certain degree American, for example the firm's illustrations were often brightly coloured perspective drawings made with magic markers, coloured pencils and pastels. This was a sharp contrast to the prevailing style among Danish architects and designers, who preferred to sketch their projects in pencil and render them in ink, possibly supplemented by a single, dreamy watercolour.

Bjørn & Bernadotte's artistic idiom was also different. They had both been to the US, and Bernadotte had also studied in New York. They would eventually work with Boeing and McDonald Douglas on fitting out SAS aeroplanes. They designed irons and other appliances for General Electric. Their artistic idiom was characterised, but not dominated, by the soft American lines, which are apparent in their Margrethe bowls for Rosti. They also designed a transistor radio that had a relatively tight geometric style for Bang & Olufsen. For the company Contex they designed a series of mechanical calculators in 1960.

Their collaboration with Contex began in the late 1940s, and Bjørn & Bernadotte started with a very soft and organic artistic idiom, which they later tightened up, but never completely abandoned.

▾ *Although the Contex 10 from 1957 (right) has a more angular casing over its mechanics than the Contex A from 1946, the shape still has slightly curving forms. And this can be done when working with casting, as in this case, where Contex A is cast in metal and Contex 10 is moulded in plastic. If the casings had been raised in metal sheets as Eskofot's photocopier (see page 359), all the lines and surfaces would have been straight. So the chosen material determines very much the form of what is to be designed.*

THE LASAT MODEM. The sharply cut 'black box' aesthetics still has its persistent advocates. Jacob Jensen's architectural practice, which has been run by his son, Timothy Jensen, since 1990, uses straight lines and clean geometry almost as their hallmark. The style was perfected while working on Bang & Olufsen's products throughout the 1960s and 1970s. In 1993 Jacob Jensen Design created a series of modems for the Danish firm Lasat. Jacob Jensen's modem drew heavily on the very same B&O look, and did so to such a degree that one was tempted to think that it was a Bang & Olufsen product. In this case, the role of design was to make the product inspire more confidence in the user so that one trusted that it worked and was well thought out, and that one didn't have to be a geek to figure out how to use it. The futuristic design was emphasised by Lasat's logo whose typeface looks just like what NASA used in its logo for many years.

The mechanical calculator, as the name indicates, was completely mechanical, and especially the sound it made was very characteristic. Every touch or rather hit of the big cycle bar emitted a short but loud clatter, and the result was shown on the display. The casing was cast in plastic, and on the later models from the 1950s and early 1960s, the casing completely covered the mechanics inside. Today we find this type of machine completely outdated, but in the post-war era it was advanced machinery, and 90 % of the calculators were exported, and pirated copies started turning up in places like the Soviet Union.

The 'German' inspiration

If anyone is the representative for unsentimental and geometric design in Denmark, it's Jan Trägårdh (see page 84). One of the biggest clients in his career was Eskofot, a company that for decades has made photocopiers for office use and printing equipment for the darkroom. In Jan Trägårdh's design these previously very technical and slightly disorganised products became clarified machines in raised and lacquered steel plates with rather sharp edges.

Planocop F7 from 1964 was the first of over 80 products that he designed for Eskofot throughout the years. From a technical and user point of view it was a very advanced photocopier. The Planocop copier was typical of Trägårdh's artistic idiom which was to construct a box of well-proportioned panels that were spray painted in a dark grey. The variation of colours on the copier emphasises where the controls are and draws one's attention to it. There's a knob to adjust the lightness and darkness of the copy, small circular warning lights, and on the side there's a little handle for the paper feed.

Jan Trägårdh's starting point is that the user isn't interested in the technical goings-on inside the machine, but only in getting a copy of a document. And therefore he plays down any reference to the internal mechanics. The product becomes an almost anonymous box whose appearance hardly denotes its function. But what Trägårdh and Eskofot achieved by this was to make people curious to find out what was inside this expensive-looking thing with its delicately enamelled surfaces. When Planocop F7 came on the market, its design was so different from anything else in the office that it was the object of fascination. You could just as well have placed a japanned jewellery box in the office, for the effect would have been the same, namely that you had to check out what it was and touch it.

And that's probably what Trägårdh wanted to achieve. Instead of a flashy intricate machine with lots of buttons and lights, he made an inconspicuous apparatus in a simple artistic expression. The question is whether the machine-aesthetic design in Trägårdh's version is so radically different from Bjørn & Bernadotte's modelled version of a calculator. On a functional level the two artistic idioms aren't far apart. It was probably a question of personal style in combination with the spirit of the times changing from the 1950s to the 1960s. As far as Contex is concerned, the competition from the big electronics companies' calculators got too stiff in the 1970s, and Contex had to close down shortly after Trägårdh had designed his first electronic calculator for them in 1973.

Desk equipment

Not everything you need in an office has to be high-tech, but it can still be well designed. In the mid-1970s, designer Henning Andreasen (b. 1923) designed a stapler for the Folle company which won the ID prize in 1978.

▾ *Eskofot's Planocop 505, an improved version of the F7 photocopier from 1964, was designed by Jan Trägårdh. Its artistic expression is a true product of the European functionalist style. Everything on the product is geometric – all rectangles and circles. The colours are also toned down and elegant, and in its entirety exudes something deeply serious.*

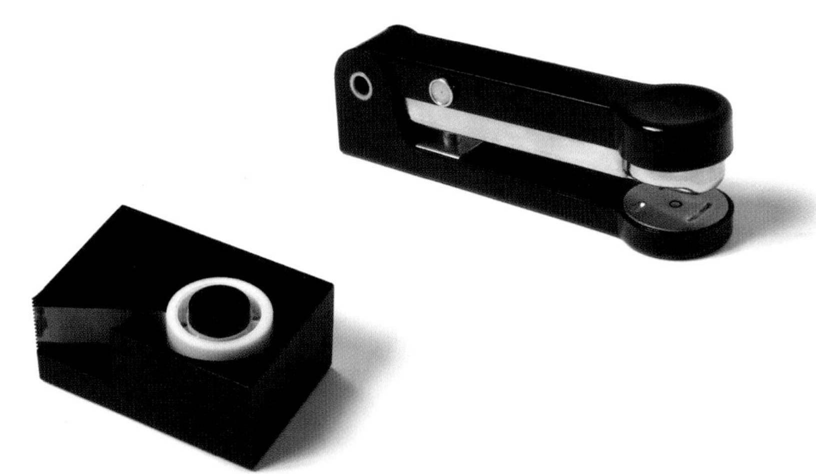

◂ *Design for the desk undergoes development just like other products. From Henning Andreasen's sturdy Folle stapler from the 1970s (top), to Torben Holmbäck's razor-sharp milled aluminium blocks from the 1980s (far left) and finally to the mysterious, floating Wave series, designed by Steve McGugan in the 1990s (below). All three examples are products that splendidly fulfil the task they're designed for. The difference is in the artistic idiom, which changes over time and expresses the designer's personal style.*

This desk equipment is designed in a typical seventies' style with rounded edges on the pressed metal pieces. The combined geometrical forms, a circle combined with a rectangle, create a clarified and sensible shape. The colours are also typical of the time – white, black and bright red – and later it came in stainless steel. This article can stand on any desk and look friendly and useful. A nice design without being conspicuous.

About ten years later, Torben Holmbäck (b. 1933) designed a series of desk accessories in a completely different artistic idiom. He took on the production and marketing of the products called the Block Series. The fundamental idea behind the very geometrical series is that all the pieces are milled from aluminium blocks, and he made a tape dispenser, paper clip holder and a pencil holder. Torben Holmbäck started with the tape dispenser, and here you can see the concept most consistently applied. A space for the roll of tape has been milled as well as one for your finger to grab the tape from underneath. Teeth have also been milled on one side so you can easily rip the tape off. The weight of the material combined with the rubber pads on the bottom make the dispenser stay in one place when you pull the tape. The aluminium is anodised in either black or its natural colour. Very distinguished.

Back in 1992, industrial designer Steve McGugan started working on the desk set called Wave for Georg Jensen. In the beginning there were seven products, but the number soon rose to 19 and includes everything you need on your desk – from a tape dispenser to a letter tray and letter opener. The materials in the series are a rubber base with a wavy top made of stainless steel. The recurring motif is, as the name suggests, a wave in the form of the gently undulating steel top. Like Torben Holmbäck's series, the many accessories can be combined however you like. The artistic idiom is also typical of its time, exclusive and a little like an instrument panel on the boss' desk. The discreet and dark rubber base makes many of the accessories look like the stainless steel top is floating above the desktop. This is an artistic idiom that has also been used by Bang & Olufsen, whom Steve McGugan also has designed for.

WORK INTERIORS

While you need tools and machines to do your work, this work has to take place somewhere and be organised in the form of a workshop, factory or an office. The conception of what constituted a workplace has undergone huge changes throughout time. In the last few decades in particular, the norms of a good interior for a workplace have changed radically. The interior decoration of a workplace is more than just furnishing the rooms in a creative way. How a company works, what it produces and the values emphasised by management can either inhibit or enhance the physical environment of the workplace. As mentioned in chapter 2, the normal power structures in society are reflected in architecture and the interior decoration of rooms and milieus in many ways.

This is very much true of the workplace as well. In the past, the location determined how the work was done. The farmer had to go out in the field to sow or harvest, the fisherman's workplace was his boat out on a lake, and the hunter had to venture into the forest or out on the moor to bag his food. The rest of the work took place in and around the home, such as grinding the grain into flour or cleaning and salting fish. When an emerging division of labour began, things like the workshop for the blacksmith or the lumberyard for shipbuilding came about. Later on in history, large

◂ *Dehn's Steam Laundry was designed in 1936 by architect Poul Henningsen. It was meant to be a model workplace, but the picture reveals the conventional view of the workplace at that time. There are no amenities here, no sitting areas, no pictures on the walls and only general lighting from high-hanging pendants. The work environment is very sterile, and one gets the impression that the workday was just a chore you had to get through so you could go home and relax.*

workshops arose, or factories if you will, with many employees, and a greater need for administration emerged. The factory and the office were born, and while some people carried out mostly physical work, others took care of the administration.

In the early days of industrialisation, factory work was often a difficult and sometimes dangerous way to make a living. The agricultural sector didn't need so many workers, so there was a surplus of manpower. The alternative to working in a factory was often not working at all, so the employers got away with offering terrible working conditions. If you look at old pictures from the early days of industrialisation, you can see how close the machines were to each other, how an exposed driving belt could catch a coat sleeve and how little light there was. The trade unions that emerged at that time were mainly concerned with raising wages and reducing working hours. Demands for the physical environment were not high on their list, although they did try to improve highly dangerous working conditions. The general view even up to our time was that you couldn't expect to influence your workplace. There were people in charge, and people who did what they were told whether it was the best way of doing things or not. This view of the hierarchy of industry was also reflected in the way the workplace was designed.

Dehn's Steam Laundry

In 1936, architect Poul Henningsen designed a modern industrial laundry, Dehn's Steam Laundry in Gladsaxe. It was the largest privately owned laundry in Denmark at the time, and the owners' ambitions were great. The laundry had become too big for the old buildings in downtown Copenhagen, and when moving to the new building on an open field outside town, there was an opportunity for further expansion. This was only one of the points described in the building project that Poul Henningsen was to follow. Moreover, it was expected that the building could be expanded and machines could be replaced without disrupting the daily operations of the laundry. They also wanted good worklight in the form of daylight and electric light as well as a comfortable temperature, but 'without the use of artificial heat'.

Dehn's Steam Laundry was considered a humane and relatively progressive employer back in the 1930s. The factory was described in a contemporary newspaper under the headline: 'Laundry done to music' and 'the factory has light, air ventilation and social arrangements'. There's no doubt that Dehn's was a good place to work especially if you compare it to many other companies of that time. But if you take a closer look at the almost 70-year-old photo from the laundry room, it is clear that not even PH could perform miracles. Manual labour wasn't all fun and games. The picture was published with an article by Poul Henningsen about the building project in Arkitektens Ugehæfte (The Architect's Weekly) in 1938. He must have thought that the photo was a suitable illustration.

The laundry hall is an open iron construction with asbestos cement boards lining the walls and ceiling. Apparently these are unpainted since the boards make a checked pattern on the walls and ceiling. Glass-encased PH lamps provide artificial light, but there isn't much daylight. There isn't special lighting at the machines and other workstations, and this would have been a help and could have varied the boring look of the big room. The art-loving PH didn't manage to include any art or other kind of decoration. The room is typical functional architecture: sober, unsentimental and without much variation. Pride of place is given to the rational, to the almost boring, during this period of time, even by Poul Henningsen. He would probably say that the architecture and furnishings are at least honest and not pretentious; there's no decoration, no cornices or stucco on the ceiling.

But what is puzzling is the physical working conditions on the floor, so to speak. There doesn't seem to be much room between the machines and not even much room for folding sheets. All the work seems to be done on one's feet, and even though PH writes in the aforementioned article that the flooring in most of the laundry is beech parquet, the workday must have been hard. There isn't a chair or a bench to be seen where the female employees could take a short rest. There was only room for work, even in a model workplace. Of course there are plenty of things you can't see in the photo. Maybe the women had plenty of freedom to organise their work. Maybe, as the newspaper headline states, music is played on loudspeakers that aren't included in the picture. Maybe the employees have lots of breaks. We don't know, but the design of the workplace isn't very inviting considering our standards today.

The office as a workplace

Working in an office has certainly been less dangerous and perhaps not quite as physically taxing, but it definitely had its own hierarchy too. Even in industrial times, administrative work has been characterised by a lot of routine jobs in both the private and the public sector. Many years passed before anything remotely automated, like computers for word processing and accounting, entered the office scene. Until then all correspondence, accounting and writing were done by hand. Most of them were routine jobs, and just like the industrial workers weren't asked to think for themselves; the menial officer workers weren't expected to be creative or take independent initiatives. If anyone was supposed to think, the bosses would take that upon themselves.

This division of labour set its mark on the design of office buildings and the way they were furnished for a very long time. The boss had his own private office, his secretary had one in front of his, and the menial personnel sat in a joint office space. The boss was the only one who had the privilege of shutting the door for a confidential meeting or conversation on the phone, while the rest of the personnel could easily be supervised. The furniture was often placed in rank and file, and sometimes the furniture was even fastened to the building, such as desks that were placed perpendicular to a wall and mounted on it. The opportunity to be more flexible or use other work methods in rooms with this type of furnishings was very small. Far into the 20th century, this was the most common way of organising and setting up office work, and it still exists in the most conventional Danish companies.

During his long career, Arne Jacobsen designed a large number of office buildings for the private and the public sector including several city halls. Søllerød City Hall is one of them, and he designed it with Flemming Lassen in 1939, just a few years after PH had planned Dehn's Steam Laundry. The building in Søllerød is very similar to Aarhus City Hall, which Arne Jacobsen and Erik Møller had designed around the same time. Here you also see the traditional office interior – private offices for the bosses and rows of desks for the office clerks. The whole building is very aesthetically thought out. The building is faced with Norwegian marble like the city hall in Aarhus, it has a copper roof and windows that flush with the façade in order to give the whole building a very compact and tight expression. It's a very presentable city hall, and both simple and modernist without a lot of frills. It must be one of the first city halls in Denmark that doesn't even have a hint of a tower or steeple on it.

But modernity doesn't pervade the whole building since the interior reflects the hierarchy of the personnel in the same way it has for centuries. The formal design of the building is emphasised by the fact that there is no solar screening on the windows on the southwestern façade. The desks were placed by the windows where the sun beat down all afternoon. It would have been too great a departure from the architectural expression to put up something like awnings on the façade. As it says in a report from the Danish Building Research Institute in 1983 about the historical development of office environments: 'At Søllerød City Hall everything from door handles and lighting elements to furniture and curtains were designed by architects, which was described in detail in the article about the project in The Architect's Weekly in 1943, while, for example, the conditions of the indoor climate and work functions are not mentioned. The same aesthetic view of administration buildings was dominant in the 50s and 60s.'

Gori

Democracy in the workplace, influence on one's workday and autonomous groups were just some of the concepts that emerged from the societal debate after the youth revolution in the 1960s and 1970s. For example, the daily Danish newspaper Information introduced equal pay for all employees, at least for a number of years. In other companies, the individual departments were allowed to plan the work themselves, and flexitime was introduced. In the interior decoration of offices, office landscapes began to be used. They aren't necessarily very democratic or very appropriate either. If nothing else, the large open-plan offices are often a symbol of wanting fellowship, and furthermore one has heard that collaboration and teamwork are good things. Few companies made major architectural or interior design changes as a consequence of 'tearing down the pyramids' as it was popular to say a few years later.

One of the exceptions was Gori in Kolding. In 1978–79 they built a new factory just outside town, and all the functions were under one roof. Normally a company would be proud if there were no walls and doors in the office area whereas the physical production should preferably be some distance away in a traditional factory building. But Gori went the whole nine yards and realised the vision of having the entire company under the same roof. The company manufactures chemicals for wood protection and was founded in 1902. It expanded in the 1960s so much that new buildings were needed in the mid-1970s. A process was initiated to clarify how this should take place. The owner and day-to-day manager of Gori, Niels Oluf Ehrenskjöld, described how it worked in a subsequent interview:

'We held several staff meetings on the layout of the building and many of its details. We also went to see the building site before it was bought, and all the staff visited the building several times during its construction where we discussed the placement of the individual functions and each employee. When the new building was finally finished, all the employees went straight to their new places and started working. It took less than a day to move in.' About the background of this special initiative Ehrenskjöld also said, 'We have an organisational structure that consists of only three levels; most decisions are left to the individual employee. I think the little,

▾ *Søllerød City hall was designed by Arne Jacobsen and Flemming Lassen in 1939. It is a piece of office architecture with great internal contradictions. Seen from the outside, the building has a modern artistic idiom, but the walls are faced with marble and the roof is copper, and inside the old-fashioned office hierarchy has been maintained. At this time the flat, democratic project organisation and flexible interiors lie far in the future.*

daily decisions are the core of a company. If you do one little thing better every day, 220 days a year for 30 years, then the 'big' decisions come of their own accord at the right time.'

The architect was Tormod Olesen, who had a background as an industrial designer. He had previously worked with the professor of industrial design at the Royal Academy of Fine Arts, Erik Herløw, who in the early 1970s had developed a colour program for Gori's wood protection products. So Tormod Olesen knew a bit about the company that needed a new headquarters. In principle, the building was, however, developed from a standard factory hall from the construction company Rasmussen & Schiøtz. So it was far from being an Arne Jacobsenian solution, and the building was even a bit anonymous in its architectural expression. However, there's a lot more wood in the building, both inside and out, than is normally used. But a company whose business is wood protection must by definition be fond of wood. The building's façade elements were prepped for future moves and extensions, and there aren't any room dividers in the factory. The almost 200 staff members all sit in the same 14,000 m^2 room.

Instead of an office landscape at Gori you could say that they tried to create a company landscape. The aim of this architecture was to stimulate the democratic forms of co-operation in a company that was already very group-oriented to begin with. The sense of perspective is increased and the individual employee's insight and responsibility could be raised to the benefit of the company, of course, but this also gave the employees a sense of security. The feeling of communality was also expressed in the fact that there was only one entrance to the building, one canteen and one common room in the middle of the building, and it could be used for sports, lectures, large meetings and parties. Since Gori manufactured chemical products to protect wood, you would think that this made the project impossible, or at the very least that the indoor climate would be poor. But this challenge was seen as a positive thing in that they were forced to solve a number of problems with noise, dust, fire precautions, threshold limit values for chemicals etc. The production itself of the chemical wood protectors ended up taking place in some closed systems that were well ventilated.

Deloite

It is difficult to find Danish companies that have gone to such extremes as Gori in integrating the staff in a kind of pastoral tribalism. Oticon's highly flexible and paperless project office (see page 68) is somewhat similar to it, but in their case there wasn't an industrial production integrated in the milieu, it was located somewhere else. Oticon has since moved from Hellerup to a considerably larger location in Smørum. There wasn't enough space, and if there's something an organisation of this type needs, it's space.

On the whole, the business community has been changing its structure in the last decade. Where production and administration were previously often in buildings next to each other, this is changing today where the production side of a business is often partly or completely taken on by sub-suppliers, sometimes in far-off countries.

In these global times, many companies will probably be more loosely organised. If the production is located in different parts of the world, then working procedures will most likely be more complicated. The employees that still work at the main office will probably also be more flexible if for no

◂ *The large, open company room which formed the framework of Gori's unique experiment in democracy in the workplace. The French artist Jean Dewasne did the artwork on the large tank and pipe systems. Gori was acquired by the Dyrup corporation in 1991, but the brand name Gori and the factory still exist.*

▾ *The office without assigned workstations, where instead each employee finds a vacant desk every morning and clears it at the end of the day. The accountancy and consultant firm Andersen built its new headquarters in Denmark in the early 2000s. PLH architects did the interiors according to new and flexible principles. Shortly after, Andersen was taken over by Deloite, who have continued the concept here as well as in their new building on Islands Brygge in Copenhagen. The large atrium on the ground floor has sofa groups on the right for relaxation or informal meetings, while on the left and in the middle of the picture and behind the white screen walls are more non-traditional workstations, which especially the young employees prefer.*

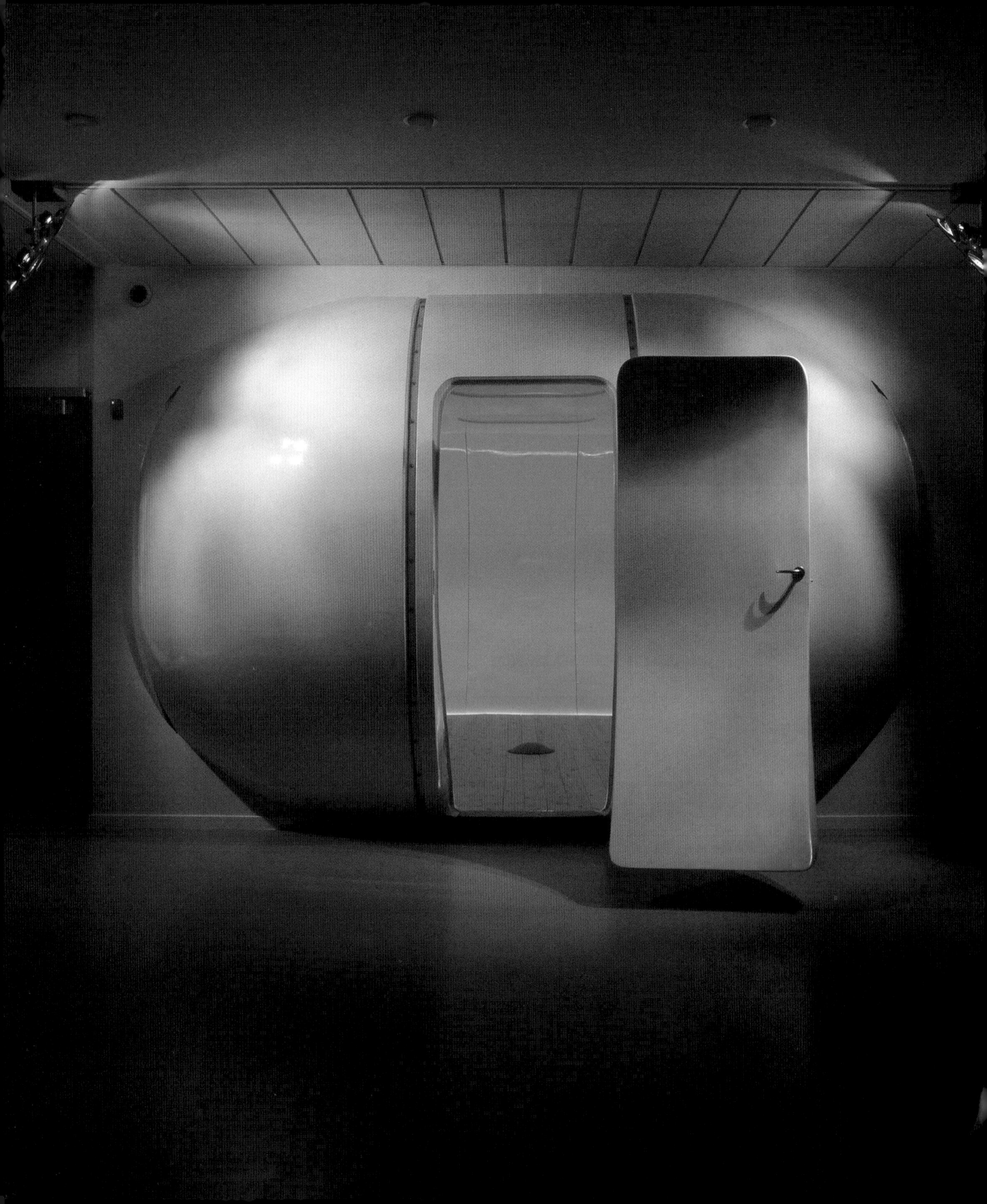

THE DEMAND FOR innovation makes some workplaces strike out on a new path. In the public as well as the private sector, initiatives are taken to make creative environments suitable for problem solving. One example is from the Danish Ministry of Economic and Business Affairs where the research unit Mindlab had a real think tank designed in 2002. It was an egg-shaped room for staging creative meetings in the ministry. The inside of the room is lined with smooth, white surfaces that can be written on, just like whiteboards. There is a table in the middle, but no chairs, and then it's just all about being creative. Unfortunately the acoustics turned out to be poor, but this has been somewhat rectified.

Another matter is whether the innovation in a company should be shut up in a room instead of being spread out in the organisation. The design and art firm Bosch & Fjord designed the egg, and they had similar commissions for several private firms.

other reason than because of travel. One example of this could be seen in the large international accounting firm Andersen. In 2001–02 they built a Danish headquarters where the employees didn't have fixed workstations. There were actually 20 % less desks than the number of employees since some of them were always travelling or visiting clients.

Andersen's headquarters was in a large, new, square six-storey building near Tuborg Havn (harbour) and it was designed by the PLH architectural firm. This was the premiere of the principle that no employee, or in the strictest sense partner, should have their own desk any more. Every morning, everyone could sit where they liked. This would be a way of counteracting the old-fashioned hierarchy, and at the end of the day everyone had to clear their desk and take their laptop with them. Andersen wanted to readjust from thinking along the lines of the old product-oriented economy to a more modern and global economy. And thus a firm that traditionally seemed closed and stiff would be transformed into a company based on openness, networking and dynamics. The building was meant to promote this process by being an office with a lot of transparency and characterised by a modern and democratic spirit for a company that had 380 employees at the time and very few limits both internally and in relation to clients and the outside world.

The interior design of the large building is distinguished by the fact that the many employees didn't have much personal space available at the workstations in the upper parts of the building. However, this was possible in the large central room on the ground floor where relaxed meetings could be held in the classic designer easy chairs. Another non-traditional feature was the coffee bar by the main entrance that was a branch of the café AMOKKA. Here was an opportunity for the employees to have a different kind of in-house coffee break and buy a cappuccino in the bar instead of using the coffee dispensers, which by the way were free, on the other floors. In the wake of the American Enron scandal, for whom Andersen was the auditor, the firm got into hot water and was taken over by another firm in the business, namely Deloite. Deloite's new headquarters in Denmark was built on Islands Brygge in Copenhagen, and here they have continued these principles of interior design.

Transport design

Every country has to have an infrastructure to create cohesion within their borders. If it's too troublesome to travel from one region to another, then the nation is difficult to rule, and the country risks falling apart. Throughout history, a prerequisite for the emergence and existence of many empires has been the ability to establish a good means of transport. Just think of the Romans in a newly conquered province: one of the first things they did was to make roads so that the legionaries and administrators could arrive soon. Or look at how the United States didn't get California and other western territories into the union until the railroad made its way across the prairies and mountains from the Atlantic to the Pacific.

Because of its unique geography, the land of the Danes has long been a challenge for the population, the Crown and the many ministers of transport. Denmark doesn't have high mountains, but it has many islands, fjords and belts that haven't made it an easy area to maintain, which the many wars and attempts at conquest are a testimony to. Nonetheless the Danes managed to create enough cohesion that for centuries we have even been able to maintain contact with Greenland and the Faroe Islands via a fairly reliable shipping route, and now also air routes.

The geography, location, nature, climate, terrain, waters and vegetation in Denmark are all factors that have played and still play a large role in our infrastructure and modes of transport, which is what this chapter hopes to shed light on. But the challenge has also resulted in a number of advantages. The Danes' inevitable association with their national waters has ultimately led to the creation of one of the world's largest seafaring nations measured in the number of ships and shipyards as well as the size of its shipping companies. Hans Christian Andersen was, of course, the author of the famous phrase 'to live is to travel', but many Danes have acknowledged the meaning behind the words.

THE VIKING SHIPS – THE ULTIMATE NAVAL ARCHITECTURE

Today sailing is considered a slow way of travelling. If you're travelling from west to east or vice versa in Denmark, then a car or train is much faster than a ship. The many bridges have also gradually replaced the ferries, so people and freight can make better time. But that has not always been the case. Long ago, transporting oneself, not to mention one's things, was very laborious by land. The belts, fjords, forests, bogs and streams usually made it heavy going and rough. There were rarely roads, and the few that existed were in very poor condition. No, back then it was easier to go by ship.

If we go back to the battle on the island of Als (see page 31), from circa 350 BC, we can see what the Hjortspring boat was an introduction to. While these early open canoes were simple and efficient for the transport of people in the Danish national waters, the ships of the new era, about 1100–1400 years later, played a dominant role in the making of the Danish kingdom. One can hardly imagine Denmark becoming a nation nor the Viking conquests in Europe, their expeditions to Greenland and North America and the extensive trade, without the Viking ships. From about the year 800 and for nearly 300 years the Nordic people, including the Danes, built some of the best sailing ships the world has ever seen.

Of course back then the field of shipbuilding was also under continued design development. It has rarely been something revolutionary, that

▸ *The Viking Ship Museum's reconstruction of a warship, Havhingsten (the Sea Stallion), at full sail.*

is, there haven't been drastic innovational changes. As a rule, a series of small improvements were gradually made. So from the relatively narrow open canoe on Als to the great ocean-going warships and cargo ships from 1300 years later, there have been built hundreds or maybe thousands of ships that have all been a little bit better than the last.

If there are any radical innovations during this millennial development, then the use of the sail must be the most important, although this accomplishment was probably imported from southern Europe where sails had been used for thousands of years. With the sail the Vikings achieved the great freedom that derives from having a choice between two ways of propelling a ship. By the way, this is a speciality that Danish shipbuilders will also cultivate later on in history (see pages 382 and 385). The sail made long journeys at sea manageable, while the oars have made it possible to navigate quickly and attack in narrow waters.

The construction

To add sails to a ship you of course need a mast, and that means going from having a central bottom plank as in the Hjortspring boat to introducing a proper keel in the construction. Otherwise there wouldn't be a solid enough foundation for the mast. And that's what also makes the Viking ships different from the Hjortspring boat, namely a sharp and high bow. This makes the ships more solid and seaworthy. The keel and the stems are the starting points of the construction. The keel is usually the largest part of the ship and is cut from one tree trunk. This part is done first and it defines, directly or indirectly, the other parts of the ship. The rest of the hull consists of planks, also called boards that are as long as possible to avoid making more joints than necessary. First the bottom planks, called garboards, are mounted directly on the keel, and then the next planks and the next again, all of which overlap the ones beneath them. This is how the characteristic clinker hull arose.

Where the boards overlap, iron rivets were nailed in at regular intervals along the ship. These rivets are called clinkers, which led to the expression 'clinker-built', signifying this characteristic construction that is still used today for dinghies and small boats. Today we even have fibreglass dinghies that have a clinker-shaped hull that makes it look like a clinker-built boat. It's a bit strange since there's no practical point to it apart from perhaps a little more rigidity in the hull. But many people still consider a clinker-shaped boat more beautiful and genuine even though the form is moulded in plastic.

When the boards are fastened to the stems and riveted together with clinkers, the hull must be braced by mounting ribs and crossbeams. Now the hull takes its final form. Wool dipped in tar was inserted between the boards to waterproof the ship. There is much that suggests that the woodwork was treated with a mixture of tar and linseed oil. And some, but not all, ships were painted on the outside; this is at least true of the largest ships. According to some illustrations, such as the Bayeaux Tapestry, every other plank was painted one colour, perhaps ochre-yellow, and every other red.

The Bayeaux Tapestry from 1070–80 is practically a comic strip of the story of how the Nordic ships were built and the major expeditions were prepared. The tapestry is 70 metres long and 50 centimetres high, and it shows how William the Conqueror prepared and sailed from France, arrived in England and then began the Battle of Hastings in 1066.

▸ Today's reconstructed Viking ships are built using roughly the same methods that they used 900 years ago. The picture clearly shows how the planks are pressed into shape in an overlapping fashion, and afterwards they are riveted together with clinks, hence the name 'clinker-built'. To keep the wood moist and supple after it's mounted, it's quickly treated with a sticky substance containing linseed oil giving it a brown colour. The special construction of long, hewn planks that are riveted together gives a flexible and tough hull that won't break in the waves, but bends under pressure.

The Viking as a lumberjack

Paradoxically, a prerequisite for building a Viking ship was to know the forest well. Back then, logging was an art in itself and probably a job for specialists, and it was laborious to find the right disease-free and whole trunks that could become the best planks. Equally impressive is that the curved elements in the ship's construction such as the curved bow and the ribs were made from crooked trees that were carefully selected for this purpose. This means that the lumberjacks looked for a tree that had a thick branch that grew at a suitable angle. The principle of finding the right pieces of wood for the purpose was also followed in the production of the many parts, such as the ribs.

The Vikings were masters of the material, and they followed the grain of the wood in their work. Therefore they needed many kinds of axes, knives, planes, awls and augers. However, they didn't use saws even though we know they were in use at the time, among other things, for fashioning bone and walrus tusks into jewellery. But saws would ruin the good properties of the wood because this tool doesn't follow the grain of the wood. By following the grain instead of cutting across it, they could reduce the dimensions of the wood without losing the strength. That's how they achieved the flexibility that the ships needed, especially in high seas.

While building the Viking ships, they worked with unseasoned wood or 'green' wood as experts would say. There are two reasons for this. First of all, when you're working only with axes like the Vikings did, and you don't use saws, it's much easier to work with wet wood. It would actually be almost impossible to use the seasoned wood that we prefer using for furniture and buildings today. Secondly, the long, wide planks have to be pliable when you're building this type of ship, and wet wood is much more flexible than dry. So instead of sawing the planks, the shipbuilders back then split the trunks with axes and wedges. There were, and still are, two ways of making planks. Either by radially splitting the wood or by tangentially splitting it. When you split the wood radially, you first split the log into two halves, then in quarters, eighths and finally you have 16 wedge-shaped sections of the trunk that can be shaped with axes and scrapers into finished planks. This was the most common way of making planks in the Viking Age, since this was how you got the best and most planks out of a log. Tangential splitting is used when you need very wide planks. Here the trunk is split down the middle, and a slice as wide as the diameter of the trunk is cut. This resulted in two wide planks (up to 50–60 cm), but a lot of wood is wasted using this method since it's chopped off. In Denmark the Vikings mostly used oak for shipbuilding, but other types of wood were used for the smaller parts of the ships, such as the ribs, oars etc.

The sail

Between the years 400 and 800, the use of sails on ships became gradually more common. This is the characteristic square sail that is hung from the mast on a long, horizontal spar called the yard. In contrast to what was previously believed, tests with reconstructed ships show that this ship can cross against the wind with a square sail. It's not the best way of working the sail, but it can be done. If you have a strong headwind, you'll make better time if the sail is taken in, the mast is laid down, and the oars are used. However, if you have a tailwind, the square sail is ideal. With a good easterly wind they could sail from Ribe on the west coast of Jutland to England in three days.

Unfortunately there isn't much original sailcloth from the many ship finds. So what we do know is based on the Viking Ship Museum's attempts to recreate what has been lost. The sail on the Viking ships was hand-spun wool, flax or perhaps hemp that was then hand-woven. After it was woven in wide strips, the strips were sewn together and hemmed, and the sail was then treated with something that would make it windproof and water resistant. This was probably a mixture of fat, ochre and tallow. To prevent the sail and rigging from rotting, they were possibly also treated with an extract made of birch and oak bark. After proofing, the Viking ship sails probably had a chestnut colour.

A lot of work went into making a good sail. Weaving and sewing a 100 sqm sail for a large ship most likely took as many man-hours as it took to build the whole ship. The ropes for the ship's rigging were laid of either lime wood bast or horsehair. During the Viking Age they also made braided cords of walrus hide which was very strong and durable. Later on they also used ropes of hemp.

▸ *The large warship Havhingsten (the Sea Stallion) in front and followed by a large cargo ship called Ottar. The Sea Stallion, which was first named Skuldelev 2 after the place near Roskilde Fjord where four Viking ships were found, was built near Dublin around 1040. With its length of almost 30 metres and a crew of 60–100 men it is one of the largest Viking ships that we know of. And since it has crossed the North Sea at least once, it's proven its seaworthiness.*

Sailing qualities and use

It's hard for people today to imagine that someone crossed the Baltic Sea, North Sea or the Atlantic in open ships like the Vikings actually did. Despite being subjected to storms and high seas that threatened to smash the ship to smithereens, the kings, warriors and merchants of the time braved the elements. We don't understand because we imagine the waves crashing in over the ship's sides and constantly threatening to fill it with water. But this probably seldom happened, and that's because of the ship's basic construction and design.

Unlike our experiences when we see big, heavy steel ships sail through a storm with waves pouring over the sides, the Viking ships were very light and rode the waves. Furthermore their ships were very flexible thanks to the way they were built. Almost everything on these ships was sturdy and could bend; the pliable planks, the clinkers made of soft iron that could give a bit and wouldn't gnaw the planks, and even the mast was supported by ropes and wasn't a stiff construction. During test runs with the modern copies of Viking ships it's been observed that some of the large ships have virtually changed shape in accordance with the waves, as if they were made of thick rubber. Even the people must have been made of stern stuff because riding out a storm was like constantly being on a rollercoaster.

There are several advantages to the lightness of these ships; among other things, they were easy to pull ashore. So it was possible to sail on some of the major rivers in Europe, and if the ship came into unnavigable waters, it could be emptied and dragged over land and past the danger zone. This is how the Vikings reached places like Central Europe, deep into Russia and all the way to Istanbul. The ships could also be beached if they wanted to attack or seek shelter from a storm. They rarely sailed in winter, and then the ships were pulled ashore and many of them were probably were stored in special boathouses.

A ship for every purpose

One archaeological find in particular has been crucial to the understanding of Viking ships and the Viking world. This is the find of five ships from the early 1000s near Skuldelev in Roskilde Fjord, discovered from 1957–59. In addition to archaeologists learning a lot about how the Vikings built their ships, the find also reveals another interesting thing. The five vessels are all very different in size and function. The shipbuilders of the day let the purpose of the vessel determine its design and size. There were cargo ships, warships, and large and small fishing boats. Some were built for the Danish national waters and others were oceangoing.

All good properties cannot be combined in one ship, and therefore the design is always a struggle to add the right properties to the specific ship. For example, the oceangoing ships had a chubby form and higher sides which made them resemble a cork on the water, but thus they could avoid taking in water even in high seas. Ships in safer waters had less freeboard and sharper lines. Furthermore, the ships that were primarily used as rowing vessels had a hull with an almost circular cross section, so as little as possible of its surface was in the water, and thus there was the least amount of resistance. Conversely, sailing ships had a cross section that was more pointed at the bottom (a bit like a wineglass with a stem) so that it had some keel to counteract the drift. Such diverse functions, and their associated designs, are apparent in the Skuldelev ships, which comprise an oceangoing cargo ship, a coastal cargo ship, a large warship, a small

▾ Skuldelev 1 or Ottar is the Viking Ship Museum's largest cargo ship. It is from 1030, and with a length of 16.5 metres it can carry about 20 tonnes payload. It isn't quite as spectacular in size or as colourful to look at as the Sea Stallion, but it's probably the type of ship that in its day could sail to Iceland and maybe on to Greenland. The ship has a square sail that is mounted on the horizontal yard. Traditionally it was thought that a square sail made it harder to manoeuvre, especially when crossing against the wind, but tests have shown that this type of sail can actually give the ship a good speed even if the wind doesn't hit the sail directly from behind.

warship and finally a fishing boat that had been converted into a little cargo ship.

The merchant ships are wide compared to their length and this makes room for a large cargo area amidships. This is clearly seen in the large cargo ship from Skuldelev. It's only 16 metres long, but 4.8 metres wide and can carry up to 24 tonnes of cargo. The crew numbered about 6–8 men, and depending on how much room the cargo took up, 2–4 of them could row when it was strictly necessary. Ships of this type could cross the North Sea, and perhaps larger models could navigate the North Atlantic with up to 50 tonnes of cargo onboard.

The cargo ships sailed at a slower pace than the small, slender warships, which didn't have room for much more than the large crew and their personal possessions and weapons. The other large ship from Skuldelev is an almost 30-metre long and 3.8-metre wide warship. This is a longship and one of the largest ever found. It had a crew of about 70–80 warriors of whom 60 could row at a time. This meant the ship was very flexible and had a top speed of 25–30 km/h. It was a dreaded weapon, since it could attack in all kinds of weather and on the coast which normally couldn't be navigated. The reconstruction of this large warship, which was launched in 2004, required 153 cubic metres of wood, 400 kg of iron, 3000 m of rigging and a 118 sqm sail.

A unique design

The image of the Vikings used by the tourist industry is characterised by kitsch. If you visit the Tivoli Gardens in Copenhagen you will see the odd dolls and ship models, not to mention the plastic helmets with horns, despite the fact that Viking helmets did not have horns. The Viking Age is often reduced to ridiculous folklore, and the myth about the primitive, yet good-natured pirates is kept alive, just like the Danish football supporters' hat with hands that clap. In reality, the Vikings were probably pirates from time to time, and they did conquer large areas, especially in England and northern France, but at the same time they were merchants and they built markets, towns and nations. Denmark began to become a united country during the Viking Age.

And nothing was more important to this development than the Viking ships. People were oriented towards the sea and what was out there. And ships were the tools that could grant this urge to travel. The world changed along with the Vikings and their ships. In the beginning they were primarily pirates who with a single ship sacked innocent towns and monasteries, but then the Vikings became a nation that waged wars of conquest and colonised large areas of land. But in the wake of these conquests came trade. And the advance of the ships follows this development closely.

In the last part of the Viking Age it is the merchant ships that develop the most, and at the end of the Viking Age, around the year 1100, another society emerges. Denmark has had its first kings, so an emerging central power is slowly consolidated. The world has changed. And the ship that began its history as one of the most versatile vessels is now refined into a number of specialised ships, which the Skuldelev finds also show. As a type, the Viking ships are a fantastic concept, an excellent example of functionalist design from a time long before the word design even existed. In many ways it's a perfect design without superfluous frills. And seen from

▸ *One of Hohlenberg's ship models that can be seen today at the Royal Danish Navy Museum in Copenhagen. The pinched stern is evident, and this gave the officers less comfortable quarters onboard, but the design improved the ship's chances of survival during battle.*

an aesthetic point of view, the Viking ship is very beautiful and simple. It has clean lines that make the characteristic beautiful curves at the stems. It is almost without ornamentation – only a dragonhead and its tail on the longships. They are optimised for their use, durable and quick, and they follow the overall principle to build as minute and light as possible without affecting the strength. You could put it like this: you can't remove anything or add anything to the design of these ships without ruining the final result.

THE WARSHIPS OF POSTERITY

While the Viking Age was a unique era for Danish and Nordic ship design, the next hundreds of years weren't quite as exciting. Danish shipbuilding became very much a part of the common European tradition and practice. Throughout the Middle Ages and the Renaissance, warships changed dramatically from the simple, open Viking ship to even bigger and more sophisticated vessels. Two factors in particular promote this development. One factor is that the large European countries need oceangoing ships to conquer overseas colonies and maintain contact with them.

The other factor that is dependent on bigger ships is the introduction of cannons. These are heavy and require a very stable basis to function properly. So this determines the need for sturdier constructions, flat decks and closed cargo holds. The latter are to be used as places for the crew to stay, to store gunpowder, cannon balls and provisions as well as to accommodate the cargo sent to and from the colonies. This resulted in ships that were much too big to row, but instead are provided with more and bigger sails than the light Viking ships of former times.

But even though the Danish national waters were badly suited to the typical European ships, for hundreds of years the Danish kings wanted to be in fashion and therefore built ships like they did abroad. A tradition in shipbuilding almost became a dogma, namely that the ships had to be big and thus draw a great deal of water and moreover be fitted with expensive and heavy ornamentation. In addition the ships had a large stern where the officers' quarters were. This large and richly decorated part of the ship looked very impressive and elegant, but was a very vulnerable part of the ship's construction.

At regular intervals, foreign naval architects were invited to Holmen Naval Base in Copenhagen so they could design Danish warships. Or talented Danish shipbuilders were sent on long study trips to the foreign naval dockyards to bring back the latest international ideas and principles.

One of these emissaries was the Danish naval architect Frantz Christopher Hohlenberg, whom after a seven-year-long trip to Holland, England, France, Italy and Sweden returned to Denmark in 1795. He brought back a lot of knowledge about shipbuilding in Europe and his own ideas on how to build better ships that were partly based on the specific Danish conditions. Among other things, he sought to make the ships more uniform and rounded at both ends. This would make it possible for more cannons pointing backwards and thus reduce the blind angle that the stern created.

The consequence of innovation and using more functional principles instead of keeping the old, ornamental conventions was that the stern was made quite a bit smaller. Hohlenberg met a lot of resistance from the officers' ranks, who could expect less living space in the future ships.

◂ *The frigate Jylland, which is now in dry dock in Ebeltoft. It is a strange design that combines the fully rigged ship with a steam engine (note the funnel).*

▸ *A drawing of the frigate Jylland during the launch from the Danish Naval Dockyards in Copenhagen in 1860. This would be the last, large wooden warship with sails in the Danish fleet. Afterwards steel and machines were used.*

This innovative naval architect tried to demonstrate the inconceivable by combining 'round corners' on the ship's stern with a 'pinched transom'.

After the bombing of Copenhagen in 1807, when the English took off with the Danish fleet, the victors noticed a new type of ship, and no later than the following year, in 1808, a drawing of the stern on the Danish warship the Christian VII was reproduced in the English periodical *Naval Chronicle*. In very short time the English fleet adopted this innovative ship design. Later on, the French fleet also followed these principles. Hohlenberg became the only Danish naval architect from this whole period to achieve international recognition for his foresight.

Hohlenberg had other ideas about how Danish ships should be designed. Among other things, he was a spokesman for getting rid of all the heavy ornamentation, which was common on the warships of the time. Together with the idea of cutting down on the number of cannons on each ship, this would enable the Danish fleet to consist of lighter, yet more manoeuvrable and efficient ships in a matter of years.

A most likely unintentional added bonus of Hohlenberg's ideas was that the new ships had a simpler and more elegant design than before. The ships' traditional heavy stern, which had an exaggerated appearance at times, was toned down to give a more natural rounded stern. Removing the ornamentation and cannons on one deck made the new ships more modern, including in their appearance.

Hohlenberg wanted very much to break with the dogmas and tendency to copy foreign practices, and instead create a fleet of warships that was partly based on what was needed, and partly on the actual conditions in the Danish waters. This is how he came to lead a common-sense trend in ship design where it's about solving problems and creating innovative solutions rather than following foreign trends and traditions.

The frigate Jylland

If you want to see what Hohlenberg intended and the result of the development, then the frigate Jylland is a very illuminating example. When the ship was launched in 1860, it was the end of the wooden ships' era at the Naval Dockyards in Copenhagen as well as in the Danish fleet. From now on ships were made of iron and called armoured vessels. Even while the frigate was being built, there was a heated debate about whether this was the right ship to build, but it was built anyway.

Since the Jylland was built in tough competition with the iron ships, it was the acme of what could be done in the field of building wooden ships. Most importantly, the stern is obviously constructed in accordance with Hohlenberg's principles. It is rounded without the large window sections that had been the norm and almost without the traditional heavy ornamentation. It was a frigate, meaning it had only one gun deck with cannons, apart from a few extra cannons on the open top deck. So this would also have pleased Hohlenberg – if he had been alive at the time.

The Jylland was the culmination of an extremely long development in the building of wooden ships. It was actually impossible to develop the technique further, and the upper limit of how long a wooden ship could be was reached. If it was any longer, the hull would break in two in the first storm it encountered.

Today the museum ship Jylland is fully restored and in dry dock in Ebeltoft, and it's actually the world's longest preserved wooden ship. When the ship was finished, 35,000 cubic feet of oak had been used and this corresponds to more than 54 acres of oak. In total, the weight of the ship was 2456 tonnes.

The ship's length of 71 metres could be ascribed to the use of iron elements in the wooden hull, especially in the form of so-called knees that are large brackets that fasten the deck to the inside of the hull. Traditionally these knees were made of crooked lumber, but in the Jylland's case they were made of wrought iron.

But although the frigate Jylland was mainly a wooden ship in a traditional sense, it also had a design that tried to bridge the gap with the future. This is because it was a screw-propelled steam frigate. This means that the ship not only had the traditional sails to propel it, but also a coal-fired steam engine under the deck. This engine could be engaged when needed, and when the wind was favourable, the sails were used. However, in unfavourable conditions and during battle, the engine could supply the necessary driving power.

Since there was only room onboard for 248 tonnes of coal, and the engine used 1.8 tonnes per hour, this was only enough for 137 hours under steam power. So most of the time they managed with the sails, especially if they didn't regularly have time to call at a port and bunker. The engine was the first of its kind that was manufactured in Denmark. It was built by Baumgarten and Burmeister and weighed 105 tonnes and could produce 400 horsepower. That made it possible to sail 11–13 knots by the engine alone (over 20 km/h). This may not sound impressive when comparing to what the Viking ships could manage, but it's fairly good for a ship of its size, and it was an advantage to not be dependent on the wind.

When the engine wasn't engaged, the screw was a problem. If it was left alone, it would create resistance in the water and reduce the speed significantly when the Jylland was under sail. Therefore an ingenious system was constructed so that the 8 tonne, two-bladed bronze screw with a diameter of 4.80 m could be released from the axle and retracted into a shaft in the stern and thus be out of the water. The funnel could also be lowered like a telescope below the deck, and then the Jylland looked like a genuine sailing ship.

The lines of the ship are simple and very beautiful. The restrained use of artistic decorations such as the figurehead and the ornamentation on the stern are suggestive of modern times and a simplified ship design. But there's no hiding the fact that when the Jylland was built, it had already been surpassed by progress. And that's in spite of the fact that a few years later, the ship did well in what would be the world's last major battle between wooden ships.

On May 9, 1864 the Jylland and two other Danish screw-propelled steamships were in battle with three Austro-Hungarian ships whose design and construction were very similar to the Danish ones. The battle went on for a couple of hours and ended when the Austrian flagship caught fire, and the enemy chose to retreat. Twelve of the 400 crew members on the Jylland had lost their lives in battle, and 29 were wounded. In 1892 the Jylland was taken out of service to be used as a depot ship.

A FOLDING PROPELLER. The retractable propeller on the frigate Jylland was one way of solving the problem of water resistance. On modern sailboats the screw is also in the way when it's not used. The solution could be to construct a propeller that unfolds when it's needed and folds when it's not. The idea wasn't new, but Gori Marine in Kolding developed a brand new propeller in 1975 together with two industrial designers, David Lewis and Henning Moldenhawer. The two blades are connected by a special joint that makes the propeller unfold when the axle starts rotating. It works both when you're sailing forwards and when you want to reverse. The propeller blades automatically regulate their position steplessly at any speed to achieve the best performance in the water. When the engine is switched off, the blades fold and create the least resistance when the boat is under sail. It was awarded the ID prize from the Danish Design Council in 1976. Since then the Steel Team company in Vojens has taken over the production.

The ship without a funnel

In its outer design the Selandia wasn't much different from the other cargo steamships of the day. Seen through our eyes, the ship is a little anonymous. The only visible difference between it and its contemporaries was that the Selandia didn't have a funnel – a revolutionary thing back in 1912 when it was launched from the shipyard of Burmeister & Wain (B&W) in Copenhagen. What made it unique, however, was on the inside of the Selandia: it was the first oceangoing ship driven by diesel engines.

While a steamship uses huge amounts of coal, a diesel ship only needs a small exhaust pipe, which in principle can be inside a mast. That's why the Selandia was built without a funnel. However, this design decision caused problems. If a large iron ship without a funnel was observed at sea, it was presumed to be shipwrecked, and other ships would rush to its assistance only to discover that it was one of those new-fangled motor ships. The consequence was that in future all the diesel ships were built with a large, traditional funnel, which most ships also have today. But today's artificially enlarged funnels only serve the purposes of hiding the little exhaust pipe, being a ventilation shaft and showing the shipping company's logo.

Nonetheless the Selandia would herald a whole new era at sea, no matter how harmless its design was on the outside. While a steamship needed about 2000 tonnes of coal to cross the Atlantic, a diesel ship making the same voyage only needed 500 tonnes of oil. And the steamship's coal had to be stored on a middle deck near the engine and shovelled by hand into the furnaces under the boilers, but diesel oil could be stored in tanks at the bottom of the ship and be pumped up to the engine by machine.

So the engine crew could be reduced from 25 people to 8 and the cargo hold for coal could be used for other purposes. And as is still the case today, it was the unskilled workers who saw their livelihood disappear in a few short years, and their workplace would finally end up in a museum. That was yesterday's version of technological unemployment. The new engines wiped out a whole profession, namely the stokers, who until then had the toilsome and dirty job of feeding the steam engines coal around the clock.

Yet the introduction of diesel power produced many more opportunities to design better ships. The coal dust onboard and the annoying thick smoke were gone. The working conditions of the few sailors left in the machine room were greatly improved. The furnishing of the cargo holds was easier and the utilisation of them was better. It was easier to get fuel aboard. But of course it was mainly the financial aspect of the new technology that had encouraged the East Asiatic Company to take such a big gamble. In this case, as so often before, the technological breakthroughs gave new freedom of choices and opportunities in design.

It was a young 30-year-old engineer employed at Copenhagen Municipality, Ivar Knudsen, who had noticed the original patent on the diesel motor. He approached Burmeister & Wain and had them buy the right to manufacture diesel engines under license. Together, they first developed engines for the production of electricity and only later for use as ship engines. However, it was the legendary owner of the East Asiatic Company, H.N. Andersen, who was one of the first to see the commercial possibilities of using a diesel engine in a ship.

The story has become a well-known tale. B&W hadn't tried to mount a diesel engine in a real ship before and wanted to give it a try first in a smaller ship of 400 tonnes. H.N. Andersen thought that if you could build a motor ship of 400 tonnes, why not one of 1000 tonnes? Yes, well, thought Knudsen, that was possible. Then why not 3000 tonnes, asked the East Asiatic Company. Or 6000 or 8000? The anecdote ended up becoming a fact. The East Asiatic Company (EAC) ordered a series of four diesel ships from Burmeister & Wain and took upon itself part of the risk if it didn't work out.

The ships were 7400 tonnes each, which was the perfect size for EAC's regular route from Copenhagen to Bangkok. They were equipped with two four-stroke engines with eight cylinders which gave the ships 2500 horsepower and a top speed of 12 knots (about 20 km/h). The ships were christened the Selandia, the Fionia, the Jutlandia and the Falstria, but the Fionia was immediately sold by EAC to the German Hamburg-America Line that couldn't get a German shipyard to build a diesel ship for them.

The Selandia (pictured above) was EAC's flagship for many years, and although it was a cargo ship, it could carry 22 passengers. The interior was kept in a moderate Victorian style and was designed by architect Carl Brummer according to the belief that the large, bright cabins and parlours would give the passengers the feeling of being in an elegant home that had large picture windows instead of the traditional portholes and a dining salon with a two-deck ceiling height. H.N. Andersen and some employees from EAC and B&W travelled on the Selandia to London in February, 1912, since this was the first stop on her maiden voyage to Bangkok. Here the ship was to be properly shown to the public and the world and was to advertise both the shipping company and the shipyard. Among others, Winston Churchill, who at the time was First Lord of the Admiralty, came aboard for lunch to see this wonder. After his visit he congratulated Denmark on being the old seafaring nation that had shown the way and had taken the lead with a development that would create a new era in shipping. He found this new type of ship to be the century's most perfect maritime masterpiece.

On its return to Copenhagen, the Selandia got a jubilant welcome from thousands of excited people that had heard and read about the new, fantastic ship without a funnel. The ship remained in service on the Copenhagen-Bangkok route for almost 25 years. During that time it sailed a distance equivalent to 55 times around the world. And this was done without serious problems with the ship or the engines. In 1936 the Selandia was sold to a Norwegian ship owner, but in 1942, while under a Finnish shipping company, it ran aground and sank off the coast of Japan.

THE DANISH FERRY

If anything, the Danish ferry is a symbol of travelling within Denmark's borders. When you have to visit another part of the country, you have to cross water, and for ages it has entailed short or long crossings. Not until the last 75 years have some parts of the country been connected by bridges. The waters are an old symbol of what separated the parts of the country; the ferry is conversely a symbol of what unites the country.

For one of Denmark's great authors, Johannes V. Jensen, it came easily to him in his novel *The Fall of the King* to use a trip on a ferry as an image of Christian II's doubt and irresoluteness. On the night of February 10,

▲ *The Selandia, the world's first oceangoing ship with diesel engines, was also known as the ship without a funnel.*

AT HOLMEN IN Copenhagen lies a museum ship. It's the frigate Peder Skram (below), the hitherto largest warship in the Danish fleet. She was commissioned in 1966 and decommissioned in 1988. When it was built, it was a bit of a sensation since it was a very fast ship in relation to its size. This is because the Peder Skram had two different kinds of engines; two ordinary diesel engines and two gas turbines. So just like the Viking ships and the frigate Jylland, it had two different kinds of horsepower to use.

When a high speed was necessary, the gas turbines could be engaged instead of the diesel engines, and the top speed was 32–34 knots (almost 60 km/h). A gas turbine guzzles a lot of fuel, and therefore was only used when necessary. From the outside there's nothing special about the Peder Skram, which looks like most warships in its class. The Peder Skram's first trip was to the US. Here the ship caused a sensation and the US Coast Guard immediately began to build vessels with the same engines. The Peder Skram and her sister ship the Herluf Trolle were creative answers to the special natural and military challenges that Denmark faced at that time. In the same way that Hohlenberg (see page 379) designed ships that fit the narrow and shallow Danish waters, the two frigates are in size, armament, draft and speed a well thought out answer to the challenges of the time and place. In the event of military engagement in Danish waters, these frigates could quickly attack an enemy and disappear again.

▸ *The steam ferry Sjælland that was built at B&W transported railcars over the Great Belt from 1887.*

▾ *The picture is called 'Ships under sail in a mild breeze' and was painted in 1836 by C.W. Eckersberg (1783–1853). Before the time of the steam ferry it could be a trial to cross the Great Belt. The crossing was usually in small ships; either in a smack or, as in the picture, a mail yacht. It probably wasn't always as nice and easy as it seems to be in Eckersberg's painting. In winter when there was a risk of ice floes, it could be very dangerous. The crossing became less dependent on wind and weather with steam ferries.*

1523 the king sailed restlessly back and forth across the Little Belt. Should he stay in Jutland and continue the fight or should he go to Copenhagen and consolidate his power? Every time the ferry approached one of the coasts, the king became doubtful and commanded that it turn around. During the course of that night on the ferry on the Little Belt, he actually lost his kingdom due to desperation and indecision.

What is a ferry?

It was rarely as traumatic to sail on a ferry. For many Danes, their first memory of a ferry trip is associated with summer vacation trips in Denmark. But what is a ferry really? It's a specially designed vessel that sails in regular service with people, vehicles or cargo. Even thousands of years ago there has most likely been a kind of ferry service in Denmark. Small crafts that in many ways resemble the smallest of the Viking ships, mentioned earlier in this chapter, have transported people, livestock and cargo across fjords and sounds. A ferryman could make a living on this passage and perhaps also on a little inn nearby.

Far into the 1800s the ferries were usually small wooden ships or rather boats, since they were often rowed. The shape could be that of a rowboat, a smack with a gaff sail or a kind of barge. For very short crossings they sometimes used a solid rope that was tied to something like a tree on each shore, so the ferryman could pull his boat back and forth. On long crossings, like across the Great Belt and the Kattegat, the ferries were large, two-masted yachts with a superstructure that could give the passengers shelter and perhaps a meal. The design of these vessels wasn't much different from the other existing small wooden ships that were used for transport, fishing and other coastal sailing.

The steam ferries

In the late 1800s, the steam ferries were launched. The increased traffic between the regions and the need for a more regular service that wasn't dependent on the wind and weather was an important reason why the new ferries were introduced. But there was also another reason behind this new development, and that was the emergence of the railway, and this fact seriously changed the design of the ferries. Now the ferries had to transport railway cars across the sounds and belts. The first steam ferry in Denmark was built in Scotland and went into service on the Little Belt crossing in 1872. It was a paddle steamer with a large blade wheel on each side of the ship.

The new ferries looked like big barges with railroad tracks on the deck. They had a relatively slender superstructure and usually two big smokestacks. These ferries were called double enders, which means that the railroad cars could drive onboard at one end and drive off at the other. In appearance many of them were symmetrical, which underlined the fact that they could sail equally well in both directions. Many of these ferries also had a rudder at both ends and therefore did not have to turn when they set out. On short routes in particular, like over the Little Belt, this could be a considerable timesaver.

The first Danish-built steam ferry on the Great Belt was the Sjælland and was delivered by Burmeister & Wain's shipyard in Copenhagen in 1887. It was followed by its two sister ships, the Korsør and the Nyborg, which were built at Kockum's shipyard in Malmö, Sweden. These ships were also paddle steamers and very large for their time, over 77 metres long, which was longer than the frigate Jylland that was built more than 25 years

◀ *The motor ferry Sjælland in the 1951 version was built at Helsingør Shipyard. From 1998–2002 it functioned as a restaurant ship at quay berth 114, close to Langebro in the middle of Copenhagen harbour.*

before and was then about the limit of how long a wooden ship could be. But the new ferries were made of steel and were almost 18 metres wide over the paddle boxes, while the blade wheels were 6 metres in diameter. The machinery could yield 1200 horsepower and that gave a service speed of a good 12 knots (just over 22 km/h).

Since the blade wheels were curved, it was preferable to turn the ship around and sail forwards on the Great Belt even though the ferries were double enders. They could carry up to 1100 passengers, and under the train deck, despite the meagre daylight, there were beautiful interiors with a dining room, smoking room and a ladies' parlour as well as toilets. There were two tracks on the deck that could accommodate 120 metres of railcars. Putting these new ferries into service on first the Little Belt and then the Great Belt entailed a dramatic reduction of the crossing time for people and on equally dramatic increase in the amount of freight. Just two years after the steam ferries starting sailing across the Great Belt, they had conveyed more than 10,000 railcars.

The ferry Sjælland again

The increased industrialisation made it possible to build these large and efficient ships that before the year 1900 could transport a whole train. At the same time, an efficient and reliable ferry service was a vital part of the infrastructure that was essential if Denmark were to develop into an advanced industrial society. And in the same way that steam and coal were replaced by diesel engines in oceangoing ships such as on the cargo ship Selandia (see page 383), the same thing eventually happened to the ferries.

From 1988 till 2002 in Copenhagen, you could see a slightly dated Danish State Railways (DSB) ferry at quay berth 114 near Langebro. It was the motor ferry Sjælland that was built in 1951 at Helsingør Shipyard but under the name Dronning Ingrid (Queen Ingrid). In professional ferry circles the Sjælland is considered the last of the train ferries that was built in the classic style, for example with two low funnels on a traditional superstructure and with slim masts and an open bow and stern. During its career it sailed on the Great Belt and in the Baltic on routes to northern Germany from Gedser and Rødby, respectively.

In the postwar era, the ferries had now developed from being advanced steam-propelled barges with a slim superstructure and passenger parlours in the bottom to becoming real, integrated seagoing ships with powerful machinery, a bow port and big, bright salons with a full kitchen. These ferries were necessary in the modern age with increased automobile and train traffic, and when the citizens and business community had high expectations of being able to get from place to place effortlessly.

At this time, the ship designers looked to the big passenger ships for inspiration when building ferries. A vessel like the Sjælland resembled in many ways a little copy of an ocean liner, especially from the outside. They also tried to make the interiors as fashionable as possible with first and second-class salons, a smoking room etc. But since the crossing time was short and there were many passengers that wanted a quick meal, it was hard to maintain the illusion of being onboard an elegant cruise ship.

A ferry like the Dronning Ingrid braved almost all kinds of weather with its two B&W diesel engines that supplied 5450 hp and a speed of

▸ *The Bornholm Traffic had the Kongedybet built at B&W in 1952. Much of the design, especially the interiors, was done by Kay Fisker's architectural practice, such as the smoking room with a very special ceiling. It was made so that light would fall indirectly on the conversing passengers sitting at the architect-designed table and chairs. The winding organic forms of the ceiling were particularly eye-catching.*

16.5 knots (30 km/h). Its length was 105.5 metres and its width 17.7 metres. This ferry, like its steam ferry predecessors, had rudders at both ends to make manoeuvring in port easier, but they hadn't yet begun to install the modern bow propellers that really could make a difference in turning and tight manoeuvres. After a few years on the Great Belt the Dronning Ingrid was to sail on the Baltic Sea, but it first had to go to the shipyard to be refitted. The more open sea on the German route gave more spindrift, and to ensure the cars in the front wouldn't be drenched in saltwater, the fore body had to be raised and covered. This made the ship look more robust and compact. Some ferry enthusiasts think the original ship was the more beautiful while others think the refitting was successful and didn't ruin the ship or make it uglier.

The ferry from 1951 was christened the Sjælland in 1979 when DSB's new and latest generation of intercity ferries were put into service. One of these ferries was christened the Dronning Ingrid. Of course DSB couldn't have two ships with the same name. In 1982 the Sjælland was no longer needed as a ferry, and it was laid up for a while before it was renovated for 10 million kroner and was given the berth 114 in Copenhagen as a restaurant ship for 13 years. In 2002 the ship was sold to an English firm and towed off to an unknown destiny.

The architect-designed interior

As mentioned before, it could be difficult on the short ferry routes to ensure an exclusive experience when many people were bustling back and forth from a train or car to the dining area. But on the longer routes things were completely different. Here there was a chance to design and stage the proper voyage in tasteful interiors.

Around the same time that the Dronning Ingrid was being finished, one of the Bornholm ferries' most beautiful ships was being built at Burmeister & Wain. This was the ferry Kongedybet (the King's Deep), which was in service from 1952 to 1978 from Copenhagen to Bornholm, after which it was sold to a Chinese shipping company. Calling the Bornholm boats ferries is perhaps going a bit too far. A ship like the Kongedybet could only accommodate 24 cars on its little car deck, and they had to be eased in and out of a port on the side of the ship. Considering the fact that the ship could carry 1500 passengers, it was clear that it had been built before driving had become the norm.

The Bornholm Traffic's ferries were called The White Ships by connoisseurs since they were all painted white. Along with the Kongedybet's very classic, beautiful lines, the white colour reminded people of ocean liners under exotic skies. The prevalent streamlined forms of the time resulted in some very integrated ships where the shape of the hull and the superstructure meet in a very harmonious way. In 1958, the Kongedybet was extended by four metres at B&W's shipyard. The ship was cut in two behind the engine room and the extension was inserted. This made room for more cars and more cabins in first class, but without increasing the total number of passengers.

The design of the ship was very consistent, and it was not only beautiful from the outside. In all the years that the Kongedybet sailed to Bornholm, the passengers could enjoy the stylish interior that was designed by Kay Fisker. Fisker and his architectural practice hadn't had as much influence on the design of the outside of the ship as on the inside, but the architect did have a little influence on the shape of the funnel and the superstructure.

▼ *A Pedersen bicycle in its proper element, namely the free town of Christiania.*

Exclusive materials were used for the accommodation of the ship, such as teak, mahogany, polished walnut, leather upholstery, fine furniture fabrics, sandblasted or etched matt glass and inlaid wood decorations on the panels (so-called intarsia). The design was typified by simplicity, almost like a 'funkis' (functional) building on land even though most of the furniture was nailed down for safety reasons in high seas. In first class in particular this cultured environment could be experienced, as if at a luxury hotel, with wide staircases, indirect light, well-furnished and well-equipped cabins and a restaurant with impeccable service.

That was the way to travel for those who could afford first class, but the good design rubbed off on all of the ship's rooms. Modern design was especially apparent in the oval smoking room. This is a good example of how the democratic view of humanity in countries like Denmark results in good design for everyone, no matter what class they were travelling on. The walls here were covered in dark palisander on which all the shipping company's ships were painted. The windows were framed with light elm, and comfortable easy chairs and sofas were grouped around small tables. But the ceiling in particular drew a lot of attention with a formidable organically formed carving in dark walnut veneer. From this amoebic form the indirect light shone down on the passengers and at the same time it hid the ventilation ducts.

After the glory days of the ferries, around the time of World War II and for a few decades, the international cafeteria style has become widespread on ships, even those who sail the long routes. The pressure from other means of transport has led to an increasing cost-consciousness and demands for efficient utilisation of the capacity. New synthetic materials, cleaning-friendly solutions along with safety regulations have made it almost impossible to maintain the high standard of interiors that architects like Kay Fisker represented. While the interior of the Kongedybet endured while the ship was in service, it's not unusual today for the interior of a ferry to be totally renovated every tenth year. This is an opportunity to update the interior of the ship, but it doesn't give the ferries much patina.

BICYCLES

Mikael Pedersen's bicycle

The history of the bicycle goes back a couple of hundred years. Many odd experiments, inventions and innovations have been made before the bicycle found the basic form we still see today. Around 1900, all the major inventions had been made and the basic design was established for the so-called safety bicycle: the diamond frame, the size of the wheels, the chain drive, pneumatic tires, the freewheeling hub and efficient brakes. The next 100 years, actually the whole 20th century, were spent developing this bicycle design but without any major revolutions. Almost all attempts to significantly change the basic concept were fiascos, fashion trends or exclusive niche productions.

One of the few serious alternatives to the safety bicycle and one which to a small degree has survived the dominance of the classic bicycle is the Danish Pedersen bike from 1893. Mikael Pedersen was a talented and imaginative smith. In his younger days he invented and patented a cream separator, which was the first of its kind to work continually and reliably. This patent earned him a tidy sum that he used to build a house and to develop his bicycle. Pedersen was not satisfied with the new safety bicycle since he found the riding position uncomfortable and the fixed saddle too hard and unpleasant.

◀ *The classic delivery bike, the so-called long john, was originally black, but is now produced in many colours by the Esimex Company in Hanstholm.*

▶ *The Christiania bike has become the urban family's alternative to a car. Anything can be transported in it.*

The Pedersen bicycle is based on a different construction principle than the safety bicycle. Our bicycles today get their strength and rigidity from a closed frame, but Pedersen's is more similar to the lattice girders of a steel bridge.

The frame consists of several triangles of thin tubes that together create a stable system. This construction makes the cyclist sit in a more upright position than on a traditional bicycle. The saddle is made of braided leather strips and is strung between the two top points of the frame. This is how Mikael Pedersen's two criticisms of the existing bicycle became the basis for a new comfortable design.

In 1893 he applied for a patent for his bicycle in England. He had settled down in the town of Dursley since this is where the Lister factory that manufactured his cream separator was located. Now he started manufacturing bicycles, first in his own workshop and later at Lister's. About 30,000 of the 'Dursley-Pedersen' bicycles were manufactured in England until 1920. Up until World War I his bicycle sold well since there was a great interest in bicycles, including among the wealthy who could afford to buy something exclusive. The Pedersen bicycle was both fast and comfortable, and due to its cross-country properties it was used on gentlemen's hunting trips as well as by the British army during the Boer War in South Africa in 1899–1902.

Mikael Pedersen also invented the first three-speed hub gear. However, due to unfortunate circumstances, a competitor acquired the market. After World War I, the exclusive bicycle market was gone. The car and motorbike were the new toys and means of transport for the well off. Mikael Pedersen was broke and returned to Denmark where he died in extreme poverty some years later.

The Pedersen bicycle was reintroduced by bicycle mechanic Jesper Sølling while he was working in the free town of Christiania in Copenhagen. Today it is manufactured in Ebeltoft and is sold worldwide to enthusiasts or to cyclists who have a bad back that demands a more upright position than found on the traditional ones. In the last 25 years, more than 6000 Pedersen bikes have been made in a version with updated accessories. Due to its special construction and many parts, this bicycle will never be produced as inexpensively as ordinary bikes with diamond frames, but it is certainly a beautiful alternative as regards design.

Christiania Bikes

In 1984, a new chapter in the history of freight bikes was written in Denmark when Christiania's smithy sent the first of many thousands of Christiania bikes on to the street. In the wake of the energy crisis, in 1976 nimble-fingered people on Christiania started using bicycle trailers. At first Lars Engstrøm had developed these trailers for use in the free town, but it turned out that there was a good basis for selling it outside Christiania. During the design process, the best solution was to further develop the principles of the good, old delivery bike.

The construction of Christiania bike is rather different from that of the old long john. The most notable difference it that the Christiania bike has three wheels, and that you turn the bike by pushing the transport box and the two front wheels in the direction you want to go. While the

A LONG JOHN. Throughout the 20th century, the bicycle has been an inexpensive and practical means of transport in Denmark. But cycling hasn't been limited to personal transport; freight bikes have been developed as well and are frequently used. The well-known long john is one of the first and most resilient long-lived designs of freight bikes.

The long john, which despite its name is Danish, came on the market in 1929 when mechanic Morten Rasmussen patented a freight bike. It resembled the later long john, but it was longer and had two wheels of the same size. Shortly after, it was developed into the long john we know, apparently by bike mechanic Mathiesen from Vanløse, outside Copenhagen. The new version had a smaller front wheel and an ordinary back wheel and could carry up to 150 kg. It was a sturdy and therefore heavy bike. The steering was a bit loose, since it went through a thin bar under the freight platform. From 1936 the long john was manufactured by the bicycle factory SCO on Funen, and since then it's been a part of the streetscape, especially up until about 1970 when every grocery store had a bicycle messenger to deliver groceries. A subculture arose around these messengers who were called 'swayers' because of their reckless driving. Today the production has been taken over by a small firm in Hanstholm called Esimex that continues to improve the model, and now the original black long john also comes in other colours.

◀ *The Dolphin bike trailer is mostly for transporting young children, but there's room for a bag of shopping too.*

two-wheeled long john was used to transport freight on a low and open frame of tubes, the Christiania bike with its solid box of plywood is mostly designed for personal use: transporting the day's shopping and picking up young children from the daycare centre. But this has not prevented many tradesmen from using it, and even the postal service has bought it in large numbers.

In 1989, Christiania Bikes had already expanded so much that the firm moved from the free town to Klemensker on Bornholm where today 1000 bikes are sent through various distributors out into the world; 500 for the Danish market and the same number for export. The bike is made in four sizes, and many accessories have been developed such as hoods, leather saddles, more gears, a reverse gear, dynamo lights and racks.

The Dolphin

The stubborn Danish bicycling culture, which hasn't been wiped out by the growing number and popularity of cars, is still a good breeding ground for new developments. While the bike mechanics in Christiania focused on the three-wheeled freight bike, others felt there were still possibilities for the bike trailer. Among them was the young design student Leif Hagerup. For his graduation project at Denmark's Design School in the mid-1990s he developed a little bike trailer for luggage and shopping. In a roundabout way he got in touch with the bicycle factory A. Winther A/S in Them, and they did indeed want a trailer in their range, but the project had to undergo many changes before it took off.

In Winther's opinion it would be impossible to sell a bike trailer that was only meant for freight; there had to be room for one or two children. It would also be a good idea if it could easily be disconnected from the bike and possibly used as a stroller. The result of subsequent work was the Dolphin bike trailer that was especially developed to accommodate two young children and a little shopping. It consists of a metal frame, suspension wheels and a moulded plastic cabin with a hood. Moreover a small front wheel can be mounted on the front of the trailer so it can be used as a stroller. At this time more than 5000 Dolphins have been manufactured, and in 1997 it won the Danish Design Centre's ID prize.

The bicycle as an object of design

Like so many other products today, the bicycle has also been the object of great interest by designers and lifestyle companies. The starting point of this desire to redesign a bicycle doesn't usually have anything to do with wanting to make a bike work better or make it cheaper for the users, but rather for the company to carve itself a niche by an aesthetic styling of a bike. Thus the bike becomes a kind of accessory just like clothes, shoes, watches and many other lifestyle products that tell other people something about who you are and which give you a personal identity.

In Denmark there are at least two examples of this, and they're very different. One of them is Sögreni Bicycles whose shop and store are located in the 'Latin Quarter' in Copenhagen and has been run by Søren Gregers Nielsen since 1981.The mark of Sögreni's hand-built bicycles is the quirky logic that is apparent in almost all of their solutions from the frame to the bell. Not only are the frames very simple, but all the different components are so straightforward that they look like they could have been made on the workbench in the workshop.

▾ *Søren Gregers Nielsen's bike workshop is called Sögreni, and here he develops most of the parts for his bikes himself. The special mechanic's style of his bikes is created by using many little fittings, such as the chainguard pictured here.*

THE COPENHAGEN BIKE. Since 1995 free bikes have been available to citizens and tourists during the summer. The concept is unique and has since been used in other cities such as Aarhus in 2005. Ole Wessung and Morten Sadolin got the idea for the project in 1989. They were very irritated by the many bike thefts and wanted to find a solution. After several attempts, the existing project was launched on May 30, 1995 with 1000 bikes on the streets. And despite several hiccups such as many stolen and vandalised bikes, the project continued. The reason for the special design of the city bike, with its very sturdy massive tires, is so that they're easy to recognise if someone should want to 'privatise' or strip them, but also so that there's plenty of room for advertising and graphics on the wheels and frame.

In the summer of 2005 there were more than 2000 city bikes on the street, and there were 110 special parking places within the city bike zone in downtown Copenhagen. Every day, trucks collect runaway and wrecked bikes, and two repair trucks visit the parking zones regularly to care for the needy ones. This is all financed by grants from foundations as well as revenue from sponsorship and ads. For the city of Copenhagen this has become a popular service for tourists. When former President Clinton visited Copenhagen in 1997, he was presented with a city bike – City Bike One.

▸ *Most of Biomega's bikes are special in one way or another. One of them, pictured here, has a shaft transmission instead of a chain drive. Other models have special frames made of pressed aluminium profiles.*

For example, the Sögreni bell is just a flat, round piece of metal in polished stainless steel. The fenders can be made of a piece of aluminium floor plate that's been bent into a curve that more of less follows that of the wheel. Other fenders are made of laminated, veneered wood and treated with a durable marine varnish. Everything is mounted with small screws, bolts and bushings, which emphasise the hand-built appearance. Abroad Sögreni bikes are not normally sold by bike stores but by exclusive furniture design boutiques.

Another example of what design can do for bicycles is to be found at the Biomega company. It was founded by two philosophers, Jens Martin Skibsted and Elias Grove Nielsen, who instead of trial and error in the workshop chose to create the bikes at the drawing board and to hire well-known foreign industrial designers. Biomega has developed some very interesting alternative solutions, for example some of their models have something as exotic as a shaft transmission instead of a chain drive. Biomega also makes bikes painted in fluorescent colours that are easily spotted by nighttime drivers.

Most of Biomega's models are designed in-house by Jens Martin Skibsted, but one model called MNO is designed by the famous English furniture and lamp designer Marc Newson. The MNO has a very different frame to most bikes, in that it is cast in aluminium and glued together to make a very strong construction. This model also comes with a hydraulic fork and lots of luxury accessories, so the total price in 2005 was over 40,000 kroner. Other designer bikes are up and coming, including with Ross Lovegrove as one of the designers.

The Biomega people are very conscious of the media and their brand; among others they have developed a bike in collaboration with the sportswear company Puma. They focus on a special client base by going to design fairs and securing mentions in design magazines, like 'Wall Paper'. Like Sögreni Bicycles, Biomega's bikes are often sold by lifestyle boutiques, and in many advertisements and articles their designer bikes are featured with other designer articles like well-known brands of furniture and lamps. Bike connoisseurs criticise their bikes for not being very practical, for example, no fenders, racks or locks are found in the Biomega range.

MOTORBIKES

Some years after the ordinary bicycle made its breakthrough and gradually achieved the basic form we know today, many inventors started tinkering with the idea of putting a motor on the bike. If not the first, the Danish inventors were at the forefront in developing these machines, and a motorcycle industry was started in Denmark. In the course of time there have been over 50 Danish makes of motorbikes on the market and in addition a corresponding number of moped manufacturers. Many of these Danish motorbike makers got no further than making a very small series of bikes. A few companies have only built a couple of prototypes. But two companies in this industry stand out from the others, namely Ellehammer and Fisker & Nielsen.

About 1000 Elleham motorbikes were built between 1904–16. Fisker & Nielsen started their production in 1921, and until about 1960 they made over 14,000 in all from their two different Nimbus models. The period from 1900 to 1925 was the heyday of motorcycle development. These years were characterised by a technical and industrial boom when energetic

◂ *Jacob Christian Hansen Ellehammer (1871–1946) with his motorbike, the Elleham, which was developed and produced in the few hundreds from 1900 till 1910. Later he sold the rights and became interested in flying and other inventions.*

engineers and boisterous bike mechanics fiddled around after working hours. If the experiments went well, these aspiring inventors quit their jobs and set up shop according to the motto – if it works, it can probably be sold. These were the technological nerds of yesteryear that entered the arena. In principle they weren't much different from the computer freaks of the last few decades who also go at it hammer and tongs. So it was all or nothing.

Elleham

In the beginning the motorbike was just a bicycle with an auxiliary engine and resembled a homemade moped, at least to our eyes. Oddly enough, the very first attempts at motorisation had cyclists as its target group. These machines were to be used as pacers during cycling races, whether they were on a course or on the road. But soon these machines had a life of their own, and one of the first people to develop something useful was the inventor Jacob Christian Ellehammer. His motorbike was called the Elleham and looked like a cross between a slender moped and a powerful motorised children's scooter. And you had to run with it to start it, since the kick starter hadn't been invented yet. But otherwise the construction resembled the tubular frame of a bicycle, and the transmission of power to the back wheel was by means of a belt drive. It may sound obsolete today, but the model wasn't very primitive back then. It was continuously improved, and later it was furnished with a suspension fork and a little built-in toolbox at the bottom of the frame.

In 1907, both the Danish postal service and the Danish police got their very first motorbikes ever, and they were Ellehams, and a sidecar was developed for transporting mail and goods. Even though Ellehammer was a very talented inventor and entrepreneur, he quickly lost interest in an invention once it was finished, so in 1910 he sold the rights to the Elleham motorbike to Skandinavisk Handelskompagni (The Scandinavian Trade Company) that was also called Mundus A/S, who continued the production until 1916, whereupon it was discontinued.

Nimbus

The really big brand in the development and production of Danish motorbikes was Nimbus. It was initiated due to the strong emotional involvement of Peder Andersen Fisker, who was the founder, co-owner and director of the vacuum cleaner factory Nilfisk (see the Nilfisk vacuum cleaner on page 121). In 1919, when the production of vacuum cleaners was well on its way, he developed his first motorbike, which was put into production in 1921.

P.A. Fisker had been a bit skeptical for a while about the existing motorbikes on the market. He thought they looked like bikes with an added motor, 'a terrible mishmash' he wrote in his memoirs, which certainly wasn't completely wrong. Instead he thought that a good motorbike should be built from scratch, and that's what he did to the fullest. The end product was almost 100 % Danish. Almost everything from the frame and motors to the electrical system was developed and manufactured by the factory in Frederiksberg. One of the first machines even had tires from the Danish firm Schønning & Arvé.

The first model was only available in black and had a characteristic frame where the petrol tank was built into the upper tube. This visionary design gave it a very special appearance, so people immediately called it 'the

▼ *The first Nimbus model from 1921. The public dubbed it The Stovepipe.This version has a sidecar and the petrol tank sat at the top of the frame. It had shaft transmission and – what was relatively new at the time – suspension on both wheels.*

Stovepipe'. Fisker hated this nickname and decided to prove the worth of his machine. He did this by participating in some races, which he often won, and after a while the motorbike was the object of so much respect that even the Danish army bought it for their courier service.

You could say that the Stovepipe is more remarkable than pretty, but it wasn't a bad construction although the underframe can seem a bit flimsy in comparison to today's machines. It has four cylinders, suspension on both wheels, a kick starter, shaft transmission instead of chain drive, and it's also said to have had really good roadworthiness for its time.

In 1924, the Danish parliament introduced a sales tax that made the production uneconomic from one day to the next. The Stovepipe was still manufactured for three to four years, primarily based on the large stock of spare parts at the factory, but in 1928 after manufacturing about 2000 bikes, it was curtains for Nimbus.

The Bumblebee

P.A. Fisker's son, Anders Fisker, graduated as an engineer in 1932 and was immediately signed on by Nilfisk. And although his daily workday was all about manufacturing vacuum cleaners, father and son got going on a new motorcycle project. In 1934 they launched a new model, which was dubbed 'the bumblebee' because of its characteristic buzzing or humming sound. It quickly became a part of street life in Copenhagen in particular, where at times in the 1930s it had an impressive market share of over 60 %. With its sidecar it was a speedy alternative to a little delivery van or a delivery bicycle, and a number of companies and shops solved their transport needs in this way.

Unlike the Stovepipe, it didn't have suspension on the rear wheel, however the saddle was rather springy, and as a worldwide innovation it had telescopic suspension on the fork. The motor had four inline cylinders and transmission through a cardan shift just like its predecessor, but it was improved on several counts, among other things it now had an overhead camshaft. The relatively powerful motor and the sturdy construction made it suitable for cross-country driving and poor roads, so sales were high to the police, army and postal service during these years.

The Bumblebee is almost in every way a far more mature and systematic design than the first Nimbus bike. It's a rather heavy machine to drive and also to look at. The unenclosed motor, the big fenders, especially the front one, and the frame's structure of rather wide iron plates with the integrated petrol tank, made the bike seem rather compact. Unlike its foreign competitors from the US and England, in particular, its appearance doesn't have much style to it.

Anders Fisker jr. describes in his memoirs how the first model was built of wood and cardboard at the factory, and nothing was done to make the motorbike more appealing: 'During the construction, considerations were only taken of the practical side of things and not the desires of the public. It sounds strange – and dangerous – but it turned out well. People liked the new Nimbus, even though I must admit that the customers got their way on several counts. For example, Dad insisted that it should be boring black, but eventually we started using many colours.'

As suggested, the design wasn't very sophisticated, but more like a brute machine, and perhaps that was the charm of the Bumblebee. As

▼ *The second Nimbus model was also given a nickname, namely the Bumblebee, because of the sound of its motor. It was built in many versions, for example, for the army and the postal service, and numbered almost 13,000 in the years 1934 to 1958.*

◂ The Hammel car, which was built in a back courtyard on Nørrebro in Copenhagen in 1888, now resides at the Danish Technical Museum in Helsingør and is the world's oldest car that can still be started and driven, although this rarely happens.

▸ An advertising poster for Triangel's cars from 1928–29 (they also sold foreign makes). Architect Kaare Klint designed it and cut the linoleum that was used to print the posters. He was also slightly involved in the design of the cars, but most of his work for Triangel was as an illustrator and exhibition architect.

one English comment stated, 'It's a tractor on two wheels.' The success of this kind of aesthetics is dependent on whether the machine works satisfactorily. It's a bit like the American jeep from World War II; it's not a pretty sight, but it improves on acquaintance when you find out that you can actually trust it always.

Unfortunately it was never mass produced on an assembly line. Strangely enough, they figured it would be too expensive, but that can be due to the fact that it wasn't conceived from the beginning for mass production, and also due to the fact that it would require large sales of the Bumblebee, and that would mean banking on export. Finally, when times got better in the 1950s, small inexpensive cars came on the market, and this was a hard blow for the motorcycles.

As of 1958, no more Nimbus parts were produced, but for several years new machines were assembled using of the stock of spare parts. And that's how Fisker & Nielsen managed to make about 12,700 Bumblebees. In posterity the Nimbus has become a bit of a cult, and there are still many on the road, especially on festive occasions like races and meets. A national icon dies hard.

DANISH CARS

Triangel

Several Danish inventors and the people in the industry worked on developing cars about a hundred years ago. One of the earliest projects was the so-called Hammelvogn (Hammel car) from 1888, which was named after Albert Hammel and his machine factory on Nørrebrogade 38 in Copenhagen. Together with his foreman, Hans Urban Johansen, Hammel built an open motorised vehicle that looked like a horse carriage without the horse. Only one Hammel car was made and today it's exhibited at the Danish Technical Museum in Helsingør as the world's oldest original car that can still run.

Other people also tinkered with cars, and after a while there was a bunch of exuberant entrepreneurs that manufactured motor vehicles. Their efforts were driven more by pure enthusiasm and a pioneer spirit than sound financial backing, so eventually there were some bankruptcies and mergers in the business. In 1918, three Danish companies merged to start the United Automobile Factories, better known as Triangel. The two small companies in the merge were JAN, which had only made a few vehicles since it was founded in 1915, and Anglo-Dane, which was established in 1902 and had manufactured bicycles, motorbikes, cars, small trucks and fire engines since that time.

The big brother in this union was Thrige in Odense. Since 1909 they had manufactured cars, some of which were electric, trucks and small buses that were partly made of foreign components. For more than 40 years, the new Triangel company made a large number of vehicles, especially trucks and buses, and some have been preserved. Triangel was the name the company was known under, while the name the United Automobile Factories drifted out of the logo's design and was only used for official purposes.

Triangel quickly concentrated on manufacturing trucks and buses, among others the characteristic flat-nosed trams that were used in Aarhus from the early 1930s. Furthermore they produced special products like fire engines

and military vehicles and motor-coach trains for the private railways. These were the predecessors of the railcars we know today. The company quickly realised that it would be a risky undertaking to compete with big foreign automobile companies in making cars. Five years before Triangel started, in 1913, Henry Ford had already launched the assembly line and could manufacture inexpensive cars suited to the common man.

Apart from being the longest surviving Danish automobile company, what made Triangel special was that it was one of the first companies in the field of technical production that started working seriously with design. In 1918 Tage Klint was hired as the company director, and he brought in his father, P.V. Jensen-Klint, who is best known for his design of Grundtvigskirken (the Grundtvig Church) on Bispebjerg in Copenhagen, and later his brother Kaare Klint, who was an architect and the first professor of furniture design at the Royal Academy of Fine Arts in Copenhagen.

Both P.V. Jensen-Klint and Kaare Klint worked primarily with the visual identity of Triangel, that is, the company logo, typography, brochures and illustrations for them, advertisements and exhibitions at shows. However, if not being actual car designers, the two architects acted as kind of aesthetic consultants for the company's product development. Employing the creative members of the Klint family marks a change in course for Triangel. Without much notice being taken, the company goes from being a rather technically-inclined automobile maker to becoming a design and image-conscious company.

The somewhat small Danish market did not allow Triangel the luxury of behaving like one of the big European automobile factories. They had to concentrate partially on manufacturing vehicles for industry and other custom-made products and partially make use of other companies' know-how and semi-manufactures. So in the 1920s, Triangel also imported Fiat cars, and from 1931 Austins. The factory's design is somewhat determined by these partnerships. Therefore the Klint architects had to be creative within a limited framework.

There is some controversy in professional circles as to what degree the Klints actually designed cars for Triangel or whether the many drawings of trucks and buses made by Kaare Klint are merely illustrations for brochures and advertisements. It's apparently difficult to find photographs of the vehicles pictured in the coloured drawings apart from a couple that were exhibited at car shows. But one must keep in mind that many of Triangel's cars were made-to-order and are either manufactured individually or in a very small series. So it was hard to integrate design in this process if the company was to still make money on their vehicles.

Although the design of their vehicles was clearly influenced by tendencies from the foreign automobile industry, there is evidence that the two architects inspired the company to think more along the lines of design. At any rate, there is a change in Triangel's design when Kaare Klint takes over from his father, P.V. Jensen-Klint, around 1925. At the time, Jensen-Klint was an elderly architect who was influenced by the classic and symmetrical style of his time, and this is expressed in the radiator grills that are reminiscent of solid, Greek temples. During Kaare Klint's time the style becomes more functional with softer and more rounded corners and edges, but without becoming completely streamlined.

▸ *The Hope Whisper – before it had an accident at the presentation in 1983.*

It's debatable how well designed are the cars that the Klints and Triangel made together. Compared to the leading international models, Triangel's design isn't particularly remarkable. It's very nice, but does not have a proper understanding of the emerging automobile culture. Kaare Klint's illustrations are typical of an architect's way of working. They are often like drawings of a house, from the front and side, with accurate dimensions and are just like an elevation of the façade and end wall of a building. But at the same time they're very strong, almost supernatural, coloured illustrations and maybe an attempt to comply with the advertising media.

In 1935 Tage Klint got a new job, and at the same time Kaare Klint was no longer affiliated with Triangel. From then on the company in Odense managed its design assignments in-house and most of it looked like an effort to keep up with foreign trends.

Triangel closed in 1957 after having manufactured about 3000 vehicles of which 500 were buses. Only 15 vehicles were exported, which shows how dependent Triangel was on the domestic market, just like the motorbikes from Nimbus. The fact that this type of industry required huge investments and a very high level of production, combined with the replacement of the protected domestic market with free trade, killed these companies. Only by focusing intently on product development, design and rational production would it have been possible to compete with the terms of the international market.

And then the other guys ...

As mentioned, Triangel threw in the towel in 1957. This was just before the 1960s automobile boom, which in the following decades led to quite a few different Danish automobile projects on the drawing board. In almost every case this was a pipe dream that never amounted to more than one or two prototypes. There was never enough capital or expertise behind the projects, and when big boys want to play at being car manufacturers, they quickly lose any sense of reality on the cut-throat world market.

The electric car Hope Whisper was one of the many Danish attempts to build cars and preferably lots of them. It was an ambitious project developed by businessman and MP for the right-wing Danish Progress Party Thure Barsøe-Carnfeldt and based at his company Hope Computer in Hadsund. In 1983 Hope had developed a little electric car that got a lot of publicity when it was introduced to the world press in Forum in Copenhagen.

Unfortunately the engineer who was to drive the car on stage for all the world to see fell asleep at the wheel because he had worked around the clock during the weeks before the premiere. So in front of rolling cameras and Prime Minister Poul Schlüter he drove the car straight into a barrier and dented the front fender. Later it was rumoured that a deal had been made to sell several hundred thousands of them to a foreign business partner. It was a billion-kroner deal that later turned out to be untrue. And that's the way this adventure ended up in a museum, too.

The Ellert – the motorised bathtub

The prototype of yet another little Danish vehicle with the official name of Mini-el – or the Ellert as it was quickly christened – was ready in 1985. The Ellert was (or still is since a small number are still produced in Germany) a one-person electrically powered three-wheeled vehicle. Besides the driver, there's room for a child or the day's shopping, but since the total

▼ *The Ellert – or Mini-el as it was officially called – was a true child of Randers. The factory was located in the town, which supported the project by buying the new vehicle and installing sockets all over the municipality for the owners to use for recharging.*

◂ *Manufacturer Knud Erik Westergaard's car project from 1991 was given the name Kewet El-jet, better known as the Kewet. This project had a short lifespan before the factory had to close its doors at a great financial loss.*

weight is limited to 115 kg, it normally isn't possible to take an adult passenger. The originator of the project and the driving force for many years was engineer Steen V. Jensen, who got the idea while employed at Dronningborg Maskinfabrik (machine factory) that makes agricultural machines.

The line of thought that led to the Ellert was that since over 80 % of the Danish population has to travel less than 15 km to get to work, and over 90 % of those who drive are alone in their cars, there had to be a market for a cheaper and more energy-economical vehicle. The Mini-el was constructed to have a range of 40–70 km per charge, and then it could regain its strength overnight in the carport with a cord plugged into the mains.

The concept is an overdue result of the energy crisis, and the prototype was given a small subsidy by the Danish Technology Board, but otherwise the Ellert was launched through small-denomination shares totalling 90 million kroner from 3000 private investors. A production was started in Randers, and the first Mini-el rolled out in June 1987. When production was at its highest, the Eltrans company employed 70 people, and 10–12 vehicles were made a day. The first version of the Ellert could go 40 km/h and had to be registered as a three-wheeled motorbike. So it can be driven by someone either with a driver's license for a car or motorbike.

The Ellert was designed by the Scottish designer Ray Innes, who used to work for Dronningborg and other Danish companies. Although he was mainly experienced in designing agricultural and construction machines, the Ellert is a very beautiful little aerodynamic vehicle to look at. The size and form alone attract notice, which at first was taken advantage of by many business owners for advertising. The lines of the Ellert are also very elegant with the slanting front end. Many Danes probably thought it was cool that you opened the whole top to get in and out. And despite the sunroof opening, sitting under the clear plastic dome could be very hot on a sunny day.

In late 1987, problems began to crop up when an almost brand new Mini-el burst into flames. That meant that all the manufactured vehicles, about 150, had to be recalled to repair a relay. A few months later, an Ellert blew up, as the press so graphically put it. It turned out that a fuse had melted one of the battery's degassing tubes, which made the ox hydrogen gas explode. No major damage occurred in the vehicle, but once again all the sold Ellerts (now about 500) had to have their construction altered.

The cost of these recalls and many other complaints from Ellert owners drained the company's finances, and in October 1988 they declared bankruptcy. They managed to build up the company again when investors supplied new capital. The plan was to solve the many technical problems that had arisen and then send a fully tested version out with new electronics and a larger motor. The latter meant that the new model could drive about 50 km/h. At this point they began to export mostly to Germany, Austria and Switzerland.

But once again they encountered problems with the technology, the bad image and lack of capital, so a new company was founded in 1991 and called CityCom A/S, which made a series of open Ellerts that were used as camera cars at the Olympic stadiums in Barcelona in 1992. In 1995 the production was moved to Germany where the Ellert presumably is still in production by CityCom AG. It looks the same, but has been continuously updated. About 4500 Ellerts have been manufactured and for a long period of time it was the best selling electric vehicle in the world.

The Mini-el got the ID prize from the Danish Design Centre in 1988 despite its technical difficulties. The panel of judges substantiated their choice by saying that they thought it was 'a good solution to a complex task.' This means that they liked the idea and the good intentions behind the creation of an environmentally friendly, alternative vehicle, and furthermore it had a good design.

The problem with the Ellert, and almost all the electric car projects that have been initiated around the world, is that the originators of the project underestimate the problems and the necessary capital and overrate the potential market for this type of car. The thing is that it seems extremely logical to many eco-friendly car enthusiasts that there should be a market for small electrically-powered cars with room for two. And with the driving needs of most Europeans it should in principle be enough with a range of about 50 km per charge.

But theory and what in principle should be enough is one thing, and practice and the actual consumer wishes are another. Few of us would sacrifice the possibility of taking one or several passengers. And we also want room for luggage or shopping in bulk. So at the end of the day, we're either not environmentally friendly enough or the price is too high considering what we have to do without for us to choose a politically correct car. If such an initiative had been good business, Ford's electric vehicle Th!nk or Daimler-Chrysler's Smart would have amounted to more.

The Kewet El-Jet

When the Ellert project was at its zenith, another Dane began his adventure with electric cars. This was manufacturer Knud Erik Westergaard, who in 1988 sold his life's work, KEW Industries, which made industrial washing machines and high-pressure cleaners, and then took up the development of the Kewet El-Jet. Westergaard invested about 25 million kroner in the project, and in 1991 the first Kewet rolled out of the factory in Hadsund.

The project suffered roughly the same fate as the Ellert. The project got plenty of attention, there were technical problems with the battery and electronics in particular that were somewhat solved along the way, and it ended in bankruptcy in 1998. Since then production was continued in Norway under the model name of Kewet Kollega by ElBil Norge that makes about 50 cars a year.

The lack of capital and the large amount of manual labour that went into the production made it necessary to use well-known and cheap technology in the Kewet to keep the sales price down to an acceptable level. And this was in spite of the fact that electric cars in Denmark are heavily subsidised through tax exemptions. The first Kewet El-Jet was sold in Denmark, but the car attracted much interest abroad, and of the 1000 units that were produced, about two-thirds were exported to various countries. Yet it was far too little to base a more industrial production on.

The Kewet, just like the Mini-el, got an ID prize from the Danish Design Centre in 1995 on pretty much the same grounds, namely that the idea was a good attempt at solving the traffic and environmental problems in the big city. The car attracted a lot of attention in town, and some might

◂ *Knud Valdemar Engelhardt's streetcar from 1908. It was in service on line 18 in Copenhagen, and Engelhardt had also designed the signs on them. Everything on the streetcars had his desired rounded edges since they would end up that way anyway from everyday wear and tear, and this extended even as far as the typeface on the signs.*

even use with word cute about it. It was designed and modelled in full size by industrial designer Lars Kjærulff, who had previously worked for KEW in designing high-pressure cleaners. But the point is that once again the concept couldn't hold its own in actual practice. A two-person car with very limited trunk space, just like in the Ellert's case, isn't an attractive car for many people. When it came on the market, the design seemed very angular, and the details and finish left much to be desired.

STREETCARS

About 100 years ago, public transport, and thus also streetcars, was run by local initiative. This also applied to establishing and running streetcar lines and other forms of public transport. In many cases, private companies took this on and ran public transport on ordinary market conditions. But this gradually came under the auspices of a municipal company that ran the streetcar and bus lines, and in some cases was also responsible for the design and manufacture of the material.

In Copenhagen this meant that far into the 20th century either the municipality or a privately operating company was responsible for designing, constructing and sometimes even building their own streetcars. Streetcars were put into service in 1863 as horse-drawn cars, and in 1897 the first electric cars were launched. In the meantime, several independent companies developed steam-driven streetcars. Electrically powered cars didn't get their power from overhead wires until about 1901. Until then the energy came from accumulators built into the motor car.

The horse-drawn streetcars were similar to horse carriages that were just put on rails. Perhaps that isn't so strange since in many areas you can see how brand new products at first borrow some of their design and construction from the past. The first cars also looked like horse carriages, just without the horses. And just like the cars of the time, it took a while before the electric streetcars got their own independent artistic idiom. Until then they were very much like the design of a classic carriage.

Until 1910 the streetcars had a relatively slim build and had open front and rear platforms. Most were also well supplied with ornamentation, decorations and frills. Among architects these streetcars were condescendingly called 'Chinese birdcages'. But that was the Victorian style of the time that characterised the old design of streetcars which meant that it was almost more important that things looked grand than that they functioned well.

Engelhardt's streetcar

Around 1908 something new happened in the arena of streetcar design in Denmark. Knud Valdemar Engelhardt was 26 years old and still a student at the Royal Academy of Fine Arts, School of Architecture when he was given the assignment of designing new streetcars for the private firm A/S De Københavnske Sporveje (The Copenhagen Streetcar Line). He attacked the assignment with such zeal that his working methods influenced generations of Danish designers afterwards. Everything on this new streetcar, down to the flush-mounted screws, was the object of his undivided attention, and the result of his efforts is a radical break with everything in the field of design up to that time.

Some people think that K.V. Engelhardt earned the status of Denmark's first industrial designer when he designed his streetcar. On the one hand,

KNUD VALDEMAR ENGELHARDT, 1882–1931. An architect and designer who began his career by almost being a permanent student, instead became Denmark's first functionalist designer. Engelhardt was accepted at the Royal Academy of Fine Arts in 1903 and attended the school until 1915; the last four years were in the Department of Decoration under Professor Joakim Skovgaard. While still a student, Engelhardt began his groundbreaking work in 1910 by designing a whole new streetcar for Copenhagen. He also designed the city fixtures and street signs for Gentofte Municipality, which were different and functionally well thought out in comparison to the usual ones. K.V. Engelhardt liked using rounded forms according to his motto of 'why put something on things that the user is going to wear off?' He also made his mark as a graphic designer. His logo, a little red heart, is almost always to be found somewhere on his designs.

he was completely absorbed in the details, and on the other hand, he consciously worked on making the streetcar a harmonious whole. In a way, Engelhardt was probably also the 20th century's first functionalist since he was extremely determined that the design of the streetcar be as appropriate as possible. During his work process he gave up the old Victorian style. Things had to be sensibly designed, he thought and started from scratch in designing a new streetcar.

He began by covering the front and rear platforms. It wasn't fair that standing passengers in a crowded streetcar should stand outside in all kinds of weather – or the conductor for that matter. Engelhardt made the windows in equal widths and at the same time emphasised the load-bearing parts of the body. The result was that the new streetcar came to look much more solid and sturdy than its predecessors. When the vertical elements are emphasised in their construction and colouring, the new streetcars were also given a more dynamic appearance. They simply looked more like a modern means of transport.

The design was both straightforward and yet sophisticated, this was true also on the inside where he simplified and rectified what he thought was old-fashioned nonsense. His philosophy was that things would quickly be affected by the use of many daily passengers. According to Engelhardt, this wear and tear could be taken into consideration beforehand. As he said himself, 'Why put something on things that the user is going to wear off? Why not from the beginning give them the form they'll get from the wear and tear of life? Then they'll be easier to use, and as for their appearance, one must learn from wear: the right wear gives things beauty!'

▾ *Architect Ib Lunding's bogie streetcar from 1930 is here on line 10 over Fredens Bro in Copenhagen.*

What this meant in practice was that Engelhardt designed all the edges, handles and fittings in soft and rounded contours. The most beautiful example is the metal handle that was carefully integrated in the backrest of the benches. The floor moulding and corners inside the streetcar were also in soft and rounded forms. That made cleaning easier and faster. Another reason for the rounded design was that it also prevented a lot of ugly scratches and harm to the material.

Engelhardt followed his philosophy of design to the letter. He even designed new tickets and the signs for the cars, and here the numbers and letters also had rounded corners as if they too would be subjected to wear and tear. Engelhardt was also progressive in his choice of colour scheme. According to legend, he walked around the streets of Copenhagen picking up bits of street dust here and there. They were then mixed, and the light grey colour they resulted in was the colour of the paint for the bogie and undercarriage. The logic was that they would eventually turn that colour anyway, so why not use it from the start so the dirt wouldn't be so visible and a lot of cleaning could be spared?

Engelhardt's streetcars were ready to roll in 1911, around the same time that Copenhagen Municipality took over the private company A/S De Københavnske Sporveje. Only ten of these motor cars were manufactured at Scandia in Randers, and this was the only streetcar that Engelhardt designed. But when the trailers were made, his principles were followed, and for decades all the streetcars were indebted to Engelhardt's groundbreaking work. In 1941–42, the original cars were extended by one metre on the platforms so there was room for 23 more standing passengers. These streetcars were in service as late as 1962 whereupon most of them were converted to salt cars with a snow plow mounted on them.

Lunding's streetcar

In the late 1920s it was time to design a new streetcar for the Copenhagen streets, and this was done by the Copenhagen Municipality itself. The 30-year-old architect Ib Lunding was hired by the Municipal Architect's Directorate in 1925, the same year that Poul Holsøe took up office as the municipal architect. In the following years, they would together put their mark on public transport in the capital. This was in the form of signs, streetcar stops, buses and, as their main work, a streetcar. The municipality's own workshop manufactured most of the 118 motor cars and 83 trailers that began in service in 1930, and the last one in 1941.

There had been many technical advances since Engelhardt designed his streetcar in 1908–10. The new cars were the first of the new bogie type. This means that instead of two axles on each car, there were four. These were arranged in pairs in two bogies that could turn independently of each other just like on train cars. This construction made longer streetcars possible and gave a more comfortable ride.

The second advance was that the seats were upholstered and could be turned so the passengers could always face the direction of travel, or a family could make their own little compartment in the streetcar so they could sit and talk. In other words, the seats were adjustable in both the angle of the seat and the position of the backrest. In addition it was the first streetcar in which noise reduction had been addressed. This was done, for example by using cork to line the walls.

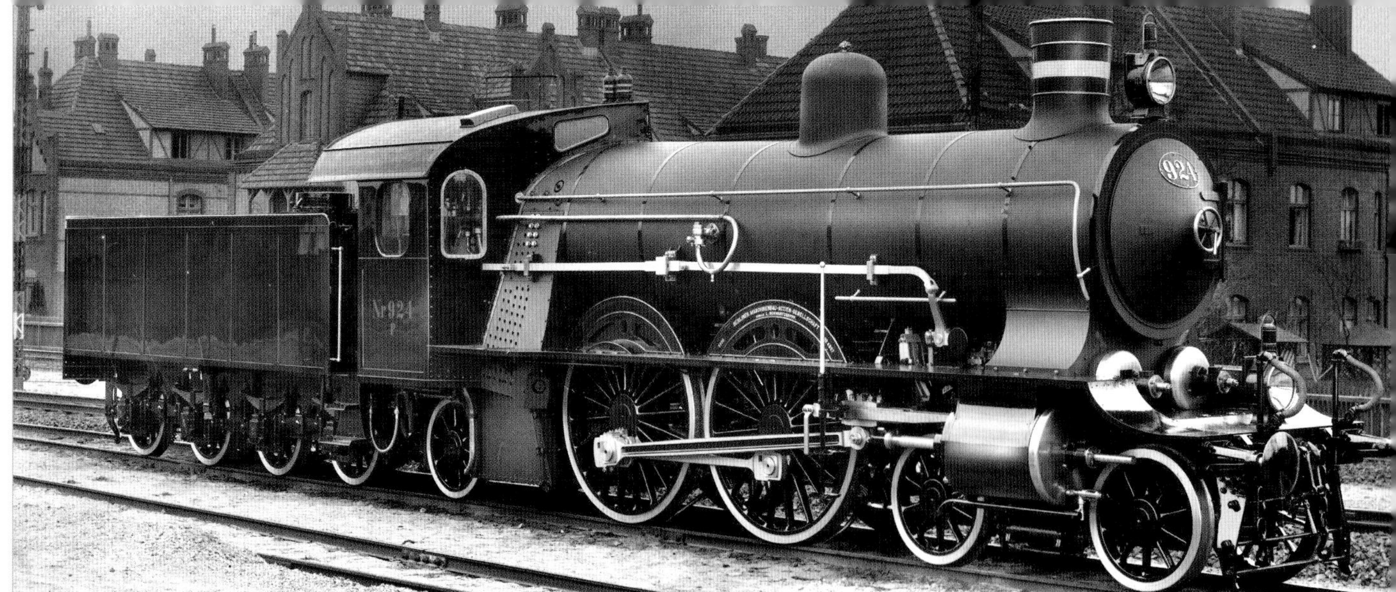

Ib Lunding was the architect responsible for the project, and as regards design he was inspired by nautical things and the functionalist style of the time; the one that was also called funkis. The nautical aspect was apparent in the streamlined window design whose rounded corners call to mind ships and ferries. The funkis aspect is most evident in the interior.

While Engelhardt set the handles into the back of the backrest, Lunding's solution was round, black, bakelite knobs with a little leather strap. The lamps and the design of the typeface also reflect the style of the time in a different way than did Engelhardt.

Although one could say that Lunding's streetcar in a very quality-conscious way continues the rational and common-sense line that Engelhardt started 20 years earlier, the design of the new streetcar is also an example of conforming to a style. Engelhardt did everything he could to eliminate the fashionable, especially the Victorian, from his design, which was very unsentimental, while Lunding sneaks in some elements that were typical of the time and were inspired by the Bauhaus style. Lunding is obviously more interested in designing something modern than Engelhardt was.

In an article in Nyt Tidsskrift for Kunstindustri (New Periodical for Art and Design) from April 1930, Poul Henningsen thought that Ib Lunding cultivated individuality and was influenced by German modernism. However, PH emphasised Engelhardt and his streetcar with the words: 'The bigger the personality that erases itself in an assignment, the greater the artistic result. He anticipated the development. He created a type at a time when one wasn't conscious of the fact that the typical was valuable. His originality made him independent of the prevailing fashion.' So in a way he thought that Engelhardt's streetcar from 1910 was more modern in its design that Lunding's from 1930.

THE DANISH TRAIN DESIGNERS

The history of the Danish railroad begins in earnest in 1847 with the opening of the first stretch from Copenhagen to Roskilde. This was also the start of Det Sjællandske Jernbaneselskab (The Railway Company of Zealand). In Denmark there have always been several companies in the railway business, and until the Danish State Railways (DSB) was established in 1885, there were two large state-owned companies; one on Zealand and a joint one for Jutland and Funen.

The first great constructor of trains was mechanical engineer Otto Busse, who was born in 1850. In 1882 he was chief engineer at the State Railways in Jutland and Funen. Today he is considered a legend in the development of early Danish trains. He was responsible for the construction and design of countless locomotives in the course of his career, first at the Jysk-Fynske Jernbaner (The Railways of Jutland and Funen), and later at DSB where he was appointed director of the machine department and member of the railway board in 1904. Furthermore he was responsible for the establishment and organisation of DSB's central workshops and played a role in the design of the new train ferries.

In Busse's time many locomotives were designed in Denmark. As mentioned, there were many companies on the market, and some developed their own material, as it was normal to customise locomotives to specific purposes and special sections of the line. Even after the partial centralisation at DSB, it was necessary to have a large range of different

◀ The then technical director of DSB was Otto Busse, who became the renowned constructor of steam locomotives in Denmark around the turn of the century. One of his first big projects was the relatively little A locomotive (right) of which 31 copies were manufactured in 1882–88. Later he headed the construction and design of the huge P locomotive (left). 33 of them were built from 1907 to 1910. When it was ready to roll, it weighed 120 tonnes.

locomotives depending on whether they were to be used for freight trains or express trains, for the hilly Jutlandic cross lines or the long, flat sections on Zealand.

In the period around 1900, Otto Busse was here, there and everywhere when the material needed improving. One of his first locomotives was litra A, of which 31 were built at several German factories. They were used by the Jysk-Fynske Jernbaner on their main lines. Litra A was manufactured from 1882–88, and five of them survived World War II, and the last one was retired in 1956. A lifespan of more than 70 years is pretty good going.

Busse's A locomotives were very modern when they were built, and they were possibly inspired by the well-known American locomotive that we know today from western movies. The locomotive's characteristic feature was the little bogie with the small wheels in front that gave the locomotive a more stable run on the tracks. Eventually the trains got longer, and the A locomotive wasn't powerful enough despite its weight of about 55 tonnes. New and more powerful locomotives relegated it to smaller passenger trains on the branch lines.

The big P locomotive

Otto Busse retired from DSB in 1910 at the early age of 60 and since then earned the reputation of not following the times. Among other things he thought all solutions should be familiar and well tested before they could be put into practice. The result was that DSB was perhaps a bit behind the times technologically until World War I in comparison to the leading foreign railways. But one of his last projects doesn't seem very old fashioned. This is the litra P locomotive that was a large and up-to-date machine built to pull express trains on DSB's main lines and on lines abroad.

The litra P was built in 1907–10, and meanwhile Busse was a busy boss who was also on the railway board, so in actual fact it was two of his employees, engineers H.G. Dorph and R. Olsen, who were responsible for a great deal of the design and construction. The 33 locomotives were built in Germany and each weighed almost 120 tonnes with a full tender. So they were huge machines that were very impressive in their day. For example, the large traction wheel on the litra P has a diameter of 1.98 metres, the largest ever on a Danish locomotive.

The locomotive had a maximum authorised speed of 110 km/h during normal service on the Danish tracks, but during the factory's test runs in Germany they reached 160 km/h. When the litra P machine was introduced, it attracted much attention in Denmark and acclaim abroad for being a beautifully designed and well-running express locomotive, but in 1963 the P locomotive was taken out of regular service. One model is still used to haul heritage trains and for royal funeral services, the last one being Queen Ingrid's in November 2000.

When Otto Busse retired, DSB changed the procedure for acquiring new locomotives. Instead of planning everything themselves, they listed a number of requirements for the new machine and let a foreign factory build a couple of them for DSB to test. Once the worst hiccups were dealt with, they had Danish factories build the number needed. Scandia in Randers or Frich's Factories in Aarhus could get the final order, whereas, for example, Triangel in Odense built some of the light motor cars for the local lines.

◂ *The IC3 train's interior was partly designed and colour schemed by Nanna Ditzel. It was meant to be a luxury train on the long distance routes in Denmark, and therefore the floors have carpets, the seats can be adjusted, and once there were plugs for earphones so you could listen to the radio.*

▸ *The IC3 train is made of aluminium, among other things, to make it light, and the diesel engines are decentred – four in each three-car train set. This gives good acceleration and high speed.*

But after Busse's time, DSB didn't undertake much independent design of trains, at least not for a good while.

Jens Nielsen

Almost 60 years would pass before Danish train design really got going again. Throughout the years, from about World War I and until prosperity became widespread, the large government institution muddled along as best as it could using its horse sense. When Otto Busse retired in 1910, the railway and the associated ferries almost had a monopoly on transportation over long distances. These were DSB's golden days, but in the late 1960s there was tough competition from other means of transport, especially cars and flights.

In 1970 something happened. This was the year DSB got a new director general, Poul Hjelt, and the year before Ole Andresen had been hired as the planning manager. Under their leadership design was put back on the agenda, and they were assisted by a book that was published about the same time called *Offentlig Design* (Public Design). It was edited by publisher Christian Ejlers, architect Niels Kryger and graphic designer Erik Ellegaard Frederiksen, and published by Christian Ejlers' publishing company. The book stimulated a debate about the public environment and led to a seminar in Vejle on this very subject. The newly appointed Poul Hjelt participated in the seminar, and in 1971, DSB hired the 34-year-old architect Jens Nielsen as their first chief designer.

Jens Nielsen attended the Royal Academy of Fine Arts from 1958–66 and specialised in industrial design. Besides being an excellent designer, he could also think in the long term and was good at communicating his visions. Although he initially was an industrial designer, he had a very broad view of design, and his total design concept for DSB attracted a lot of attention at home and abroad. He worked on the design of almost everything; from the new logo, the typeface and signs to the design of new trains, as well as buildings and furnishings (see page 480).

The design of trains was only part of what the newly appointed chief designer had to deal with, but it was most likely the aspect he found the most exciting. Since Otto Busse's day this area had been somewhat neglected. When the first high-speed trains were introduced in 1935 and the Little Belt Bridge was opened, DSB was hit by a breath of fresh air since it was now easier and quicker to get across the country, but the red high-speed trains were patterned on a German model.

In 1974, DSB introduced the system of the intercity trains, which departed every hour at set times. On that occasion, the material was slightly renovated and modernised as a visible manifestation of this new product. The concept put more passengers on the trains, but DSB still had rather outdated material. The large MZ locomotives still hauled a row of passenger cars whose new paint and newly upholstered seats couldn't quite hide the fact that the trains were worn. It was high time to get new trains. Several attempts were made in the design department before Jens Nielsen and his team got a good grip on the problem.

The IC3 train

Denmark is not a typical railway country. It's a country that even in the 1980s was divided in half by the Great Belt, and a ferry trip was always necessary when going from the capital to other major cities in the country.

JENS NIELSEN, 1937–92, Danish architect who graduated from the Royal Academy of Fine Arts, School of Architecture in 1966 with a dissertation on industrial design. In 1971 he was appointed chief designer for DSB, where Director General Poul Hjelt gave him an opportunity to work on every aspect of design from trains and ferries to stations and signs. His design concepts attracted attention, including at foreign railways and among design experts. He was an entrepreneur and took the initiative for many new design projects at DSB.

That meant the intercity trains spent a lot of time getting through this bottleneck. The train had to be split up and shunted on to the ferry before the locomotive could be disengaged and the ferry could sail. And on arrival the whole process was repeated in the reverse order. When a train going from Copenhagen towards Aalborg got to Fredericia, some of the cars had to be disconnected and sent west to Esbjerg or south to Padborg. All these manoeuvres took time, and lots of locomotives were needed to haul the small trains to their final destinations.

It wasn't very rational, and much time was wasted. Jens Nielsen's solution to these problems was to design a new train, the IC3. Each end of the train had its own engines and control panel, so the only thing needed to divide the train and go in separate directions from Fredericia was an extra locomotive driver. It was also easier and quicker to get off and on the ferry at the Great Belt. The new train was an intelligent answer to Denmark's unique geography.

In the summer of 1984 the concept was ready to be realised. Scandia in Randers constructed the new train. Every train set consists of three cars with bogies shared between the cars to save weight. That means that the smallest unit DSB could run was one train set that could be coupled to another or several if need be. Due to the length of the platforms, there can be a maximum of three train sets in one train.

Every train set has four truck engines, two at each end. That gives 1600 hp and a high speed and good acceleration. The weight of each train set is 90 tonnes, which is much less than what an MZ locomotive weighed alone.

The appearance of the IC3 train was at first the cause of some skepticism, since it didn't have the traditional sloping front. The criticism was that the air resistance must be very great since the train had a flat front. It's true that the IC3 train looks different, but the front isn't completely flat. The big rubber ring is soft and rounded in its form, but also most of the air resistance on a train set is along the sides, the roof and the bottom. So by making the roof and bottom smooth and the windows flush with the sides, a far better aerodynamics was achieved than if the designers had made a sloping front.

The inflatable rubber ring at the front also makes it possible to couple two train sets and walk from one set to another since the control panel and front windshield can be folded away. In practice, only the train personnel walk back and forth because passengers could risk being at the wrong end of the train during uncoupling at places such as Fredericia. The train's materials were chosen with an eye to achieving great strength and low weight, and that's why the sides of the train and many of the load-bearing parts are made of aluminium profiles, for example.

The IC3 train is a splendid example of total design that was thorough and headed by DSB's design department under the leadership of Jens Nielsen. Even the interior is custom made with adjustable seats that look like they're floating, so it's easy to clean under them. Furniture designer Nanna Ditzel was responsible for the colour scheme and textile design (see page 169). There is also a specially designed reader-friendly electronic typeface for the displays that keep passengers updated with relevant information (see page 522).

The new trains were put into service in 1989, albeit with some teething problems. The risk of being innovative and using new unfamiliar solutions is, of course, that some hiccups will occur. This also happened to DSB in this case, for example, the computers in each train set crashed when they were coupled to another train set. Which one was in control? It was just like a science-fiction film. The computers blacked out when they had to work together, since they weren't programmed to be subordinate to another one. But problems of this kind were quickly solved, and after the Great Belt Bridge had been opened, a trip from the capital to Odense takes only 75 minutes, and Aarhus can be reached in less than three hours. Much has happened since one had to take two ferries to get from the mainland to the capital. DSB and the IC3 train were awarded the ID prize from the Danish Design Centre in 1991, but unfortunately Jens Nielsen didn't get to rest on his laurels for very long because the following year, in 1992, he died at the age of 55.

AEROPLANES

Ellehammer planes

The inventor Jacob Christian Ellehammer had lots of irons in the fire. He was the type that couldn't stop inventing things, and in total he patented 400 of his many inventions. Many of them could be relegated to curiosities such as a cigarette machine, the boats that are powered by compressed air for the lake in the Tivoli Gardens, and a beer barrel that also functions as a dispenser, so after inserting 25 ører you get a glass of beer. His more serious inventions count – including a phonograph cylinder, a movie projector and a wind motor that powered a pump. A number of his inventions can be seen now at the Danish Technical Museum in Helsingør.

Most Danes remember him for his planes. On September 12, 1906 he was the first European to rise above the Earth's surface in a motorised machine that was heavier than air. This took place on the island of Lindholm, a small, normally uninhabited island off the north coast of Lolland where he could work undisturbed by onlookers. However, the flight was not acknowledged internationally since there weren't enough witnesses, and it was a tethered flight. The 42 metres of flight, about half a metre off the ground, took place on a cement strip, and the plane was tethered to a pole. He was thus helped by centrifugal force – in other words it wasn't free flying.

Many experiments and wrecked models went before this, and the flight in 1906 was followed by more attempts, which in January 1908 led to a 170-metre flight at 2–3 metres height on a plain north of Copenhagen. In 1908 he won a flying contest in Kiel and 5000 German marks since his machine was the only one that left the ground. He was originally a watchmaker, and now he became one of the pioneers of flight. In 1912 he was the first person in the world to get a manned helicopter into the air. After that he gave up flying and worked on other things, and it was during this time that he worked on his Elleham motorbike (see page 398).

When Ellehammer was a young boy he built kites and flew them, and this might be where his interest in flight comes from. If you look at his planes, there is also something unmistakably kite-like about their construction, especially the wings. As an introduction to his work with planes he studied birds and particularly the relationship between their weight and their wingspan. If you compare Ellehammer's planes to those of his contemporaries, it's clear that he was more inspired by nature's flying

creatures than they were. Many of the other planes were more inspired by box kites and had a more square and geometrical appearance.

If we look at how the aeroplane developed in the years after the first flights, you could think that the geometrical design had won. The planes used during World War I and for a long time afterwards had a very boxy fuselage and perpendicular wings on the body of the plane. But if you look further into the future, for example to the Concorde and jet fighters, the angular appearance is no longer prevalent. And in today's ultra light planes, hang gliders, paragliders etc. the kite and bird-like appearance is paramount. Ellehammer's plane design was perhaps more ahead of its time than we thought, even though he didn't get the greatest results from his efforts.

Ellehammer's plane constructions also have similarities to other designs and technical breakthroughs of the time. Compare Ellehammer's plane with the Pedersen bike on page 390. These lattice constructions in thin steel tubes are very similar. And it's no coincidence that J.C. Ellehammer worked on aeroplanes and motorbikes at the same time. First he developed a one-cylinder engine for his motorbike, and based on that he built the world's first radial engine for his plane. At first it had three cylinders, and later there was a 12-cylinder model with a specially developed carburettor for his last plane experiments. The design of the radial motor was undoubtedly Ellehammer's greatest contribution to the continued development of aeroplanes.

Scandinavian Aero Industry – Kramme & Zeuthen

In Denmark building aeroplanes has never been a big business, unlike in the US and many European countries. For many big countries it's been important to have a national aeroplane industry that was independent of other countries. There were military, technological and industrial-political reasons for this. Having one's own aeroplane factory also secured a lot of jobs. Sweden has for many years had its own production of fighter planes because of Saab, but this is not the case in Denmark.

However, some planes were produced in Denmark over the years. At the naval dockyard, of all places, 40–50 planes were built from 1914 to 1940, and they were primarily seaplanes for military use. The army's flying troops had a workshop on Kløvermarken on Amager, where about 75 planes were built for what later became the Danish Air Force.

Despite many attempts by enthusiastic Danes, there is really only one private company that distinguished itself in Danish aeroplane history. This was Scandinavian Aero Industry (SAI) or better known by the public as Kramme & Zeuthen (KZ). The company started in 1935 as a haphazard partnership between Viggo Kramme, an aircraft mechanic who had left the Naval Air Service and established a workshop to repair and maintain private aircraft at Kastrup Airport, and the young, recently graduated aeroplane enthusiast K.G. Zeuthen. Over a period of about 20 years Kramme & Zeuthen built almost 200 planes, many of which were sports or private planes.

Kramme & Zeuthen's planes were good, solid machines, but one cannot claim that they were groundbreaking in any way when you compare them to contemporary foreign planes. But two KZ planes should be pointed out for their elegant design. The first plane made by the two enthusiasts is known as KZ 1. It's an exquisitely built little one-engine plane with an open cockpit and a rather small 38 hp motor.

▸ *Here Jacob Ellehammer makes his first hop in his many attempts to build an aeroplane. The plane was half a metre off the ground and flew 42 metres. It wasn't acknowledged as a proper flight because the plane was tethered to a pole, and thus Ellehammer took advantage of the centrifugal force in gaining speed.*

◂ *Kramme & Zeuthen's first real plane, KZ 1, of which there were only one or two. They don't exist anymore. This is a copy in flight.*

▾ *A copy of Ellehammer's famous flying machine is at the Danish Technical Museum in Helsingør.*

The plane's proportions are very good – the fuselage, the wings and the tail merge very beautifully, and the integrated appearance is emphasised by the aeroplane's matt, silver finish. Unfortunately, only one original KZ 1 was built, plus many years later a copy, which is now at the Danish Collection of Vintage Aircraft at Stauning Airport in west Jutland.

However, two KZ 4's were built and this is also a very beautiful plane. It's a two-engine ambulance plane that oddly enough was designed and built during World War II and delivered to the ambulance service Zonen. In its white ambulance paint the two-engine plane seems very well proportioned, just like KZ 1, KZ 4 had to be able to land and take off on very short strips on the Danish islands, and that's why it has a relatively large tail plane and large wings. The integration of the wheels in the engine's casing increases the feeling of stability and quality.

◂ *Aircraft mechanic Kramme in his best suit and tie ready to be photographed next to one of his planes.*

▾ *KZ 4 was specially designed as an ambulance plane for the ambulance service Zonen in 1944. One was made available during World War II for the Swedish Count Folke Bernadotte's flights to Berlin to negotiate the release of Danish and Norwegian Jews from concentration camps. After the war, another model of this beautiful plane was built for Zonen – it is now part of the Danish Collection of Vintage Aircraft at Stauning Airport in west Jutland.*

Public design

When you consider the fact that the government dispenses over half of the Danish economy, it's interesting to see what the citizens get for their taxes, and often there isn't much attention paid to design in the government's decision-making. Most of these billions of kroner aren't spent on commodities, but on wages, pensions and subsidies for this and that. Yet it isn't small change that is spent on forming the public environment, designing urban spaces, putting up road signs and buying equipment for the health sector. But there was a time when the government played a much smaller role in Denmark. Once in a while you can still hear the words 'night watchman state' to refer to the minimal public sector of the past, which mostly dealt with upholding law and order and protecting the country's borders.

Exactly what articles or works were used first publicly is hard to say. In prehistoric times a clear division between the private and the communal wasn't possible in the same way it is today. Making a burial mound had to be a joint effort of a local society, but at the same time it was the burial site of a single person or family. Some of the earliest public design has been a way of staging communality, and the burial mound is just one example of this. The circle of seats that was often granite boulders in the thingstead is another interesting example. Not only public negotiations took place here in a type of budding democracy, but also court cases and disputes were settled. The design of sitting in a circle is a strong symbol of equality and is suitable for the purpose.

In the Middle Ages, very little of the government and city's money was spent on improving the public utilities in cities. They had a public well in the square, a watchman who patrolled at night and maybe a scaffold. But this doesn't mean that the citizens didn't use the public space. On the contrary, the streets were used as a dump and an open sewer for long periods of time. Not until the 1800s was it generally accepted that there were several shared challenges, and for the citizens, the fairest and most effective way of doing something about it was communally. The local government was of course dependent on having sufficient funds to do something about the conditions that caused epidemics in the towns, and this societal wealth did not arise until recent times.

THE CITY FLOOR

Throughout the ages, one of the large tasks in the public space has been to build roads, streets and squares. While the Romans had already created an advanced system of roads and paved their way to the farthest reaches of their empire, the road system in Europe fell into disrepair in the Middle Ages. In Denmark the roads weren't too good either, and as mentioned, the city streets were open sewers. In Copenhagen this miserable situation led to a decree in 1764 that prescribed cobbling the streets 'from one end to another when necessary'. Based on foreign design, the streets were given sidewalks and gutters on both sides, however, sewers and drainage weren't installed, so in rainy weather the gutters overflowed.

The paving stones weren't as nice to walk on as the ones we use today since they mainly used roughly hewn fieldstone (rounded cobblestones). Yet in some places the sidewalks were paved with flat, rectangular granite slabs that are still found in old sidewalks and squares in many places. The cost of this work was imposed on the street's homeowners as a group. Later they used more carefully hewn stones that we know today as the biggish, square cobblestones with flat sides, and even later, in the late

GRÅBRØDRE TORV (the Grey Friars' square) in the heart of Copenhagen wouldn't be the same place if it was asphalted instead of being paved with granite stones. Here the classic cobblestones are combined with rectangular granite slabs. Road surfaces are an often overlooked aspect of the city environment where old surfaces have been replaced with new ones. But now it seems that the authorities as well as homeowners are more attentive to the design qualities of good surfaces.

1800s, the cities also began to use the small cobblestones called setts in areas where there wasn't too much heavy traffic.

Later both asphalt and cement tiles were seen in the streetscape. Asphalt is a genuine product of the 20th century. It is very suitable for the automobile era since it's cheap, practical and comfortable to drive on as well as being easy to repair. But old asphalt full of potholes is not a vision of beauty, especially not in a town where the cracked and patched asphalt indicates that the town has cut down on maintenance.

From an aesthetic point of view, the worst case is when asphalt is used to patch other road surfaces. Many municipalities used special flagstones with pebbles embedded on the surface in their pedestrian streets. The material character of these flagstones has a certain charm, but unfortunately they can't bear the weight of the heavy trucks that are allowed to drive on these streets. The flagstones crack. And a cobblestone street or one paved with flagstones looks terrible with dabs of asphalt here and there. The very widespread cement flagstones, just like asphalt, are a relatively new phenomenon. They are often used on sidewalks and are well suited for that purpose. But while stone surfaces, such as granite, get more beautiful with wear, the same can't be said of new industrial materials like cement and asphalt that don't stand the test of time with as much grace.

Author and professor at the Royal Academy of Fine Arts, School of Architecture Steen Eiler Rasmussen wrote about the problem many years ago in his book *Experiencing Architecture*:

'In Denmark today sidewalks are often paved with several rows of concrete slabs separated by rows of granite cobblestones. It is undoubtedly practical, when necessary to lift the slab of concrete, to be able to rest the crowbar against hard granite, which is less likely to crumble. But the combination gives a singularly inharmonious surface. Granite and concrete do not mix well; you can almost feel how unpleasant it is right through the soles of your shoes – the two materials are of such different grades of smoothness. And when, as sometimes happens, this pavement is flanked by broad strips of asphalt or gravel and edged with kerbstone, the modern Danish sidewalk becomes a veritable sample collection of paving materials, not to be compared with the pavements of more civilised eras, which are pleasing to the eye and comfortable under foot. The Londoner calls his sidewalk the "pavement", and a more cultivated example of paving can hardly be found.'

Surface variations

In recent years it's become common to use the horizontal surfaces of the city to create new experiences. The surface on, for example, Gammeltorv/Nytorv in Copenhagen has been used to indicate the history of the place. This was done by showing the outline of the previous city hall with granite slabs and small changes in the level of the cobblestone surface of the square. And the city's old scaffold is also outlined in another type of stone. The rest of the square is also paved with cobblestone, and especially during the summer it's a colourful place, not least around the Caritas Fountain on Nytorv where the of bike messengers gather during their breaks.

Nytorv/Gammeltorv is intersected by Strøget, which was made into a pedestrian street in 1962. At the time it was a unique initiative since Strøget became one of the first and largest of this type of pedestrian streets in Northern Europe. At the time it was met with great resistance, especially by business owners who feared they would lose their business. Some experts felt that Copenhagen lay too far north for it to be as successful as the southern European squares that teemed with life. Nevertheless the plans were realised. In the beginning, the municipality did nothing about the surface – the road and sidewalks were still there. But since then the street has been paved with cement flags of the type that has a pebble finish.

In 1996 the business owners around Amagertorv and Copenhagen Municipality took the initiative of enhancing the square. Had they followed a traditional line, they would perhaps have suggested putting up a work of art or designing other forms of spectacular street fixtures. Instead they followed another idea, namely to clean up Amagertorv and make the large, horizontal surface a work of art in itself. Artist Bjørn Nørgaard (b. 1947) designed a beautiful and delicately patterned surface on the square. Using tightly packed small and large stone flags, Amagertorv has created a surface whose finish resembles a carpet. One can only hope that it will be a very long time before some public works has to dig up the area to get to some installations.

But in the city streets other things take place that also involve a form of design. In the course of time, lots of cables and pipes have been laid out underground, and sometimes these have to be accessed. Manhole covers and cast-iron grates in various sizes and shapes are the traditional and often obvious solution to this problem. For more than a hundred years, designing the manhole covers has been a job for city architects and other

◀ *If you look down when you're in the city, you'll see many variations in the design of cast-iron manhole covers.*

▼ *On Amagertorv in Copenhagen the stone surface is a work of art by artist Bjørn Nørgaard, and it was financed by the local business owners. The patterned surface is delicate, almost like an oriental rug, and it gives the square a particularly exclusive identity.*

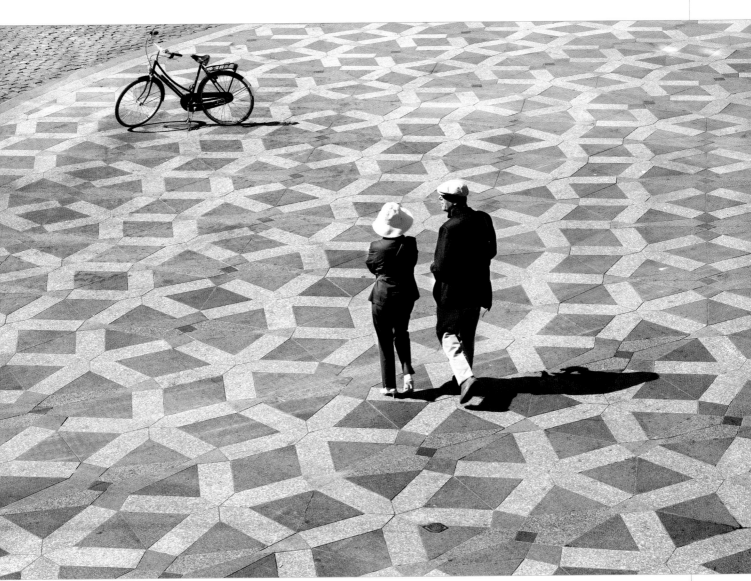

TRAFFIC ALSO MAKES noise, which is an increasing problem that Danes try to design their way out of in different ways. Various solutions with noise barriers have been developed in recent decades to create a barrier between the heavily trafficked roads and residential areas. Some of these barriers are advanced systems of industrially manufactured components of glass, metal or combinations of stone, brick or cement. A little company called Pilebyg (Willow-build) had a different solution for a noise barrier. On a farm outside Hjørring in northern Jutland they build windbreaks out of willow branches, and shortly after they are put up, the branches start to sprout and become a living fence.

Two parallel rows of these prefabricated fences are put up just close enough for a layer of rock wool to be laid in between. This system, which is called the Green Element, gives an effective noise reduction. At least 98 % of the willow branches take root and begin to sprout, and after just a year, the two-metre-high fence has grown to almost four metres. So maintaining this fence is just a matter of pruning. The fence can last at least 25 years, and all the materials in the product can even be reused or recycled.

▲ *Guidelines for the visually impaired can become a discreet part of the public environment. This is Pictoform from the company GH form and designed by Knud Holscher Industrial Design.*

artistic consultants for the municipalities and the companies that needed and installed the covers on public streets. This has resulted in a huge variety of different sizes, geometries and patterns that give large and small towns character. The motifs on these manhole covers vary from patterns, often with classical symbols like six-pointed stars and old Greek meander patterns, to pictures of animals or company logos cast in the metal.

Palpable stripes

When we're talking about the design of surfaces in a city, we are not thinking only of their visual impression. Acoustics, too, are influenced by the choice of materials in the urban space, including the surfaces of streets and squares. But it's especially our feet that feel the surfaces of the city. There's a great difference between walking on cobblestones, asphalt, gravel, grass or wood, and this is something that one can take advantage of. In the mid-1990s Knud Holscher Industrial Design developed a guiding system for the blind. This was for the company GH form in Borup, and the system is based on little cast-iron studs, some oblong and some round, set into the city streets. These guidelines are more easily interpreted by a cane than by our feet. The studs are available in either special cast-iron flagstones on which the studs are embedded or as individual studs that can be mounted on existing surfaces with nails, screws or glue. The narrow cast-iron flagstones with studs have the right dimensions to replace the little setts between the flagstones on sidewalks and squares.

Also car tires can sense surfaces as the Danish Road Directorate realised and made use of with the design of rumble strips that have since the early 1990s been frequently used on the Danish road systems, not least on highways and main roads. For most drivers the principle is familiar since you can both feel and hear when you cross one of these strips that are laid like a kind of relief on the surface. Originally they were merely an attempt to develop road strips that were more visible when the roads were wet, and the sun shone brightly. But an added bonus was that the texture of the strips can be felt in the car. This is like an alarm going off when the driver is inattentive or maybe even nodding off. The rumble strips are far more effective than a visible road marking alone. The strips are laid on the road like a thick coat of paint, and the idea won the Danish Design Centre's ID prize in 1994.

CITY LIGHTS

In the past, the city was pitch black at night. Neither public lighting nor the light from shop windows that we are used to today existed in the Middle Ages. At most there was a faint glow from the candles and oil lamps in private homes. If you were going out in the evening, you had to either make do with moonlight and starlight or you had to carry your own lantern. People of rank might have a servant to accompany them and hold the lantern, or if they were in a horse carriage, it might have lamps, but the common man had to provide these things himself. And when you consider how badly the roads were paved back then, it's no wonder that many people probably stayed indoors after dark.

In 1680 Copenhagen got its first streetlamps, and they were train-oil lamps. This was at the initiative of copper engraver Johan Huusmann at the University of Copenhagen. He had suggested to the municipal authorities of Copenhagen that streetlamps should be put up, and this was tested first in Købmagergade and on Højbro Plads (a street and a square). It was an instant success, and the following year Christian V issued a decree for

▸ *Chief architect in Copenhagen Municipality, Ludvig Clausen (1851–1904) designed lots of city fixtures for the capital around the year 1900. Among them is the Clausen lamp of which about 10,000 copies were manufactured. It was used with various lampposts such as Vilhelm Dahlerup's (1836–1907).*

the introduction and maintenance of streetlamps in the capital. The lamps were made of copper, and since glass was in short supply, they used horn. The light from these train-oil lamps wasn't exactly bright, but it was better than letting the citizens stumble around in the dark.

Under Struensee's rule in 1791 the horn was replaced with glass, and even later the capital switched to using gas in the streetlamps, as the rest of Europe had done. This happened in 1857, more than 40 years after gaslights were introduced in London. At this time there were over 1800 train-oil lamps in use in Copenhagen, and they were substituted by 2200 gaslights. Along with the industrialisation of the 1800s it became more common to make streetlamps out of cast iron, which is more resistant to rust and corrosion than the old type that was made of iron plate by plumbers. These are the cast-iron fixtures that can still be found here and there in Danish cities and that now have electrical wiring and bulbs instead of gas. In the late 1800s and early 1900s, many architects designed streetlamps. One of the best known examples is architect Vilhelm Dahlerup's model of which eight still exist on Dronning Louise's Bridge that connects Nørrebro to downtown Copenhagen.

◂ *The rumble strips are more than a traditional visual road marking. The ribbed pattern makes a humming noise and gives vibrations in the car when it's crossed. An effective way of getting drivers to pay attention and perhaps even to wake up.*

HERRENS·ORD·BLIVER

▾ *The Copenhagen lamp is a true work of industrial design. City architect at Copenhagen Municipality Eivind Lorenzen designed it in the late 1970s. It's brown like the street dust that will accumulate on it anyway, it doesn't emit a blinding light and it has all the qualities one could ask for from a public streetlamp. It's not exactly beautiful, yet very well thought out in its functionality.*

The Copenhagen lamp

The train-oil lamps were substituted with gas lamps, which in turn were replaced by incandescent lamps in the 1890s, and afterwards came the various energy-saving sources of light such as the fluorescent tubes. For many years it was all about getting the most light for your money, and it didn't matter much where the light shone. When fluorescent lighting became widespread in the cities, on the suburban ring roads and on the main roads, they quickly started hanging the fixtures high up so the individual source of light could illuminate as much of the road as possible. On the wide roads outside urban areas wooden telephone poles were used first and then often tall steel masts, while in the cities the lamps were suspended by wires between the façades and directly over the roads. Unfortunately, the rather primitive industrial light fixtures for the fluorescent tubes gave off a garish and blinding light. Even from a distance one could see the whole dazzling light source.

Another type of fixture was also very common, and this was a round milky glass shade that used an ordinary type of bulb. It was more pleasant to look at and the light it emitted wasn't poor, but on the one hand it was made of glass that could easily break, and on the other hand, the light could be blinding.

In Copenhagen Municipality, city architect Eivind Lorenzen (1918–94) started developing a new type of fixture in the late 1970s. Instead of the flat, boxy shade for the long fluorescent tube, he designed a bowl-shaped hemisphere that originally housed a mercury-vapour lamp. This light source is also energy saving, but its rendition of colours, like in the fluorescent tube, isn't fantastic; however, the form of the fixture gives a better light

THE PRIVATE LIGHT. Besides the lighting that the public sector provides in urban and rural areas after dark, there is the light that comes from private sources, and it is increasingly important in certain neighbourhoods in our cities. This is the light that comes from the shop windows, but also surplus light from offices and private homes. And then there's the most interesting light that comes from neon advertising signs that in some places almost turns night into day – just think of Strøget in Copenhagen.

From the point of view of design, neon signs are a particularly interesting subject, not to mention the partly animated neon signs. For example, the chocolate frogs from Galle & Jessen are still jumping around on the night sky by Vibenshus Runddel on Østerbro in Copenhagen. One of the most beloved of these neon signs is the so-called Irma hen near Dronning Louise's Bridge in Copenhagen. This narrative ad began its life as early as 1936 and with only a few breaks (neon signs were prohibited during the occupation and during the energy crisis in the mid-1970s) it has laid seven eggs a minute ever since. In the course of time the sign has been renovated and slightly changed; it got bigger eggs in 1950 and coloured eggs in 1953. When Irma was incorporated in FDB in the 1980s, the hen was in danger of being slaughtered, but so far it has survived. Today it is a Copenhagen icon whose commercial value certainly can't be overrated. A piece of excellent commercial urban design that has become a national heritage.

◂ *The light installation Stjernedrys (Stardust) on Torvegade in Esbjerg. This is a different way of illuminating a street, although this type of lighting can't do the job on its own, but must be supplemented by other light sources. The project was designed by architects Helene Plot and Kirsten Frederiksen from Esbjerg Municipality and lighting architect Gunver Hansen as external consultant.*

on the road. Furthermore, the light doesn't dazzle you unless you stand directly below it and look up, and not many people do that after all.

Today it also comes with an energy-saving bulb. With regard to the colour scheme, Eivind Lorenzen followed the same principle as Knud V. Engelhardt did when choosing the colour of the streetcar bogies. He chose a matt, brown colour that for one thing didn't need cleaning to look clean, and for another, merged reasonably well with the many façades in Copenhagen. The round form also suits most urban environments, not least the old neighbourhoods in Copenhagen.

The Albertslund lamp

In 1960, Danish towns started expanding intensely. Finally the country had put the meagre years after the war behind it, and construction escalated, especially in the suburbs. Among other places, the Copenhagen satellite towns built a lot of public housing, and sometimes it was quite visionary. The large building estate called Albertslund Syd (South) was designed by Fællestegnestuen (the Common Architectural office) headed by architect Viggo Møller-Jensen among others. The estate was finished in 1963 and had 486 identical atrium houses surrounded by streets and walkways. The young designer Jens Møller-Jensen (b. 1938) designed a lamp for this

▸ *At first the Albertslund lamp was pieced together of standard elements, which made the price one third of what it would have cost to manufacture specially designed components. For designer Jens Møller-Jensen, who had a background as a metal worker, it was important to develop a good and inexpensive lamp for the public housing estate that his father, architect Viggo Møller-Jensen, was designing. At first the lamp was made in true blacksmith fashion of enamelled or galvanised iron, but later models have been made of fibreglass and plastic.*

area that became known as the Albertslund lamp. The fixture later became a very tenacious series of about ten different outdoor and indoor lamps that are manufactured by Louis Poulsen. The variations in the product line range from outdoor post top lamps to wall lamps, ceiling-mounted models and indoor pendants. In 2000 the Albertslund lamp was awarded the Danish Design Centre's Classic prize, which is given to well-designed products that have been in production at least 25 years.

Jens Møller-Jensen was an instrument maker before he was the first graduate in industrial design from the Royal Academy of Fine Arts in 1965, two years after he designed the Albertslund lamp. The lamp is very simple, and the prototype was mainly made of standard elements: a jam jar, board bolts, antenna tubes and a round street sign for a shade. Only the base had to be specially made and this was cast in iron. This lamp may not have the same sophisticated way of treating light as the PH lamp, but there is nonetheless some similarity between them. It is said that Poul Henningsen was so fond of young Møller-Jensen's lamp that the old master had one put up in his garden. In actual fact, the Albertslund lamp is a further development of PH's Slotsholm lamp from 1920 that was a very early predecessor of the later PH lamps. Today the Albertslund lamp is one of Louis Poulsen's largest commercial successes besides the PH lamp.

Stardust

Public lighting can also take on other forms than the traditional fixtures hung from lampposts or wires. In Esbjerg there is a couple hundred metres of street from Torvet (the square) to the performing arts centre-cum-art museum on Havnegade. Here you can see the interesting lighting of the public space called 'Stardust'. The cobblestone street isn't heavily trafficked, and between the cobblestones are little luminous fixtures that sit flush with the stones, hence the name. The special thing about this installation is that all the small, luminous dots on the road surface are a copy of the night sky over Esbjerg as it was at midnight on January 1, 2000, that is, the turn of the millennium. So you can find parts of the Milky Way and constellations like the Great Dog, Cassiopeia, Ursa Minor etc.

The luminous dots are made with fibre optics. In several places along the stretch of road, light generators have been installed under the ground, 14 in all, and all the metal fixtures are wired from them. Inside each fixture is a lens that sends the light upward. Another subtlety of the project are the coloured filters in the light generators that constantly change the colour of the light from blue to green, yellow, white and red. In all there are 288 points of light. These lanterns aren't the only street lighting, but are supplemented by more traditional fixtures. Project Stardust can interest the passer-by even if he doesn't know about the constellations.

CITY FURNITURE

In the classical era of the city everything was sturdily made. The city fixtures could last for many decades, sometimes even for centuries. The choice of material is one of the secrets of these long-lasting successes. What couldn't be made of stone was often made of cast iron, which is almost indestructible. This is due to the large amount of carbon that is added to the metal alloy which prevents the iron from rusting as easily as steel. A drawback is that the iron loses some of its elasticity, which is why it has to be cast in sturdy dimensions to make it durable. Grates, lampposts, fire hydrants and hand rails were often made of oil-painted cast iron.

▸ *The old Copenhagen bench (below) and Nanna Ditzel's bench called City (right) are now manufactured by GH form in Borup. Cast iron is a suitable material for city furniture since it can withstand wind and weather and the rough treatment that things in the public space are subjected to.*

One example of a solid piece of city equipment in cast iron is the more than 100-year-old Copenhagen bench. The Copenhagen bench is from the 1880s, and the designer's identity is a bit hazy. Some say the artist Thorvald Bindesbøll had a hand in it somehow, and others say the design originates from a Norwegian factory. But the fact of the matter is that there are many variants of the archetypical bench with sides of dark green-painted cast iron and a seat and back of wooden planks that are still painted green today, but in a slightly lighter tone. These benches, and especially the ends, are designed in the Classicist style of the time with a sweeping principal form and details inspired by nature. Casting these pieces in iron makes it possible to add decorative elements to the form, including flower motifs and the town arms, which can be seen on some of the models. In the early 1970s the Copenhagen bench was slightly redesigned by the Office of the City Architect, but the bench still has a very classic expression.

Yet cast iron can also have a more up-to-date appearance. A public cast-iron bench with a modern expression is manufactured by the same company, namely GH form. The new design from the mid-1990s was created by Nanna Ditzel and is very much inspired by her Trinidad chair (see page 269), which she designed a short time before this bench. The load-bearing parts, the ends and the top of the back rest and front of the seat are made of cast iron, while the seat and back are in different hardwoods. The iron parts of the bench are painted a glossy dark grey colour.

The new redesigned mailboxes were introduced in 1986 and onwards. Some functional improvements were included. The new design in aluminium made it easier to block the letterbox, for example on New Year's Eve. As well, the box is easier for the mailman to empty, and finally it can be repaired on the spot since it's built of replaceable components.

The private bus stop

In the Social Democratic welfare state, the notion has always existed that there should be a clear distinction between what the public sector should do, and what private market forces could attend to. That's why it was very distressing when many cities finally decided to let a private company take over the bus stops of city buses and the accompanying signs, bus shelters, seats and wastebaskets. In return for the French company with the difficult name of AFA JCDecaux financing the development and production of this city fixture as well as operating, maintenance and cleaning, they were allowed to sell the advertising space on one end of the bus shelter. The other side was to be used for public information, such as a map of the city or other forms of public service.

The various municipalities in the country with the capital leading the way had other requirements as part of entering the agreement. The new city fixtures should be specially designed for each individual city and painted in their municipality's colours. In Copenhagen this was relegated to Knud Holscher Industrial Design after competition on designing bus stops in 1995. And the outcome was a very satisfactory system, which, of course, was spray painted in the municipality's official dark blue colour. The system of private financing seems to work so well that it has put to rest the fears of commercialisation. The bus stops used to be in a terrible state and were a heavy strain on the municipality's budget, and now they are clean and proper for the bus passengers.

Holscher's design was based on the model that AFA JCDecaux had used in a number of other big European cities. It's a modular system that makes it possible to vary the size and equipment according to how much room there is on the sidewalk and how popular the bus route is. The bus stop sign usually stands alone like a totem pole with the route sign and schedule. The shelter consists of two pillars and a roof of enamelled metal and tempered glass sides and back. The roof has small hidden gutters, and inside there's a bench that isn't big enough to lie down and sleep on. Finally there's a wastebasket integrated into the system. AFA JCDecaux' service vans come by regularly to clean and change the advertising posters and do minor repairs.

The Danish mailbox

The tradition of letting other 'services' than the municipality's put a stamp on the street scene is much older than the new bus stop financed by advertisements. The postal service is a half-public/half-privatised company – in the beginning it was a government service, but in recent years it's been increasingly liberalised from government ownership. Nonetheless the red mailboxes are some of the most officially Danish articles one can imagine, a kind of national property. However, the mailbox as a concept isn't so very old. Not until the system of stamps was introduced in 1851 were all post offices ordered to put up mailboxes on the wall or door of the building, and in 1860 the red colour was chosen as the standard. Shortly after, the mailboxes began to resemble the ones we have in Denmark today with a curved top, so the rainwater can run off, and the letterbox has a large opening and there's a list of pickup times.

But the old mailboxes were impractical in at least one way: they couldn't be emptied by using the bottom hatch as is done today. That meant that the mailman had to stick his hand in and pull out the letters with the risk of missing some or getting them wet in rainy weather. So emptying from

MANY PRIVATE COMPANIES contribute to the furnishing of the public space, not least businesses such as petroleum companies with their many petrol stations. One of the more imaginative designs that is characteristic of the recent period could be seen at the Uno-X stations around 1980. It was a specifically Danish design for a city fixture that is normally a standardised international product. Artist Paul Gadegaard (1920–96) and silversmith Allan Scharff (b. 1945) were included in the design process that came about because of the need for new electronics in the pumps as well as to make them easier to use. The swivelling arm at the top of the cylinder made pumping easier from both sides of the pump. And now the customers had the electronic display on the arm itself. The blue and black colours were chosen by a process of elimination, since yellow means danger and red means fire. The green colour was used for the other parts of the petrol station, such as the pillar that supported the roof. These pumps were a strong visual signal.

the bottom had to be introduced, and after having evaluated several solutions in 1870, among others from the postal assistant Louis Pio, who later became the first Socialist leader in Denmark, the new model was introduced in 1876. The model was almost identical to the one we have today. Yet much has been changed since then, especially after an extensive redesign in the mid-1980s. This modernisation was done by the Danish Mail Service with S.H. Nissen at the helm.

The old mailbox was made out a large piece of iron plate that was raised into the shape. This was an expensive way of doing it, and it was difficult to repair without having to replace the whole box. The new construction simplified both the production and the appearance. In the production process, the mailbox was now built of individual parts that could easily be replaced so the mailboxes could often be repaired on site and were easy to empty for the mailman. The new components were made of aluminium, so the box couldn't rust anymore. Aesthetically there has also been a simplification in that some of the protruding edges were removed, and the words and typeface were simplified and modernised, for example the word 'Mail letter box' was changed to 'mailbox'. But the colour was maintained and the redesign was so mild that only the keenest customers noticed that the box had changed. Sometimes a new design can be so discreet and well executed that no one notices that it's new.

▸ *The erection and maintenance of bus shelters in a number of Danish cities are financed by advertisements. The concept was developed by the French company AFA JCDecaux, but the design is by the Danish architect Knud Holscher and his architectural practice.*

▾ *The Question Mark (below) is the nickname that professionals and the public quickly gave the new telephone stands. Architect Klavs Helweg-Larsen (b. 1939) won first prize in a large design competition to find a replacement for the old telephone booth (upper right) that the Bomber from Gladsaxe had made unsafe. After handicap organisations protested, the Utzon model (lower right) was adopted. Perhaps a bit more boring, but at least the phone could be reached by everyone.*

The telephone booth

The postal service may be half or completely owned by the state, but the telephone companies were privatised, although until recently they were protected by a concession agreement with the government that gave them a monopoly on telephony in their geographical area. One of the world's first telephone companies was the Copenhagen company KTAS that began operating in 1881. But in 1879 there were already so-called 'conversation stations' established in the capital by Kjøbenhavns By- og Hustelegraf (Copenhagen City and House Telegraph). From these stations one could phone in messages that were either sent as telegrams or delivered by messenger. In 1896, the telephone kiosk appeared; a combination of public telephone and kiosk. An independent company, Kjøbenhavns Telefonautomater (Copenhagen's Telephone Automatons), started installing pay phones in apartment houses in 1898.

The first free-standing telephone booths that could take coins were introduced in the early 1930s. The first model was designed in 1931 by an architect at KTAS, Jens Ingwersen (1871–1956), and the first ten were put up in Copenhagen's streets and ten more in Gentofte Municipality in 1934. According to the requirements of Copenhagen Municipality, this telephone booth had the same measurements as the newspaper kiosks, and even its matt glass windows had to be the same size as the newspaper flyers of that time. Otherwise it was painted green and had a door that kept the traffic noise and driving rain out. The approximately 600 copies of this classic, designed booth lived a stable life until 1978, when the so-called 'Bomber from Gladsaxe' began to vandalise and place his bombs in them. Subsequently the doors were taken off the old booths, and later KTAS arranged a design competition for a new public telephone.

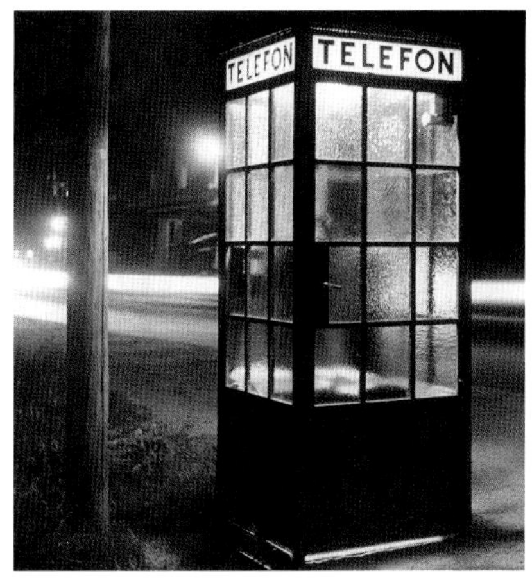

The result of the competition was determined in 1980, and architect Klavs Helweg-Larsen won first prize. The premise for the new telephone booth was that it wasn't a closed booth (because of the bomb scare). Helweg-Larsen's proposal was an advanced construction in matt-polished stainless steel with sides of tempered glass. From the side the design looks a bit like a question mark, which was its nickname from then on. The load-bearing construction looks like it has sprung from the pavement. It's a sandwich construction consisting of two folded plates of stainless steel, that is a front and back plate that have been welded together with end pieces. The space between the plates is filled with foam material, and all together the construction is strong enough for an elephant to sit on top of. The lighting in the Question Mark is in the form of two lanterns that go through the roof and both emit light on the inside of the stand and show its location after nightfall.

In general, the Question Mark was well received as a successful and innovative design of a traditional city fixture. KTAS started manufacturing the new stand, but a new problem arose. The handicap organisations approached the Minister for Transport, Arne Melchior, and complained that the Question Mark couldn't be used by people in wheelchairs. This came as a surprise since the same organisations were consulted previously and didn't have major objections. The minister resolutely threw the whole project out. The factory that was to be a sub-supplier of the new stand were left holding the baby after having invested in new factory equipment worth millions of kroner. Only Copenhagen Municipality had the guts to maintain that this was the public payphone they wanted. Therefore the Question Mark is still seen in Copenhagen's streets.

THE SPHERICAL MAIL COACH – DENMARK'S first design competition? Regular mail routes have existed in Denmark as far back as 1624. For over 150 years it was the duty of local peasants to be responsible for the transport in their region, but in the late 1700s proper mail coaches were introduced. Their quality wasn't particularly good, so in 1814 a competition was arranged between two Copenhagen coachbuilders for the design of a new mail coach. The General Post Management had three requirements: the coach should be as light as possible; it should protect the mail from the weather; and passengers would not be allowed. The final requirement was a matter of delivering the mail and newspapers quickly. The postal service had previously taken passengers, but now time was of the essence, so the drivers were no longer allowed to make money on the side by taking passengers.

Everywhere else in Denmark there are phone booths that have been rather quickly developed by Utzon Architects. Although this more traditional booth doesn't have a bad design, it's far from being an innovative city fixture like the Question Mark. The Utzon booth is made in several colours depending on which municipality it's in. It is found in green, red, blue or grey. The sides are made of glass with a lattice of expanded metal on top that partly prevents vandalism of the worst kind, and partly makes life miserable for people who want to put up posters. The little pyramid roof gives the booth what one could call a rather cute appearance. In the long run the question is how long phone booths will be a part of the townscape. High cost, vandalism and the huge predominance of mobile phones make it unprofitable to maintain many public telephones.

PUBLIC PLAY

In the spring of 1980, the playground Byggeren (the Builder) was to be removed to make room for public housing close to Blågårds Plads on Nørrebro in Copenhagen. Several hundred residents and housing activists blockaded the area for weeks to preserve this popular playground as a breathing space in an area that had never been pampered with many recreational or green areas. It resulted in a Social Democratic city council headed by Lord Mayor Egon Weidekamp refusing to negotiate or make any concessions, and large police forces had to clear the protesters off the playground. Today the area is considered an overdeveloped ghetto that has so many social problems that the police at times say they can't patrol the area.

Ten years prior to this, in 1970, the company Kompan was founded when graphic artist Tom Lindhardt (b. 1935) was assigned the task of making playground sculptures for the public housing estate Vollsmose in Odense. The work gave Tom Lindhardt two ideas. One was to add round and colourful details to the grey and square environment around the cement buildings, and the other was to systemise the playground equipment. The classic Kompan equipment, which among other things is made of thick plywood and is spray painted in primary colours, was rather typical of the artistic idiom of the 1970s. Of the company's products, the most long-lasting is the little hen that is a spring rider with a large spring that can move the hen in all directions when the child is sitting on it.

Kompan quickly expanded and began selling a large number of its products on the export market. In 1986 the company was listed, and LEGO's holding company, Kirkbi, took majority control of the company in 1996. In the course of its history, Kompan has bought up several of its foreign competitors, including in Holland and the US. As one of the first playground toy manufacturers in the world, Kompan began to design and proportion its playground equipment with a view to safety. The company's products are modular, so the elements can be combined to fit any size of playground and any age group. Thus many different types of playgrounds can be built, featuring castles and bridges and little hiding places, tables and benches, ladders, slides, ropes to climb and much more.

In 1997 Kompan launched a new type of playground under the name Galaxy, which was to stimulate physical activity in older children. Galaxy is more like gym equipment that you can climb on and it has built-in challenges to develop the children's sense of balance. The materials used are primarily galvanised steel combined with sturdy details in materials like plastic and rubber.

The two competitors were Fife and Dreyer, and Fife designed a coach with a square box mounted on it costing 1080 rix dollars. However, Dreyer designed a coach with a round, pumpkin-shaped container for the mail, and his proposal cost only 800 rix dollars. For technical and cost reasons Dreyer won. The design of the spherical coach prevented the possibility of taking passengers, and in later versions little spikes covered the roof of the barrel to prevent stowaways. The new spherical coach attracted attention wherever it went. The speed was one Danish mile an hour (7.5 km) which was rather high for a horse carriage on the poor roads back then. According to the decree, the trip from Copenhagen to Hamburg should be covered in three days.

The sphere was made of wicker with a canvas cover, and it had good suspension. The first spherical coach had four wheels and two harnessed horses, and later two-wheeled versions with one horse were also used. The colour chosen was a warm yellow that was very similar to the colour the Danish mail cars have today. When quicker stagecoaches that also carried mail were introduced in the 1830s, and the railroad arrived in the 1840s, the spherical coach was phased out, and the last one made its final run in 1865.

▲ *The idea behind Kompan's playground equipment from the 1970s was partly based on the visual art movement called pop art. Graphic artist Tom Lindhardt founded the company Kompan together with Hans Mogens Frederiksen in Ringe on Funen. Here is some of their colourful playground equipment.*

THE ARCHITECTURAL PRACTICE BBP Architects won a design competition in 1999 for new lifeguard stations for the Danish beaches and open-air public swimming pools. TrygFonden was behind the initiative and financed the project. The first-prize winners designed a tower built of box-like modules that could be stacked. Since the modules slope outward, they have two advantages: first of all they can be stacked and thus create a very visible landmark on the beach. Secondly, when the tower is dismantled at the end of the season, they fit together like a Chinese box and only take up slightly more room than the bottom module.

The plywood box modules are alternately painted red and white, which beautifully emphasises the significance of the tower. Furthermore, slots are cut on one side making a ladder to the top of the tower. The lifeguard tower is erected on a number of Denmark's most popular beaches as well as the Copenhagen Havnebad (Harbour pool), which has been a huge success since 2002 and is a clear indication that the water in Copenhagen Harbour is clean enough to swim in.

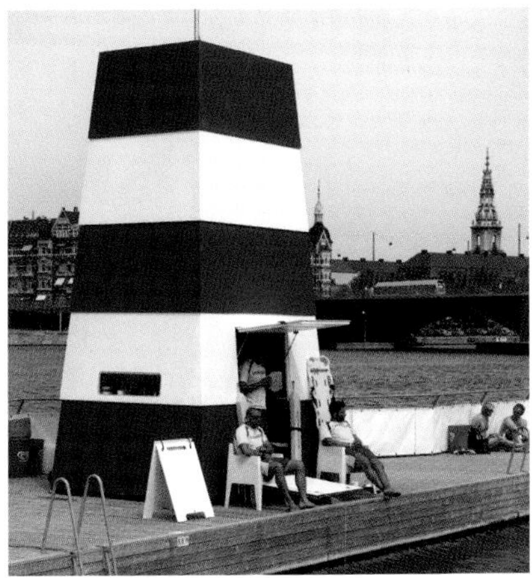

Today the company has expanded, but they have carefully maintained their original concept of designing and manufacturing expressive playground equipment. If there was anything lacking in Kompan's universe it would be to challenge the children to be more creative and take part in designing their play and the playground that rightfully should be their domain. When you walk by a playground today with Kompan's products, you can't help thinking that there's not much rebellion or 'Builder' playground in the concept, and at the end of the day, the playground looks how the adults think it should.

DESIGN FOR FINDING ONE'S WAY

In 1771, the same year that streetlamps had real glass installed, Struensee also decreed that all houses in town had to have visible title numbers. It was not until 1859 though that today's consecutive numbers were introduced, with the even numbers on the right side of the street, and the odd ones on the left. Furthermore, the owners of buildings on a corner were required to paint the street name on the wall. Until this time it hadn't been easy to find one's way around town. Since 1624, in Christian IV's time, the mailmen had been notified to put a sign with a white horse on their homes, but otherwise the only means of orientation were the craftsmen's guild signs.

In the Navy's old neighbourhood in Copenhagen, Nyboder, you can still see the painted street signs on the walls of corner houses. Gradually other solutions were found since painting directly on the walls wasn't very wear-resistant and was maintained by the house owners. In the late 1800s, the oven-baked enamelled metal signs began to be common, and this type of street sign is still seen in many places in the capital. And although new signs were developed a few years later, now of cast iron and still very common today, Copenhagen Municipality didn't organise a proper design program that would determine the type of signs desired in the city. And typographically there is a great difference in the designs. Numerous typefaces are used in the municipality, and while white letters on a blue background seem to be preferred, other solutions can be found here and there.

The diversity of the designs can of course be charming in itself. Some people get the impression that they're in a dynamic big city that has arisen in an entrepreneurial spirit of enterprise. Others see it as just a mess that along with the poor maintenance of the city's public areas and the lack of cleaning in the streets only confirms the impression that something's wrong in the city of Copenhagen. It is a difficult balancing act whether a city should choose a spirited expression in its public design and let relatively many things emerge by themselves, or whether it should take control and adopt a well-organised public design that indicates that they have thought things over and provided a certain standard for everything under the auspices of the local authorities.

One can easily see the merits of both points of view. On the one hand, there are many cities in the world whose growth is sprawling, and most of us like some of these cities for the very reason that they're unpredictable and dynamic. London, New York, Barcelona and many others could be mentioned. These cities would be boring to live in and visit if they were too neat and tidy with consistent design in every area.

On the other hand, there are also cities that have lost all their charm, if they had any at all, because no one has taken the overall responsibility, and progress and market forces have been given free rein. Some large cities in the US midwest are examples of this, but also a few Danish provincial towns have let the local pedestrian streets become an ugly hodgepodge of store fronts without any consideration for the big picture.

Signs with hearts

In Gentofte Municipality you can see one of the most consistent and successful Danish sign programs. Back in 1923, a competition was held the same year that architect Knud V. Engelhardt (known in professional circles as KVE) started working in the field of design. The project took many years, and the most notable result of his work is the cast-iron street signs that are still standard in the municipality. All the signs including the stands and the bell-shaped top are charcoal coloured. The letters, which are in relief, are painted white and furnished with Engelhardt's little heart logo as the dot over the letter J in the word 'vej' (street) painted red. The design of the sign is also very practical because Knud V. Engelhardt was a person who thought along industrial lines. For example, all the signs have two rings at the end that are slid onto the stand, and two screws that are tightened so the sign is turned in the best angle in relation to how the streets intersect.

The street signs in other municipalities aren't nearly as flexible. They can be mounted on bent and galvanised tubes that have to be dug into the ground at the correct angle. Or they can be designed so the signs are perpendicular to each other even if the streets don't intersect at a right angle. Engelhardt's system was ahead of its time and as a total system it hasn't been surpassed yet. He was an architect who took pride in working for the public sector. According to graphic designer Erik Ellegaard Frederiksen's biography, Engelhardt wanted to reach as many people as possible with his design, and he felt that the government and municipalities had a great responsibility to lead the way with good design in the public space. In the case of Gentofte Municipality, one could say that KVE's design of city fixtures has made the area well known. Otherwise Gentofte is a municipality that merges imperceptibly with its neighbouring areas such as Copenhagen Municipality. A distinct street sign system lets one clearly see where one is. You could say that in a fine way Engelhardt anticipated much of the later talk about design programs and the branding of Danish cities.

The typeface that KVE designed for the signs looks at first very different from what Danes are used to seeing on public signs. Some of the letters were very distinctive for the time in which they were designed, and they haven't become less characteristic over the years. Some of the letters even seem to be very wide. There may be a purely practical explanation in that when you see a sign from an angle, the letters are pushed together, but you still have to be able to read them. The typeface isn't like those that are inspired by either the classic Times or the modern Helvetica typefaces. KVE's typeface is robust and almost old Danish and bold. The inspiration has more likely come from Art Nouveau and the graphic design that Thorvald Bindesbøll and others worked on back then. And yet it's more simple and straightforward than most of its time's typefaces.

Engelhardt loved to round corners off on almost everything he made. It was one of his trademarks that things get worn down anyway at some point, so why not design them that way from the beginning? But typefaces and letters don't get worn, do they? Nevertheless, KVE often designed his

▾ *Architect Knud Valdemar Engelhardt designed the street signs for Gentofte Municipality. The name Engelhardt (angel heart) became his logo and was always included in his works. In Gentofte, almost all the street names end with the word '-vej' (street). And ingeniously Engelhardt's little heart is the dot over the letter J and now also a symbol of Gentofte Municipality. This is good branding before we even learned to use the word in Denmark.*

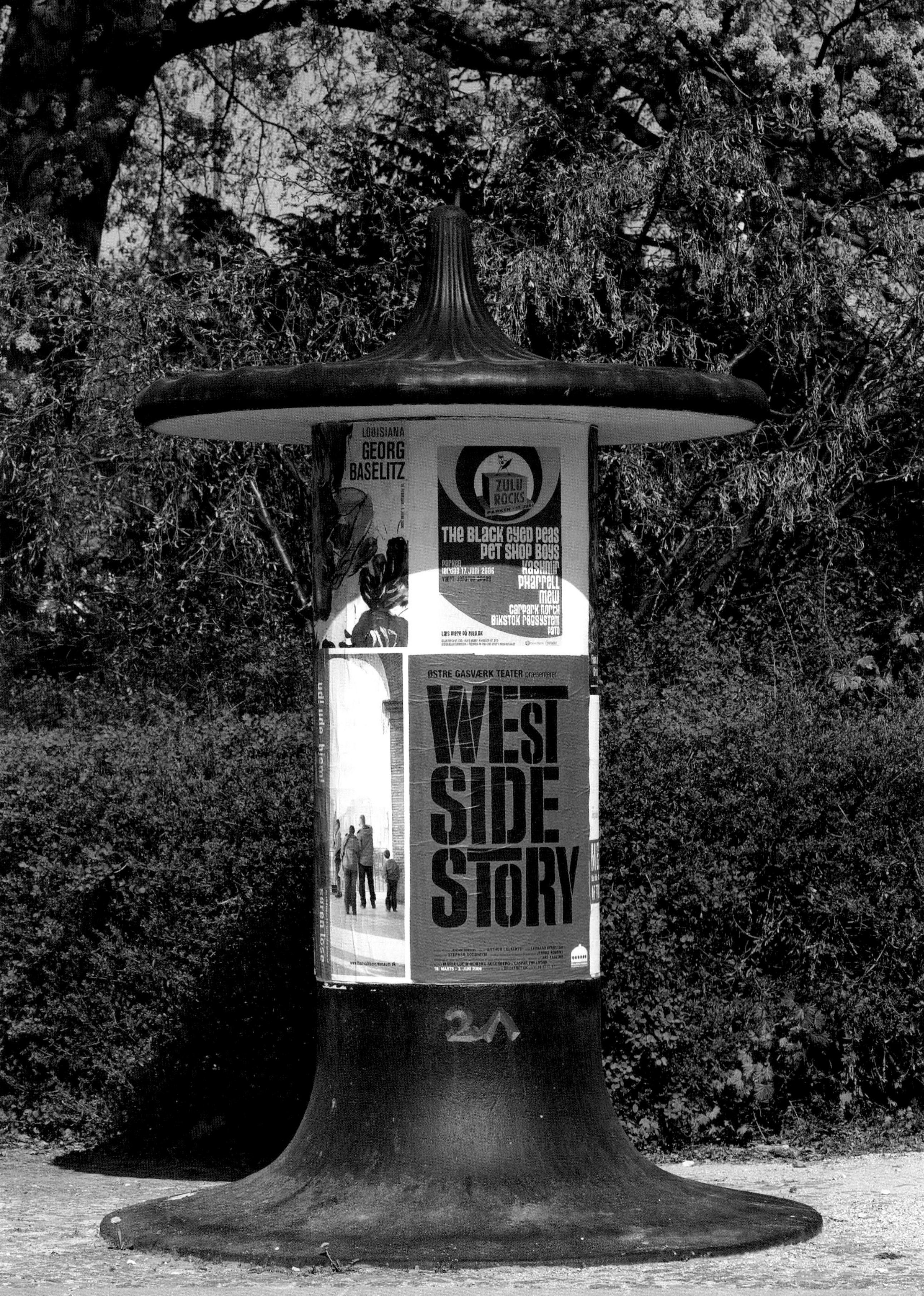
LOUISIANA
GEORG
BASELITZ
ZULU
ROCKS
THE BLACK EYED PEAS
PET SHOP BOYS
PARKEN
lørdag 17. juni 2006
KASHMIR
PHARRELL
MEW
CARPARK NORTH
BIKSTOK RØGSYSTEM
PATO
Læs mere på zulu.dk
ØSTRE GASVÆRK TEATER præsenterer
WEST
SIDE
STORY

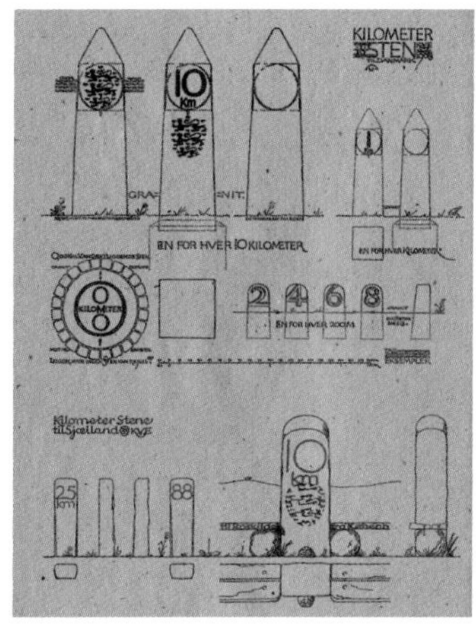

◀ The advertising pillars for Gentofte Municipality, like everything Engelhardt designed, are strongly characterised by the soft and rounded artistic idiom. The wide, rounded lip at the bottom is to prevent dirt from collecting there and dogs from relieving themselves on it.

▼ The kilometre stones on Zealand were designed by P.V. Jensen-Klint, and they start with the zero point stone in large cities – here at Amagerport in Copenhagen. The design is from 1910 and is based on extensive preliminary work, some of which is pictured right, by Knud V. Engelhardt.

sign typefaces in this way, see for example the Copenhagen streetcars. It's as though he thought that signs could be visually worn with time. But whatever the reason, his typography continues to be very humanist and warm.

The advertising pillars

Street signs weren't the only things that Engelhardt designed for Gentofte Municipality. Concurrently he designed the municipality's advertising pillars that have also gone down in Danish design history as being a groundbreaking way of working with city fixtures. The 30-odd pillars are manufactured at a factory and made of reinforced concrete and delivered on site. Already at this point KVE demonstrates his practical way of thinking. In order to save driving expenses he designed the individual elements of the pillar – the base, body and top – so they could fit on the bed of a truck. And thus only one trip was necessary. The function of the rounded lip at the base is to prevent dirt from accumulating where the pillar meets the ground. Moreover, it discourages dogs from relieving themselves on it. Once again everything in this design is round and soft.

KVE was also active outside of Gentofte in designing for the public sector. He designed lots of signs for Copenhagen Municipality and in 1910 a series of streetcars for the capital (see page 408). In the beginning of the 20th century, there arose a need for kilometre stones along Denmark's main roads. They were to replace the old, existing Danish milestones with the new unit of measurement that had become the norm. Knud V. Engelhardt argued for many years that there should be completely new stones to mark the number of kilometres from city to city.

◂ In recent years, Køge has carried through a comprehensive revision of the shop fronts in the city centre. This managed to get even traditionally vociferous chain stores to be more discreet for the benefit of an improved visual urban environment. Later it turned out that the turnover in stores with a more discreet and aesthetic signposting did not fall, something the business owners had feared.

From 1907 to 1909 he compiled several proposals. The final proposal was for roughly hewn stones of light granite from Bornholm. The design of the typeface and numbers was typical of Engelhardt, organic and functional. A simple design full of soul.

In 1909 he finally convinced the authorities of the significance of the project, but things went awfully wrong for KVE. First the counties in Jutland and on Funen decided on their own particular solution, and then a competition was arranged for the design of the stones on Zealand. Five architects participated, but since Engelhardt had already publicised his proposals, everyone else could look over his shoulder, and P.V. Jensen-Klint won in the end. His proposal was based so much on KVE's preliminary work that there was talk of blatant plagiarism. This bad luck threw KVE into such despair after having worked so hard and so passionately that he ended up in the mental ward of Frederiksberg Hospital for an entire year. Luckily he recovered, and afterwards he immediately designed his groundbreaking streetcars for Copenhagen Municipality.

The private signs

The public sector isn't the only one that makes signs. Just like the private operators who supply the public space with various forms of city fixtures, there are private company signs that also have a great visual impact, as do the designs of store fronts. In the past one could manage with a signboard that informed people that here was a cobbler, a barber or a baker. But gradually the need to make one's mark on the street scene has developed into a kind of visual arms race. For a long time many cities, especially those with old city centres worth preserving, have had to put up with their existing buildings and façades being remodelled, often beyond all recognition.

In the last few decades, the large chain stores have in particular become visually intrusive. With reference to their brand and the accompanying extensive design manuals, some of them have practically turned the whole façade into one big sign, and in many cases they've even boarded up the windows to make more room for signs. Some cities have realised that this development will eventually entail a deterioration of the quality of street life and have resorted to regulating the private enterprise in this area, sometimes very strictly. Cities like Køge and Helsingør, but also in other municipalities, have strictly regulated the signage of the shops. Some Danish municipalities have gradually adopted an approach for the collective design of the urban environment, street equipment and the graphic identity. In many cases the regulation of the pedestrian areas is done in close collaboration with the business owners and trade associations, but in some of the more obstinate cases, direct orders or bans were necessary.

Many stores and chain stores have admitted their own responsibility for the urban environment, and that in the long run it isn't to their advantage if the city's distinctiveness is ruined by exaggerated signage. Research in the area also suggests that it doesn't pay to advertise too conspicuously, as it doesn't attract more customers. On the contrary, a less commercial milieu with more amenity value and diverse experiences results in more people coming to the area and thus also more customers in the shops.

ANOTHER SIDE OF PUBLIC DESIGN

Not only on the streets can one find products that the public sector has had a considerable influence on. This effect is achieved by the various authorities' purchasing policies and by the many demands and

▼ *At an early point in time, many municipalities had district plans and various restrictive covenants that they could use to intervene if a façade was overly decorated. For example, the Deres shop on Strøget in Copenhagen was ordered in November 1967 to change its façade, since the municipal authority felt that their signposting was at odds with the general street scene. However, the following year Deres, Nørgaard på Strøget and Butikken Uden Navn won the PH prize for their store fronts and were thus saved by public opinion. Today this would hardly raise an eyebrow for there aren't many places in Denmark where the municipalities enforce their right to weed out the thistles of ugly and intrusive signposting. During this period, the façade of the Deres stores were redesigned every year, and the picture below shows the Deres façade from the late 1960s. It was partly inspired by the Beatles album 'Yellow Submarine'.*

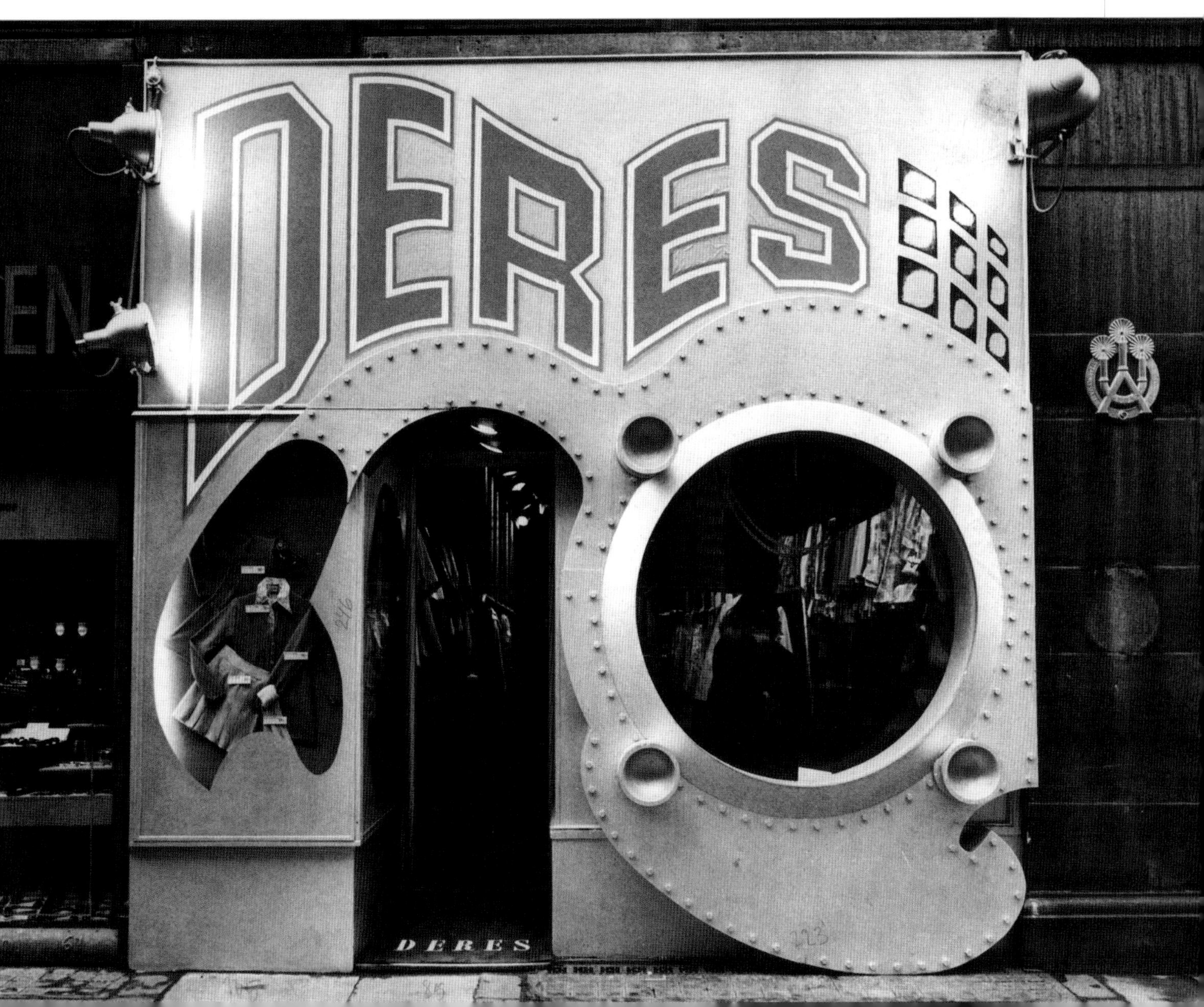

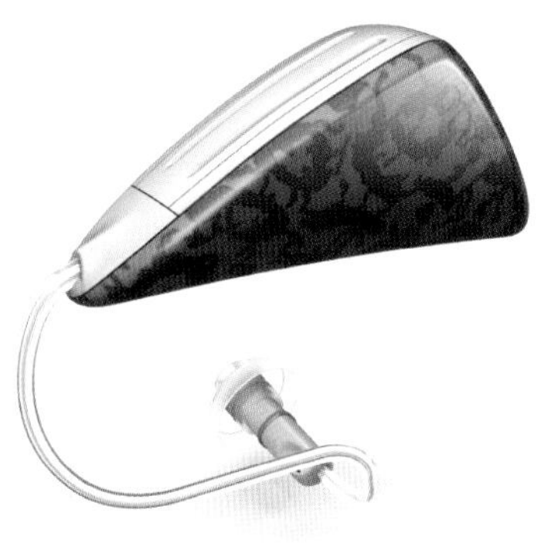

◂ *Oticon's digital hearing aid from 2006 is called Delta and is worn behind the ear. It is as small as technically possible and comes in 17 different colours and patterns. This is how the new generation of hearing aids is disguised as a kind of jewellery.*

specifications for products and procedures that legislation demands of suppliers and operators in many different areas.

This is especially true of purchases in the health sector, but equally so to a great degree in the fields of interior design and the furnishing of various public institutions and the like. The government and municipalities don't have any part in the production itself of these products. On the contrary, this is left almost solely to the private companies, but the way in which the public sector can exert this influence can vary quite a bit. It doesn't have to take place only through direct public spending, but also by giving tax advantages in some areas. This has helped, among other things, to build up the Danish windmill industry which is a global leader in the field.

In addition, the government is able to stimulate the development and spread of new and well-designed products in the areas of the treatment of illnesses and assistive technology for the handicapped. For example, Denmark was one of the very first countries that subsidised hearing aids for the hearing impaired. In 1951, permanent residents of Denmark could get a free hearing aid if they needed it, and to ensure that the patients got the best aid and at a reasonable cost, the order was put out to tender. Based on this good domestic market the Danish manufacturers of hearing aids had a perfect basis for developing new products. This means that today three out of five of the largest companies in the field are Danish.

New technologies make it possible to design better products. It is an old truism that this also applies to the public environment. Light emitting diodes (LEDs) have been in the pipeline for many years before they were powerful and stable enough to be used in things like traffic lights, but in the late 1990s this was possible. A small company on Funen with the international name of Technical Traffic Solutions developed a Danish traffic system along with the design company Harrit og Sørensen. The many LEDs replace one incandescent bulb. This has a number of advantages with regard to economy, safety and not least aesthetics. A lot of energy is saved with the new sources of light, since they used one third of the electricity of the old bulbs. An ordinary intersection that has about 20 traffic lights is comparable to the amount of electricity consumed by an average house. Furthermore, the new lights require much less maintenance, especially because the lifespan of an LED is about ten times that of an ordinary bulb.

There are also safety advantages. The light sources consist of about 125 to 180 LEDs in the circular area of about 200 mm in diameter. Even if some of the LEDs should go out before the normal lifespan of 10,000 hours, no great harm is done since there are plenty left. The luminosity is also ample, depending on the colour of the signal, since it's double the minimum requirement of 200 candelas.

Aesthetically it has also been possible to improve the old traffic lights. Among other things, the LEDs take up less room than ordinary bulbs, so the depth of the traffic light as been reduced. Another advantage is that the traditional cap peaks aren't needed anymore. Along with a general modernisation and streamlining of the design, the small dimensions have given the new traffic lights a more up-to-date look. In 2000 the company and designers received the ID prize from the Danish Design Centre, and in 2002 they were awarded the EU's environmental prize.

THE DANISH HEARING aid industry began to expand slowly after World War II, but the real boost came in 1951 when hearing aids were made free of charge in Denmark. Until 30 years ago, only standard hearing aids were produced. They were relatively big and placed behind the ear and had few, if any, adjustments. They consisted of a microphone, an amplifier and an earphone, that is, they not only reproduced the sound in the frequency area that the user needed, but also a lot of noise.

In the 1990s, digitally programmable hearing aids were introduced, and they can be adapted to the individual user. It's a technologically ongoing process, and the aids are also getting smaller in size. Some of them are clearly visible and look almost like a piece of jewellery, while others are fitted invisibly in the ear canal and adapted to the individual ear. This type of hearing aid is moulded for the individual ear by first taking an impression of it.

▲ *The traffic lights from the company Technical Traffic Solutions here in the new Copenhagen neighbourhood of Ørestaden. The new LEDs do not require the usual 'cap brim' to shield the light from sunlight.*

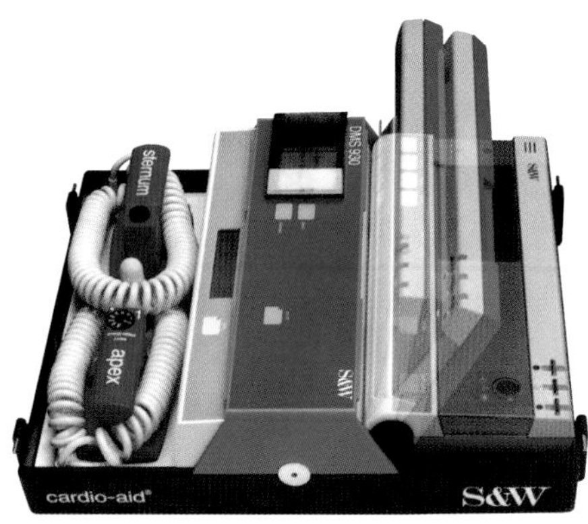

◂ *Simonsen & Weel is one of the oldest and largest Danish companies in the field of hospital and healthcare equipment. The firm was founded in 1817 in Copenhagen and mainly sells other companies' products, but they also manufacture things such as surgical equipment. The DMS 930 defibrillator is from the late 1980s and was designed by Simonsen & Weel's own designer, Harry Haun.*

Help in a suitcase

Industrial designer Jan Trägårdh designed an emergency case for the company Ambu in the early 1980s. It is designed to contain various equipment for resuscitation – oxygen mask, medicine, tubes, hypodermic needles, scissors, bandages etc. Until this particular case was designed, ordinary suitcases were used that could be mistaken for other suitcases. Ambu's new model was specially made so it didn't resemble ordinary suitcases and could furthermore be supplied with Red Cross labels or similar graphics. In this type of design tasks, much emphasis isn't put on the aesthetic expression; the product is about saving lives, and this is what the design should contribute to. The great task in the design is to make the product as suitable and manageable as possible, so the risk of confusion or mistakes being made is not possible in an emergency. Therefore the quality of this product is on the inside, even though the outside exudes quality and efficiency.

The large parts, such as the oxygen tank, can be strapped in, and otherwise the case is divided into sections with transparent lids which make it easy and logical to organise. The point is to prevent the doctor or paramedic from having to hunt for something. The compartment sizes and sectioning can be customised to suit individual needs, but otherwise every compartment has the size and form that matches the contents. This is also a help when the emergency situation is over because you can see if something's missing, and if the bandages need to be restocked when returning to base. The case, which was mainly designed for use on ships and in the military, is made of robust plastic shells with rounded corners and reinforced with ridges on the sides. The handles and spring lock are simply designed with nylon bands. It comes in orange or black.

Resuscitation

When someone is in cardiac arrest, help is needed quickly and preferably with electricity in the form of a defibrillator. Designer and Chief of Construction Harry Haun (b. 1936) took part in developing a defibrillator for Simonsen & Weel in the mid-1980s. The model DMS 930 is a portable defibrillator for use in hospitals and ambulances. The device is in a wall-mounted charger when not in use, but in an emergency it can be taken anywhere. Simplicity and clarity are of the essence in saving lives as the example of the Ambu case shows. Therefore all important handles, buttons and graphic instructions are large and unmistakable. Since the defibrillator is a dangerous device to use, there is a colour code that assists the use of the individual parts. During resuscitation the paddles on the electrodes are used.

The DMS 930 is enclosed in a case with handles and two hinged covers. Under the first cover are the two electrodes, and under the second is a screen that shows the characteristic graph of the heart rhythm. This display can be tilted upwards for easy reading and can also be detached so it can go with the patient for continued monitoring and alert during further transport. In the middle console of the device there is a small printer that can print a short or long recording of the heart rhythm. Compared to the Ambu case, the design is rather angular, sharply edged and serious while the primary colours contribute to taking the drama out of the situation. DMS 930 is no longer manufactured, but when it was introduced in 1998, it was awarded the ID prize.

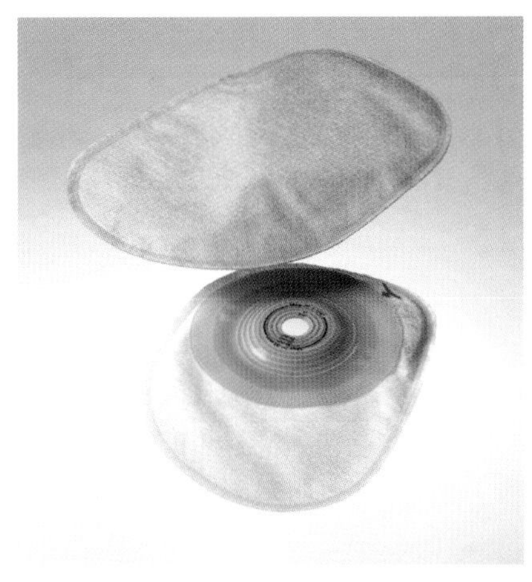

COLOPLAST IS ONE of Denmark's large industrial companies that for 50 years has designed and manufactured groundbreaking aids for people who suffer from incontinence or have had an ostomy operation. It started when nurse Elise Sørensen's sister was operated on for colon cancer and was given a colostomy, that is her faeces were let out on her abdomen. There weren't proper aids to prevent leakage and odour, so Elise Sørensen had the simple idea of making special plastic bags supplied with double adhesive tape to be put directly on the body. The small company of Dansk Plastic Emballage (Danish Plastic Packaging) saw the sense of the idea, and in 1957 they began manufacturing the new bags that quickly became an export item. Two years later, more than two thirds of the ostomy bags were sold abroad. The continuing development and design of new solutions, as well as in other medical areas, have created a workplace for 6000 employees in a company called Coloplast. Today 97 % of their products are exported, and the company has received a number of design awards.

▲ *The Ambu company was established in 1937 to develop and manufacture various kinds of life-saving equipment. Industrial designer Jan Trägårdh has designed several different products for the company over the years, including this emergency case. Although the aesthetic appearance isn't of the first priority when an emergency case is designed, it nonetheless ended up being a bold, robust and very beautiful, quality product. The Ambu emergency case got the ID prize from the Danish Design Centre in 1985.*

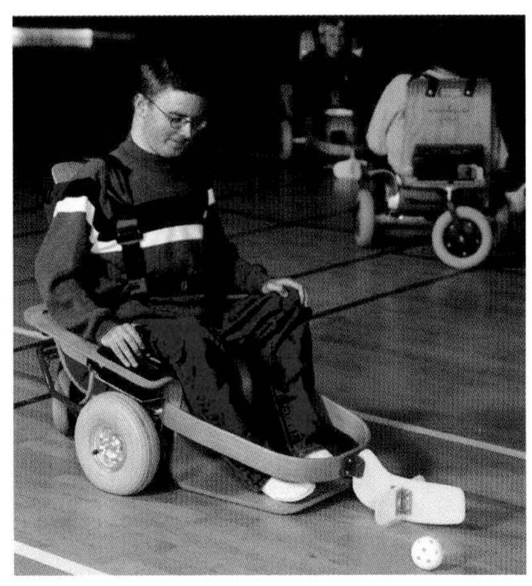

WHEELCHAIR FOR POWERHOCKEY. In 1988 architect Mogens Holm-Rasmussen won a large design competition for sports equipment for the disabled. His suggestion was a little, low, electric sports wheelchair for severely disabled children. The wheelchair's basic structure consists of several laminated wood shells that are screwed together. The speed of the electric motor and steering are controlled by a joystick, and in most cases the wheelchair is supplied with a kind of fibreglass hockey stick in front. This stick is used for playing PowerHockey, which is one of the few sports that severely disabled children and young people can play as a team. The chair can go 14 km/h, and the most important part of the chair as regards the ball is the stick that is shaped like a cross so the ball can both be dribbled and hit. But it is the movement of the chair that gives the ball speed and direction. The sports wheelchair costs about 60,000 kroner, and it can be customised to suit the user's needs. The wheelchair gives the severely disabled a fantastic opportunity to participate in sports. It was awarded the ID prize in 1994.

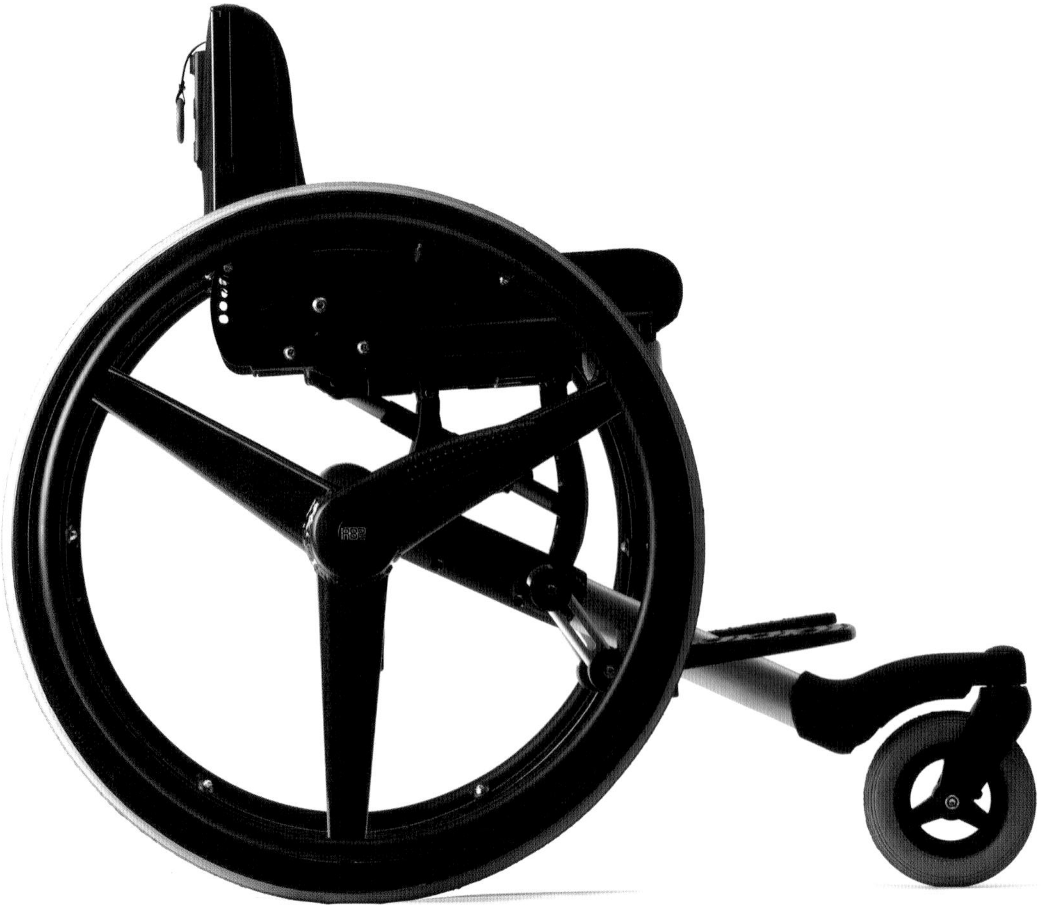

▲ *The Cheetah wheelchair.*

CHEETAH, THE WHEELCHAIR for children. In 2003, the company R82 launched the Cheetah, a wheelchair for children. Compared to the PowerHockey chair, Cheetah is designed for those who are less severely disabled. It was designed by the design office 3PART in Aarhus whose assignment was 'to design for children an extremely flexible wheelchair of the future', as R82 put it. The company wanted a product that would set a new standard for all their future products. They wanted new thinking and innovation in materials and production.

The Cheetah is the result of a comprehensive collaboration between R82, 3PART, occupational therapists, physical therapists, users and handicap helpers. The design is based on materials like aluminium and glass-reinforced plastic which make the chair light and safe at the same time. The construction of the chair is so flexible that it can grow along with the child, both in length and width, and furthermore, three or four wheels can be mounted. The chair exudes play and activity. The Cheetah got the Danish Design Prize for 'personal use' in 2004.

S
Sol gi'r varme.
Sol gi'r sved.
Sol gi'r næsen fregner.
Sol står op
og sol går ned
osse når det regner.

Graphic design

Communication requires form. And if the communication isn't oral, then it often consists of writing or images or a combination of the two. Graphic design is about giving visual communications a recognisable form. For example, the letter A can be designed in many ways, but it still has to be recognisable as the letter A. In other less linguistic forms of expression, such as posters or book covers, one can work more freely with the graphic expression and the symbols used. But the signs also becomes more imprecise and ambiguous, and this allows for interpretation.

Some of the first graphic expressions we know from archaeological finds in Denmark are symbols, and most of them are open to interpretation today. We do not have any written sources that can give us the key to understanding the characters and figures that were cut or scratched on tools and weapons thousands of years ago. What was their purpose? Who made them? How and in what connection were they made? We have to guess and dig deeper in an attempt to understand the message. But we needn't go far back in time to find very ambiguous graphic signals. Just think of Mona Lisa's smile or the many interpretations of Peter Blake's cover for the Beatles album 'Sergeant Pepper's Lonely Hearts Club Band' from 1967. The more veiled and mysterious a message is designed, the more room there is for various interpretations.

◂ *'The sun makes heat*
The sun makes sweat
The sun makes freckles on your nose
The sun rises
And the sun sets
Even when the rain flows.'
This nursery rhyme is from 'Halfdan's ABC' (1967) by Halfdan Rasmussen and illustrated by Ib Spang Olsen.

THE JELLING STONE. The large rune stone in the little town of Jelling is an important Danish monument from the Viking Age. It's from circa 985 AD, and is very much identified with the birth of the kingdom of Denmark and of its conversion to Christianity. The large carved picture is so pivotal to the history of Denmark that a slightly adapted version adorns page two in Danish passports, which, by the way, are designed by the design company Bysted. The picture depicts Christ entwined by serpentine bands of ornamentation. However, it is a rather different image of Christ than the one we're presented with today. It's not a suffering Jesus, but a victorious Jesus, and he isn't visibly crucified although the pose might indicate it. The image has a couple of important messages. First, that Christianity is a faith of strength, as the image of a humiliated Jesus would not have caught on with the Vikings. Secondly, the mixture of the Christian figure with the Vikings' traditional serpentine ornamentation indicates that the new religion was compatible with their lifestyle until then as well as with certain heathen traditions. The whole concept of the stone and the graphics emphasise Harold Bluetooth's (see page 482) message about a Danish nation with a central leadership and a new Christian religion. The 2.5 m tall rune stone was most likely been painted in bright colours in its day. Small fragments of pigment were found in tiny cracks, and a reconstruction was made by archaeologists at the Danish National Museum. Although the reconstruction may be subject to uncertainty, there is no doubt that the Viking Age was much more colourful than we now imagine.

PETROGLYPHS

Some of the more mysterious messages from Denmark's ancient history are the so-called petroglyphs. The word is from Greek, where *petra* means rock and *glyphe* carving. The petroglyphs are not carved in the stone, but have been made by painstakingly hitting the rock face with a smaller stone. The Danish petroglyphs are for natural reasons mostly on Bornholm where the bedrock is above ground. They're also found elsewhere, especially in northern Zealand and on the northern coasts, but here the figures are carved into large stones that the Ice Age left behind in the landscape. The Danish petroglyphs are from the Bronze Age, around 1700 to 500 BC. The figures are surprisingly alike, both petroglyphs from various parts of the country and from different periods during the Bronze Age.

The most common image among the petroglyphs is the bowl sign. It is a flat, circular depression in the stone, whose size varies greatly. There is no unequivocal interpretation of this motif since the sign is so simple and can mean many different things. Perhaps this sign did have different meanings depending on the context and the situation. It could be a symbol of the sun, which we know was worshipped back then (for instance, the Trundholm sun chariot). It could also have been a kind of fertility symbol. Of all the figure motifs, the ship is the most common; this was also the main religious symbol in the Bronze Age. In Denmark alone there are hundreds of petroglyphs that picture ships, and even more in the rest of southern Scandinavia, whereas ship motifs are virtually unknown further south in continental Europe.

The ship also had a great practical and symbolic meaning for the prehistoric people in this area. Impulses came from the south; not only spiritual impulses but also the more material ones such as raw materials for the new material of the time, bronze. And the Danish regions, not least the island of Bornholm, were very dependent on vessels to maintain contact with the outside world. With this in mind it's no surprise that they worshipped the ship in the same way that many people nowadays practically worship the car as an icon of freedom. The practical meaning of the ship was transferred to a symbolic and religious meaning. Various depictions from that time even describe the ship as the carrier of the sun. They imagined that the sun was on a ship that sailed across the sky in the course of a day, and at night it sailed back through the netherworld to re-emerge the next morning. Some petroglyphs have even merged the sun and the ship in one figure so one can almost imagine the sun as a ship. In areas far from the coast, the ship was replaced by a horse, and in some cases the ships had a horse head as their figurehead. The ship was considered the horse of the sea.

The graphic expression of the petroglyphs is extremely simple, and when you look at them today, they almost have a modern look, a bit like naive art. The simplistic expression is due not least to the way there were made, namely by hitting a stone against a rock face for a long time. The possibility of adding details to the images was limited by this technique. The purpose of making petroglyphs is not clear. They can have been used as a form of teaching or passing on traditions, and maybe rituals were used, for example when initiating young people into adult life. Perhaps they marked holy places, gathering places for religious acts or rituals or were merely to mark a tribe's territory.

However, there is some indication that rituals did have great significance, since in some places a new image was added every generation, and in certain cases over a period of 300–400 years.

▸ *A copy of the large Jelling stone, which once was in the courtyard of the Danish National Museum, but now no longer exists.*

In 1987, Denmark held the EU presidency that was then called the EEC, and for that occasion a symbol was designed that was based on a petroglyph. This represented a ship with 12 people onboard symbolising the then 12 EEC countries. The ship is similar to the Hjortspring boat (see page 31) that is some hundreds of years younger than this petroglyph. The original petroglyph is from the Gilleleje area, and graphic designer Peter Blay interpreted the old symbol. The original petroglyph had only 11 people onboard, so in order to represent all 12 member states, Blay had to add a person. The logo was so popular that it was reused in 1993 when Denmark again held the EU presidency.

COATS OF ARMS

In the early Middle Ages, that is in the beginning of the 1100s, graphic images of a more personal nature began to turn up. These were the knights' coats of arms that still exist as a type and were the predecessors of what we today know as trademarks or logos. The tradition of designing these coats of arms with their easily recognisable figures in bright contrasting colours arose because princes and noblemen needed to identify themselves. When these persons of rank wore full body armour during war or in jousts, they were unrecognisable. Therefore they had to have a clear and characteristic mark that also had the shape of a shield. The coat of arms also quickly attained a more general and symbolic meaning, and soon it was reproduced on seals, buildings, sepulchral monuments etc. as the visual identity of the whole family as well as the towns and areas of land that were the nobleman's property. Soon the clerics adopted the custom, and the king's coat of arms also became the country's coat of arms.

The expertise in coats of arms, the rules for their design and the graphic art that renders them is called heraldry. It originates from the time when a so-called herald was in charge of holding jousts and the etiquette pertaining to them. There are still strict heraldic rules for the correct design of the content, colouring and composition of a coat of arms. These rules have been upheld since the art arose and are still very much subject to their medieval origin. So if the figures are to be correct, they have to be drawn flat, that is without the use of perspective, and they mustn't be natural, which means the animals and plants should be simple and stylised. The figures that are used on coats of arms have the greatest graphic strength and character when they take up as much space as possible. Therefore there is rarely much space between the graphic elements. A well-designed coat of arms uses as few colours and as simple figures as possible.

Many of the graphic rules that were established originally as good form in the Middle Ages still apply today. For example, you have to use particular colours such as red, blue, black and green. Yellow and white are also used, but they can be replaced by the metallic colours gold and silver. Furthermore there are rules for tincture that require that certain colours may not be placed on each other, such as a gold lion may not be on a silver background. This made it easier to make out the figures on a coat of arms at a distance. These old heraldic rules correspond very well to the graphic ideals we practice today, although many of today's designers try to challenge these rules to achieve eye-catching effects. Today's forms of graphic identity, like a company's trademark and logo, stem from the tradition of designing these noble coats of arms.

The country's coat of arms

The knights had their coats of arms, so the king also had to have his own, and obviously it had to be very special since it represented the country and the regent. This duality is expressed in the fact that Denmark's coat of arms is found in two versions, the little coat of arms, also called the national coat of arms, and the large royal coat of arms.

Danes see the national coat of arms most often. It is found in more or less modernised versions on stationery from state authorities, on the enamel signs outside the Danish embassies abroad and other similar official connections. In principle the national coat of arms with its three

◄ In the last 20 years, several versions of the little royal coat of arms have been designed. In 1986, heraldic painter Aage Wulff made a rather traditional version, whereas architect and professor Claus Achton Friis in 1991 designed a more simple royal coat of arms for the newly created Told og Skat (Customs and Taxes). These are two different solutions to the task. The reason why there have always been lions on the Danish royal coat of arms is that the lion has always been a symbol of strength in Europe, and it's also king of the beasts. So although no one had even seen a lion in medieval Denmark, it was included on the royal and national coats of arms. The royal coat of arms (left) was digitally drawn in the mid-1990s by designer Henrik Darlie.

lions surrounded by hearts is from the time of the Valdemars. The royal coat of arms is more complex with two savages (woodwoses) armed with clubs and surrounded by the collars of the orders of the Elephant and the Dannebrog. This is used by the royal family, the court and the Royal Danish Life Guards, while all other government authorities use the national coat of arms. To the royal coat of arms belongs also the crown in the Baroque style. It was designed in 1671 and based on Christian V's crown.

At regular intervals the national coat of arms and the crown are redesigned and newly interpreted or 'tightened up' as graphic designers would say. These modernisations have been made as a part of the natural course of events. Today there are several versions of the little national coat of arms that are used by various institutions. In 1986, heraldic painter Aage Wulff redesigned the coat of arms in a style that is very loyal to the historic original while several graphic designers have made versions that are more simplified. In recent years it's as if there has been an explosion of new interpretations of the royal symbols.The crown in particular has been designed in a multitude of variants where almost each ministry and state body must have its own version.

Post Denmark, 1993

The Ministry of Culture, 1994

The Royal Danish Theatre, 1996

The Ministry of Finance, 1999

The Town and Housing Ministry, 1999

The Central Business Register, 1999

▲ During the 1990s the graphic design company Kontrapunkt had been almost permanently employed with designing crowns for various state institutions, from the ministries to DSB. There were so many that the Danish Design Centre in 2000 published a book entitled 'Kronen på mærket' (The crown on the cake) filled with Kontrapunkt's many versions of the crown and identity programs for government institutions. Here is one page from the book with six different crowns. Notice how the Royal Danish Theatre's version is similar to a fool's cap and the Town and Housing Ministry has houses integrated in the crown motif.

The question is whether the Danish state couldn't have made do with one authorised version of the crown. As things are now, Danish citizens as well as countries abroad might wonder who has a right to use the crown and for what purpose. In the last 20 years, the various Danish governments have let the individual ministries, boards and public institutions devise their own graphic identity to distinguish themselves from each other. Whether this is a good idea depends on your point of view. Should it be clear who represents Denmark or should the different public authorities be allowed to brand themselves independently and distinguish themselves more clearly to the citizens?

AS FAR AS we know, the first town arms in Denmark was Varde's, which dates back to the early 1200s when the town was given as a dowry to Valdemar the Victorious' sister Helene when she married the German Prince Vilhelm of Lüneberg. His coat of arms was a single yellow lion on a blue background, and this is still the town arms of Varde. In the course of time, many have used the whole coat of arms or parts of it for other purposes. For example, the three towers on their own can be a symbol of Copenhagen. The concept of 'three-towered silver' is an old Copenhagen stamp of quality on silverware with a millesimal fineness of 830. The Copenhagen porcelain factory Bing & Grøndahl has, since 1895, used the three towers as their hallmark on their products, again a public act of respect for the capital.

▲ *The Copenhagen town arms is among the oldest in the country. The first time it was seen was on a seal from 1254. The arms consist of three stylised towers in the fortified medieval town and the wavy lines symbolise the waterfront it lies on.*

Town arms

Very early on, the Danish market towns began to make their own town arms. In some cases they more or less willingly took over the local nobility and feudal overlord's coat of arms. The arms of the princes were often identified with their territories. In many other cases, they designed their own town arms. And although the use of these painted coats of arms eventually ceased with the demise of chivalry, they continued rendering coats of arms in the form of a shield primarily for traditional reasons and because they had become a visual expression that was immediately recognisable.

Today the town arms are still actively used in many places in Denmark such as on signs on city halls, on official printed matter, on the municipalities' cars or cast on the city's manhole covers. Depending on the municipality's size and point of view, this symbol is more or less prevalent. After the many municipal fusions in connection with the municipality reforms in 1970 and again in 2006–7, many town arms have been redesigned and some will be gone forever when a small community merges with a larger one. And still other communities discontinued using the system of shield-shaped symbols and have a more modern trademark or logo designed.

Oddly enough, traditional heraldry is in many ways a freer form of expression than that of logos or trademarks. The heraldry is only determined by the symbols included in the coat of arms, and they must be respected when the town arms are redesigned. If it's an age-old custom to have symbols like an eagle and a tower on the town arms, they should still be included, but they can be redesigned in a new and more modern expression, if desired.

▸ The entire Copenhagen town arms is used in the logo of the publishing company Krak's. This version is from 1989 and was redesigned by Erik Ellegaard Frederiksen.

▸ In 1995 graphic designer Erik Ellegaard Frederiksen redesigned the town arms of the capital in white and blue. The same elements are included in the simplified version as in the original, but the wavy lines in particular have raised an eyebrow or two since some people think they look more like a tent canvas than waves.

In contrast to this, the logos of organisations and companies must be very precisely designed to be legally protected from plagiarism and other unlawful use. In some cases, companies, especially abroad, have used their hometown arms as the company's logo. For example, Porsche uses Stuttgart's town arms as the hood ornament on their cars.

The coat of arms as a form is not protected. Any individual or company can design their own private coat of arms that contains the graphic elements and colours they want, as long as they don't copy someone else's coat of arms. For example, the National Association for Danish Enterprise that was established in 1908 to promote the production and sale of Danish products had a logo in the shape of a shield.

The version depicted here was designed by Claus Achton Friis around the year 1958. The design is a bit odd since the main motif is Thor's hammer, which is a symbol from the pre-Christian Norse mythology while the shield originates from the Christian crusades during the age of chivalry. So there is a peculiar contradiction in the graphic elements of the logo, which, despite this, is a fine example of graphic craftsmanship.

The National Association for Danish Enterprise merged in 2002 with the Danish Trade Group and no longer exists under that name. In its time the association arranged exhibitions and made lists of Danish products, and the association's logo has always been used by manufacturers as a guarantee for consumers that the product was made in Denmark.

▲ *The logo for Landsforeningen Dansk Arbejde (The National Association for Danish Enterprise) strikes all the patriotic chords possible; the only thing missing is a crown on the top. The coat of arms is an old chivalric symbol that most Danes know from the royal coat of arms and their town arms. Thor's hammer is an old Danish-Nordic symbol and the shield is held in the colours of the Danish flag, red and white. The message is clear: be a patriot and buy Danish products.*

◀ *Here is Margrethe II's monogram on a sentry box at Amalienborg. It was designed by Professor Claus Achton Friis according to the queen's own draft.*

▶ *The graphic artists of the past such as Joakim Skovgaard and Thorvald Bindesbøll made ex libris for themselves and others. On the right is Thorvald Bindesbøll's own ex libris bookplate.*

LOGOS AND MARKS

Just as booklovers feel the need to mark their own books and therefore have an 'ex libris' designed, the craftsmen, businesses and companies also needed marks of their own. Some of the world's first manufacturers' marks were probably the potter's signature or symbol made on the bottom of ceramics when it was still wet. Much later, the goldsmiths and silversmiths followed suit by stamping their products, and then the cabinetmakers started doing so too. In some periods it was compulsory for certain professions to sign their products, and if it wasn't a law, then the guilds had rules stating that their members had to guarantee the quality by signing whatever left their workshop. These signatures could take the form of a stamp or a wax seal, such as that used by the Royal Furniture Magazine (see page 212). It is still a custom in some of the fine furniture factories that the individual craftsman signs the furniture that she/he has made, normally with a pencil mark. The porcelain painters at Royal Copenhagen still sign their work in a similar manner. This is done on the bottom of the product next to the company stamp and production number.

Apart from the tradition of coats of arms and town arms, the need eventually arose for individual companies to have their own, easily recognisable sign. Since olden times, the various professions had their own symbols indicating their profession. This is how you could tell where a cobbler lived since there was a boot hanging on the façade. And that was often the only way you could tell since the shops didn't have shop windows until much later.

This is how the original signboards arose. One of the few professions in Denmark that still uses this custom is the baker, who still hangs a golden

MONOGRAMS AND EX LIBRIS. Besides the royal coat of arms that belongs to the monarch and court, the Danish regents have long had their own more personal monograms. They consist of very fixed elements, such as the regent's first letter, which in our present Queen Margrethe's case is a capital M. Also included was the number in the name list of regents; in Queen Margrethe's case the number two. And the last thing is a new interpretation of a crown designed in the style of the time. The monogram at left was designed by Claus Achton Friis based on the queen's own draft. Commoners could also have a personal graphic identity designed.

In the late 1400s in Germany, ex libris were being made. Ex libris means 'from the library of'. These were bookplates or stamps that indicated the book's owner. Usually an artist made this little piece of graphics that also contained the person's name or initials. In the late 1800s ex libris were popular collectors' items just like other kinds of graphics such as stamps and postcards.

pretzel perpendicular to the façade. And moreover, the bakers have the time-honoured right as the only craftsmen to use the crown on their sign. But in time and especially after industrialisation, the craftsmen's guilds lost their dominance, and the individual firms needed to have their own mark or logo.

When we say that somebody made their mark, it originally meant that instead of writing their name or initials they made a mark or a symbol. These marks originate from the Middle Ages when people were illiterate and often used a little picture to sign a document or mark their personal property. Craftsmen as well as others used marks as their signature or stamp of quality when they made or sold products. This is the basis for the practice by which many companies nowadays use a mark to represent their company in every conceivable way; on stationery, signs, ads, delivery vans, uniforms etc. In many cases you can recognise a particular company's stores, cars or ads at a distance by spotting their symbol; you don't even have to be close enough to read the name. When the logo is used on the company's products you can call it a trademark, but the words trademark and logo are often used interchangeably.

The word logo comes from Greek and means word. This word is used to denote the company symbols that consist of words (like Carlsberg) or abbreviations (like SAS). These signatures can be graphically designed just as distinctly as marks and can create a unique identity for the company solely by means of their typographical treatment. And marks that only consist of a symbol are practically nonexistent (the Red Cross is one exception). In practice, a name is always connected to the mark even though one can often recognise the company by its graphic symbol alone – just think of Nike's famous 'swoosh' symbol. But even a firm like Nike has to have a special signature that goes with the symbol when necessary. For convenience the word logo is therefore often used as a collective term for every form of identity-creating graphic mark.

Designing a logo is an exceedingly demanding discipline for graphic designers, and it's not just about being a good graphic craftsman, as they work with the whole identity and soul of a company. The atmosphere that is created and the associations that customers and the public get when seeing a logo can be essential to the company's image and success. For firms that manufacture distinctive products, a good design can to some degree replace a logo. For example, Bang & Olufsen don't have to stamp their logo loud and clear on their products. But for companies that manufacture standard products like batteries, the graphic design might be the only thing that clearly distinguishes two products from each other in the store. And companies that sell services, such as phone companies, the success of the visual identity can be the difference between life and death.

Hellesen

In the early days of industrialisation, which took place in the late 1800s and early 1900s in Denmark, many new companies were established that had no connection to the old guild system. They were often based on industrial mass production and therefore had a need to make their mark on a competitive market. Sometimes the new industries and their products were based on inventions, and therefore an extra effort had to be made to alert the customers' attention to this new product. However, the new industrialists did not always have their attention focused on this

LOGO FOR THE Ministry of Culture. As an extension of the design office Kontrapunkt's mass production of crowns for various state institutions, they also designed a new identity for the Ministry of Culture in 1994. This ministry has almost always had to balance between being, on the one hand, a central state authority, and on the other hand, a representative of the artistic, dynamic and creative segment of society. In this logo the contrast between the two worlds is illustrated quite literally. It is the combination of the word 'culture' written in loose and informal handwriting, and the word 'ministry' written with capitals in an almost exaggerated classic typeface. And added to this is the relatively traditionally designed crown. The contrast is emphasised by the crown and the 'ministry' being symmetrical in relation to each other while the world 'culture' is almost carelessly added asymmetrically on the left.

important side of the business; they were often busy with the technical and manufacturing side.

Gradually, many companies got better at communicating, by, among other things, having a logo designed and everything that that entails. One example of this is the battery factory Hellesen that was established in 1887, but did not get its famous signature and frightening tiger until some years later. The company was founded when Wilhelm Hellesen (1836–92) after many experiments finally made what we today call a battery, but back then was called a dry cell. Until then, one had to use liquid-filled glass containers that certainly weren't easy to insert in a bike light. In 1887 Hellesen and Valdemar Ludvigsen opened a factory in Copenhagen. The new batteries were a huge success, and in the 1890s they were already exported to 50 countries and manufactured in factories abroad.

In the beginning, the factory's products were furnished with an ordinary black and white label on which the name Hellesen was written in a thin typeface along with the type and model number and without any frills of any kind. And many years would pass before something was seriously done about it. Not until around World War I did Hellesen begin to work with graphic designer and architect Knud V. Engelhardt. He quickly created the well-known tiger logo, although Engelhardt himself didn't design the original tiger. Who did has passed into oblivion. However, he was responsible for the very different lettering written in bold capitals with peculiar details in the signature. For example, the large S's that are shaped like lightning and the middle of the E's that looks like a light bulb.

Engelhardt redesigned the logo several times, and when he died in 1931, his employee took over. This was Gunnar Biilmann Petersen (1897–1968), who later became a professor at the Royal Academy of Fine Arts. He was an eminent illustrator and designed a new tiger for the logo. Actually he sat outside a tiger's cage at the zoo for several days so he could make the best drawing of one. The new tiger was far better than the slightly thin and pale version that Engelhardt had made. At first only the tiger was redesigned, but after a few years Biilmann Petersen also designed a new signature for the company, but it was very much based on his old mentor's. Among other things, Engelhardt's lightning S's were discredited when the runic S's of the Waffen-SS became known. But finally in about 1939, Hellesen's graphic identity was established – more than 50 years after the company had been founded.

Nonetheless the logo has become a fixed element in many Danes' consciousness; especially among older Danes the Hellesen batteries are known as 'the ones with the tiger'. The choice of a tiger for the symbol of Hellesen's products is said to be because they wanted the batteries to be associated with the 'silent and powerful burst of energy' that the big cats could muster.

Today Hellesen is an example of Danish industrial history which in its heyday in the early 1900s had more than 100,000 distributors on 60 markets all over the world. In 1959 the company was bought by Store Nordiske, and in 1972 a new battery factory was built in Thisted – on Tigervej (Tiger Street). Afterwards the brand languished for some years until it was bought by Duracell. The trademark is still the same, although the tiger doesn't look as ferocious and the lettering is very different.

GUNNAR BIILMANN PETERSEN, 1897–1968, was an architect and graphic designer who became Denmark's first professor of design. Biilmann Petersen studied at the Royal Academy of Fine Arts in Copenhagen from 1915–1922 and worked with Knud V. Engelhardt, among others. Biilmann Petersen very much embraced Engelhardt's philosophy of design and work methods that focused on the architectural approach and rational aesthetics in work assignments. Biilmann Petersen primarily designed logos (such as FDB's) and typefaces, but he also made posters and illustrations (such as the Hellesen tiger). Along with illustrator Ib Andersen, Biilmann Petersen designed the Danish banknotes from the 1950s. In 1951 he was appointed professor of industrial art at the Royal Academy of Fine Arts, School of Architecture. In 1959, industrial design was assigned its own professorship which Erik Herløw got, while Biilmann Petersen continued to head the department of industrial graphics, as graphic design was then known.

▲ *This Hellesen poster from 1937 is a hybrid. The lettering was Knud V. Engelhardt's with S's like those of the runic alphabet and little bulbs in the middle of the E's and H's. But this natural-looking tiger with shining eyes like headlights was designed by Gunnar Biilmann Petersen.*

◀ *The publishing company Gyldendal's crane evolves. The first version on the left is from 1953 and designed by Erik Ellegaard Frederiksen, then there's Austin Grandjean's design from 1975 and finally the latest version by e-Types in 2000.*

▲ *Kristian Kongstad (1867–1929) was an artist, illustrator and book craftsman and was hired as an artistic consultant by Gyldendal in 1916. In 1920 he made a rendering of Søren Gyldendal's signet from the 1770s and used the motif in his logo (top). Below is a logo designed by Frederik V. Hegel (1817–87) from around 1850 that also includes a crane.*

Animal symbolism

Animals are often used on logos, and not only for pet stores or manufacturers of dog food. Animals are often attributed positive qualities that can be used as a symbol of a company or organisation. As in the case of Hellesen's tiger it was the animal's great strength, silence and efficiency that they tried to use to market the batteries. Of course, the discount supermarket Netto chose to use a Scottie as its logo for different reasons. There is more humour and an indirect symbolism based on the prejudice that Scots are stingy, and therefore a Scottie must also be price-conscious as it sits holding its shopping basket in its teeth. In reality most of us just think the dog is cute, and we don't think about its symbolism. Since 1955 the Danish Booksellers' Association used a stylised owl designed by Erik Ellegaard Frederiksen as their logo. The point here is, of course, that the owl is traditionally seen as being a wise and clever bird that is characterised by wisdom and intelligence, and these are qualities that buyers of books and booksellers would like to be associated with.

Ever since the publishing company Gyldendal was established in 1770, it has used a crane as its logo, and that might be puzzling because what qualities does a crane have that a publishing company would want to identify with? There are at least two explanations for the use of the crane as its symbol. The first one is that the founder of the publishing company, Søren Gyldendal, had a crane on his signet ring, and that's why the bird was used in the logo. The crane is an old European symbol of care and watchfulness, and when the bird stands on one leg with a stone held in its lifted claw, the myth says that if it should fall asleep, the stone would drop and wake it up. The second explanation for the logo is perhaps more straightforward, namely that the street called Klareboderne, where the

ERIK ELLEGAARD FREDERIKSEN, 1924–97, was a prominent Danish graphic designer. Shortly after graduating as an architect he was employed as an assistant to graphic designer and architect Gunnar Biilmann Petersen from 1946–48. From 1948–50 he worked in London for the German-born book artist Jan Tschichold at Penguin Books. When he returned to Denmark in 1950, Erik Ellegaard Frederiksen worked as a freelance graphic designer and continued to do so until his death. He had lots of work that covered many facets of the trade, but logos and book designs were his primary areas. He also wrote articles, features and debate articles about design and even wrote several non-fiction books on the subject.

company moved to in 1787, lies in an old Copenhagen neighbourhood called Rosenborg. And this part of town had a crane as its hallmark, and the crane motif was embroidered on the neighbourhood pennant.

Gyldendal's logo has been modernised several times. In 1953, Erik Ellegaard Frederiksen redesigned the crane in a rather detailed version that, however, could be reproduced using only one colour. The founding year of 1770 was also included in the logo which was a negative (white crane on a coloured background) and with a thin frame around it. In 1975 it was time to simplify the crane again, and this was done by graphic designer Austin Grandjean (1930–2006), who for many years was Gyldendal's main book designer. The logo now became a positive, with the frame and year retained. Here the crane is a silhouette in contrast to Ellegaard Frederiksen's version in which one can see the bird's eye and feathers. The logo in Grandjean's version is more stylised and not particularly like a 'real' crane; this is typical of the development in this period when things were constantly simplified. Finally, in 2000 the latest version so far of the crane was designed by the graphic design office e-Types. They removed the year, made the frame thicker in the line and narrower and reintroduced some of the details on the bird and the claw and stone have also been simplified. The latest version is a little more robust in its lines than Grandjean's crane so it can better stand reproduction and will be clearer in even small versions in print and electronic media.

IDENTITY

Many companies invest large sums in the design of their identity to distinguish themselves from their competitors. And if they take a professional approach, then a logo isn't something you 'just have to have because everybody else does'. Graphic identity programs, which the whole system of logo, stationery, signs etc. are also called, must express the company's core values. Naturally this has to be done so that customers as well as employees can clearly see what the company's core values are. For example, it's not good communication when a toy store has a sign that looks like a bank's, and the opposite could be just as disastrous. If you look at bank logos, you'll notice that many of them are blue since it is considered a slightly conservative colour that also inspires confidence, and when people are entrusting their money to a company, confidence is essential.

Another aspect of identity design is that the logo shouldn't be too smart and trendy, especially if it's to be used for more than a couple of years. The more modern you try to be, the more likely your company logo will appear outdated in a few years. This does not mean that a good logo doesn't need to be modernised and tightened up every now and then. There are good examples of companies that have kept their original identity programs for many years, and regularly send them in for a checkup at the graphic designer's or at a design bureau. Gyldendal's logo is a good example of this.

The design of a company identity sometimes starts with something as simple as finding a good name for the company. An example of this was when the Dansk Mobil Telefon (Danish Mobile Telephone) began its existence in Denmark. At first the challenge was to design a new logo, but as the graphic design firm Linneballe Designers got deeper into the project, they realised that they also had to find out under what name Dansk Mobil Telefon was to do business. The acronym DMT was very anonymous and risked being mistaken for TDC (a rival company). Instead of competing with

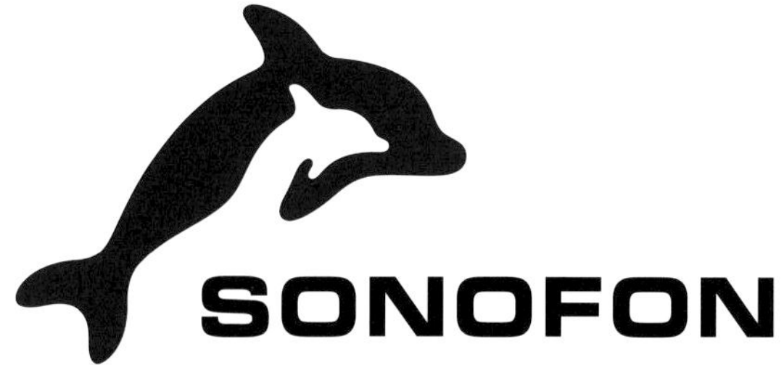

◂ *Sonofon is a word that was developed together with the leaping dolphins as the identity for the second-largest mobile phone company in Denmark. The dolphin is good at communicating with the help of sound waves, and this association was used when Linneballe Designers, now Scandinavian Branding, designed the name and logo. The soft lines and values in the picture of the dolphins were a creative contrast to the angular and technical typeface. On the one hand, Sonofon creates good communication between people – the soft values. On the other hand, a competent system is needed to back it up – the technical values.*

the previously state-owned TDC's well-established reputation, it would be better to be the naughty boy in the class that conducted business in a new and different way. The design office quickly honed in on associations to the animal kingdom, for example, drawings were made of the fire-bellied toad (in Danish 'a bell toad') since one of the owners of the new company was the American company Bell South, but toads and telephony didn't seem to go together.

They continued to think along the lines of animal logos, like grasshoppers that also communicate over long distances. In that case the name would have been Unison, but because many people don't like insects and other creepy crawlers, the idea was given up. The idea of a flock of birds and the name Symfon also had to be dropped since the name was already taken by another company. Finally they settled on the name Sonofon and a logo consisting of two dolphins. The dolphin is an intelligent and likeable animal that is known to communicate with high sounds that the human ear can't detect. The logo had to have two dolphins since two are needed to communicate. The word Sonofon consists of sono, which means 'something with sound and tone' and fon, which is used in telephone and means 'speech sound' or 'loudness'. In any case, the name Sonofon sounded good. The big blue dolphin and its little partner in the logo have a strong graphic expression, and together with the characteristically modern signature it became one of the best known logos of the 1990s.

The development of Sonofon's identity took place at the beginning of the 1990s. In 2005, Sonofon merged with the internet company Cybercity, and although the name Sonofon is still an independent brand, the dolphin logo has been replaced by a more anonymous amoebic symbol made by the English design firm Wolff Olins. There used to be a connection between the meaning of the word Sonofon and the dolphin logo, but now it's lost with the new logo. Graphically the new identity doesn't seem to be a step forward either. But this development is typical of the many acquisitions and mergers that have taken place in the telecom industry in the last 10–15 years. Good, incorporated brands are replaced by new ones resulting in a huge loss of goodwill and subsequent high expenses upon launching new names and logos on the market.

Whereas the private companies' development of logos was basically inspired by the coats of arms and heraldry of the Middle Ages, much time passed before the public sector began to develop their town arms into a more modern form of communication and branding. State and municipal authorities as well as various public works and organisations saw themselves as a cut above this kind of thing. Identity programs were for firms that competed on market terms and had to advertise. The local gasworks or the municipal road administration didn't have to do that.

This attitude was gradually replaced by the understanding that public institutions also had to make themselves visible in the consciousness of the citizens as a part of their service. It is also thought-provoking that the companies in the public sector who first started branding themselves were the ones who competed most with other suppliers. The wave of privatisation that started in England during Thatcherism in the 1980s and subsequently came to Denmark also moved this development forward. State-owned companies like the postal service, the telephone companies, the Danish State Railways and others had to be made ready to be sold, which also included from a graphic point of view.

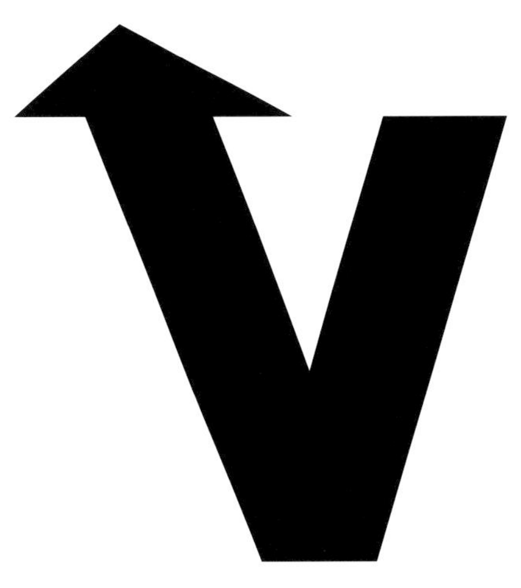

THE DANISH LIBERAL PARTY (called 'Venstre' in Danish) had its logo redesigned several times, and for some years the letter V, which is also the party's symbol on electoral lists, had an arrow pointing upwards. To some Danes it was a bit confusing (or affirmative?) that the arrow pointed backwards seen from the direction you read in. If the symbol was to be seen as a growth curve that points towards progress and economic growth, which is a natural conclusion, then the arrow should surely have been on the right side of the V? Graphic designer Erik Ellegaard Frederiksen designed the logo with the backward pointing arrow that was used until 2001. Graphic designer Finn Nygaard has designed the latest logo for the party without moving the arrow to the other side. Instead he made the V look more like a checkmark like when you check something off on a list because now it's okay. The logo and the signature are graphically strong which is something many other parties and political organisations could learn from.

Among the public companies that are in close competition with the private firms every day are the energy suppliers. In principle, many Danes can choose between gas, electricity, district heating or heating oil to heat their homes. In practice, most consumers don't have such a wide choice, and therefore many wrinkle their nose when they see large, public energy companies spending huge amounts on image advertisements and similar initiatives. It's very amusing to see the Great Belt Bridge spend astronomical sums on TV commercials. How much competition do they actually have from the ferry company Mols-Linien? For the many commuters that would rather see a cut in the bridge toll, money spent on branding can seem offensive. So it can become a balancing act when public actors profile their company and services.

One of the ways for old state or municipal services to signal innovation and modernisation is to have a new graphic identity designed. And making this new identity into a more visible event can be done by arranging a design competition. This was what Hovedstadens Trafikselskab (HT: the Greater Copenhagen Transport Authority) did in 1985. The result of the process was that the old HT logo, which mostly looked like a crude coat of arms in yellow and black, was substituted by a new logo where the capital letters H and T were merged in one continuous line. The letters HT were written in italics, and at the same time the figure looked like a route through the city streets. The first-prize winners were graphic designers Peter Hiort and Janne Iglsø Andersen, and their logo still adorns buses, signs, tickets, etc.

▾ *In the 1985 book called 'The Spirit of a Trademark' from the Danish Design Centre, you can see two pages about the different ways of designing a logo for HT (The Greater Copenhagen Transport Authority). One page lists the stringent proposals where the letters H and T look like streets or a route through town. The winning proposal is the upper left one whose form was slightly changed into the final one (the lines were made thicker). On the opposite page are some of the more crazy and humorous proposals that self-evidently weren't chosen since HT is a much too 'serious' organisation.*

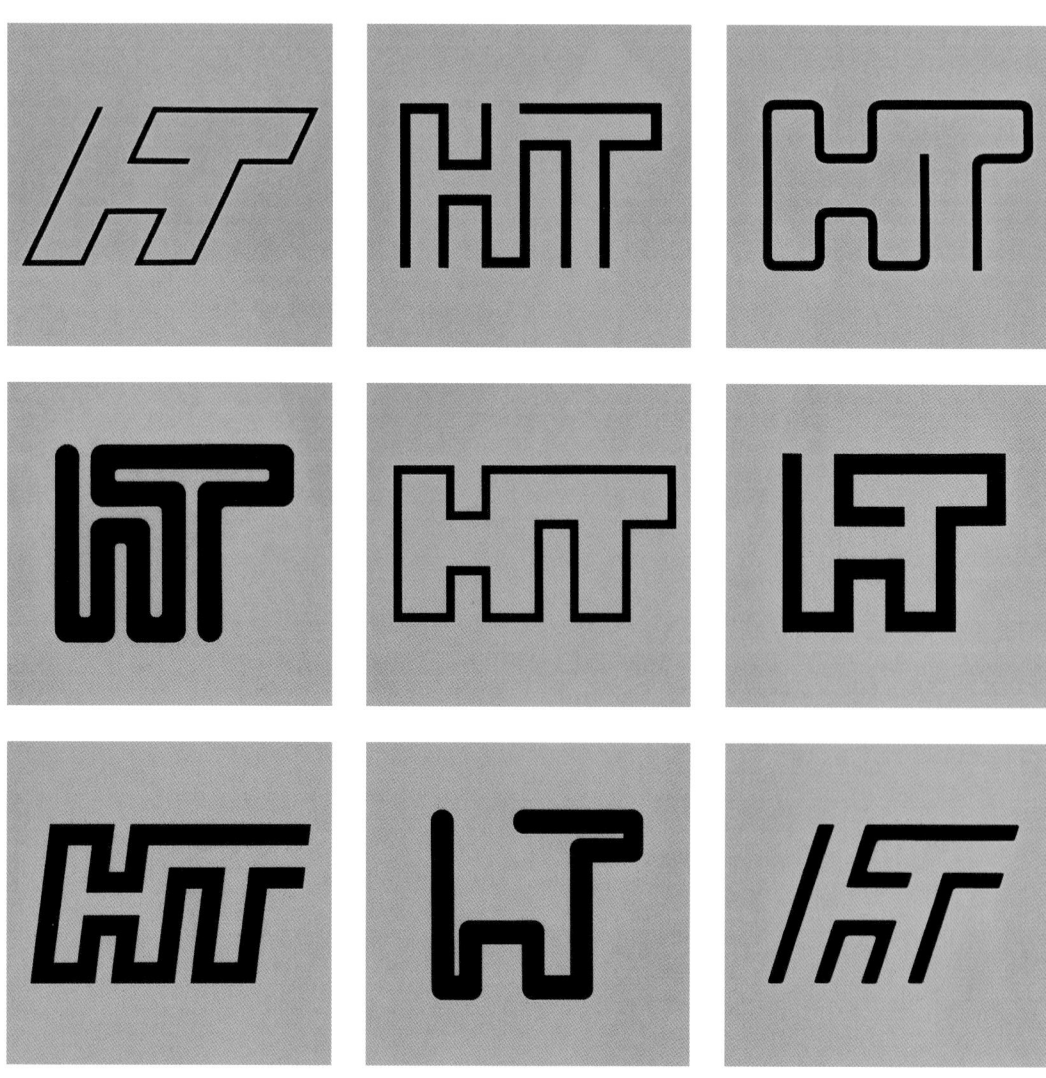

HT

▾ The logo of the General Workers' Union in Denmark (SiD) from 1996 was the result of a large design competition which the design office Etcetera won. In 2005, the men from SiD and the women from the Women Workers' Union were joined in the United Federation of Danish Workers, known as 3F, so once again a new design had to be made. The result was that the graphically interesting SiD logo from 1996 was substituted by a new and not as strong graphic element designed by the Datagraf company.

The competition fetched 2,222 proposals from near and far, from professionals and interested citizens. The great interest in the competition surprised the organisers. This was partly due to the high prize money (100,000 kroner for first prize, and 75,000 kroner to be distributed among the second- and third-prize winners), and partly due to the great interest taken by professionals and laymen in putting their mark on such a noticeable public service. The results of the competition are nicely documented in a little book that includes 300 of the proposals and was published by the Danish Design Centre. The proposals shown here are categorised according to type, so that the proposals that more or less use the same motif and form as the winner are shown on the same page. Correspondingly, the proposals that use the wheel as their inspiration are put together etc. The book is both an interesting documentation of the many ways to approach the task and an interesting insight into the way a jury of professionals thought when picking a winner, an approach that was typical of the time.

In the same way that the public authorities were slow to realise the need for modern, graphic communication, many large and small organisations have had a safe and stable existence by not jumping on the design bandwagon. Trade unions in particular have for a long time had a hard time modernising their visual signals. If you look at the many trade union banners and the logos embroidered on them, you'll clearly see that they are from a very different time. The classic mark for a trade union in the traditional crafts and industrial professions seems to have got its artistic idiom from the heraldry and coats of arms of the past. The large federations of trade unions have, however, supplemented the old symbols with new logos, yet without using groundbreaking graphic design. One of the good exceptions

Kræftens Bekæmpelse

THE DANISH CANCER SOCIETY's red, abstract, bow logo is the organisation's third logo. It was designed in 1977 and is still used, and there is no reason to change it since the majority of the population (88 %) recognises it. The logo is so distinctive and pure in style that it can stand alone without lettering and still be recognised. In 1980 is was awarded the Danish Design Centre's prize for good graphic design, the so-called IG prize. On the left is the old logo with St. George beheading the cancerous dragon.

is the Danish Metalworkers' Union's stylised anvil logo, which Jette Löfvall designed in 1973, and it is still used.

In 1996, the General Workers' Union in Denmark (SiD) arranged a design competition for a new graphic identity to replace the old logo from the 1970s. This was on the occasion of SiD's 100th anniversary, although the logo wasn't meant to reflect this directly since it would have a longer lifespan. More than 1100 proposals were submitted to the jury that primarily consisted of graphic designers and SiD's union president. As so often when arranging a competition of this kind, the competition rules listed a number of requirements of the design, for example that it should work well in a small or large size while remaining recognisable. In addition the logo should be able to be reproduced in both a positive and negative version, and if it was designed in colour, it should also be able to be reproduced in black and white.

The competition was won by the graphic design office Etcetera that had made a very simple but also surprising logo. On the one hand, it was a traditional typographic solution with the letters in a modern typeface. On the other hand, the surprising thing was the letter S was laid down, and thus there was graphic tension in the logo. Now it could be used horizontally and vertically. In the horizontal version the large S resembled the infinity sign, and so it signalled stability and 'eternal values'. But in a vertical position the logo looked a bit like a coat of arms, and now the heraldic symbolism on the red banners wasn't so far fetched. In addition there was some humour, self-irony and thoughtfulness in the design, which perhaps don't characterise the trade unions very much.

The bow against cancer

A society that fights cancer and supports patients and their relatives can have a hard time deciding how their cause should be expressed graphically in a logo. Cancer is not clear-cut, much less a very visible disease, and the fight against it isn't easy to symbolise. The Danish Cancer Society was established in 1928, and since then they have chosen several different ways, each of which are interesting, to illustrate cancer and the fight against it. In the beginning the disease was seen as a monster that had to be fought by a strong person. This was quite literally illustrated by a logo that represented St. George whose raised sword was ready to strike the dragon (above left). Later, and until 1977, the society had another logo in the form of a red bow with the text 'The fight against cancer'. This logo was meant to remind members and others to support the cause, just like tying a bow on your index finger.

In the mid-1970s, the shape of the bow inspired the logo that the Danish Cancer Society still uses. It was designed by graphic designer Rolf Lagersson and the design office Plan Design that simplified the old logo into a more abstract symbol for the society. It's a very characteristic and easily recognisable symbol, albeit it's connection to the fight against cancer isn't blatantly clear. The logo could only represent the Danish Cancer Society by being publicised a lot. This was apparently successful since 88 % of the Danish population recognises it. This a very high recognition value compared to other logos. Graphically you can see it as a stylised red bow that, like the latest SiD logo, trades on the mathematical symbol for infinity. However, the logo is so abstract that many people probably don't notice the bow, but it doesn't really matter when it's as easily recognisable as it is.

CONTROL OR FREEDOM? A large company that has many different products spread over many divisions can find it necessary to use design to help its employees, customers and suppliers to orientate themselves in the organisation. Therefore it can be an advantage to have a special type of design manual that gives each individual line in the company its own identity. A corporation like Coloplast has a handful of primary business areas such as ostomy, incontinence, wound treatment and skin care. Each of these divisions have their own colour that they use on printed matter, packaging and their homepage, but otherwise they use the central elements of the corporation's design, such as the logo and typeface. In this way both the employees and outsiders can quickly see who they're dealing with, and yet there is no doubt that they're still a part of Coloplast.

In a small company you don't have to divide the organisation into systems like this. However, other considerations can be important. A design office is full of inventive individuals, many of whom feel the need to assert themselves. How can this be done when the company also needs to keep track of the signals it sends? In the early 1990s, the design company Kontrapunkt found a system that simultaneously ensures a consistent branding and gives the

BRANDING

Logos and other traditional graphic expressions aren't the only things that give a company identity, although they have a great significance. Other factors also play a role when we form an impression of a company and its products. For example, this can also be smells and sounds. One of the more peculiar examples of this is the airline Air France. They have had a special aroma made that they use in every room and area where their customers and passengers congregate; in the planes, waiting rooms and sales offices. In this way, they create an extra experience that their passengers can recognise when flying Air France. Of course, this aroma should be pleasant to the vast majority of people since it would otherwise backfire. The same consideration applies to automobile manufacturers. It's no use that their new cars interiors are beautiful and durable if they have an awful smell. And the same thing applies to sounds. It is said that car doors on a Mercedes, for example, make a special sound when you close them, and that the factory has worked hard and single-mindedly to get just the right quality of sound.

When companies have a clear strategy for the products and services they want to supply and are determined to live up to this and communicate it to their customers, employees and the outside world, they're well on their way to branding themselves. In principle, branding is a kind of promise that the company gives its customers and other working partners that they will set certain standards and do everything to live up to them. Basically, branding is about trust, and design can be used on many levels to build up this trust. The word branding comes from American English and originates from the cattle farmers' branding of cattle so they could tell their cattle from the neighbouring farm's. This meaning has been symbolically transferred to today's companies, but the sense is still the same: branding is a combination of symbols and content that helps to identify the company and its products.

Branding is usually expressed through a number of elements that range from the choice of name and design of the logo, products, packaging, colours and much more. For instance, the airline SAS under the leadership of Jan Carlsson in the 1980s decided to paint all their aeroplanes white in addition to having designed a new logo which would give them a lighter and simpler appearance. But branding can begin in a company with the way the phone is answered. All of this contributes to the identity of the company and the brand. If a company is good at branding itself and delivering the goods in accordance with the promises that lie in the branding, the customers will have a good experience and they will be more interested in dealing with the company and paying a higher price for their products.

The Green Bike Messengers

Branding often has an ethical aspect which is increasingly an important part of the signals that a modern company sends, namely that it isn't only interested in making money, but it's also willing to consider the customers, society and the environment. If these considerations become a part of the collective business concept, they can be an important part of the company's branding. The organic fruit and vegetable supplier Aarstiderne (see the Seasons, p. 546) is one of the new and more distinctive examples of this. Another example is the Green Bike Messengers in Copenhagen. They started their bike messenger service in 1988 when four students, who were inspired by the bike messengers in New York City, decided to reintroduce the old delivery bikes called 'swayers' into the Copenhagen

employees the freedom to act. The solution was a modular program of printed matter in which the only fixed elements were the name and location of the firm. The rest was self-adhesive labels that the individual employee could use. Stationery and business cards were plain and basic; the rest was a DIY system of names, titles etc. in Danish or English, depending on the recipient.

▲ *The different divisions at Coloplast each have their own colour, and at the same time they emphasise that they are part of a whole.*

◂ *In the beginning, the people behind the Green Bike Messengers were in charge of the design of the graphic identity and uniforms and bags. From the start they were very conscious of their image, for example, they had the professional cyclist Hans-Henrik Ørsted take the first trip. In 1997 they were one of the first clients of the design and advertising bureau Raffinaderiet (The Refinery), which made an image brochure that this picture is from.*

streetscape. They hired seven messengers, but on their first day they only had 21 trips, and that wasn't nearly enough to keep all the messengers occupied. But these four guys had caught the spirit of the times, and soon it became fashionable for the advertising agencies and design bureaus to use the eco-friendly messengers and 'call one of the greens'.

Gradually it became a decent business, and for a number of years it was fashionable and trendy for young people to be a bike messenger and thus get into shape instead of sitting on their behinds as a taxi driver in a Mercedes. The branding of the Green Bike Messengers became gradually more systematic with a specially designed neon green cycling outfit, matching backpack and a microphone clipped on to one of the shoulder straps. In this way the product became the brand, and by cleverly knowing how to market themselves, the company started making advertising campaigns that were directed at the receptionists who were the messengers' primary customer contact persons. At their high point the Green Bike Messengers had 120 messengers in Copenhagen, and in 1997 they opened a branch in Aarhus, and a few years later one in Odense. At the same time they bought up some of the other messenger services that had emerged in Denmark in the wake of the Green's success, such as Den Blå Kurer (the Blue Courier) and Postrytterne (the Mail Riders).

At one point the need arose to be able to offer customers transport over long distances. But investing in and maintaining cars would compromise the eco-friendly concept that the Green's had branded so well. So, initially, they bought electric cars to supplement the bike messengers. They were painted in the same green colour, and in large letters on the cars it said that they were 'clean' transport. However, problems in running them and their short range made the company finally bite the bullet and switch to ordinary gasoline-powered vans. Because the four founders had different views on the development of the business, the Green Bike Messengers was taken over in 2001 by a large courier service called Box Delivery, so now the company is called 'Box Green Bike Messengers'. Similar bike messenger services started in the rest of Scandinavia as well. Many of them are now in the joint Box corporation, so today there are more than 1000 green Box messengers in 17 cities in Denmark, Norway and Sweden.

DANSKE STATSBANER

◂ The symbol of the winged wheel is originally German and dates to about 1850. DSB used it for the first time on the Limfjord bridge in 1879. The logo here is from 1887, but it was redesigned many times throughout the years. In 1972 under chief designer Jens Nielsen it was given up in favour of using only letters as shown on the opposite page. In 1998 the winged wheel was back in favour, below, but in a radically new form, which the design office Kontrapunkt had designed. The question is whether it has become too abstract a symbol for many people to see it as a wheel with wings.

▸ A page from DSB's large design manual from 1972. It describes in detail how all the moving material on roads and tracks, the so-called livery, should be painted, and where the logo should be placed.

DESIGN MANUAL

In order for large companies to coordinate their efforts regarding design, it's become increasingly common to have a so-called design manual made. This is usually a large book or binder that today might just as well exist in the form of a CD-ROM or lie on the company's intranet. In the design manual all the employees can see the design standards used by the company. This includes everything from what typeface and size of type to use for writing letters to what colour the company's official vehicles should be painted. Depending on what the company does and how ambitious they were when the manual was made, there can also be standards for signposting in the company, the quality of paper as well as the design of packaging and the width of the margin in printed matter. Often the design manual is made by company appointees in collaboration with an external design bureau.

One of the first companies in Denmark to throw itself seriously into getting a design manual made was the Danish State Railways (DSB). In 1971, DSB hired architect Jens Nielsen as their first chief designer, and the same year work was started to develop a comprehensive design program. As Director General Poul Hjelt wrote in the preface of the subsequent design manual: 'First of all, it has great commercial value that DSB presents itself as a modern and well-run business. Secondly, there is a need to rationalise, simplify and standardise the elements that create the company's face and environment. In both cases, planning has economic effects – partly in increased sales and partly in savings ... in a large company like DSB it is necessary to subject every aspect of design to collective planning.'

At that time, DSB's design manual was already a bulky ring binder that among many things determined exactly where the company's new logo should be placed in the corner of a Danish flag of the swallow-tailed type. The first manual took three years to make, and in the meantime DSB's graphic design was totally renewed. The old winged wheel was dropped and replaced by a new and greatly simplified logo where only the abbreviation DSB was written in a modern Helvetica typeface. The old crimson colour of the trains was changed to a brighter red colour, and this is how things were changed and tightened up throughout the organisation. Naturally all the changes couldn't happen from one day to the next; redesigning stations in particular and repainting all the transport material had to take place gradually when there was time and money.

The new program was developed under the leadership of Jens Nielsen in collaboration with, among others, graphic designers Niels Hartmann and Find Rinds as well as architect Niels Kryger. Regarding the colour scheme, artist Gunnar Aagaard Andersen and architect Svend Limkilde were included in the work, while architect Jens Møller-Jensen developed a modular sign system for DSB, which cost about a fourth of the existing signs. Using a ring binder for the design manual was deliberate since extensions and changes would gradually come, and then they were easy to insert into the correct place. The new company design steadily trickled through the organisation and also into new areas, such as new uniforms for the personnel and the interiors of ferries and passenger cars. This design manual was used until 1998 when Jens Nielsen's successor, architect Pia Bech Mathiesen, replaced it with a brand new design line. Among other things, the old winged wheel was back in favour, and a new special typeface was made by the design company Kontrapunkt.

Begrebet liberi omfatter den udvendige bemaling m v af tog, automobiler, skibe og andet materiel i DSB.

Det er af stor betydning for virksomhedens ansigt, at disse ting fremtræder på en tiltalende måde, og at de har et ensartet præg. Både det umiddelbare indtryk og den senere genkendelse skal være med til at opbygge billedet af DSB som en effektiv, landsdækkende transport-organisation, hvor man end møder virksomheden.

Samtidig skal liberiprogrammet så vidt muligt tjene til vejledning af kunderne, og til rationalisering af virksomhedens eget arbejde med planlægning og udførelse af materiellets udvendige bemaling.

Disse krav ligger til grund for udformningen af liberiprogrammet som benyttes ved al bemaling m v af DSB materiel.

Programmet er baseret på design-programmets grundelementer. Det omfatter placeringsmoduler, grafiske moduler, farvenormer og redaktionelle normer.

En konsekvent anvendelse af designprogrammets grundelementer er en forudsætning for, at DSB kan præsentere sig som en velordnet og velsoigneret virksomhed overalt.

DSB rød er virksomhedens kendingsfarve sammen med sort og hvid. Alt materiel til persontransport, samt førerhuse o lign er DSB røde. Maskinvæsen kendetegnes ved sort bemaling.

Materiel til godstransport kan være DSB brunt, hvidt eller sort. Ejere og faste lejere af vogne m v kan bemale deres materiel i egne firmafarver.

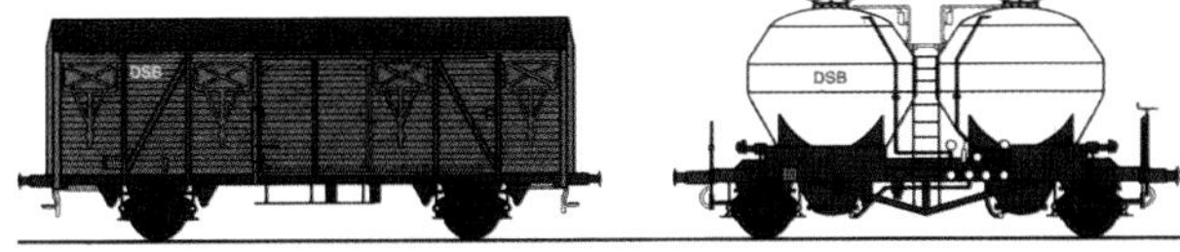

Entreprenørmateriel er DSB gult med sort påskrift.

◂ *The large Jelling stone has three sides (see page 458–9) and one of them has a runic inscription that says: 'King Haraldr ordered this monument made in memory of Gormr, his father, and in memory of Thyrvé, his mother; that Haraldr who won for himself all of Denmark and Norway and made the Danes Christian.' The Harold that ordered the stone is Harold Bluetooth, who also had the four circular forts built (see page 58). The lettering on this stone has a better design than most of the other runic inscriptions in Denmark. For example, it's the only stone in Denmark where the lines of the text are horizontal, and something as modern as spaces between the lines is used. Yet compared to the beautiful images on the stone the lettering is somewhat thin and irregularly designed.*

THE DESIGN OF LETTERING/WRITING

In Denmark, the runes were the first real writing we know of, and they began to appear around the year 300 AD. We mostly know of runes from those carved in stone, but they were also frequently carved on tools and ceremonial articles, such as those found on the famous Golden Horns. The inspiration for the runes was a Mediterranean language, most likely Latin. It is the first alphabetic writing that reached our neck of the woods, and it's impossible to say where in Europe it got its final form, but it was possibly in the Nordic area. In Scandinavia the runes were used for over 1000 years. The runic alphabet is also called futhark after the first character letters of the alphabet ('th' is one character in this system). Almost all the runes have a vertical stave and some diagonal cross lines. All the characters in the alphabet consisted of straight lines which made it easier to carve or hit them into the stone.

In the beginning, one could write in the direction one wanted, from right to left or vice versa, and the rune writer could start at the bottom of the stone and work his way up; whatever worked best. Later the 'right-oriented' runes were the most common. They didn't use spaces between the words like we do, but it became common to use one or more dots as a sign of separation between words or groups of words.

The futhark alphabet consisted of 24 characters and has roughly the same letters as the Latin alphabet although the characters were very different. Some time around 640 AD, a type of language reform took place and these first runes were replaced by a younger futhark. This contained only 16 characters, many of which were ambiguous, so that the rune for the letter I also represented the sounds E and J, and the K rune was both a K and a G. Thus the runes became both easier to write but harder to read for the few people that could read at all.

The Danish runes that were written around the year 700 AD were often memorial stones, but letters and other more everyday texts were also written on pieces of wood and parchment. When Christianity was introduced, the runes were replaced by the Latin alphabet. In Denmark the two types of writing existed concurrently until the Latin one won out. Runic writing was in many ways a rather primitive design, especially compared to the sophisticated typefaces we have today. The thin lines that were cut into rather uneven stone or carved into materials like wood or bone are often not easy to read. Traditionally there wasn't any space between the lines or between the words, as mentioned before, so one's main impression is that it's quite cramped. And even runes written on parchment aren't very legible, among other things because of the lack of variation in the form of the letters and their thickness.

One could object by saying that everything is difficult at first, and establishing a script culture takes a long time. Seen in that light, criticism that is based on practical demands for reader-friendliness may seem a bit harsh. On the other hand, the Vikings made the world's most advanced ships at the same time, so we are not talking about an underdeveloped society as regards technology or craftsmanship. And at this point in history, the Romans had carved some of the most beautiful and reader-friendly texts in marble for hundreds of years. The conclusion must be that at the time when runes were being carved in the far north, not many of the Danes concerned themselves with academic studies, and instead were content to sail off and conquer the world.

▸ *Here are two examples of Gothic script in book print. Notice how back then they used more different sizes of type on the page than we would today. The most important information is naturally in the largest type. Perhaps this was just a way of making a page look more varied.*

The book on the left is entitled: 'Thoughts about abundance and its effects by Christian Sommerfeldt, corresponding member of the Royal Rural Household Society, Sorøe, 1772. Printed by Jonas Lindgren's Widow.'

On the right: 'Former Count and Royal Danish Privy Council Cabinet Minister Johann Friderich Struensee's story of conversion as well as his own description of the way in which he came to change his way of thinking as regards religion. Seen through the press by D. Balthasar Münter. Translated from the German. Copenhagen, printed by Nicolaus Møller, by appointment book printer to HM the King. 1772.'

Tanker

om

Overdaadighed

og dens

Virkninger.

ved

Christian Sommerfeldt,

Correspondende Medlem i det Kongelige Landhusholdings-Selskab.

Sorøe, 1772.

Trykt hos Jonas Lindgrens Enke.

Forrige

Greve

og Kongelig Danske Geheime

Cabinetsminister

Johann Friderich Struensees

Omvendelses-Historie,

tilligemed

hans egenhændige Efterretning

om Maaden, hvorledes han er kommen til Forandring i sin Tænkemaade, i Hensigt til Religionen.

Til Trykken befordret

af

D. Balthasar Münter.

Oversat af Tydsk.

Kiøbenhavn,

Trykt hos Nicolaus Møller, Kongl. Hof-Bogtrykker.

1772.

Towards more modern typefaces

The alphabets that in time replaced the runes were partly the Latin alphabet based on the old Roman alphabet, and partly the later Gothic alphabet. The antique Roman scripts were called majuscule, where only capital letters of the same height were used. Afterwards came the minuscule letters that were only lowercase letters. This alphabet roughly corresponds to what we use today where some letters have ascenders and descenders. For example, a small 'a' has neither an ascender nor a descender, but 'b' has an ascender and 'g' has a descender. The minuscule script dominated the development of the Latin script in southern and western Europe from the end of the year 200 AD. From about the year 800 the so-called Carolingian minuscule was developed and for a period of time it was the prevailing script. It is characterised by rounded letters that are separate and regular.

From the beginning of the 12th century the Gothic script was developed, and it was to some degree based on the Carolingian minuscule. Gothic script was very common in the Middle Ages. It emerged in northern France and was given the name because it has shapes that are similar to those found in Gothic architecture that also emerged at the time (the style is characterised by windows with pointed arches, for example). However, it was given this name by posterity since the Italians during the Renaissance found it ugly and barbaric. The Gothic script is also called 'fracture' among typographers. The Italian humanists preferred the Latin script and during the Renaissance they went back to the Carolingian minuscule, which they erroneously thought was an antique script. This script gradually gained a footing in the 1500s, and ever since the minuscules have been the lowercase letters in our script system.

The Gothic script lasted for a long time in Northern Europe; in Denmark as 'Danish script' and in the German-speaking countries as 'deutsche Schrift'. Although for practical handwriting one could use a more common cursive that was easier to both read and write, the Gothic letters were the dominant printing script in Denmark for hundreds of years. In 1875, Gothic handwriting was no longer taught in the Danish schools, but up until the 1930s it was customary to teach Danish schoolchildren to read the Gothic script. In this way Denmark was under German influence for a long time, while in southern Europe, England and Holland they developed much more legible Antiqua scripts. The word Antiqua means 'the old letter', and ever since it ahs bedome the most common typeface. It was a kind of fusion script where Roman capitals and the lowercase letters from the Carolingian minuscule were combined. Today the word Antiqua is used for scripts where the letters have feet or serifs, as they're also called.

DANISH SCRIPT DESIGN

The long and the short of it is that the Danes used the stiff, German-inspired Gothic script for a surprisingly long time. Unlike the English and Dutch in particular, the Danes didn't design independent scripts until the beginning of the 1900s. Danish script designers did not enter the scene until the Danes had extricated themselves from the German influence.

In the beginning it was mostly architects who were interested in graphic design as regards the typeface, and they were greatly inspired by the English typeface tradition in particular. Furthermore, around the year 1900 they were very much influenced by the Art Nouveau style that in England was called 'Arts and Crafts', in France 'Art Nouveau' and in Germany 'Jugend'.

ANTIQUA SCRIPTS ARE still designed today even though the origin of the script goes back to the Renaissance. The Danish graphic designer Poul Søgren designed the typeface Jante Antiqua in 1992 to have a classic typeface that worked with the new digital production process. For example, the minuscules or lowercase letters are a bit taller and a little more open in order to create a calm text image and to increase legibility. Poul Søgren is a graduate of the Graphic Arts Institute of Denmark and has worked with type design for the large graphic company Purup Prepress. In 1994 Jante Antiqua got the Danish Design Centre's IG prise for graphic design.

ABCDEFGHIJK
LMNOPQRSTU
VWXYZÆØÅ
abcdefghijk
lmnopqrstu
vwxyzæøå
1234567890
$&£*(.,:;)?!

ABCDEFGHIJK
LMNOPQRSTU
VWXYZÆØÅ
abcdefghijk
lmnopqrstu
vwxyzæøå
1234567890
$&£(.,:;)?!*

▲ *Jante Antiqua Bold*

▲ *Jante Antiqua Regular Italic*

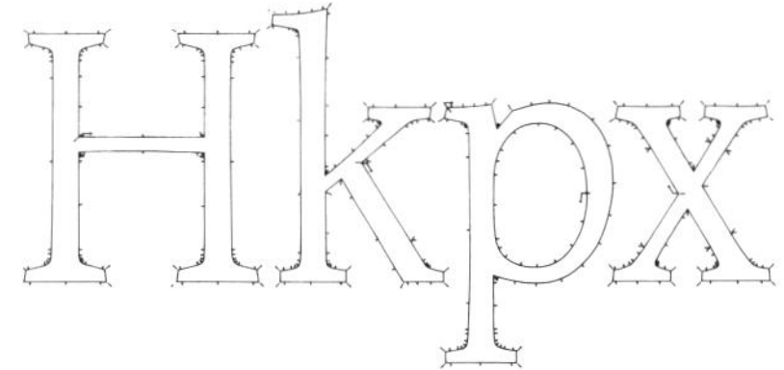

JANTE ANTIQUA WAS the first Danish designed typeface that was especially made to be used in the digital production process. This means that it is a typeface that takes advantage of the benefits of laser technology. Among other things, more of the fine details of the design of the letters can now be rendered in the reproduction and printing process. The new font Capitolium, which the newspaper 'The Politiken' began to use as its body typeface on October 1, 2006, is also an example of this.

When a typeface is designed today, it is no longer done by a graphic designer writing the letters in ink and using a scalpel or correction fluid to reduce the thickness of a line. Now most of the design work is done digitally, and the type is constructed using vector graphics. On the left is a draft of Jante Antiqua. The ticks on the letters are like digital handles that the designer can use to adjust the form of the letters. It corresponds somewhat to the working drawings used in other professions.

One of the first Danes to work with typefaces in this winding and organic style was Thorvald Bindesbøll, and the most well-known result of his efforts was the Carlsberg logo from 1904, which is still used, and the bottle label for the brewery's pilsner beer Hof (see page 524). The design of a whole typeface in a modern design first began with Knud V. Engelhardt's signposting typeface for the Danish section of the Baltic Exhibition in Malmö, Sweden in 1914. This typeface was without serifs (sans serif), and therefore it is called a grotesque typeface. It was designed in Engelhardt's traditional robust style with a hint of inspiration from Art Nouveau, and it resembles the typeface used on the street signs he designed for Gentofte Municipality some years later (see page 445). The grotesque typefaces are a product of the new modern points of view that state that everything superfluous must be done away with. However, in the early 1800s some English type designers had already designed sans serif typefaces, though they weren't popular at the time. Yet the German design school Bauhaus used these typefaces since they were very much symbols of the modernism they subscribed to. Bauhaus even went so far as to use only lowercase letters since it made the text more uniform and beautiful. The fact that this made it much less legible didn't matter much to them.

Far into the 20th century Danish type design was a speciality of architects. Not until later did graphic designers from the schools of arts and crafts and the Graphic Arts Institute of Denmark begin to work within this discipline. After Engelhardt, Gunnar Biilmann Petersen carried on the tradition of type designing for signs and other purposes. Biilmann Petersen was actually Denmark's first professor of design when he was given the professorship in 1951 in the Department for Industrial Art at the Royal Academy of Fine Arts in Copenhagen. Kaare Klint, as head of the Furniture School, had been 'only' associate professor, and when he was appointed professor in 1944 it was in architecture. Biilmann's department stressed graphic design although the students were also assigned other tasks such as designing lamps, radios and buses. A separate department for industrial design was not established until 1959 when Erik Herløw, who had taught under Biilmann, was made professor of the new department of industrial design.

Besides working at the Royal Academy, Gunnar Biilmann Petersen had many assignments in all types of graphic design including type design. Particularly in the beginning of his career he owed a great deal to Engelhardt from a professional point of view. Several of Biilmann's early typefaces bear a distinct mark of the influence that Engelhardt had on the entire design milieu in the period up until his death in 1931. Biilmann carried on the robust style of designing solid typefaces with rounded corners and relatively wide letters. His typeface for labels for the company P. Rønning & Gjerløff, which was the result of a design competition that Biilmann won, is clearly a sophisticated version of Engelhardt's typeface from 1914. In the jury's statement when awarding first prize in 1932 it said, 'like the most beautiful block letters, easy to read and easy to make. For writing as well as painting with Rønning's ink, skiltol and dekanol.'

Type design is a special discipline among graphic designers, and designing a complete typeface is considered to be one of the most demanding tasks. In a way, graphic designers feel the same way about type design as furniture designers feel about designing a chair, it is the pinnacle of disciplines in their field. Today there are thousands of active fonts on the market that are used by newspapers, magazines, publishing companies, companies and graphic designers. Some of these fonts are designed for

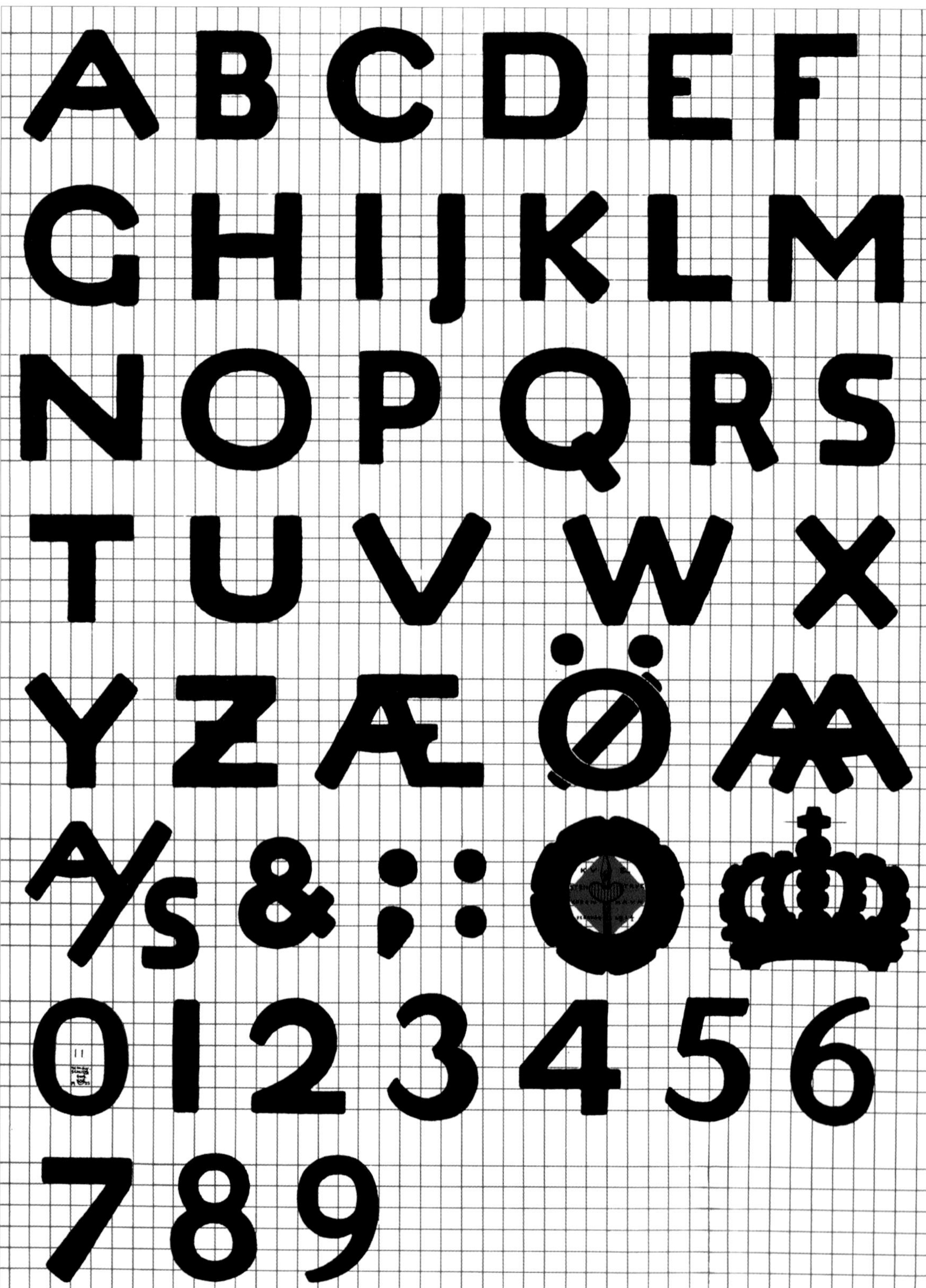
ABCDEF
GHIJKLM
NOPQRS
TUVWX
YZÆØÖÅ
A/S & ; :
0123456
789

◄ Knud V. Engelhardt's solid block letter typeface designed for signposting in the Danish section of the Baltic Exhibition in Malmö, Sweden in 1914. There's something consistent and thoroughly sturdy about the design of this alphabet. As everything else from Engelhardt's hand, a common sense approach seemed to reign: the corners were rounded, the lines were thick and therefore it was both easier to make and to see at a distance.

general use and are found in thingd like word processing programs for computers or can be purchased at a reasonable price. Other fonts can be ordered at a type designer's, for example if a company wants their own special typeface for their printed matter, signs or other graphic identity, just like the typeface that Biilmann Petersen designed for P. Rønning & Gjerløff.

For example, in 1985 DSB had a special typeface designed for their freight division by the design office Mollerup Designlab. This typeface is a stencil typeface, which means that is it solely comprised of open shapes. In this way sign stencils can be cut out of materials like cardboard and used to spray paint texts directly on cardboard boxes and freight cars. There probably aren't very many signs today that are made in this way, but the typeface is characteristic and image-creating for a freight company. It was also used in other contexts where the company communicated in writing such as advertisements, printed matter and of course signposting.

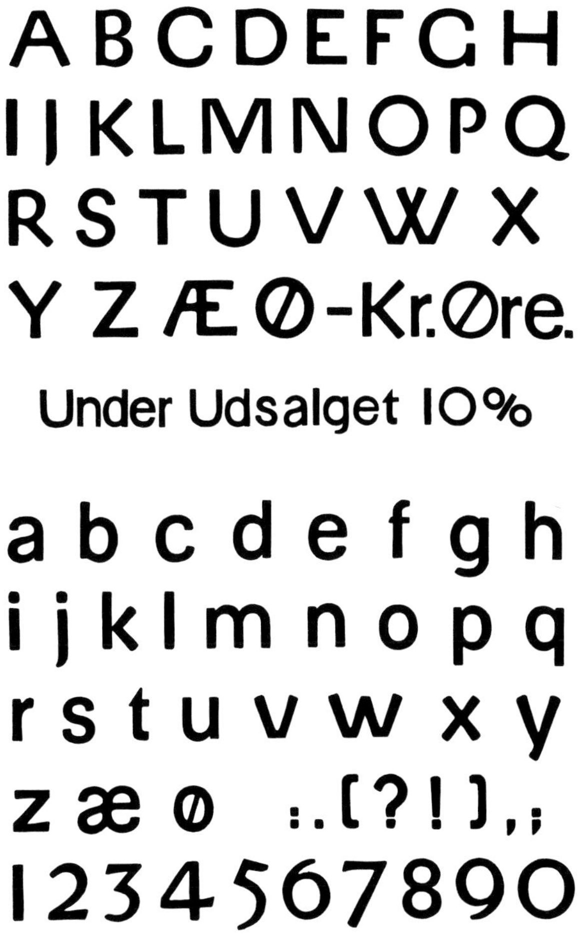

A B C D E F G H
I J K L M N O P Q
R S T U V W X
Y Z Æ Ø -Kr. Øre.
Under Udsalget 10%

a b c d e f g h
i j k l m n o p q
r s t u v w x y
z æ ø :.(?!),;
1234567890

▲ Gunnar Biilmann Petersen's typeface of the grotesque type – that is, without serifs – won first prize in a competition for typeface for labels in 1932 for the paint company P. Rønning & Gjerløff. Engelhardt's legacy is obvious.

▼ DSB's ordinary typeface was based on Helvetica, and the stencil typeface from DSB's Freight Division is therefore based on the same typeface. But when Mollerup Designlab in 1985 were commissioned to design a special typeface for DSB's Freight Division, it needed something that signalled heavy transport in a bold way. That is how the DSB Cargo alphabet came about.

OLE SØNDERGAARD (b. 1937) is an architect and a graphic designer who attended the Royal Academy of Fine Arts, School of Architecture from 1961–64. Afterwards he worked at Naur Klint's architectural practice until 1971. Søndergaard established his own practice in Helsingør in 1971 and has since been a prolific graphic designer of signs, pictograms, typefaces and logos. He took an interest in Helsingør's street signs and proposed new ones for the downtown area. From 1985–95 Ole Søndergaard was a partner in the design company Eleven Danes A/S.

A TYPEFACE CANNOT be designed letter by letter, so before the type designer is finished, he has worked with the whole typeface again and again, so that the shapes of all the letters go together. And afterwards versions in italics and bold have to be designed, and everything has to go together, and preferably the typeface will look good and be legible in both the small and large versions. Then the result is digitised to a modern production technique, which is to ensure that the typeface both looks good in print and as images on a screen. Type design often appeals to the nerds of the design field. In 2000 graphic designer Ole Søndergaard designed the typeface FF Signa, which has become the house alphabet at the Danish Design Centre as well as being included in the catalogue of the distributor of typefaces FontShop International. It was achieved with the help of a three-year work grant from the Danish Arts Foundation. The result was a grotesque typeface that isn't very distinctive but still has some of Knud V. Engelhardt and Gunnar Biilmann Petersen in its soul. Notice for example the lowercase g's.

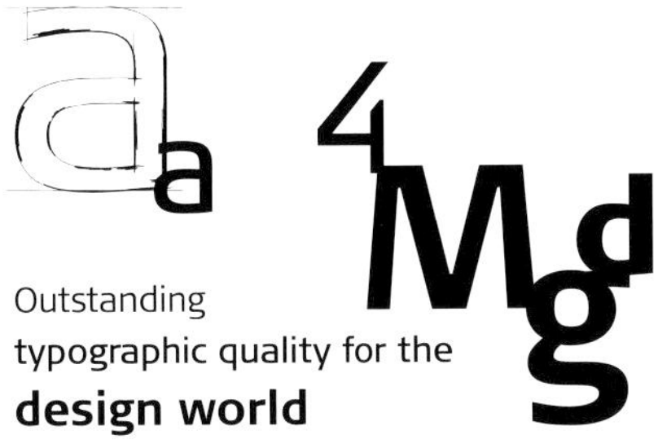

a b c d e f g h i j a b c d e f g h i j
k l m n o p q r s k l m n o p q r s
t u v x y z æ ø å t u v x y z æ ø å
1 2 3 4 5 6 7 8 9 1 2 3 4 5 6 7 8 9
+ ? ! =) (% & / + ? ! =) (% & /

OTHER SIGNS

Danish licence plates are also a kind of sign, and the ones in use today were designed in 1975 by the Professor of Graphic Design at the Royal Academy of Fine Arts, School of Architecture, Naur Klint (1920–78). At the time, after Denmark had entered the EEC in 1972, new licence plates were needed, and the Ministry of Justice made its own proposal first. This was rejected by the Academy Council, which was and still is the state's supreme council in artistic and aesthetic matters. Therefore it became Professor Naur Klint's job to design a new proposal during the summer of 1975 because now it was an urgent matter. The reason for this urgency was said to be because the old factory that had manufactured the black and white licence plates used until this time was bankrupt, and therefore the supply of the old models would soon run out. Together with a group of employees Naur Klint made the present design where the typeface and numbers were designed and the sizes, proportions and colours were determined.

The result is a very legible licence plate. The letters and numbers are in the spirit of Engelhardt and solidly designed, among other things they are very open in their shape and have slightly rounded corners. Unlike the old enamel plates, the new generation was made of aluminium plate that was pressed in relief and painted with fluorescent white paint, and then the black numbers and letters were painted. A thin red frame helps form a whole, and the choice of colours emphasises the Danish affiliation. The only thing one could possibly criticise is that the combination of two letters and five numbers probably isn't the easiest thing to read and remember, but it is most likely a decision made by the ministry and not the designers. When the Danish parliament in 1992 decided that one could buy custom-made plates, some of the letters were missing. They hadn't been designed in 1975 since they weren't deemed necessary. Some of these letters were W, Q and the Danish letters Æ, Ø and Å, which were thought too inconvenient to use since they resembled other letters or weren't international enough to have on Danish cars when driving abroad. The alphabet was supplemented by Naur Klint's son, Lars Klint (b. 1947), who today is an associate professor in graphic design at the Royal Academy of Fine Arts, School of Architecture. So now one could have a license plate that read BRIAN.

MODULEX

In the early 1960s, the LEGO bricks were so successful that the company began looking for new business opportunities. It was one thing that construction toys apparently could be manufactured ad infinitum, but could the principle of the hollow plastic elements that were connected by studs have a further use? In the beginning they worked on developing a special module system that could be a tool for architects in building models, but it wasn't a success. Later on the creative people in Billund, encouraged by LEGO owner Godtfred Kirk Christiansen, thought of making planning boards for companies. The principle was large boards with studs and lots of LEGO elements in all sizes and colours but completely flat on the surface so they could be imprinted with numbers and letters. This system was suited for making and visualising production plans, work schedules and vacation lists. In 1963 this resulted in the establishment of a subsidiary company called Modulex in the LEGO corporation.

Since then the idea has been developed to become what is the main business of Modulex, namely making signs of all kinds.

▾ *The design of the current Danish licence plates is from 1975 and was done by Professor Naur Klint. One can see at a distance that it's a Danish licence plate from the combination of colours, the typeface, the grouping of letters and numbers as well as the frame around it. At the time of writing this, a new design for licence plates is still being considered since the Ministry of Justice is running out of letters that haven't been used before.*

Jones
t
Mark
e

◂ *The Modulex Interior 10 system from 1974 is based on the idea that the LEGO bricks could be transposed to a flexible sign system. Designers Jan Trägårdh and Niels Hartmann worked with in-house developers from Modulex to find the best possible way of getting the system to work both as industrial design and as a good graphic solution.*

Not until 1972 was it decided to focus seriously on the idea, and industrial designer Jan Trägårdh and graphic designer Niels Hartmann were hired for the project. The principle of the sign system is a bit similar to the old-fashioned lead type that could be picked out of the printer's type case and combined for the desired text. Modulex was awarded the ID prize in 1974 for its Interior 10 system, and they continued to develop new sign systems, but over the years they have departed from the original modular concept to make all kinds of signs, including for outdoor use. Modulex is still indirectly connected to LEGO, but otherwise it functions as an independent company. The company has sales in over 35 countries and is today the world's largest company in architectural signage.

Copenhagen Airport

Properly informing one's customers about how find one's way is not just about putting up some signs that randomly direct them to this and that. No matter how graphically well-designed signs might be, the total signage in a traffic junction such as an airport requires more precision. Many passengers arriving at an airport are in a hurry and perhaps aren't used to flying and can therefore be a bit nervous. Furthermore they have to pass through several bottlenecks such as check in and security control in addition to maybe going to the restroom and shopping at the airport stores. In a situation like this, signage has to be extremely thorough. The job can't only be reduced to graphic design, but it demands that the designers seriously take on the responsibility of thinking things through and planning the routes through the building, and preferably in several languages.

Per Mollerup's company Mollerup Designlab did this for Copenhagen Airport around 1990, and they apparently did a good job since they were awarded

Terminal
Terminal 3
Ankomsthal
Arrival hall
Told VAT Tax free
Customs VAT - Tax free
Garderobe/Information
Left luggage/Information
Valuta veksling
Exchange
Garderobe/Information
Left luggage/Information
Udgang
Exit
Afgang
Departures
Toilet
Toilet

◂ Mollerup Designlab's signage at Copenhagen Airport, also known as Kastrup Airport. The typeface was designed for the occasion and is called Airfield. It's in white for the Danish text and yellow for English. In planning the signs, the designers tried to avoid more signs than necessary, and to place the signs exactly where they were needed. Mollerup Designlab has subsequently transferred this graphic line to the airport logo and stationery, vehicles and employee uniforms etc.

an IG prize the following year and the signage hasn't been significantly changed since then. Furthermore the design office has done the same thing for other airports, especially in Scandinavia. The main principle is to tell the travellers how to get from one place to another. It sounds trivial since what else should they do? But many traditional sign systems don't concentrate on telling travellers the most important thing, namely exactly how to get where they want to go. For instance there is a tendency to inform people of everything; for example, signs which tell them which doors they do not have access to. Mollerup Designlab worked on paring down the amount of irrelevant information including incomprehensible colour codes and ambiguous images called pictograms.

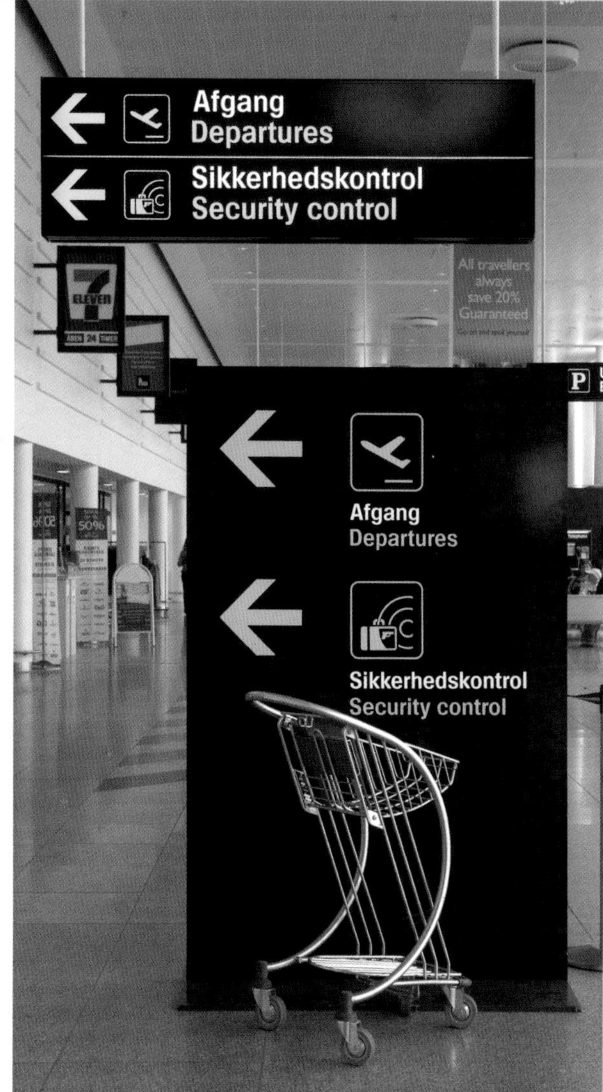

The previous traffic signs at Copenhagen Airport were yellow with the Danish text in black, which was fine because the contrast was so great, but the English text was white which is often almost illegible on a yellow background. Instead Mollerup Designlab made all the signs dark blue, which is a different colour to the many advertisements that an airport normally have and furthermore, the colour has an authoritative and conservative feel to it. The Danish text was then printed in white on the dark blue background, and the English in yellow. The typeface Airfield was specially designed by Mollerup Designlab's employee Trygve Hansen for maximum legibility in both the positive and negative version. Pictograms were only used on the signs to the extent that they improved communication. The signs were manufactured by cutting self-adhesive foil in the relevant colours, and in many cases by mounting them on light boxes that were backlit.

PICTOGRAMS ARE CAREFULLY and meticulously designed in almost the same way as typefaces are. Often very small margins determine whether a stylised picture of a coffee cup in an airport is understood by the travellers, no matter where they come from. On the other hand, it's often not only about showing the way to a cup of coffee, but also suggesting that it's a good cup of coffee. If the coffee cup used by the graphic designers in the pictogram resembles one from the Great Belt ferries of the 1970s, it might not look so appealing. And then the promise of a good cup of coffee in a café might suddenly turn into a warning of a rather dismal canteen.

Throughout the 1990s, graphic designer Ole Søndergaard designed a large system of symbols for use on both pictograms and traffic signs. The customers were at first the Danish Road Directorate and later on other authorities and DSB. Ole Søndergaard's pictograms are often a much needed update of older versions that have had their day. In the case of the traffic signs, traffic safety is a necessary consideration in that the signs must be easy to read at a glance.

▲ *Pedestrian crossing, new and old.*

▲ *Children, new and old.*

▲ *Roadworks, new and old.*

▾ Valdemar Andersen (1875–1928) was a painter, who like many other artists back then went freely back and forth between art and craft-based graphics. Apart from posters, he also made illustrations, advertisements, packaging and did interior design. He was inspired by many things, but his advertising poster for 'The Politiken' from 1908 has something unmistakably French about it. His style is often light and decorative, normally with a sophisticated use of coloured surfaces, such as the way the woman's dress spreads out over the surface of the poster. Valdemar Andersen's wife is believed to be the model for the poster's liberated woman who is reading 'The Politiken'.

POSTERS

Posters are also a type of signs, but their purpose is usually not to show the way, at least not in a physical sense. This is actually an old form of communication that goes back hundreds of years to when they were mostly used as notices and government ordinances. In this sense one could call Martin Luther's famous 95 theses that he nailed on a church door in Wittenberg in 1517 as an early poster and even as a (church) political one. And just look at what it led to. The first real Danish poster that is verifiable is from 1722 and advertises for the opening night of a play. The play was a comedy by Molière entitled *The Miser*. It was performed at Lille Grønnegade Theatre in Danish, which wasn't the norm at the time. The poster was completely typographical, that is there weren't any illustrations, so the only way of attracting attention and spicing it up was to vary the size and type of the typeface. This type of poster is called a playbill, and we can sometimes see it used in today's theatre, variety and circus posters in which only text is used, set in different characteristic typefaces.

The posters that we know today, that is large pieces of paper with colourful motifs, arrived when lithographic printing was invented and later came to Denmark. The invention of lithography (*lithos* means stone in Greek) took place in Germany in 1796, and the first Danish lithographic prints were made in 1811. For many years, probably only rather small prints were made since the large lithographic stones were very difficult and expensive to manufacture.

▸ *Aage Rasmussen's (1913–75) poster from 1937 of the express train racing through the night was an impressive piece of work for a debutante in the field. Aage Rasmussen had attended technical college in Copenhagen and at the age of 24 he approached DSB's advertising department with an almost print-ready poster under his arm. He worked for DSB for several decades, and he also designed tourist posters. The express train poster was very modern for its time. The slanting writing and the speedometer drawn on the night sky were proof that this was a high-speed train. It was so fast that the train leaned into the curves. Aage Rasmussen's style during this period was somewhat inspired by Bauhaus, but also by the American Streamline, exemplified in the American automobile design of the time.*

In making original lithographs the artist draws his motif, reversed, directly onto the stone with a special greasy ink or oil, and then a series of identical pictures can be printed from the image. A qualified lithographer can also transfer an original picture to the stone, and in recent times this can also be done with the help of a special photographic technique. It was probably not until around 1885 that authentic lithographic posters were printed in Denmark, and even then, only in small numbers.

The tradition

The artistic tradition of lithographically printed posters originated in France in the 1860s and then came to Denmark. But not until around the year 1900 did good quality Danish poster production begin. For example, artist J.F. Willumsen designed a beautiful exhibition poster with lots of symbolism in the motif for the Den Frie Udstilling (The Free Exhibition) in Copenhagen in 1896. Two years later, in his capacity as an architect, he designed the famous wooden exhibition building that is still located on Oslo Plads in Copenhagen. At this time, large lithographic printing works were established particularly in the capital, and the atmosphere in these places was important to the quality of the continued development of the poster as an artistic and design-related medium. The poster designer could come and take part in the printing process and thus make sure he got the result he wanted. Some of these printing works, especially abroad, have gone down in history as very inspiring workplaces for poster artists, and in some cases they have set a fashion.

In the beginning of the 20th century, the poster continued to thrive. It was a good medium at the time since many Danes didn't subscribe to newspapers or read magazines, and the 'modern' media we know today (movie theatres, radio, TV and the internet) didn't yet exist. The poster was therefore one of the few media that was colourful and eventful. It was something that especially the business world made use of, and therefore most posters, back then as well as today, were made to sell something or at least brand a company or an organisation. Political posters were made too (see page 78). The poster was also used to educate the public, for example in campaigns for traffic safety or to encourage the public to be tested for tuberculosis. And finally, art posters were also printed; they weren't normally hung in public spaces, but were usually numbered lithographic prints for sale for art lovers.

The poster was and primarily is an information medium since there is some kind of message behind it. An invitation to buy something or do something (vote for a particular political party), or to be aware of something (such as traffic safety). All of these types of posters could be seen from around World War I up until about 1960, which was the absolute heyday of the poster. During this period Danish poster designers were often influenced by foreign trends and poster artists. The French poster artist Cassandre (see page 54) and the German design and art school of Bauhaus up until World War II had a great influence on Danish poster people like Ib Andersen, Aage Rasmussen and several others. However, Aage Sikker Hansen was very inspired by the Soviet Social Realism. Gradually, as other media began to make their mark, the poster lost some of its footing as a medium.

Advertisers had other channels through which to influence the public, especially with the increasing competition from magazines and periodicals that now were printed to a high quality. But the poster still exists although it has competition from billboards that are often seen on the approach

AAGE RASMUSSEN
1937

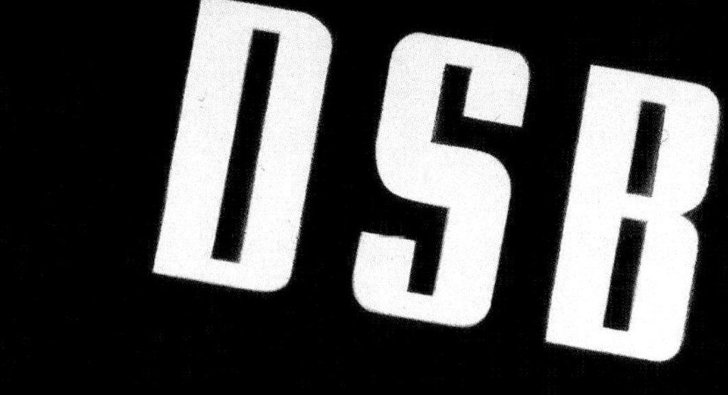
DSB
120

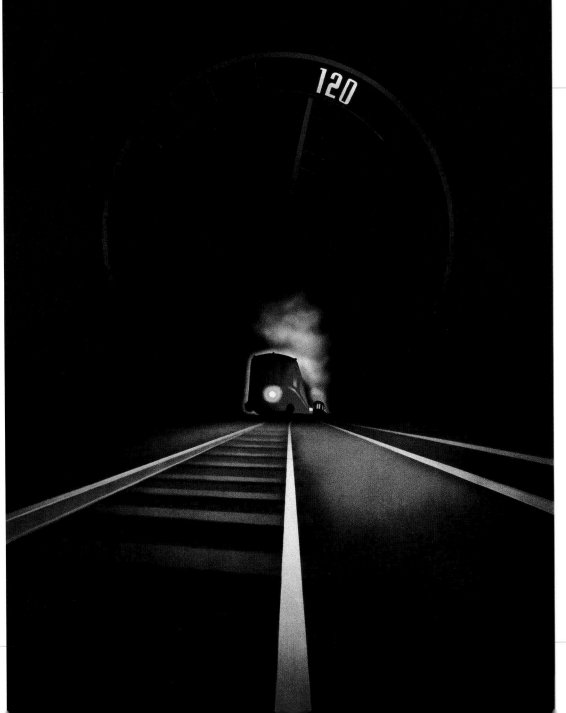

IB ANTONI JENSEN (1929–73) was a Danish illustrator and poster artist, who had many jobs in Denmark, but also a great deal of work in both Europe and the US. He made several graphic works, especially numerous posters for the Danish Foreign Ministry and their export campaign. He was internationally renowned for his posters. The poster for Circus Schumann with Charlie Rivel, the clown, is one of his major works; it's poetically moving while also being a little monumental.

ARNE UNGERMANN (1902–81) designed the poster 'Use your eyes and the pedestrian crossing' in 1941. The inspiration from Miró is quite obvious in this excellent example of poster design. Ungermann qualified as a lithographer in 1922 and had the technical skills of basic poster printing in his blood. From 1924 he worked for The Politiken's advertising department, and from 1930 until his death he was an illustrator at the same paper. From 1946–52 he was also co-editor of the Sunday supplement 'The Magazine'. In 1979 he received the Eckersberg Medal.

FINN NYGAARD (b. 1955) was, among other places, educated at the Design School Kolding and is known for his many posters. Jazz posters in particular are his hallmark. This one was for Aarhus International Jazz Festival in 2001 and is entitled 'A tribute to a fictive drummer'. His poster style is often imaginative and 'loose', unlike his identity programs and other graphic works that are often more stringent. Finn Nygaard and Finn Sködt are the only Danes admitted in the prestigious association Alliance Graphique Internationale.

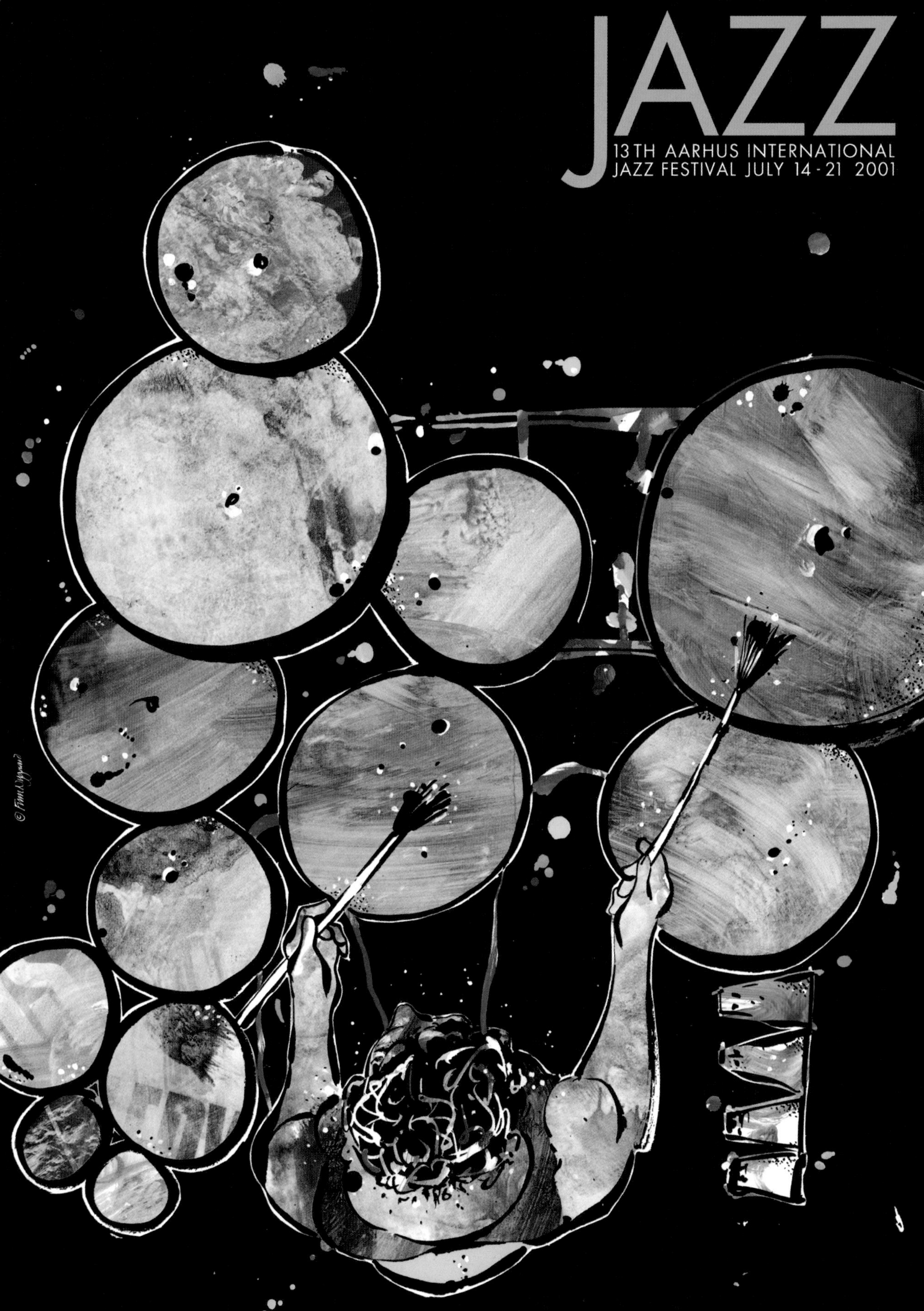
JAZZ
13TH AARHUS INTERNATIONAL
JAZZ FESTIVAL JULY 14 - 21 2001

▼ *Per Arnoldi (b. 1941) is a self-taught Danish artist and graphic designer. Arnoldi works in an easily recognisable style with the same colours (blue, yellow and red) in the same hues, which have become his artistic signature. Arnoldi works in a very precise and often geometric style that can be traced back to the Bauhaus style. He is internationally renowned for his posters. The poster 'October 1943' was designed for the 50th anniversary of the Danish Jews' flight to Sweden.*

roads to cities and are usually just newspaper ads that have been blown up in size. This reflects a development in which poster design has mainly become a job for advertising agencies. In the poster's glory days it was a job for artists, graphic designers and architects. Danish poster design has been characterised by a solid high quality over the years, even though it didn't set the fashion like, for example, the strong Polish graphic tradition. There is still a Danish poster milieu albeit a very specialised niche that mainly designs posters for special occasions such as music festivals, exhibitions and the like.

OCTOBER 1943
THANKS TO SCANDINAVIA THE 50TH ANNIVERSARY OF DENMARK'S RESISTANCE TO THE NAZI OCCUPATION – THE RESCUE OF THE DANISH JEWISH COMMUNITY – SANCTUARY IN SWEDEN

NEWSPAPER GRAPHICS

By their very nature newspapers have always been large consumers of typography although they haven't always used the most advanced typefaces. Yet sometimes newspapers have been groundbreaking, such as when the London paper 'The Times' had a typeface designed that many people use today to write letters with on their computer. Newspapers have probably been most graphically innovative in the area of layout. Denmark got its first newspaper in 1749, and today it is known as 'The Berlingske Tidende'. For 200 hundred years, that is until the post-war era, newspaper layout was mostly just about typesetting page after page. An authentic new Danish design on a large daily paper did not come until the early 1960s when Austin Grandjean started working for 'The Ekstra Bladet' in his spare time as a book designer for the publishing company Gyldendal. From 1961–64, along with the newspaper's editorial office, Grandjean developed a new look for the newspaper.

The result was a brand new and thoughtful layout that coincided with 'The Ekstra Bladet' switching from the traditional broadsheet format to the tabloid format. The little newspaper on Rådhuspladsen (The Town Hall Square) was in a crisis at the time since its circulation had dropped by about 50,000 and its competitor, 'The B.T.' was far ahead. The solution was a re-launch that the owners had the courage to wait three years for until Grandjean had finished his work. The result was a big success editorially and with regard to design and circulation. The newspaper was given a new heading, which is roughly the same today, and the number of typefaces was reduced to three. Furthermore, many superfluous elements such as lines, frames and other special plates were discarded. At the same time, the technical manufacturing process was simplified while the editor-in-chief, Victor Andreasen, struggled to make the editorial line more forceful. The new design was much clearer especially because there was more space between the columns, pictures and headlines, and also because the layout of the articles was in individual blocks and not like before when the articles were almost jumbled together on the page.

Once baby brother had been 'converted', after a couple of years it was the main newspaper's turn, 'The Politiken'. Austin Grandjean was again asked to do the redesigning. And also in this case it was important that the employees were motivated to walk the path of change, so the project took two years. In many ways the new layout was based on the experiences with 'The Ekstra Bladet': setting out the articles in clearer blocks, using fewer typefaces and more space, and getting rid of the many unnecessary lines between the articles and columns. Moreover a bolder typeface was used for the headlines, and a fixed left margin gave the paper a less messy look. This line was introduced in 1968 and has been more or less maintained, and in some ways it has even been strengthened.

▾ *'The Magazine' was the Sunday supplement of 'The Politiken' from 1922 till 1962. During these years, leading Danish artists made good illustrations that could survive duplication by the paper's rotary press. Often the best illustrations were used as posters in Danish homes – that's how good the graphic quality was. The illustration below from the front page of the supplement was drawn by Arne Ungermann.*

POLITIKEN

REDAKTØRER: JØRGEN BODE og ARNE UNGERMANN

MAGASINET

KØBENHAVN 12. MAJ 1951 PROVINSEN 12. MAJ

VORES LILLE TOG

Af Ove Brønnum - Tegning af Ungermann

Hvor mennesket endnu er teknikens herre og ikke dens slave, kører de smaa tog ad private baner, og sære skæbner fuldbyrdes i deres spor

VORES lille tog har to grønne vogne paa høje hjul, og et lille, sort lokomotiv. Inden i vognene er der træsæder og en forskrækkelig masse støbejernsstolper med kruseduller paa. Over sæderne og imellem støbejernskrusedullerne er der sejlgarnsnet, og i hver vogn er der to ventiler, som rigtigt kan dreje rundt. I den bageste vogn er der ogsaa et centralfyr, som to jernbanemænd med mellemrum fylder med tørvesmuld. Om aftenen, ved vintertid, ser det malerisk og truende ud, naar de røde flammer slaar ud af fyret og lyser i vifter fra døren, paa hvirvlende sne eller regn, eller taage, og inden for de to jernbanemænds skygger flyver over væggene, bliver kæmper og dværge, i takt til skovlenes gang over gulvet. Senere, naar toget sætter sig i gang igen, kommer de ind og er helt sorte i ansigterne og spørger, om der er kommet nye rejsende, og maa jeg se billetterne. Det er egentlig to overkomplette sønner fra et husmandsbrug, som man har knappet uniformen paa, for at de skulle faa en slags eksistensberettigelse, og de kender gud og hvermand langs linjen fra gamle dage. Derfor er der temmelig mange mennesker, som kører gratis med vores lille tog, for det ville være uhøfligt at bede om at maatte se deres billetter, det ville være at insinuere, at de snød, og det kunne aldrig gaa an. Dertil kommer, at mange slet ikke er saadan, at man kan tale til dem: nogle svarer simpelthen ikke, andre svarer alt for meget og faar en ud i lange samtaler, som man ikke kan slippe fra igen, førend toget holder, og

POLITIKEN

Søndag

Ejsa

Skjult mesterværk

Fogh lægger luft til Dansk Folkeparti

Asylbørn lider uret

122 år og stadig i fuldt format

Berlin 199,-

ON OCTOBER 1, 2006 'The Politiken' made a major change in its design. After having followed Grandjean's concept from 1968 with minor adjustments along the way, the time had come to tighten it up. The signature in Egyptienne typeface has been kept, but the font is larger and thicker. The old body typeface Century was replaced by Capitoleum. It was designed by the Dutchman Gerard Unger in 1998 for the Catholic church in 2000 and is based on the Italian calligraphist Cresci's work from the 1500s.

The new typeface is thus a continuation of an old tradition, but otherwise much of the new layout was drawn from modern newspaper usage. The pages have a more airy appearance, with a larger point size for the body typeface, but also because there is more open space between the elements on the pages. A new addition was the news bar above the heading. Quotes are extracted in bold as the essence of an article, and this slightly resembles the design of an electronic media.

POLITIKEN

KØBENHAVN, TIRSDAG 6. JUNI 1967

Omringet – Voldsomme kampe – Stormagterne „neutrale"

Israel ene i krig med 11 lande

ISRAEL holdt endnu i aftes ud mod overlegne arabiske styrker efter daglange kampe ved grænserne og i luften. Den krig, som begge parter hævdede, den anden startede, har allerede kostet store ofre, men ingen tabslister forelå i nat. På kampens første dag erklærede 11 lande Israel krig eller lovede Ægypten tropper til hjælp. Israelerne har ingen løfter fået – derimod erklærede stormagterne sig neutrale, også USA.

Israel: Første angreb afvist

„Vi kan holde os dem fra livet"

Af Herbert Pundik

Eshkol: Vi rykker frem på Sinai

Krigen og krisen

INDE I BLADET

Sikkerhedsrådet strides om to resolutions-forslag:

FN straks kørt fast

Danmarks Hans Tabor leder hemmeligt møde for at få kompromis i stand

Af Daniel Viklund

Hemmeligt møde

Krav om retræte

Jubelråb i Cairos gader

Trods meddelelser om store israelske grænseangreb

Af Anders Johansson

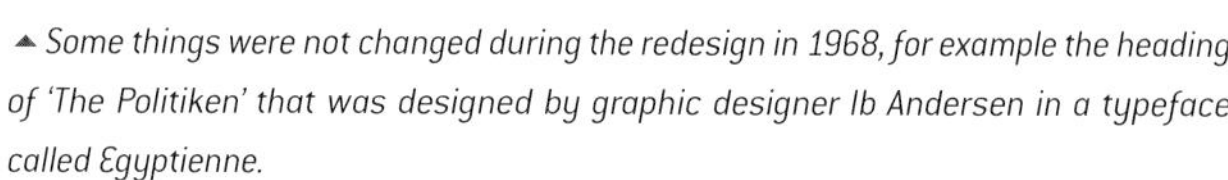

▲ *Some things were not changed during the redesign in 1968, for example the heading of 'The Politiken' that was designed by graphic designer Ib Andersen in a typeface called Egyptienne.*

POLITIKEN

KØBENHAVN, MANDAG 19. OKTOBER 1981

General skal styre Polen

Jaruzelski alene med magten efter Kania

Vejret

13 rigtige

Feriestart med 6 dræbte

Svensk sejr i blomsterkamp

Dansk par stjal alt

Billigrejse hele ferien

Barn i tørretromle

Fårenes fødselsdag

Dræbt mod traktor

Sejrherren

Socialisten Papandreou vandt det græske valg

Borg-mester: Politiet skal ikke blande sig

Tager trusler om sag roligt

Gravfred krænket på havets bund

Gulddykkere i unåde

SPORT

AGF øjner guld

Fire hold slås om mesterskabet

KRONIKKEN

Forskningens vilkår

AUSTIN GRANDJEAN, 1930–2006, was a graphic designer with a solid background in typography. Originally he completed an apprenticeship as a compositor in 1953. After a stint at an advertising agency in Aalborg, he was headhunted by Gyldendal in 1954 and worked there until 1996 as a graphic designer and head book designer. Grandjean's contribution in rationalising and systemising book design and production has resonated in many parts of the graphic business and the publishing world. Apart from working for Gyldendal, he also had the energy to work seriously on newspaper layout and typography. First at 'The Ekstra Bladet' in 1964, and then at 'The Politiken' in 1968.

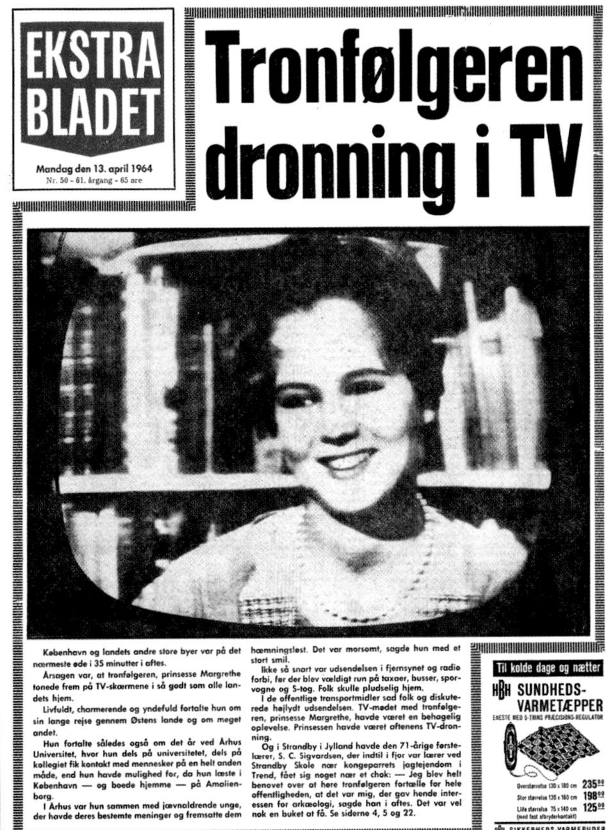

EKSTRA BLADET

Mandag den 13. april 1964
Nr. 50 - 61. årgang - 65 øre

Tronfølgeren dronning i TV

København og landets andre store byer var på det nærmeste øde i 35 minutter i aftes.

Årsagen var, at tronfølgeren, prinsesse Margrethe tonede frem på TV-skærmene i så godt som alle landets hjem.

Livfuldt, charmerende og yndefuld fortalte hun om sin lange rejse gennem Østens lande og om meget andet.

Hun fortalte således også om det år ved Århus Universitet, hvor hun dels på universitetet, dels på kollegiet fik kontakt med mennesker på en helt anden måde, end hun havde mulighed for, da hun læste i København — og boede hjemme — på Amalienborg.

I Århus var hun sammen med jævnaldrende unge, der havde deres bestemte meninger og fremsatte dem hæmningsløst. Det var morsomt, sagde hun med et stort smil.

Ikke så snart var udsendelsen i fjernsynet og radio forbi, før der blev vældigt run på taxaer, busser, sporvogne og S-tog. Folk skulle pludselig hjem.

I de offentlige transportmidler sad folk og diskuterede højlydt udsendelsen. TV-mødet med tronfølgeren, prinsesse Margrethe, havde været en behagelig oplevelse. Prinsessen havde været aftenens TV-dronning.

Og i Strandby i Jylland havde den 71-årige førstelærer, S. C. Sigvardsen, der indtil i fjor var lærer ved Strandby Skole nær kongeparrets jagtejendom i Trend, fået sig noget nær et chok: — Jeg blev helt benovet over at høre tronfølgeren fortælle for hele offentligheden, at det var mig, der gav hende interessen for arkæologi, sagde han i aftes. Det var vel nok en buket at få. Se siderne 4, 5 og 22.

Boligfilmen vi ikke måtte se — Side 2

Ekstra Bladet

tør - hvor andre tier

TORSDAG 17. JANUAR 1991
Nr. 329 - uge 3 - 87. årg. - 6,50 kr.

USA bomber Irak

KRIG

Klokken 00.36 i nat begyndte operation Ørkenstorm. 2500 fly bombede atom-anlæg, fabrikker for kemiske våben, olie-raffinaderier og kommunikationscentre i Irak og Kuwait. Vi er gået ind i kampen, sagde George Bush i Washington. – Slaget over alle slag er startet, svarede Saddam Hussein i Bagdad

SE SIDE 4, 5, 6, 7, 8, 9, 10, 11 OG BAGSIDEN

▲ *Austin Grandjean's finished changes for 'The Ekstra Bladet' that forced its arch rival 'The B.T.' onto the defensive. Until 'The Ekstra Bladet' was re-launched in 1964, 'The B.T.' had been one of the newspapers with the best design and layout in the Nordic countries. It wasn't renovated and was consequently overtaken in circulation by its rival.*

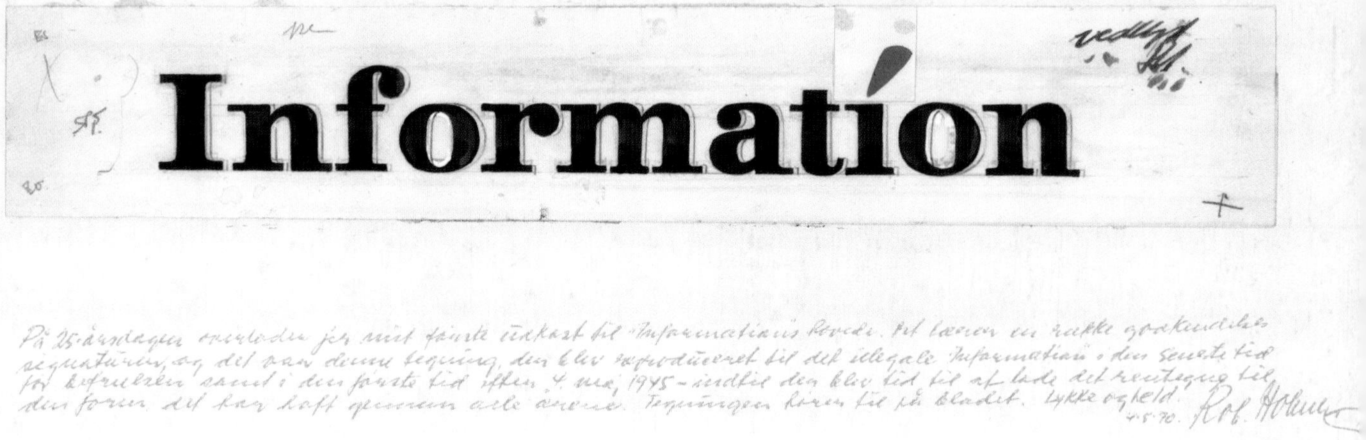

Among other things, the front page of the first section has fewer articles than before, but on the other hand, they undergo a more thorough treatment, this is true also for the graphics and pictures. In this way 'The Politiken' signals that it is a very serious newspaper with longer and more feature articles.

'The Politiken' has tried to be a serious newspaper since it was started in 1884. 'The organ for the highest enlightenment' was one of the pompous slogans that set the tone in its early days. And in order to live up to that, something had to change in a time before there was television and many of the other media and offers we have today. So from 1922 to 1962, 'The Politiken' had a Sunday supplement 'The Magazine' with short stories and illustrations by some of the best Danish artists at the time, including Ib Spang Olsen, Des Asmussen, Aage Sikker Hansen, Ib Andersen and Arne Ungermann. The latter was also co-editor of 'The Magazine' from 1946–52, and the graphic quality was in general very high in the years the supplement was published.

BOOK DESIGN

Designing books is done in roughly the same way as a newspaper, since it entails information in the form of text and sometimes also pictures for the reader. The scope and character of this job depend on the book. Does it have illustrations, or like many novels, does it only consist of text? The book as a medium has developed enormously since the monks copied them by hand. The largest leap forward was the printer Gutenberg's invention of movable type that resulted in his 42-line Bible from 1454. This art of printing quickly spread to Denmark, and textbooks became rather easy and relatively inexpensive to print. If the book was to have illustrations, they were still very complicated to print for several hundred years. Not until blocks were invented and later offset printing was developed did it become more affordable to print books as we know them today.

Book design was characterised by traditions far into the 20th century. There virtually weren't any publishing companies that employed graphic designers with a further education in design. Instead many books got their appearance from the usual practice and from a more or less qualified collaboration between the publishing company's editors and typographers. If a book cover needed a little more pizzazz, a freelance illustrator was hired for the occasion. But just as often they managed with a typographical solution for this part of the book as well. Nonetheless, in many cases good book covers were made. This was possible largely because of the typographer's basic education and their many rules for making good lead type and letterpress printing that did not allow for many mistakes in the final production. But very little creativity was mobilised, and if it was, it was usually because an architect or artist had written the book and wanted to see it through to the end with their own design and layout.

Ellegaard Frederiksen and Grandjean

After World War II, the Danish book printing and therefore also the Danish publishing companies were in a bad state. Investments in new equipment in the form of printing machines and new typefaces were needed. But the crisis was also of a creative nature since back then there were only a few professionally trained book designers working in the business.

In 1950, graphic designer Erik Ellegaard Frederiksen came home from London where he had worked at Penguin Books for the renowned

DOTTING THE I. It wasn't only Politikens Hus (The Politiken's House) that made a difference through the graphic style of their publications. As of May 5, 1945 (the day after the liberation of Denmark) one could see the characteristic red dot over the letter i in the heading of the daily newspaper 'Information'. It was quickly designed by the first director of the newspaper and consultant in printed matter, Robert Holmberg. He was inspired by the typeface on the posters of the time. Even seen as an isolated dot most people recognise it, such is its brand value.

The standardisation of the book production at Gyldendal led to the launch of Tranebøgerne (the Crane books) from 1959 and onwards. This was a concept where literary classics especially and other good, modern novels were published in inexpensive paperback form. The goal was that the books in the series should not cost more than a pack of cigarettes. The paperback below is Johannes V. Jensen's Nobel Prize winning book 'The Fall of the King' in an edition from around 1980, and the price is still in pencil on the inside: 15.25 kroner. And although the price reflects that the book is cheap, its type and print are of good quality, and the company could still afford an illustration by Aage Sikker Hansen on the cover.

German book artist Jan Tschichold. Here he had learned much more than he could have done in Denmark at the time, and he didn't hesitate to pass his knowledge on in Copenhagen. He told anyone who bothered to listen that something had to be done in the business. He set up as an independent graphic designer and also worked on several book design assignments.

JOHANNES V. JENSEN
Kongens Fald
,,Kongens Fald" er det bedste, Johannes V. Jensen har skrevet. - Den sandeste bog, der er skrevet om det danske sind.
TOM KRISTENSEN
GYLDENDALS TRANEBØGER

Around the same time, in 1953, Austin Grandjean got his apprenticeship as a compositor in Copenhagen. After a couple of years at an advertising agency in Aalborg, the 23-year-old was headhunted by Gyldendal's new technical head Jokum Smith, who had heard Ellegaard Frederiksen's points of view. The publishing company had a new owner now that Knud W. Jensen (who later established the Louisiana Museum of Modern Art) had taken over the controlling interest in Gyldendal. A new management triumvirate was hired because now something had to be done, and Jokum Smith was one of them. So from 1954, for the next 42 years Grandjean was the man responsible for the company's book design. His job was not only to design books, but also to simplify and standardise the book production so it could be more cost-effective. Standardisation was met with much resistance both among the in-house typographers and in the rest of the book business. It was thought that this would take away the typographers' opportunity for being creative, and furthermore it would lead to books being more boring. But the introduction of new typefaces and new paper formats based on the golden section did not lead to boring books, but liberated energy in the publishing company to be creative in other ways, and soon a large part of the publishing business followed the same model. Rational industrial production had come to stay, not least in the publishing world.

A PURELY TYPOGRAPHICAL treatment of a book cover. Knud V. Engelhardt's design for the telephone book from KTAS (Copenhagen Telephone Company) from 1909 is in the Art Nouveau style and contains a nod to his older colleague Thorvald Bindesbøll and his graphic works, which we still know today from the Carlsberg Hof label. One objection to the design could be that it isn't easy to read, but what does that matter once you know that this is the telephone book? You'll recognise the handsome design without have to read the writing.

THE CHILLING SCIENCE-FICTION novel '1984' by George Orwell was graphically designed by Austin Grandjean for Gyldendal. Here the typographic cover is designed in an ideal and illustrative way. It would almost be too difficult to find a picture that could illustrate the book. Grandjean's typographical treatment of the cover speaks volumes compared to plain text. Just look at the way the word 'Gyldendal' is squashed between the huge numbers '1984'. It says everything about this gloomy book.

A COMPLETELY DIFFERENT cover that also uses typographical effects to indicate the theme of the book is 'Manual til dansk samtidskunst' (Manual for Danish contemporary art'), published in late summer 2006 with analyses of new Danish art. The artists, groups and works portrayed are very different in their expression and media, not to mention artistic approach. It would have been hard for graphic designer Camilla Jørgensen to find illustrations that could do the contents justice. And since the title 'Manual' was definite, it was logical to play on the idea of a user's guide, since art, just like technology, can require a guide. The typography is quite new; the typeface is called NB55, and it's also used inside for headlines. Since a manual breaks things down into smaller bits of information, the same way of thinking is used in the division of the word manual. And the use of slashes instead of hyphens emphasises the future-orientated contents of the book. The soft cover in cartridge paper contributes to the impression of a book whose contents are matter-of-fact and perhaps unpretentious.

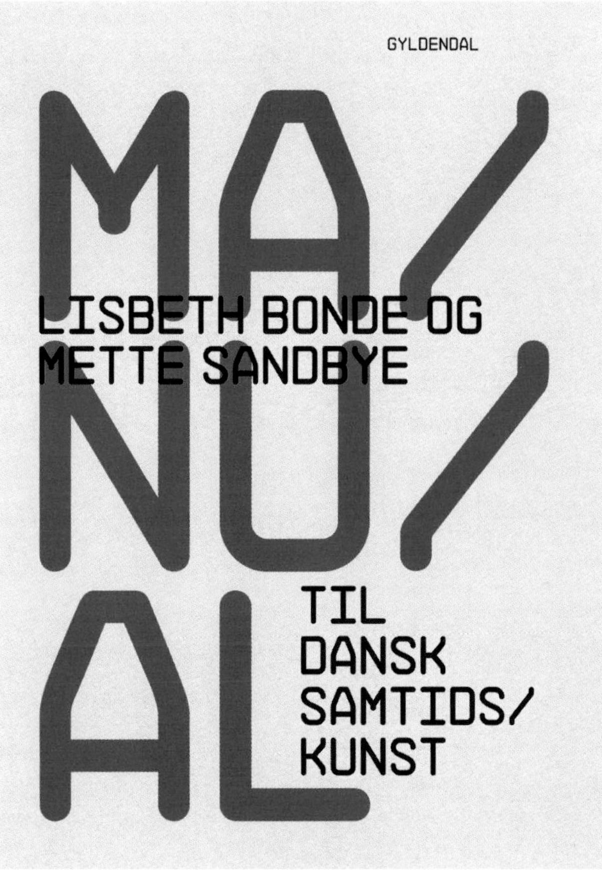

▾ The illustrated cover has the advantage over the typographic cover that it can say something about the contents in a more direct way. But there's the risk of not creating the correct image in the recipient's head, and then the reader will be very disappointed. A good example is Ib Andersen's cover for Anders Bodelsen's novel 'De lyse nætters tid' (The time of light Northern nights) from 1959. This drawing reveals so little about the contents that one can read anything into it. And if one knows Bodelsen's books, one can sense that the poetic cover probably has several layers of meaning in it. Ib Andersen (1907–69) studied architecture, but never designed many houses. Instead he was known as an excellent illustrator and poster designer as well as for working with Gunnar Biilmann Petersen on designing the new series of Danish banknotes, also in 1959.

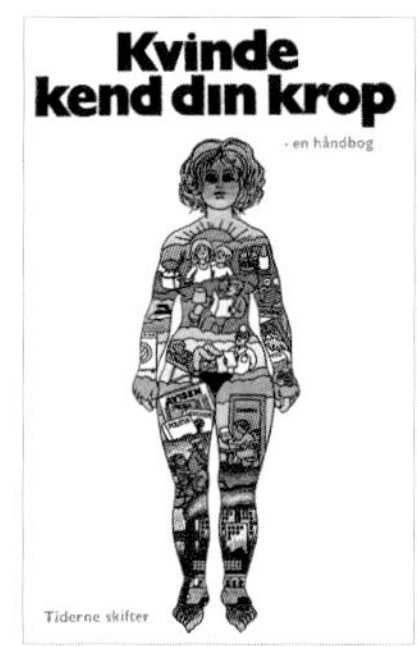

1975.

1983.

1992.

TIDERNE SKIFTER (Times Change) is a publishing company founded in 1973 and whose director has been Claus Clausen ever since. The company has made its mark with alternative publications, of which the user's manual 'Kvinde kend din krop' (Woman, know your body), which was first published in 1975, has sold over 200,000 copies over the years. It's been revised three times, and the different covers show how the times have changed. The first edition was according to the preface 'written, drawn, photographed and criticised by a large group of women and a few men'. The cover was a collage-like, naive drawing of a woman's body that contained all the contradictions in a modern woman's world. The book was almost synonymous with Women's Lib that rejected superficial female glamour. The second edition from 1983 was still produced by a work commune, but the cover now had a photo of a naked woman on a bike. The time had passed for Social Realism. The graphic design is by Anne Houe and Tove Ulstrup Rasmussen. In 1992 the third edition was published, and sensuality was rife with young, naked women floating in water. The same working group was behind the book, but now they were denoted as 'authors and contributors'. Graphics and cover by Anne Houe. The latest edition is from 2001, and the cover hides more than the previous edition – perhaps influenced by a new modesty? Graphic design is by Michala Clante Bendixen.

▸ *When jazz musician Niels-Henning Ørsted Pedersen (NHØP for short) died in 2005, only 58 years old, a memorial biography was quickly written about the great Danish contrabassist. The cover photo, like the rest of the book's pictures, was taken by Jan Persson, and sensitively shows the artist and man in deep and loving concentration, alone with his instrument. The book and its simple cover were made by graphic designer Bettina Kjærulff-Schmidt – showing that a charismatic photograph can stand alone and have a very strong effect with a minimalist approach to the graphic design.*

▾ *The world-famous children's book 'Paul is alone in the world' is a classic example of an intelligent children's book that is both brilliantly written and no less brilliantly illustrated. It was first published by Gyldendal in 1942, and came about through a close collaboration between author and teacher Jens Sigsgaard and illustrator Arne Ungermann. The story of Paul's experiences is based on Sigsgaard's conversations with his pupils about what they would do if they were invisible. But in real life it might not be so fun to be all alone and drive a streetcar and raid a candy store. The text and pictures support each other in the most sublime way, and the book was sold for publication in 30 countries, and has even been pirated.*

Palle er så glad, fordi han er alene i hele verden. Nu kan han gøre lige, hvad han vil.

Palle kører i sporvognen lige til Rådhuspladsen. Så kan han ikke komme længere, for der holder en anden sporvogn på sporet.

Palle kan ikke standse, og så kører han lige ind i den anden vogn.

BANG!

22

▸ *Another classic children's book is 'Halfdan's ABC', which is illustrated by Ib Spang Olsen (b. 1921) and contains nonsense rhymes by Halfdan Rasmussen (1925–2002). It was first published in 1967 by Carlsen publishers and has been in bookstores ever since. In this case the illustrations are equal to the design of the book, since all illustrations by Ib Spang Olsen completely fill the pages, and even the letters in the individual rhymes are drawn by hand and form part of the total design. The catchy verses and crazy illustrations are a big hit with both children and adults.*

Bagfacaden af Slotskirken, der vendte mod Vogngården Efter Samling …

Slotskirkens facade mod Slotspladsen. 358 x 261 mm. KAB.

som fandtes, men de fordeles på en måde. Facaden må opfattes som en underdel til kuplen. Fire vinduesfag i stuen gøres til to, som anbringes i fremspringende murflader, der i facaden markerer kirkerummets udstrækning inde i bygningen. I facadens midte er der tre fag vinduer mellem de lukkede flader. De tre vinduer findes svarende til stue- og mezzaninetagerne; ovenover, tilsvarende Kongeetagen, ses et stort halvcirkulært vindue. Dette parti af facaden er lige under kuplen, og dets vinduer giver lys til rummet under denne. Takten i de to gange tre vinduer i facadens endepartier er overtaget fra den gamle bygning, og de har ingen relation til det egentlige kirkerum.

Kuplen er bemærkelsesværdig. Det er ikke en halvkugle, men en mindre del af en kugleflade, som hviler på en murcylinder, der er helt lukket. Den kugleflade, som kuplen er et udsnit af, har større diameter end en halvkugle, som ville dække cylinderen, og virker derfor større; man tror, kuppelrummet inde i kirken er mere imponerende, end det er i virkeligheden. Det var ganske almindeligt at opføre kupler med dobbeltskal, men sjældent at forskellen på de to skallers krumningsradius er så stor som her.

Den ovenfor citerede bemærkning om kirkens relation til omgivelserne gør det mindre forbavsende at iagttage, hvorledes Hansen lader denne øjensynlig strenge logiske bygning tilpasse sig bybilledet. Den udgør et markant hjørne af Slotsholmen set fra Højbro. I modsætning til sin forgænger har den sin egen ræson i forhold til slottet uden derfor at løsrive sig. Det er en konsekvens heraf, at den på langsiden, som vender mod slottet, har bevaret en ubrudt vinduesflugt, kun den halvcirkulære åbning midt i overetagen bryder takten. Det er på denne side mod Prins Jørgens Gård, at man erkender, at stueetagens vinduer sidder lavere end i slottets facade overfor. Forklaringen er, at Hansen projekterede den ny slotskirke uden kælder. Derved opnåede han at øge kirkens indvendige højde med et par meter, hvilket naturligvis bidrog til rummets anselighed. Tricket afsløres alene af det enlige vindue, som sidder i facadedelen mod Slotspladsen, det er nemlig anbragt i højde med løngangens vinduer og dermed slottets. Inde i kirken bemærkes det ikke, da det giver lys til trapperummet.

Kirkens bagside skulle vende mod Vogngården. Der var ingen facadetegning til denne side i projektmaterialet, muligvis fordi det endnu på dette tidspunkt har været uafklaret, hvad der skulle ske med den ruinerede Vogngård. Af planerne fremgår blot, at arkitekten havde regnet med, at der skulle være to par vinduer omkring en midtdør i stueetagen, og fem ovenover.

Enten synes Hansen at have være stensikker på, hvordan kirken skulle være, eller også må næsten alle forarbejder være gået tabt. Selv de få tegninger, som man må anse for præliminære, viser entydigt mod den endelige løsning. Af samme grund er det ikke fristende at beskæftige sig ret meget med de i alt tre tegninger det drejer sig om: en plan, nogle snit på ét blad og en facade.[96] Planen meddeler kun et lidt længere kirkerum og to pilastre i stedet for to søjler, snittene, to på tværs og to på langs, viser blot et par forslag uden synderlig interesse

Længdesnit af Slotskirken. Efter Samling …

356 CHRISTIANSBORG SLOT

CHRISTIANSBORG SLOT 357

▴ *The book can also be a graphic work of prestige, almost a monument for a person who died long ago, such as the large work about the Danish Classicist architect C.F. Hansen, who designed The Church of Our Lady, Christiansborg Slotskirke (Castle church) and the Courthouse in Copenhagen, among others. Published by Arkitektens Forlag in 1996, this book sold out long ago. This magnificent work designed by Anne Rohweder is a classic coffee table book, which those interested in culture can display with ease for guests. In this book, the text, original drawings and new photographs all graphically come together, and nothing was skimped on as regards scope, quality of paper or colour prints.*

UNTIL STEPPEULVENE'S ONLY LP 'Hip' was released in 1967, the Danish album covers had been rather traditional. The design on the new cover corresponded rather well to the music on 'Hip', which was a milestone in Danish music history since Steppeulvene was the first band with original Danish lyrics.

From a graphic point of view the album was an eye-opener, designed by the rather unknown Anders Bull Clausen, who hasn't since attracted notice in this area. The style of the cover fit the times to a T with its acid hippie look and references to Buddhism and psychedelic drugs. The cover set new standards for the design of covers and posters in the music business, but was in line with contemporary trends abroad.

The task of designing an album cover is in many ways similar to designing a book cover. The front of an album, just like a book, has to reflect the contents in a way that contributes to the big picture. There has to be some relationship between contents and packaging, although sometimes it can be hard to see for those who are outside the target group or subculture. Peder Bundgaard's cover for the album 'Verden er vidunderlig' (The world is wonderful) from 1982 was an example of an ambiguous cover that, just like the band TV2, reflected an ironic distance to the world – a feeling shared by those who were young in the 1980s.

The expressed opinions should not always be taken at face value, and graphic design can help stage this.

Designed by Anders Bull Clausen, 1967.

Designed by Peder Bundgaard, 1982.

New interpretations of old songs and old graphics are a different kettle of fish. John Ovesen, who worked for both Gyldendal and the record company Exlibris, changed the old photo of the ageing Grundtvig into a strongly-coloured cover inspired by Warhol. This was in 1983 when Erik Grip made new interpretations of Grundtvig's hymns. The cover was a clear indication of the contents on the one hand – it was staying true to the original – and on the other hand, it was a modern record. By using a well-known, original photo as the basis for Ovesen's painted illustration, there wasn't any need for text on the front or back of the album.

Another solution to elaborating on a photograph is Peter Ravn's cover for the album 'Alle Vore Håb' (All Our Hopes) recorded in 1983 by the band Tøsedrengene (Sissies/Wimps). As a graduate in industrial design from the School of Architecture in Copenhagen, Peter Ravn was used to thinking in holistic terms regarding a product and brand. And Tøsedrengene was definitely a brand in the 1980s. Therefore the concept for all of their album covers was to reuse old, powerful black and white photos from 1950s' magazines. In their slightly coloured versions the photographs became mischievous comments on the group's name. That is how the group attained their own graphic identity along with their individual musical profile.

▲ *Designed by John Ovesen, 1983.*

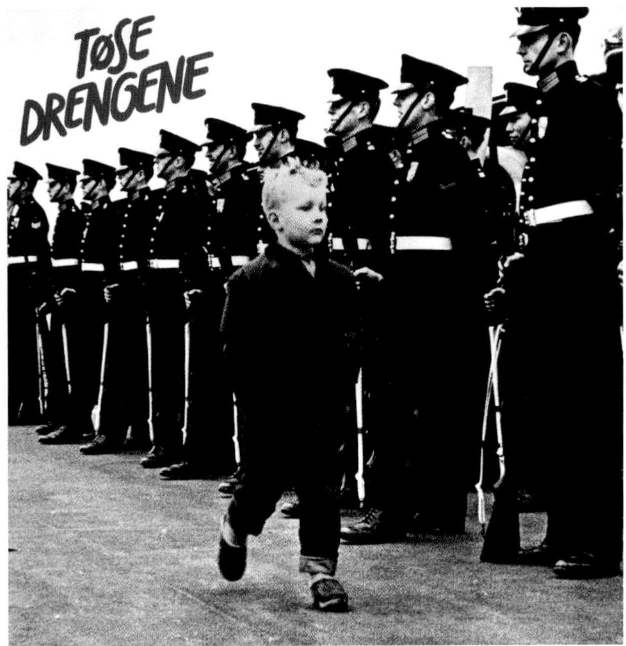

▲ *Designed by Peter Ravn, 1983.*

IN 1990 THE sale of music definitively switched from the old LPs to CDs. The 30 x 30 cm format of the old covers changed to the CD's 12 x 12 cm, which of course limited what the graphic designers had at their disposal. However, this was no hindrance to creativity, which can be seen on the covers below.

The first example is Aqua's super hit from 1997 designed by Art Director and advertiser Peter Stenbæk. His beginnings in the advertising world influenced the look of the cover. Stenbæk saw the cover and music video as tools to be used in promoting Aqua and their music rather than decorative art as an extension of the artists' music. The cover was meant to sell and brand Aqua instead of sending subtle messages. The 'Aquarium' album was launched as naïve and positive pop with a capital P and with a cartoonish twinkle in the eye in the letter Q.

Some years later, in 2004, Peter Stenbæk got the job of designing the cover for Bent Fabricius-Bjerre's album Jukebox. Once again the graphic design seems to be inspired by cartoons, this time from the 1950s and 1960s. At the time when this cover was designed, the retro look was very popular among graphic designers. But nevertheless, the design of the cover suited the contents, since it played on the tension that lay in the fact that the almost 80-year-old Fabricius-Bjerre, whose hip-hop stage name for this

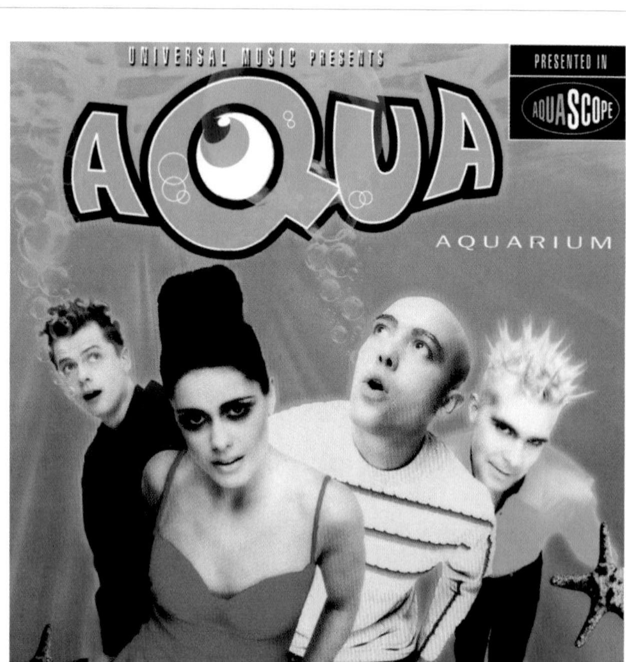

▲ *Designed by Peter Stenbæk, 1997.*

▲ *Designed by Peter Stenbæk, 2004.*

occasion was Bent Fabric, made a modern album and simultaneously maintained a connection to his musical past.

In 2003, Jesper Dahl, alias Jokeren, released his debut album 'Alphahan' (Alpha male). The aggressive lyrics and raw hip-hop music were given a corresponding graphic expression in the aggressively over-painted photo of Jokeren. Here there's tension between the styled photo and the severe graphics surrounding it. Behind the cover was the original 80 x 80 collage by concept artist Kristian von Hornsleth. In the summer of 2006 he was noted for giving several hundred Africans in a village in Uganda a goat in return for taking his surname. Tine Knudsen from Jokeren's bureau Art Management did the art direction.

'Karen – En til en' (Karen – one to one) was the title of the first R&B album in Danish recorded by singer Karen Rosenberg in 2001. The expression 'one to one' manifests itself in the graphic design with a full-size close-up of Karen's face. By zooming in, the portrait becomes more immediate, honest and personal, perhaps a bit invasive as if it's insistent on saying: 'I am Karen, now listen to my music.' And if you disregard the discreet makeup, it comes across as an honest and 'unstyled' cover. The design, including the choice of transparent lettering, was made by Sille Aasmul.

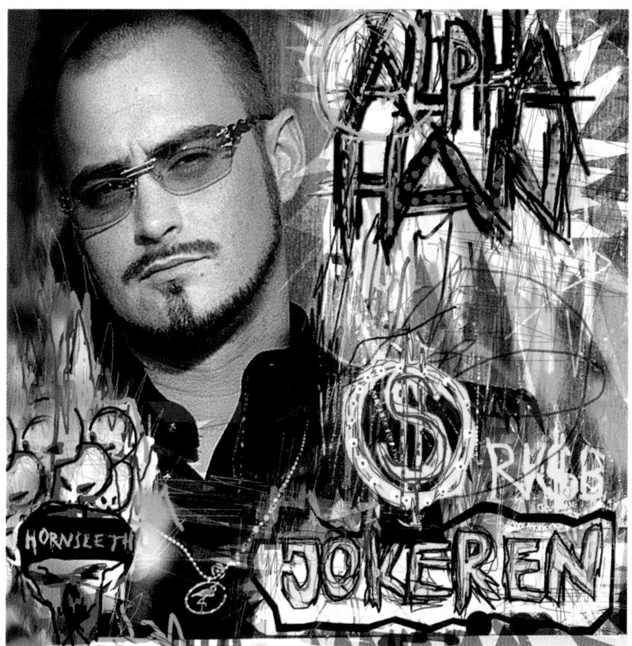

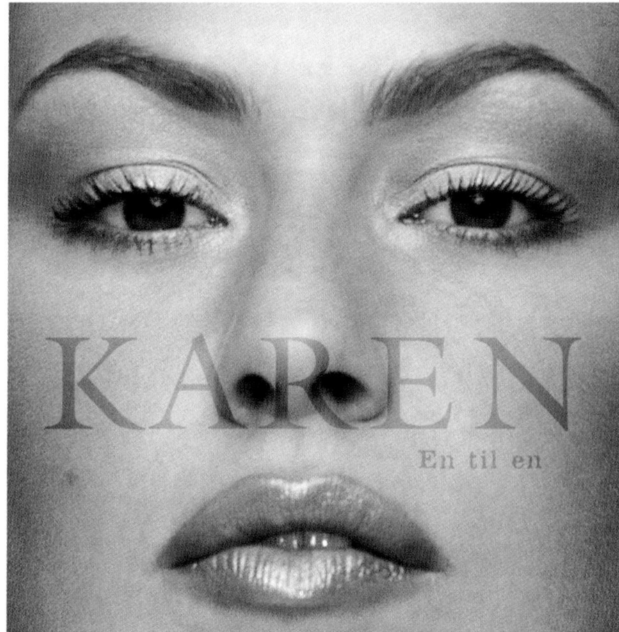

▲ *Designed by Kristian von Hornsleth, 2003*

▲ *Designed by Sille Aasmul, 2000.*

THE WAVE POSTAGE STAMP. One of the smallest graphic products is the stamp. Since it has a denomination, almost like a currency, is has to be made using security printing and designed so that it's difficult to counterfeit. For technical reasons and cost-efficiency, the Danish postal service used to print stamps in one or at most two colours. The stamps were steel-plate printed so the amount of detail in the patterns was so fine and complicated that they were hard to copy. One example is the old Danish wavy stamp that is the second oldest in the world, and which is still available. It was the result of a 1902 design competition that was won by architect Julius Therchilsen, who received 500 kroner for his first prize place. It was also the first stamp in Denmark printed with the new and more secure method of steel engraving. The motif has elements from the royal coat of arms – lions, crown and hearts. Then there are the wavy lines that are normally associated with the Copenhagen town arms, but in this case are probably meant to symbolise the Øresund and the two belts. The typeface is still in the original Art Nouveau style, and if you use a magnifying glass, you can see the dots in the steel engraving. Leter, graphic designer Torben Skov designed modern versions of the wavy stamp. They were to celebrate the new millennium, so the year 1999 is disappearing off the top and the year 2000 is emerging from the bottom. The old symbols of waves and hearts are included, one on each stamp, while the crown and lions are left out. These stamps were printed with offset printing, with several colours as well as silver to safeguard the stamp from counterfeit.

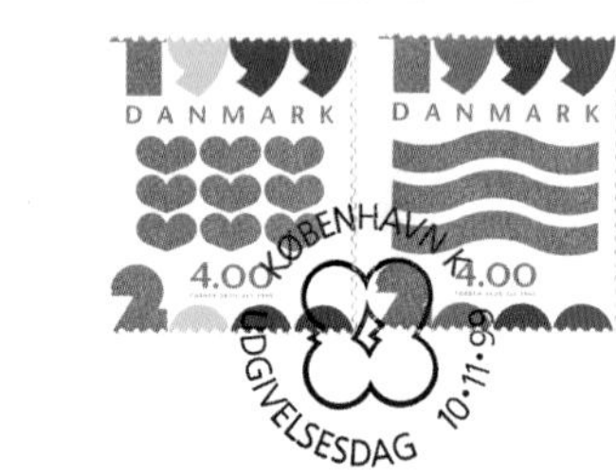

▾ *Radio Denmark's logos – from the first one designed by Connie Linck in 1964 and to Mollerup Designlab's radical screen signature from 1994 to DR's own designs from 1996 and 2005, respectively.*

ELECTRONIC DESIGN

Ever since moving pictures became common, the challenge has existed to design relevant graphic expressions for these media. In the early days of film, making rolling credits was a lot of work, while today it's relatively easy to do. In the beginning it was done in a low-tech way where the graphic artist in extreme cases drew and coloured directly onto the celluloid film. But they quickly changed to photographing the printed words and drawings on paper, and this can be seen in old silent movies where the scenes are interrupted by fastidious typography on signs that explain the plot or recounts the actors' primitive dialogue. They also started using drawings to animate the stories, and this is what we know as cartoons.

While the pictorial medias gradually developed, not least in the area of television, the aesthetics of book printing and the old design methods from the paper era were no longer suitable. The graphics on the TV screen soon got a life of its own in the form of the symbols and logos of TV stations that at first were only used between programs. Later they were also used as a permanent identification mark somewhere on the screen, so that viewers could immediately tell what station they had tuned in to.

On the only TV station that Danes could watch for many years, Radio Denmark (DR), things got off to a slow start. In the pioneering days of the 1950s, when DR was still called the State Broadcasting Service, they used a screen graphics with wavy lines, where the word Denmark was written in classic cursive. It resembled something on the Danish banknotes or stamps. It wasn't until 1964 that the national TV station got its first real logo that was designed by the graphic artist at Radiohuset (Radio Denmark's House), Connie Linck. It has large voluminous rounded forms, and it is said that she was inspired by 1950s stamps from Bolivia, Chile and Costa Rica. It is a robust graphic design that was maybe a bit too classic and conservative for such a new media.

From the 1960s and onwards, an awful lot happened in television, and although DR had never called itself TV1, one day there was a channel called TV2. Perhaps that's why they started considering their identity at the old station. The result was that DR in 1994 asked an external design firm, Mollerup Designlab, to design a new symbol to display in the upper right corner of the screen. The new logo was a 'negative number one'. Negative in the sense that the number one isn't drawn, but the shapes around it are. The new logo caused quite a stir in the public. It was said that the viewers couldn't tell what the figure was supposed to be and what it said.

But the advanced visual design of the logo wasn't the only thing that met resistance. DR's reason for wanting a new simplified logo was that all the other stations used theirs like a constant signature on the screen during programs. Yet despite this, the logo wasn't well received by all the viewers. They just didn't like the idea of having a logo in the corner of a TV program. And directors of old Danish movies tried to have it prohibited for their films to be shown with the new logo on the screen, since they thought it was visual vandalism. Some of the objections to the new logo were perhaps not due to its design but to that fact that it was on the screen all the time.

The protests and the debate were interesting since once again it was clear that sometimes there are narrow limits to how innovative one can be.

◂ *The Hitman character at work in the digital game of the same name.*

Seeing as Radio Denmark is an institution that many people consider a part of the national identity, people find it unsettling when such a giant leap is made. When a switch is made from using a slightly antiquated graphic expression to something that resembles avant-garde art, one is asking for it. One can't help thinking back to the words of the American designer Raymond Loewy about designing 'Most Advanced, Yet Acceptable' (see page 112).

Two years later, in 1996, two graphic designers at DR, Morten Noer and Mark Gry Christiansen, made a new signature for the radio and television corporation. It was a modernisation of Connie Linck's logo and was used in relevant places with Per Mollerup's number 1 until 2002 when they switched to a new number 1 and a number 2 for DR2. It might seem strange to do away with Mollerup Designlab's symbol when it had finally been accepted and considered by many to be a very good design, for example the number 1 got a design prize from the Danish Design Centre in 1994. But the desire for a more homogenous corporate identity seems to have carried weight.

In 2005 the logo was redesigned again by DR Design. The reason for the new design was partly the same as in 2002, namely that the image of DR as an all-round media company needed to be strengthened, and partly that the 1996 logo wasn't suitable for the internet and other digital media. The new logo is more angular in its expression although there are some similarities to its predecessors. Concurrently with the ongoing development of the logo, a number of other graphic elements were introduced. In the old days, the station used the famous 'break fish' (a picture of an aquarium with goldfish swimming around), but between the programs they now showed animated graphic jingles and little cartoons that were produced for that purpose. In this way not only DR but other TV stations try to brand their range of programs and all their media activities.

The digital assassin

Digital design is increasingly important in our modern society. It's not only about the ordinary design of graphic icons for use on computer screens, but also numerous new media and products that use a radically different artistic idiom. More specifically not only are websites designed, but also the new types of electronic signage in the public space and the graphics on the small displays of cell phones. This has created new conditions for working with graphic design, and the field has been split into those who specialise in the print media and those who work in the new digital arena. Even graphic design bureaus are internally split into departments for one or the other discipline.

So the area is in rapid development, and as regards things such as websites, it's a media that is hard to assess as well as to find really good examples of. On the one hand, it seems like web designers who have a background as graphic designers focus very much on good aesthetics whereas functionality and user-friendliness can be lacking. Designing websites is not just about transferring the layout of a paper brochure to a screen image. The media on the internet function far more dynamically and have new possibilities for interactive communication, which won't be fully explored for years. Conversely, the websites where the technical functioning has been prioritised often don't have a very appealing appearance. The correct balance between the two considerations doesn't seem to have been found yet.

The digital products that seem to be the most advanced are games, both those which can be played on the internet and those that demand special hardware. Among the most successful Danish designed digital games we find the computer game *Hitman*. There are now four versions, the latest from 2006, and there is a movie from 2007 with Timothy Olyphant in the title role. Digital computer games are often designed as interactive environments with a plot or a narrative. When you play a game like *Hitman*, you're playing an active part in the story, and you experience the plot in a credible way through the assassin's eyes. The point of the game is to play Hitman and survive all the battles against his adversaries and to complete his mission.

When you design and manufacture a computer game, you construct the interactive universe that includes scenography, animations, movie sequences, sound and graphics. By being interactive, the digital medium allows the designer unique opportunities for creating a whole world of game possibilities. The user can experience the complex stories and take an active part in them. Often it is primarily the aesthetic experience of the environment and the participation that makes a game fascinating and attractive, and not so much the story itself. In the development process, the work on the design of the atmosphere and the environment is mostly done first while the story is written afterwards to fit the scenography and the effects.

The *Hitman* games were developed by the Danish company IO Interactive. Even though it was purchased in 2001 by the English game corporation Eidos, much of the development and programming still takes place in Denmark. The *Hitman* game has at this point been sold in eight million copies worldwide, but many games have to be sold to recoup the investments. The development expenses alone for the fourth version of the game were around 100 million kroner. What makes it so expensive is that *Hitman* is very realistically designed so the surroundings are almost true to life. That's what makes it a very credible game. It's another thing entirely if one likes the plot about a bald hired gun that goes around blowing people away, and if one would like to play such a character.

DSB's Dot alphabet

While the IC3 trains were being developed and were gradually put into service in the late 1980s, DSB wanted to furnish the trains and the passenger areas with an electronically controlled information system. However, they weren't satisfied with the crude electronic typefaces that were on the market at the time and that's why they chose to develop their own alphabet. This type of electronic lettering is based on every letter consisting of many small dots. In this case a number of light emitting diodes that are used to create the typeface almost like a raster image.

Back then, the norm in the field of electronic moving messages that produced electric newspapers and the like was to use 7 or 9 dots in the height to make the letters. This is a very crude raster that renders some 'choppy' letters. In the Dot alphabet they instead used 13 dots on the vertical plane which gives a more reader-friendly lettering and makes it possible for DSB to use its standard signage typeface without too much distortion. The final result was a very legible information system. DSB was responsible for the development along with one of their regular partners in graphic design and communication, namely Damsgaard & Lange, who have also designed many of DSB's traffic maps and boards.

▼ *DSB's Dot alphabet from 1988 that is still used on long-distance and regional trains. The sign reads: To Frederikshavn, Car 12.*

▾ Thorvald Bindesbøll's Hof label from 1904 is one of the most long-lived packaging designs in the world, and its form is almost the same today. Actually, the shape of the bottle has changed more than the label since the Danish breweries in 1949 switched from the old type with rounded shoulders to a new standard bottle of the 'Viennese type' that was more robust and therefore better suited to the Danish system of recyclable bottles. The formal occasion for Carlsberg wanting a new label was that the brewery was now 'By appointment to the royal Danish Court' (in Danish, the word for court is 'hof', hence the name). Therefore a new label with a crown on it was designed. Many years later, in 1976, Faxe Breweries designed their own special bottle that was popularly called 'The little chubby one'. Faxe played a joke on the beer magnate by writing on their label 'By appointment to the Danish people'. The Professor of industrial design at the Royal Academy's School of Architecture Nils Fagerholt designed the bottle, but not the label. The reason behind this design was, apart from standing out, the little brown glass bottle provided better protection for Faxe's special pasteurised beer from the destructive effects of light. Faxe's little chubby one was taken out of production in early 2006.

DANISH PACKAGING

The design of packaging is an interesting cross between the flat, two-dimensional graphic design on paper and the three-dimensional product design. Packaging has fulfils only the function of being practical containers for products and protecting them on their way to the consumer, but there must also be a place for communication with the users. Particularly because of the latter function, graphic designers normally work on the design of packaging, but sometimes product designers are also involved. The communication on the box or bottle often takes place on several levels. It can be on the supermarket shelf as a seductive object whose job it is to sell the product as well as possible, and it can also be the place where the consumer has to find all the E numbers and other information about the product. The packaging in successful cases has an experience and user value that goes beyond its original function. The vanilla girl (on the package of vanilla extract) may remind us of childhood dreams of faraway places, and the cigar box can be used to contain mementos from these travels long after grandfather has smoked the last cigar.

The modern sealed packaging that we know today was slowly developed during the industrialisation. Products were standardised and the production was centralised in fewer factories and this led to a greater need for both packaging for transport and easily recognisable wrapping. However, the modern self-service principle in the supermarkets has caused the development of packaging to accelerate. Furthermore, the increased focus on branding in recent decades has made companies concentrate more on the role of packaging. Before all this happened, it was common for the buyer to bring his own packaging to the store. For example, even in the 1900s in Denmark one had to bring one's own pitcher to the dairy store to buy milk. And fish was perhaps wrapped in a piece of old newspaper before being put in the basket next to the unwrapped loaf of bread. Modern industry, long transports and increased demands on hygiene have changed this forever.

Carlsberg

Funnily enough, some the most well-known Danish packaging is in the area of food, drink and other stimulants. In this context one of the most famous Danish examples of packaging is the Carlsberg label for the Hof beer bottle. It was designed in 1904 by architect, artist and designer Thorvald Bindesbøll (1846–1908), who otherwise didn't design much commercial art, but had since the 1880s been the aesthetic advisor and graphic designer for the Carlsberg Brewery. The timing of the design for the Hof label wasn't random, for at that time the breweries in Denmark had agreed to standardise their bottles. This was the beginning of the recyclable bottle system which Danes still use today. But this also made the bottles identical, and thus the labels of the individual beer brands became far more important for marketing and branding the beer. For his design of the label Bindesbøll received 5000 kroner, at the time a very high payment for something that didn't seem like a very big job.

Bindesbøll also designed other labels for Carlsberg, but only the Hof one has survived unscathed till this day. It was a great success, since the design is estimated to have been printed on more than 10 billion bottles and beer cans. The way in which Bindesbøll wrote the word Carlsberg was shortly after used as the brewery's logo and is still used on stationery, cars, uniforms and in all the brewery's advertisements. So the designer's fee has been recovered many times over.

◂ *FDB's logo designed by Gunnar Biilmann Petersen in 1951 and diligently used until 2002, when it faded into the background in favour of Co-op Denmark's new logo. The classic logo with the initials FDB in a closed bow symbolises harmony and agreement on the joint task of getting the customers and thereby the members good products at good prices.*

The label was designed in the Art Nouveau style in which the romance of nature was the hot style. The style can be recognised in the way the writing winds around and especially the G's tail. Furthermore the little hops leaves are placed here and there. In comparison to other artists and graphic designers of the time, Bindesbøll had a rather simple expression; not very messy or overly decorative. He was one of the best representatives of Art Nouveau, although he didn't like to be pigeonholed as regards style.

Yet the design of the signature breaks many of the traditional rules for good type design. It's neither a real typeface for writing nor for printing, and the letters are strangely dissimilar, for example, the two R's are rather different. Nonetheless the logo is powerful and full of vitality, and although the label and the signature have been redesigned and slightly simplified many times, this has been done slowly and surely so that consumers have hardly noticed. Bindesbøll was one of the first artists in Denmark to put his mark on industrial commercial art while still doing his own artistic work. Thus he came to set a fashion for people like Engelhardt and those who followed him. The label also set the fashion for other breweries, since before Carlsberg's design, the labels on the market had looked very different from each other. Some were square, some were rectangular, but after Bindesbøll's design the norm became oval labels.

The cheerful 1950s

The first decade after World War II was a good time for Danish packaging design. Retailing had been developed in the tender years of welfare by a number of companies of which some were conscious of the value of design. In this context, new brands were sent on the market, and new packaging was designed, which we see today as classics. In particular the company FDB (the Danish Consumers' Co-operative Society), which at the time was a true giant in Danish retailing, did its best to raise the bar. As an extension of the co-op's focus on manufacturing and selling well-designed quality furniture to its members, they also focused on design in other areas. For example, newly appointed Professor Gunnar Biilmann Petersen from the Royal Academy's Department of Graphic Design designed a new logo for FDB in 1951. This three-winged bow-like logo that is reminiscent of the graphic works of the Dutch graphic artist M.C. Escher (1898–1972) had a great graphic strength and was used by FDB until it merged with the Swedish co-ops, and then they primarily used the name Co-op Denmark.

While FDB was working with Biilmann Petersen, they also hired illustrator and poster designer Aage Sikker Hansen to illustrate packaging and posters for, among other products, the oatmeal brand Davre-gryn and Cirkel Kaffe (Coffee). The poster for Davre-Gryn has gone down in history as an almost permanent fixture in Danish children's rooms, but it is no longer used actively by the co-ops. One that is used is the illustration with the Cirkel coffee girl from 1954 that still adorns the coffee packages in the co-op's stores in Denmark. Sikker Hansen's illustrations exude sunny Danish summers and people from exotic places. Besides the coffee girl, he had already designed in 1945 a mysterious pipe-smoking Indian woman with tobacco leaves on her head as an advertisement for FDB's own tobacco factory in Esbjerg. Sikker Hansen's style was poetically dreamy with softly toned drawings of romantic figures, whether they were children or natives from some other country. It was a very special style to use for the normally rather forceful retailer and gave FDB the distinctive image of being an idealistic enterprise, which it was to some extent, being a customer-owned company.

▾ *The Cirkel coffee girl has become synonymous with not only the coffee but also as a symbol of the classic post-war FDB that imported exotic products to Denmark and their customers. Aage Sikker Hansen, who designed the poster in 1954 was very interested in foreign peoples. He also designed other posters and illustrations with the same kind of motifs, always with an almost touching solicitude and respect for 'the noble savage'.*

◂ Claus Achton Friis designed the original King's pack in 1948. The pack was white, which was unusual for a cigarette pack in those days, and moreover the design was simple with a lot of space around the graphics. Thus the pack had a slightly distinguished look, which apparently appealed to the intellectuals of the time. In 1995 two new variants were added, namely one with a filter and a light cigarette with a filter. On that occasion the old design was changed by Plan Design, much to Achton Friis' regret. He was paid 2500 kroner for his work in 1948, which corresponded to six months' pay for a recently qualified graduate.

King's

Another example of the 1950s creative abundance in the field of packaging design is the cigarette packs that were made by Claus Achton Friis. The graphic design on the packs of the Danish brands Cecil, Prince, Queen's and King's was designed for what was then known as Chr. Augustinus Factories, but which today are part of the Scandinavian Tobacco Company. The pack of King's cigarettes has in particular been noted for its graphic qualities. It's a white pack with a distinguished signature and furnished with a little emblem that contains a coat of arms. The pack is almost British in its elegant expression. Because of the image that the individual cigarette brands have, they are directed at certain target groups on the market, or segments as they're also called. While Cecil has traditionally been a working-class brand, King's have appealed to more intellectual consumers, which the design also had to reflect. Or perhaps it was the other way round. The difference in the design of the brands sends certain signals that more or less were instrumental in making certain people prefer one brand over another.

This differentiation between brands, signals and segments is something that a designer has to be conscious of when designing a cigarette pack. He can't just design what would appeal to him as a consumer; he must immerse himself in the task and put himself in the place of the people who are presumed to buy and use the product. Claus Achton Friis wasn't fond of cigarettes. He smoked a pipe if he smoked at all, but this didn't stop him from designing the packaging for cigarettes. Sometimes you'll hear a designer say in an interview that they only 'design something that they would like to have or buy for themselves'. A designer who expresses this sentiment is not a good designer. If a designer or architect can't put his or her self in another's place and design solutions for them, then they haven't understood the nature of the profession. Claus Achton Friis could therefore easily design a number of very different cigarette brands and do it well. It's not the same as saying that a good designer can't have points of view and strong opinions about how things should be done or what is good or bad. Achton Friis was later appointed professor of graphic design for a short period of time at the Royal Academy of Fine Arts, School of Architecture. And anyone who met him there in his professional capacity sensed his clear opinions and points of view. He formed an opinion of every design he cast his eye on, but he didn't judge them in terms of whether he would like to have them or not, but in terms of whether they were designed well for their purpose and the target group.

CLAUS ACHTON FRIIS, 1917–1999, was an architect and graphic designer and was qualified both as a ceramicist and carpenter before entering the Royal Academy of Fine Arts in 1940 and graduating in 1944. He worked with Gunnar Biilmann Petersen for some years before setting up his own architectural practice in 1950. From 1964–68 he was an assistant to Professor Biilmann Petersen, and from 1980 to 1985 he was professor of graphic design at the Royal Academy's School of Architecture. Friis worked in a classic method with design and never used a computer for this purpose. His works ranged from the very official heraldry to signs, logos, typeface and designing cigarette packs for the Scandinavian Tobacco Company as well as designing over 40 Danish stamps. Among other things, he designed Queen Margrethe's monogram according to her own draft.

THE BUCKET OF bricks from LEGO. If the packaging can be a part of the product, a company can hit two birds with one stone. Not only do you solve your packaging problem, but the customers feel they're getting extra value with the product. Since 1987, LEGO has sold bricks by the bucket along with their construction sets in cardboard boxes. The bucket works both as packaging in the stores where it's sealed with a nylon band to guarantee the correct contents, and as a storage space in the children's room or in the daycare centre. The buckets were developed in-house at LEGO and are available in different versions with different contents. However, the large labels on the outside were designed by the design office Plan Design, who have also done the graphics for many of LEGO's other boxes over the years. The LEGO bucket is one of the corporation's most successful and best-selling products, and unlike other construction sets, it's been a permanent part of their range since it was introduced.

THE IRMA BAGS. In the late 1960s, Irma was a supermarket chain store with a slightly luxurious image, and it hadn't yet been taken over by FDB; that didn't happen until 1982. It was actually a competitor to FDB, and FDB's image that it had gradually built up through collaboration with poster designers and graphic designers was something Irma wanted to match. In 1970, Irma's chief of advertising, Thomas Brandt, along with a group of young artists, had the idea of putting art on Irma's shopping bags. At the same time, Irma started charging 25 ører for a bag. But now the customers didn't have to advertise for Irma on their way home, so the idea of art on the bags was implemented. Since then, 400 different versions of their art bags were printed, which these days have a print run of 700,000. So now about 100 million bags have been printed. However, the price of the bag has risen to 2.25 kroner.

New times and a new type of design

The way in which designers work has naturally changed continuously. This has happened as society, technology, the conditions and the tasks have changed. So in this respect, design isn't different than other professions – everyone has had to adjust to survive the changing challenges. Many of these changes have taken place over a long period of time and some of them have, of course, had their origin in technological and economic development, but they have also come about through man's new life circumstances and the changing views in society about what is good or bad. Although the word design is rather new in the Danish language, the practice of designing is an old discipline. Design is much more that just giving industrial products a form. This was the case centuries ago before industrialisation, and this is still the case today.

Far back in history people made decisions about design. Of course, someone has directed the work of building, designing and planning Viking ships and the circular forts. And when visiting the Royal Naval Museum in Copenhagen, one can find numerable ship models from the 1600s and 1700s, and many of them were not made merely for decoration after the large ship was built. These models played an important role as design tools. They were used by naval architects to show the admirals and the king what a specific design would look like and to get their approval. And afterwards these models were used to show the shipbuilders and workers how the ships should be built. The scale model as a tool in the design process isn't something new. It has long been used as a means of getting an idea of what the final ship design or the finished house would be like.

DESIGN AS A CRAFT

In earlier times, design and craftsmanship were closely related. Often craftsmen such as cabinetmakers, ceramicists and tailors were the ones who decided on and carried out the final design. These designs usually weren't groundbreaking, but were often limited to decorating and modifying the furniture/pot/clothes to the needs and tastes of the customer. The development of design from prehistoric times till modern times consisted mostly of an endless row of tiny steps of progress based on experiences and minor technical breakthroughs. For example, it could be a tool that the practising craftsman constantly refined until it was perfectly suited to its purpose and the user's needs and ergonomics. The large leaps came in very special situations. The most significant progress could happen, for example, when new materials or technologies were introduced, such as when bronze in prehistoric times replaced stone.

New tools and machines also led to new work methods. This happened when the saw was developed and gained ground in carpentry. And then the axe, including the previously mentioned broadaxe, faded into the background as the preferred tool. A corresponding change took place when the saw was motorised, and then new working procedures were introduced into carpentry. Other changes have been made as a result of the advent of new materials, such as when traditional lumber was supplemented, or even replaced, by new products such as chipboard, plywood, beams of laminated wood and plasterboard. Each time the carpenters have had to adjust and get used to working in new ways. The same thing happened later on when many designers were inspired by new materials and technologies.

THE FURNITURE COMPANY Montana specialises in a bookcase system designed by the company owner Peter Lassen (b. 1930). The Montana system is based on roughly the same modular principle as Mogens Koch's bookcase system from 1928. That is, a square element that can be turned to accommodate either big or small books. However, it's possible to order custom-made Montana elements with various pre-mounted shelves, drawers and doors. Montana's bookcases are made of both MDF that is spray painted and comes in various colours, or in different types of wood. Peter Lassen, who had previously been the director of the furniture factory Fritz Hansen, established Montana in 1970 and has since branded the simple, and not especially original, product fantastically well. For example, at exhibitions and for the use of catalogues, the company has let young graffiti artists loose on lots of their bookcases. One of the latest initiatives has been to manufacture a version of the Montana bookcase in recycled plastic instead of MDF. The plastic boards are from a German company that has specialised in collecting and reusing household plastic, especially soda bottles and other packaging. The materials are sorted according to colour, melted and moulded into the shape of the boards. The flecked pattern arises since the plastic isn't thoroughly sorted, and among other things, the screw caps are left on the bottles. At the Copenhagen furniture fair at the Bella Centre these plastic bookcases where exhibited at Montana's stand as an effective eye-catcher. They can be bought by consumers, just like the wooden bookcases, however only in the measurements 69.6 x 69.6 cm.

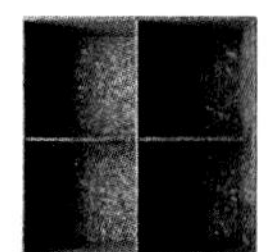
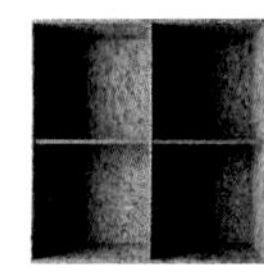

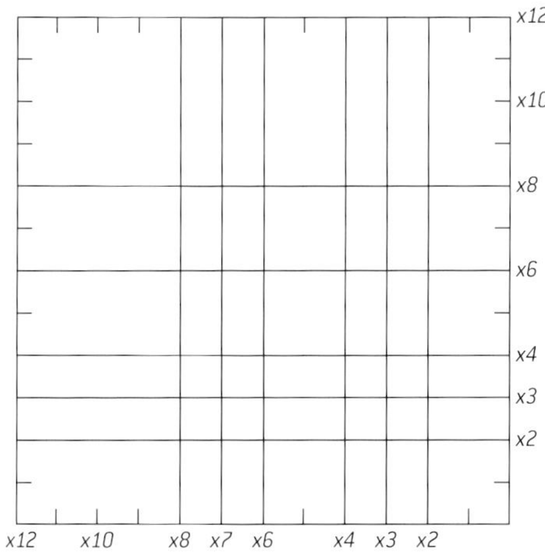

▸ *The drawing shows Montana's modular system. The basic module's 69.6 x 69.6 cm is divided into twelfths so the system's smallest unit is the so-called cardinal number, 5.7 cm. Within these numbers, any kind of element can be manufactured. Furthermore, one can choose between four depths: 20, 30, 38 and 46.8 cm.*

▾ *Industrial designer Henrik Holbæk (b. 1960) and Claus Jensen (b. 1966) have designed some kitchenware in the Eva Solo sub-brand for the company Eva Denmark. In their designed products they often use new and different materials in a surprising way. This is perhaps most noticeable in their pot holders made of solid-coloured silicone rubber. At first it might seem an odd choice of material, and people might ask questions like: Can this rubber take the heat? Won't the hot dish slip out of my hands? Despite these fears, they work well and have the advantage of being easier to clean than grandmother's old homemade crocheted versions.*

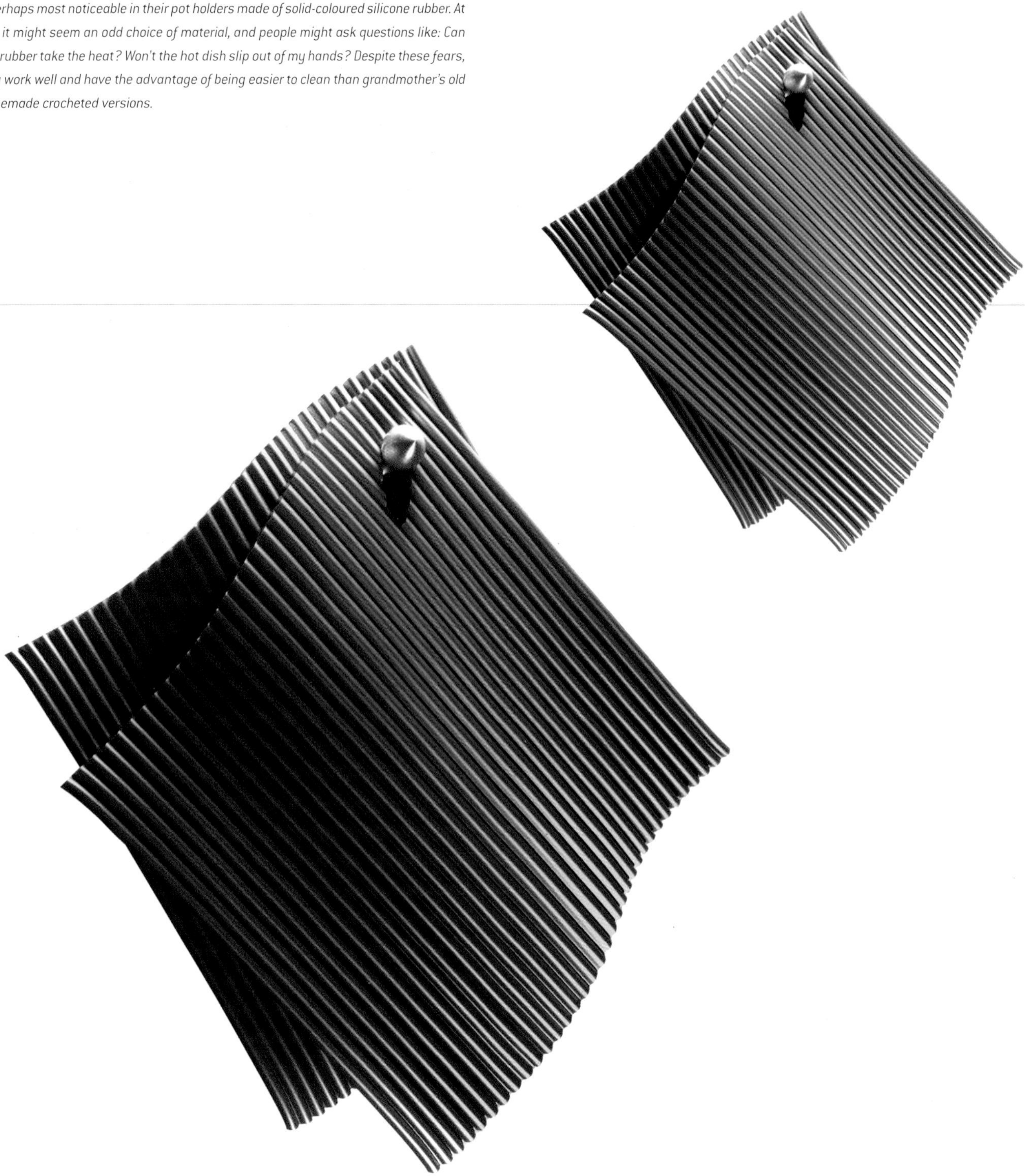

▸ *Ceramicist and designer Ole Jensen has also worked with rubber in an untraditional way for the design of his dishpan. The reason why he made the dishpan out of pliable rubber was that it is gentler on porcelain and glass during dishwashing. Furthermore, the user would have a different sensuous experience than with a traditional dishpan. Ole Jensen moulded the first copies himself in silicone rubber in 1996, but since then the company Normann Copenhagen has taken over the production and sale of the dishpan, which comes in many colours.*

Often new products have been made by taking existing models and giving them a new expression with the help of a new material or a new manufacturing process. A classic example of this is the Margrethe bowls from 1951 (see page 94) that back then were manufactured of the new plastic material called melamine resin. The form of the bowls themselves was not actually groundbreaking in comparison to earlier bowls made of ceramics, glass or metal, but the tough plastic material with a high breaking point meant that a little handle could be added on the rim, which was difficult to do in ceramics or glass. In their day, the designers Bjørn & Bernadotte and their young employee Jacob Jensen were some of the most internationally oriented designers in Denmark. They did not shrink from using new materials at a time when not only the Danes generally, but also many Danish designers thought along traditional lines, and plastic was considered an inferior material. The entire success of Danish designer furniture in the 1950s was very much based on things such as the traditional cabinetmaker's craft although it was executed in a very high quality.

CRAFTSMANSHIP AS DESIGN TODAY?

It was indeed the sublime craftsmanship that became Danish design's hallmark in the successful post-war years. And in many ways it is this image that is still Danish design's and especially furniture design's claim to fame. The current cultivation of the functionalist classics, where cabinetmakers' furniture like the Egg and the Swan are sold at auctions at exorbitant prices, bears testimony to this. Why was this period so successful and full of vitality for Danish design? The answer is not exactly clear cut, but can probably be found in a combination of a really good aesthetic sense, excellent craftsmanship and respect for the materials. At the same time, designers contributed with their products to the vision of a civilised and humanist society. In this arena, the cultivated person could put the barbarity of the world war behind him in designed surroundings that reflected the dream of a future characterised by new humanist and aesthetic values. That this actually came to pass is both a result of the Danish designers' talent and their timing, which perhaps a bit haphazardly turned out to be perfect.

But around 1970, extensive changes had gradually been made in the way Western society worked. There were no longer low wages and a shortage of resources – quite the contrary. Buying traditional craftsmanship was now expensive, while new and cheaper materials had come on the market, such as plastic, plywood, chipboard and aluminium. However, these materials required new ways of designing and new methods of production. And not many Danish designers could immediately adjust to this. The only Danish designer that seriously had something new in the offing in the 1970s was Verner Panton. His colourful and organic style suited both the spirit of the times and the new economy.

The success of the 1950s was a bit of a mystery to both designers and the design-based industry. There hadn't been any timely research and analysis done that could make the businesses aware of their strengths and weaknesses and chart a new course for the profession. On the contrary, they held on to the dream of reviving the previous glory of expensive craftsmanship. It was just a matter of designing even more exquisite and exclusive furniture. But it was not only the new technology and the cost of labour and materials that had changed and made new demands on designers. The times had also changed regarding the way people

SOMETIMES YOU SEE products, which were originally designed in wood, be redesigned and made of plastic. The opposite is the case with the Gubi chair from 2003. The design office Komplot Design took its starting point from a 50-year-old American plastic chair designed by Ray and Charles Eames. From 1948 and onwards, it had been manufactured in fibreglass by the company Herman Miller. Since 1971 it was also made in a newly designed mould-injected version. In 1948, the Eames chair was the world's first chair in which the seating shell (all-in-one back and seat) had been made of plastic, while the frame was made of chrome-plated wire (Verner Panton's plastic chair from 1967, on page 266, was, however, the first chair completely moulded out of a single piece of plastic).

Komplot Design, which consists of Poul Christiansen (b. 1947) and Boris Berlin (b. 1953), has designed the Gubi chair for production in a brand new laminating technique, developed by a German professor. Normally you can't bend laminated wood as much as is done here where it goes in two directions at the same time. The technique is to make many small cuts in the layers of veneer before gluing them together. That makes the shell very flexible, and when the glue dries, you have a chair shell that couldn't have been made before without breaking. The seating shell is strong enough to be made very thin, about 5 mm, and the total weight of the chair is consequently also very low. Despite the technique being German and the design based on an American chair, the Gubi chair got the ID prize from the Danish Design Centre in 2004.

lived, their family structures, work methods and their social intercourse. In time there was a need for completely new types of furniture. Just think of the fact that many people today work at home one or several days a week.This makes demands for a development of new types of furniture that people can work at, without making the living room or bedroom look like an office.

But naturally these visions cannot be realised by designers alone, and that's why companies, buyers of design in the public sector and consumers have a responsibility too. The fruitful years in the 1950s and 1960s have certainly shown that good design and commercial success go hand in hand. Nonetheless it appears that many designers are trying to revive the golden years of Danish design by focusing on craftsmanship, form and materials, which were the principle qualities of the classics seen from a superficial point of view. But by doing that one overlooks first of all that one of the reasons why the golden age waned was that traditional hand-crafted furniture became too expensive for most Danes, and second of all that good design requires insight into the situation and the users' circumstances. Some of the furniture classics as well as the latest Danish design have become so elitist and expensive that whatever market is left has been reduced to museum curators and a little group of well-off design nerds.

DESIGN AS A CULTURAL PHENOMENON

Apart from being propelled by new materials and new technologies, new developments in design and style can emerge as reflections of the great cultural upheavals that have taken place over the years. These new impulses frequently came from abroad, for example when the Renaissance replaced the Gothic style of the Middle Ages and reached Denmark from Italy in about 1535, about 130 years after it had first emerged. In Denmark, the Renaissance made its entry around the same time as the Reformation, and from a design point of view that is quite interesting. For this religious division of Europe has contributed to defining and clarifying the Danish artistic idiom as something that is typically Northern European. When designers talk about various national and regional distinctions in European styles of design, sometimes the expression 'the rye bread border' is used. This border runs east to west through Central Europe, and it received its name because north of this border rye bread is eaten, while it isn't on the southern side. The same border marks roughly how far the Reformation of the Christian church progressed. Interestingly, since time immemorial this border also divided the mostly beer-drinking northern Europe from the wine-drinking southern Europe.

But what does this have to do with design? All these factors, not least the religious ones, have over the years been the basis of what we northerners consider to be good solutions to our various needs in life. It has simply been a result of a different view of design in our neck of the woods, and this is still expressed to some degree in the difference between Danish and Italian furniture, clothing and architecture, for example. At the risk of lapsing into a repetition of stereotypes, one can say that Nordic design is typified by minimalist horse sense, while the Southern European design is often more colourful and typified by a little more show. As mentioned in chapter two, it is possibly the hard, dark and life-threatening winters as well as a certain scarcity of natural resources that are reflected in this artistic design idiom. At any rate, the Nordic and thus also the Danish designers often seek minimal and maybe even puritan solutions where materials are economised on and simplicity takes pride of place.

THE MINIMALIST AND Apollonian designs have often been a characteristic of Danish and Nordic design, and have sometimes been taken to the utmost extreme. An example of this is the Air Titanium glasses that were designed in the mid-1980s by Arne Jacobsen's old architectural practice Dissing & Weitling for the Aarhus-based eyewear company Lindberg Optics. Using thin wires of titanium they have designed an ultra light frame that only weighs 3 grams. Combined with lenses made of synthetic material, the Air Titanium is the closest you can get to a weightless and invisible pair of glasses. The titanium wire is treated, bent and coiled so that the wire itself becomes the hinges, bridge and holders of the lenses. Moreover, the ability of titanium to change colours when subjected to electricity while in a chemical bath was taken advantage of. Thus frames are available in many colours, even rainbow. The Air Titanium glasses have attracted attention in Japan where they also traditionally cultivate minimalist design.

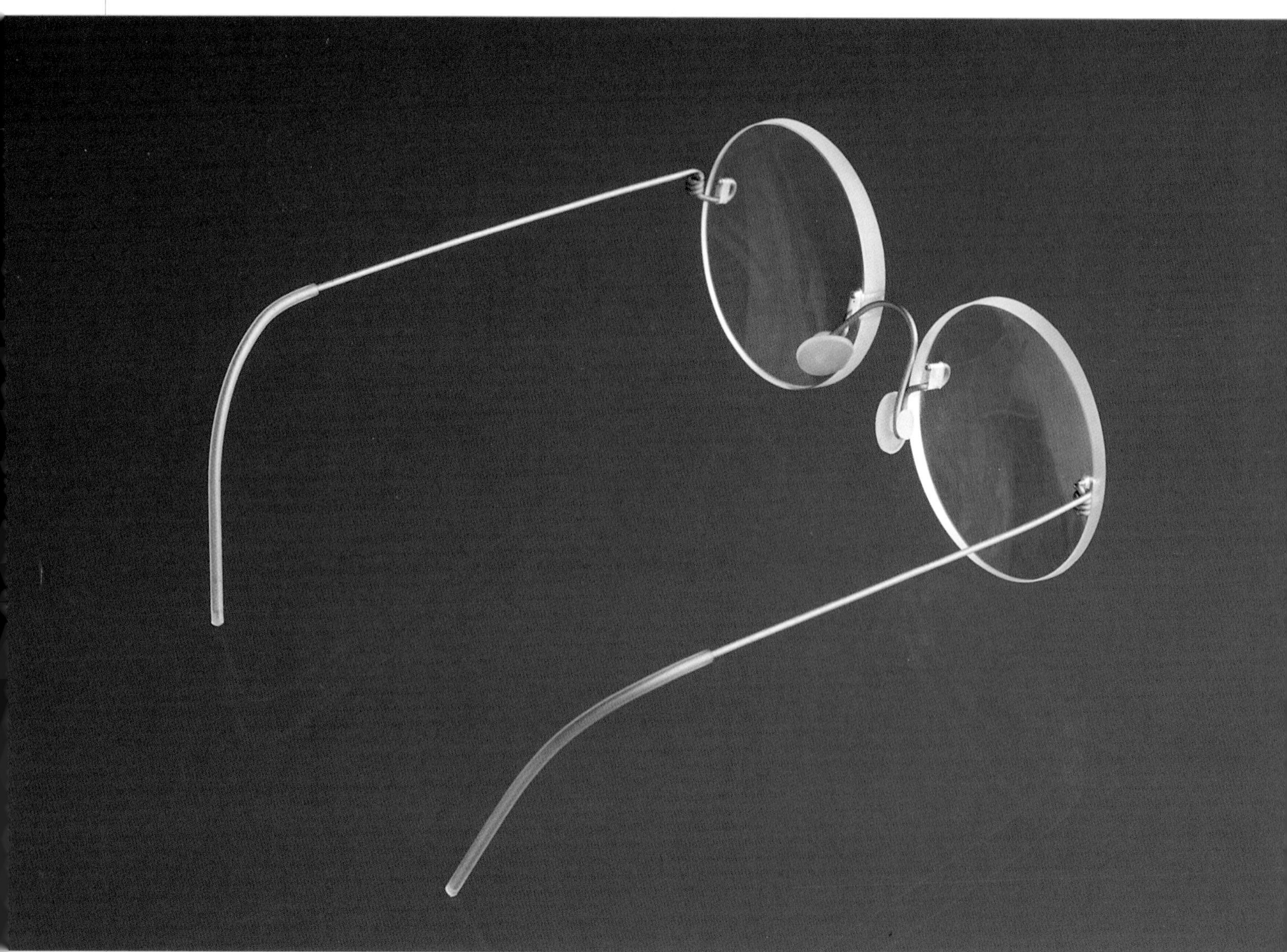

WHILE DISSING & WEITLING were designing the minimalist Air Titanium glasses, architect Ernst Lohse (1944–94) designed a number of proposals for decorative city gates in Copenhagen. With a starting point at the capital's old gates that had been in use until the ramparts collapsed around 1850, Ernst Lohse imagined in true Dionysian fashion new landmarks at the entryways to downtown Copenhagen. Executed in a deconstructivist artistic idiom, one gate was built and erected on Rådhuspladsen (the Town Hall Square) at the entrance to Strøget where it stood during the summer of 1887. However, Copenhagen Municipality did not want this colourful version of Vesterport (the western gate) to remain there permanently, so later it was moved to the square in front of the exhibition hall Brandts' Klædefabrik in Odense.

PRODUCT SEMANTICS. In the old days there was a clear correlation between how a product looked and how it worked. Then the users could intuitively understand how to operate it. Before the washing machine was invented, we washed clothes by firing up the cauldron and otherwise using elbow grease and a washboard. Then the clothes were put through a wringer. Anyone could understand this, even the most slow-witted husband. In a modern washing machine all these function are hidden behind white-enamelled iron plates. Somehow we have to figure out what buttons to push to get the machine to run. If the control panel isn't logical, we have to read the instruction manual, and if we don't understand that either, we have to hope there's someone around who we can ask for help.

The problem of designing machines that are logical to operate is something designers have increasingly had to relate to since many products have become more and more electronic. Perceiving the form of an everyday article as something one can read and unconsciously interpret was known in the 1980s in particular as 'product semantics'. Semantics is the study of the meaning of language, and product semantics is the study of shaping and understanding the artistic idiom of the products.

For many years at the schools of architecture this has been expressed in a differentiation between the Apollonian and the Dionysian principles in design, artistic idiom and art.

These concepts are from classical Greek mythology and refer to the two gods Apollo and Dionysus. While the Apollonian artistic ideal is clarified, well-shaped, well-proportioned and rather stringent and reserved, the Dionysian is in many ways an expression of the opposite view of life and art: the imaginative, chaotic, ecstatic, lively and transcendent. Throughout history, Nordic architecture and design has had a clear tendency to seek the Apollonian idiom. Even when consistent foreign styles, such as the Rococo, have been imported to Denmark, they were usually moderated and were not used to the same degree as in southern Europe. And this is most likely one of the reasons why the clean, geometric and clarified artistic idiom from the two German design schools Bauhaus and Hochschule für Gestaltung in Ulm became so popular within the Danish design milieu.

FROM INVENTION TO INNOVATION AND DESIGN

In the beginning of industrialisation in Denmark 100–150 years ago, technology and inventions were the driving forces in the creation of new products. At one point it was primarily a matter of reining in technology and converting it into useful products. Among other things, it was about creating industrial growth and getting a foothold on the new international markets. The cream separator that is described on page 350 was just one of the examples of an innovative product that formed the basis for progress in another business, namely the dairy business, which in turn made it possible to export butter on a large scale to countries such as England. At this time design had, on the one hand, a very technical character that mainly served to get the technology to work, and on the other hand, the designers had to furnish the products with aesthetics. Thus the visible design often was about decoration and ornamentation. (For example, the meander band that adorns the cream separator on page 350). Much design work was embellishment, which is true far into the 20th century, but it wasn't particularly innovative in itself.

In order to achieve a pivotal role in the development of new products, designers had to work hard to gain respect. In the beginning of the 20th century, talented professionals like Knud V. Engelhardt, Kaare Klint and several others made huge pioneering efforts to create room for the design profession in industry, the public sector and in further education. There was plenty to sink their teeth into. After the first technological wave of industrialisation had swept over Denmark, it was clear that design was also needed, and not just to make the products more beautiful. But in order to solve some of the emerging welfare society's great challenges, good architects and designers had to be included in the picture. There were tasks like ensuring proper housing for everyone and furniture for it, and all the other products that were needed to make a modern society function; from trains and streetcars to kitchen utensils and effective graphic communication. Organisations like the Cabinetmakers' exhibitions and the Danish Consumers' Co-operative Society also did their part in focusing attention on good design. In the inter-war years, Denmark was slowly becoming a design country.

The general conditions for the Danish business community were historically characterised by a certain shortage of natural resources, which necessitated a focus on innovative product development in order

▸ *The Tess bike light.*

The ideal for many industrial designers has since become that it shouldn't be necessary to read a manual in order to use a device. The product should be self-explanatory. This design discipline is still important today; just ask anyone who has ever tried to program a DVD player.

Sometimes products come out that belong to whole new categories and are therefore not always easy to understand. When the fax machine came out, the user had to understand the function first, that is, that one could send texts through the telephone lines. And it was a great challenge for designers to design them so they were easy to operate. And once in a while, new interpretations of known products come out that at first glance seem peculiar. This applied to the bike light Tess that was designed by architect Niels Tessing (b. 1944). When you first saw it, it wasn't clear how to use this bike light unless it was already mounted on a bike. But as soon as it was demonstrated, it was obvious that this design could provide light on your bike in a new way. A special holder was no longer needed since a thick rubber band did the trick. Tess was so different that Danish manufacturers wouldn't buy the concept, so Niels Tessing put it into production himself and ended up selling several hundred thousands of these lights.

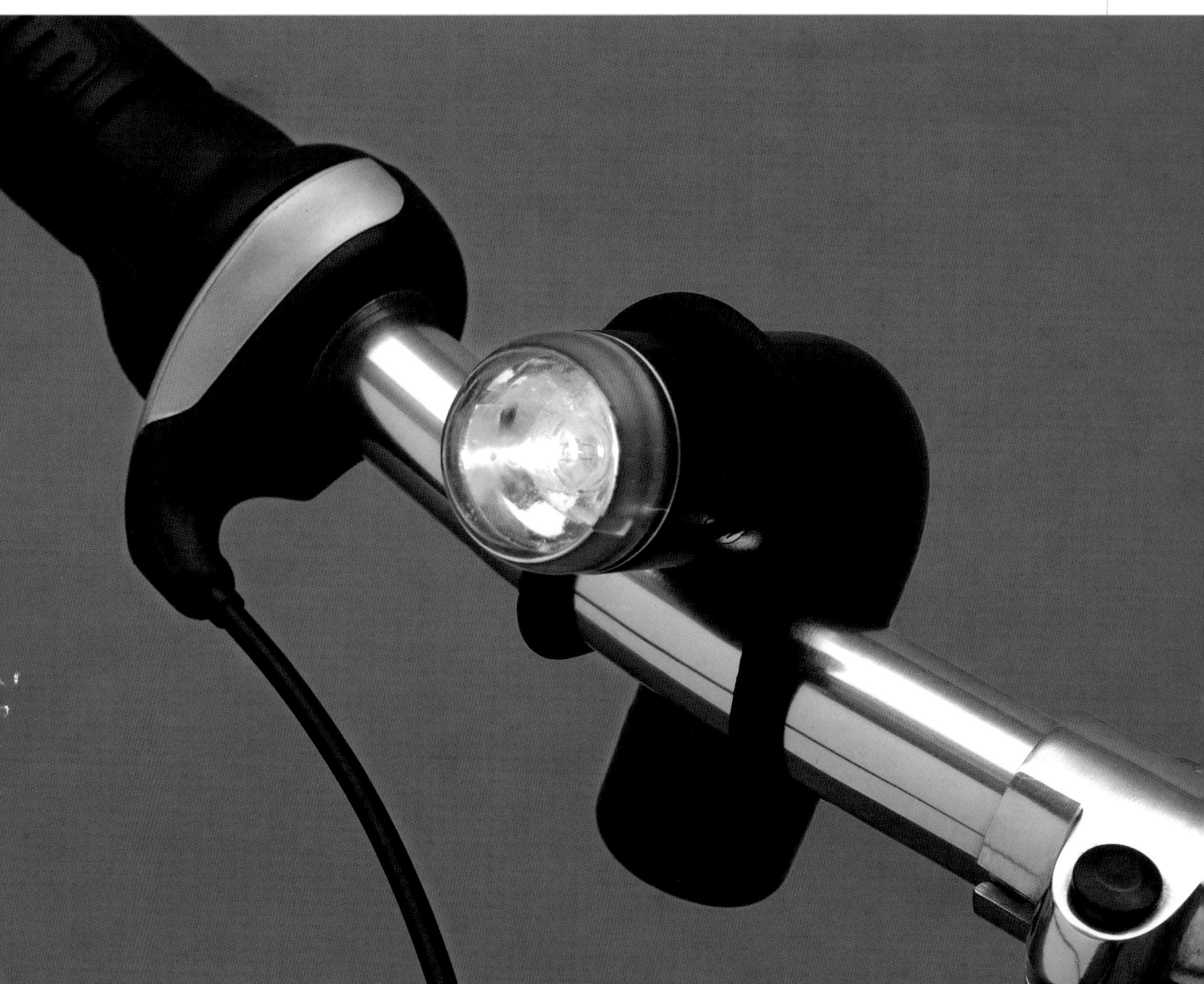

A LOT OF good innovation starts with the perfect identification and definition of the problem. Manufacturer Michael Remark (b. 1941) noticed that there was an irritating problem in the shipping business, namely that many padlocks on containers had to be cut with a bolt cutter at their final destination because the key had been lost on the way. A good padlock is expensive though it doesn't guarantee that the container hasn't been opened during transport. Therefore Michael Remark envisaged a cheaper disposable lock that could replace the traditional customs seal, as well. The result was the product OneSeal, which is a lock that has to be opened with a bolt cutter and is thus ruined. Furthermore the lock has a unique number engraved with a laser, which also protects the contents of the container from being disturbed. OneSeal's construction consists of a type of bolt that can easily be pressed into the coupler, but it takes a force of more than 1100 kg to pull them apart again. The bolt has a piece of wire embedded in it so it can't be broken with someting like a sledgehammer, instead it just bends. At the factory in Kokkedal over 20 million of these disposable locks are made annually, and they're all furnished with a security number engraved with a laser on the coupler. OneSeal is a cheaper solution than a padlock and has significant benefits.

to compensate for this handicap. Some areas of the Danish design tradition are a clear extension of this necessity. When K.V. Engelhardt in 1910 used his abilities to create a rational and sensible streetcar, it was an expression of Danish distinctiveness.

And when Kaare Klint in 1924 sent his students out to measure all the things that a kitchen cupboard should contain, it was an expression of the same thing. The same is true of Poul Henningsen when he analysed the character of electric light and then designed fixtures that emitted both good and cosy lighting for rooms in the northern hemisphere. It has largely been this legacy that has contributed to establishing for posterity the Danes' innovation culture.

FOCUSING ON THE USERS

What has been the driving force in Danish design? Perhaps it was the professional and craftsmanship-based ambitions, perhaps the desire to make beautiful things, or the dream of a society that was secure and prosperous. Perhaps it is the same enterprising spirit that has characterised other Danish entrepreneurs. Danish design has always been part of the collective movement that has contributed to making the Danish version of the welfare state, which is symbolised by the folk high schools and the co-operative movement. Danish companies and designers have made many innovative products and solutions over the course of time. They have found ingenious ways of tackling new tasks, solving problems or of finding new methods of production. The unifying principle in many of the solutions that Danish craftsmen, designers and companies have developed through the centuries is that they have looked beneath the superficial surface of the problem. Cosmetic solutions are rarely appreciated by Danish designers. Styling in the sense of superficial design, as mentioned earlier, is not very popular in the profession.

One of the strengths of Danish design is the tendency to delve deeper into problems to find the truth in a given task and then develop more genuine solutions than the traditional ones. This is one of the good qualities to have, not least today where the world is becoming increasingly complicated and globalised. The ability to put oneself in someone else's place is also a good quality for a designer to have. This quality is especially important in a country like Denmark where equality and democracy are often taken for granted. Anyone who changes the physical environment or designs new products is essentially changing the circumstances of other people's lives. And for many Danish designers this has eventually led to feeling a certain degree of modesty about working with the tasks that were to be done. Among other things, this has manifested itself in the many high-quality solutions that have often been developed for the Danish public environment. For example, this is one of the reasons why Danes have relatively well-designed public transport, and why PH lamps hang in the nursing homes, and why talented architects are often chosen to design public buildings.

But this development has not been limited to the public sector. Back in about 1950, the pharmaceutical company Novo hired architect Arne Jacobsen to design their new factory plant. Here the very first copies of a chair, which later became famous, were used. This was the Ant and 200 of them were used as canteen chairs for the workers. A large part of Danish industry has considered it a hallmark to prefer quality, and not only for their white-collar workers and management. Later on, Novo merged with Nordisk Gentofte and became Novo Nordisk, the world's leading manufacturer of insulin for the treatment of diabetics. The company spent exorbitant amounts of money over the years on research and in their endeavours to develop the best possible human insulin. But at one point, people in the organisation began asking the essential question: why do we do what we do?

All this research money, which was billions of kroner a year, was of course spent on helping patients as much as possible by manufacturing the best medicine technically possible. But it wasn't so simple. Diabetics have to take their medicine in carefully measured and regular doses, and preferably before main meals, or otherwise they risk an acute lack of insulin. On the other hand, they mustn't take too much insulin either. In the past, insulin was sold in ampoules, and the diabetic had to leave the room and use a syringe to take his medicine. This was a bother and led to incorrect dosages with subsequent side effects and discomfort for many people. Many patients felt that they were slaves of their disease, and their quality of life was unnecessarily reduced because of these circumstances. The question put by the people at Novo led to the realisation that they shouldn't see themselves as insulin manufacturers, but as suppliers of a good everyday life for diabetics.

The result was a whole new insulin system developed by Novo Nordisk, so diabetics had an easier time taking their medicine when needed. The new design is called a NovoPen and comes in various versions. Basically it looks like a ball-point pen that combines the traditional insulin ampoule with a newly developed injection system. Among other things it has a very fine needle, a number scale and a dial system that makes dosage easy. What used to be time consuming is now over with in no time, and the pen is easy to transport anywhere. It fits in a breast pocket and looks just like a pen, or it can lie in a little handbag. The NovoPen led to a different view of innovation in the company itself, and the mindset behind the development of this product has since been used for the company's other products.

In design and business circles, Novo Nordisk has ever since been perceived as one of the companies in Denmark that has made the most successful and visionary use of design. The company's consistent work with design-oriented solutions culminated, at least so far, in the mid-1990s with the production of an internal information video about design. Its sole purpose was to explain to Novo's employees how the company wanted to work with design and innovation. On the video, the CEO at the time, Mads Øvlisen said, 'For about 60 years we have been the world's foremost insulin producers, but then our people decided, 'No, no, no we had to supply diabetic *care*.' And when you make that statement, you make a mental leap from trying to supply the correct quality of insulin with the correct specifications to thinking in terms of what is important for the person with diabetes. And when you put yourself in their place, you start thinking not in terms of perfect vials, but you started to think in terms of normal everyday lives. And that was of significance to us at Novo Nordisk. I believe that in all our pharmaceutical history as a company, this is the first time we really, really identified with the customers, and it paid off handsomely in terms of recognition from people with diabetes, but also in the market place where we very, very quickly could brand this market, make it our market and turn it into a handsome business.'

▾ *The bestselling version of the NovoPen, called the NovoLet, was introduced in 1989 (below). It was designed by Steve McGugan and was awarded an ID prize in 1990. The NovoLet was the world's first disposable insulin syringe and was soon the bestselling pen for insulin injection worldwide at the time. In 2005 the NovoPen 3 was the most used insulin pen in the world.*

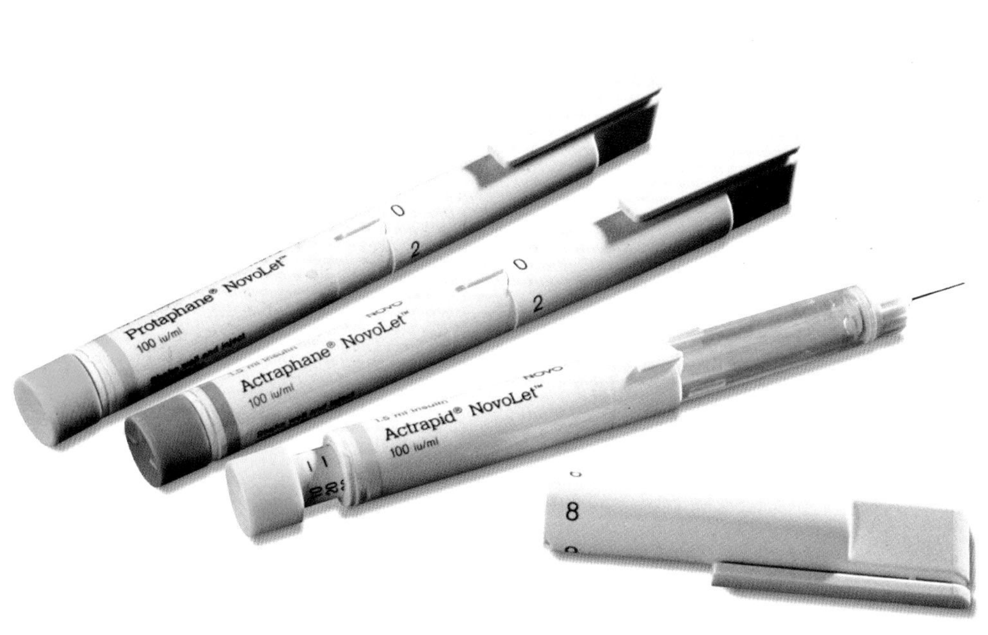

ORGANIC VEGETABLES ON your doorstep. In the new economic world order where there is a growing focus on users, companies and designers have to see themselves not so much as manufacturers of material things, but as suppliers of intelligent solutions.

A good example of what that can lead to is the company Aarstiderne (the Seasons) that started in 1996 with the idea of supplying organic vegetables to its customers. If the company had thought along traditional lines, they might have opened a chain of greengrocers in large Danish towns.If so, they would have been in direct competition with the existing greengrocers and would most likely have vied with them on prices and the best locations in town. Instead they thought creatively and combined internet shopping with delivering crates full of fruit and vegetables in season on the consumer's doorstep. Aarstiderne didn't really get going until 1999 as that was when the concept was launched on the internet so customers could shop there.

By 2006 the company had 120 employees and more than 35,000 customers all over Denmark, and they also began selling other types of products, such as fish, wine, bread from Emmery's (another exclusive food retailer) and processed foods. Apart from the way Aarstiderne developed their business using intelligent system design, one can say that their design is visible in their graphic identity, for example on their homepage, on their delivery vans and on their packaging. Customers are also offered recipes of the week and cookbooks.

IN THE EARLY 1990s, architectural student Steen Mandsfelt Eriksen identified a problem that has its root in the area of cleaning. Many of the places that need vacuuming are hard to reach with traditional vacuum cleaners. For example, movie theatres, trains, buses and aeroplanes, but also long flights of stairs can be a problem for ordinary vacuum cleaners. At DSB they had tried to solve the problem by mounting a traditional vacuum cleaner on a backpack iron frame, but the Danish Working Environment Authority wouldn't approve it.

Steen Mandsfelt Eriksen interviewed people who cleaned in cramped spaces, and meanwhile he made experimental models. Experts were consulted, such as a physiotherapist and employees at the Technological Institute. The result was a backpack vacuum cleaner that was divided into two main parts with a special rubber coupling in between for ergonomic reasons. The flexible harness allows the user great freedom of movement while working. Mandsfelt's consultants at the Technological Institute saw the possibility of patenting the concept.

So when he graduated as an industrial designer, he looked for a manufacturer for his product. It was easier said than done. However, right before the expiration of the first year of the patent, a deal was made with the Danish company Nilfisk, who today market the backpack vacuum cleaner in many countries under the name Backuum. Steen Mandsfelt Eriksen was awarded the Vision prize from the Danish Design Centre in 1996 for his original product, and two years later, in 1998, he and Nilfisk were also awarded the ID prize for Backuum.

ETHICAL DESIGN

In the basement of Hornbækhus, the large housing block from 1923 on Nørrebro in Copenhagen (see page 228), the housing co-operative association has a boardroom. There is a bronze sign that ceremoniously states that Copenhagen Municipality has bestowed it the honour of being an especially well-built building. But why isn't this sign displayed on the façade as it was meant to be? This is because Kay Fisker, the architect of the building, didn't want the sign on public display. His explanation was that the building wasn't constructed to the standard he had desired, namely that all the apartments were not furnished with a bathroom, but only 85 % were. The rest had to do without what we take for granted, but back then it was a new-fangled luxury, and there was probably also the original building owner's lack of funds.

This anecdote is only one example of how the relatively high professional standard and ethical mindset in much of the architect and designer milieu could be expressed in prior times. Of course the question is whether today's architects and designers would adopt the same attitude. One can be a bit doubtful now and then, since the many designer prizes and various awards for good design and good architecture are a calculated factor in the marketing of design offices and individual practitioners. If one does not wish to accept an award for 'best this' or 'most excellent that' because one has high moral standards, then one loses ground to the competitors in the battle for the next assignment. Nonetheless, the ethical debate in the design profession seems to be relevant again. This is not least because in recent years the rest of the business community has increasingly had to relate to politically-conscious consumer demands. These consumers' desires are about having access to products that live up to their expectations of being eco-friendly and not being manufactured in third-world countries under unreasonable conditions where there is child labour or the rain forest is over-exploited etc. However, sometimes the desire for certain ethical standards originates from the deep convictions of a company's owners. For example, LEGO would never make war toys, which is an old decision made by the Kirk Christiansen family and still deeply rooted in the values of the company. What they mean by war toys are modern weapons, tanks and cannons from the 20th century's bloody wars. They do make construction sets of older historical situations that include castles and pirate ships, and the same is true of science-fiction sets with Star Wars' starships including laser cannons. Their explanation for the latter is that it's a fictitious media world that doesn't relate to an existing world where real people are killed.

DESIGN CREATES A FRAMEWORK

One hundred years ago, when you needed a new piece of furniture for your home, you went to the local cabinetmaker and ordered, say, a cabinet. He would then talk to you about what it should look like, its design and in what style it should be made, and then it was custom-made to fit the spot it was meant for and with the storage space needed. In the same way we can still visit a tailor and get a tailor-made suit or a party dress. Later on, this was replaced by clothes off the rack and standard furniture that were cheaper and able to be delivered faster. And then standardisation became a virtue in the beginning of the industrial age, since then one could avoid the irregular and unpredictable element that was inherent in the old hand-crafted production.

THE DEBATE ABOUT the quality of our food and the ethical aspect of farming animals has raged for quite a few years. It has mostly been a question of whether one can get consumers to pay extra for organic meat. But good meat is not only about the quality of animal fodder or how much medicine they're given, but also about how it tastes. Free-range animals spend more time in their natural surroundings than in a pen, and in the mid-1990s architect Bent Hindrup Andersen (b. 1943) from the Research Centre Bygholm designed a tent system that made it possible to keep pigs outdoors all year round. The tents are manufactured by the company Aug. Olsens Eft. A/S (Aug. Olsen's Successor) that also makes tents and tarpaulins for other commercial purposes.

The principle is that the distinctive tents provide shelter from rain and other kinds of weather. The many bales of straw give the pigs an opportunity to make cosy nooks, for example when giving birth. The tents are designed in either 12- or 16-sided models of reinforced polyethylene with a mast that ensures stability. Ventilation is provided by the hole in the top of the tent, and the sail is whitewashed in summer to deflect sunshine and prevent overheating. In the fall the whitewash has been worn off, and when the sun shines during winter, it can more easily heat the tent. The only apparent drawback of this system is that it requires a lot of space, but since the tents are relatively easy to move, the system can be a part of the ordinary rotation of crops. The climate tent got the ID prize in 1998.

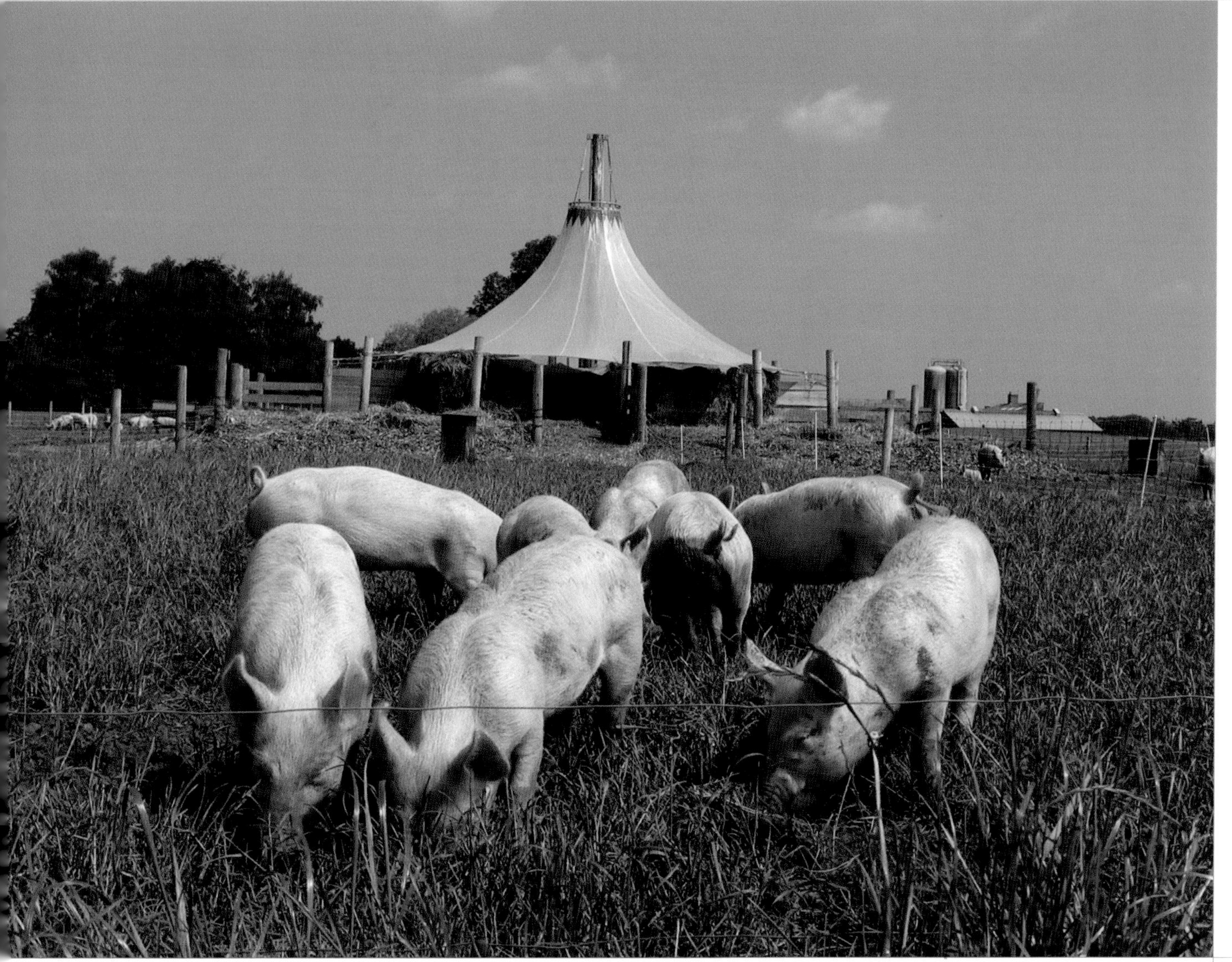

THE COMPANY VESTERGAARD Frandsen in Kolding develops functional textiles. They make mosquito nets that are treated with insecticide, and these nets can be washed ten times before the insecticide is ineffectual. For a number of years, Vestergaard Frandsen has worked on a solution to the lack of clean water in third-world countries. Drinking water is a significant source of serious diseases. In the beginning the company tried to solve the problem by developing special textiles, but realised later that the solution lay elsewhere. The answer came in 2005 and was called the LifeStraw, a large plastic tube with filters and active ingredients that purify the water and kill bacteria and viruses. It prevents diseases like cholera and typhoid fever – which annually kill millions of people. The lifespan of one straw is about 700 litres of water, so with a consumption of two litres a day, the straw can last for about a year. Unfortunately the LifeStraw isn't furnished with an indicator that shows when the active ingredients no longer work, so it's up to the individual user to keep tabs on its use. The price is about US$3, and this allows you to drink at any watering hole. It's hardly the ultimate solution to the third world's problem with clean drinking water. That would take large treatment plants that can clean the water for whole villages at a time. But in emergencies the LifeStraw can be a lifesaver. At the large design festival Index 2005 this product was the only Danish design to be awarded one of the five prizes of 100,000 Euros.

In recent years, designers have also rediscovered the unique user and have begun to study people's needs in a more systematic way. The NovoPen is just one example that demonstrates how the business community is also thinking about accommodating their customers in a better way. And of course not only are the ethical and humanist considerations the basis of the development and design of these user-friendly solutions, but they're also demonstrating that at the end of the day they can be really good business. Perhaps these two things, ethics and business, don't have to be opposites, which we're otherwise likely to believe. Designers today must get used to working in this field of tension.

To a great degree, design is about creating a framework for a good life, be it for the individual diabetic, for a family in their home or for citizens in the public space. This is what the progressive design movements were all about in the beginning and middle of the 20th century, and among them were FDB, the Association of Better Architectural Design, Poul Henningsen, Critical Revue and several other exponents.

But if designers are to contribute to creating the framework of a good life, then they also have to have ideas about what this good life should contain without resorting to old-fashioned guardianship and a tyranny of taste. Long ago, designers and architects were primarily people who shaped things and were aesthetic consultants for their clients and building owners, and in many cases one could probably call them arbiters of taste. But today few people would allow an opinion of what is beautiful, ugly or good taste to be fobbed off on them. We want to make up our own minds, since design, like so many things in our society, is a free and democratic matter. Therefore design is increasingly about creating the best basis in which users can create their own surroundings freely, and as they please. In other words, what will be needed in the future is a broader scope of design competencies where the designers should not focus on their own unique works, but rather be good at working together in a network, and take part in solving complex problems and creating meaningful connections for other people along with other professional groups and ultimately with the users themselves. When it comes down to it, we are all designers ...

Concepts of style

[1]

[2]

[3]

[4]

In this book various styles are referred to. For the sake of clarity, very short descriptions are given below of the major styles used in the book.

PREHISTORIC TIME [1]

Even in ancient times, people decorated their things with pictures and signs that often were typical of the time. Today inspiration is drawn from these early times. One example is the current Danish coins that are decorated with the same spiral ornamentation as found on the Egtved girl's belt disc from the Bronze Age. About 1000 years later, the Viking Age was characterised by winding animal ornamentation, which we today find on objects such as Danish passports as security printing.

ROMAN STYLE [2]

This style is also called the round arch style because of the hemispherical arches above windows and doors as well as the barrel vaults of the churches. The name refers to ancient Rome, which the style was influenced by. It is the first common European style, and it included all of the Roman Catholic area. In Denmark the entry of the style coincides with the introduction of Christianity, about the year 1000, and it lasted until about 1250. Early Roman architecture was simple and calm with large flat walls, but later, in the 1100s the style became more detailed. Most Danish village churches are primarily built in the Roman style, but often finished in the Gothic style. Ribe Cathedral is in the Roman style. Smaller objects from that time, like furniture, goblets and jewellery, are more ornamental.

GOTHIC STYLE [3]

This is popularly called the pointed arch style and it gradually replaced the Roman style from about the year 1200. In Denmark it lasted until the beginning of the 1500s. The large leaded stained glass windows – the cartoons of the time – and the vertical lines that strive towards the heavens are a product of the Gothic style, in which elegant constructions in stone were especially cultivated. The Gothic style was given its name by the Renaissance – the style of the Goths, the barbarians' style – since they considered the style mysterious and dark. Roskilde Cathedral is Gothic, and the Grundtvig Church (completed in 1930) is Gothic-inspired and the most recent example of the style in Denmark.

THE RENAISSANCE (THE 1500s) [4]

This means rebirth, for at the time they put the Middle Ages behind them and cultivated the architecture and art of Classical Antiquity. The style often seems lighter and simpler than the Gothic. Furniture was no longer built-in, but was free standing on the floor. In architecture, lines were horizontal, and buildings were well-proportioned and not quite as tall as in the Gothic style. In Denmark, the Dutch Renaissance dominated; materials were local red bricks and imported sandstone. The castles Kronborg, Frederiksborg, Egeskov and Rosenborg are all examples of this style.

BAROQUE (CIRCA 1600–1720) [5]

This is a more symmetric style in architecture, horticulture as well as in furniture design. In Denmark, the Baroque period was one of the greatest construction periods in our history when castles like Eremitagen, Fredensborg and Frederiksberg were built, as well as quite a few stately homes and mansions. The Baroque style has a little of the Gothic drama in it with picturesque sweeping ornaments and lavish wood carvings in both architecture and furniture. Not only is the architecture colourful and full of contrasts – bombastic in our view – but so is the jewellery and clothing.

[5]

[6]

[7a]

[7b]

[8]

[9]

ROCOCO (CIRCA 1720–70) [6]

This is a transitional style that particularly as regards architecture is related to the Baroque. Otherwise the Rococo was to a great degree an interior style for the upper class; a scene for the elegant social life; a light style with a gradual transition between indoors and outdoors and between architecture and decoration. Seen from the outside, the architecture was rather tight and symmetrical, as can be seen at Amalienborg, but in the details it's a nature-loving and asymmetrical style. Many pieces of furniture from this time resemble the violin with forms that wind in and out and with curved surfaces that harmoniously meet. The spiral tower of Frelserkirken (Our Saviour Church) is from the Rococo period.

CLASSICISM [7A+B]

This style has emerged regularly and was originally characterised by simple, harmonious and symmetrical forms inspired by Antiquity. The Renaissance was a form of Classicism, and it re-emerged again around the 1800s as Neo-classicism. The style suited the new bourgeoisie's desire to signal individualism, freedom and democracy. Classicism survived until about 1920 (for example the Copenhagen Police Headquarters). At the time, it was seen as old-fashioned and fake, while in Germany and the Soviet Union the style was used to pay homage to dictatorships.

19TH CENTURY STYLES [8]

These changed a lot, but they were often variants of Neo-classicism. From the early 1800s till about 1825, the style called French Empire was prevalent and inspired by the Roman Empire (which Napoleon took inspiration from). At first, the French Empire style was mostly a simplification and smoothing out of the Rococo style. In Denmark the style wasn't quite so imperial, but in both architecture and design it was a rather simple and sparsely decorated style. C.F. Hansen was the great Classicist architect of this period and designed Vor Frue Kirke (the Church of Our Lady) and the Copenhagen courthouse on Gammeltorv in the French Empire style. The simplicity of the style eventually became so marked that it has since been called a predecessor of functionalism. Up until and including the French Empire period, the styles succeed each other consecutively, but from the mid-1800s different styles begin to exist side by side.

HISTORICISM AND STYLE IMITATION [9]

Throughout the 1800s, Neo-classicism continued to have a great influence. In time, artists, architects and interior designers drew on some of the other styles, so one can talk about Neo-Gothic, Neo-Baroque and Neo-Rococo. Sometimes they changed styles from one assignment to another. At the end of the 1800s, the style was called Victorian because of all the fringes and little tassels on furniture, curtains and lampshades. The period was very much characterised by things being in order on a superficial level while the content didn't always have any substance. For example, the large pillars that looked like they were made of sandstone could be made of plastered wood, and wood fixtures could be painted in the so-called trompe d'oeil technique to look like marble or precious wood. The Royal Danish Theatre on Kongens Nytorv and the Glyptotek are Copenhagen examples of this style in architecture.

ART NOUVEAU ETC. [10]

Gradually, industry replaced craftsmanship. For example, wrought iron was substituted by cast-iron imitations, which we can see in things like the old treadle-powered sewing machine. The reaction to this came in the

[10]

[11]

[12]

[13]

[14]

form of a movement that cultivated craftsmanship, and in some cases they looked to the Gothic plant ornamentation of the Middle Ages for inspiration. This aversion to 'soulless machine production' emerged first in England with Arts and Crafts movement around 1860. The style spread to the rest of Europe in the following decades and culminated around the year 1900 as Art Nouveau in France, and Jugend in Germany. In Denmark the style is known from about 1890 till 1920. The most important practitioners were Thorvald Bindesbøll (the Carlsberg Hof label), Georg Jensen (silver jewellery) and Martin Nyrop (Copenhagen City Hall). Knud V. Engelhardt was influenced by the style in his graphic design.

FUNCTIONALISM [11]

Throughout the 20th century there were two prevalent schools of thought in design: the innovative form and the reusable form. While Art Nouveau was a reaction to industrialism and delved into the past, a movement arose in the 1900s that was far more positive about new technology and mass production. The well-known German art, architectural and design school Bauhaus was the origin and the hub of the first functionalism after World War I. The leading principle of this style, which is also known as modernism, was that there mustn't be decorations on either buildings or products. For example, as early as 1908, the Austrian architect Adolf Loos wrote in an essay that ornamentation was nothing less than a crime. The functionalist movement was not only a style, but also a social and political manifestation of the times that praised industry. Mass production would provide the population with good housing as well as inexpensive and high-quality everyday articles. Functionalism was also called 'machine aesthetics'. Arne Jacobsen's building complex Bellavista in Klampenborg, north of Copenhagen, was a distinctive example of this style, while his Stelton service and Vola fixtures were corresponding product designs. Jan Trägårdh was influenced by the original Bauhaus style and its successor in the post-war years at the school in Ulm.

STREAMLINE [12]

This was an American-inspired fusion of functionalism and the Jugend style. Cars, aeroplanes and ships were designed so that they could more easily glide through the air or water. These elegant forms were transferred to furniture such as the Panton chair and products like the Ballerup mixer and the Contex calculator.

POSTMODERISM [13]

From around 1970 a reaction to modernism arose. In many circles, not least among architects and designers, it was felt that functionalism had gone too far and had become a cold style. Postmodern architecture and design borrowed from every period and often used historical and particularly Classic elements such as pillars, cornices and imitations of precious materials. It was often perceived as ironic and slightly kitsch. It didn't gain much acceptance in Denmark.

DECONSTRUCTIVISM [14]

Like Postmodernism, this was a style that broke with Functionalism. The style arose around 1980 and is especially known in the field of architecture. Deconstructivism is often characterised by the body of a building being broken up in irregular elements and fragments. A Danish example is the art museum Arken in Ishøj. Ernst Lohse's temporary city gate on the town hall square in Copenhagen is also an example of the style. In graphic design deconstructivism in a layout practically 'explodes' in fragments.

Timeline

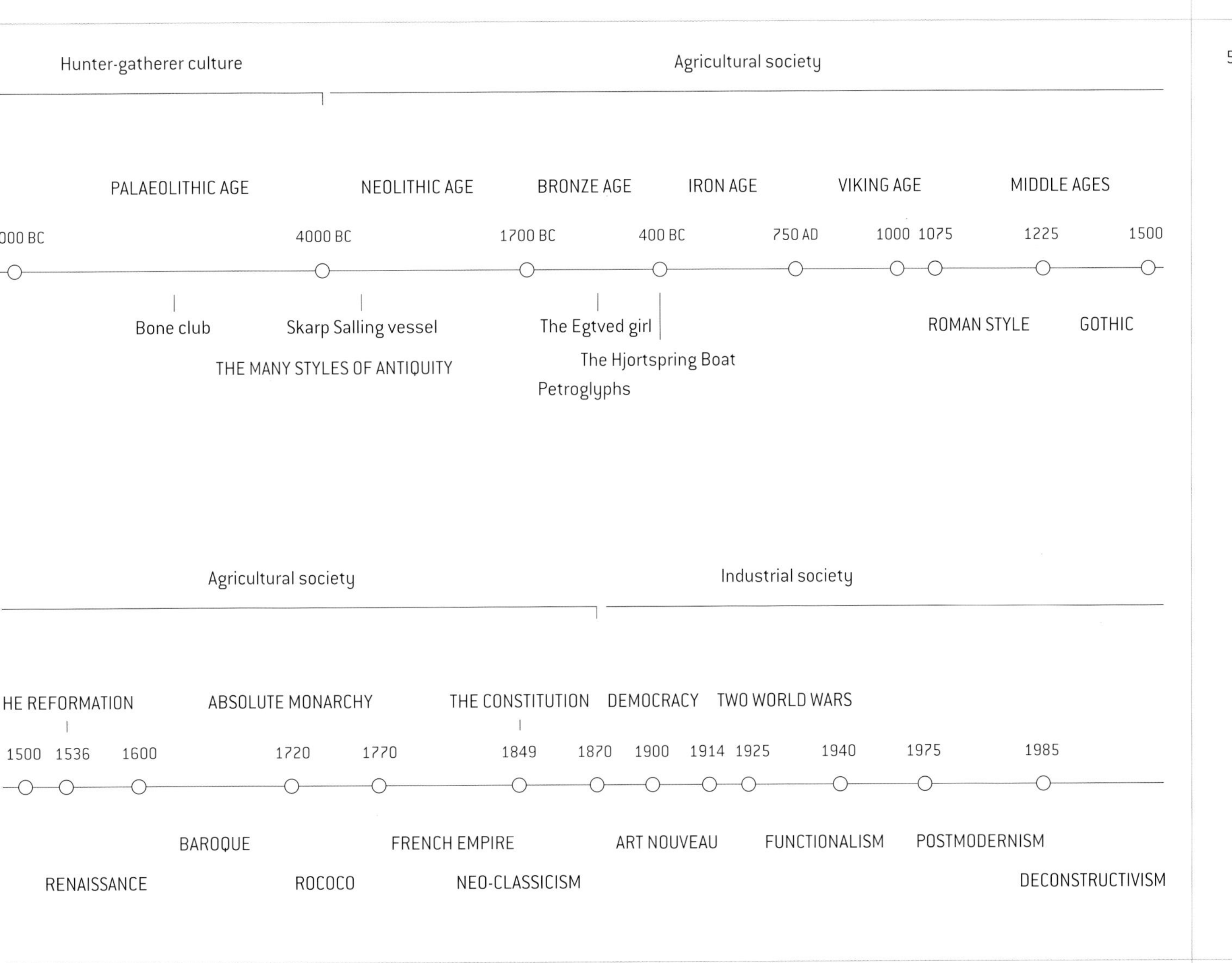
Hunter-gatherer culture
Agricultural society
PALAEOLITHIC AGE
NEOLITHIC AGE
BRONZE AGE
IRON AGE
VIKING AGE
MIDDLE AGES
000 BC
4000 BC
1700 BC
400 BC
750 AD
1000
1075
1225
1500
Bone club
Skarp Salling vessel
The Egtved girl
ROMAN STYLE
GOTHIC
THE MANY STYLES OF ANTIQUITY
The Hjortspring Boat
Petroglyphs
Agricultural society
Industrial society
HE REFORMATION
ABSOLUTE MONARCHY
THE CONSTITUTION
DEMOCRACY
TWO WORLD WARS
1500
1536
1600
1720
1770
1849
1870
1900
1914
1925
1940
1975
1985
BAROQUE
FRENCH EMPIRE
ART NOUVEAU
FUNCTIONALISM
POSTMODERNISM
RENAISSANCE
ROCOCO
NEO-CLASSICISM
DECONSTRUCTIVISM

Bibliography

The literature below is meant as a help for those who would like to know more about the subjects or specific products in the book. Therefore the literature is listed according to the chapters. However, the first books and periodicals are of a more general nature for those who want to get a general introduction to the subject.

BOOKS

Bernsen, Jens and Schenstrøm, Susanne (ed.): 100+3 Great Danish Industrial Designs. ID prisen 1965–85, Dansk Designråd, Copenhagen 1985

Dybdahl, Lars: Dansk design 1910–1945. Art déco & funktionalisme, Kunstindustrimuseet, Copenhagen 1997

Dybdahl, Lars (ed.): De industrielle ikoner: Design Danmark, Kunstindustrimuseet, Copenhagen 2004

Frederiksen, Erik Ellegaard: Knud V. Engelhardt, Arkitektens Forlag, 1965

Gyllan, Peter and Kindt, Svend: Design Jan [Jan Trägårdh], Dansk Design Centre, Copenhagen 1999

Jensen, Jørgen: Danmarks Oldtid, vol. 1–4, Gyldendal, 2002–04

Jeppesen, B. a.o.: Dansk design – fra kirke til café, Systime, 1993

Rasmussen, Steen Eiler: Om at opleve arkitektur, Gads Forlag, 1957

Roesdal, Else: Vikingernes verden, Gyldendal, 2001

PERIODICALS AND MAGAZINES

Arkitekten. Published since 1898 with articles about architecture, design and related subjects.

Arkitektur DK. Periodical published by Arkitektens Publishing Company.

Design DK. The Danish Design Centre's magazine published from about 1977 till 2002 and replaced by the design periodical Designmatters.

Mobilia. Design periodical published from 1954–84. A rich source of information on all types of new design.

Rum & Form. Public members' magazine from the Association of Furniture Architects and Interior Architects (MMI) and later for the Association of Danish Designers (MDD), merged in 2003 with Design DK and became Designmatters.

Scandinavian Journal of Design History. Trade periodical in English. Published annually by the Rhodos publishing company.

Tools. Design magazine in newspaper format published 1984–1988 in a varying number of editions each year.

FURTHER READING – CHAPTER BY CHAPTER

Chapter 2, Where does Danish design come from?

Andersen, Steen Wulff: Vikingeborgen Trelleborg, Museet ved Trelleborg, Slagelse 1998

Bernsen, Jens: Hans J. Wegner, Dansk Design Centre, Copenhagen 1995

Cousins, James: British Rail Design, Dansk Design Centre, Copenhagen 1986

Faber, Tobias: Dansk Arkitektur, Arkitektens Forlag, 1977

Floris, Lene: Bedre Byggeskik. Bevægelse og bygninger, Holbæk Museum/Thaning og Appel, 2005

Gelfer-Jørgensen, Mirjam: Guldalderdrømmen: dansk nyklassicistisk møbelkunst 1790–1850, Forlaget Rhodos, 2002

Gleeson, Janet: Arkanum, Rosinante, 1998

Henningsen, Poul: Om smag, stil og kunst. Artikelsamling, Forlaget Rhodos, 1984

Hiesinger, K.B. og Marcus, G.H.: Design Since 1945, Philadelphia Museum of Art, 1983

Krogh, Erik: Jørgen Gammelgaard. Udstillingskatalog, Kunsthallen Brænderigårdens Forlag, Viborg 2001

Mollerup, Per: Offspring. Særnummer af Mobilia: nos. 315/316, Mobilia Press, Copenhagen 1983

Møller, Svend Erik: På Wegners tid, Poul Kristensens Forlag, 1989

Chapter 3, Product design

Bang, Jens: Bang & Olufsen, Forlaget Vidsyn, 2000

Bloch, Michael: Dansk presset glas 1850–1950, Sesam, 2003

Buchwald, Gunnar and Schlüter, Mogens (ed.): Kastrup og Holmegaards Glasværker 1825–1975, Nyt Nordisk Forlag Arnold Busck, 1975

Heath, Adrian & Ditte, and Jensen, Aage Lund: 300 Years of Industrial Design, Herbert Press, London 2000

Herløw, Erik: Gode ting til hverdagsbrug, Det Schønbergske Forlag, 1949

Hiort, Esbjørn: Moderne dansk keramik, Gjellerups Forlag, 1955

Kaiser, Niels-Jørgen: Henning Koppels verden, Gyldendal, 2000

Larsen, Alfred, Riismøller, Peter and Schlüter, Mogens: Dansk Glas 1825–1925, Nyt Nordisk Forlag Arnold Busck, 1996

Lassen, Erik and Schlüter, Mogens: Dansk Glas 1925–1975, Nyt Nordisk Forlag Arnold Busck, 1975

Lassen, Erik: Keramik, Branner og Korch, 1968

Lassen, Erik: Ske, kniv og gaffel, Høst & Søn, 1960

Laursen, Bodil B. and Nottelmann, Steen (ed.): Dansk Porcelæn 1775–2000, Nyt Nordisk Forlag, 2000

Lütken, Per: – glas er liv, Nyt Nordisk Forlag Arnold Busck, 1986

Mogensen, Thomas: Et fuldt møbleret liv – en bog om Børge Mogensen, Gyldendal, 2004

Møller, Henrik Sten: Dansk design, Forlaget Rhodos, 1975

Møller, Viggo Sten: Dansk kunstindustri 1850–1900, Forlaget Rhodos, 1969

Møller, Viggo Sten and Henrik Sten: Kay Bojesen. Christian Ejlers' Forlag, 1983

Nielsen, Teresa: Ursula Munch-Petersen, Forlaget Rhodos, 2004

Olesen, Christian Holmsted: Jacob Jensen, Aschehoug, 2003

Schou-Christensen, Jørgen: Moderne glas 1890–2000. Collection catalogue for the Danish Museum of Art & Design.

Schäfer, Paul: Jacob Jensen Design. Katalog til udstilling på Kunstindustrimuseet, Forlaget Rhodos, 1993

Thau, Carsten and Vindum, Kjeld: Arne Jacobsen, Arkitektens Forlag, 1998

Thulstrup, Thomas: Georg Jensen. Sølv & design, Gads Forlag, 2004

Uldall, Kai: Keramik, Fra Frilandsmuseets samlinger, Nationalmuseets 7. afdeling, København 1959

Chapter 4, Textile and clothing design

Andersen, Ellen: Moden i 1700–årene. Danske dragter, Nationalmuseet, Copenhagen 1977

Andersen, Paulli and Christensen, Ruth: Stoftrykker- & Væverlauget, 1946–1986. Jubilee publication.

Bech, Viben: Historien om moden. Fra antkken til det 20. århundrede, Politikens Forlag, 1994

Broby-Johansen, Rudolf: Krop og Klær, Gyldendal, 1966

Christensen, Ruth: Stoftryk. Historie, farver og teknik, Gyldendal, 1975

Cock-Clausen, Ingeborg: Moden 1890–1920, Nationalmuseet and Nyt Nordisk Forlag Arnold Busck, 1994

Cock-Clausen, Ingeborg: Tekstilprøver fra danske arkiver og museer 1750–1975, Borgen, 1987

Hansen, Henny Harald: Klædedragtens kavalkade, Politikens Forlag, 1972

Hamre, Ida and Meedom, Hanne: Tøj og Funktion, Borgen, 1978

Hvass, Lone: Egtvedpigen, Sesam, 2000

Krag, Anne Hedeager (ed.): Dragt og magt, Museum Tusculanums Forlag, 2003

Lorenzen, Erna: Tråde bagud. Tekstilers kulturhistorie, Poul Kristensens Forlag, 1985

Manufakturhandlerforeningen (ed.): Tekstil og modegennem 300 år, Manufakturhandlerforeningen, 1988

Mogensen, Thomas: Et fuldt møbleret liv. En bog om Børge Mogensen, Gyldendal, 2004

Nielsen, Henning (ed.): Folk skaber klæ'r. Klæ'r skaber folk, Nationalmuseet, Copenhagen 1971

Nørgaard, Mads (ed.): Modeleksikon. Fra couture til kaos, Politikens Forlag, 2002

Paludan, Charlotte: Vævekunst. Dansk håndvævning i det 20. århundrede. Kunstindustrimuseet, 2003

Salicath, Bent and Karlsen, Arne: Modern Danish Textiles, Landsforeningen Dansk Kunsthåndværk, 1959

Sieck, Frederik (ed.): Bogen om Bum! Galskabens triumf, Kvadrat Boligtekstiler A/S, 1984

Thau, Carsten and Vindum, Kjeld: Arne Jacobsen, Arkitektens Forlag, 1998

Chapter 5, Furniture and interior design

Abrahamsen, Povl: Den danske enkelhed, Christian Ejlers' Forlag, 1994

Andersen, Rigmor: Kaare Klint møbler, Kunstakademiet, Copenhagen 1979

Broby-Johansen, Rudolf: Hverdagskunst – verdenskunst, Gyldendal, 1977

Clemmensen, Tove, Nørregaard, Georg and Søgaard, Helge: Københavns Snedkerlaug gennem fire hundrede år. 1554–1954, Copenhagen 1954

Dahlsgård, Inga, Michaelsen, M.K. and Møller, Viggo Sten (ed.): Bosætningsbogen, Statsradiofoniens grundbøger, Schultz, 1953

Engholm, Ida: Verner Panton, Aschehoug, 2004

Faber, Tobias: Dansk Arkitektur, Arkitektens Forlag, 1977

Gelfer-Jørgensen, Mirjam: Danske nyantikke møbler. Collection catalogue, The Danish Museum of Art & Design, Copenhagen 2003

Gelfer-Jørgensen, Mirjam: Guldalderdrømmen: dansk nyklassicistisk møbelkunst 1790–1850, Forlaget Rhodos, 2002

Harlang, Christoffer, Helmer-Petersen, Keld and Kjærholm, Krestine (ed.): Poul Kjærholm, Arkitektens Forlag, 1999

Hiort, Esbjørn: Arkitekten Finn Juhl, Arkitektens Forlag, Copenhagen 1990

Horsfeld, Hanne: Nanna Ditzel, Aschehoug, 2005

Jalk, Grete: Dansk møbelkunst gennem 40 år. Københavns Snedkerlaugs møbeludstillinger 1927–1966, vol. 1–4, Teknologisk Instituts Forlag, 1987

Jepsen, Anton: Danske empiremøbler, Thaning og Appel, København 2002

Jepsen, Anton: Det kongelige Møbelmagasin og københavnersnedkerne, Poul Kristensens Forlag, 1991

Juhl, Finn: Hjemmets indretning, Thaning og Appel, 1954

Kaiser, Birgit: Den ideologiske funktionalisme, Gads Forlag, 1992

Karlsen, Arne: Dansk Møbeldesign, Christian Ejlers' Forlag, 1994

Karlsen, Arne: Dansk møbelkunst i det 20. århundrede, vol. 1–2, Christian Ejlers' Forlag, 1990

Karlsen, Arne: Krydsklip i en arkitekts dagbog, Arkitektskolens Forlag, Århus og Christian Ejlers' Forlag, 2002

Laursen, Bodil Busk and Matz, Søren: Mesterværker. 100 års dansk møbelsnedkeri, Kunstindustrimuseet, Copenhagen 2000

Møller, Henrik Sten: Bevægelse og skønhed. Bogen om Nanna Ditzel, Forlaget Rhodos, 1998

Møller, Svend Erik and Kaiser, Niels-Jørgen: Verner Panton, Dansk Design Centre, Copenhagen 1986

Møller, Viggo Sten: Dansk kunstindustri 1850–1900, Forlaget Rhodos, 1969

Møller, Viggo Sten and Møller, Svend Erik: Dansk møbelkunst 1927–51, Rasmus Navers Forlag 1951

Mørch, Søren: Den ny Danmarkshistorie 1880–1960, Gyldendal, 1982
Sieck, Frederik: Nutidig dansk møbeldesign, Nyt Nordisk Forlag, 1990
Steensberg, Axel and Lerche, Grith: Danske bondemøbler, Nyt Nordisk Forlag, 1989
Thau, Carsten and Vindum, Kjeld: Arne Jacobsen, Arkitektens Forlag, 1998
Tøjner, Poul Erik and Vindum, Kjeld: Arne Jacobsen. Arkitekt & Designer, Dansk Design Centre, Copenhagen 1994
Wanscher, Ole: Møbelkunstens historie, Thaning og Appel, 1941
Wivel, Henrik: Finn Juhl, Aschehoug, 2004
Waagepetersen, Christian: Danske Møbler før 1848, Forum, 1980
Zahle, Karen, Monies, Finn and Christiansen, Jørgen Hegner (ed.): De gamle mestre, Arkitektens Forlag, 2000

Chapter 6, Building and design

Bernsen, Jens (ed.): Danish Building Design, Dansk Designråd, Copenhagen 1984
Dahl, Torben and Wedebrunn, Ola: Københavns murede huse i det 20. århundrede, Forlaget Tegl, 2000
Engholm, Ida: Verner Panton, Aschehoug, 2004
Faber, Tobias: Dansk Arkitektur, Arkitektens Forlag, 1977
Floris, Lene: Bedre Byggeskik. Bevægelse og bygninger, Holbæk Museum/Thaning og Appel 2005
Ganshorn, Jørgen: Murværk i blank mur. Historie og vedligeholdelse, Raadvad Centreet, Lyngby 2000
Hammerich, Paul: Lysmageren. En Krønike om Poul Henningsen, Gyldendal, 1986
Henningsen, Poul: PH om lys. En artikelsamling, Forlaget Rhodos, 1974
Jensen, Thomas Bo: P.V. Jensen-Klint, Kunstakademiets Arkitektskoles Forlag, Copenhagen 2006
Jørstian, Tina and Nielsen, Poul Erik Munk (ed.): Tænd! PH lampens historie, Gyldendal, 1994
Møller, Henrik Sten: Dansk design, Forlaget Rhodos, 1975
Møller, Jonas (ed.): Mur og rum, Centralforeningen af Murermestre i Danmark, København 1985
Møller, Svend Erik and Kaiser, Niels-Jørgen: Verner Panton, Publisher not known, 1986
Skriver, Poul Erik: Knud Holscher. Architect and Industrial Designer, Edition Axel Menges, Stuttgart/London 2000
Thau, Carsten and Vindum, Kjeld: Arne Jacobsen, Arkitektens Forlag, 1998
Tøjner, Poul Erik and Vindum, Kjeld: Arne Jacobsen. Arkitekt & Designer, Dansk Design Centre, Copenhagen 1994

Chapter 7, Design for the workplace

Bernsen, Jens: Innovation via design. ID prisen 25 år, Dansk Design Centre, Copenhagen 1990
Beuse, Ejvin a.o. (ed.): Vedvarende energi i Danmark. En krønike om 25 opvækstår 1975–2000, OVEs forlag, 2000
Buhl, Hans and Nielsen, Henry (ed.): Made in Denmark? Nye studier i dansk teknologihistorie, Forlaget Klim, 1994
Christensen, Benny: Fra husmøller til havmøller. Vindkraft i Danmark 1862–2002, Danmarks Vindkrafthistoriske Samling, 2002
Christensen, Benny: Mindre danske vindmøller 1860–1980, Danmarks Vindkraft-historiske Samling, 2001
Dahl, Børge: Gammelt værktøj, Ledreborg Tømmerhandel AS, Roskilde, 1973
Flagstad, S.M. og Laustsen, S.: Kontormiljøets historiske udvikling, SBI-rapport: 140, 1983
Heath, Adrian & Ditte, and Jensen, Aage Lund: 300 Years of Industrial Design, Herbert Press, London 2000
Hyldtoft, Ole and Johansen, Hans Chr.: Teknologiske forandringer i dansk industri 1896–1972, Syddansk Universitetsforlag, 2005
Jensen, Ib Konrad: Mænd i modvind – et dansk industrieventyr, Børsens Forlag, Copenhagen 2003
Jørgensen, K.O.B.: Danske foregangsmænd indenfor teknik og naturvidenskab, Strandbergs Forlag, 1986
Lebech-Sørensen, Anne Marie: Vindmøller og Vandmøller i Danmark, vol. 1–2, Skib Forlag, 2001
Meyhoff, Peder and Mouritsen, Peter: Teknologihistorie, Systime 2005
Olesen, Christian Holmsted: Jacob Jensen, Aschehoug, 2003
Rud, Mogens: Bayeux-tapetet og slaget ved Hastings 1066, Christian Ejlers' Forlag, Copenhagen 2002
Schäfer, Paul: Jacob Jensen Design. Exhibition catalogue from the Danish Museum of Art & Design, Forlaget Rhodos, 1993
Sestoft, Jørgen: Danmarks arkitektur. Arbejdets bygninger, Gyldendal, 1979
Thau, Carsten and Vindum, Kjeld: Arne Jacobsen, Arkitektens Forlag, 1998
Thorndahl, Jytte: Gedsermøllen – den første moderne vindmølle. Elmuseet, Bjerringbro 2005

Chapter 8, Transport design

Andersen, E. a.o..: Roar Ege – Skuldelev 3 skibet som arkæologisk eksperiment, Vikingeskibshallen i Roskilde, 1997
Bell, P. and Olesen, M.N.: Færgen Sjælland, Lamberths Forlag, Copenhagen 1990

Bjerg, H.C. and Erichsen, J.: Danske orlogsskibe 1690–1860, vol. 1–2, Lademann, 1980
Christiansen, Hans Gerner: Damplokomotiver. En grundbog, Forlaget Stavnsager, 1986
Dannesboe, Erik: Kølvand. 1000 år under sejl og med motor, Skib Forlag, 2001
Filholm, Bjarni Åkesson: De hvide skibe, Forlaget Nautilus, 2000
Frederiksen, Erik Ellegaard, Kryger, Niels and Nielsen, Vibeke Lassen (ed.): Jens Nielsen, Dansk Design Centre, Copenhagen 1996
Hansen, Ole Steen: Danskernes fly, Aschehoug, 2003
Jensen, Niels: Danske Damplokomotiver, Aschehoug, 2001
Mygdal-Meyer, Toni: Da danskerne fik vinger, Gyldendal, 2002
Olesen, Mogens Nørgaard: Danske jernbane-dampfærger, Lamberths Forlag, Copenhagen 1988
Olesen, Mogens Nørgaard: Enten nu eller aldrig, Danmarks Færgemuseum, 1995
Olesen, Mogens Nørgaard: Over Storebælt i 1000 år, Lamberths Forlag, Copenhagen 2000
Olesen, Mogens Nørgaard: Over sund og bælt, Lamberths Forlag, Copenhagen 1993
Palsbo, Søren and Zeeberg, Nils Kr.: Byens nips, Sporvejshistorisk Selskab, 1974
Peter, Bruce: Danish Ship Design, Ferry Publications, Isle of Man, 2004
Poulsen, Villy: Danske motorcykler, Forlaget Classic, 1987
Poulsen, Villy: Nimbus. Danmarks motorcykler, Forlaget Notabene, 1986
Trier, Hans and Erlandsen, Helge: Design – fra sporvogn til metro. 1910–2000, Ørestadsselskabet, 1999
Vinner, Max: Vikingeskibsmuseets både, Vikingeskibshallen i Roskilde, 2002

Chapter 9, Public design

Andersen, Kim Meyer, Bernsen, Jens and Damsgaard, Jørn: Offentligt design på dagsordenen, Dansk Design Centre, Copenhagen 1993
Bernsen, Jens (ed.): KTAS i gadebilledet, Dansk Designråd, Copenhagen 1985
Ejlers, Christian, Frederiksen, Erik Ellegaard og Kryger, Niels: Offentligt design, Chr. Ejlers' Forlag, 1970
Gehl, Jan: Livet mellem husene. Udeaktiviteter og udemiljøer, Arkitektens Forlag, Copenhagen 1996
Møller, Ib: Hestevogne i Danmark, Skib Forlag, 2002
Møller, Svend Erik (ed.): KTAS i hundrede år, Kjøbenhavns Telefon Aktieselskab, Copenhagen 1981
Nielsen, Anker Jesper: Lysene over København. Hovedstadens lysreklamer 1898–1994, Borgen, 1994
Nørhald, Stig: Byens skilte. Et vigtigt træk i byens ansigt, Kunstakademiet, 1993
Palsbo, Søren and Zeeberg, Nils Kr.: Byens nips, Sporvejshistorisk Selskab, 1974
Skude, Flemming: Byens gulv, Dansk Design Centre, Copenhagen 1999
Skude, Flemming: Byens inventar, Dansk Design Centre, Copenhagen 2000
Trier, Hans and Erlandsen, Helge: Design – fra sporvogn til metro. 1910–2000, Ørestadsselskabet, 1999

Chapter 10, Graphic design

Achen, Sven Tito: Danmarks kommunevåbner, Forlaget Komma, 1982
Andersen, Kim Meyer a.o.: Kronen på mærket, Dansk Design Centre, Copenhagen 2000
Arnoldi, Per: Per Arnoldi 250 plakater etc., Aschehoug, 2003
Bekker-Nielsen, Hans: Fra runeskrift til trykte bogstaver, Foreningen for Boghaandværk, 2002
Bertelsen, Lise Gjedssø (ed.): Vikingetidens kunst, Kongernes Jelling, 2002
Dybdahl, Lars: Den danske plakat, Borgen, 1994
Dybdahl, Lars a.o.: Ungermann, Gyldendal, 2002
Ejlers, Steen: Claus Achton Friis. Skrift & brugsgrafik, Arkitektens Forlag, 1996
Ejlers, Steen: Ib Andersens Brugsgrafik, Chr. Ejlers' Forlag, 1980
Frederiksen, Erik Ellegaard: Bogstavelig talt, Chr. Ejlers' Forlag, 1994
Hansen, John Juhler: Gadens blikfang. Danske emaljeplakater gennem 100 år, Forlaget Jelling, 2002
Hvass, Steen: De kongelige monumenter i Jelling, Fonden Kongernes Jelling, 2000
Jensen, Pernille: Ungermann & bogen, Foreningen for Boghaandværk, 1991
Karlsen, Arne (ed.): Dansk design ved årtusindeskiftet. Fem udstillinger, fem essays, Christian Ejlers' Forlag, 1997
Kaul, Flemming a.o.: Helleristninger, Forlaget Wormianum, 2005
Kaul, Flemming: Masser af skibe. Bronzealderens skibsbilleder på sten, Nationalmuseets Arbejdsmark, Copenhagen 2005
Kroman. E.: Skriftens historie i Danmark, Dansk Historisk Fællesforening, Viborg 1970
Mollerup, Per: Mark of Excellence. The history and taxonomy of trademarks, Phaidon Press, London 1997
Mollerup, Per: Wayshowing. A Guide to Environmental Signage, Lars Müller Publishers, Baden 2005
Nygaard, Finn: Visual Voice, Forfatteren and Kannike Graphic, 1990
Reimer, Eli: Skriften, vort vigtigste værktøj, Grafisk Litteratur, 2003
Rohde, Bent (ed.): Det er bare typografi. En samling artikler tilegnet Eli Reimer, Den Grafiske Højskole, Copenhagen 1983
Sejerkilde, Henrik: Den visuelle legekammerat. En bog om grafikeren Austin Grandjean, Poul Kristensens Forlag, 2002
Wisler-Poulsen, Ian: Hvad er meningen med virksomhedens logo?, Grafisk Litteratur, 2005

Index

▼ Juno 2, the classic children's bed, designed by architect Viggo Einfeldt in the mid-1940s.

photo credits: 3F (SiD) 474l, 474r **3Part** (photographer: KAT studio; manufacturer: R82 A/S) 454b, 455 **3xN** 299 **Ahm, Kim** 10-11, 253, 264, 284t, 307b **Arkiv Sporvejshistoriske Selskab** 408, 410 **BAM** (photographer: Jørgen Schytte) 349 **Banedanmark** 55t **Bang & Olufsen** 50t, 50b, 123t, 123c, 127t, 127b, 128, 129, 130, 131l, 131r, 132t, 132tr, 132b, 133, 134, (photographer: Ib Sørensen) 123r, (photographer: Søren Solkær) 136, (photographer: Jesper Jørgen) 137 **Baum und Pferdgarten** (photographer: Signe Vilstrup) 197 **Biofoto** (photographer: Leif Schack-Nielsen) 346 **Biomega** (photographer: Dorte Krogh) 397 **Bloch, Jacob** 114t **Bonacina Pierantonio** 268b **Brahl, Erik** 30t, 34, 41tr, 41b, 41tl, 46 (on the far right), 47b, 69b, 203, 224, 232, 236, 239, 241, 242bl, 244, 247, 254, 255, 257, 266 **Brandt, Erik & Margit** 188 **Brüel & Kjær** 353t **Børge Mogensens Tegnestue 76, 229h, 233, 238ø, (photographer: Peter Mogensen) 242t** **Campbell, Louise** (photographer: Erik Brahl) 282 **Carlsberg A/S Archives** (photographer: Dorte Krogh) 534 **Christian Bjørn Design** (manufacturer: Bates ventilsække A/S) 351 **Christian Dior** 186t **Clausen, Anders Bull**/Copy-Dan 514l **Coloplast** 477b, 453t **Dagbladet Information** 506 **Danmarks Jernbanemuseum** 387, 412, 413 **Danmarks Radios Arkiver** 103 **Danmarks Tekniske Museum** 354, 398, 402 **Darlie, Henrik** 461tl **Daughters of Style** (photographer: Rasmus Mogensen) 198 **De Danske Kongers Kronologiske Samling, Rosenborg Slot** 108 **Deichmann, Henning** 21t **Den Gamle By** 182 **Den Hirschprungske Samling** (artist: C.W. Eckersberg) 386 **Deres Design A/S** 449 **Designskolens Arkiv** 75, 229l, 234, 304, 409t, 409b **Det Kongelige Bibliotek** 183, 225, 231b, 480t, (photographer: Michael Hjuler) 529t **Det Kongelige Danske Møbelmagasin** 212 **Det Konservative Folkeparti** 79l **Dickson, Thomas** 539 **Dissing & Weitling + Poul-Jørn Lindberg** (photographer: Finn Christoffersen; manufacturer: Lindberg) 538 **DR** 519 **DSB Fotoarkiv** 481, 484, (photographer: Torben Dragsby) 414 **ECCO** 193 **Ekstra Bladet** 505 **Elmuseet** (photographer: Johannes Juul) 347 **Ergomat Danmark A/S** 355 **Erik Herløw Design** (photographer: Dorte Krogh) 97b **Erik Jørgensen Møbelfabrik A/S** 26b, 271, 276 **Esimex** 392 **Eva Denmark A/S** 534 **Faber Danmark A/S** 170l **Finn Nygaard Design** 501 **Forlaget Carlsen** 456-57 (Ib Spang Olsen/Copy-Dan), 513t (Ib Spang Olsen/Copy-Dan) **Forskningscentre Bygholm** 549 **Fredericia Furniture A/S** 17t, 237b, 237t **Frederiksborgmuseet** (photographer: Lennart Larsen) 57, 209, (photographer: Ole Haupt) 69t, 181, (fotograf: Kit Weis) 180b, 213 **Frederiksen, Jens** 393 **Frihedsmuseet** (the colours have been added) 70 **Fritz Hansen A/S** (photographer: Egon Gade) 28t, 46cl, 100-01, (photographer: Piotr Topperzer) 262, 284-85 **Furiosa** (photographer: Lene Mendel) 204t **Faaborg Museum** (photographer: Mogens Winther) 218 **Georg Jensen A/S** 104br, (photographer: Piotr Topperzer) 20, 21b, 27, 80-81, 104t, 104bl, 105, 106-07, 110t **Georg Jensen Damask** 159t **Gram A/S** (photographer: Erling Jensen) 120 **Grundfos A/S** (photographer: Morten Rasmussen) 344t, (photographer: Misfeldt Reklamefotografi) 345 **Grønlunds Forlag** (photographer: Fotodanmark.dk/ Jørgen Grønlund) 180t **Gyldendals Billedbibliotek** 58, 68, 71, 179, 221, 231t, 272, 344b, 381, 419t, 468, 483, 507 (Aage Sikker Hansen/Copy-Dan), 509l, 510bl, 512, 509r, 511, (photographer: Thorkild Jensen) 175, (watercolour by Kornerup) 176t, (illustrator: Carl Jensen/Copy-Dan) 220, (photographer: John Jedbo) 482 **Handels- og Søfartsmuseet** 389 **Hansen, Ole Steen** 418, 420-21 **hummel** (photographer: Nikola Novic) 190-91 **IKEA A/S** 280, 281 **IO-Interactive** 523 **Jacob Jensen Design** 121t, 358 **Kannik, Preben** 153 **Knoll Inc.** 49 **Koch, Mogens S.** 74 **Kontrapunkt** 477t **KRAK** 463t **Krogh, Astrid** (photographer: Torben Eskerod) 171 **Krogh, Dorte** 8, 15, 16, 17n, 22v, 22-23, 25, 26ø, 28n, 29, 33, 36-37, 38, 39, 43, 48n, 51, 60-61, 61, 62, 63, 64-65, 66n, 67, 72-73, 73h, 77, 78, 79r, 83, 86, 89, 90, 91b, 92b, 93b, 93t, 94, 95t, 95b, 96t, 98b, 98t, 100, 101, 102n, 110b, 111, 112, 118, 119, 121b, 122, 124, 126, 135t, 138, 139, 140, 142, 143, 144, 145, 155, 161, 172-73, 178, 204, 206, 208, 211, 217, 219, 222, 227, 228, 230, 238n, 249, 250-51, 251t, 252, 259, 260, 261, 263, 268t, 269, 270t, 275b, 275t, 277, 283r, 288, 289, 291, 292, 293, 296, 286-87, 300, 301, 305, 306, 307t, 308b, 309, 310, 314, 319l, 320, 323, 325, 328, 329, 334, 336, 337, 338, 339, 340t, 341, 342t, 342n, 343, 330-31, 348, 353b, 357, 359, 360tr, 360tl, 360b, 367, 380, 390, 395, 396, 399, 401, 404, 405, 406, 419b, 423, 424, 425t, 425b, 426, 427, 428, 429, 430, 431, 432, 433, 435t, 435b, 436, 437b, 438, 439b, 441, 442, 443, 445, 446, 447b, 448, 451, 464, 466, 494, 495, 527 (Aage Sikker Hansen/Copy-Dan), 529b, 531, 537, 541, 546, 547, 571 **Kræftens Bekæmpelse** 475 **Kunstakademiets Bibliotek, ARKI-samlingen** 223, 203, 447ø **Kunstindustrimuseet/ Pernille Klemp** 45, 46yv, 54, 91ø, 92ø, 96n, 109, 113, 114n, 115, 117ø, 154, 156, 158-59, 162-63, 164, 165, 215, 245, 246, 270b, 302, 318, 350, 403, 463b, 465, 467b, 497, 499, 500r, 500v, 502, 508, 526, (photographer: Dorte Krogh) 160 **Kvadrat A/S** (photographer: Poul Ib Henriksen) 168, 169 **Københavns Stadsarkiv** 462, 463c **LEGO Koncernen** 146, 147, 530 **Länsmuseet Varberg** (photographer: Arne Persson) 177 **Lauritz Knudsen** 329t, 329c (to the far right) **Le Klint** (photographer: Dorte Krogh) 326b, 326t, 327 **Linie Design A/S** 170r **Louis Poulsen** front page, 313, 316, 317, 319r, 362, (photographer: Dorte Krogh) 322, 324 **Magnussen, Arne** 297 **MAN B&W Diesels historiske fotoarkiv** 384 **MindLab** (photographer: Magnesium) 368 **Modulex A/S** 492-93 **Moesgård Museum, Foto/Medie Afdeling** (photographer: Preben Dehlholm) 150, (photographer: Søren Christiansen) 207t **Munthe plus Simonsen** (photographer: Henrik Bülow; model: Lykke May Andersen, 2pm modelmanagement) 194-95 **Nanna Ditzel Design** (photographer: Louis Schnakenburg) 141, 207b **Nationalmuseet** 214, (photographer: Lennart Larsen) 9, 19, 30b, 85, 174b, 459, (photographer: Kit Weiss) 40, (photographer: Niels Elswing) 176b **Nielsen, Søren** 478 **Normann Copenhagen** 102t, 116b, 116t, 535 **Novo Nordisk** 545 **Nørgaard, Mads** 196 **Olesen, Magnus** (photographer: Dorte Krogh) 274 **OneSeal A/S** 542 **Orlogsmuseet** (photographer: Dorte Krogh) 379 **Oticon** 450 **Piotr Topperzer** 20, 21b, 27, 80-81, 104t, 104bl, 105, 106-07, 110t **PLH arkitekter as** (photographer: Erik Brahl) 65r **Polfoto** 47t, 44, 469, 385, 439t, (photographer: Jacob Maarbjerg) 84, (photographer: Lars Hansen) 185, (photographer: Camilla Bloch) 187, (photographer: Erik Petersen) 190l, 248, 415t, (photographer: Annelise Fibæk) 191r, (photographer: Jørgen Sperling) 192, 504, (photographer: Morten Langkilde) 205, (photographer: Lars Skaaning) 267, (photographer: Peter H. Petersen) 415b, (photographer: Peer Pedersen) 467t, (photographer: Niels Peter Jakobsen) 491 **Politiken** 504, (illustrator: Arne Ungermann) 503 **Post Danmark** 518l **Post- og Telemuseet** (illustration: A. Blom) 440 **PP Møbler** (photographer: Jens Mourits Sørensen) 242br **Pressalit A/S** 308t **Rohweder, Anne** 513b **Royal Copenhagen** 35t, 35b, 88 **Salto, Kasper** (photographer: Søren Nielsen; manufacturer: Stærk Design) 283l, (photographer: Søren Nielsen; manufacturer: Fritz Hansen A/S) 283m **Scanpix** 66ø, 420ø, (photographer: Søren Steffen) 12, (photographer: Birte Melchiors) 48ø, (photographer: Willy Henriksen) 250t, (photographer: Bjarke Ørsted) 265, (photographer: Keld Navntoft) 388 **Simonsen & Weel** 452 **Skandinavisk Tobakskompagni A/S** (photographer: Dorte Krogh) 528 **Skov, Torben** 518r **Sonofon** 470 **SONY BMG Music Entertainment/Genlyd 2000** 517r **SoundShip** (photographer: Stine Heger) 352 **Statens Museum for Kunst** (artist: Frederik Vermehren) 152 **Superflex** 18 **Søgren, Poul** 484 **Søllerød Rådhus** 365 **Søndergaard, Ole** 489 **Thornvig, Peter/I2U** 53, 488, 521 **Tiderne Skifter** 510br, 510tr, 510tc, 510tl **Told & Skat** 461t **U-B-Let A/S** (design: Mogens Holm-Rasmussen) 454ø **Universal** 516 **Vadstrup, Søren** 332**VELUX A/S** 294, 295 **Venstre** 471ø, 471n **Verner Panton Design, Basel** 166 **Vestergaard Frandsen A/S** 550 **Vibskov, Henrik** (photographer: Asger Carlsen) 199t, (photographer: Shoji Fujii) 199b **Vikingeskibsmuseet** (photographer: Werner Karrasch) 371, 373, 374-75, 377 **VIPP AS** (photographer: Anders Hvid) 340b **Voigt, Zarah** 148-49, 189 **Voss, Morten** (photographer: Dorte Krogh) 279 **Winther Cykler** (photographer: Dorte Krogh) 394 **Aasmul, Sille** 87, 174t, (photographer: Diana Nilsson) 517r

Published in 2008 by Murdoch Books Pty Limited
First published by Gyldendalske Boghandel 2006

Murdoch Books Australia
Pier 8/9
23 Hickson Road
Millers Point NSW 2000
Phone: +61 (0) 2 8220 2000
Fax: +61 (0) 2 8220 2558
www.murdochbooks.com.au

Murdoch Books UK Limited
Erico House, 6th Floor
93–99 Upper Richmond Road
Putney, London SW15 2TG
Phone: +44 (0) 20 8785 5995
Fax: +61 (0) 20 8785 5985
www.murdochbooks.co.uk

Translator: Karen Margrete Wiin
Chief Executive: Juliet Rogers
Publishing Director: Kay Scarlett

Consultant: Mette Strømgaard Dalby
Non-fiction editor: Lil Vad-Schou
Photo consultants: Annette Ekstrand and Lilja Hardt
Graphic design and cover design: Sille Aasmul/Asap Design
Photos: Dorte Krogh a.o. See page 572
Vignette and silhouette illustrations: Sille Aasmul
Repro: Narayana Press, Gylling

National Library of Australia Cataloguing-in-Publication Data
Dickson, Thomas
Dansk design/Thomas Dickson
ISBN: 9781741963175 (hbk.)
Includes index.
Design, Denmark.
Designers, Denmark.
Decorative arts, Denmark.
745.409489

A catalogue record for this book is available from the British Library.

Printing: South Sea International Press Ltd. Hong Kong.
PRINTED IN CHINA.